The History of Beaufort County, South Carolina

Volume 1, 1514–1861

Lawrence S. Rowland
Alexander Moore
George C. Rogers, Jr.

UNIVERSITY OF SOUTH CAROLINA PRESS

The authors wish to accord special recognition to administrative assistant Mrs. Mary Gaffney Allen for her work on this book.

Published in Columbia, South Carolina, by the
University of South Carolina Press

Manufactured in the United States of America

00 99 98 97 96   5 4 3 2 1

Library of Congress Cataloging-in-Publication Data

Rowland, Lawrence Sanders.
  The history of Beaufort County, South Carolina / Lawrence S.
Rowland, Alexander Moore, George C. Rogers, Jr.
    p. cm.
  Includes bibliographical references and index.
  ISBN 1-57003-090-1
  1. Beaufort County (S.C.)—History. I. Moore, Alexander, 1948–
  II. Rogers, George C. III. Title
F277.B3R68 1996
975.7'99—dc20   96-10078

Contents

Illustrations

MAPS

Acknowledgments

This book has taken more than a decade to complete. During that time, the greatest resources available to the authors have been those institutions which have preserved, protected, published, and disseminated the history of our state.

Since its founding by James Louis Petigru in 1855, the South Carolina Historical Society in the Fireproof Building at 100 Meeting Street in Charleston has been dedicated to collecting, preserving, and publishing the records of South Carolina. Two of this volume's authors served as presidents of the society and the third is its current executive director. Many members of the society's staff have assisted with the research for this volume over the years. Past directors David Moltke-Hansen and Mark Wetherington were both supportive and generous with their time. Former staff members Mary Giles, Harlan Greene, and Susan Walker all helped with sections of this manuscript. Current assistant director Daisy Bigda has been supportive in numerous ways, and current staff members Peter Wilkerson, Patton Hash, and Rhonda Hunter have assisted with the research. Mr. Steven Hoffius, director of publications for the society, has been a friend and supporter for several years. These dedicated professionals, and the vast treasure of South Carolina history that they manage, are of incalculable value to all those interested in the history of South Carolina.

The South Carolina Department of Archives and History is the principal repository of the public records of South Carolina. It has been the home of the proprietary, colonial, and state records of South Carolina since its establishment in Columbia in 1909. Its search room is a beehive of activity and the necessary haunt of every scholar of South Carolina history. Two of this volume's authors have served at different times as members of the South Carolina Archives and History Commission. Past staff member Wylma Wates, who has assisted so many scholars over the years, helped with the research for this volume as well. Archives staff members Charles Lesser, Robert McIntosh, and Terry Lipscomb all shared important pieces of their own ongoing research. Alexia Helsley, director of public programs, former director of the search room, and a native Beaufortonian, has been an important and valued friend to this project and its authors. Judy Andrews provided invaluable technical assistance, and the maps are the result of the computer graphics wizardry of Tim Belshal.

Two of this book's authors are career employees of the University of South Carolina; without the support of this institution this book would not have been started, let alone finished. Robert M. Weir, Walter Edgar, and Daniel Hollis of the Department of History assisted in the early stages of this project. From the Department of Geography, Charles Kovacik and John Winberry provided important perspective. David Chesnutt, James Taylor, and Peggy Clark have provided professional advice and technical assistance throughout the many years of this endeavor. Robert Weir and James Taylor read, criticized, and substantially improved this manuscript.

Thanks are due also to the University of South Carolina Press, particularly former director Ken Scott, current director Catherine Fry, acquisitions manager Warren Slesinger, and managing editor Peggy Hill for their assistance. Their commitment to publishing the stories of South Carolina's historic counties and their patience in waiting for this manuscript are much appreciated.

The South Caroliniana Library is the oldest freestanding college library in America. It was built in 1840 under the direction of the president of the South Carolina College, Robert W. Barnwell of Beaufort. The library houses nearly every book published on South Carolina history as well as a large and valuable manuscript collection. Allen Stokes, director of the South Caroliniana Library, has been a friend and professional resource for this project over many years.

The Beaufort County Public Library, which dates its origin to the founding of the Beaufort Library Society in 1803, holds many treasures of local history. The library's collection of rare photographs was the principal source of illustrations for this volume. Library director Julie Zachowski has been a supporter of local history and this project for many years. Library staff members Dennis Adams and Hillary Barnwell were always helpful and informative.

The Georgia Historical Society was founded in Savannah in 1838. Its valuable collections, particularly the Savannah newspapers dating back to colonial times, were also a major resource for this volume. The authors particularly thank the former director of the society Lila Hawes for her patient and helpful assistance.

Several institutions and individuals in the Beaufort area have been important sources of local history. Mr. Gerhard Spieler, local historian and columnist for the *Beaufort Gazette,* and his wife, Ruth DeTreville Spieler, have been regular contributors and steady friends of this project over the years. Robert E. H. Peeples and Cora Peeples, founders of the Hilton Head Historical Society and longtime students of that island's history, have contributed many useful facts. At the Bluffton Historic Preservation Society, the longtime contributions of Betsy Caldwell and the late Ben Caldwell to the history of St. Luke's parish have been invaluable.

Mary Pinckney Powell, many times president of the Beaufort County Historical Society, added her expertise in genealogy and local church history to this task. Cynthia Cole Jenkins, former executive director of the Historic Beaufort Foundation, has been an especially valued friend and colleague over many years. Her numerous contributions and constant encouragement have been crucial to the completion of this volume. Her husband, Robert Jenkins, added his expertise as a photographer and is responsible for many of the illustrations. The many hours spent with these friends, sharing the minutia of local history and the genealogical links so important to understanding the South Carolina lowcountry, have been among the greatest pleasures of this endeavor.

Numerous colleagues at the University of South Carolina at Beaufort made contributions, both directly and indirectly. From the administration, former deans Darwin Bashaw and Ron Tuttle and current dean Chris Plyler were generous and patient supporters of this ongoing work. Dean of students Vincent Mesaric has always been a counselor, friend, and confidant. Another supportive friend has been John Kent, director of financial aid. Academic dean Lila Meeks maintained her sense of humor and her patience regarding the seeming endlessness of this work. Wenda Graves, faculty secretary, was always efficient and helpful. Tom Odom and Mark Palombo of the USCB computer lab were also very helpful in preparing the final draft. Mary-David Fox very willingly rendered expert technical assistance.

The moral and intellectual support of the faculty at USCB has also been instrumental to the completion of this book. Of particular note is the help of Stephen R. Wise, director of the U.S. Marine Corps Museum, Civil War author, and adjunct professor of history at USCB. Somers Miller of the history department, Jane Upshaw from mathematics, Rod Sproatt from education, Ed Caine from marine science, and Joan Taylor and John Blair from the English department offered encouragement, humor, and sometimes both over many years.

From the library at the University of South Carolina at Beaufort, former librarian Joe Malloy and current staffers Geni Flowers and Mae Mendoza have helped in many ways. Interlibrary loan specialist Catherine Carr has been particularly patient and helpful. Current librarian Ellen Chamberlain has been a friend, supporter, adviser, and cheerleader without whose counsel and good humor this task would have been far more difficult.

Thanks go also to my wife, Margot, and our three children, Lawrence, Katherine, and Margaret, for the support and patience they provided and the neglect they suffered in the completion of this project.

Lawrence S. Rowland

The History of Beaufort County, South Carolina

Volume 1, 1514–1861

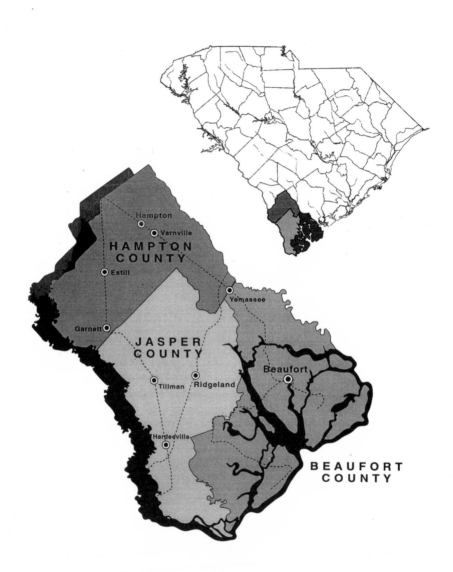

Hampton

○ Varnville

HAMPTON COUNTY

○ Estill

○ Yemassee

Garnett ○

JASPER COUNTY

○ Tillman ○ Ridgeland

○ Beaufort

Hardeeville ○

BEAUFORT COUNTY

Introduction

THE LIMITS OF BEAUFORT COUNTY

This is the story of the people who lived in the geographical region which is now Beaufort, Jasper, Hampton, and part of Allendale Counties. In 1682, the Lords Proprietors of Carolina gave directions for the laying out of three counties: Berkeley, Craven, and Colleton. These three original counties were north of the Combahee River. The land between the Combahee and the Savannah Rivers was considered the northern part of a no-man's-land lying between the English at Charleston and the Spanish at St. Augustine. When the Scots came in 1684 to 1685 to settle on the sea islands between St. Helena Sound and the Savannah River, the region was called Port Royal County. Around 1705 it became Granville County, the fourth of the original South Carolina counties. Granville had a mainland component which hugged the northern side of the Savannah River up to a point northwest of present-day Augusta. On January 17, 1711, the port of Beaufort was created.

South Carolina is traditionally divided into lowcountry, middle country (midlands), and upcountry. Almost all of Granville County was in the lowcountry, except for that portion that skirted up the Savannah and thus pierced the middle country. Granville County was cut from northwest to southeast by a number of rivers, but only the Savannah River, which marks its southwestern boundary, rises in the upcountry and flows to the ocean. It was subject to freshets, a phenomenon of some consequence once the uplands had been cut over, and was therefore considered a red river. The Savannah River was the chief highway in the colonial period between the Indian country of the Cherokees and Creeks and the lowcountry.

The other rivers between the Combahee-Salkehatchie and the Savannah flowing from north to south were the Bull (Coosaw), Pocotaligo, Chuleyfine, Coosawhatchie, May, New, and Wright. These arise below the sand hills; are slow moving; and are black rivers. The tides affect these rivers to a considerable degree from the coast and thus were ideal for the culture of rice.

The tongues of land that jut out between the rivers and the creeks were known as necks, most valuable configurations of land as the landward side could be fenced and the whole turned into a cattle ranch. The necks were named after early settlers or landowners with large properties. Keans Neck lay between Wimbee Creek and South Wimbee Creek; Grahams Neck between Pocotaligo and Tulifiny Rivers; Gregorie Neck between Tulifiny and Coosawhatchie Rivers; and Scotts Neck between Huspa Creek and Pocotaligo River.

An early human-made feature of the whole lowcountry scene was the cut which sliced through a neck in order to join two bodies of water and form an inland waterway. The first of these was Wappoo Cut which joined the Stono River to the head of Wappoo Creek and the Ashley River. A statute of June 7, 1712, stated that the cut was to be 10 feet wide and 6 feet deep. A series of cuts was thereafter made which linked the Ashley with the Savannah, the last two being Wall's and Fields Cuts, thereby creating an early inland waterway.

Beyond the rivers, necks, and cuts were the sea islands. These are the most distinctive geographical features of the Beaufort region, making it very different from the Georgetown region north of Charleston. One might group the sea islands into two divisions: one division lying between St. Helena Sound and Port Royal Sound, and the other between Port Royal Sound and the Savannah River. Another more helpful organization might be to consider the islands in terms of use. The barrier islands were never used to produce crops, but the sea islands behind the barrier islands were used for the production of indigo and cotton. Finally the islands that almost seemed a part of the mainland itself were suitable for rice culture.

The barrier islands between St. Helena Sound and Port Royal Sound are separated from the other sea islands by Harbor River on the east end and Station Creek on the west end, with Story River running through the middle of the marsh and emerging into Fripp Inlet. Harbor Island to the east is small and lies between Harbor River and Johnson Creek. It is across this island that the road now runs to Hunting, Fripp, and Pritchard, and was formerly known together as the Hunting Islands. Hunting Island was at one time called Reynolds Island. Fripp Island, named after an early surveyor, lies between Fripp Inlet and Skull Inlet. Pritchards Island lies between Skull Inlet and Moon Inlet and was formerly known as Chaplin Island. Capers Island lies between Pritchards Inlet and Trenchards Inlet, and the tip of Capers Island is named Bull Point. St. Phillips Island is across Trenchards Inlet, bounded on the north and west by Station Creek, and was formerly known as Eddings Island. Bay Point Island is the southern tip of St. Phillips separated by Morse Island Creek and was formerly known as Jenkins Hunting Island.

St. Helena Island, Lady's Island, and Port Royal Island, along with their auxiliary islands, dovetail so completely that they might be pieces in a jigsaw puzzle. Together these are the heart of the sea island region. St. Helena Island next to Port Royal Island is the largest of this group. It runs 22 miles from St. Helena Sound to Port Royal Sound. The northeast end is pierced by Village and Eddings Creeks; the southwestern end by Capers Creek which brings its tides almost to Frogmore. There had been an Indian village at Frogmore, and the earliest settlements by Nairne and Stewart were on the northeastern tips. Three small islands snuggle into the northwest side of St. Helena: Polawana, Datha, and Warsaw. Polawana Island is almost at the center of the area. Matthew Smallwood and James Cochran were the earliest settlers, but this island was put aside as a reservation for the Indians from 1707 to 1784. Datha Island was once called Westbrook's Island as it was here that Caleb Westbrooke had his Indian trading post. This island rests between Jenkins Creek and Morgan River. Charles Odingsell obtained a grant for it in 1699 and assigned it to Joseph Boone in 1702. Warsaw Island was granted to Jonathan Norton.

Morgan Island is surrounded by St. Helena Sound, Parrot Creek, Morgan River, and the mouth of the Combahee River. Coosaw Island is next to the west between Parrot Creek and Lucy Point Creek, Morgan River, and Coosaw River. Lady's Island abuts on Coosaw River on the north and then lies between Lucy Point Creek on the east and Brickyard Creek on the west, tapering to the southward into three islands: Distant, Cane, and Cat. Lady's Island was named after Lady Elizabeth Axtell Blake and is sometimes called Combachee, Combee, or Comber Island. Port Royal Island, as a continuation of Parris Island, is the largest land mass among the sea islands. Whale Branch Creek is to the north and Broad River and Beaufort River to the south and east. The island contains McCalleys Creek, Middle Creek, Albergotti Creek, Archer Creek, and Battery Creek. The long elongation (peninsula) to the eastward was to be the home of Beaufort, Stuart Town, and Port Royal. Parris Island was the site of the early French and Spanish settlements.

To the north and west of Coosaw River and Whale Branch Creek are islands which are more a part of the mainland than they are of the sea islands. Their inner reaches would make good rice plantations. From the east moving to the west are Combahee River and Bull River with a tongue of marsh in between. Williman Island lies between Bull River and Wimbee Creek. This was once Poatinka Island and was first granted to Richard Harris. Keans Neck lies between Wimbee Creek and South Wimbee Creek. Chisolms Island is between South Wimbee Creek and Coosaw River. Horse, Oak, Halfmoon, and Ballast Islands are all really a part of Chisolms Island. Between Huspa Creek and Pocataligo River are a number of marsh islands: Little Barnwell, Barnwell, Ball, Hall, and Bray's. William Bray, the Indian trader, gave his name to Bray's Island. The land between is Scott's Neck.

More islands lie south of the Broad River. Pinckney Island lay between Mackay Creek and Skull Creek. It was originally Mackay's Island. Hilton Head abuts northward on Port Royal Sound and to the southward on Calibogue Sound; fringing the west side are Skull Creek, the mouth of the May River, and Calibogue Sound. Broad Creek flows into Skull Creek and almost divides Hilton Head. Between May River and Cooper River, which also empties into Calibogue Sound, are three small islands which make one large mass. Barataria Island is the easternmost and separated from Bull Island by Bryan Creek, which in turn divided Bull from Savage Island. Daufuskie lies between the Cooper River and the New River. Turtle Island is between New River and Wright's River, but was created as an island by the digging of Walls Cut. Jones Island which lies between Wright's River and the Savannah River was similarly created as an island by the digging of Fields Cut. There is also Cook's Cut and Barnwell Island. The ownership of these last islands is still in dispute between the states of South Carolina and Georgia.

When the Church Act of 1706 divided the lowcountry into parishes, none was laid out for this region of the sea islands. But on June 7, 1712, the parish of St. Helena was created, including St. Helena, Lady's, and Port Royal with their dependent islands and the mainland portion of Granville County.[1] On May 25, 1745, the parish of Prince William was carved out of St. Helena. On February 17, 1746, the parish of St. Peter was designated to include "the township of Purrysburg and all that part of St. Helena's Parish which lies to the westward of a division line to be run due north from the bridge near the head of the main branch of Day's Creek until it meets King-creek."[2]

On May 23, 1767, St. Luke's Parish was established "by a line from the bridge over New river or Day's Creek, North ten degrees, West until it intersects the line of Prince William Parish, and from thence to be bounded by the Southwest side of Coosawhatchee river, Port Royal, Broad river, the Sea, Callibogy Sound, and New River or Day's Creek, up to the bridge on the said river or creek, including all the islands to the south and west of Port Royal, Broad River and Callibogy Sound."[3] In 1769, these four southern parishes were included in the Old Beaufort Judicial District, the limits of which are the limits of the area discussed in this book.

The earliest visitors noted that the waterways were the main highways of the region; the tides made the network of waterways work as one. Captain William Hilton noted the tide: "It flowes here S. E. and N. W. seven foot and a half, and eight foot at common Tydes." Hilton also noted that "fresh water at low Tide" was "within two leagues of the Mouth." Captain Sandford and his men said that they found the innumerable estuaries "to crumble the Continent into Islands." Sandford was aware that the tides could help navigation, "and by it into the Sea again, though by the Travers I tooke of our Course I found it perform-able with light boates in one tide of flood and an Ebbe." Thus, from the very beginning the Europeans realized that the sea islands with their tides higher than elsewhere on the coast and their cross-currents could begin to make use of their waterways for navigation and transportation.

In 1738, James Michie advertised land on Daufuskie Island which was one tide from Port Royal and two from Savannah. In the British Public Records Office report there is a statement about Purrysburg Island being so many tides from Port Royal. The earliest settlers were immediately aware that they could take advantage of the tides.

It would not be long before South Carolinians would try to understand the geological evolution of the region. John Drayton in *A View of South Carolina* wrote of the short rivers and the bays. Benjamin Reynolds, who owned one of the barrier islands, explained to David Ramsay in a letter of December 1, 1808, that the sea islands had been formed underwater with all the valleys and rising grounds running northeast and southwest. The hunting islands, on the other hand, were new lands formed above water, and the sand hills were formed from the erosion of the prevailing winds. Ramsay was aware of this constant erosion: "That the Atlantic waters have encroached upon the whole line of this coast, is a fact notorious and confessed."[4]

South Carolinians, both black and white, came to know these waters and respect them. I. Jenkins Mikell in his classic, *Rumbling of the Chariot Wheels,* said that St. Helena Sound "was as though a prehistoric monster had come out of the sea and with a Gargantuan mouth had bitten out of Carolina a jagged mouthful of some eight miles in length by four in width, leaving the wound ever raw, resentful, treacherous and dangerous." Mikell also described a forty-mile dash from Edisto to Charleston through Wappoo Cut on the family's twelve-oared boat on the eve of the Civil War.

In the seventeenth century, the inland waterway from Charleston to Savan-nah was the main highway of the southern frontier. Frederick Jackson Turner, in a classic description, compared standing in Cumberland Gap in the Great Smokey Mountains in the late eighteenth century to standing almost a hundred years later in South Pass in the Rocky Mountains. In both instances, one could have observed the movement of the frontier in procession. One could have stood at any one of the cuts in the early days of South Carolina and seen a similar move-ment of the frontier in procession—Indian traders, rice planters, indigo planters, sea island cotton planters, slaves being transported to develop new lands or pad-dling away to Florida, Confederate and Union forces, yachtsmen, or planters out to shoot boar and deer on the hunting islands.

NOTES

1. Thomas Cooper and David J. McCord, eds., *The Statutes at Large of South Carolina,* 10 vols. (Columbia: A. S. Johnston, 1836–1841), 2: 372.

2. Cooper and McCord, eds., *Statutes of South Carolina,* 3: 668–69.

3. Cooper and McCord, eds., *Statutes of South Carolina,* 4: 266.

4. Cooper and McCord, eds., *Statutes of South Carolina,* 2: 281n.

1

American Indians
in Beaufort County

EARLY HUMANS IN BEAUFORT COUNTY

Paleo-Indians, ancestors of North America's native peoples, were the first inhabitants of lowcountry South Carolina. Fifteen thousand years ago Paleo-Indians crossed the North American land bridge that connected Siberia and Alaska at the Bering Straits. In the following millennia they migrated southward and populated the North American and South American continents. Archeological evidence reveals that the Paleo-Indians and their prehistoric descendants created a distinctive culture along the Atlantic Coast from the Santee River in South Carolina to the St. Johns River in Florida. The presence in South Carolina of Clovis, Dalton, and Suwannee projectile points—the oldest known kinds in America—indicates that Paleo-Indians lived along the middle portion of the Savannah River in the late Pleistocene Age, as early as 10,000 B.C.[1]

At that time the climate of South Carolina was considerably cooler than at present, and the mouth of the Savannah River was 50 to 100 kilometers further out to sea than it is today. This latter fact is important to keep in mind when considering the earliest evidence of human habitation in South Carolina. Fossil remains and artifacts found today along the coast are in fact the archeological remains of humans who lived in mixed-growth hardwood forests some distance from the ocean. Post-Pleistocene inundation of the old Atlantic seacoast has obliterated all possible traces of coastal habitation.[2]

In addition to Clovis and Dalton points, another remarkable fossil relic helps to place early inhabitants in South Carolina. In March 1983, Robert Mackintosh was searching for fossils on Edisto Beach shortly after a violent storm. He discovered a fossilized elephant rib with cut marks along one edge. This relic, now on display at the South Carolina State Museum in Columbia, links South Carolina early prehistory with that of early humans throughout North America. Here in South Carolina, nomadic Paleo-Indians hunted and killed mammoths and mastodons just as they did in Alaska and Montana.[3]

THE ARCHAIC AND WOODLAND PERIODS
IN THE LOWCOUNTRY

Scanty archeological evidence along the coast suggests that Paleo-Indians may have been only occasional visitors to lowcountry South Carolina. But by the Archaic Period (8000 B.C.–1500 B.C.) human beings, now referred to as Indians, had become regular seasonal inhabitants of the coast. During the intervening two millennia (10,000 B.C.–8000 B.C.), North American glaciers had receded; the polar ice cap had melted considerably; and the Atlantic coastal shoreline had risen to approximately its present location. The climate and landscape of the lowcountry came to resemble present-day conditions: semitropical with salt-laced breezes—a land of creeks, marshes, and islands.[4]

During the Archaic and Woodland Periods (1500 B.C.–A.D. 500), Indians left a rich archeological legacy in Beaufort County and along the Georgia–South Carolina coast. Ceramic and lithic artifacts, floral and faunal remains, ceremonial objects, village sites, and human burials provide archeologists with sufficient evidence to create a vivid picture of lowcountry life thousands of years before Europeans reached the New World.[5] During this long expanse of time, agriculture, pottery-making, religion, and political institutions made their appearances in South Carolina.[6]

Coastal shell rings and shell middens mark the locations of aboriginal settlements during the Archaic and Woodland Periods. Composed of myriad oyster, clam, mussel, and other shellfish remains, the rings and middens were built from the refuse of thousands of years of shellfish consumption by Archaic Indians who moved their village sites to the coast during the summer.[7] Remnants of grains and other floral foodstuffs in the shell rings document the emergence of agriculture in the region. Fish hooks made of animal bone and stone net weights demonstrate that inhabitants possessed a variety of fishing techniques to harvest coastal waters and marsh and creek banks.[8]

Ceramic shards, Kirk-stemmed, and Savannah River projectile points testify to a shared Indian culture that encompassed lower South Carolina and Georgia. Fiber-tempered pottery—pots made of clay infused with vegetable fibers to ensure even firing—was first discovered at Stallings Island, in the middle Savannah River region. This is the earliest known pottery in North America, and its prevalence along the Savannah and adjacent coastal regions suggests that the region may have been a technological cradle of civilization. Stallings Island pottery and its successor styles—known as Thoms Creek, Refuge, and Deptford—were found abundantly in shell rings.[9] There are three possible explanations for the presence of these styles, each being a significant clue to Indian life in prehistoric Beaufort County. Inhabitants near shell rings probably migrated back and forth from the

Savannah River to the coast carrying the pottery with them. They may have traded local products with Savannah River inhabitants for their pottery. Or possibly fiber-temper technology was shared by all residents of the Southeast. Other archeological evidence suggests a regional Archaic and Woodland culture. Projectile points made of Allendale County chert were found in coastal shell rings. In this case, there is no question that coastal and inland tribes either migrated back and forth or had commercial links between middle Savannah River villages and coastal dwellers.[10]

Shell rings were inhabited throughout the Archaic and into the Woodland Period. Archeological excavations revealed not only cultural continuities among coastal inhabitants but also social evolution towards settled groups and increasing dependence upon agriculture for subsistence. Ornamental bone and shell objects found in rings, mounds, and human burial sites of the Woodland Period attest to aesthetic and religious dimensions of Indian life in the South Carolina lowcountry.[11] Village sites and sites of post-constructed buildings gave evidence of year-round habitation on the coast in the last years of the Woodland Period.

THE MISSISSIPPIAN PERIOD AND EUROPEAN CONTACT

The Mississippian Period (A.D.1150–A.D.1600) was a time of great cultural and political change in South Carolina. Not only did Native Americans develop sophisticated political, cultural, and religious institutions but they also confronted for the first time a totally foreign culture—the Europeans.[12] In addition to archeological evidence, written accounts in French and Spanish describe the last years of Mississippian culture.

Whether driven by agricultural changes, increasing populations, organized military campaigns, or other factors, Indian tribes throughout the southeast coalesced into political institutions known as ranked chiefdoms. Ranked chiefdoms were hierarchical in character and based upon exchanges of tribute and protection. Small tribes were led by chiefs or headmen who commanded respect and obedience in their villages. These chiefs and headmen in turn owed allegiance to paramount chiefs, who ruled larger geographical areas and greater numbers of people. Subordinates paid tribute to their superiors and looked to them for protection and food supplements in times of dearth.[13]

Populous, fortified towns and large earthen mounds were the hallmarks of the Mississippian Period. Mounds, whether single or built in complexes, were religious and political centers of southern ranked chiefdoms. Built laboriously by large numbers of workers, they are the best evidence that paramount chiefs enjoyed considerable power and authority over their subordinates.[14]

Mississippian culture had reached its apogee before the time of Hernando De Soto's *entrada* in 1540. He visited many towns and several paramount chiefdoms of the Southeast, and his scribes recorded in considerable detail the names of towns and their rulers. Juan Pardo's explorations in 1566 and 1567 added more information on coastal and inland tribes.[15]

At the time of first European contact two important paramount chiefdoms in Georgia and South Carolina were Guale and Cofitachequi. Guale was located on St. Catherine's Island and its chief held several villages as tributaries.[16] However, Guale's authority seems not to have extended across the Savannah River into Beaufort County. The paramount chiefdom of Cofitachequi, centered at Mulberry Mound, near Camden, was ruled in 1540 by a queen whose authority was largely inland and north of the Edisto River.[17] But Cofitachequi was known by coastal tribes to be a rich, powerful nation that commanded respect throughout the Southeast. Cofitachequi was still an important center in 1670 when the English settled at Charles Town, but its power had diminished considerably.

Locally in the Beaufort area there is some evidence that coastal tribes were within the sphere of two hierarchies, lesser paramount chiefdoms called Orista (Edisto) and Escamacu-Ahoya. Throughout the sixteenth century and up to the time of English settlement, these tribes had tenuous connections with Guale and Cofitachequi; by that time the authority of these two and all paramount chiefdoms in the Southeast had begun to collapse in the face of European settlement.[18]

European accounts suggest that numerous coastal tribes had considerable independence from their superiors but enjoyed less security in their daily lives. During the last years of the Mississippian Era—the time of European contact— eleven tribal groups lived between the Savannah and Edisto Rivers. From south to north these tribes were: Hoya, Witcheough, Escamacu, Wimbee, Toupa, Mayon, Stalame, Combahee, Kussoh, Ashepoo, and Edisto.[19] Linguistically and culturally these tribes were of Muskhogean stock, that is, related to the large southeastern tribes later known as the Creeks, Chickasaws, and Choctaws. Governed according to European parlance by caciques, micos, kings, captains, and queens, these tribes had complex political interactions both as equals among many and as subordinates to local paramount chiefs. A notable example of local independence and a concomitant lack of security was the readiness with which coastal tribes sought alliance with Europeans.

The brutal struggle between Spain and France to establish strongholds in the Port Royal area hastened the decline of coastal tribes. The Spanish at Santa Elena and St. Augustine, Florida, Christianized coastal and inland tribes. They had fair success among Georgia tribes, but considerably less among the South Carolina tribes. However, given the tumultuous history of Santa Elena and the Port Royal region, it must be assumed that the Spanish sought less to save souls than to secure allies.[20] Chapter 3 recounts an important event in Indian-Spanish relations, the Escamacu War of 1576 to 1579, in which tribes from Guale, Orista, and Escamacu united to drive the Spanish from Santa Elena. They succeeded briefly and sought to consolidate that success by an alliance with French visitors to the coast. But the Spanish returned in force. They hunted down the French hiding among the Indians and rebuilt Santa Elena. In 1587, the Spanish abandoned Santa Elena and consolidated their new-world capital at St. Augustine.

English exploration and settlement in South Carolina added another source of information on the coastal tribes. But it also injected a third, and the most disruptive, factor in lowcountry Indian life. From the beginning the English planned to erect permanent, expanding settlements in South Carolina. One element in their design was to form alliances with coastal tribes. Captain Robert Sandford reported in 1666 that Indians at St. Helena Sound sought English protection from the Westos, an Algonquin tribe that had recently entered the Southeast and harried settled tribes. Indeed, one factor in the English decision to establish Charles Town at Albemarle Point, not Port Royal, was the importunities of the cacique of Kiawah.[21] In 1671, Maurice Mathews, one of the first settlers and an agent for the Lords Proprietors, named the coastal tribes south of Charles Town that were "our friends" as the St. Helena, Ashepoo, Wimbee, and Edisto.[22]

In the face of a permanent and growing English settlement, coastal tribes lost their lands and suffered from imported diseases, enslavement, and forced emigration. By the end of the seventeenth century most of these small tribes were close to extinction. Maurice Mathews purchased large tracts of land from chiefs and caciques in the Port Royal region in 1684. Bounded by the Stono and Westo (Savannah) Rivers, the "Apalathean Mountains," and the Atlantic Ocean, the tract contained all of the territory that would become Beaufort County. In addition to being an important political document, this deed of sale demonstrated the formal character of early English-Indian relations. Also, the marks of the Indian signers revealed which tribes still had some territorial and political integrity in 1684. The signers included two Ashepoo caciques, two Witchow caciques, two Stono caciques, an Edisto queen and captain, a Kussah cacique and captain, a St. Helena queen and captain, and two Combahee captains.[23]

By the American Revolution, disease, enslavement, and amalgamation had melted the coastal tribes even closer to extinction. Pervasive English settlement destroyed the post-contact archeology of these tribes but, in exchange, immortalized them in the names of lowcountry geographical features. Guale and Cofitachequi exist today only in European records and archeological evidence, but the Edisto, Ashepoo, Coosaw, and Combahee Rivers; Edisto, Datha, and Daufuskie Islands; and Salkehatchie, Yemassee, Pocotaligo, and Coosawhatchie towns bear constant testimony to the Native Americans of Beaufort County.

THE YEMASSEE IN SOUTH CAROLINA, 1684–1715

The Yemassee Indians were late arrivals in lowcountry South Carolina. Called the Tama in Spanish records, this Muskhogean group lived on the Altamaha River in central Georgia in the 1660s. At that time their tribal organization may have been a ranked chiefdom with the town of Ocute on the Altamaha River the abode of the paramount chief.[24] As the Spanish and English competed for control of the regional tribes they encouraged Indians to move closer to the European towns of St. Augustine and Charles Town. This encouragement likely induced the Tamas to move to the coast in the 1670s and then to South Carolina after 1684. In the late 1670s, the Spanish pressured those Tamas who had moved to Guale to move even closer to St. Augustine, but they refused. Instead, Yemassee groups contacted the English at Charles Town and, in 1684, began moving to the Port Royal region.

The simultaneous settlement by Scottish Covenanters at Stuart Town, Port Royal, was likely another magnet drawing the Yemassee to that region.[25] The Yemassee quickly became important allies and trading partners both of the English and the Scots. Both Scots and Yemassee were placed on Charles Town's southern frontier to act as buffers between the English and the Spanish. But both failed at the task. In 1686, Spanish forces destroyed Stuart Town and ravaged settlements on Edisto Island. The Yemassee abandoned the coast and moved inland to the upper reaches of the Ashepoo River.

Despite South Carolinians' best hopes, the immigration of the Yemassee into the Beaufort region proved to be a prescription for disaster. English traders and Scots before 1686 ruthlessly and heedlessly exploited the Yemassee by drafting them to fight the Spanish and their Indian allies, cheating them in trade, and despoiling their fields and villages. The Lords Proprietors of Carolina and wiser English heads at Charles Town sought to halt or mitigate abuses against the Yemassee. In 1707, the General Assembly of South Carolina, encouraged by the Proprietors, passed a comprehensive law to regulate Indian trade by requiring traders to acquire licenses and appointing a commission to supervise the trade. A second law established a large Yemassee reservation to segregate Indians from whites.[26] The reservation was bounded by the Combahee and Savannah Rivers and contained a large tract of good land and accessible waterways known in the colonial period as the "Indian Land."[27] These efforts failed disastrously.

In 1715 there were ten Yemassee towns in the Port Royal and St. Helena region: Pocotaligo, Altamaha, Pocosabo, Ocute, Salkehatchee, Euhaw, Huspa, Tomatly, Chechesee, and Tuscagy. At that time, the population of these towns was 1,220, of whom about four hundred were warriors.[28]

The Yemassee bore the brunt of English expansionism, border warfare, and demographic decline for thirty years. By 1715, they despaired of survival and retaliated with remarkable violence in April of that year. The war that bears their name lasted from 1715 to 1717, and was followed by a decade of border raids. But the Yemassee War was not solely an uprising of the tribe nearest South Carolina. It was waged by a Muskhogean-speaking confederation that included most of the tribes of the Southeast—the Creeks, Choctaws, Natchez, Yemassee, and others. The defeat of the French and Spanish in Queen Anne's War in 1713 left the English dominant throughout the Southeast. Indians in the region realized that the English were now the greatest threat to their survival, and the Yemassee War quickly followed that realization.

NOTES

1. Albert C. Goodyear III, James L. Michie, and Tommy Charles, "The Earliest South Carolinians," in *Studies in South Carolina Archaeology: Essays in Honor of Robert L. Stephenson,* ed. Albert C. Goodyear III and Glen Hanson, Anthropological Studies 9, Occasional Papers of the South Carolina Institute of Archaeology and Anthropology (Columbia: South Carolina Institute of Archaeology and Anthropology, 1989), 19–24, 34–39.

2. Goodyear, Michie, and Charles, "Earliest South Carolinians." See also Kenneth E. Sassaman, *Early Pottery in the Southeast: Tradition and Innovation in Cooking Technology* (Tuscaloosa: University of Alabama Press, 1993), 45–48, for a discussion of the environment of the Southeast during that era.

3. Goodyear, Michie, and Charles, "Earliest South Carolinians," 26–27; James L. Michie, *An Intensive Shoreline Survey of Archaeological Sites in Port Royal Sound and the Broad River Estuary, Beaufort County, South Carolina,* Research Manuscript Series No. 167 (Columbia: South Carolina Institute of Archaeology and Anthropology, 1980), 14–21.

4. Charles F. Kovacik and John Winberry, *South Carolina: A Geography* (Boulder and London: Westview Press, 1987), 18–27; Mark J. Brooks, Peter A. Stone, David J. Colquhoun, and Janice G. Brown, "Sea Level Change, Estuarine Development and Temporal Variability in Woodland Period Subsistence Patterning on the Lower Coastal Plain of South Carolina," in *Studies in South Carolina Archaeology,* 91–100.

5. Keith Derting, Sharon Pekrul, and Charles J. Rinehart, *A Comprehensive Bibliography of South Carolina Archaeology,* Research Manuscript Series No. 211 (Columbia: South Carolina Institute of Archaeology and Anthropology, 1991), lists thirty pages of published archaeological reports of sites in Beaufort County. See Alan Calmes, "Indian Cultural Tradition and the European Conquest of the Georgia-South Carolina Coastal Plain, 3000 B.C.–A.D. 1733: A Combined Archaeological and Historical Investigation," Ph.D. diss., University of South Carolina, 1967, passim, for a comprehensive interpretation of early South Carolina.

6. Michael B. Trinkley, "An Archaeological Overview of the South Carolina Woodland Period: It's the Same Old Riddle," in *Studies in South Carolina Archaeology,* 73–89.

7. David R. Lawrence, ed., *Studies in Southeastern Aboriginal Shell Rings, Five Parts* (Columbia: Department of Geological Sciences, University of South Carolina, 1989–1991) includes numerous research papers, printed and manuscript, on shell rings. See

especially James L. Michie, "The Daws Island Shell Midden and Its Significance during the Shell Mound Formative," part 2: 284–91.

8. See Trinkley, "Archaeological Overview," and Lawrence, ed., *Studies in Southeastern Aboriginal Shell Rings,* on bone pins and incised shells.

9. Sassaman, *Early Pottery,* 16–20.

10. Goodyear, Michie, and Charles, "Earliest South Carolinians," 29–44.

11. Trinkley, "Archaeological Overview," 75–76.

12. David G. Anderson, "The Mississippian in South Carolina," in *Studies in South Carolina Archaeology,* 101–32.

13. Charles Hudson and Paul E. Hoffman, *The Juan Pardo Expeditions: Explorations of the Carolinas and Tennessee, 1566–1568* (Washington, D.C.: Smithsonian Institution, 1990), 75–104, discusses well-identified paramount chiefdoms in the southeast, the character of governance, and their geographical extent.

14. Clarence B. Moore, "Certain Aboriginal Mounds of the Coast of South Carolina," *Journal of the Academy of Natural Sciences of Philadelphia,* 2nd series, vol. 11, part 2 (1899): 147–66, identifies and describes excavations of mounds in Beaufort County.

15. Chester B. DePratter, "Explorations in Interior South Carolina by Hernando DeSoto (1540) and Juan Pardo (1566–1568)," *South Carolina Institute of Archaeology and Anthropology Notebook 19* (Columbia: South Carolina Institute of Archaeology and Anthropology, 1987); Hudson and Hoffman, *Juan Pardo Expeditions.*

16. Hudson and Hoffman, *Juan Pardo Expeditions,* 81.

17. Chester B. DePratter, "Cofitachequi: Ethnohistorical and Archaeological Evidence," in *Studies in South Carolina Archaeology,* 133–56; Hudson and Hoffman, *Juan Pardo Expeditions,* 75.

18. Gene Waddell, *Indians of the South Carolina Lowcountry, 1562–1751* (Spartanburg: Reprint Co., 1980), 126–68 for Orista (Edisto) and 168–98 for Escamacu. See also David Andrew McKivergan, "Migration and Settlement among the Yamasee in South Carolina," M.A. thesis, University of South Carolina, 1991, 30.

19. Waddell's *Indians of the South Carolina Lowcountry* is a compendium of data on lowcountry Indians. For information on these eleven tribes, see them listed alphabetically in Waddell.

20. Lawrence S. Rowland, *Window on the Atlantic: The Rise and Fall of Santa Elena, South Carolina's Spanish City* (Columbia: South Carolina Department of Archives and History, 1990), concisely narrates the struggle for hegemony in lowcountry South Carolina and the Indian roles in that struggle. See also chapter 3 in the present volume.

21. Verner Winslow Crane, *The Southern Frontier, 1670–1732* (Durham: Duke University Press, 1928), 5–6.

22. Maurice Mathews to Lord Ashley, August 30, 1671, in Langdon Cheves, ed., *The Shaftesbury Papers and Other Records Relating to Carolina and the First Settlement on Ashley River Prior to the Year 1676,* vol. 5 of *Collections of the South Carolina Historical Society* (Charleston: South Carolina Historical Society, 1897), 334.

23. A. S. Salley, ed., *Records in the British Public Record Office Relating to South Carolina,* 5 vols. (Columbia: Historical Commission of South Carolina, 1928–1947), 2:170.

24. William G. Green, "The Search for Altamaha: The Archaeology of an Early 18th Century Yamasee Indian Town," M.A. thesis, University of South Carolina, 1991, is a history of the Yamasee Indians before they entered South Carolina and of their residence there. McKivergan's thesis, "Migration and Settlement among the Yamasee in South Carolina," referred to in note 18 above, is a definitive history of the Yemassee in South Carolina. The narrative in the present volume is derived from both works.

25. George Pratt Insh, *Scottish Colonial Schemes, 1620–1686* (Glasgow: Maclehose, Jackson, 1922), 201–7, 209–11.

26. "An Act for Regulating the Indian Trade and Making it Safe to the Publick," in Thomas Cooper and David J. McCord, eds., *The Statutes at Large of South Carolina,* 10 vols. (Columbia: A. S. Johnston, 1836–1841), 2: no. 269, enacted July 19, 1707; "An Act to Limit the Bounds of the Yamasee Settlement, to prevent persons from disturbing them with their stocks, and to remove such as are Settled within the limitations thereafter mentioned," in Cooper and McCord, eds., *Statutes of South Carolina,* 2: no. 271, enacted November 28, 1707.

27. McKivergan, "Migration and Settlement," map 3.

28. Green, "Search for Altamaha," 33–34; McKivergan, "Migration and Settlement," 62.

2

Window on the Atlantic
The Rise and Fall of Santa Elena, 1514–1618

THE EARLIEST SPANISH VOYAGES

In 1496, the Spaniards planted the first permanent European colony in the New World at Santo Domingo on the island of Hispaniola. There the handful of Spanish settlers mined for gold, cultivated sugar cane, and raised cattle while their adventuresome agents fanned out across the Caribbean in search of land, gold, and labor. One of the major problems of the Spanish enterprise on Hispaniola and neighboring Puerto Rico was the lack of an adequate labor force to work the mines and cane fields. The fearful decimation of the small, indigenous population of Arawak Indians by disease and overwork led the Spanish colonists to look for sources of native labor in other lands. This was the motivation for the voyage of Pedro de Salazar between 1514 and 1516.

Salazar was the agent of Lucas Vasquez de Ayllon, a sugar planter on the northern coast of Hispaniola and major political figure in the colony. He was a member of the Audencia in Santo Domingo and *alcalde* (mayor) of the town of La Concepcion. Rather than sailing west or south as most previous Spanish expeditions had done, Salazar sailed north. He sailed past the Bahama Islands and continued northward until he made landfall somewhere between the coast of Georgia and Cape Fear. Salazar called this new land the "Land of the Giants" because the stature of the Indians he met was superior to the Arawak or Lucayan Indians of the islands. He also discovered that the only objects of value these natives could produce were pearls from the oysters which were a staple of their diet. Pedro de Salazar reported his discovery to Lucas Vasquez de Ayllon and thereby set in motion the events which led to the establishment of the first European colony in what is now South Carolina.[1]

In 1521, another expedition financed by Lucas Vasquez de Ayllon and led by Captain Francisco Gordillo set out for the "Land of the Giants." Gordillo sailed through the Bahama Islands in search of Indian slaves. While there he encountered another Spanish ship from Hispaniola commanded by Captain Pedro Quexos. Both captains agreed to proceed north in company and since Quexos had been a pilot on Salazar's expedition six years earlier, his experience would be useful. On June 24, 1521, the two Spanish ships made landfall at a prominent headland which protected a large bay. Gordillo and Quexos managed to coax some of the nervous Indians aboard their two caravels where they exchanged gifts and learned that the natives called their country Chicora. The two ships then put to sea with some of their Indian guests on board and set sail for Hispaniola. On the return voyage, Quexos's ship was lost in a storm, but Gordillo's ship returned safely to Santo Domingo.[2]

Among the Indian captives brought from the South Carolina coast was Francisco Chicora who was destined to become one of the most celebrated and influential native Americans of the time. Francisco Chicora became the instant favorite of Lucas Vasquez de Ayllon, adopted the Catholic faith, and quickly became fluent in Spanish. The wondrous tales that Chicora told the Spanish of his native land excited Ayllon to embark on further adventures on the American mainland. Ayllon returned to Spain with Francisco Chicora in 1523 in order to convince the crown and the Council of the Indies in Seville, which governed events in the Spanish colonies of the New World, of the value of a colonial enterprise on the mainland of North America.

During this trip Francisco Chicora entertained the Spanish Court with his stories and was extensively interviewed by two of the most widely read chroniclers of the New World: Pietro Martire D'Anghiera (known as Peter Martyr), the Italian secretary to the Council of the Indies whose *Decades 1455–1526* recorded all the reports of discoveries brought to Seville, and Gonzalo Fernandez de Oviedo whose *Natural History of the West Indies* was first published in Toledo in 1526. These stories were the origin of the Chicora legend of a vast and fruitful land in the interior of the Southeast which the Spanish equated with the Iberian plain of Andalucia.

These early publications on the New World recorded Francisco Chicora's stories of a huge Indian king named Datha who ruled a race of giants that grew to great size by stretching the limber bones of their infants and stories of another race of men who grew long tails and had to dig holes in the ground in order to sit. More believable was the Indian practice of raising young deer in their villages and producing cheese from the milk of the does. Later confirmed was the Muskohegan Indian ritual of drinking the black juice of the holly plant (*Ilex vomitoria*) which made them vomit and feel better. Also later confirmed were the descriptions of the flora and fauna of the South Carolina coast and the large amounts of pearls derived from the coastal Indians' main protein staple, oysters. These stories helped convince the Spanish authorities to award Ayllon the title of *adelantado* (governor) of La Florida and encourage his exploration and settlement of the South Carolina coast.[3]

By 1525, Ayllon and Francisco Chicora were back in Santo Domingo making preparations for the expedition. That year Pedro Quexos was dispatched with his kinsman Fernandez Sotil, who had been the pilot for Gordillo on the 1521 voyage, to reconnoiter the coast in advance of Ayllon's expedition. It was on this voyage of 1525 that Quexos, on May 22, encountered a prominent headland on the coast and named it La Punta de Santa Elena after St. Helena, virgin martyr of Auxerre, France, who is honored on that day. Known by its anglicized version, St. Helena is one of the oldest continuously used European place names in the United States. La Punta de Santa Elena became a well-known name in the Old World and an important landmark for European mariners of many nations. Its precise location in 1525 remains in doubt, but the most likely location is Tybee Island, Georgia. In the sixteenth century, La Punta de Santa Elena was the landfall not for the Savannah River, whose entrance was blocked by sandbars, but for what the Spanish later called the harbor of Santa Elena. Today, the harbor is known by its French name, Port Royal.

In 1526, Lucas Vasquez de Ayllon, Francisco Chicora, and five hundred colonists left Santo Domingo aboard six ships. Among the colonists were several Negro slaves and three Dominican friars including Father Antonio Montesino, the first priest to preach against the genocidal practice of Indian slavery on Hispaniola. Significantly, the Royal Cedula (certificate) awarding Ayllon his titles and grants specifically forbade the practice of Indian slavery.[4]

Ayllon's fleet made landfall somewhere on the coast of South Carolina in the summer of 1526. While trying to enter the mouth of a large river they named the Jordan, Ayllon's flagship and most of the supplies were run aground and lost. The fleet then proceeded southwestward approximately 40 leagues to a large river called the Gualdape. There, on low sandy soil in a country that was flat and swampy, Ayllon constructed the first Spanish municipality within the territorial limits of the United States: San Miguel de Gualdape. The location of this Spanish colony has been a matter of much debate among historians in recent centuries. The common assumption among nineteenth-century historians is that San Miguel de Gualdape was located at Spanish Punta de Santa Elena, now called Port Royal.[5] Early twentieth-century historians have favored a location near Winyah Bay.[6] The most recent scholarship, however, suggests that San Miguel de Gualdape may have been further south near the mouth of the Savannah River or St. Catherine's Sound, Georgia.[7]

The settlers established a municipal government with an *alcalde* to manage the affairs of the town. They set about building their houses and constructing public buildings which included a common storehouse and perhaps a church. Also built was a ship to replace the one that had been wrecked. Instead of building a large ocean-going caravel, however, they constructed a shallow-draft open vessel that could be propelled by either oars or sails and was well suited to the shallow coastal waters. This was the first instance of a ship being built by Europeans in the territory of the United States.

Sickness ravaged the settlers during that summer. In fact, Lucas Vasquez de Ayllon was stricken and died on October 18. Francisco Chicora abandoned the settlement to return to his native relatives. He was never heard from again. Francisco Gomez was left in charge and he was unable to prevent a mutiny among the unhappy colonists led by Ginez Doncel and Pedro de Bacan. Gomez and other leaders were imprisoned. Doncel and his confederates mistreated the Indians who retaliated by killing some of the settlers. Some of the Negro slaves, who had also been mistreated, conspired in turn against Doncel and burned his house during the night, thus fomenting the first of many Negro slave revolts in South Carolina history. Francisco Gomez was freed from prison while the rebels, Doncel and Bacan, and some of their followers were executed.

Faced with the onset of winter with no supplies, surrounded by hostile natives, and thoroughly demoralized, the settlers of San Miguel de Gualdape abandoned their colony and set sail for Hispaniola. On the bitter cold passage home seven men froze and one man, driven insane by hunger, ate the frostbitten flesh from his own bones. The body of the *adelantado,* Lucas Vasquez de Ayllon, was lost at sea; of the 600 original colonists only 150 survived to return to Hispaniola in 1527. Of the survivors, the most credible witnesses to the tragedy were the three Dominicans, Father Antonio Montesino, Father Antonio de Cervantes, and Brother Pedro de Estrada.[8]

The sad fate of the first colony of the South Carolina coast did not prevent Spanish adventurers in America from maintaining a continued interest in the land of Chicora. Ayllon's own son and namesake kept alive his father's claims to the North American continent as late as 1563, but the enormous family debts he had inherited prevented him from achieving his father's ambition. In 1540, Hernando De Soto passed near the Santa Elena area on his overland journey from Tampa Bay to the Mississippi and crossed into what is now South Carolina at Silver Bluff on the Savannah River. At the village of Cofitachequi on the Wateree River, he was entertained by the queen of the region who wore many pearls that had been brought from the coast. There he also found the Indians in possession of iron axes, a dagger, a rosary, and a cross, all of which they had gotten from the Christians who had settled on the coast many years before. These artifacts are generally considered to have been remnants of the Ayllon settlement. The Indians reported that these objects had been gathered within a two-day journey from Cofitachequi.[9]

De Soto's expedition also ended in failure and it was nearly twenty years before the Spanish again returned to Santa Elena. But at least one English expedition arrived at Santa Elena in the 1540s. In 1560, the Spanish picked up an English castaway on the coast of Florida who testified that as a cabin boy many years before, he had shipped out with a Bristol fleet bound for America to intercept the Spanish treasure ships from the Indies. The fleet had left Ardmore in 1546 and was hit by a storm in latitude 37 degrees. From there they sailed south to 33 degrees latitude and went ashore at "Punta de Santa Elena." There they traded tools and weapons for skins "and some pearls." If the testimony of John of Bristol, or as the Spanish called him, Juan el Ingles, is correct then this was the first English expedition to land at Santa Elena and one of the first English voyages to the southern coast of North America.[10]

Thus, by the middle of the sixteenth century, two European nations had knowledge of and interest in Santa Elena. In the 1550s, however, it was not the English but the French who mounted the most serious challenge to Spain's claim to "La Florida." The occupation of the South Atlantic coast by any power hostile to Spain posed a danger to the safe passage of Spanish treasure fleets from the New World. It was bullion from the mines of Peru and Mexico which maintained Spain's position as the preeminent political and military power in Europe during the sixteenth century, and any threat to the flow of that wealth demanded immediate attention at the highest levels of the Spanish court. Spanish activities and correspondence in the 1550s demonstrate their early recognition of the strategic importance of Punta de Santa Elena.

The harbor at Santa Elena (Port Royal Sound) was the deepest and most accessible harbor on the southern coast of North America. More important to the Spanish, it was on the westward flank of the route of their galleons transporting gold to Spain. Spanish convoys in the sixteenth century commonly rendezvoused at Havana from Colon, Panama, and Vera Cruz, Mexico. From Havana they would follow the Gulf Stream through the Bahama Channel until they encountered the prevailing westerly trade winds. Then they would head east across the Atlantic for Cadiz. The westerly trades were first encountered off the North American coast between Jacksonville, Florida, and Wilmington, North Carolina. Thus, Santa Elena, lying on the "hinge" of the convoy route, was ideally located for protecting or plundering Spanish gold.

It was this realization that prompted Phillip II of Spain to order the expedition of Tristan de Luna y Arrellano and Angel de Villefane to "La Florida." Rumors had been reaching the Spanish court for some time of French interest in North America, and the Spanish expressed concern about the settlement of French fishermen at "Los Bacallos" (literally "Codfish Country" or modern Newfoundland). In 1557, Phillip II sent orders to Luis de Velasco, viceroy of New Spain, to appoint his friend Tristan de Luna as governor of "las provinces de la Florida y Punta Santa Elena." Luis de Velasco replied from Mexico in 1558 that de Luna's

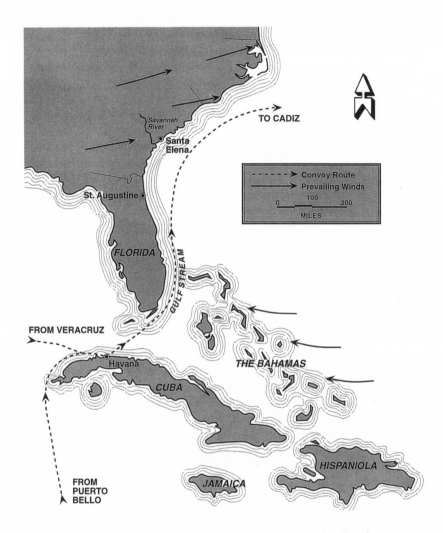

Sixteenth-century Santa Elena and the route of the Spanish convoys

expedition would embark from Vera Cruz that year and that they were already having problems with French intruders.[11] The expedition was delayed for many months and when it did finally plant a settlement, it was on the Gulf coast of Florida and not on the Atlantic coast where Phillip II urgently repeated that it would do the most good. In 1559, the king wrote directly to Don Tristan de Luna: "As you know from being told, it was fitting and very necessary to make a strong settlement at the Punta de Santa Elena . . . to bring the people of that land to our Holy Catholic faith, and in order that ships which come from New Spain and other parts of the Indies to this Kingdom . . . may find shelter instead of being lost . . . and also in order to prevent people from France or any other foreign country from entering there to settle or take possession in our lands . . . the first of all the settlement we have ordered must be made at the Punta."[12]

Sensing the king's impatience, the viceroy further clarified the orders to de Luna: "There are suspicions and some indications that the French who have settled Los Bacallos, which is not far from Punta de Santa Elena, are trying to come and take the . . . ports and settle them so as to impede the passage of the Bahamas Channel. They will be able to do this easily if they find a port."[13] Thus, the king and the viceroy expressed their concern that de Luna's settlement on the Gulf coast was of little strategic value and that the real object of their intentions was Santa Elena. Though de Luna's colony was another expensive failure, his assistant, Angel de Villefane, was dispatched with a small fleet to find and secure Santa Elena on the Atlantic coast of "La Florida."

The orders from Luis de Velasco in Mexico which dispatched Villefane in 1560 again reflected the concern of the highest Spanish officials that a foreign power might occupy Santa Elena and threaten the route of the Spanish treasure fleets. Velasco reminded de Luna and Villefane that the king himself ordered that "a settlement be made with all haste at Punta de Santa Elena, for it is suspected, notwithstanding there is peace with France, that either the French or the Scotch may enter there and take possession of the lands of his majesty and occupy them."[14]

Villefane proceeded from the Gulf coast to Havana to reprovision. From there he sailed north with two caravels and two shallow draft frigates. Among the hundred men who accompanied Villefane were two Dominican friars, John de Contrerars and Gregory de Beteta. In 1561, Villefane's fleet found Santa Elena, entered the harbor, and explored the sea islands. A violent hurricane, however, wrecked three of the ships and killed twenty-six men. This prevented Villefane from establishing the colony the king had ordered and again frustrated Phillip II's desire for a "window on the Atlantic."[15]

THE RIBAUT COLONY

The suspicions of the Spanish monarch were confirmed the next year when a French expedition led by Captain Jean Ribaut of Dieppe arrived on the coast of Florida. This French adventure was sponsored by Gaspar Coligny, admiral of France and leader of the Protestant Huguenot faction at the French court. Coligny had several purposes for Ribaut's voyage. First, he hated the Spanish who incited Catherine de Medici, queen mother and real power within the French government, to violent persecution of his fellow Protestants. Second, he saw a French colony in Florida as a useful bargaining tool in the ongoing diplomatic maneuvers between France and Spain in Europe. Third, a successful colony in the New World would provide an avenue of escape for the persecuted Huguenots in France. And last, Coligny was an ardent nationalist who believed, as many Spanish, Portuguese, and English of the age also believed, that colonial expansion was one of the best means of realizing national ambitions.[16]

Ribaut sailed from Havre de Grace in Normandy in February 1562. He had two ships, one of 160 tons and the other of 60 tons, and 150 men. They were well supplied with arms and provisions. Ribaut arrived on the coast of Florida on April 30, 1562. The Frenchmen rowed ashore and met the local Indians. Not finding a good harbor in the vicinity, they set sail and proceeded up the coast to the north. As they slowly explored the coast of Florida and Georgia, they named the many inlets and rivers that they found after rivers in their homeland. The St. Johns River was the River May (the month it was discovered). The St. Mary's River was called the Seine and the Savannah River was called the Gironde. In the second week in May, they entered a harbor "so large and magnificent that they named it Port Royal."

Between May 15 and 20, the enterprising Frenchmen built a substantial fort that was 160 feet long by 130 feet wide with a moat and a log blockhouse. The Indians they met reported previous Spanish presence on the coast, but Ribaut was not deterred. Ribaut explored the waterways and ordered a stone column with the arms of France chiseled on it to be placed on "a small island formed by a creek which left the main stream and a little farther on rejoined it." This island 3 miles to the west of their camp they called Libourne. Its description conforms to the present circumstances of modern Dawes Island. Ribaut then decided to return to France for supplies and asked for volunteers to remain at Charlesfort and hold the land for France. Every one of the soldiers wished to stay, but Ribaut chose twenty-eight men under the command of Captain Albert de la Pierria. With assurances that he would soon return, Ribaut sailed away on June 11, 1562.[17]

The French outpost at Port Royal did not fare well. The soldiers were so confident of Ribaut's return that they did not bother to plant any Indian corn or other crops to see them through the winter. After they had completed the fort they spent their time hunting, fishing, and fraternizing with the Indians. Months went by and the long summer began to turn to winter with no sign of Ribaut's return. By January 1563, all their food had run out and famine was sapping the morale of the garrison. The local Indians became less generous with their contributions, and a party of Frenchmen traveled up the Combahee River to visit with Chief Quade and seek aid. Chiefs Quade and Couexis, the major Indian lords of the region, were generous with their supplies and filled two canoes with maize and beans for the garrison at Charlesfort. The Frenchmen's luck, however, was not to last. The supplies and part of Charlesfort were destroyed by fire and the men "found themselves in such extremity that without the aid of Almighty God . . . they had been quite and clean out of all hope."

Hunger and despair broke down the discipline of the garrison and Captain Pierria responded harshly. He hanged one man, Guernache, with his own hands when the garrison refused to assist him. Guernache was an old veteran of the French guards and his offense had been minor. Then Captain Pierria humiliated young La Chere and marooned him on a neighboring island without food or water. When Pierria next threatened to kill anyone who did not obey him, the soldiers mutinied. They chased Pierria through the woods until they caught him and murdered him. Then, they rescued the half-starved La Chere and chose Nicholas Barre as their leader. Barre was an experienced New-World adventurer and had served with Villegagnon on his expedition to Brazil in 1556.

The Frenchmen then set about to build a ship and return to France. They had little experience in shipbuilding but they constructed a twenty-ton sloop of local materials. They caulked the seams with the abundant Spanish moss and prevailed on the local Indians for cordage. The Frenchmen then contributed their own shirts and bedding to fashion sails. By April 1563, all was ready. When the ship was provisioned from the diminished supplies of the local Indians, the craft set out on its perilous voyage across the Atlantic. One young Frenchman, Guillaume Rouffi, remained with the Indians rather than risk a transatlantic passage in a leaky vessel with no experienced navigator.

The ship became becalmed at sea, and the food and water ran out. The men then ate their leather shoes and jerkins in desperation. A storm battered the craft, and the crew lay helplessly in the hold waiting for the end. At that point a grisly plan for survival was suggested; they would kill one of their comrades in order to eat his flesh and blood. The lot fell to La Chere who was killed and his flesh divided among the remaining men. This allowed the survivors to sail on until they were within sight of the coast of Europe. There they were picked up by a passing English ship. The most feeble of the survivors were put ashore at Corunna and the rest were taken to England where the Elizabethan court learned first-hand the fate of the first Protestant colony in the New World.[18]

In the meantime, the Spanish had been informed of the French expedition to Florida and belatedly ordered measures to counter the French Protestant intrusion in the New-World empire of Catholic Spain. Phillip II sent orders to Havana for Governor Mazariego to dispatch a force from Cuba to find and destroy the French settlement and mete out whatever justice they thought fit for the Protestant trespassers. Governor Mazariego sent Don Hernando de Manrique Rojas in command of the frigate *Nuestra Senora de la Concepcion* to find and destroy Charlesfort. The Spanish expedition left Cuba in May 1564, more than a year after Nicholas Barre and the French garrison had left Port Royal. In June, they arrived at Santa Elena and found the column Ribaut had left. They symbolically knocked it to the ground and then loaded it on board their frigate to take back to Havana. On June 11, 1564, the Spanish found young Guillaume Rouffi living with the natives and "clothed like the Indians of that country." Rouffi led the Spanish to the location of Charlesfort which they promptly burned.

Captain Rojas took Guillaume Rouffi back to Cuba for detailed interrogation regarding the French intentions for settling "La Florida." No doubt Rouffi told the Spanish what they wanted to hear in order to save his own neck, and some of his information conflicts with the French accounts by Laudonniere and others. Rouffi's account, on the other hand, is no more self-serving than others and does contain more detail on Ribaut's Port Royal expedition than most others. Rouffi stated that the Ribaut expedition was paid for by Monsieur de Vendome and the queen mother of France. They were ordered to settle at Santa Elena because it was "a good location for going out into the Bahamas Channel to capture the fleet from the Indies." Rouffi claims this was common knowledge among the crew. While most of Ribaut's crew were French Protestants, there were some Catholics and one was English. The pilot, in fact, was a Spanish man named Bartolome from Seville. Rouffi, as might be expected, claimed that he was one of the few Catholics on the expedition.

When the French arrived at Port Royal they built a fort which consisted of an "enclosed house of wood and earth covered with straw with a moat around it, with four bastions and on them two brass falcones and six small iron culverines." Of the men who were left at Port Royal, Rouffi claimed that two were drowned crossing the river in a canoe and Captain Pierria was killed in a fight with another soldier, rather than as a result of a general conspiracy. When the French garrison left with Barre aboard their makeshift sloop, the only valuable item they took from the sea islands was "a hatful of pearls." Rouffi remained with the Indians because the French crew had no experienced pilot.

Rouffi reported that there had been no ships entering the harbor in the fourteen months since Charlesfort was abandoned, but the Indians reported four ships to the north and remnants of a French ship were found off the coast. The Indians also reported that a large ship came to the coast to the north more than two years before and killed many Indians. Guillaume Rouffi remained with the Spanish in Cuba and was later to serve Pedro Menendez de Aviles in his permanent conquest and settlement of Florida.[19]

Ribaut's failure to return to Port Royal was due to the outbreak of religious civil war in France. He was unable to get the money, supplies, or political support he had expected in France. He traveled to England in search of aid to relieve the garrison at Charlesfort. In May 1563, Ribaut had an interview with Queen Elizabeth who remained publicly neutral but who secretly agreed to fund Ribaut's relief of Charlesfort if he would deliver Florida into English hands. In desperation, Ribaut agreed. Later, he reconsidered and tried to escape to France. He was caught and thrown into prison.

In France, the religious wars had temporarily ceased, and Admiral Coligny was back at the French court making preparations for a second expedition to Florida. With Ribaut in prison in England, he chose Rene de Laudonniere to lead the expedition, as Laudonniere had been Ribaut's second in command on the voyage to Port Royal. Laudonniere left Havre de Grace with three ships and three hundred men on April 22, 1564. Few of them would ever see France again.[20]

While the French had been preparing to settle and fortify Florida, the Spanish were just as busy preparing to eliminate the intruders and make a permanent settlement of their own. The man personally chosen by Phillip II to succeed where Ayllon, de Luna, and Villefane had failed was the decisive and energetic Pedro Menendez de Aviles. Menendez was an experienced seaman whose first command had been in the Mediterranean fleet of Phillip II. He had also fought against French corsairs in the Bay of Biscay off the coast of his native Asturias. In 1554, he had visited England as one of the officers accompanying Phillip II on his state visit to marry the English queen, Mary Tudor. In the late 1550s, Menendez developed substantial mercantile interests in the Indies, but in 1563, he lost a fortune and his only son off the coast of Florida when a September hurricane scattered the Indies fleet. This new expedition to Florida offered Menendez a way to recoup his losses, search for information about his lost son, and provide a valuable service for his king and his church. Another principal motive for Menendez was the belief that to the north of Santa Elena lay the large Bahia Santa Maria (Chesapeake Bay) which many thought was the entrance to the northwest passage to the Pacific and the "way to the Orient." Discovery and conquest of such a place would allow Spain to dominate the Asian trade and would immortalize Menendez.[21]

There now occured on the beaches of Florida a wilderness drama that was to capture the attention of all of Europe and affect history of the southern coast for more than two centuries. Laudonniere had arrived on the coast of Florida on June 22, 1564. There on a bluff overlooking the St. Johns River, he established the second French Huguenot colony in North America, Fort Caroline. The French colonists spent the fall and winter months exploring the country of north Florida and establishing relations with the local Indians. In August of 1564, the English privateer, Sir John Hawkins, arrived to trade with the fledgling French settlement. Finding little of value, Hawkins offered supplies to the garrison and transportation back to Europe to the disaffected. News of this visit of the English caused additional concern in the Spanish Caribbean, where the rumor was spread and transmitted back to Spain that Fort Caroline was a joint English and French Protestant enterprise of more than one thousand inhabitants.[22] This unwelcome news spurred the Spanish monarch to urge the rapid deployment of Menendez's fleet to the Indies. Menendez left Cadiz on June 29, 1565, with more than one thousand men on several ships led by his huge nine-hundred-ton flagship, *San Pelayo*.[23]

Jean Ribaut, released from his confinement in England, had already left Dieppe on May 22, 1565, with a fleet of ships, supplies, and reinforcements for the French colony at Fort Caroline. Though he wasted two weeks across the Channel in England waiting for favorable weather, Ribaut was still two weeks ahead of Menendez's fleet in the transatlantic race to Florida. While Menendez was aware of Ribaut's departure, Ribaut was not specifically aware that a Spanish fleet was headed, via the Canary Islands, for the same destination bent on the destruction of Fort Caroline and the permanent removal of the French from Florida. While Ribaut's voyage was uneventful, Menendez's was not. Ribaut arrived off the mouth of the St. Johns River in July to the joy and relief of the settlers at Fort Caroline. Menendez's fleet, on the other hand, had been scattered by a hurricane in the mid-Atlantic. Two ships were wrecked and the great *San Pelayo* limped into San Juan, Puerto Rico, under a gerry rig. Despite this setback, Menendez set out almost immediately for Florida and risked his flagship in the shorter, but treacherous, route through the Bahama Islands in hopes of beating Ribaut to Fort Caroline. He was too late. The day Menendez sighted Cape Canaveral, Ribaut's fleet anchored off the St. Johns River. Menendez coasted northward until he spied the French fleet anchored offshore. After exchanging a few shots with the French, he withdrew down the coast and established a Spanish beachhead at the next negotiable inlet. There, Spanish officers went ashore, claimed the land for their king, and named the port St. Augustine.

On hearing of the arrival of Menendez's forces, Ribaut acted decisively. He set out with four ships and six hundred men, nearly three-quarters of the total French forces in Florida, in order to strike first at the Spanish. Only a small garrison was left to protect Fort Caroline. Ribaut's aggressive move met with disaster. As he led the small fleet down the coast aboard his flagship *Trinite*, a summer thunderstorm blocked his view of the Spanish forces as he passed St. Augustine inlet. He sailed too far south and before he could retrace his course, the fleet was struck by a huge storm, possibly a hurricane. All four ships were wrecked in the surf with most of the French artillery aboard. Ribaut's main force was stranded on the Florida beaches in two separate parties.

Menendez, in the meantime, had also acted decisively. He was determined to lead a striking force overland to capture Fort Caroline before Ribaut could return. Under the cover of the heavy rains that accompanied the hurricane, he led five hundred men through the marshes and tangled undergrowth in back of the beaches. After an arduous two-day march, they rested in a grove of live oak trees only 3 miles from Fort Caroline. On the morning of September 20, 1565, the Spanish attacked. The French garrison was weak, and the sentinels were both sleepy and distracted by the rain. The fort was quickly overrun, and those members of the garrison who had not been able to escape into the woods were put to the sword. Menendez ordered that the women and children in the fort be spared, but 132 Frenchmen were killed. Forty-five others ran into the woods and escaped onto the two ships anchored in the river. Among the survivors of the massacre at Fort Caroline who eventually returned to Europe aboard the *Pearl* and the *Levriere* were the carpenter Le Challeux, the cartographer Le Moyne, Rene de Laudonniere, and Jacques Ribaut, son of the Huguenot commander.

After securing the position on the St. Johns River, Menendez returned to St. Augustine to protect his own position against an expected assault by Ribaut. He learned from the Indians to the south that the first group of French castaways had arrived at Matanzas Inlet 18 miles south of St. Augustine. Menendez marched to meet them, and after receiving the surrender of the desperate Frenchmen, he had nearly all put to the sword. Jean Ribaut and a second group of Frenchmen, however, still lived, and it was not until October 11 that the half-starved survivors arrived at Matanzas to negotiate with the Spanish. Unaware of the fate of their comrades, they also surrendered to the mercy of Pedro Menendez de Aviles. Seventy Frenchmen along with their commander were executed. The fate of "La Florida" had been decided in favor of Spain.[24]

The first accounts to reach Europe of the events of the Florida coast were those of the French survivors of Fort Caroline. While Laudonniere and Le Moyne had landed in England, Le Challeux had gone directly to France; his was the first account of the tragedy to be published. Laudonniere reached France later, and his account, largely an attempt to justify his own actions, was not published in France until 1586. Jacques Le Moyne remained in England where he produced numerous engravings of the natural surroundings and native inhabitants of Florida. In the highly charged religious atmosphere of late-sixteenth-century Europe, the accounts of this clash of Protestants and Catholics for mastery of a tropical empire, along with the explicit engravings by Jacques Le Moyne of the exotic land of "La Florida," made these publications among the most widely read and sensational accounts of the New World. Between 1565 and 1591, these accounts were published in four different countries in northern Europe and in the English, French, Latin, and German languages.[25]

THE SETTLEMENT OF SANTA ELENA, 1566–1576

After the elimination of the French forces in Florida, Pedro Menendez de Aviles set about establishing the settlements and military posts that would finally secure the southern coast and protect the eastward route of the Indies fleet. Menendez maintained his position at St. Augustine and fortified the previous French position on the St. Johns River, calling it San Mateo. On his way to Havana, he discovered that ships could conveniently sail south to Cuba in deep water bucking the powerful Gulf Stream by staying close to the Florida beaches.[26] This navigational information began to alter the Spanish strategy for the protection of their easterly trade route. In the age of sail, this two-way communication made the otherwise uninviting coast of Florida more important to the Spanish. By contrast, the Punta de Santa Elena, which had been the focus of Spanish interest for the previous half century, became less important.

Other strategic factors in the late sixteenth century contributed to this gradual shift in Spanish emphasis on the continent away from the South Carolina coast and toward the Florida peninsula. In the first two decades of the sixteenth century when Spanish discovery of the continent occurred and nascent colonial interest was generated, the locus of Spanish power in the New World was the islands of Hispaniola and Puerto Rico. These were the first permanent European settlements in the New World. Pedro de Salazar in 1516, Francisco Gordillo and Pedro Quexos in 1521, and Lucas Vasquez de Ayllon in 1526, all launched their expeditions from Hispaniola. Ponce de Leon discovered Florida from Puerto Rico in 1512. The settlement of Cuba and the conquests of Mexico and Peru, however, shifted the center of Spanish power westward. By midcentury, Mexico had become the seat of the vice-royalty of New Spain and Havana had become the port of rendezvous for the Indies fleet. Thus Tristan de Luna y Arellano launched his expedition from Vera Cruz in 1554 and consequently settled on the wrong side of Florida; Angel de Villefane left from Havana in 1561 to try again to settle at Santa Elena.

Spanish navigators in the early sixteenth century, sailing from Hispaniola before southeasterly trade winds in deep water east of the Bahama Islands, would naturally first encounter the North American continent somewhere along the Georgia–South Carolina coast. This was the experience of Pedro de Salazar, Francesco Gordillo, and Pedro Quexos. Thus, while Hispaniola and Puerto Rico were the bases of Spanish colonial enterprise, Punta de Santa Elena was the most likely place for a Spanish continental foothold. When the center of Spain's Caribbean empire shifted westward to Cuba and Mexico, Santa Elena became more difficult to reach. This was the experience of Tristan de Luna and Angel de Villefane.

Menendez's initial attack on Florida originated from Puerto Rico. Almost by accident he discovered a useable port at St. Augustine and two-way communication by sea with Havana. Despite some political resistance from the governor of Cuba, Menendez, in 1565, shifted his base of support for the Florida colony from Hispaniola and Puerto Rico to Havana. As the Florida settlements began to emerge in the late sixteenth century, the natural base for their support became Cuba, not Hispaniola, and the focal point of Spanish settlement became St. Augustine, not Santa Elena.

A half century of strategic assumptions, however, do not quickly disappear. In 1565, Menendez set about establishing a strong settlement and fortifications at Santa Elena as his king had long desired. And Santa Elena with its huge harbor and safe seaward approaches would still make the best northern haven for Indies ships before the long Atlantic passage to Spain. Menendez reported to the king in October 1565 on the events and conditions in Florida. He was concerned particularly with the influence that the remnants of the French colony would have on the Guale Indians of the Georgia coast and with reports that French corsairs were already lurking in the Santa Elena area. On April 1, 1566, he left St. Augustine with one large ship, two shoal draft frigates, and 150 soldiers to secure the coast as far north as Punta de Santa Elena. Menendez's kinsman, Esteban de Las Alas, an experienced Atlantic seaman, was given command of the flagship. Gonzalo Guyon, who had been the pilot on the Villefane expedition in 1561 and the Rojas expedition of 1564, was the pilot for the small fleet. Guillaume Rouffi, the young French castaway from Ribaut's Port Royal colony in 1563 and the man who had led Hernando Manrique Rojas to the destruction of Charlesfort in 1564, accompanied Menendez as his Indian interpreter. With these experienced counsellors, Menendez explored the Georgia coast and landed at Santa Catalina de Guale on the south end of St. Catherine's Island long enough to learn of a war between the Guale Indians and the Indians of the Santa Elena area. He managed to convince the Georgia Indians to turn over to him two captive Santa Elena Indians. Leaving Guale he sailed north until he found La Punta de Santa Elena and entered its huge harbor.[27]

At Santa Elena, Menendez found the local Indians of Orista busy rebuilding their villages after having been burned out by a recent raid of Guale warriors. The appearance of the captive Indians returning with Menendez's party quickly put the Orista Indians on good terms with the Spanish. The Orista chief entertained Menendez and joined him on the short trip downriver to the site of the former French colony of Charlesfort. There on the southern point of Parris Island, with a commanding view of the harbor at Santa Elena, Menendez erected Fort San Felipe. Antonio Gomez, a master carpenter from Havana who had been temporarily assigned to Menendez to build permanent fortifications in Florida during the summer of 1566, was in charge of the construction of the fort. The stockade was built of earth, stakes, and facings. Six bronze cannons were placed around the earthworks for defense. When the fort was complete, Menendez set out for St. Augustine via the inland waterway with a small party of soldiers and two local Indian guides.[28]

Esteban de Las Alas was left at San Felipe with 110 men. Trouble, however, quickly visited the new settlement. When a supply ship from St. Augustine arrived at Santa Elena in June, sixty men mutinied, commandeered the ship, and set sail for Cuba. Of the remaining forty-five soldiers, twenty deserted to the interior leaving Las Alas with a desperate band of twenty-five men to hold the continent for the king against the expected attacks of French corsairs. The farmers who had been left at Santa Elena to try to develop an independent food supply for the garrison were not successful. They planted on low ground that was subject to saltwater intrusions; the crops that were not destroyed by the tide were ravaged by the abundant wildlife. The Spanish soldiers were in the precarious position of dependency on the meager food supply of the friendly Indians.

In July 1566, relief for the beleaguered garrison arrived under the command of Captain Juan Pardo. Pardo had arrived at St. Augustine aboard the fleet of Sancho de Archiniega fresh from Spain. While Menendez was in Havana, Archiniega dispatched Captain Pardo with three ships and three hundred men to reinforce the new fort at Santa Elena. The arrival of Pardo aboard the galleon, *San Salvadore,* temporarily eased the severe shortage of supplies but was attended with some problems of jurisdiction. Las Alas with his small band was at first reluctant to allow Pardo's overwhelming force access to the fort until he was first assured of his loyalty to the *adelantado* Menendez. Pardo was a professional soldier who quickly perceived the reasons for Las Alas's misgivings. With mutinies and desertions at both Santa Elena and San Mateo and with well-known misgivings about the Florida adventure by the governor of Cuba, Las Alas had good reason to be suspicious. Pardo assured Las Alas that the orders his commander Archeniega had brought from Spain were complimentary of Menendez's efforts and supportive of the *adelantado*'s continued command of the Florida enterprise. Pardo carefully deferred to Governor Las Alas in all matters of command at Santa Elena, and the two soldiers began a healthy working relationship that was to last for several years. Together they set about to reinforce the fort and restore order so that by the time of the arrival of Menendez on August 20, 1566, the *adelantado* was well pleased with the circumstances at Santa Elena.[29]

Menendez stayed at Santa Elena for only eight busy days. Deputations of caciques from the sea islands and the interior came seeking to adopt Menendez as their brother and thereby cement an alliance with the obvious power of Spain. Menendez ordered the expansion of Fort San Felipe to accommodate the larger garrison and left orders to be alert to the danger of French corsairs. Then he reordered the command structure and, reinforced by the royal support brought to America by Archeniega, appointed his kinsman, Esteban de Las Alas, as governor and captain-general of all Florida. Las Alas was to exercise his jurisdiction from Santa Elena which became, in August 1566, the capital of the new province.[30] Thus, Menendez finally accomplished what King Phillip II had been specifically requesting since 1557, that La Punta de Santa Elena should become his "window on the Atlantic."

Menendez also wanted to reconnoiter the interior in order to find additional sources of wealth and supplies for the Florida colony. Accordingly, he left orders for Captain Juan Pardo to take 150 men on an expedition to the interior. Pardo was to assure the many chieftains of the *adelantado's* friendship and fortify the overland route to Mexico. On December 1, 1566, the Pardo expedition left Santa Elena probably proceeding up the Coosawhatchie River and then overland to Cofitachequi. From there he proceeded to the mountains in what is today North Carolina. At the foot of the Appalachian Mountains, he built Fort San Juan near the Indian village of Joada. There he left Sergeant Boyano and a small garrison. Pardo then headed east until he reached the village of Guatari where he received word from Las Alas to return immediately to Santa Elena to help defend Fort San Felipe against French corsairs that had been sighted on the coast. Pardo returned quickly across the midlands until he reached the Coosawhatchie River. He arrived at Santa Elena four months after he had started, having been the first European to explore the backcountry of South Carolina.[31]

The French threat against Santa Elena did not materialize, but Sergeant Boyano, who had been left in charge of Fort San Juan in the Piedmont, had started a war of his own. With his small band of soldiers he moved across northern South Carolina into Georgia where he attacked an Indian village and, according to his report to Las Alas, killed one thousand natives and destroyed their town. Las Alas gave Boyano permission to continue his aggressions. Boyano then reported attacking a large town in the mountains and killing fifteen hundred Indians with injuries to only nine of his own men. After these highly exaggerated exploits, Boyano moved west to the Indian country of Chiaha in western Georgia. There he built another fort for his party to await the arrival of Captain Pardo in the fall of 1567.

Before Pardo could set out on his second expedition from Santa Elena in 1567, *Adelantado* Pedro Menendez de Aviles made another arrival and departure from the port. He had completed the construction of several forts along the coast of Florida, had arranged for supplies for the colony from Governor Osorio of Cuba, and had received word from Sancho de Archiniega of the pleasure of the king on his conquest and settlement of Florida. He was determined to return to Spain to receive his just rewards and accolades and seek additional royal support for his still tenuous enterprise in the New World. Menendez departed from Santa Elena on May 18, 1567, on his triumphant return to Spain.[32]

Pardo began his second expedition into the interior on September 1, 1567. He proceeded up the Savannah River to Cofitachequi and then struck out overland to relieve the garrison at Fort San Juan. When he found it he then marched through the rolling hills of the South Carolina and Georgia piedmont until he found Sergeant Boyano at Chiaha. According to Juan de Vandera, who served on Pardo's second expedition, the entire Spanish force was impressed with the abundance of grain and wild fruit in the backcountry, and Pardo was determined to establish posts in the interior. He placed garrisons in blockhouses at Chiaha, Joada, Cauchi, and Guatari. Pardo then took the remainder of his force and returned to Santa Elena. These wilderness outposts did not last long and their fate is not well known. Only a fifer and his family was able to escape a general massacre by the Indians probably in the spring of 1568.[33]

Conditions at Santa Elena had also deteriorated in Pardo's absence. In spite of the reduction of the garrison at Fort San Felipe and the discovery of a fertile backcountry, the Santa Elena settlement was near starvation during the winter of 1568. Supplies from Mexico arrived at St. Augustine and were distributed at San Mateo on the St. Johns River and at Santa Elena just in time to avert a mutiny. In the midst of this crisis, the long suspected attack by French corsairs finally came. The French force led by Dominique de Gourges bypassed Santa Elena to attack the weakened garrison at San Mateo, site of the former French Fort Caroline. De Gourges overwhelmed the outposts of San Mateo and, on April 14, took the fort. There he executed all his Spanish prisoners to avenge Menendez's massacre of the Huguenots in 1565.[34]

The garrison at Santa Elena hung on through the year, and in 1569 a Jesuit missionary to the Indians, Father Juan Rogel, arrived at the settlement. Rogel was a native of Pamplona and was highly educated with a licentiate of arts and a bachelor of medicine, as well as advanced studies in theology. He had been received into the Jesuit Order at the College of Valencia in 1554. He left Spain for the New World in 1566 and spent some time in Havana studying the Indian language before striking out for Santa Elena. Rogel arrived at the settlement in June 1569 and almost immediately set out for the Indian town of Orista to instruct the natives in the Catholic faith. He spent two busy but ultimately fruitless years among the Indians.[35]

Father Juan Rogel recorded many of the habits of the local Indians of the Santa Elena area. Rogel found that the Indians had a habit of wandering: they rarely stayed in their villages for very long, spent long periods in the woods, and, when he provided them with maize to plant around the village, only two of all the families in the village actually did any planting. These Orista Indians were obviously still a hunting and gathering population, while many of the tribes of the interior had already developed productive systems of agriculture. These local Indians had much more in common with the Guale Indians of the Georgia coast than they had with the tribes of the interior. The Spanish found that training in the Guale language was sufficient for work among the Orista Indians. Indeed, Rogel himself had spent six months at St. Catherine's studying the Guale language before arriving at Santa Elena. The Indians of the lower South Carolina coast also shared marriage habits with the Guale Indians. While most of the families were monogamous, the chiefs and powerful leaders were normally allowed several wives. Father Rogel, of course, condemned this pagan practice among the Orista Indians, thereby alienating himself from the power structure and hampering the Indians' acceptance of Christian dogma. As Rogel was trying to instruct the village in the Christian attitude of monogamy and general restraint, the Indians asked if God had a wife. Rogel answered that of course He did not. The Indians then laughed at him and mocked God, much to the mortification of the good priest. Almost immediately they scattered into the woods and returned to their old ways. This incident apparently cost Rogel his credibility with the Indians who thereafter generally ignored him. At one point Rogel implored them to renounce the devil and his ways, to which the Indians replied they would not; in fact, there was nothing better than the devil and they preferred his ways. This was the final blow. On July 13, 1570, Father Juan Rogel abandoned his mission to the Indians and returned to Santa Elena.[36]

Rogel was at Santa Elena in September 1570 when the ill-fated Spanish expedition to the Chesapeake left after reprovisioning at the port. Pedro Menendez de Aviles had long felt that the Indian country of Axacan or, as the Spanish called it, Bahia de Santa Maria, might be the long sought passage to the Pacific. The expedition led by Captain Juan de Carrerra contained a small body of soldiers, one ship, and four Jesuit priests led by Father Juan Bautista de Segura. The expedition also had a converted Indian captive from the Chesapeake region, Don Luis. At Santa Elena they picked up a young boy named Alonso, the son of one of the Santa Elena settlers who had been trained to assist at mass. The expedition left Santa Elena on August 5, 1570. The ship that transported them stayed at Axacan for a few weeks and then departed, leaving the Jesuits, Don Luis, and young Alonzo to struggle alone. In February, Don Luis fomented a plot to murder the entire party, and only Alonso was saved from the massacre by Don Luis's brother. Alonso eventually returned to Santa Elena to relate the details of the tragedy to Father Rogel and the other settlers.

Rogel then accompanied Menendez on his last tour of Florida after his return from Spain in the spring of 1571. While touring the struggling colony with the *adelantado*, Rogel speculated on the failure of the Jesuit missions among the Indians of Florida. He left Menendez some suggestions which were to form the basis of the more successful operations of the Franciscan friars in Georgia and Florida in the late sixteenth and seventeenth centuries. Rogel noted that the most difficult obstacle to the effective conversion of the Indians was their habit of wandering about in search of food. If they could be forced to settle down and become productive farmers and gardeners then the missionary work would bear more fruit. This procedure must be gradual and patient, Rogel counseled, because the Indians had been pursuing their way of life for thousands of years and could not easily change. Also, the soil of the southeastern coast had proven to be somewhat infertile, and the Indians, as well as the Spanish, were skeptical of its ever supporting a large population. Nevertheless, the settled mission system which was later developed by the Franciscans on the Georgia coast and across north Florida and which lasted until its destruction by the English during Queen Anne's War followed very much the same pattern that Father Juan Rogel had suggested to Pedro Menendez de Aviles in 1571.[37]

This last visit of Menendez to Florida provides a glimpse of the dismal conditions of the colony at Santa Elena. In 1572, the settlement at Santa Elena consisted of a garrison at Fort San Felipe and forty-eight farmers and their families. Many of the Santa Elena settlers were from the region of Asturias on the north central coast of Spain. This was Menendez's homeland, and in characteristic medieval fashion, much of the leadership of the Florida colony were relatives or in-laws of the *adelantado*. These settlers had been encouraged to emigrate to Florida by promising them a grant of farmland as good as that of the Andalusian plain and an assignment of livestock. The farmers planted corn, wheat, oats, pumpkins, chickpeas, beans, and sugar cane. They raised stocks of cows, horses, pigs, sheep, and goats. Their efforts, however, were not very successful. The land was low and subject to flooding, and the soil proved to be sandy and unproductive. In addition, they suffered from several years of heavy frosts which damaged their spring planting. The abundant wildlife, which was such a boon to the woodsmen and sustenance for the southern Indians, was another hazard for the Santa Elena farmers. Worms, moles, and rats devoured the wheat seeds and the freely ranging cattle destroyed the corn once it began to grow. Only melons and pumpkins were successfully harvested on a regular basis. Much of the stock perished or was eaten by the garrison and the settlers. The pigs went wild in the forest and were freely hunted by the Indians. The settlers and the garrison, unable to sustain agriculture and finding little in the way of support from the natives, spent their time looking out to sea across Port Royal Sound in search of supply ships from Havana or St. Augustine. These ships became fewer as the other settlements in Florida experienced similar failures, and finally the settlers began to search the woods for natural foods and scour the shores for oysters.[38]

In addition to the constant problem of food, the colony was experiencing serious political problems. Juan de la Vandera, who had replaced Esteban de Las Alas as governor of Santa Elena, was systematically plundering the colony. He commandeered provisions intended for the use of the whole colony and sold them for his own gain. He had some settlers beaten for refusing supplies for the garrison, and he imprisoned some settlers for asking to be removed to Havana. The frequent petitions of the inhabitants for redress or escape went unheeded.[39]

The complaints against Vandera finally made their way back to Spain where they prompted a full-scale investigation by the Council of the Indies which was frequently looking for an excuse to examine the business of Pedro Menendez in Florida. Martin Diaz, a Santa Elena settler, testified in Madrid on February 4, 1573, that Menendez had not fulfilled his contract to provide the settlers with cattle and that instead of allowing them to colonize the interior lands, he "kept them on the seacoast which is all sand and not fruitful." Diaz reported the outrages of Juan de la Vandera and added that he had ordered one man back to Spain in order to appropriate his wife. Then after Vandera was tired of her he cast her out, much to the mortification of the settlement. This scandalous behavior was confirmed by the testimony of several other witnesses. The investigation embarrassed Menendez just as he was preparing another fleet to return to Florida and reorder the colony. Before the fleet could leave, however, Menendez died in Spain. The great *adelantado* and founder of Florida was buried at Lianes in September 1574. Years later, his remains were removed to the church of San Nicholas in his native Aviles.[40]

The loss of Menendez's leadership and political influence at the Spanish court meant that the Florida colony was largely neglected for the next few years. Don Diego de Valasco was sent to replace Juan de la Vandera as lieutenant governor at Santa Elena. Velasco did little to revive the moribund settlement at Santa Elena and instead tried to enrich himself by appropriating property that belonged to the estate of Menendez. When the king gave a commission to General Hernando de Miranda in 1575 to become captain general of the Florida colony, he set about to end the corruption and establish his own leadership over the colony. On February 24, 1576, General Miranda arrived at Fort San Felipe to conduct his examination of the state of the colony.

Miranda's investigation revealed that Governor Velasco had appropriated considerable sums from the estate of Menendez on the pretext that he had owed at least that much to Velasco before his death. This was enough for General Miranda to have Velasco arrested and replaced as governor of Santa Elena by one of Miranda's own lieutenants, Alonso Solis. The most damaging testimony against Velasco came from his own treasurer, Bartelomeo Martinez, who reported misgivings about the improper procedure employed by Velasco, but was briefly arrested himself on suspicion of complicity.

The report of Martinez also revealed that it was not so much the land but the governmental system the Spanish employed which accounted for the lack of success in the Florida colony. Martinez reported that he had traveled for thirty leagues around Santa Elena and that "this country whereof everyone speaks ill is marvelously good, for where I have gone there are the richest lands for cultivation and cattle-raising; mighty fresh water rivers, great plains and mountain ridges inland, very great indications of there being therein very fine pearls and mines of silver.... in Santa Elena I planted with my own hands grape vines, pomegranate trees, orange and fig trees; wheat, barley, onions and garlic. All the vegetables which grow in Spain were raised in that fort." Martinez asserted that if enough funds were placed at the disposal of loyal governors in Florida, a vast and abundant land could be added to the empire of Spain.[41]

THE ESCAMACU REVOLT AND RESETTLEMENT OF SANTA ELENA, 1576–1587

Before Martinez's report even reached Spain, however, disaster struck the Santa Elena settlement. Alonso Solis made even more serious mistakes in leadership at Santa Elena than his predecessors had. Solis began to tyrannize the Indians and abuse them beyond their endurance. He killed a cacique named Humalo for no apparent reason. Humalo had been to Spain in the company of Menendez de Aviles and had returned to Santa Elena to lead his village, presumably, to a closer understanding of Spanish ways. Solis followed this crime by killing one of the Guale chieftains and hanging a third Indian leader at Santa Elena. These cruelties led the Indians of Guale and Orista (Santa Elena) to rise in rebellion in the summer of 1576.

The rebellion began without warning on June 17, when Ensign Hernando Moyano along with twenty-one soldiers from the garrison of Fort San Felipe were ordered to the village of Escamacu to demand food from the Indians. When the Indians, who were in the middle of a festival, replied that they had none to give him, Ensign Moyano threatened them with his sword. The Indian warriors and their women fled to the woods, and the soldiers warned Moyano that it was dangerous to remain. Moyano laughed at them and ordered them to remain there with fuses of their arquebuses lit in case the Indians should return to attack them. An old cacique then came out of the woods and asked Moyano why he wished to make war on the Indians. Moyano replied that he had no desire to make war, but only to lodge his soldiers with them and obtain food for the garrison at Fort San Felipe. The old cacique then asked why, if he intended no hostile action, had the soldiers kept their fuses lit. The Indians would return to host the Spanish if they would extinguish their fuses, according to the cacique. Moyano then ordered the soldiers to put out their fuses; when the cacique saw that the order was carried out, he gave a great shout. The Indians then rushed from their hiding places in the woods and slew Moyano and twenty of his men.

Only one Spaniard escaped the massacre at Escamacu: Calderon, who reportedly swam eight leagues to bring the news of the disaster to Santa Elena.

Word of the uprising passed quickly from the Oristan Indians in South Carolina to their Guale cousins in Georgia, who seemed equally anxious for revenge against their Spanish overlords. The Guale Indians seized and murdered Governor Pedro Menendez (the Younger) along with several high-ranking officials of the colony who were traveling up the inland passage from St. Augustine to Santa Elena aboard a shallow draft shallop. News of these events to the north encouraged the Timucuan Indians of Florida to rise in revolt, and by the fall of 1576 nearly all the Spanish settlements in the province of "La Florida" were in flames.

At Santa Elena, the warning brought by Calderon had given the settlers time to repair Fort San Felipe. For three days, the soldiers and settlers waited for the expected Indian attack and foraged in the nearby woods for food. During that time, General Hernando Miranda arrived by boat from St. Augustine, having escaped the murderous intentions of the Guale Indians of Georgia. When the son of settler Rodrigo Menca failed to return from a foraging party, General Miranda ordered Captain Solis to take a troop of nine soldiers to search for him. Leaving before dawn on June 21, Solis's party searched the length of Parris Island to determine if the Indians were already on the island and if there was any hope for young Menca. The first warning of the Indian attack came when the now tiny garrison and frightened settlers huddled in Fort San Felipe heard reports of the Spanish arquebuses in the distance, followed by a long and ominous silence. The Indians had surprised and massacred Captain Solis and all but one of his soldiers, meeting out a terrible revenge for his brutal insults.

The next morning more than five hundred Indians attacked the fort by showering it with burning arrows and destroying most of the thatched huts outside the walls. The garrison and settlers responded from the fort with arquebus and cannon fire. The Indians retreated to the safety of the woods and waited for reinforcements. This standoff lasted for two or three days when the women of Santa Elena could stand it no longer. They petitioned the general "with great weeping and wailing, telling him that they were left alone, that their husbands had been killed, that he must take them away from there." General Miranda refused to abandon the fort despite the fact that he had only fifteen or twenty soldiers remaining to oppose a force of five hundred Indian warriors. The desperate women then seized General Miranda and forced him aboard one of the two small boats in the creek by the fort. They rowed him out to the vessel moored in the river on which he had arrived. The general then ordered Fort San Felipe abandoned and all the garrison, settlers, and their belongings removed. The artillery pieces which had defended the settlement for a decade were buried near the fort. As the ship lay at the mouth of Port Royal Sound awaiting a favorable wind to carry them south, the forlorn passengers could see a large number of Indians attack and burn Fort San Felipe and the remnants of the Santa Elena settlement.[42]

The Indian revolt, which had begun at Santa Elena, had spread throughout the province by the fall of 1576. At the close of that year, only the fort at St. Augustine was still holding out. Most of the Santa Elena settlers were sent to Cuba, and the remaining able-bodied men from Fort San Felipe were kept at St. Augustine.[43]

In the summer of 1577, Pedro Menendez Marques returned from Spain with orders from King Phillip II to reoccupy Santa Elena and rebuild the fortifications there. Spanish strategic preoccupation with Santa Elena had not lessened in twenty years, and the king saw his northern bastion of Florida as vital to the protection of his New-World wealth from an increasing array of seaborne marauders. Menendez Marques arrived at Havana in June and reported that the former settlers from Santa Elena were either gone to New Spain or largely unfit for the rigors of rebuilding the settlement in the wilderness. He left for Santa Elena without them and arrived at Port Royal Sound in the late summer. Menendez Marques left the most precise navigational description of the harbor at Santa Elena of any of the Spanish commanders: "It is 40 leagues from the bar of San Mateo [St. Johns River] to Santa Elena which is 32½; the coast runs northeast-southwest and because the shoals extend into the sea from the many good bars . . . [one must] not venture in less than nine or ten fathoms, except there was a wind from the land." These sailing instructions kept the Spanish ships almost ten miles off shore until they "saw land ahead of the prow to the north, which is an island south of the entrance of Santa Elena; it forms a point projecting into the sea, and [is] very thickly wooded." This corresponds to the northwest point of Tybee Island, Georgia, which is the easternmost point of land in the vicinity. The high dunes topped with tall sea pines were evidently visible in advance of the low land surrounding it and were a navigational aid for coastal mariners for three hundred years to come. This landmark was known as La Punta de Santa Elena. The harbor bore north-northeast from that point. Menendez Marques entered the harbor of Santa Elena, being careful to avoid the dangerous bars to the north of the entrance. The harbor itself was "half a league wide with no heavy seas" and had a sounding of ten to twelve fathoms.[44]

Menendez Marques landed at the same place where Fort San Felipe had been located, but chose somewhat higher ground just to the north for the second fort. Fort San Marcos was constructed during the summer of 1577, barely fifty yards from the location of Fort San Felipe. Fort San Marcos was a rectangular fort with a moat on three sides and a small creek on the east. The west wall had a bastion in the center and three cannons mounted on it to protect the side facing the woods where an attack by Indians was most likely to come. The two corners of the fort on the northeast and southeast were also protected by raised bastions each mounted with two cannons that could face either the woods or the river. Within the wall was a long fortified barracks with three more cannons mounted on top. The whole structure was made of earth, heavy timbers, and boards made by the soldiers on the site. Stationed at the fort was a garrison of fifty men. The larger, better armed and better garrisoned Fort San Marcos was to remain the focus of Spanish settlement in the area for the next decade.[45]

While the new fort was still under construction, Menendez Marques had to aggressively reassert Spanish claims to the area. He learned that there were more than one hundred Frenchmen living among the Indians of Guale and Santa Elena, forty of them in one village to the north of the Spanish settlement. They were a constant threat to Spanish control of the area. The Indians of the immediate vicinity seemed to desire peace with them and refused the plans of the Guale Indians and Frenchmen to join in an attack on the new Spanish fort. Before the fort was complete, Menendez Marques went to Guale in two launches with twenty-three men to try to arrange peace with the Indians and to warn the Frenchmen there to flee. The mission failed as the Indians evaded his suggestions and the Frenchmen replied that they were afraid to leave because the Indians would then hang them. With too few forces to both staff Fort San Marcos and mount an offensive against the Guale Indians, Menendez Marques could only express concern over the presence of so many Frenchmen residing among the Indians of the coast. "This has troubled me, owing to the evil seed they sow among those Indians. . . . I would greatly like to break the spirit of those Indians, because, although they have greatly felt the power of Santa Elena, yet they are much on their mettle, as they see that I have not enough men to go hunt for them in their houses."[46]

Even within the vicinity of the Spanish fort, the Indians were found skulking in the woods. Spanish patrols were unable to catch them because when they were spotted they "took to the woods for they are like deer." To add to Menendez Marques's troubles with the natives, at least three large ships were spotted off the coast during the summer months. One was a suspected French vessel which anchored off Port Royal Sound but was blown offshore by a storm during the night. The other two were known corsairs. Menendez Marques knew that to hold Santa Elena for long, he had to make a quick and decisive demonstration of Spanish power. He therefore dispatched parties to search for the Indian village to the north where forty Frenchmen were reportedly living. These Frenchmen, it turned out, were the survivors of the wreckage of a large French ship called *El Principe* in St. Helena Sound. It was in that area that Menendez Marques found the French fort.[47]

Menendez Marques found the large French fort in the woods near a river. It was triangular and sixty-three paces (200 feet) on a side. It was built of earthen embankments topped with a wooden palisade. On each of the corners was a raised bastion. Within the fort were five houses and one large bronze cannon that had been salvaged from the wreck. The fort was deserted because the Indians had already taken the Frenchmen to their villages. Menendez Marques found only the body of one man they later learned was a Spaniard who had been hanged by the French. The Spanish commander burned the French fort and returned to Santa Elena. He began negotiations with the cacique of Cosapoy for the custody of the Frenchmen, but the quarrelsome chief refused his offers three times. Realizing that he could not attack a village of four hundred Indians and forty Frenchmen with his paltry force of eighty-three men, Menendez Marques left the now finished Fort San Marcos under the command of Captain Vincent Gonzales and returned to St. Augustine for supplies and reinforcements.

While in St. Augustine he was delayed in returning to Santa Elena by the arrival of an official deputation of inspectors led by Captain Alvaro Flores. Flores was commissioned to inspect all the military installations, royal arms, garrisons, and supplies in the Florida colony and submit a detailed report to the king. Flores did not arrive at Santa Elena until October 12, 1578, but his report remains the most complete description of the Santa Elena settlement and Fort San Marcos for the entire Spanish period.

Captain Flores began his inspection "in the city and fort of San Marcos, province of Santa Elena" on October 14, 1578. He found there a garrison of fifty-two men. In addition to Captain Vincent Gonzales there was one lieutenant, Tomas Bernaldo, one ensign, one sergeant, and three corporals. Father Francisco del Castillo served as chaplain. Alonso Diaz was the drummer and Gonzalo Vicente was the blacksmith for the fort. All the rest of the garrison were ordinary soldiers. Prudencio de Arrieta, the keeper of supplies, and Juan Mes, the notary for rations, both served as ordinary soldiers. Juan Garcia was the master gunner for artillery. All the ordinary soldiers were equipped with the same arms. Each carried an arquebus with powder flask and bullet, a sword, and a dagger. Rather than the heavy metal breast- and backplates that were standard for the Spanish army in Europe, the soldiers in Florida were equipped with a quilted linen tunic called an *escaupiles* which provided some protection from light arrows and were much more comfortable on long marches in hot weather.

In addition to inspecting the soldiers of the garrison, Captain Flores also reported that the ten pieces of artillery placed around the fort were in good working order and well maintained, although he suggested some changes in their placement because he felt that one of the platforms was not heavy enough to withstand the shock of firing the large cannon placed on it. Flores found the supplies and armaments, including many pikes and javelins, to be well ordered and accounted for. He also inspected the living quarters of the garrison which consisted of many small rooms behind the walls of the fort. Each room was equipped with a raised cot and four nails on which to hang the soldier's arms and clothing. The only entrance to Fort San Marco passed underneath the northeast bastion. In the west wall, there was a "secret door for bringing in and taking out people, when necessary."

Within the walls of the fort was a long building which housed the food storage (including three casks of wine and twelve casks of flour), the armory, and the powder magazine. One end of this long building was used as the central mess hall and living room for the garrison. By the time Flores had completed his thorough inspection, he was well pleased with the condition of Fort San Marcos.[48]

These official deputations, however, had distracted Governor Menendez Marques from his chief concern about the continued residence of the forty Frenchmen with the defiant cacique of Cosapoy. During 1579, Menendez Marques returned to Santa Elena from St. Augustine with supplies and pay for the garrison only to find that the local Indians would not come to the settlement to talk as was customary on the return of the governor. Suspecting that a plot was being hatched and that the French at Cosapoy were behind it, he dispatched a boat with twelve men to talk with the Indians. The natives, however, defied the Spanish party. When the Spanish called for a meeting, the Indians "answered that they did not desire friendship and began to shoot arrows at them." A second party of twenty men was sent by boat to the north but they had no more success than the first and the Indians proved "so rebellious that the soldiers grew angry and the Indians wounded five men." Realizing that peaceful overtures were to no avail, Menendez Marques was determined to personally lead a punitive expedition of sixty men against the village of Cosapoy.[49]

Menendez Marques led the expedition to the river landing where the Indians had challenged the Spanish boats. There, he found a large party of armed warriors who "waited with great courage, so much so that I marvelled, and wounded fourteen of my men, but no one was killed." He landed his forces in the face of this opposition and killed many Indians before they fled to the woods. Menendez Marques then returned to Santa Elena for reinforcements and immediately set out to attack the village of Cosapoy fifteen leagues to the north in the midst of a swamp. The Indians were not expecting the Spanish to return so quickly, and when Menendez Marques's forces attacked the well-fortified town at midnight, they caught the French and Indians unprepared. The Spanish killed forty Indians, captured the family of the rebellious cacique, and burned the village. They also captured two Frenchmen but learned that twelve others had escaped to the woods with the Indians, among whom was a French pilot named Felix who had escaped capture by the Spanish seven years earlier. These men had to be captured; to allow the pilot to return to France would only permit more and larger French expeditions against Santa Elena.[50]

With this demonstrative victory behind him, Menendez Marques began to receive some grudging cooperation from the local Indians. He arranged to trade his women hostages for their French allies when he went to the south to confer with the still-independent Guale tribes. They had already heard of his victory over Cosapoy and readily turned over to the Spanish the leader of the French expedition. This turned out to be a highborn Florentine named Nicholas Strozzi. Strozzi was a very wealthy young adventurer and a cousin of Catherine de Medici. His wealth and political connections were of little use in dealing with the determined Menendez Marques who, following the tradition of his uncle, showed them no mercy. He hanged all of the captured Frenchmen at Santa Elena, leaving only two young men, Julian and Martin, to serve as interpreters. More Frenchmen remained among the Indians of the backcountry, however; later in 1579, a party of Indians from the coast traveled 120 leagues to the west to lay their hands on a group of four Frenchmen who were living with the Cherokee Indians "on the other side of the mountain ridge." The French leader was a young native of Rouen named Captain Roque who was described by Menendez Marques as "very warlike, and of very fine appearance." These Frenchmen were delivered to Santa Elena where they suffered the same fate as Strozzi's party. Though a few Frenchmen remained lurking in the woods, this demonstration of Spanish power at Santa Elena broke the back of the Indian resistance and made the whole southeast unsafe territory for French interlopers.[51]

Nevertheless, the Spanish settlements along the Atlantic coast continued to be harassed by French corsairs throughout the summer of 1580. In the months of July and August, no less than fifteen French ships were seen on the coast between Santa Elena and St. Augustine. The Indians, however, remained friendly to the Spanish and reported these sightings promptly. The most serious incursion was that led by a Corsican named Captain Gil who was killed along with most of his crew in a sharp battle with Menendez Marques on the St. Johns River. These victories by the Spanish at Santa Elena in 1579 and on the St. Johns River in 1580 seem to have discouraged further French expeditions against Florida, and the Santa Elena settlement settled into a few years of well-earned peace.

With these threats swirling around them, the Spanish colonists had been busily rebuilding the settlement at Santa Elena. By 1580, there were more than sixty houses in the village, half of them constructed of wood and mud covered with lime, with flat roofs of lime. The Spanish had learned how to make lime from the abundant oyster shells. By plastering the walls of the houses with it, they made each appear to be fortified. It also made them much less susceptible to attack by burning arrows than the previous thatched huts had been. Menendez

Marques remarked to the king that "we are building the houses in such manner that the Indians have lost their mettle." The years between 1580 and 1586 were relatively peaceful. In the spring of 1579, Menendez Marques had sent Captain Vincente Gonzales from Santa Elena as commander of the ship, *Nuestra Senora de la Concepcion,* to Santo Domingo to load cattle to feed the settlers and try to reestablish the herds at Santa Elena.[52] In addition, corn was successfully planted. Some of the garrison began to make permanent investments at the settlement and began petitioning the king for grants of land in the area. Captain Gutierrez de Miranda, who was serving as *alcalde* of the city of Santa Elena and commander of Fort San Marcos, replaced Menendez Marques as governor of Florida when Menendez Marques returned to Spain in 1581. He made considerable personal investments in the settlement, and in 1580 he had petitioned the authorities for permission to bring a black slave to Santa Elena to serve as the drummer. Despite the relative peace at Santa Elena, political and strategic considerations in the Spanish Main began to shift. Locally, a rivalry developed between Pedro Menendez Marques and Gutierrez de Miranda over control of the Florida colony. Strategically, many Spanish colonial officials began to question the usefulness of maintaining a Spanish bastion so far north on the Atlantic coast, especially since these fixed land fortifications proved so ineffective in halting the continuing parade of French, English, and Dutch pirates who plagued the Spanish Main.

This realization caused the Spanish authorities to shift gradually from a policy of fixed land fortifications to a more mobile defense based on naval patrols. Information provided by a veteran of Santa Elena, Domingo Gonzales, in 1584, first suggested this shift. He pointed out that good relations between the French and Indians threatened the Florida foothold and that if Florida was lost to the French, it would present a serious threat to New Spain. He suggested populating the ports on the Florida coast and guarding them with permanently stationed ships. By April 1585, Juan Mendez was able to report to the king from St. Augustine that the frigates *Santa Clara* and *Santa Elena* were already under construction. In June, Governor Gabriel de Lujan of Cuba wrote to the king that he had dispatched two galleys to the coast of Florida to discourage corsairs. This was the genesis of the system of *guarda costas* which was to be the most effective Spanish defense of Florida for the next two hundred years. This change, however, had long-range consequences for the Santa Elena settlement. The need for a land-based installation at Port Royal Sound naturally diminished as time went on.[53]

Momentous events in the New World, however, forced the Spanish to make their decision sooner than expected. The establishment of Sir Walter Raleigh's Roanoke Colony in North Carolina in 1585 and the arrival of Sir Francis Drake's powerful English fleet in the Caribbean in 1586 posed the most serious threats to Spanish control of Florida since the days of Ribaut. Political and economic circumstances in England were favorable enough by the 1580s to make the idea of an English colonial venture in the New World attractive to many merchants and seamen. Considerable literature was published in the early 1580s relating the New-World adventures and discoveries of such English sea dogs as Sir John Hawkins and Sir Humphrey Gilbert. The English colonial planners were only vaguely aware of the situation of Spain's Florida colony at that time, but intended to stay well north of Spanish territories to avoid a confrontation. Spanish-English relations broke down in 1584 when Queen Elizabeth expelled the Spanish ambassador. The next year, Spanish authorities seized English ships in Spanish ports and open, though undeclared, naval war ensued. These hostilities, which culminated in the defeat of the Spanish Armada in the English Channel in 1588, relieved any hesitation English adventurers like Sir Walter Raleigh might have had about intruding in Spanish territory in North America. The patent for Raleigh's Roanoke Colony was confirmed by Parliament in December 1584, and the next spring the expedition was under way. English documents confirm Spanish fears that one of the chief aims of the Roanoke adventure, as Ribaut's before it, was to establish a fortified base from which privateers could operate against Spanish shipping.[54]

Within a few months of the English arrivals in the western Atlantic, the Spanish were aware of their presence. In July 1585, Governor Gutierrez de Miranda of Santa Elena was told that English corsairs were on their way to Florida. In January 1586, Menendez Marques at St. Augustine reported that ten English ships were off the Florida coast. And by the spring of that year, Spanish authorities were aware that the specific threat to the Caribbean in 1586 was the arrival of the powerful fleet led by Sir Francis Drake. The thinly defended ports of Santa Elena and St. Augustine were prime targets for Drake's privateers.[55]

Drake attacked St. Augustine on June 6, 1586. Governor Menendez Marques in command of the Spanish defenses reported that Drake's fleet consisted of twenty-three large ships and nineteen small ones, clearly the largest armada yet seen on the Florida coast. The Spanish garrison held out for a few days but decided to abandon the fort when the English landed with a force of two thousand men. Drake's men looted the town for seven days, carried off all the moveable goods including the artillery, cut down all the fruit trees, razed the fields, and burned the settlement on their departure. The ships headed north on June 13, bent on wreaking the same havoc at Santa Elena. Drake's fleet passed Santa Elena on June 26. Some accounts reported that Drake was kept offshore by a storm and others say he passed Santa Elena at night and simply could not find the harbor. Whatever the reason, the settlement on Parris Island was spared certain destruction by Drake's fleet. Drake sailed north and stopped at the outer banks long enough to remove the English colony at Roanoke led by Ralph Lane. The English colony was in desperate circumstances by the summer of 1586, and they could hardly refuse what Lane described as "the very hand of God . . . stretched out to take us from thence."[56]

The Spanish in Florida, however, were not aware that the English colony at Roanoke had been removed by Drake. They still feared that it was a powerful nest of pirates permanently located just to the north of Santa Elena. Menendez Marques's first report to the king following the reoccupation of the smoldering ruins of St. Augustine reflected Spanish fears that the English presence in North America was permanent. A Spanish sailor named Pedro Sanchez, who had been captured by Drake's fleet off Hispaniola and who had escaped during the attack on St. Augustine, reported conversations among the English sailors of their plan to reinforce the Roanoke colony. It was this knowledge that prompted Menendez Marques to suggest to the king as early as July 17, 1586, that all the Spanish forces in Florida should be concentrated in one location further south. Captain Juan de Posada, who arrived with reinforcements from Cuba during the summer of 1586, seconded this advice. He noted that Indian reports told of the English colony to the north, and he reflected Spanish fears that English privateers were still searching for Santa Elena. He recommended that the Spanish abandon Santa Elena and rebuild St. Augustine. He pointed out that in order to maintain both Santa Elena and St. Augustine, the crown would have to provide many more soldiers. By September 1586, word of the destruction of St. Augustine had reached the Council of the Indies in Seville. The council agreed with Menendez Marques and Juan de Posada, but suggested a single fortification on the Florida Keys to protect the Bahama Channel.[57]

The only objection to the idea of abandoning Santa Elena came from Gutierrez de Miranda, the commander at Fort San Marcos, who reported in the fall of 1586 on the defensive measures he had taken at Santa Elena and on the passing of Drake's fleet. Miranda pointed out that the fort was in good condition, the houses were well fortified, and the Indians were peaceful. Independent reports in 1587 indicated that the Indians at Santa Elena were indeed friendly and obedient to Gutierrez de Miranda. The plan to concentrate Spanish forces at one location in Florida, however, had reached too high a level in the Spanish bureaucracy. In the summer of 1587, Menendez Marques ordered the removal of Spanish forces from Parris Island over the objections of Gutierrez de Miranda. In June 1587, Menendez Marques led a Spanish expedition up the coast to destroy the Roanoke colony. He searched as far north as 37 degrees latitude, but could find no sign of the English. In August, Maestro de Campo Juan de Tejeda was sent to Santa Elena to dismantle Fort San Marcos and carry the timbers, artillery, supplies, soldiers, and settlers to St. Augustine. This marked the end of the permanent Spanish presence in South Carolina.[58]

The settlers who were evacuated from Santa Elena in 1587 petitioned the king for redress for their losses and asked to be resettled in other parts of the New

World. Tomas Bernaldo de Quiros was a sailor who had served in several Indies fleets, including one commanded by the *Adelantado* Pedro Menendez de Aviles, before being assigned to the Santa Elena colony. He was present when Menendez Marques captured the survivors of the French ship, *El Principe,* near Santa Elena in 1579 and served at both Santa Elena and St. Augustine during the 1580s. He asked to be resettled in New Spain.[59]

One of the most experienced veterans of the Florida colony was Domingo Gonzales, who served in and out of Florida for twenty-three years. He claimed to be the first soldier to learn the Indian language. He was evacuated when the Indians burned Santa Elena in 1576 and resettled in New Spain. He was ordered to return after the building of Fort San Marcos to help pacify the Indians. He had hoped to make considerable investments at Santa Elena, but the tenuous military situation and a rivalry with Menendez Marques discouraged him. He later returned to New Spain.[60]

Martin de Estueta Lezcano was a master carpenter who had come to Florida with Pedro Menendez de Aviles and had fought the French at San Mateo in the company of Captain Martin Ochoa. As a master carpenter, he had been instrumental in building the forts at St. Augustine and Santa Elena. While in Florida he had sent his wife and children back to Spain, but their ship had been captured by pirates. Though his family was freed, he lost all his property. He asked to be resettled in Peru as a *gentilhombre.* His request was granted.[61]

Gutierrez de Miranda also petitioned for redress for his losses at Santa Elena. He detailed his long service in Florida, pointed out again his objections to the decision to abandon the northern post and remarked on his commendable record in maintaining friendly relations with the once dangerous Indians of the Santa Elena region. He asked that he be compensated for his financial losses at Santa Elena. The reward for his service came when he was appointed governor of Florida over his rival Menendez Marques in 1589.[62]

INDIAN MISSIONS AND THE ARRIVAL
OF THE ENGLISH, 1587–1607

Though the permanent Spanish settlement at Santa Elena was abandoned, the influence of the Spanish on the Indians of the region lingered for many generations. The Spanish missionary work among the American natives, begun by the Jesuits in 1568, was carried forward by the Franciscans after 1573.

The Spanish policy toward the Indians became more sensible as their experience at Santa Elena advanced. Initially, the Spanish tried to impose their will on the Indians by force such as the tactics employed by Pardo and Boyano in the Georgia and South Carolina backcountry in 1567 and by Governors Solis and Menendez Marques at Santa Elena in 1575 and 1579. This behavior, however, proved very costly when the Indians revolted in 1576 and destroyed the colony.

Even the Jesuit missionaries, who intended no harm to the Indians, incurred their displeasure by trying to impose their Christian dogma in too imperious a manner. The Indians who resisted the Spanish authority seemed duplicitous and untrustworthy to the Spanish. Perhaps the worst Spanish attitude toward the Indians was expressed by Escalante Fontaneda in 1575. Stating that the Indians would never submit to Spanish rule in Florida "less they will become Christians," he recommended the following policy: "Let the Indians be taken in hand gently, inviting them to peace; then putting them under decks, husbands and wives together, sell them among the islands. . . . In this way there could be management of them and their number diminished."[63]

Such a genocidal policy was not adopted in Florida, however, and in time the Spanish authorities developed a system which the Indians found to be generally tolerable. To the credit of the Spanish colonists, they always adhered to the royal prohibition against Indian slavery which had been part of every charter for the colonization of the mainland since the days of Lucas Vasquez de Ayllon. The shift in Spanish policy toward the Indians was first suggested by the Jesuit Father Juan Rogel and later put into practice by the Franciscans. Rogel had reported to Pedro Menendez de Aviles that the best way to pacify the Indians was to settle them in mission communities and teach them more productive methods of agriculture and gardening. He thought that this policy would cause them to settle into village life and cease their wandering ways: they could then become good Christians and develop the habits of civilization. This settlement policy could be implemented in a gentle and humane manner so as not to arouse the Indians' warlike inclinations. Thus, Rogel thought, it would be better accomplished by priests than soldiers.[64]

The wisdom of Rogel's advice to Menendez became apparent to the colonial authorities in Florida over the years. They realized it too late to save the Jesuits from the massacre at Axacan and too late to prevent the disastrous rebellion of 1576. In 1573, however, Spanish policy toward the Indians began to change with the arrival of Franciscan friars at Santa Elena sponsored by Pedro Menendez himself, probably for the purpose of putting Juan Rogel's ideas into action. Diego de Velasco, the powerful viceroy of New Spain, reported to the king in 1575 that the work of these first Franciscan missionaries was already having a beneficial effect. The Indians in Florida were in a better mood toward the Spanish than ever before, and the cacique of Guale and his wife had traveled to Santa Elena in 1574 to receive baptism. These first Franciscans, however, did not stay at Santa Elena after they learned of the death of their sponsor, the *adelantado.* Shortly afterward, their good start was aborted by the highhanded behavior of Governor Alonso Solis.[65]

The establishment of a Franciscan friary in Havana in 1577 opened a new era of missionary influence in Florida. Franciscans were active in Florida in that year. When Captain Alvaro Flores came to Santa Elena as a visitor in the fall of 1578, he reported the presence of Father Francisco del Castillo, a native of Marchena, as the chaplain of the garrison of Fort San Marcos. Mendendez Marques expressed concern over the lack of support from the leaders of the Franciscan order in New Spain who could withdraw their friars from Florida whenever they felt they were needed in other parts of the New-World empire. In 1584, there were still only two Franciscans in Florida: one in St. Augustine and one in Santa Elena. Menendez Marques was anxious to proceed with the task of christianizing the Indians, but could not without more support from the missionary orders.[66]

The real expansion of the Franciscan mission system in Florida began with the arrival, in the summer of 1584, of Father Alonso Reynoso and two other Franciscans. Father Reynoso returned to Spain in 1586 to recruit more friars and more support from the crown for the missionary enterprise. Reynoso and the thirteen friars he hired landed at St. Augustine on October 4, 1587, and immediately set out to establish their mission villages on the coast. By 1588, they had established five active mission villages: Nombre de Dios on the upper St. Johns River, San Juan on Talbot Island, San Pedro on Cumberland Island, San Sebastian on Jekyll Island, and San Antonio on St. Simon's Island. Later, the mission of Santa Caterina at the Indian town of Guale on St. Catherine's Island became the center of Franciscan activity on the Georgia coast. All this admirable work, of course, came too late to be of any benefit to the Santa Elena settlement, which had been abandoned the year before.

These Franciscan missions became centers of Indian activity on the coast, and the christianizing process worked for a decade almost as Father Juan Rogel had envisioned it. Not only did the Christian Indians gather around the missions, but also several Franciscans were dispatched to the mainland villages to minister to the more heavily populated towns. It was at the inland town of Tolomato on the Altamaha River in 1597 that a young prince of the Yemassee tribe named Juanillo aroused the latent resentment of many of the Indians against the accumulated insults of the Christian Spaniards toward the Indian's traditional beliefs and customs. Juanillo specifically objected to the attempts of the Franciscans to prohibit the pagan custom of polygamy among the leaders of the tribes. The Juanillo revolt of 1597 was a mortal blow to the permanent missions on the Georgia sea islands. Most of the Franciscan missionaries were massacred, and the missions, as far south as Cumberland Island, were laid waste. The loyalty of the Timucuan Indians of north Florida stemmed the tide of the rebellion and gave the Spanish at St. Augustine time to organize a counterattack. Finally, a party of Timucuan Indians hunted down the rebel prince and his coconspirators in central Georgia and returned with his scalp to St. Augustine. This ended the Juanillo revolt and began a historic enmity between the Timucuan Indians of Florida, who remained loyal to the Spanish throughout the seventeenth and eighteenth centuries, and the Guale or Yemassee Indians of Georgia and later South Carolina, whose traditional hatred of the Spanish and the Timucuans was exploited in the next century by the Scottish and English colonists in the Port Royal area.[67]

After the destruction of the Georgia missions in 1597, the Spanish began to concentrate their mission and agricultural efforts westward across north Florida to the Gulf of Mexico. During the seventeenth century, these north Florida missions became the centers of flourishing Indian villages based on the traditional Spanish activity of cattle raising and the continuing labors of the Franciscan friars. With their efforts redirected in the seventeenth century, and with the Florida colony for the first time developing a successful indigenous economy, Spanish attention toward the sea islands of Georgia and South Carolina became sporadic.[68]

While trying to settle down the Indians and recover one of the captive priests, a Spanish party led by Captain Ecija traveled to Santa Elena in 1598 with gifts to buy the aid, or at least neutrality, of the cacique of Escamacu. The chief's warriors delivered to Ecija four scalps taken in a raid against the Guale rebels and brought the welcome news that one of the Franciscans of the Guale missions, Father Avila, was still alive. Eventually the Spaniard secured his release. Thus, the Indians of the Santa Elena area remained on good terms with the Spanish twelve years after the evacuation of the settlement on Parris Island.

Franciscan missionaries slowly returned to the friendly villages of the Georgia coast during the next few years under the encouragement of the expansionist governor at St. Augustine, Gonzalo Mendez de Canzo. It was Canzo who first encouraged the westward thrust of the Spanish effort with his scheme to plant a major settlement at Tama, 200 miles to the west. Tama was to be the first step in a fortified land route all the way to New Spain. In addition, Canzo revived Spanish interests to the north by proposing a settlement at Jacan (Roanoke). He believed he had evidence in 1600 that the English colony still existed in that vicinity. His evidence came chiefly from the testimony of a Catholic Irishman named David Glavin who was a soldier at St. Augustine.

Glavin was a sailor aboard a French ship out of Nantes in 1584 when he was captured at sea by Sir Richard Grenville. Grenville sailed to the New World and left Glavin off at the newly founded Roanoke Colony in 1585. The next year, Glavin, along with the rest of the colony, was picked up by Sir Francis Drake after he had burned St. Augustine and bypassed Santa Elena. He was taken to England and shipped out the next year with Drake's English fleet sent to harass the Spanish main. Glavin managed to escape from the English at Puerto Rico. He was subsequently pressed into service as a Spanish soldier and assigned to the presidio at St. Augustine in 1595. It was his belief that the second expedition of the English had successfully planted a colony at Roanoke. This belief that the Roanoke colony still existed was erroneously confirmed by information from the cacique of Escamacu at Santa Elena. Canzo proposed to the king that, in addition to a settlement at Tama, Spanish forces should seek out and destroy the English colony at Jacan and plant one of their own. This grand design of Governor Canzo's, stretching from the Chesapeake to Mexico, could not be accomplished with the paltry force of three hundred men at St. Augustine. It would require, Canzo estimated, one thousand soldiers with supporting ships and supplies. The funds were never granted by the crown, and Canzo was replaced as governor of St. Augustine in 1603.

His replacement, Pedro de Ibarra, continued Canzo's concern for the northern missions and, in November and December 1604, conducted a tour of inspection of the Spanish domains to the north. He traveled through the Timucuan country and into the heart of the now pacified Guale country. Ibarra entertained the chiefs and presented gifts in exchange for their professions of adherence to the crown and the church. He officially re-established the missions of Sapelo Island and St. Catherine's Island, which was as far north as his party traveled. At St. Catherine's Island he received the obedience of most of the Guale caciques and learned that many of the young chiefs who were subordinate to the cacique of Aluste had renounced their allegiance to him and declared their allegiance to the cacique of Orista, "a good Indian who did not abuse them nor speak harshly to them and who was, besides, the heir of Aluste." Ibarra ordered these young caciques to return to their rightful allegiance to the old cacique of Aluste and bring their complaints to the governor at St. Augustine in the future.[69]

In 1605, the armed merchant vessel *Castor and Pollux* appeared on the coast near Santa Elena. Through coastal reports and reconnaissance patrols of two Spanish frigates, *San Josephe* and *Asuncion,* the Spanish learned that the ship was lying in St. Helena Sound, known as the Bay of Shoals to the Spanish. The *Castor and Pollux* was a joint English and French expedition commissioned by the French King Henry IV to establish trading contacts along the American coast. In St. Helena Sound they were trading for sassafras root, believed by the European medical community of that time to have great medicinal powers. The Spanish suspected they had less peaceful purposes. The two Spanish frigates, led by Captain Fernandez Eciga of the St. Augustine garrison, defeated and captured the *Castor and Pollux* in St. Helena Sound. They returned the ship and its crew to St. Augustine for imprisonment and interrogation. It was learned that one of the stops of the *Castor and Pollux* was to have been at "Crotuan" where they thought some remnant of the lost colony still survived. Captain Fernandez Eciga was to lead two more expeditions along the coast north of Florida. In 1606, he coasted northward in search of the "lost colony" but failed to find any trace of the English. In 1609, after hearing reports of a new English settlement at Bahia Santa Maria, Captain Eciga again headed north along the coast. On July 24, he spied the ship of Samuel Argall in the James River of Virginia. Eciga took no action against the English, but he was the first Spanish commander to confirm the location of the Jamestown settlement.[70] It was a little noticed, but significant, turning point in early American history. The English had come to stay.

In 1606, the most colorful event of the early Spanish missions among the sea islands occurred: the visit of Bishop Juan de las Cabezas Altamirano of Cuba. The bishop, having been persuaded of the benefit to the faith of a visit to the Florida frontier, arrived at St. Augustine just before Easter in 1606. After observing Holy Week at the capital, he proceeded with an impressive party up the inland passage to visit the missions and confirm the faithful as far north as St. Catherine's Island in the heart of Guale. During this ceremonial procession throughout the province, Bishop Altamirano confirmed 2,074 Indians, 756 of them natives of Guale. None, however, came from as far away as Santa Elena.

Bishop Altamirano's visit renewed missionary activity, and more Franciscans arrived in 1608, 1612, 1615, and 1617. But their attentions were directed westward where the mission villages were able to develop a more self-sustaining economic system. While the western mission villages began to raise cattle successfully in the seventeenth century, the Spanish were reluctant to introduce cattle to the Atlantic coast missions for fear that the cattle would eat the Indians' gardens and corn patches and that the cattle would be stolen by the non-Christian Indians of the interior. Thus, while the western missions became self-supporting and provided much needed beef for the garrison and settlers at St. Augustine, the Guale missions were always an expense. This naturally discouraged further expansion to the north, and the Santa Elena area was ignored except for occasional military patrols and indirect contacts with the Cusabo Indians of Orista through their Guale cousins. The name, however, remained prominent as the entire Florida frontier was made into the Franciscan ecclesiastical province of Santa Elena in 1612.[71]

The last attempt to revive the Spanish foothold at Santa Elena was made in 1618 by Father Luis Jeronimo de Ore. Father Ore was sent on an official visitation of the ecclesiastical province of Santa Elena, which comprised all of Spanish Florida, but whose northernmost permanent mission was at Guale on St. Catherine's Island. In his inspection he was very impressed with the possibility of extending the missionary activity even further to the west and north. To anchor the northern missions, he proposed that the presidio at Santa Elena be rebuilt so that the small villages of Guale and Orista could be reduced to one large town to allow more efficient use of the limited number of Franciscan priests available for duty in the New World.[72] Father Ore's suggestion was never acted upon. The Spanish withdrawal from South Carolina was permanent.

NOTES

1. Paul E. Hoffman, "A New Voyage of Discovery: Pedro de Salazar's Visit to the 'Land of the Giants,'" *Florida Historical Quarterly* 58 (1979/80): 415–26; C. H. Haring, *The Spanish Empire in America* (New York: Harcourt, Brace and World, 1947), 7–8.

2. Peter Martyr, *De Orbe Novo*, 22 vols., trans. Augustus Francis MacNutt (New York: G. P. Putnam's, 1912), 2: 56; Woodbury Lowery, *The Spanish Settlements Within the Present Limits of the United States 1513–1561* (New York: Russell and Russell, 1959), 153–55; Edward G. Bourne, *Spain in America 1450–1580* (New York: Harper, 1906), 138; David B. Quinn, ed., *New American World: A Documentary History of North America to 1612,* 5 vols. (New York: Arno, 1979), 1: 248. The authoritative new work on this era is Paul E. Hoffman, *New Andalucia and a Way to the Orient: The American Southeast during the Sixteenth Century* (Baton Rouge: Louisiana State University Press, 1990), 3–11.

3. Martyr, *De Orbe Novo,* 2:258–67; Paul E. Hoffman, "The Chicora Legend and Franco-Spanish Rivalry in La Florida," *Florida Historical Quarterly* 64 (1984): 419–38; Lowery, *Spanish Settlements,* 161–62; Alfonso Trueba, *Expediciones a la Florida* (Mexico City: Editoreal Campeador, 1955), 9–10.

4. Hoffman, *New Andalucia,* 54; Quinn, ed., *New American World,* 1: 258.

5. Edward McCrady, *The History of South Carolina under the Proprietary Government, 1670–1719* (1897; rpt., New York: Russell and Russell, 1969), 42; William J. Rivers, *A Sketch of the History of South Carolina* (Charleston: McCarter, 1856), 15–18; "Memoire of Fontenada" (typescript), 56–57, Buckingham Smith Collection, P. K. Yonge Library, Gainesville, Fla.

6. Lowery, *Spanish Settlements,* 166; David Duncan Wallace, *The History of South Carolina,* 4 vols. (New York: American Historical Society, 1934), 1: 6–31; Paul Quattlebaum, *The Land Called Chicora: The Carolinas under Spanish Rule with French Intrusions, 1520–1670* (Gainesville: University of Florida Press, 1956), 23; J. G. Johnson, "A Spanish Settlement in Carolina, 1526," *Georgia Historical Quarterly* 7 (December 1923): 339–45. The most authoritative voice is Hoffman, *New Andalucia,* 70, who establishes the St. Catherine's site.

7. David B. Quinn, *North America from Earliest Discovery to First Settlement: The Norse Voyages to 1612* (New York: Harper and Row, 1975), 148, and Quinn, ed., *New American World,* 1: 260; Carl O. Sauer, *Sixteenth Century North America: The Land and the People as Seen by the Europeans* (Berkeley: University of California Press, 1971), 73.

8. Lowery, *Spanish Settlements,* 165–68; Quinn, ed., *New American World,* 1: 260–73; Martyr, *De Orbe Novo,* 2: 254–71; Sauer, *Sixteenth Century North America,* 72–76; Andreas Gonzalez Barcia, *Ensayo Cronologico, Para la Historia General de la Florida De Sole ano de 1512,* trans. Anthony Kerrigan (Gainesville: University of Florida Press, 1951), 7–8; Hoffman, *New Andalucia,* 60–83.

9. Garcilaso de la Vega, *The Florida of the Inca: A History of the Adelantado, Hernando de Soto, Governor and Captain General of Florida and Other Heroic Spanish and Indian Cavaliers,* trans. and ed. John G. Varner and Jeannette J. Varner (Austin: University of Texas Press, 1951), 302; Sauer, *Sixteenth Century North America,* 166–68; Herbert Bolton and Mary Ross, *The Debatable Land: A Sketch of the Anglo-Spanish Contest for the Georgia Country* (Berkeley: University of California Press, 1925), 6; Wallace, *History of South Carolina,* 1: 30–33; John R. Swanton, *Indians of the Southeastern United States* (Westwood, Conn.:

Greenwood Press, 1946), 157; Quinn, ed., *New American World,* 2: 90–187. For the location of Cofitachequi, see Charles Hudson, Marvin T. Smith, and Chester B. DePratter, "The Hernando DeSoto Expedition: From Apalachee to Chiaha," *South Carolina Institute of Archaeology and Anthropology Notebook 19* (Columbia: South Carolina Institute of Archaeology and Anthropology, 1987), 18–28.

10. Herbert R. Priestley, ed., *The Luna Papers. Documents Relating to the Expedition of Don Tristan de Luna y Arrellano for the Conquest of La Florida in 1559–1561* (Deland: Florida Historical Society, 1928), 1: 177–79; La Relacion del Ingles, October 1560, Calendar of the Stetson Collection, P. K. Yonge Library, Gainesville, Fla.

11. Priestley, ed., *Luna Papers,* 1: 123; Luis de Velasco to Tristan de Luna, August 20, 1560, Calendar of the Stetson Collection, P. K. Yonge Library, Gainesville, Fla.

12. Priestley, ed., *Luna Papers,* 2: 16–17.

13. Priestley, ed., *Luna Papers,* 1: 195.

14. Priestley, ed., *Luna Papers,* 1: 123.

15. Herbert R. Priestley, *Tristran de Luna: Conquistador of the Old South* (Glendale, Calif.: Arthur Clark, 1936), 191–95; Quinn, ed., *New American World,* 2: 271–75.

16. Paul Gaffarel, *Histoire de la Floride Française* (Paris: Librarie de Fermin-Didot, 1875), 143; Charles Andre Julien, *Les Voyages de Decouverte et les Premiers Etablissements* (Paris: Presses Universitaires de France, 1948), 222–304.

17. Jean Ribaut, "The Whole and True Discoverie of Terra Florida," in Quinn, *New American World,* 2: 285–94; also in William A. Courtenay, ed., *The Genesis of South Carolina, 1562–1670* (Columbia: State Printing Co., 1907); Stefan Lorant, ed., *The New World: The First Pictures of America Made by John White and Jacques Le Moyne and Engraved by Theodore De Bry; with Contemporary Narratives of the Huguenot Settlements in Florida, 1562–1565, and the Virginia Colony, 1585–1590* (New York: Duell, Sloan and Pearce, 1946), 6–8; Quattlebaum, *Land Called Chicora,* 45–49; Julien, *Voyages de Decouverte,* 229.

18. Gaffarel, *Histoire de la Floride,* 20–40; Lorant, ed., *New World,* 8; Quattlebaum, *Land Called Chicora,* 49–51; Woodbury Lowery, "Jean Ribaut and Queen Elizabeth," *American Historical Review* 9 (1904): 456–59; Quinn, ed., *New American World,* 2: 307–08.

19. Manrique Rojas, "Report on the French Settlement in Florida in 1564" (typescript), July 9, 1564, P. K. Yonge Library, Gainesville, Fla.; also in Quinn, ed., *New American World,* 2: 308–16.

20. Julien, *Voyages de Decouverte,* 234–36; Lorant, ed., *New World,* 10; Paul E. Hoffman, "Diplomacy and the Papal Donation, 1493–1585," *Americas* 30 (1973): 170–71.

21. Eugene Lyons, *The Enterprise of Florida: Pedro Menendez de Aviles and the Spanish Conquest of 1565–1568* (Gainesville: University of Florida Press, 1976), 19–38; Gonzalo Solis de Meras, *Pedro Menendez de Aviles: memorial,* trans. Jeannette Thurber Connor (Gainesville: University of Florida Press, 1964), 39–64. On the way to the Orient, see Hoffman, *New Andalucia,* 232–33.

22. "Gov. Carasa (Puerto Rico) to King," April 14, 1565; "Council of the Indies to King," May 12, 1565; "Council of the Indies to Casa de Contratacion," August 14, 1565; "Information Presented to Alonso de Caceres . . . by . . . Luis Hernandez, Pilot of the ship San Antonio," August 30, 1565, Calendar of the Stetson Collection, P. K. Yonge Library, Gainesville, Fla.; Lorant, ed., *New World,* 11–20.

23. Lyons, *Enterprise of Florida,* 88–99.

24. Lorant, ed., *New World,* 70–86, 98–116; Charles E. Bennett, *Laudonniere and Fort Caroline: History and Documents* (Gainesville: University of Florida Press, 1964), 13–41; Lyons, *Enterprise of Florida,* 101–30; Barcia, *Ensayo Cronologico,* 82–97; Quattlebaum, *Land Called Chicora,* 53–56; Quinn, ed., *New American World,* 2: 389–463.

25. Lorant, ed., *New World,* 30–31; Rene de Laudonniere, *A Notable History Containing Four Voyages Made by Certain French Captains unto Florida,* ed. Martin Basanier, trans. Richard Hakluyt, facsimile of the edition printed in London in 1587 with a survey by Thomas R. Adams (Larchmont, N.Y.: Henry Stevens and Sons, 1964), viii–xvi.

26. Lyons, *Enterprise of Florida,* 131; Solis de Meras, *Pedro Menendez de Aviles,* 129–30.

27. Lyons, *Enterprise of Florida,* 153–57; Bartolome Barrientos, *Pedro Menendez de Aviles, Founder of Florida,* trans. Anthony Kerrigan (Gainesville: University of Florida Press, 1965), 101; Herbert E. Bolton, ed., *Arredondo's Historical Proof of Spain's Title to Georgia* (Berkeley: University of California Press, 1925), 9; "Probanza of Gonzalo Gayon," July 5, 1566, Calendar of the Stetson Collection, P. K. Yonge Library, Gainesville, Fla.

28. Lyons, *Enterprise of Florida,* 157; Barrientos, *Pedro Menendez de Aviles,* 102–3; Barcia, *Ensayo Cronologico,* 117; Quattlebaum, *Land Called Chicora,* 62–63.

29. Lowery, *Spanish Settlements,* 260–61; Lyons, *Enterprise of Florida,* 167; Barcia, *Ensayo Cronologico,* 128; Quattlebaum, *Land Called Chicora,* 65.

30. Lyons, *Enterprise of Florida,* 166; J. G. Johnson, "The Spanish Period of Georgia and South Carolina History, 1566–1702," *Bulletin of the University of Georgia* (May 1923): 2.

31. Chester B. DePratter, Charles Hudson, and Marvin Smith, "The Route of Juan Pardo's Explorations in the Interior Southeast, 1566–1568," *Florida Historical Quarterly* 61 (1982/83): 125–58. See also "Memoria de Juan de la Vandera en que se hace Relacion de los Lugares y Tierra de la Florida por donde el Capitan Juan Pardo entro a Descubrir Camino para Nueva Espana por los Anos de 1566–1567," in B. F. French, ed., *Historical Collections of Louisiana and Florida* (New York: Albert Mason, 1875), 289–93; Bolton, ed., *Arredono's Historical Proof,* 336–37.

32. Lyons, *Enterprise of Florida,* 182.

33. DePratter, Hudson, and Smith, "The Route of Juan Pardo's Explorations," 142–58; "Juan Pardo Narrates His Conquest of the Interior," in Eugenio Ruidaz y Caravia, "La Florida, Su Conquista y Colonizacion por Pedro Menendez de Aviles" (Madrid, 1893) (translated typescript), 2: 154–60, P. K. Yonge Library, Gainesville, Fla.

34. Lyons, *Enterprise of Florida,* 198–201; Lowery, *Spanish Settlements,* 324–33.

35. Felix Zubillaga, *La Florida: La Mision Jesuitica y la Colonizacion Espanola* (Rome: Institutum Historicum, 1941), 340, 370, 375, 421; Ruben Vargas, "The First Jesuit Missions in Florida," *Historical Records and Studies: U.S. Catholic Historical Society* (New York: U.S. Catholic Historical Society, 1935), 60; Lowery, *Spanish Settlements,* 270.

36. "Juan Rogel's Account of the Florida Mission, 1569–1570" (typescript), P. K. Yonge Library, Gainesville; see also "Father Juan Rogel to Pedro Menendez de Aviles," December 9, 1570, in Ruidaz y Caravia, "La Florida."

37. Lowery, *Spanish Settlements,* 359–66, 372.

38. Barcia, *Ensayo Cronologico,* 156; Lowery, *Spanish Settlements,* 367–86.

39. Lowery, *Spanish Settlements*, 376.

40. Jeannette Thurber Connor, ed. and trans., *Colonial Records of Spanish Florida: Letters and Reports of Governors, Deliberations of the Council of the Indies, Royal Decrees and Other Documents*, 2 vols. (Deland: Florida State Historical Society, 1925–1930), 1: 85; Quattlebaum, *Land Called Chicora*, 69–70.

41. Connor, ed., *Colonial Records*, 1: 147–53, 239, 246–47.

42. Connor, ed., *Colonial Records*, 1: 193–203.

43. Bolton and Ross, *The Debatable Land*, 8–15.

44. Connor, ed., *Colonial Records*, 1: 327, 329; Quattlebaum, *Land Called Chicora*, 74.

45. Connor, ed. and trans., *Colonial Records*, 2: 153–57; Bolton, *Arredondo's Historical Proof*, 336; Robert L. Stevenson and Stanley South, "Bienvenido a Santa Elena: Report on the Santa Elena Site on Parris Island, South Carolina," paper presented at 16th Annual Military History Conference of the Council on America's Military Past, Charleston, South Carolina, 1982.

46. Connor, ed., *Colonial Records*, 2: 81–83.

47. Connor, ed., *Colonial Records*, 2: 89.

48. Connor, ed., *Colonial Records*, 2: 157–63.

49. Connor, ed., *Colonial Records*, 2: 253; "Informacion de Tomas Bernaldo," March 24, 1579, Calendar of the Stetson Collection, P. K. Yonge Library, Gainesville, Fla.

50. Connor, ed., *Colonial Records*, 2: 195.

51. Connor, ed., *Colonial Records*, 2: 283; "Service of Captain Vincente Gonzales," March 29, 1579, Calendar of the Stetson Collection, P. K. Yonge Library, Gainesville, Fla.

52. "Royal Cedula," June 10, 1579; "Cedulario," February 9, 1580; "Juan Menendez to King," April 6, 1584; "Governor Gabriel Lujan to King," June 5, 1585; and "Gutierrez de Miranda to King," August 8, 1585, Calendar of the Stetson Collection, P. K. Yonge Library, Gainesville, Fla.

53. David B. Quinn, ed., *The Roanoke Voyages 1584–1590: Documents to Illustrate the English Voyages to North America under the Patent Granted to Walter Raleigh in 1584* (Nendeln, Liechtenstein: Kraus Reprint, 1955), 6, 118.

54. "Informacion de Gutierrez de Miranda," July 12, 1585, and "Diego Fernandez de Quinones to King," January 18, 1586, Calendar of the Stetson Collection, P. K. Yonge Library, Gainesville, Fla.

55. "Pedro Menendez Marques to King," June 17, 1586, and "Same to Same," July 16, 1586, Calendar of the Stetson Collection, P. K. Yonge Library, Gainesville, Fla.; Quinn, ed., *Roanoke Voyages*, 292.

56. "Pedro Menendez Marques to King," July 17, 1586; "Testimony of Sailor Pedro Sanchez," September 1586; "Juan de Posada to King," Sept. 2, 1586, and "Consejo de Indias to King," September 10, 1586, Calendar of the Stetson Collection; "Pedro Menendez Marques to King," August 31, 1586, Buckingham Smith Collection, P. K. Yonge Library, Gainesville, Fla.

57. "Report of Gutierrez de Miranda," November 11, 1586; "Reply from Gutierrez de Miranda," August 16, 1587, and "Report of Pedro Menendez Marques," June 22, 1587, Calendar of the Stetson Collection, P. K. Yonge Library, Gainesville, Fla.

58. "Tomas Bernaldo de Quiros to King," July 19, 1582, and "Same to Same," September 6, 1580, Calendar of the Stetson Collection, P. K. Yonge Library, Gainesville, Fla.

59. "Informacion de Domingo Gonzales," 1584, Calendar of the Stetson Collection, P. K. Yonge Library, Gainesville, Fla.

60. "Martin Estueta Lezcano to King," March 29, 1585, Calendar of the Stetson Collection, P. K. Yonge Library, Gainesville, Fla.

61. "Gutierrez de Miranda to Consejo de Indias," August 20, 1580, Calendar of the Stetson Collection, P. K. Yonge Library, Gainesville, Fla.

62. John Tate Lanning, *The Spanish Missions of Georgia* (Chapel Hill: University of North Carolina Press, 1935), 14–15; Charles W. Arnade, *Florida on Trial, 1593–1602* (Miami: University of Miami Press, 1959), 26.

63. "Cedulario," August 10, 1574, Calendar of the Stetson Collection, P. K. Yonge Library, Gainesville, Fla.; Vargas, "First Jesuit Missions," 81–95; Lowery, *Spanish Settlements*, 354.

64. Maynard Geiger, *The Franciscan Conquest of Florida, 1573–1618*, vol. 1 of Catholic University of America Studies in Hispanic-American History (Washington, D.C.: Murray and Heister, 1936), 39–40.

65. Lanning, *Spanish Missions*, 66–67; Geiger, *Franciscan Conquest*, 46.

66. Lanning, *Spanish Missions*, 82–110; Geiger, *Franciscan Conquest*, 71–116.

67. Robert A. Matier, "The Spanish Missions of Florida: The Friars vs. the Governors in the Golden Age," Ph.D. diss., University of Washington, 1972, 64–88.

68. Geiger, *Franciscan Conquest*, 127–28.

69. Lanning, *Spanish Missions*, 136, 144–45.

70. Quinn, ed., *New American World*, 5: 108–27, 141–51.

71. Geiger, *Franciscan Conquest*, 237; Lanning, *Spanish Missions*, 153, 160.

72. Geiger, *Franciscan Conquest*, 256.

3

English, Scots, and Yemassee
at Port Royal

English claims to North America originated from John Cabot's 1497 landfall at Cape Breton, Newfoundland. He had sailed from Bristol, England, but
failed to return from his second voyage in 1498. At that time, his son, Sebastian
Cabot, also explored the New World for the English. His 1509 search for a
northwestern passage may have led Sebastian Cabot into Hudson's Bay in Canada.
One group of English explorers followed the Cabots in seeking a northwest
passage. They concentrated their settlements in the New England region. Another group, inspired by the exploits of Sir Francis Drake and John Hawkins,
explored and settled the Caribbean and southern coast of North America. They
were motivated by anti-Spanish zeal and the lure of the Spanish treasure fleets.

Some of England's southern ventures included Sir Walter Raleigh's ill-fated
Roanoke Colony, the Virginia Company's settlement at Jamestown in 1607, and
the Somer's Island Company's colonization of Bermuda in 1609. Sir William
Courteen and the Courteen Association sponsored a voyage to the Caribbean in
1626. John Powell, leader of the Courteen expedition, made landfall at Barbados
in 1626 and claimed the island for the English. Courteen and Powell's small
Barbados colony was the beginning of the English Caribbean empire.[1]

The South Carolina coast first stirred English interest in 1629. Sir Robert
Heath, Charles I's attorney general, obtained a royal charter to settle "Carolana,"
a vast region that extended from Virginia to Spanish Florida. He intended to
sponsor a Huguenot, French Calvinist settlement on the southern mainland. To
that end he outfitted a ship, in 1633, bound for South Carolina, but it landed in
Virginia instead.[2] In 1632, Captain Henry Taverner, in the *George,* explored the
South Carolina coast looking for a suitable place for Heath to found a colony.
He sailed as far south as St. Helena River.[3]

The pace of English settlement slowed but did not stop during the civil wars
and interregnum. In the 1640s and 1650s, Congregationalists looked westward
across the Atlantic for religious asylum, and in 1655 Oliver Cromwell's army and
navy captured Jamaica from the Spanish. But the New-World settlement blos-

somed after the 1660 restoration of Charles II to the English throne. In 1663, eight prominent royalist supporters of Charles II acquired a charter to the lands formerly contained in Heath's patent of 1629. Heath's charter was voided, and the southern mainland, including some Caribbean Islands, became the property of the Lords Proprietors of Carolina.[4]

Barbados was part of the South Carolina grant. Strongly royalist during the Civil Wars, Barbados had prospered by being left alone. Well supplied with African slaves and heavily engaged in sugar production for export, Barbadians quickly outstripped the resources of their small island. By 1663, Barbadians looked to the southern mainland to expand their enterprises. To this end the Company of Barbados Adventurers sponsored a voyage of exploration to the South Carolina coast. On August 10, 1663, Captain William Hilton sailed from Speight's Bay, Barbados, in the *Adventure*. He entered St. Helena Sound on September 3 and explored the area for nineteen days. There he met caciques of the Edisto and Escamacu Indian tribes and examined the rivers and inlets of Port Royal and St. Helena Sound. Hilton's *A Relation of a Discovery lately made on the Coast of Florida*, published in 1664, recounted his experiences:

> On Sunday the sixth, several Indians came on Board us, and said they were of St. Ellens; being very bold and familiar; speaking many Spanish words, as, Cappitan, Commarado, and Adeus. They know the use of Guns, and are as little startled at the firing of a Peece of Ordnance, as he that hath been used to them many years; they told us the nearest Spanyards were at St. Augustins, and several of them had been there, which as they said was but ten days journey; and that the Spanyards used to come to them at Saint Ellens, sometimes in Canoa's within Land, at other times in small Vessels by Sea, which the Indians describe to have but two Masts. They invited us to come to St. Ellens with our Ship, which they told us we might do within Land.[5]

Hilton visited the Escamacu town on the tip of Parris Island where he saw the Indians' great meeting house and a raised watchtower. The Indians' lodge was

> builded in the shape of a Dove-house, round, two hundred foot at least, compleatly covered with Palmeta-leaves, the walplate being twelve foot high, or thereabouts, and within lodging Rooms and forms; two pillars at the entrance of a high Seat above all the rest: Also another house like a Sentinel-house, floored ten foot high with planks, fastned with Spikes and Nayls, standing upon substantial Posts, with several other small houses round about. Also we saw many planks, to the quantity of three thousand foot or

thereabouts, with other Timber squared, and a Cross before the great house. Likewise we saw the Ruines of an old Fort, compassing more than half an acre of land within the Trenches, which we supposed to be Charls's Fort, built, and so called by the French in 1562 etc.[6]

The ruins that Hilton and later Robert Sandford viewed were probably those of San Felipe and San Marcos, not Charlesfort. Hilton wrote glowingly of South Carolina's coastal beauty.

The lands are laden with large tall Oaks, Walnut and Bayes, except facing on the Sea, it is most Pines tall and good: The Land generally, except where the Pines grow, is good soyl, covered with black Mold . . . with Clay underneath mixed with Sand; and we think may produce any thing as well as most part of the Indies that we have seen. The Indians plant in the worst Land, because they cannot cut down the Timber in the best, and yet have plenty of Corn, Pumpions, Water-Mellons, Musk-mellons: although the Land be overgrown with weeds through their lazinesse, yet they have two or three crops of Corn a year, as the Indians themselves inform us. The Country abounds with Grapes, large Figs, and Peaches; the Woods with Deer, Conies, Turkeys, Quails, Curlues, Plovers, Teile, Herons; and as the Indians say, in Winter, with Swans, Geese, Cranes, Duck and Mallard, and innumerable of other water-Fowls, whose names we know not, which lie in the Rivers, Marshes, and on the Sands: Oysters in abundance, with great store of Muscles; A sort of fair Crabs, and a round Shel-fish called Horse-feet; The Rivers stored plentifully with fish that we saw play and leap. There are great Marshes, but Most as far as we saw little worth, except for a Root that grows in them the Indians make good Bread of.[7]

Leaving Port Royal, Hilton sailed north to Cape Fear and was back in Barbados by January 1664. As a result of Hilton's voyage, the Company of Barbados Adventurers planted a settlement called Charles Town at Cape Fear, North Carolina.

In 1665, Charles II granted the Proprietors a second South Carolina charter that enlarged the size of the Proprietors' territory.[8] The next year the Proprietors commissioned Robert Sandford to explore the coast. Sandford sailed southward from Charles Town at Cape Fear in a ship of 15 tons with a three-ton shallop. He published *A Relation of a Voyage on the Coast of the Province of Carolina* in 1666 describing his voyage. By the end of June 1666, Sandford had reached the North Edisto River. There he met Shadoo, "Capt. of the Edistow that had been with Hilton att Barbados." Sandford also met a cacique of the Kiawah Indians, who wanted to show Sandford the benefits of Kiawah (present-day Charleston Harbor). Unwilling to retrace his steps, Sandford insisted that he must visit Port Royal first. The cacique of Kiawah sent a message ahead to the cacique of Port Royal to prepare a welcome for Sandford and then accompanied Sandford as a guide.[9] Sandford described the coast from Edisto to Port Royal as

> nothing else but severall Islands made by the various intervenings of Rivers and Creekes, yett are they firme good Lands (excepting what is Marsh) nor of soe smale of sieze, but to continue many of them thousands of acres of rich habitable wood land, whose very bankes are washed by River or Creek, which besides the fertillity adde such a Comodiousnesse for portage as few Countryes are equally happy in.[10]

On July 3, 1666, Sandford reached Port Royal Sound. The next day he anchored off the same Escamacu town on Parris Island that Hilton had visited two years earlier. He saw the ruins of Charlesfort and a bowling green whereon stood "a faire woodden Crosse." The captain and his crew were entertained in the Escamacu's large meeting house.[11]

Sandford explored Port Royal Sound by proceeding up the Broad River to the confluence of Tullafinny and Coosawhatchie Rivers. Later he entered Calibogue Sound between Hilton Head and Daufuskie Island. He noted the myriad waterways and observed that "if the Sound goe through to such a great River as the Indians talk off (which seems very probable) it will but in addiconall value upon the Settlemts that shal be made in it."[12] The great river of the Indians may have been the Savannah. Nisquesalla, the Escamacu cacique, boarded the English ship as it was about to return to Cape Fear and offered to let his nephew stay with Sandford and be educated in English ways. In exchange, Sandford placed Henry Woodward in Nisquesalla's care in order to learn the native languages and make trade contacts for the Proprietors.

> The Cassique placed Woodward by him uppon the Throne, and after lead him forth and shewed him a large feild of Maiz which hee told him should bee his, then hee brought him the Sister of the Indian that I had with mee telling him that shee should tend him and dresse his victualls and be careful of him that soe her Brother might be the better used amongst us.[13]

Henry Woodward remained with the Escamacu and had the distinction of being the first permanent English settler in South Carolina.[14]

Robert Sandford published *A Relation of a Voyage on the Coast of the Province of Carolina* (1666) and dedicated it to the Lords Proprietors. His pamphlet and

Hilton's *Relation of a Discovery* aimed to whet English interest in South Carolina.[15] By 1669, the Proprietors were ready to undertake an expedition of settlement bound for the state. The Proprietors wished to place their first settlement
at Port Royal. In August 1669, the *Carolina,* the *Port Royal,* and the *Albemarle*
embarked from London with about 150 settlers. The *Albemarle* wrecked off Barbados, and the *Three Brothers* took its place in the fleet. Governor Joseph West,
named by the Proprietors to govern the colony, was replaced at Barbados by Sir
John Yeamans. The fleet set sail under Yeamans's command but misfortune struck
again. A storm wrecked the *Port Royal* at Abaco in the Bahamas and forced the
Carolina to make port at Bermuda. The *Three Brothers* was blown so far out to sea
that it landed at Virginia and made its way separately to South Carolina. William
Sayle, a longtime Bermuda resident and founder of the Bahama colony, replaced Yeamans as governor of South Carolina. Under Sayle's command, the
settlers finally reached South Carolina. The *Carolina* and the sloop that replaced
the *Port Royal* made landfall in mid-March at Bulls Bay, north of present-day
Charleston. Nicholas Carteret, a passenger on the *Carolina,* wrote that the Seewee
Indians at Bull's Bay:

> understanding our business to St. Hellena told us that the Westoes, a rangeing
> sort of people reputed to be the Mandatoes, had ruinated that place, killed
> severall of those Indians, destroyed and burnt their habitations and that
> they had come as far as Keyawah doeing the like there, the Casseka of
> which place was within one sleep of us (which is 24 hours for they reckon
> by that rate) with most of his people whome in two days after cam aboard
> of us.[16]

The cacique of Kiawah sailed with the *Carolina* from Bull's Bay down to
Port Royal, where the Indians reported that the Westoes had indeed been raiding the coastal towns. Governor Sayle sent the Bermuda sloop up to Kiawah to
investigate that harbor. When it returned with a favorable report, the South
Carolina fleet left Port Royal in April and settled at a low bluff called Albemarle
Point on the Ashley River upriver from Charleston Harbor. The land around
Kiawah was judged "more fit to plant in than St. Hellena," and the proximity of
the Spanish at St. Augustine made a small settlement there a dangerous proposition.[17]

Maurice Mathews reported that the *Three Brothers* had reached St. Catherine's
Island (Spanish Guale) on May 15, 1670. It was there that four Spanish soldiers
armed with muskets and swords commanded the English to yield to the
sovereignty of Santo Domingo. But the English returned to their ship and

sailed northward. On May 20, they met cacique Shadoo of Kiawah and another Indian, Captain Alush, who told them that the English had been at Port Royal but had moved up the coast to Kiawah.[18] By the end of May 1670, all of the settlers had reached Kiawah and planted their colony, Charles Town, at Albemarle Point.

Henry Woodward was a member of the first fleet of Charles Town settlers. He had enjoyed his sojourn with Nisquesalla and made an alliance with the local tribes where he took "formall possession of the whole Country to hold as Tenant at Will" of the Lords Proprietors. However, the Spanish soon learned of Woodward's presence. They captured him in 1667 and took him to St. Augustine. The English privateer, Robert Searle, attacked St. Augustine in 1668 and liberated Woodward and other English prisoners. Woodward then joined Searle's crew as the ship's surgeon, but soon thereafter their ship wrecked at Nevis. The South Carolina fleet picked up Woodward at Nevis in December 1669 and returned with him to Port Royal. Woodward contributed much to the English settlement of South Carolina and Beaufort: scientist, linguist, and explorer, he established South Carolina's trade with the native peoples—the first source of revenue for the province—and was progenitor of several lowcountry families, including the Barnwells, Elliotts, and Rhetts.[19]

THE BAHAMA CONNECTION

The Bahama Islands played an important role in the English settlement of South Carolina. Indeed the South Carolina-Bahama connection continued throughout the eighteenth and nineteenth centuries, long after South Carolina's more celebrated links to Barbados had snapped. During and after the American Revolution, the Beaufort region had especially strong ties to the Bahamas. English projectors of colonial expansion thought of South Carolina and the Bahamas simultaneously. Sir Robert Heath's 1629 Carolana grant had included the Bahamas as well as the southern mainland. And when Heath's patent was extinguished both South Carolina and the Bahamas were free to be regranted to the Lords Proprietors of Carolina. English settlement in the Bahamas preceded the Proprietors' South Carolina charters. The first Bahamian settlers were Bermudians driven by religious enthusiasm, factious republicanism, and economic opportunism. William Sayle, a native of the Isle of Man, Independent Congregationalist, and future governor of South Carolina, had settled at Bermuda in the 1630s. He and a group of his fellow Dissenters projected a Bahamian settlement as a haven for Independent Congregationalists and a source of new land to relieve overcrowding at Bermuda. Sayle founded a small settlement at Sayle's Island, later called New Providence, but the colonists chafed under the control of the old Somers Island Company of Bermuda. To remedy this, Sayle visited England in 1647 and founded the Company of Eleutherian Adventurers. The company canvassed for settlers and patronage to establish a Nonconformist colony in the Bahamas. Despite support from London and the Massachusetts Bay Colony, Sayle and the Eleutherian Adventurers failed to obtain a charter.

Undeterred by this factor, however, they began settling the Bahamas without a charter. In 1648, the Sayle's company placed a colony on Eleuthera which expanded slowly to nearby islands. In 1666, Sayle founded Charles Town (later known as Nassau) on Sayle's Island. By 1670, there were nearly eleven hundred whites and African slaves on the islands of Eleuthera, Abaco, and New Providence; however, the Bermudians still governed the Bahamas.[20]

After 1660, Sayle knew that he had no chance to acquire a charter from King Charles. So in 1670, he approached the Lords Proprietors of Carolina and suggested that they acquire a Bahamas' charter. The Proprietors were about to send a fleet to South Carolina so their commitment to colonization was unquestioned. They had also gone to great lengths to advertise that religious toleration would be the order of the day in all of their colonies. This latter element doubtless appealed to Sayle.[21]

Two other Eleutherian Adventurers also made a case for acquiring the Bahamas. John Dorrell and Hugh Wentworth met the South Carolina fleet at Bermuda in February 1670 and wrote to Lord Ashley extolling the merits of the Bahamas. Bermuda was overcrowded, and many inhabitants, particularly Nonconformists, wanted to emigrate to the Bahamas. In addition, the Bahamas provided the first line of defense for South Carolina, and the islands were already settled and under cultivation. According to Dorrell and Wentworth, the islands produced provisions and cattle useful to South Carolina and "as good cotten as ever grew in America and gallant Tobacco."[22] With this mention of cotton, Dorrell and Wentworth might be called prophets of Beaufort's magnificent sea island cotton kingdom. Writing from Albemarle Point in September 1670, Governor Sayle also suggested to the Proprietors the wisdom of acquiring the Bahamas. The islands would provide salt to South Carolina and supply brazilwood for export to England.[23]

On October 29, 1670, Lord Ashley informed Dorrell and Wentworth that he and five of the Carolina Proprietors had obtained a charter for the Bahamas. The other Bahama Proprietors were Earl Craven, Lord John Berkeley, Sir George Carteret, the second duke of Albemarle, and Sir Peter Colleton.[24] The Proprietors added these islands to their mainland territory hoping that the two would prove mutually beneficial. Their hope was long deferred but was eventually fulfilled when the first crops of sea island cotton were harvested in Beaufort District.

Sayle personified the link between the Bahamas and South Carolina. He died at Albemarle Point on March 4, 1671, but by that time the South Carolina colony was off to a good start. The first parliament had met at Port Royal in March 1670 and begun a South Carolina tradition of wary self-government. Sayle also promulgated the first known South Carolina law—an ordinance against "prophaning the Sabbath."[25] Before his death, Sayle named Joseph West as provisional governor. A fellow Dissenter, West had been the Proprietors' first choice as governor but had been replaced in 1669 by Sir John Yeamans. West served three terms as governor, and during those years the colony received new immigrants, slave and free, and organized a profitable Indian trade. In 1680, Charles Town moved from Albemarle Point to Oyster Point—the peninsula in Charleston Harbor bounded by the Ashley and Cooper Rivers. By 1683, there were about one thousand people in South Carolina, and two hundred families resided in Charles Town.[26]

THE SOUTH CAROLINA INDIAN TRADE, 1674–1686

Henry Woodward was one of the earliest English explorers to trade with the Indians of the southeast. In summer of 1670, Woodward traveled from Charles Town to Cofitachequi on the Wateree River, the central town of an inland chiefdom, which both Hernando De Soto and Juan Pardo had visited in the sixteenth century. Woodward reported to the Proprietors that he had made an alliance and trade agreement with the "emperor" of Cofitachequi and hinted at the existence of pearls, silver, and mines in the region.[27] However, little came of this venture. Cofitachequi and its tributary towns were in rapid decline, and South Carolinians soon realized that a more profitable trade lay westward with the populous Muskhogean tribes—the Creeks, Chickasaws, and Choctaws.

On October 10, 1674, Woodward traveled to St. Giles Kusso, Lord Ashley's plantation on the upper Ashley River. There he met a group of Westo Indians and accompanied them back to their village, Hickauhaugau, on the west bank of the Savannah River near present-day Augusta, Georgia. To reach the town, Woodward and his guides crossed the Edisto River and traversed "divers spatious Savanas, seeming to the best of my judgment good Pastorage." This region later became Colleton County, long known for its cattle ranches.[28] Woodward passed above the headwaters of the Port Royal or Combahee River and arrived at Hickauhaugau. Upon reaching the town he discharged his firearms in greeting. The Westos replied with a volley of "fifty or sixty" small arms—startling evidence that the Westos had easy access to firearms. The town was on the riverbank, double palisaded on the land side with a single palisade by the river. Nearly a hundred canoes lay on the bank "ready upon all occasions." The Westos had already established trade links both with the Spanish to the south and the English from Virginia. They exchanged furs, deerskins, and Indian slaves for metal tools, cloth, and firearms.[29]

By November 6, 1674, Woodward was back at St. Giles Kusso where he, Lord Ashley, Maurice Mathews, Andrew Percival, and other South Carolina settlers overtook the Indian trade from Virginia, Spanish, and French traders. They directed the trade through St. Giles Kusso and Charles Town, making it the province's first economic enterprise.[30] Woodward, Lord Ashley, and their partners knew the political and diplomatic character of the trade and manipulated these elements to their best advantage. Among the Westos, Woodward had also formed a trade agreement that served as a diplomatic alliance. For the next six years, the Westos traveled to the Proprietors' trading station at St. Giles Kusso. Not only did the Westos trade their own products, but they also acted as middlemen trading on behalf of the more populous Muskhogean tribes west of the Savannah River. In effect the Westos and the Proprietors established an exclusive trade monopoly.

From 1674 to 1680, the Westo alliance was the cornerstone of South Carolina Indian trade and diplomacy. The Westos taught South Carolinians what products to seek and provide and how to negotiate. All these skills were important elements in South Carolina's rise to wealth and power in the eighteenth century. But the Westo alliance did not last. The trade grew so lucrative that the Westos, a small nation, could not keep up the pace of heaving trading. The envy of private trades in Charles Town, which chafed against the Proprietors' monopoly, was another element in the collapse of the Westo alliance. By its nature Indian trade was harshly exploitative, especially when one article of trade was Indian slaves. As demand increased for slaves, the Westos grew less discriminating in which tribes they attacked. Some South Carolinians began to look upon the Westos themselves as a nearby source of slaves. Private traders sought an opportunity to disrupt the Proprietors' monopoly and have a war with the Westos, which could have ended the monopoly, unclogged the Westo bottleneck that hampered Indian trade with the southwest, and provided a new, nearby source of slaves.

Henry Woodward strongly opposed war against the Westos. In April 1680, the Grand Council of Carolina placed an embargo upon Westo trade and found Indian allies, the Shawnees, to attack the Westos. The war was one of extermination, and within three years there were reportedly less than fifty Westos left alive. A few survivors migrated westward and found a home among the Lower Creeks.[31] According to Verner Crane, the Proprietors lost interest in Indian trade after the war, and the trade was wide open to all by default.[32] Immediate gains from Indian trade were considerable, but warfare, enslavement, and aggressive expansionism built a large blood debt on the part of southeastern Indians. In 1715, Native Americans organized a large confederation to collect that debt.

THE SCOTS AT STUART TOWN

In 1682, the Carolina Proprietors, frustrated with the Charles Town colony, sought to place a second settlement in their domain, this time at Port Royal. This settlement would also provide the Proprietors an opportunity to assist Scottish Presbyterians who were being persecuted in England. From the Proprietors' point of view, the Westo War had ruined the Indian trade. South Carolinians' aggression against small coastal tribes, along with the Spanish at St. Augustine, gave them considerable cause for alarm. By 1682, they had reaped no profit from their South Carolina enterprise. They believed that a second settlement further south might be the new beginning needed in order to restore some measure of control over their colony. At the same time many Scottish Presbyterians were eager to leave Scotland and find a safe haven in the New World.[33]

In the late 1670s, Scottish Presbyterians were under the thumb of a repressive, persecuting Church of England regime. Scottish Covenanters, Presbyterians who had signed the Solemn League and Covenant in 1638 and 1643, had joined the English Long Parliament in opposition to Charles I. They had been instrumental in fomenting and prosecuting the English Civil War and had supported Oliver Cromwell's Protectorate. In 1660, when Charles II returned to the throne of England, Scotland, and Ireland, he took strong measures in order to subject the Covenanters to the political and spiritual authority of the Church of England. The Clarendon Codes, statutes enacted from 1661 to 1665, along with the Corporation Act (1661), Act of Uniformity (1662), and Conventicle Act (1664) caused great hardship among Scottish Presbyterian clergy and lay people. All ministers—English, Irish, or Scottish—who refused to accept presentation and collation to their parishes were removed. Some excluded clerics fled with their congregations to Holland; others held illegal conventicles in private homes or in remote areas. Arrest warrants were issued for Robert Montgomery, brother of the earl of Eglinton, and Sir George Campbell of Cesnock for their open resistance to the Anglican establishment.[34]

Despite persecution, the Covenanters enjoyed considerable support among common folk, particularly in southern Scotland. In 1666, the Covenanters organized a revolt, the Pentland Rebellion, and marched on Edinburgh with the aim to remove the archbishop. The rebels were defeated at the Battle of Rullion Green on November 28, 1666, and many captured rebels were sentenced to transportation to the New World.[35]

Henry Erskine, Lord Cardross, was fined for permitting house conventicles on his Perthshire estates and several of his tenants were prosecuted for attending illegal Presbyterian services. On May 3, 1679, the assassination of James Sharp, archbishop of Saint Andrews, was the signal for a rebellion in the western parts of Scotland. This "Western Rising" was defeated on June 22, 1679, by English troops commanded by James, duke of Monmouth, at the Battle of Bothwell Brigg. Among the Covenanters implicated in the Western Rising were several who became involved in the Stuart Town settlement: William Dunlop, John Erskine (half-brother of Lord Cardross), Lord Cardross himself, Sir Robert Montgomery of Crevock, and Sir George Campbell of Cesnock.[36]

In the months leading up to the rising, the earl of Shaftesbury, Anthony Ashley Cooper, had spoken in Parliament against repression in Scotland. His advocacy of lenity and his position as a Carolina Proprietor soon engaged the interest of Cardross, Campbell, and Dunlop. James, earl of Dalkeith, petitioned the Lords of Trade to acquire a charter for "Florida, Cape Florida, and Guiana" but was unsuccessful. Among Dalkeith's confederates were Lord Cardross, Sir John Cochran, and Sir George Campbell.[37]

In the meantime, Shaftesbury and the Proprietors undertook a campaign to promote South Carolina to English and European Protestants. During early 1682, Shaftesbury's political newspaper, the *True Protestant Mercury,* published announcements of ships sailing to South Carolina, news from the province, and other information of interest to prospective immigrants. Thomas Ashe's *Carolina; or a Description of the Present State of that Country;* Robert Ferguson's *Present State of Carolina with Advice to Settlers;* Samuel Wilson's *Account of the Province of Carolina,* and Joel Gascoyne's "New Map of the Country of Carolina" (all 1682) were published extolling the climate, soil, liberal government, and religious toleration found in the Proprietors' American colony.[38]

Perhaps the best evidence that the Proprietors were anxious to encourage settlement was their revision of the Fundamental Constitutions, the "fixed and unalterable" plan of government they had devised for South Carolina and the Bahamas. They amended the constitutions in January 1682, giving the South Carolina General Assembly the authority to create landgraves and caciques and increasing the Assembly's political power in other ways. For the first time the Proprietors authorized the outright purchase of land in South Carolina and further liberalized their policies regarding religious toleration.[39]

In spring 1682, Cardross and other leading Covenanters corresponded with the Proprietors concerning a Scottish settlement in South Carolina. The lairds were impressed with reports of the Port Royal region and believed they could obtain strong assurances of religious toleration in South Carolina. Sir John Cochran and Sir George Campbell visited the Proprietors during the summer to negotiate terms for the enterprise. The Scots sought more changes in the Fundamental Constitutions and the Proprietors quickly acceded.[40]

The Proprietors revised their fundamental constitutions again in August 1682. The Scots then sought authority to tax their Dissenter congregations to support their ministers as did the Anglicans in South Carolina. Other revisions lessened the power of manorial courts, authorized per diem payments to jurymen, and forbade clerics from holding public office.[41]

On September 16, 1682, Cochran reported to Cardross that he and Campbell had "made a bargain" for two counties in South Carolina south of the English settlement. The land was to be divided into thirty-two square plats each containing 12,000 acres. Cochran, Campbell, and other subscribers had agreed to settle 36,000 acres per year for eight consecutive years. At this point the investors included Callender, Cardross, Haddington, York, Patrick Hume of Polwart, Archibald Cockburn, Archibald Douglas, George Lockhart, and Alexander Gilmour. Cochran had arranged to send a ship to South Carolina to locate a site for the new colony and take possession of the territory for Cardross and the undertakers.[42]

The *James of Erwin* sailed for South Carolina in October 1682. John Crafford, supercargo, wrote an account of the voyage and did his part to promote the charms of South Carolina. His *A New and Most Exact Account of the Fertiles [sic] and Famous Colony of Carolina,* published in Dublin in 1683, had a lengthy subtitle extolling the "advantages accruing to all Adventurers" in this "most Healthfull and Fertile of His Majesties Territories."[43] Crafford's voyage to Bermuda lasted twelve weeks. The *James of Erwin* remained there for sixteen days before heading to Charles Town, where it landed in early March 1683. After gathering information and visiting local notables, Crafford left Charles Town on March 23 and arrived at Port Royal two days later. The ship and crew spent a month taking soundings of the harbors and river channels and exploring the region. Crafford visited local Indians of whom there were "not above eight Score" in the area. His statement regarding the Indian population provided us with an overview of the area prior to the Yemassee migration.[44]

The stage was now set for the Scottish settlers to embark, but domestic political events imperiled their venture. In summer 1683, English Whigs, Nonconformists, and Scottish Covenanters sought to curb the crown's expanding prerogatives. The incident that set off this movement was the successful *quo warranto* proceeding that voided the charter of the city of London. The earl of Shaftesbury and other Whig magnates were heavily involved in this movement. But the Whigs were completely overthrown when the opposition became confused with the spurious "Rye House Plot" to assassinate Charles. The consequences of this political fallout were that Shaftesbury and Monmouth fled to Holland where Shaftesbury died shortly thereafter. Lord Russell and Algernon Sydney were executed for treason and the earl of Essex committed suicide.[45]

All of this threw the Covenanters' plans for South Carolina into disarray, but by March 1684, Cardross, Campbell, and Cochran had recovered their political standing sufficiently enough to proceed with the South Carolina venture. The

Proprietors informed Governor Morton at Charles Town that the Scottish settlers would soon arrive to establish a colony at Port Royal. Morton was instructed to "afford them all manner of countenance and advice in their undertaking."[46]

In late 1683 and early 1684, public announcements informed prospective settlers that the venture would soon get under way. Walter Gibson, a Glasgow merchant, and his brother, James Gibson, captain of the *Carolina Merchant,* were engaged to transport settlers to Port Royal. Walter Gibson published a broadside "Proposals" stating that the coast of passage was to be fifteen pounds sterling for men and women and fifty shillings for children aged two to fourteen. In addition to carrying paying passengers, Gibson offered to transport settlers free of charge. In exchange for terms of labor from three to five years, Gibson would convey settlers to Port Royal and maintain them during their terms of indenture. All free South Carolina settlers were entitled to a fifty-acre headright grant, and when servants had completed their indentures, they would receive the land grants. Gibson was ready to advise all prospective settlers how to prepare for their new homes in America. "And those who go in this vessel will have the occasion of good company of several sober, discreet persons, who intend to settle in Carolina, will dwell with them, and be ready to give good advice and assistance to them in their choice of their Plantations, whose Society will be very helpful and comfortable, especially at their first settling there."[47]

Another group of prospective South Carolina settlers were convicts sentenced to banishment to America. These convicts were mostly rebels involved in the Pentland Rebellion and the Western Rising or Presbyterians sentenced for crimes against the Anglican establishment. Walter Gibson took a prominent role in arranging passage for these convicts when he obtained crown contracts to ship these prisoners to the plantations. The terms of Gibson's contracts suggest that in exchange for their transportation these prisoners were "gifts" to Gibson; that is, they were indentured to him for terms of service in South Carolina. Gibson posted surety bonds for the prisoners' departure from the realm and their safe delivery to America.[48]

Robert Wodrow, the Covenanters' hagiographer, collected the names of prisoners assigned to Gibson for transportation to South Carolina. His thirty names correspond with other observers' statements that thirty-five prisoners traveled to South Carolina in the *Carolina Merchant.*[49] Gibson's prisoners were James McClintock, John Buchanan, William Inglis, Gavin Black, Adam Allan, John Galt, Thomas Marshal, William Smith, Robert Urie, Thomas Brice, John Syme, Hugh Syme, John Alexander, John Marshal, Matthew Machen, John Paton, John Gibson, John Young, Arthur Cunningham, George Smith, John Dowart, John Dick, John Smith, William Laing, James White, John Harper, Gavin Muirhead,

John Gardner, David Jameson, and James Balfour. Robert Malloch of Edinburgh also obtained contracts to transport prisoners to South Carolina. Only briefly mentioned by Wodrow, Malloch was as assiduous as Gibson in acquiring indentured servants for exile. The fate of Malloch and his passengers is not known, perhaps another of the tragic mysteries that make up Stuart Town's brief history.[50]

John Erskine recorded last-minute preparations for the ship's departure in July 1684. The *Carolina Merchant,* captained by James Gibson, met its passengers at Gurock, near Glasgow in the Firth of Clyde. The vessel shipped 170 tons and carried sixteen cannon for defense. There were 149 passengers representing all ranks of Scottish society. Gibson's thirty-five convicts, William Dunlop, Lord Cardross and his servants, Robert Montgomery and his son, and Alexander Ure crowded aboard the ship. One more passenger, Elizabeth Lining, had been kidnapped by Captain Gibson. The rest of the passengers were freemen or indentured servants bound to Gibson or other passengers.[51]

On July 21, 1684, the ship stood ready to embark. Erskine left the ship a little before noon and wrote in his journal that the settlers were leaving Scotland because of "corruptions and antichristian latitude of bishops and their dependents, the now pretended officers of the church, and because of the tyranny and usurpations of both which was daily growing, and all this tending to promote [Papist?] interest by extirpating Presbyterians out of Scotland."[52] Soon thereafter the *Carolina Merchant* weighed anchor. It stopped briefly at Cumbrae Island and put out to sea on July 24, 1684. Malloch then sailed on August 14, 1684, with 150 prisoners bound for exile in South Carolina.[53]

Gibson's ship and its passengers reached Charles Town on October 2, 1684, after ten weeks at sea. None of the 149 passengers died, but one, John Alexander, died soon after landing. Unfortunately, Charles Town was "so extraordinarie sicklie" when they arrived that most of the immigrants, including Cardross and Dunlop, soon fell ill. Although the settlers were well received many of them grew discouraged. The Spanish threat weighted heavily upon the metropolis, and news that another ship bound for Port Royal and bearing Scots from Belfast had been lost, probably Malloch's, further depressed their spirits.[54]

Another incident may have boded trouble. Elizabeth Lining had boarded the *Carolina Merchant* at Gurock to visit some of the departing prisoners. Captain James Gibson had kept her aboard against her will and when she escaped, sent his crew to hunt her down and bring her back to the ship. Arriving at Charles Town, Lining petitioned the governor and council for help. On October 17, Governor Joseph Morton investigated her complaint and ruled that she had been kidnapped and transported to South Carolina under false pretenses. He ordered her released from Gibson's authority and received as a free woman of Charles Town.[55]

Despite these early setbacks, Cardross and Dunlop persisted. In November their party, reduced to fifty-one in number, sailed down the coast to Port Royal and chose a site 1.5 miles south of present-day Beaufort. They named their settlement Stuart Town in honor of Catherine Stuart Erskine, Lord Cardross's wife.[56] Dunlop and Cardross informed Sir Peter Colleton that "we have so framed the modell of the toun that everie toun lot hath a garden adjacent to it, and two ackers of toun land lying near the toun. We have devyded it into two hundreth and twentie lotts; the toun itselfe, the streets and ackers of toun land, will in all consist of six hundreth ackers of land, Inglish measure; there are already fourty one toun lots takin up by ourselves and severall Inglish who have resolved to setle with us."[57]

As part of the Scots' agreement with the Proprietors, Stuart Town had considerable political autonomy. It was to be the seat of justice for Port Royal County, and the Scots could name their own justices and sheriffs. But the political relationship between Charles Town and Stuart Town was too ambiguous. In March 1685, Dunlop and Cardross wrote to Sir Peter Colleton requesting that the Proprietors send blank commissions to name proprietary deputies at Stuart Town. A separate proprietary council at Stuart Town would *de facto* and *de jure* place the new colony on an equality with Charles Town, for virtually all authority in South Carolina in the 1680s flowed from the governor and council.[58]

An important source of conflict between Stuart Town and Charles Town was the question who—Governor Morton or Lord Cardross—had authority over Indian traders living and plying their trade in the Port Royal-St. Helena region. Some English had established plantations and trading posts there and clashed with the Scots. Caleb Westbrooke was the most prominent of these early Port Royal settlers. He established a plantation on Datha Island and, by 1684, was trading with the Indians. Westbrooke operated independently and outside the Proprietors' trade monopoly and likely welcomed the Scottish challenge to Charles Town's authority. Rather than fight the Scots, he allied with them and used the changing situation in Port Royal to his advantage.[59]

In a portentous coincidence the Port Royal area saw another, considerably larger, immigration from 1684 to 1685. The Yemassee Indians' migration to Port Royal has been described earlier. However, the implications of the Scots' and Yemassees' simultaneous arrivals have not been examined. The Yemassees had begun their migration from central and northern Georgia, and during the mid-seventeenth century their travels had led them to St. Augustine. They sought to move their whole confederation north of the Savannah River into South Carolina.[60] In addition to their numbers, almost two thousand by 1686, the Yemassee had the potential to succeed the recently defeated Westos as middlemen for the southeastern Indian trade. Charles Town and Stuart Town competed to ally themselves with the Yemassee, and it appeared that the Scots were winning in 1685.

Westbrooke played a significant role in cementing the alliance of the Scots and Yemassees. Altamaha, chief of the Yemassees' lower towns, visited Westbrooke in January 1685, and delivered to him a letter from the Spanish governor of St. Augustine. A month later, Altamaha told Westbrooke that his people had fully settled Hilton Head and were expanding into other locations in the Port Royal region.[61]

In March 1685, Cardross, Dunlop, Westbrooke, and John Hamilton, another Scot, sponsored a slave-catching raid southward toward St. Augustine. The Yemassees attacked the Spanish mission Santa Catalina de Afuica, and, according to the testimony of an Indian who participated in the raid, "burnt several Towns and in particular the Said Chappell and the Fryers house and killed Fifty of the Timechoes [Timucuans] and brought away Two and twenty Prisoners which they delivered to the Scotts as slaves." Dunlop and Cardross disingeniously reported that they had been exploring the Savannah River and "went near" the mission. They said that the Spanish had deserted the area because the Scots had settled so near. Henry Woodward roundly condemned the Scottish policy as reckless.[62] Other conflicts arose over territorial jurisdiction, and these too were linked to control of the Indian trade. The Scots stopped John Edenburgh, a South Carolina trader, as he proceeded to the Yemassee towns. Held briefly at Stuart Town, Edenburgh was informed that the Scots had authority from St. Helena to the Westo (Savannah) River and from the Savannah to St. Catherine Island. The next month, Westbrooke and Hamilton arrested Woodward, Reuben Willis, George Franklyn, William Parker, and John Wilson as they passed through Port Royal. Cardross questioned them at Stuart Town and reiterated the Scottish claim to territorial control.[63]

In May 1685, Governor Richard Quary and Deputy Governor John Godfrey, Henry Woodward's father-in-law, ordered the arrest of Cardross, Hamilton, and Westbrooke. Charles Town Provost Marshal Griffin proceeded to Stuart Town where he learned that Westbrooke and Hamilton had fled and that Cardross was too ill to travel. Angered by Cardross's refusal to leave Stuart Town, the governor and council issued a second arrest warrant on June 2. In July, Cardross still could not leave Charles Town because of his continuing illness but hinted that he might adopt a more conciliatory attitude toward English authority. He stated that he desired "to uphold your authority." Dunlop wrote to Quary in Cardross's behalf, apologized for arresting Woodward, and requested the governor to appoint magistrates in Port Royal County.[64] But the damage had been done: tough competition for the Indian trade and the Scottish highhandedness had led Charles Town to grow indifferent to the fate of Stuart Town.

Spanish revenge for the Scots-inspired attack upon Santa Catalina de Afuica arrived on August 17, 1686, when three Spanish "Perreaugoes or half Galleys" appeared in the Port Royal River. In them was a force of one hundred Spanish soldiers and a complement of Indians commanded by General Thomas De Leon. The Spanish and Indian forces took the town by surprise, forcing the Scots, most of whom were sick with fever, to flee into the woods. After routing the inhabitants, the Spanish spent three days plundering houses and killing livestock. Finally, they burned Stuart Town to the ground. The troops then sailed northward toward Charles Town. They burned Paul Grimball's home on Edisto Island and plundered Governor Joseph Morton's plantation farther north on Edisto Island. But Charles Town was spared when a sudden hurricane wrecked De Leon's fleet. His flagship, the *Rosario,* was cast ashore, and the Spanish general drowned. Another of his vessels was beached and burned. According to one source, Governor Morton's brother-in-law had been captured by the Spanish and was burned to death in this second ship. The third vessel returned to St. Augustine where it reported a qualified success of the mission.[65]

Stuart Town was no more. The settlement had been dispersed, the town and fortifications burned, and the long-held risk of settlement at Port Royal had proven to be true. Scots Covenanters directed their colonizing sights elsewhere for thirty years, settling Darien on the Isthmus of Panama and in east New Jersey. However, in 1720, Sir Robert Montgomery, son of a Stuart Town projector, Montgomery of Crevock, obtained a charter from the Proprietors to settle a colony in Georgia just south of the Savannah River. He wished to found the "Margravate of Azilia," a frontier garrison colony designed to protect the southern frontier and be a haven for Nonconformists. As planned, Azilia would be placed in the southernmost region of Stuart Town's two "colonies."[66]

A lesser-known result of De Leon's destruction of Stuart Town was the Yemassees' brief abandonment of Port Royal and St. Helena. As agents of the Scots, the Yemassees were also targets of Spanish vengeance. Their Port Royal towns suffered the same fate as Stuart Town. Soon after the 1686 Spanish invasion, the Yemassees moved northward to the banks of the Ashepoo and Combahee Rivers to be closer to Charles Town. William Dunlop, who had escaped from Stuart Town, visited Cacique Altamaha on the upper Ashepoo River in April 1687.[67]

The Spanish destruction of Stuart Town answered the question of which Europeans would control the southeastern Indian trade. South Carolina traders spread throughout the south, from the Santee River to the Mississippi River. South Carolinians cooperated briefly with the Yemassee, especially in slave-catching raids, but within twenty years the Yemassee were at war with Charles Town. Cardross was in Scotland at the time of the Spanish raid but he never returned to South Carolina. Instead, he expatriated to Holland and returned to England, in 1689, as an ally of William of Orange. He served the Protestant king in battle at Killiecrankie, July 17, 1689.

When Cardross died in 1695, his son was made the earl of Buchan.[68] William Dunlop resided in Charles Town for a few years after 1686. In addition to his 1687 expedition to the site of Stuart Town, he undertook a diplomatic mission to St. Augustine. He then left Charles Town and returned to Scotland. In 1690, William III appointed him principal of the University of Glasgow, and he became a director of the Scots Darien Company.[69]

Not all of the Stuart Town settlers were killed or returned to Europe. A few joined the South Carolina settlers and made lasting contributions to the Proprietors' province. John Stewart was a notable Stuart Town survivor. He was an early planter on St. Helena Island and a prominent Indian trader; he even experimented with cotton a century before its general introduction to the sea islands. According to his statements, he had traveled 930 miles west from Charles Town, 240 miles farther than Woodward had traveled. His letters to William Dunlop reveal Stewart to be an astute politician and avid controversialist.[70] If his claims were true, Stewart had followed Woodward's path westward, established a trade with the Lower Creek tribes at Kashita, and pushed even farther to trade with the Talapoosas and the Chickasaws.

Thomas Nairne, a native of Scotland, may also have been a Stuart Town settler. One of the most remarkable South Carolinians of his era, Nairne was a scholar, soldier, politician, explorer, frontier diplomat, and Indian slave catcher. For most of his public life Nairne tried to meliorate exploitation of the southern Indians. He failed at this impossible task, and in April 1715 he perished under horrible torture when the Yemassee and other southern Indians rose up to kill all the English in the Southeast.[71]

During the American Revolution British soldiers at Port Royal unearthed Lord Cardross's seal—most likely buried by Stuart Town officials during the Spanish attack in August 1686. In 1794, Lord Buchan, Cardross's grandson, gave the seal to Governor William Moultrie who placed it at the Charleston Library Society. That silver seal is one of the historical treasures of the Library Society today.[72]

The Stuart Town settlement failed but some of the Scots' attitudes and ambitions—good and evil—persisted in South Carolina. For example, the South Carolinians developed a taste for slave-catching raids against Spanish Indians. Thomas Nairne and Governor James Moore mingled the Scottish imperialist vision and expediency when they commanded Indian allies and white volunteers in raids against the Apalachee and the Timucua in the first years of the eighteenth century. The Yemassee migrated from their temporary homes on the Ashepoo and Combahee Rivers and reclaimed their old towns at Port Royal. There they began a troubled, unsuccessful attempt to coexist with the English South Carolinians at Charles Town and the new town of Beaufort.

NOTES

1. Vincent Todd Harlow, *A History of the Barbadoes, 1625–1685* (Oxford: Clarendon Press, 1926), 12–16.

2. Paul E. Kopperman, "Profile of a Failure: The Carolana Project, 1629–1640," *North Carolina Historical Review* 59 (January 1982): 1–23.

3. Kopperman, "Profile of a Failure," 14.

4. Mattie E. E. Parker, *North Carolina Charters and Constitutions, 1578–1698* (Raleigh: North Carolina Tercentenary Commission, 1963). The Carolina Proprietors were Anthony Ashley Cooper; Sir George Carteret; Sir John Colleton; George Monck, Duke of Albemarle; William Lord Craven; Sir John Berkeley; Edward Hyde, Duke of Clarendon; and Sir William Berkeley. See William S. Powell, *The Proprietors of Carolina* (Raleigh: Carolina Charter Tercentenary, 1963), for biographies of the original eight Proprietors and their successors.

5. William Hilton, "A Relation of a Discovery, 1664," in *Narratives of Early Carolina, 1650–1708,* ed. A. S. Salley (New York: Charles Scribner's Sons, 1911), 39.

6. Hilton, "A Relation of a Discovery," 41.

7. Hilton, "A Relation of a Discovery," 44–45.

8. Parker, *North Carolina Charters,* 90–104.

9. Robert Sandford, "A Relation of a Voyage on the Coast of Carolina, 1666," in *Narratives of Early Carolina,* 90.

10. Sandford, "A Relation of a Voyage," 101.

11. Sandford, "A Relation of a Voyage," 91, 100.

12. Sandford, "A Relation of a Voyage," 103.

13. Sandford, "A Relation of a Voyage," 105.

14. Henry Woodward has been the subject of considerable research but remains an elusive presence in South Carolina history. Verner Winslow Crane's *The Southern Frontier, 1670–1732* (Durham: Duke University Press, 1928) is the best study of his activities. Josephine Pinckney's *Hilton Head* (New York and Toronto: Farrar and Rinehart, 1941) is a historical novel that incorporates most of the factual information known about Woodward. Also of interest is Alexander Moore, "Henry Woodward's Twenty Years among the Southeastern Indians," paper presented at the Society for American Ethnohistory Annual Meeting, Charleston, South Carolina, November 1986, on file at the South Carolina Historical Society.

15. William S. Powell, "Carolina in the Seventeenth Century: An Annotated Bibliography of Contemporary Publications," *North Carolina Historical Review* 41 (January 1964): 84.

16. Nicholas Carteret, "Mr. Carteret's Relation of Their Planting at Ashley River, '70," in *Narratives of Early Carolina,* 118.

17. Carteret, "Mr. Carteret's Relation," 119.

18. Maurice Mathews, "Mr. Mathews's Relation of St. Katherina," in *Narratives of Early Carolina,* 116.

19. Effie Leland Wilder, *Henry Woodward, Forgotten Man of American History* (N.p., n.d.), 29–31, lists many of Woodward's illustrious descendants.

20. Wilder, *Henry Woodward*, 79.

21. Langdon Cheves, ed., *The Shaftesbury Papers and Other Records Relating to Carolina and the First Settlement on Ashley River Prior to the Year 1676*, vol. 5 of *Collections of the South Carolina Historical Society* (Richmond, Va.: William Ellis Jones, 1897), 160–61; William Sayle, "Letter of Governor Sayle and Council," in *Narratives of Early Carolina*, 124.

22. Cheves, ed. *Shaftesbury Papers*, 160–61;

23. Sayle, "Letter of Governor Sayle," 124.

24. Cheves, ed. *Shaftesbury Papers*, 207–8; Daniel W. Fagg Jr., "Carolina, 1663–1683: The Founding of a Proprietary," Ph.D. diss., Emory University, 1970, 253–61, describes the Proprietors' acquisition of the Bahama Islands. The Bahamas charter and other early documents are published in Malcolm Harcourt, ed., *Historical Documents Relating to the Bahama Islands* (Nassau: Nassau Guardian, 1910).

25. Cheves, ed., *Shaftesbury Papers*, 291–92, 296.

26. M. Eugene Sirmans, *Colonial South Carolina, A Political History, 1663–1763* (Chapel Hill: University of North Carolina Press, 1966), 24.

27. Cheves, ed., *Shaftesbury Papers*, 191, 194; Kathryn E. Holland Braund, *Deerskins & Duffels: The Creek Indian Trade with Anglo-American, 1685–1815* (Lincoln and London: University of Nebraska Press, 1993), 28–29.

28. Henry Woodward, "A Faithfull Relation of My Westoe Voyage," in *Narratives of Early Carolina*, 130–34.

29. Woodward, "A Faithfull Relation," 130–34.

30. Converse D. Clowse, *Economic Beginnings in Colonial South Carolina, 1670–1730* (Columbia: University of South Carolina Press, 1971); Crane, *Southern Frontier*, 16–17, 18–21.

31. Crane, *Southern Frontier*, 18–21; Robert M. Weir, *Colonial South Carolina, A History* (Millwood, N.Y.: KTO Press, 1983), 26, 62.

32. Crane, *Southern Frontier*, 20.

33. The standard history of Stuart Town is found in George Pratt Insh, *Scottish Colonial Schemes, 1620–1686* (Glasgow: Maclehose, Jackson, 1922), chapter 6. The lack of and presumed destruction of Stuart Town records has hampered research on this episode in South Carolina and Beaufort County history.

34. Maurice Ashley, *England in the Seventeenth Century (1603–1714)* (Baltimore: Pelican Books, 1963), 125–27, describes the Clarendon Codes. Robert Wodrow, *History of the Sufferings of the Church of Scotland from the Restoration to the Revolution*, 4 vols. (Glasgow: Blackie, 1836), records the effects of the Restoration and Church of England hegemony on Scotland.

35. C. S. Terry, *The Pentland Rising and Rullion Green* (Glasgow, 1905).

36. See J. G. Dunlop, *The Dunlops of Dunlop: and of Auchenskaith, Keppoch, and Gairbraid*, vol. 2 of *Dunlop Papers* (Frome and London: Butler and Tanner, 1939), 119–47, for a biography of William Dunlop. See John Erskine of Carnock, *Journal of the Hon. John Erskine of Carnock, 1683–1687*, ed. Walter Macleod (Edinburgh: T. and A. Constable, 1893), introduction, for biographies of Henry Erskine, Lord Cardross, and John Erskine of Carnock.

37. Crane, *Southern Frontier,* 26.

38. John Carter Brown Library, Providence, Rhode Island, has numerous issues of the London, England, *True Protestant Mercury,* 1681–1682. See nos. 125, 126, 129, 174, 175, 178, 180, 186, 187, published in 1682, for articles relating to Carolina. See also Powell, "Carolina in the Seventeenth Century," 92–99, listing eight publications in 1682 and 1683 that promote immigration to Carolina.

39. Parker, *North Carolina Charters,* 186–207, publishes the January 1682 Fundamental Constitutions.

40. Insh, *Scottish Colonial Schemes,* 194; Great Britain Historical Manuscripts Commission, *The Manuscripts of the Duke of Roxburgh, Sir H. H. Campbell, Bart., and the Countess Dowager of Seafield* (London: HMSO, 1894), 113–14.

41. Text of the August 1682 Fundamental Constitutions is in Parker, *North Carolina Charters,* 208–33.

42. Wodrow, *History of the Sufferings of the Church of Scotland,* 3: 368–69; Insh, *Scottish Colonial Schemes,* 195–96.

43. John Crafford, *A New and Most Exact Account of the Fertiles* [sic] *and Famous Colony of Carolina (on the Continent of America) . . . Together with a Maritine* [sic] *Account of Its Rivers, Barrs, Soundings and Harbours: also of the Natives, their Religion, Traffick and Commodities . . .* (Dublin: N.Tarrant, 1683), photocopy in the South Caroliniana Library at the University of South Carolina, Columbia. See also Powell, "Carolina in the Seventeenth Century," 97–98.

44. Crafford, *New and Most Exact Account,* 6.

45. K. D. H. Haley, *The First Earl of Shaftesbury* (Oxford: Clarendon Press, 1968), 706–7, 710–17, 735–36.

46. Insh, *Scottish Colonial Schemes,* 201.

47. Walter Gibson, "Proposals," in Insh, *Scottish Colonial Schemes,* 278–79.

48. Henry Paton, ed., *Register of the Privy Council of Scotland,* 3d series, vol. 9 (Edinburgh: H. M. Register House, 1924), 12, 111, 208.

49. Wodrow, *History of the Sufferings of the Church of Scotland,* 4: 8–10; Erskine, *Journal,* 69.

50. Paton, ed., *Register of the Privy Council of Scotland,* 9:15–16, 28, 69–70.

51. Erskine, *Journal,* 69, 71–72; Wodrow, *History of the Sufferings of the Church of Scotland,* 4:11.

52. Erskine, *Journal,* 72.

53. Erskine, *Journal,* 73, 76.

54. George Pratt Insh, "The *Carolina Merchant:* Advice of Arrival," *Scottish Historical Review* 25 (January 1928): 102.

55. Wodrow, *History of the Sufferings of the Church of Scotland,* 4:11.

56. Insh, "*Carolina Merchant,*" 102.

57. Insh, "*Carolina Merchant,*" 102.

58. Insh, "*Carolina Merchant,*" 103.

59. Crane, *Southern Frontier,* 25–26.

60. David Andrew McKivergan, "Migration and Settlement among the Yamasee in South Carolina," M.A. thesis, University of South Carolina, 1991; James W. Covington, "Stuart's Town, the Yamasee Indians and Spanish Florida," *Florida Anthropologist* 21 (March 1968): 8–13.

61. Crane, *Southern Frontier*, 25–26; J. W. Fortescue, ed., *Calendar of State Papers, Colonial Series, America and West Indies, Volume 12, 1685–1688* (London: HMSO, 1899), no. 28.

62. Crane, *Southern Frontier*, 31; Insh, "*Carolina Merchant*," 103; Fortescue, ed., *Calendar of State Papers*, no. 83.

63. Fortescue, ed., *Calendar of State Papers*, nos. 173, 194.

64. Fortescue, ed., *Calendar of State Papers*, nos. 286, 287.

65. Accounts of the Spanish destruction of Stuart Town are few. See Insh, *Scottish Colonial Schemes*, 210–11; J. G. Dunlop, "Spanish Depredations, 1686," *South Carolina Historical Magazine* 30 (April 1929): 81–89; J. G. Dunlop, "Paul Grimball's Losses by the Spanish Invasion in 1686," *South Carolina Historical Magazine* 29 (July 1928): 231–37; "Statements Made in the Introduction to the Report on General Oglethorpe's Expedition to St. Augustine," in *Historical Collections of South Carolina*, ed. B. R. Carroll, 2 vols. (New York: Harper, 1836), 2:350–51.

66. Sir Robert Montgomery and John Barnwell's *The Most Delightful Golden Isles. Being a Proposal for the Establishment of a Colony in the Country to the South of Carolina* (1717; rpt., Atlanta: Cherokee Publishers, 1969) is a history of the Azilia plan. Sir Robert Montgomery's plan was a forerunner of the Georgia colony.

67. J. G. Dunlop, "Capt. Dunlop's Voyage to the Southward, 1687," *South Carolina Historical Magazine* 30 (July 1929): 127–33.

68. Erskine, *Journal*, introduction.

69. J. G. Dunlop, *The Dunlops of Dunlop*, 119–47.

70. Crane, *Southern Frontier*, 46, 103; J. G. Dunlop, "Letters from John Stewart to William Dunlop," *South Carolina Historical Magazine* 32 (January–April 1931): 1–33, 81–114, 170–74.

71. Thomas Nairne, *Nairne's Muskhogean Journals: The 1708 Expedition to the Mississippi River*, ed. Alexander Moore (Jackson: University Press of Mississippi, 1988); the introduction includes a biography of Nairne.

72. J. G. Dunlop, "Spanish Depredations, 1686," 81.

4

Settling the Southern Frontier

South Carolina faced destruction three times during the proprietary era: in 1686 by the Spanish, in 1706 by the French and Spanish, and in 1715 by the great Yemassee uprising.[1] The second assault came in October 1706 as a campaign of Queen Anne's War. A combined force of French and Spanish soldiers made an amphibious landing near Charles Town and marched against the metropolis. The enemy fleet bypassed the Beaufort and Colleton region in order to catch the Carolinians by surprise. The plan failed, and the attackers were driven off.[2]

The final and gravest threat South Carolina faced was the Yemassee War, begun in April 1715, in which Indian tribes throughout the Southeast united to drive the English from the colony. The Yemassees and their allies advanced toward Charles Town from the south and west, killing and pillaging as they proceeded toward the city. Through a combination of good fortune, military skill, and adroit diplomacy, the English prevailed, but the experience marked the colonists' lives for generations. Once again the Port Royal and Colleton regions were depopulated.[3]

The point of this brief narrative is to emphasize that South Carolina's southern frontier was a dynamic, dangerous place to live. Settlers might grow prosperous from the Indian trade and find opportunities to undertake the colony's first agricultural enterprise—livestock raising—but they also risked economic ruin and death. Despite the loss of life and property, the Spanish destruction of Stuart Town had solved a problem that had vexed the English at Charles Town. The Scots at Stuart Town had weakened the hegemony of Charles Town in South Carolina and had begun to compete successfully against them in the region's blossoming Indian trade. Now that the Port Royal area had been scoured of settlers—both white and Indian—the English at Charles Town could take up the land and establish the Indian trade to suit themselves. During the next thirty years (1686–1720) South Carolinians acquired land grants on the islands near Port Royal and St. Helena Sounds. From their frontier plantations they conducted Indian trade and erected the foundations of lowcountry plantation society.[4]

INDIAN TRADERS ON THE SOUTHERN FRONTIER, 1686–1715

In April 1685, a year before the Spanish struck Stuart Town, Henry Woodward undertook his last and greatest venture among the Indians. Carrying a Proprietors' commission to explore the southeast region of South Carolina and make contacts with western tribes, Woodward began his journey. But he immediately ran into trouble. Along with other Indian traders, he was arrested in the Port Royal area, detained at Stuart Town, and questioned about his activities.[5] This event exemplified the discord between Charles Town and Stuart Town. The Scots had placed their settlement directly astride the new westerly trading paths and, through the energies of Caleb Westbrooke and John Stewart, had begun to exploit that trade.[6] Woodward threatened the Scots' growing interest in Indian trade. Hence his arrest and the concern of Charles Town officials a year later when the Scots were driven from their settlement.

Woodward was quickly released from custody and, by the summer of 1686, had reached Coweta and Kashita—two Muskhogean towns on the Chattahoochee River. There he forged trade links with the Creeks that lasted—with the notable exception of the Yemassee War—until the American Revolution. He and his party then journeyed even deeper into the continent.[7] Writing in 1708, Thomas Nairne reported that "when Doctor Woodward about 20 years agoe made peace with the Ochesees and Tallapoosies these people having Then Freindship with the Chicasaws he sent two of his men hither, who brought them aquanted with the English. Ever since they have traded with Carolina."[8] Evidently by 1685, South Carolinians had nearly reached the Mississippi River and had begun to direct the vast trade of the southeast to Charles Town. Twelve years later, in 1698, Thomas Welch and Anthony Dodsworth had founded a trading station at the mouth of the Arkansas River, on the west bank of the Mississippi River.[9]

By 1700, the geographical limits of the Carolina trade extended west from Charles Town to the Mississippi and north to the Tennessee River. The entrepot of this great trade network was Savannah Town, later called Augusta, the former site of the Westo town of Hickahaugau. However, there were two routes from Savannah Town to Charles Town—the older of the two routes went overland from the Ashley River and the newer route employed travel down the Savannah River to Port Royal and north through the inland waterways of the coast to Charles Town. This was the Scottish route and was appropriated by the English after 1686.

There was another facet of the Carolina Indian trade—the nearby trade with the Yemassee and the Cherokees. Beginning in 1686, the Yemassee established ten towns in the Port Royal and St. Helena region. They were a populous nation with a considerable volume of trade with their English neighbors but they also played a role as middlemen in the far-flung western trade. This numerous tribe aided South Carolinians in wars against the Spanish and other Indian nations, acted as slave catchers, and as family hunters for local whites. The relative stability of the region and nearby markets led many traders to take up lands in the Beaufort area.

Thomas Nairne was among the earliest South Carolinians to acquire land in the area after the sack of Stuart Town. He owned land at a place later known as Dulamo, St. Helena Island, before 1698 and, by the time of his death in 1715, had accumulated nearly 3,600 acres there. John Stewart, a Stuart Town survivor, obtained a warrant in 1698 for 1,000 acres adjoining Nairne's lands. Their property was well situated in such a way as to take advantage of the new inland trade route.[10]

In 1698, Governor Joseph Blake took a warrant for Combahee Island, which was later named Lady's Island for his widow, Elizabeth Axtell Blake. She and her mother, Rebecca Axtell, each acquired another 500 acres on the island in 1707. John Pinny obtained a warrant on January 12, 1699, for a point of land on Port Royal Island. He later acquired Parris Island. At the same time Charles Odingsell, son-in-law of Paul Grimball, took a warrant for Datha Island, the site of Caleb Westbrooke's old trading post.[11]

The land rush continued through the turn of the century. Joshua Brinan acquired an unnamed island on Port Royal River; William Meggett obtained 800 acres on St. Helena Island; Robert Seabrooke took Caushee Island; and Landgrave Joseph Morton obtained Coosaw Island. Nairne, Alexander Mackay, Daniel Callahan, William Bull, James Tibb, Edmund Ellis, Richard Hatcher, and Thomas Hatter acquired grants of about 500 acres. Other grantees who later played prominent roles in Beaufort history were John Palmer Sr., who acquired a warrant for land on the Combahee River, and William Bray, who had 200 acres, perhaps on Bray's Island.[12]

John Barnwell, imperialist par excellence, was instructed in 1703 by the Commons House to prepare a plat of the Port Royal area which depicted the extent of English settlement. Apparently liking the area, he took out a warrant for 400 acres. This first acquisition was called Doctors Plantation and was the nucleus of Barnwell holdings that eventually amounted to 6,500 acres.[13] The Barnwell name became synonymous with Granville County and Beaufort.

Blessed with some prescience, Barnwell and Nairne took leading roles in trying to regulate the Indian trade. Nairne was commissioner of the Indian trade in 1707 and in 1712 was a special commissioner to his neighbors, the Yemassees. Barnwell was also a trade commissioner and in 1718 was appointed provincial trader at Port Royal.[14]

The journals of the commissioners of the Indian trade, the "Indian Books," gave a clear picture of the mechanics of Indian trade. After 1707, traders had to be licensed, and many new Beaufort patentees acquired them, including William

Bray, Samuel Hilden, John Fraser, Daniel Callahan, Alexander Mackay, Samuel Warner, Richard Hatcher, Thomas Ayres, Edmund Ellis, Alexander Nicholas, and Captain John Cochran.[15]

The influx of South Carolinians to Granville County was so great that, by 1707, conflicts regularly erupted between English and Yemassee settlers. In addition to monetary debts to traders, the Yemassees were increasingly threatened by an influx of English settlers. In 1707, in order to stabilize relations between these two groups of settlers, the General Assembly passed an act "to limit the bounds of the Yemassee settlement, to prevent persons from disturbing them in their stocks, and to remove such as are settled within the bounds described." The Yemassee reservation was called the "Indian Land," a phrase used to describe that tract throughout the eighteenth century. This region was bounded on the northeast by the Combahee River, the southeast by the marshes and islands on Coosaw and Port Royal Rivers, southwest by the Savannah River, and northwest by a line drawn from the headwater of the Combahee River to the head of the Savannah River "and also one Island lying between Pocosabo town and the North Branch of the Port Royal river commonly called Coosawache now inhabited by the Said Yamasee Indians."[16] Having been established by law, this large tract of land was now subject to the same guarantees of territorial integrity as have been all Indian reservations in America. No whites were permitted to inhabit the Indian land, but the journals of the Indian commissioners record numerous violations of that proscription. During 1711 Thomas Jones, John Whitehead, Joseph Bryan, Robert Steale, John Palmer, Burnaby Bull, Peter Hanes, Isaac DeFrance, William Bray, and Edmund Bellinger were reported for trespassing upon Yemassee properties.[17]

The South Carolina government established another reservation in 1712 for the Cusabo Indians—a small coastal tribe that had aided the first English settlers in 1670. Palawana Island, granted to James Cochran, Indian trader, was recovered from him by the province and then set aside to be a Cusabo refuge "until extinction"—a not too distant future for the shattered tribe.[18]

Indian trade was inherently exploitative, placing the Indians at a disadvantage as they grew to depend upon European products—cloth, firearms, metal tools, and utensils. Depletion of deerskins and the decline of the Indian slave trade drove Indians into great debt to South Carolina traders. By 1711, the Yemassee owed debts that amounted to one hundred thousand deerskins, and by 1715 that debt had reached fifty thousand pounds Carolina currency, or ten thousand pounds sterling.[19] Coupled with rising debts and diminishing resources to pay those debts, the Yemassee faced an influx of whites into the region they inhabited, and the two could not successfully share the land. Whites required a free range for livestock and protected areas for agriculture, while the Yemassee hunting ground required larger open spaces free from cattle and hogs and unrestricted access across property lines. The Indian land plan failed and their debts mounted. Finally, in 1715, justly fearing that they might be enslaved to pay their traders' debts, the Yemassee and other Indian tribes united to extinguish their debts by declaring war on the English.

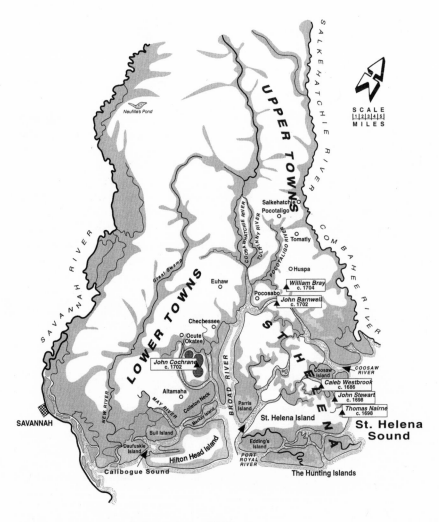

Yemassee towns and plantations, 1715

CATTLE RANCHING ON THE SOUTHERN FRONTIER

European settlers in South Carolina soon realized that the southern frontier was well suited for raising livestock, especially cattle. Mild winters and extensive savannah lands allowed owners to release their animals to graze throughout the year. Laced with numerous rivers and creeks, the lowcountry geography materially assisted cattle ranchers. Prospective ranchers acquired necks of land—small peninsulas bounded by creeks, streams, and marshes—so that their cattle could not wander too freely. Cattle owners simply had to construct a single fence across these necks to pen their animals. Occasionally they corralled their cattle at night and during bad weather, but for the most part the cattle ranged free. Early maps and plats often depict cowpens on these necks of land.[20]

Another incentive to livestock husbandry in South Carolina came from stated objectives in founding the colony—the desire to supply Barbados and other sugar islands with provisions while those islands concentrated on staple crop production. Governor John Yeamans brought the first cattle herds to South Carolina overland from Virginia in 1671, and by 1682 Samuel Wilson boasted that "cattle thrive and increase here exceedingly."[21] By that year some planters already owned herds of seven or eight hundred head of cattle. Wilson attributed their success to abundant forage and mild winter weather, which meant that, unlike northern cattlemen, they did not have to spend the summer raising winter food for their cattle. He waxed eloquent, suggesting that "an ox was raised at almost as little expense in Carolina as a hen in England."[22] In 1712, John Norris, writing as "James Freeman" in *Profitable Advice for Rich and Poor,* described how South Carolina cattle survived the winter. "Although we have . . . incredible numbers [of cattle] yet we produce no fodder for them against the winter for they gather their food in the woods at that time." The cattle ate "a sort of green Moss which the wind shakes off the trees . . . comparable to very good straw and a sort of short cane growing plentifully on the lower moist land, which bears a long green leaf in winter in which the cattle delight much to feed . . . and keep themselves in very good plight, 'till grass springs again."[23]

In addition to good climate and geography for cattle raising, early South Carolina settlers were knowledgeable cattle raisers. Many settlers came from Somerset, Exeter, and Devon, where the British cattle-raising industry had reached a high level of development. Also, some African slaves had been cattle raisers in their homelands. The slaves contributed most of the physical labor involved in animal husbandry, and their skills and methods of tending livestock are reflected in South Carolina industry.[24]

Cattle ranching and hog raising were natural occupations for the earliest settlers because these jobs were inexpensive to undertake and required little management in a sparsely settled land. The open-range system was complemented by early laws requiring that all cattle be marked with unique, officially recorded brands and ear notches. These books containing the cattle markings were important records of the early province. In 1694, Landgrave Thomas Smith began keeping these brands in "A Book for Recording Cattle Marks and Others." In 1707, William McPherson and Richard Hazzard, early settlers of the Beaufort region, recorded their cattle marks. Later records show that in 1734, Hugh Bryan, the largest cattle rancher in the Port Royal area recorded "his brand being an 'HB'... and an earmark being an upper kell in each ear and one ear cropped."[25]

During the first decades of settlement large cattle herds were kept around the headwaters of the Ashley River. Mrs. Ann Drayton, wife of Thomas Drayton, and Ralph Izard kept extensive cowpens in that region. As the Ashley River became more heavily settled, the cattle herds moved further south. When they crossed the Edisto River at Jacksonborough in 1686, and Round O a few years later, the cattlemen entered some of the best cattle country in the southeast. Between 1694 and 1715, the principal cattle-raising area of South Carolina was the broad neck of high woodland between the Edisto and Combahee Rivers in Colleton County. The area between the Stono and Edisto Rivers became St. Paul Parish in 1706, and the area called Colleton Neck, between the South Edisto and Combahee Rivers, became St. Bartholomew Parish in that year.

During these years, Colleton County was dotted with frontier cowpens. Sometimes these clearings were human-made: trees were felled, underbrush burned off, and eventually 100 or 200 acres of cleared ground was fenced. Each cowpen had a source of fresh water from a nearby spring or stream and an essential salt supply. Some cowpens were located on large natural fields known as savannahs. Godfrey's savannah in St. Paul and Round O savannah in St. Bartholomew were heavily occupied. The village of Round O, near the Edisto River, was settled by the cattle-raising families of Elliott, Sanders, and Drayton about the beginning of the eighteenth century. The village later became famous as General Nathanael Greene's encampment during the American Revolution. Godfrey's savannah was settled in the 1690s by Captain John Godfrey, and the cattle-raising families of Williamson and Bellinger began their enterprises in the neighborhood.

In 1734 a man passed through Godfrey's savannah and described it as "a large spot of cleared land where there never was any timber grew, and nothing but grass, which is exceedingly good for a stock of cattle, and on which they frequently settle their cowpens. This savannah is about one mile over and several in length."[26] Each winter cattle hunters rode through the forests to drive the herds into cowpens for slaughter.

Barrelled beef and pork were exported to the West Indies and England before the eighteenth century. Early South Carolina statutes regulated the size of shipping barrels and attempted to control the quality of exported beef and pork.

However, the extent of this early trade was difficult to assess. Reliable export statistics are not found prior to 1712, but earlier statistics are found on beef production in the plantation records of Newington, Lady Rebecca Axtell's plantation near the upper reaches of the Ashley River. In 1701, the plantation produced 4,050 pounds of beef and paid for packing barrels for shipment. The Newington journal records another expense of cattle ranching. Abram Cureton was paid three shillings in 1705 "for cattel hunting." Axtell and her daughter, Elizabeth Axtell Blake, widow of Governor Joseph Blake, were among the early Ashley River settlers who obtained large tracts of land in Colleton County and Port Royal.[27]

Official export statistics indicate that in 1712, South Carolinians exported 1,963 barrels of beef and 1,241 of pork. These numbers may represent the apogee of beef production during the proprietary era. Three years later the Yemassee War destroyed the industry so completely that it never recovered its place in South Carolina's colonial economy.[28]

The first cattle ranches were most likely temporary drovers' camps, but by 1715 these camps had developed into settlements and then into permanent plantations. The cowpens were well fertilized and became desirable farm land, so that the frontier industry really was a precursor of staple crop agriculture. Cattlemen and Indian traders planted provisions within the fenced cowpens and eventually moved their families and a few slaves to the settlement. These cattlemen joined the Indian traders as the first settlers on the southern frontier. Some Colleton County settlers whose families played important roles in the later history of Port Royal were William McPherson, Joseph Bryan, John Palmer Sr., Edmund Bellinger, William Bray, John Williamson, and Burnaby and John Bull.

Richard Harris's plantation on Poatinka Island was representative of the early settlements in the Port Royal area. The fifteen-hundred-acre island, known today as Williman's Island, was on the edge of St. Helena Sound just across the Combahee River marshes from Colleton County. Harris lived there with eight family members and nine Indian slaves. He, his brother John, his grown son and nephew, and three male Indian slaves performed the heavy work of clearing land and building cowpens. Harris's wife, his three daughters, and six female Indian slaves shared the domestic labors. The settler's main enterprise was breeding livestock. In his 1711 will, he bequeathed more than sixty cattle, six horses, and numerous hogs to members of his extended family. There is no indication that Harris grew any market crops on the island though the family doubtless raised corn, peas, and potatoes. Though isolated, the island provided protection from roaming Indian bands on the mainland and a natural boundary for the cattle. In addition, the wooded island provided game and the surrounding rivers were filled with fish and shellfish.[29]

Cattle ranching was a perfect frontier enterprise, but its success depended upon access to open-range land. Increased settlement reduced the amount of land available and led to disputes among the new landowners. Bitter though they might have been, such disputes were insignificant when compared to the impact cattle ranching had upon the Yemassees. Free-ranging cattle destroyed Yemassee crops and reduced the deer population. Surveyors' stakes and black lines on maps and plats imposed a new and exclusive kind of possession upon the lands, necks, and savannahs of the lowcountry. After 1707, the commissioners of the Indian trade were occupied arbitrating between cattlemen and Yemassees over mutual destruction of property. Burnaby Bull and John Palmer regularly drove their cattle southward across the Combahee River in search of grazing lands. They did this both before and after the demarcation of the Indian lands in 1712. As more whites moved southward, pressure grew upon the Yemassees to act. The result of this white encroachment was the Yemassee War.[30] When the war broke out the Indians took revenge upon the large herds of cattle which had helped destroy their land and food supply. Many reports of raids commented upon the destruction of livestock and, in 1722, Francis Yonge wrote that "the late Indian War . . . not only destroyed the stocks of cattle, but drove most to the southward where the greatest stocks of cattle were, from their plantations. Thus those unfortunate people have lost that branch of their trade."[31]

THE FOUNDING OF BEAUFORT

The dual motives of military necessity on the southern frontier and proprietary politics in London led to the founding of Beaufort in 1711. While the French, Spanish, and Scots had come and gone from Beaufort over the previous two centuries, the English came and stayed.

The military pressure on the southern frontier was caused by Queen Anne's War (1702–1713) between the British empire, on one hand, and the French monarchy and their Spanish allies, on the other. The turbulent southern frontier was an important front in this conflict, and this front came down to a contest between the Spanish stronghold in St. Augustine and the English stronghold in Charles Town. To complicate matters for the English, the French, under Pierre LeMoyne d'Iberville, founded Mobile on the Gulf Coast as a special check on the expansion of South Carolina. True to their aggressive nature and their expansionist ambitions, the South Carolinians attacked first. In September 1702, Governor James Moore convinced the Commons House of Assembly to fund an expedition against St. Augustine.

In October 1702, five hundred South Carolinians, three hundred Indian allies, and fourteen small ships rendezvoused at the south end of Port Royal Island. Governor Moore led the expedition with Colonel Robert Daniell as second in command. They made their camp at the large bend of the Port Royal River, at a place called the Bay. On the other side of the bay were the ruins of Stuart Town, mute testimony to the power of Spanish Florida. James Moore's expedition of 1702 was the largest event on Port Royal Island since the fall of Stuart Town in 1686, and it was the beginning of the town of Beaufort.

The expedition against St. Augustine was not a complete success. The South Carolinians destroyed the outlying mission villages and permanently ended the Spanish presence in Georgia. When they attacked St. Augustine, they were surprised and thwarted by the size and strength of the new Castillo San Marco, completed in 1680. The siege was abandoned when two Spanish ships arrived from Cuba. Moore's fleet was trapped in the harbor. Moore and Daniell burned their ships and retreated to Port Royal via the inland passage in a small fleet of peraguas. Upon their return, Moore and Daniell left a small detachment on Port Royal Island to guard the inland passage.[32]

In November 1703, the Lords Proprietors first reported to the Board of Trade that they had posted lookouts on the coast to warn of Spanish privateers and that they had also posted "a body of men at Port Royal to resist them in case they come within land." The next month, the Proprietors requested a royal navy frigate be stationed at Charles Town and noted that if the ship drew more than twelve feet of water it could be stationed at Port Royal "where a large frigate may ride with safety, which is deep water and not barred."[33]

The recognition of the strategic value of Port Royal and the necessity of defense during Queen Anne's War resulted in the founding of the town of Beaufort around the small wooden blockhouse and garrison on Port Royal Island. Between 1703 and 1706, the lookout post evolved into a two-story wooden blockhouse and a palisade enclosure on "the bay." By 1706, the garrison consisted of four officers and 112 men. It became a natural gathering place for the Indian traders and early planters of Port Royal and St. Helena Island.[34] By 1709, several merchants of the province and the traders and planters from the southern district petitioned for the founding of a town on Port Royal Island. They claimed it to be "the most proper place in the province for ships of Great Britain to take in masts, pitch, tar, turpentine, and other naval stores."[35]

At the same time, proprietary politics in London encouraged the founding of a second town on Port Royal Island. In 1694, John Granville, earl of Bath, acquired the duke of Albemarle's share of proprietary land. Albemarle had died without an heir, and his estate passed to the earl of Bath. The earl of Bath died in 1701. His eldest son, Charles (1661–1701), second earl of Bath, committed suicide after he discovered how little he had inherited. His son, William, became the third earl of Bath (died 1711). The second son of the first earl of Bath was John (1665–1707), who acquired his father's share in South Carolina and thereupon became a

Lord Proprietor of Carolina. On January 10, 1702, he became Lord Palatine. On March 9, 1702, he became Baron Granville of Potheridge, Devonshire. He married Rebecca Child (the daughter of Sir Josiah Child, a very wealthy London merchant), who was the widow of Charles Somerset (1661–1698, the son and heir of the first duke of Beaufort). When John, Lord Granville, died in 1707, his proprietorship passed to his wife, who transferred the property to her son by her first marriage, Henry Somerset (1684–1714, who became the second duke of Beaufort upon his grandfather's death in 1700).

After Lord Granville's death in 1707, William Lord Craven was elected palatine. He had been the heir of the first earl of Craven, being a great-grandson of Sir Robert Craven, a cousin of the earl of Craven. After Craven died in 1711, Henry Somerset, the second duke of Beaufort, was elected palatine on November 8, 1711. It was from this lineage that the names of Granville County and the town of Beaufort were derived.[36]

Sir George Carteret (1615–1680) was the original proprietor. Carteret's grandson George inherited the proprietorship and became Baron Carteret of Hawnes on October 14, 1681. He married Grace Granville (1654–1744), the older sister of the second earl of Bath and of John Lord Granville of Potheridge. Lord Carteret and Grace Granville had a son, John, who succeeded his father on September 22, 1695. Therefore, between 1701 and 1707, there were two proprietorships held by Lord Carteret and Lord Granville. Inasmuch as Lady Grace Carteret was to become countess of Granville on January 1, 1715, and her son, John, would succeed her upon her death on October 18, 1744, as earl of Granville, the family name of Granville seemed to be more important, and thus the use of Granville for this new South Carolina county.[37]

On February 22, 1704, John Barnwell had a grant for 400 acres on Scotts Island in Port Royal County. On October 25, 1707, John Conniers had a grant for 500 acres in Granville County. Thus, the change in names of this county took place sometime between 1704 and 1707, and it was referred to as Granville County until the Revolution.[38]

The Indian trade, the cattle industry, the emergence of an infant naval stores industry, and military necessity all dictated the importance of establishing a port on Port Royal Sound. The Indian traders who had settled on the sea islands were eager to improve the connections with Charleston and create a port. On July 19, 1707, Captain Thomas Nairne, John Cochran, Alexander Mackey, Thomas Palmenter, and Richard Reynolds were named commissioners for making highways, bridges, and cutting creeks southward of St. Helena Sound.[39] These men, most of whom were Indian traders, were undoubtedly the ones behind the movement to create a port among the sea islands. Nairne went over to London during the winter of 1708 to 1709 in order to make known to the Palatine Board the wishes of the commissioners. On April 9, 1709, several London merchants, among whom must have been Edward Crisp and several of the inhabitants of that part of South Carolina (presumably including Nairne), met at Craven House with the Lords Proprietors and urged them to make Port Royal a seaport. This was the period when the production of naval stores brought great wealth to certain South Carolinians.

These efforts resulted in a meeting on January 17, 1711, at Craven House, where the palatine (Lord Craven), the duke of Beaufort, Lord Carteret, Lord Maurice Ashley, Sir John Colleton, and John Danson (the son-in-law of John Archdale) met and ordered under their rights in the charter that Beaufort Town at Port Royal be established and declared a seaport which was to be ruled by the provisions of the Navigation Acts.[40] John Drayton said that Beaufort was named after Henry, duke of Beaufort. On February 21, 1711, the board selected Charles Craven as the governor of South Carolina.[41] On June 6, 1711, at Craven House, in the Eleventh Instruction drawn up for Charles Craven, he was required to issue warrants to eight persons, four from Colleton County and four from Granville County, "to sound the River of Port Royal & to examine which is the fittest place to fix a Town upon." On June 13, 1711, they ordered six hundred acres to be laid out for Edward Crisp as he "has given us several proofs of his good Inclinations to our Service and his earnest Endeavours to promote the general good of our province."[42] As Edward Crisp had issued his great map of South Carolina that very month, he had earned his six hundred acres. Inasmuch as the map contained two insets by Nairne, he must have been working closely with Crisp and with the Lords Proprietors.

On November 10, 1711, the General Assembly named Thomas Nairne, John Barnwell, Henry Quintyne, Edmund Bellinger, and Thomas Townsend to make one common highway, sixteen feet wide, from the islands of Port Royal and St. Helena to Ashepoo, to be made clear of all standing or lying trees, brush, and underwood and over all creeks to build strong substantial bridges.[9] Henry Quintyne was the only son of Richard Quintyne, who had been an original settler from Barbados and, in 1713, was supervisor of the Port Royal Watch. His sister married William Bull I. Henry Quintyne was murdered by Indians in July 1716.

On June 7, 1712, the parish of St. Helena was laid out to contain all of Granville County. The limits of the county were on the northeast the Combahee River and St. Helena Sound; on the northwest a line drawn from the head of the Combahee River to the Savannah River; and on the southeast by the ocean.[43] The new town was named Beaufort and its two principal streets were named Craven and Carteret, which they remain to this day. Thus, the town arose from military events on the southern frontier and meetings in London between 1709 and 1711. However, before the new town could be settled or the first lots sold, the southern frontier erupted in the most dangerous Indian war in American colonial history.

NOTES

1. J. G. Dunlop, "Spanish Depredations, 1686," *South Carolina Historical Magazine* 30 (April 1929): 81–89; "Paul Grimball's Losses by the Spanish Invasion in 1686," *South Carolina Historical Magazine* 29 (July 1928): 231–37; "Capt. Dunlop's Voyage to the Southward, 1687," *South Carolina Historical Magazine* 30 (July 1929): 127–30.

2. Joseph I. Waring, ed., "An Account of the Invasion of South Carolina by the French and Spaniards in August 1706," *South Carolina Historical Magazine* 66 (January 1965): 98–101; Kenneth R. Jones, "'A Full and Particular Account' of the Assault on Charleston in 1706," *South Carolina Historical Magazine* 83 (January 1982): 1–11.

3. David Lee Johnson, "The Yamasee War," M.A. thesis, University of South Carolina, 1980; Verner W. Crane, *The Southern Frontier, 1670–1732* (Durham: Duke University Press, 1928), chapter 7.

4. Phillip M. Brown, "Early Indian Trade in the Development of South Carolina: Politics, Economics and Social Mobility during the Proprietary Period, 1670–1719," *South Carolina Historical Magazine* 76 (July 1975): 118–28.

5. See above, chapter 3.

6. Crane, *Southern Frontier,* 26, 29–30.

7. Alexander Moore, "Henry Woodward's Twenty Years among the Southeastern Indians," paper presented at the Society for American Ethnohistory Annual Meeting, Charleston, South Carolina, November 1986.

8. Thomas Nairne, *Nairne's Muskhogean Journals: The 1708 Expedition to the Mississippi River,* ed. Alexander Moore (Jackson: University Press of Mississippi, 1988), 50.

9. Nairne, *Nairne's Muskhogean Journals,* 3–5; Crane, *Southern Frontier,* 46, 66, 74, 79.

10. A. S. Salley, ed., *Warrants for Land in South Carolina, 1672–1711* (Columbia: University of South Carolina Press, 1973), 582.

11. "Joseph Blake," in John W. Raimo, *Biographical Directory of American Colonial and Revolutionary Governors, 1607–1789* (Westport, Conn.: Meckler Books, 1980), pp. 421–22; "Robert Daniell," *Biographical Directory of the South Carolina House,* 2:180–82; "Charles Odingsell," *Biographical Directory of the South Carolina House,* 2:494.

12. Salley, ed., *Warrants,* 613, 626, 634. Index entries in *Warrants* indicate other Beaufort region grants.

13. "John Barnwell," *Biographical Directory of the South Carolina House,* 2:52–54; Stephen B. Barnwell, *The Story of an American Family* (Marquette, Mich.: Privately printed, 1969), 1–17.

14. William L. McDowell, ed., *Journals of the Commissioners of the Indian Trade, September 20, 1710–August 29, 1718* (Columbia: University of South Carolina Press, 1955), 252; *Nairne's Muskhogean Journals,* 12, 19.

15. See McDowell, ed., *Journals of the Commissioners of the Indian Trade.*

16. Thomas Cooper and David J. McCord, eds., *The Statutes at Large of South Carolina,* 10 vols. (Columbia: A.S. Johnston, 1836–1841), 2: 317–18.

17. McDowell, ed., *Journals of the Commissioners of the Indian Trade,* 11.

18. Cooper and McCord, eds., *Statutes of South Carolina,* 2: 599–600.

19. Richard L. Haan, "The 'Trade do's not flourish as formerly': The Ecological Origins of the Yamassee War of 1715," *Ethnohistory* 28 (Fall 1982): 343.

20. See Kean's Neck in Beaufort District and Bear Island in Colleton District on maps in Robert Mills, *Mills' Atlas of South Carolina, 1825* (Easley, S.C.: Southern Historical Press, 1980).

21. Samuel Wilson, "An Account of the Province of Carolina, in America," in *Historical Collections of South Carolina,* ed. B. R. Carroll (New York: Harper, 1836), 2: 29.

22. Wilson, "An Account of the Province of Carolina," 29.

23. [John Norris] *Profitable Advice for Rich and Poor . . .* (1712), in *Selling a New World: Two Colonial South Carolina Promotional Pamphlets,* ed. Jack P. Greene (Columbia: University of South Carolina Press, 1989), 102.

24. John S. Otto, "The Origins of Cattle Ranching in Colonial South Carolina, 1670–1715," *South Carolina Historical Magazine* 87 (July 1986): 121–22; Gary S. Dunbar, "Colonial Carolina Cowpens," *Agricultural History* 34 (January 1961): 125–30.

25. A. S. Salley, ed., "Stock Marks Recorded in South Carolina, 1695–1721," *South Carolina Historical Magazine* 13 (April 1912): 126–31.

26. Jessica Stevens Loring, *Auldbrass, the Plantation Complex Designed by Frank Lloyd Wright* (Greenville: Southern Historical Press, 1992), 5–6.

27. Alexander Moore, "The Daniel Axtell Account Book and the Economy of Early South Carolina," *South Carolina Historical Magazine* 95 (October 1994): 280–301.

28. Converse D. Clowse, *Economic Beginnings in Colonial South Carolina, 1670–1730* (Columbia: University of South Carolina Press, 1971), 82–83, 135, 178–79.

29. John R. Todd and Francis M. Hutson, *Prince William Parish and Plantations* (Richmond: Garrett and Massie, 1935), 2–3, 15–17.

30. Edgar L. Pennington, "The South Carolina Indian War of 1715, as Seen by the Clergymen," *South Carolina Historical Magazine* 32 (October 1931): 251–67.

31. Francis Yonge, *A View of the Trade of South Carolina with Proposals Humbly Offer'd for Improving the Same* (London, 1722), 6.

32. Crane, *Southern Frontier,* 46, 175–77.

33. A. S. Salley, ed., *Records in the British Public Record Office Relating to South Carolina,* 5 vols. (Columbia: Historical Commission of South Carolina, 1928–1947), 5: 112, 117.

34. Salley, ed., *Records in the British Public Record Office,* 5: 150–51.

35. Henry A. M. Smith, "Beaufort: The Original Town and Earliest Settlers," *South Carolina Historical Magazine* 9 (1908): 141–42.

36. George C. Rogers Jr., "Walking in the Footsteps of the Lords Proprietors," *Carologue* (a publication of the South Carolina Historical Society) 10 (Autumn 1994): 8–12, 18–19.

37. Rogers, "Walking in the Footsteps."

38. Salley, ed., *Warrants,* 626, 638.

39. Cooper and McCord, eds., *Statutes of South Carolina,* 9: 11.

40. British Public Record Office Transcripts, 6: 1, 3, South Carolina Department of Archives and History.

41. John Drayton, *A View of South Carolina, As Respects Her Natural and Civil Concerns* (1802; Spartanburg, S. C.: Reprint Co., 1972), 208–9; British Public Record Office Transcripts, 6: 10–12, South Carolina Department of Archives and History.

42. British Public Record Office Transcripts, 6: 43–47, South Carolina Department of Archives and History.

43. Cooper and McCord, eds., *Statutes of South Carolina,* 9: 14–17.

5

Yemassee War

The complex collision of cultures, interest, and raw force on the Port Royal frontier ignited the most dangerous and decisive Indian war in South Carolina history. The Yemassee War, which erupted with sudden fury on Good Friday, April 15, 1715, was much more than an isolated Indian massacre. It was a far-reaching conspiracy involving most of the tribes on the southern frontier. The principal conspirators were the powerful old Emperor Brims of Coweta, leader of the Creek nations, and the wily Huspa king of the Yemassee.

Rumors of the impending uprising spread through the white settlements during Easter week, 1715. While William Bray was tracking runaway slaves in Florida, a Yoa Indian named Cuffy came to his wife near Port Royal and warned her of the plot among the Creeks and Yemassee. The same rumor reached Samuel Warner at the Palachacola settlement on April 12, 1715. Both men hurried into Charleston with the disturbing news. Bray and Warner were immediately dispatched to Pocotaligo to assist Captain Thomas Nairne in forestalling hostilities. There they were joined by experienced traders, John Cochran and John Wright, who came to assist in the parlay.

During the day, April 14, Nairne's delegation seemed to make progress with the Yemassee headmen. After a friendly meal, the South Carolinians retired believing their assurances had averted a crisis. At dawn, April 15, however, they awoke to the terrifying sight of Yemassee braves dressed for the warpath, their bodies painted with red and black rays symbolic of war and death, "which made them resemble devils coming out of hell." Clearly the Yemassee chiefs knew while they were negotiating that the plot was irreversible. What is surprising is that they were able to deceive such experienced frontiersmen as Nairne, Bray, Warner, Cochran, and Wright.[1]

All the white traders and their families in the Yemassee villages were attacked. Between twenty-five and ninety people were killed on the first day. In addition, the Creek tribes of Georgia and Alabama massacred the English traders in their villages on the same day.

William Bray, Samuel Warner, and John Wright were killed immediately. John Cochran and his wife were held captive for a time and later murdered. Thomas Nairne, though once the Yemassee's friend and protector, was saved for a particularly refined form of torture. His flesh was pierced with slivers of resinous fat pine wood which were then set afire. Nairne endured this torture, according to reports, for four days before finally dying. With the death of Nairne, who was considered a founder of Beaufort, along with Colonel John Barnwell, the mantle of leadership on the Port Royal frontier passed to his protégé and friend, "Tuscarora Jack."

Only two white men escaped the massacre at Pocotaligo. One, a trader whose name was lost to history, hid in the marsh near the village and witnessed the slaughter of his friends. Nine days later, he appeared half-starved at Woodward's Fort on the Ashepoo River. The other man, named Seymour Burroughs, muscled his way through the crowd of Indians despite being shot twice with muskets. One shot in his back remained lodged in his chest. The other pierced his cheek taking most of his teeth with it. Despite these terrible wounds, Burroughs escaped through the woods and swam several miles down the Broad River to bring news of the disaster to John Barnwell's plantation near Seabrook, on Port Royal Island.

This heroic deed saved the families on Port Royal Island. Barnwell immediately dispatched riders to the neighboring settlements and to the new town of Beaufort. Their warning allowed the three hundred whites and a few slaves living on Port Royal Island to seek refuge aboard a smuggler's ship then impounded and in the bay at Beaufort. As soon as the settlers had gathered on board, the Yemassee appeared in town. They fired on the ship for several hours with no effect and the settlers answered with several shots from the ship's cannons. The Indians then set fire to the town, as they had to most of the plantations on Port Royal Island, and returned to Pocotaligo.[2]

While one party of Yemassee had attacked Port Royal, another had crossed the Combahee River into Colleton County where the scattered plantations had no warning. There more than one hundred settlers fell into the hands of the Indians and were killed, while the rest fled in panic toward Charleston.

The initial attack was devastating. Verner Crane states that, "At a stroke the Yemassee had massacred the traders and destroyed the border settlements." Governor Craven responded to the emergency with dispatch. He raised the Colleton Militia, threw up a hasty fort at Woodward's plantation on the Ashepoo River, and checked the advance of the raiders. Then he ordered a two-pronged counterattack. Under his own command he led the bulk of the Colleton Militia overland to the crossing at the head of the Combahee River near the present town of Yemassee. Another party under Captain Alexander MacKay and Colonel

John Barnwell gathered several boats and advanced up the Broad River to attack Pocotaligo.³

Craven's force encountered the main body of the Yemassee emerging from the eastern edge of the Salkehatchie Swamp. With a semicircular advance, the Indians nearly surrounded the militia; but Governor Craven rallied his men, and, after killing some of the Yemassee chiefs, routed the enemy, who fled through the swamp. Fearing an ambush, Craven halted his forces.

Meanwhile, Barnwell and MacKay had creeped up unnoticed on Pocotaligo, where they found many stolen items but few defenders. They routed the Indians, who fled to a more heavily defended fort about four miles away. There Barnwell and MacKay's force of 140 South Carolinians found a large fort defended by 200 Indians. It was in this battle that John Palmer distinguished himself for heroism and became, after "Tuscarora Jack" Barnwell, the most celebrated Indian fighter on the Port Royal frontier. Palmer, leading a small body of men, scaled the walls of the fort. Despite being driven from the town at first, he returned to the attack and succeeded in forcing the Yemassee warriors from the enclosure where they were killed, captured, or scattered by MacKay's troops waiting in the woods.

These dual victories on the southern frontier proved decisive. They drove the Yemassee settlements from the Port Royal area and, except for continuing forays, kept them from resettling in South Carolina. The war then shifted to the northern and western frontiers. After an ambush of the militia by the Congaree Indians, the Winyah frontier was evacuated and the whole colony was confined to a ring of forts around Charleston. The situation for South Carolina at this juncture was critical. It was estimated that the Creeks and their allies could field nine thousand warriors to oppose the twelve hundred men of the South Carolina militia. Had it not been for the intrepid activity of a few South Carolina frontiersmen—Colonel Maurice Moore, Eleazer Wigan, Robert Gilcrest, and Colonel George Chicken—in securing an alliance with the Cherokee, the Indians might well have realized their goal of driving the English into the sea. As it turned out, the Cherokee alliance, which added five thousand warriors to the South Carolina side, balanced the forces on the southern frontier and placed the Creeks and their allies in a defensive posture. By April 1716, the immediate danger to the province had passed but a period of sporadic raiding continued until the formal treaty with the Creeks was signed in June 1718.

While frontier diplomacy was ensuring the survival of Charleston, the Port Royal area remained the site of the most intense and enduring Indian raids. In July 1715, a raid of Apalachee Indians across the Edisto River prompted Governor Craven to dispatch Captain William Stone with six piraguas and one hundred men to Port Royal Island. There, Stone cut off six retreating war canoes and drove the Indians into the woods. In August, Indian war canoes were still around Port Royal Sound and the Combahee River. Colonel Fenwick marched from the Edisto River to the Combahee ferry, where he surprised a body of Indians looting Jackson's plantation. Colonel Fenwick then commandeered the Indian canoes and took his party to Port Royal to join Captain Stone, Captain John Palmer, and Captain Seymour Burroughs.

Learning that eight to ten Yemassee war canoes had come up the inland passage from Georgia and were in the Port Royal area, Fenwick, Stone, Palmer, and Burroughs proceeded with their small fleet to the southern tip of Daufuskie Island, a spot the Indians had to pass on their water route back to Georgia. There Stone went ashore, concealing his men and boats, while Palmer lay out of sight with his boats in a nearby creek, with Burroughs's long boat and its powerful swivel gun in reserve. When the Yemassee canoes rounded the inside point of Daufuskie Island, they were completely surprised by Palmer's party. Receiving heavy fire from Palmer's piraguas and Burroughs's swivel gun, they abandoned their canoes and swam for the woods of Daufuskie. There they were met by the withering fire of Stone's ambush. Thirty-five Yemassee were killed and two taken prisoner. Two canoes escaped. This was the "Daufuskie fight" of late August 1715, from which two erroneous local traditions had arisen. The first was that this was the "last stand" of the Yemassee in South Carolina, which it was not. They continued to raid the Port Royal area for the next thirteen years. The second was that this battle gave the present name of "Bloody Point" to the southern tip of Daufuskie Island. In fact, that name was not used until after the second battle in the same location in January 1728. The Daufuskie fight, however, did show that the Port Royal settlers had learned well the Indian military tactics of concealment and surprise.[4]

As a result of these defeats, the Yemassee continued to retreat south along the coast of Georgia until they found refuge and protection in Spanish Florida. In October 1715, a South Carolina expedition led by the redoubtable old enemy of the Spanish, Lieutenant Governor Robert Daniell, left Charleston bent on destroying the remaining Yemassee.[5] The South Carolinians had learned from captives taken in the Daufuskie fight that the Huspa king and the rest of the Yemassee tribe had resettled their ancestral lands on the Altamaha River. Daniell's expedition found the Altamaha village abandoned and pursued the Indians into Florida. A second expedition in February 1716 pursued the Yemassee practically to the walls of St. Augustine. Though Spanish protection prevented them from annihilating the Yemassee, they did capture thirty Indians including the Yoa king and his family.[6]

The Yemassee now made permanent settlements near St. Augustine. The Spanish welcomed them as allies and provided them with arms and provisions which they used to harass the southern coast of South Carolina. When the South Carolina authorities protested to the Spanish governor they were told that "he looked upon ye Yemassees as subjects of Spain who a long time ago revolted from the Crown and are now returned again to their former allegiance."[7] Not only did the Yemassees seek refuge in St. Augustine, but many black slaves were kidnapped or fled to St. Augustine, where, if they adopted Roman Catholicism, they were emancipated but employed as state levies to work on the Castillo San Marcos.[8] Occasionally, they were armed for raids against South Carolina. These desertions were costly. Over the next half-century, the slave refuge in St. Augustine was a constant problem for South Carolina and the southern district. During 1715, ninety-eight black and Indian slaves fled to St. Augustine. The greatest slave losses were suffered by John Cochran, John Barnwell, and William Bray.

South Carolinians were also aghast that the Spanish allowed the Yemassees to keep their captive white women and children as slaves.[9] The most famous of these was Hugh Bryan, son of Joseph Bryan, who was a slave of the Huspa king for two years before being returned as a gesture of peace. Bryan defended the Huspa king, saying he had saved Bryan's life, and wished to return to the English. The Huspa king, however, remained an elusive character. When the English sent a peace emissary to the Huspa town in Florida, the king was nowhere to be found, and the Spanish later told the English that "When he talks of going to one place, he commonly goes to another."[10]

Yemassee war canoes continued to range the inland passage with impunity. To counter these "vexatious raids," a series of lookout posts were scattered among the sea islands to complement the ring of forts on the mainland. These lookout posts were irregularly occupied by the scout boat crews who patrolled southward from the Edisto River. The most important of these camps was on the southern tip of Daufuskie Island, later named Bloody Point, at the extreme southern corner of the province. From here the scouts could observe the whole entrance to the Savannah River and the mouth of St. Augustine Creek behind Tybee Island, the old entrance of the inland passage to Florida. Posts were also located at Spanish Wells on the south end of Hilton Head Island, Look-Out Point on MacKay's (now Pinckney) Island, Cochran's Point on the north end of Port Royal Island, and another near the ruined village of Beaufort at the south end of Port Royal Island.[11] These scout camps were gradually replaced by a more efficient system of roving waterborne patrols ranging from the Stono River in South Carolina to the Altamaha River in Georgia.[12]

On August 1, 1716, the Port Royal frontier suffered a serious reversal when a party of Yemassee ambushed Major Henry Quintyne, new commander of the Port Royal scout boat, and his entire crew. Among the dead were Major Quintyne;

Captain Thomas Parmenter, one of the first settlers on Port Royal Island and a veteran scout; and Thomas Simons. Only Dr. Rose, left for dead with a cut across his nose, escaped the massacre.[13]

During 1716, the Lower Creek tribes in Georgia began to waver in their commitment to their Indian allies. One faction came to the English with a flag of truce and a promise to destroy the Yemassee, whom they accused of being "the beginners of these troubles." They even brought in three Yemassee scalps as proof of their sincerity. Thus, while the Cherokees made war on the Creeks on behalf of the English and part of the Creeks made war on the Yemassee on behalf of the English, the Yemassee made war on the English on behalf of the Spanish. This confusion was partially resolved when a formal treaty with the Creeks was signed in June 1718. This ended hostilities in the backcountry and assured the survival of Charleston.[14]

The Yemassee, however, remained intractable. They had been received in St. Augustine "amidst great rejoicing" and had been thoroughly provided for by the Florida governor. In 1720, it was reported that three to four hundred Yemassee warriors lived in four villages near St. Augustine. This number seemed too high and probably included several other refugee tribes from South Carolina and Georgia. Nevertheless, they continued to inflict damage and prevent resettlement in the Port Royal area.

During the summer of 1719, a Yemassee party led by a Huspa warrior attacked Port Royal. They killed three white men and captured the wife of Captain Seymour Burroughs and her neighbor, Mrs. McCord. They also took one of the Burroughs's children, a slave named Marcus, and a Cusabo Indian slave. Only Mrs. Burroughs made it to St. Augustine alive; the rest were slain enroute. Seymour Burroughs and his neighbors pursued the raiders and actually arrived in St. Augustine before them. There Burroughs was imprisoned as a spy despite a commission from Governor Craven. When the Indians brought Mrs. Burroughs to town, they were both released and taken as guests to Captain Romero's house. Both returned to South Carolina, where Mrs. Burroughs claimed, as Hugh Bryan had two years before, that her life was spared by the intercession of the Huspa king.[15]

This outrage prompted Colonel John Barnwell to organize a large expedition against the Yemassee in September 1719. The expedition was commanded by a Creek warrior named Oweeka and included a white man named Melvin, two half-breeds named Musgrove and Griffin, and fifty Indians including parties led by King Gilbert of the Coosa and King Foster of the Tuscaroras, both then living near Port Royal. Seven canoes left Port Royal on September 28 and reached the St. Johns River by October 10. Two days later, they attacked the Yemassee towns. They burned the Yoa town of Tolomato and ransacked the church and house of Father Pedro de la Lastras. They next attacked a nearby village of Apalachee Indians. A platoon of fifty or sixty Spanish soldiers then marched out from Fort San Marcos. Though the Creeks sent word that they came only to kill the Yemassee in retaliation for the recent murders at Port Royal, the Spanish paid no heed and continued to advance in close formation. Oweeka then divided his forces and attacked the flanks of the Spanish company. After having fourteen men killed and ten taken prisoner, the Spanish retreated to the safety of their castillo. Oweeka and his party returned quickly to Port Royal with all the plunder they could carry. On October 28, two canoes reached Barnwell's plantation and reported capturing twelve Yemassee slaves, two Spanish men, and one Frenchman.

In June 1720, the Yemassee retaliated. First, they attacked a Creek town in Georgia, killed seven warriors, and took many prisoners. Next, they attacked St. Helena Island, killed a white man, and captured Mr. June, a tanner, with twelve black slaves whom they took to St. Augustine. On August 19, 1720, William Dry wrote to Colonel Barnwell describing this raid. His conclusion was prescient: "We must never live peaceably here," he wrote, "whilst the Spaniards are in St. Augustine." Dry later moved to North Carolina.[16]

In August 1720, the South Carolinians sent a flag of truce to the Yemassee, who surprised everyone by quickly accepting it and returning Mr. June and fifty white captives to South Carolina. Thus began two years of quiet on the Port Royal frontier. The Port Royal area, though, was ruined and uninhabited. Almost all the Indians had gone, and in 1721 there were only thirty white and forty-two black inhabitants in all of St. Helena Parish. The permanence of these few settlers was very much in doubt. The lack of adequate defenses made the position of the settlers hazardous. In that year, the inhabitants petitioned for the rebuilding of the fort at Beaufort. "The fort at Beaufort is so much out of repair . . . that the same is defenseless . . . the inhabitants have no place of security for their families in time of alarm, which so dispirits them as may cause a desertion of these frontiers."[17]

In addition to repairing the old fort, the provincial authorities decided in 1722 to improve and formalize the system of scout boats which during the Yemassee War had proved far more effective against the highly mobile Indians than any fixed installation among the sea islands. Two heavily armed scout boats were stationed at Port Royal with Colonel John Barnwell as commissioner in charge. One was to cruise the inland passage between Beaufort and the Stono River and the other was to range southward into Georgia and Florida. These boats were piraguas, about thirty feet long with a crew of six men and a scout boat commander, all heavily armed with muskets, cutlasses, and pikes. The piraguas were equipped with two loose-footed sails on removable masts but used oars as their primary means of propulsion. Each boat was equipped with a heavy swivel gun. Their main function was not for defense but as an alarm system. They were to bring advance warning of attack to the Port Royal Militia. In 1722, however, it was recognized that the Port Royal Militia was understaffed and overworked. Every landowner in St. Helena Parish was, therefore, required to supply one white man for every one thousand acres he owned in order to bolster the militia on the exposed frontier. In addition, because of the frequency of alarms, all settlers living within thirty miles of Port Royal were exempt from normal garrison or scout duty.[18]

In 1723, the Palachacola Fort was established in the northwest corner of Granville County near the present town of Garnet. This was a well-traveled crossing of the Savannah River, later to be known as the Two Sisters Ferry. For years it had been an important Indian crossing, and trading posts had grown up there long before the Yemassee War. In 1723, the Commons House appropriated four hundred pounds currency for the construction of a small palisaded fort armed with light cannon. It was garrisoned by a sergeant and nineteen privates. Lieutenant William Bellinger was the first commander. From the Palachacola fort, overland patrols were to range across the pine barrens to the confluence of the Salkehatchie and Combahee Rivers near the present town of Yemassee and as far north as the road connecting Charleston and Fort Moore (Augusta). These mainland patrols were to complement the waterborne scouts from Port Royal to ensure that the Indians now stayed south of the Savannah River.[19]

To Colonel Barnwell, these acts were merely gestures. The only permanent solution for the defense of Port Royal was to move the English frontier further southward. It was at this juncture that Barnwell provided his greatest service to the settlement of Port Royal and to the future of the British empire on the southern frontier. Late in 1720, Barnwell traveled to England to promote his views on the settlement of the southern frontier to the Board of Trade. There Barnwell joined forces with Joseph Boone, the South Carolina agent in London, and established a political alliance and friendship with General Francis Nicholson, soon to return with Barnwell to South Carolina as its interim royal governor.[20]

Barnwell's influence with the Board of Trade and with many leaders of the British government was great. He was an eloquent spokesperson of the imperial vision he shared with Thomas Nairne. He was a war hero and veteran commander of frontier forces, and he had firsthand knowledge of the complex relationships among the English in South Carolina, the Spanish in Florida, the French on the Mississippi River, and the various Indian tribes caught in between. He was, in addition, the largest planter and landowner on the Port Royal frontier with a real, not speculative, interest in a permanent settlement of the southern frontier.

Barnwell outlined the facts of the southern frontier, highlighting the potential danger of French encirclement and emphasizing the importance of the royal
government's direct involvement in the defense of South Carolina. Barnwell's
plan was bold. It called for a string of forts from the middle of Tennessee to the
mouth of the Altamaha River in Georgia. These forts would be located on the
Tennessee River, west of the Appalachians; at "Savannah Town" (modern-day
Augusta), on the Savannah River; at Palachacola, on the lower Savannah; and at
the mouth of the Altamaha River (modern-day Darien, Georgia). Lands around
these forts were to be reserved for permanent settlers or for grants to the soldiers.
Port Royal would become the port of entry and the magazine of supply for the
entire frontier. Thus, South Carolina would become the southern shield of the
British colonies in North America, and Port Royal would become a strategic
port of empire.[21]

The Board of Trade was impressed by the imminent danger posed by the
French and Spanish and by Barnwell's knowledgeable and forceful presentation.
The board acted with uncharacteristic dispatch and approved Barnwell's plan in
a week. The Privy Council, however, was less enthusiastic and ultimately approved only the fort at the mouth of the Altamaha.[22] Despite this disappointment, the historic result of Barnwell's plan was far reaching. It remains one of the
best early expressions of English desire for westward expansion and continental
dominion, a destiny which was far from manifest during Barnwell's lifetime and
particularly doubtful during the awful spring of 1715. It was also the seed of
Governor Robert Johnson's Township Plan of the 1730s, which was largely the
basis for settling the South Carolina backcountry.[23] And, perhaps most important
to the Port Royal frontier, Barnwell's plan was the genesis of Georgia.

Barnwell returned to South Carolina to personally take charge of the construction of the fort on the Altamaha. On May 22, 1721, the HMS *Enterprise*
arrived in Charleston with Barnwell, Governor Francis Nicholson, and a company of royal troops. Though Barnwell was personally disappointed in not receiving a royal commission to command the new fort, the provincial government
quickly charged him, as commander of the South Carolina scouts, with the
responsibility of building it. He did not have much to work with. Instead of a
battalion of infantry, which Barnwell and Governor Nicholson had hoped for,
the home government sent only a company of old pensioners hardly fit for the
task and half sick. No engineers, carpenters, blacksmiths, or bricklayers were
provided. The task of building a regular royal fort as intended was impossible, but
Barnwell pressed on. He altered the plan to provide a temporary palisade fort
and a few huts until a more permanent installation could be constructed.[24] To
complete the task, he enlisted Captain Joseph Parmenter and the South Carolina
scouts from the posts at Port Royal and MacKay's Islands. Barnwell was further

disappointed by the behavior of the scouts in his absence. They were a "wild, idle people and continually sotting if they can get any rum for trust or money." This motley crew arrived at the Altamaha on July 13, 1721, and under Barnwell's energetic leadership managed to erect the earth and palisade fort, build the huts, move the garrison in, and set up a regular supply system from Beaufort by the end of 1721. The lookout at the fort commanded a view of the marshes and creeks of this inland passage from the mainland to St. Simon's Island. In clear violation of historic Spanish claims, the English fort now controlled the lands of the Guale missions, and Barnwell's settlement plan of 1720 replaced Father Juan Rogel's mission plan of 1572.[25]

The presence of Fort King George on historic Spanish lands occasioned lengthy diplomatic exchanges between Madrid and London and frequent negotiations between St. Augustine and Charleston. Not coincidentally, Yemassee Indians began to reappear on the South Carolina frontier. In June 1723, two years after the last raid on St. Helena Island, Colonel Barnwell was informed that a Yemassee named Istawekee was lurking in the area, harbored by a settler named Blakeway. It was suspected that Istawekee kept a canoe on the Savannah River and occasionally transported parties of Apalachee Indians into South Carolina. Since the Apalachee tribe of Chief Cherokeeleechee had been driven from their former town on the Savannah and were now allies of the Yemassee, they were not welcome intruders. Istawekee was once driven away by Barnwell's Indian scouts but returned in September 1723 and was finally captured by Captain Joseph Parmenter on Parris Island. When accused by Barnwell of trespassing on private property, the island then being the property of Provincial Treasurer Alexander Parris, it was Istawekee who defiantly asserted the Indian belief that the land ought to be free, like the air and water. Barnwell incarcerated Istawekee but allowed his companions free passage back to Georgia.[26]

At the same time, several Creek tribes began again to harass the Yemassee settlements in Florida. These minor disturbances were followed by a major Creek raiding party sent out by Emperor Brims of Coweta to destroy the Yemassee towns. The raid failed due to a premature attack on a Spanish garrison, but the Creeks claimed to have wounded the Huspa king and killed his head warrior.

In 1724, just as these disturbances began to degenerate into open warfare, Colonel Barnwell died. His death was greatly lamented in the province, and Governor Francis Nicholson wrote of the "great loss that His Majesties Province in general and more particularly that part to the southward hath sustained by the death of the Honorable Colonel Barnwell."[27] He had done more than any man, both on the battlefield and in the council chamber, to sustain the struggling settlement at Port Royal. Perhaps his tough frontier character can best be summed up in a frequently repeated quotation attributed to him many years later by his son Nathaniel, "Never trust a Spaniard, nor be afraid of an Indian."

Though Barnwell was the largest landowner in the Port Royal area, the value of his estate was rather modest, probably a result of the depredations on the frontier and a testimony to the amount of energy he expended in public service. Barnwell left only eighteen slaves and a total estate valued at less than six thousand pounds South Carolina currency. He left considerable progeny, however. Most of the natural leadership of the Port Royal area for more than a century was descended from John Barnwell's two sons and five daughters.[28]

Many of Barnwell's military responsibilities were passed on to Colonel John Woodward. He was also a large landowner in Colleton County, on Port Royal Island, and in the town of Beaufort. He was the scion of the oldest family in South Carolina and a son of Dr. Henry Woodward. Colonel Woodward was named commissioner of the South Carolina scouts, was empowered to complete the work of Fort King George, and was given the contract to supply both the scouts and the fort in Georgia from his store in Beaufort. In 1724, his concern over the Indian disturbances led the Commons House to authorize another look out at the mouth of Port Royal Sound (Bay Point) and to move the "Great Guns" from John Palmer's plantation on the Stono to Beaufort.[29]

But Woodward did not prove to be as effective a leader as Barnwell had been. In 1724, he was involved in a minor election controversy in the Commons House, and in 1725 he was accused of using his position as commissioner to hinder the military duty of the scout boats by requiring that they carry heavy loads of his provisions down the inland waterway to Fort King George to fulfill his contract. The Commons House made no fine distinction on the conflict of interest but "strongly directed Woodward not to hinder the military duty of the scout boats."[30] Provincial concern for the deteriorating condition of the Port Royal defenses prompted the Committee on Fortifications to recommend in 1726 the construction at Beaufort of a "good and substantial fort . . . built with lime, shell and sand mixed."[31] This was the genesis of Fort Prince Frederick, the ruins of which still stand on the grounds of the U.S. Naval Hospital.

Just at this juncture, the Yemassee began a fresh and terrifying series of raids. In September 1726, a small party of Yemassee attacked the plantation of John Edwards on the Combahee River. They killed Edwards and carried four black slaves to St. Augustine, in addition to plundering his home.[32] In the summer of 1727, several raids occurred, prompted, the Yemassee claimed, by the Spanish governor's bounty offer of thirty pieces of eight for every white scalp and one hundred pieces of eight for every live black delivered to St. Augustine. In June 1727, William Lavy and John Sparks were murdered and scalped by a party of Yemassee. Their wives were spared but left with the chilling news "that there was a party, both Indians and Spaniards, fitting out from St. Augustine who had received orders from the Governor to spare nobody."[33] In July, five traders were killed and scalped within sight of Fort King George. Their trading post was plundered, and three white prisoners were taken to St. Augustine. Perhaps the same raiding party continued up the inland passage to South Carolina, where they killed Henry Mishoe and Hezakiah Wood and captured ten black slaves. Captain John Bull and fifteen South Carolinians pursued them, killing a Spaniard and six Indians and wounding many of the rest. The blacks told Captain Bull that the Indians had tried to save Wood's life but that the Spaniard took a wooden club and "knocked out his brains." In September, a party of Indians and blacks from St. Augustine attacked Hilton Head Island. They killed or captured four adults and four children at the plantation of Alexander Dawson, who reported that the fugitive slaves had prevented the Indians from murdering all the whites.[34]

These raids caused the citizens of Port Royal to petition Acting Governor Arthur Middleton, expressing their fear of "Spaniards and Indians committing depredations on the settlement."[35] Middleton used this petition to urge his plan of launching an attack against St. Augustine. "I am in great pain for our settlement at Port Royal," he stated, "and apprehensive that the Spaniards from St. Augustine may suddenly destroy the same. . . . I really believe that part of our settlement will be attacked." Middleton offered to use contingency funds to pay for the expedition and the Commons House chose veteran Indian fighter Colonel John Palmer to lead the expedition.[36]

Palmer had settled along the Combahee River in Colleton County before the Yemassee War. He first gained fame as the hero of the assault at Pocotaligo in 1715 and was generally thought to be the mastermind of the successful "Daufuskie fight" later that year. Palmer was not as politically active as other leaders of the Port Royal frontier, such as Thomas Nairne or John Barnwell. Palmer's interest in St. Helena Parish increased after his marriage to Elizabeth Bellinger, daughter of Landgrave Edmund Bellinger, who held title to a twelve-thousand-acre barony in what was later to become the mainland parish of Prince William. Palmer held many local offices—commissioner of the High Roads south of the Combahee (1721), commissioner to lay out the road from Port Royal to Purrysburg (1733), and commissioner of the Port Royal and Combahee ferries. Palmer represented St. Helena Parish in the Commons House in 1728.[37] Palmer's death defending Fort Moosa during Oglethorpe's siege of St. Augustine in 1740 was one of the principal causes of the hostility between Georgia and South Carolina at that time.

Before Palmer's expedition could get under way, one of the Yemassee raiding parties massacred the entire crew of one of the South Carolina scout boats on Daufuskie Island. Captain Barnabas Gilbert and his crew were camped at the look out on the southern tip of Daufuskie Island in January 1728, when they were surprised by a Yemassee war party. The entire crew was put to death except Captain Gilbert, who was carried to St. Augustine as a prisoner. This was the massacre which gave the name "Bloody Point" to the southern tip of Daufuskie Island. It also spurred the Commons House to step up preparations for Palmer's expedition.

Colonel Palmer's force consisted of 110 of the South Carolina Militia and an equal number of Indians from various friendly tribes. Captain John Hunt and Captain William Peter commanded under Palmer. The South Carolina expedition was constrained to attack only the Indians since any attack on the Spanish would precipitate an international incident. Knowing this, the Yemassee had abandoned their outlying villages and established a town virtually under the guns of the Castillo San Marcos in St. Augustine. Nevertheless, Palmer was able to approach the town at night, on March 9, 1728. At dawn his forces surprised the village and routed its defenders, killing thirty warriors and capturing fourteen prisoners. For three days, Palmer's army besieged the castillo while plundering and destroying at will outside the walls. The Spanish answered with an ineffective artillery bombardment and then sent an accommodating message to Colonel Palmer asking him to lift the siege. Palmer demanded beef and provisions for the return voyage and when that was provided, began the long trek back to South Carolina. Palmer had suffered light casualties, with only two Indian allies wounded.[38]

Almost as soon as Palmer could make his report, a debate arose in the Commons House as to the value of the raid. It was argued that Palmer had not eliminated the source of the Yemassee raids, namely the Spanish base at St. Augustine, and may have only succeeded in further arousing the hostility of the intractable Yemassee. No action was brought against Palmer by the Commons House. He could hardly have been expected to attack the strong Spanish fortress at St. Augustine without artillery or naval support. The men of St. Helena Parish, on the other hand, did not question the efficacy of Palmer's raid.[39] In spite of the controversy, they returned Palmer to the Commons House immediately following the expedition. And, as it turned out, Palmer's raid finally ended the Yemassee War.

The Yemassee raids on Port Royal ceased. The Spanish in Florida lost considerable prestige among their Indian allies because of their inability to defeat Palmer's small army, and even in Havana many Spanish "privately condemned" the governor at St. Augustine as the aggressor.[40] Not only did the Yemassee raids end, but the lower Creeks of Georgia were now more than ever on the side of the English. The Port Royal area was more secure than it had been for thirteen years.[41]

The Yemassee disappeared from South Carolina and soon disappeared as a tribe altogether. During the eighteenth century, they continued to maintain one village, named Pocotaligo, under the walls of St. Augustine and, as late as 1761, were still considered a distinct tribe with about twenty men.[42] The remnants of theYemassee gradually merged with other bands of Lower Creek refugees to whom they were related. Collectively these tribes were known as Seminoles, a Creek Indian word meaning "runaway" or "vagabond."[43]

In the Port Royal area the effects of the Yemassee War were momentous. Early in the war, the large herds of cattle which preceded planting on the frontier were destroyed. The Yemassee War also removed Beaufort from the normal pattern of the Indian trade. Most of that commerce now flowed through "Savannah Town" and Fort Moore near present-day Augusta.[44] It is speculative to try to imagine what role Beaufort might have played as a commercial center in the early colonial period had it not been for the alterations wrought by the Yemassee War. But the earliest settlers in the Port Royal area—Henry Woodward in the 1670s, Lord Cardross and Caleb Westbrooke in the 1680s, and Thomas Nairne and John Barnwell at the turn of the eighteenth century—were all Indian traders. It was on this trade that their initial hopes for commercial development at Port Royal were pinned. The fact that Port Royal never achieved much commercial importance in the colonial period may be partly attributable to the changes brought about by the Yemassee War.

The most important result of the Yemassee War to the settlers of the Port Royal frontier, however, was its lingering memory. Well into the 1750s, the most prominent topic in the public life of the Port Royal area was defense. The fear of horrible massacres, lurking savages, and the memory of the kidnapping, torture, and bloody destruction of wives, husbands, and children was not removed for a generation.

The elimination of the Yemassee threat to the Port Royal frontier by Palmer's raid of 1728 issued in a period of stability and economic growth during the 1730s. The development of rice plantations among the mainland swamps encouraged the settlement of the Purrysburg Township and brought the first large influx of African slaves to the Beaufort District. But the memory of thirteen years of murderous raids by the Yemassee and costly counter expeditions by the South Carolina scouts and militiamen left a strong impression on a whole generation of settlers in the Port Royal area.

NOTES

1. Larry E. Ivers, "Scouting the Inland Passage," *South Carolina Historical Magazine* 73 (July 1972): 25; Chapman James Milling, *Red Carolinians* (Chapel Hill: University of North Carolina Press, 1940), 90.

2. Katherine M. Jones, ed., *Port Royal Under Six Flags* (Indianapolis: Bobbs-Merrill, 1960), 99; Verner W. Crane, *The Southern Frontier, 1670–1732* (Durham: Duke University Press, 1928), 169.

3. Crane, *Southern Frontier,* 169.

4. Ivers, "Scouting," 117–29.

5. Crane, *Southern Frontier,* 178–79.

6. Ivers, "Scouting," 128.

7. Milling, *Red Carolinians,* 153.

8. Samuel Proctor, ed., *Eighteenth-Century Florida and Its Borderlands* (Gainesville: University Presses of Florida, 1975), 3.

9. Milling, *Red Carolinians,* 153, n62.

10. Milling, *Red Carolinians,* 154.

11. Crane, *Southern Frontier,* 171–86; David Duncan Wallace, *The History of South Carolina,* 4 vols. (New York: American Historical Society, 1934), 1: 207–13; Edward McCrady, *The History of South Carolina under the Proprietary Government, 1670–1719* (1897; rpt., New York: Russell and Russell, 1969), 534–46.

12. Ivers, "Scouting," 117–29.

13. Milling, *Red Carolinians,* 151.

14. Milling, *Red Carolinians,* 152.

15. Milling, *Red Carolinians,* 154.

16. Dry to Barnwell, August 19, 1720, British Public Record Office Transcripts, 8: 86, South Carolina Department of Archives and History; Ivers, "Scouting," 126.

17. M. Eugene Sirmans, *Colonial South Carolina: A Political History* (Chapel Hill: University of North Carolina Press, 1966), 116; Crane, *Southern Frontier,* 185–86; Wallace, *History of South Carolina,* 1:219–20; Brown, "Early Indian Trade," 122.

18. Crane, *Southern Frontier,* 189.

19. Crane, *Southern Frontier,* 189.

20. Crane, *Southern Frontier,* 228–31.

21. Crane, *Southern Frontier,* 230–31.

22. Sirmans, *Colonial South Carolina,* 135.

23. Crane, *Southern Frontier,* 231.

24. Crane, *Southern Frontier,* 235.

25. Joseph W. Barnwell, ed., "Fort King George: Journal of Colonel John Barnwell in the Construction of the Fort on the Altamaha in 1721," *South Carolina Historical Magazine* 27 (October 1926): 189–203.

26. Milling, *Red Carolinians,* 157–58.

27. Barnwell, "Fort King George," 189–203; Ivers, "Scouting," 128–29.

28. J. H. Easterby, ed., *Journal of the Commons House of Assembly, 1741–1742* (Columbia: Historical Commission of South Carolina, 1953), 137; "Will of John Barnwell," June 16, 1724, *Charleston County Wills* 1 (1722–1724): 94–97, South Carolina Department of Archives and History.

29. "Inventory of the Estate of John Barnwell," appraised June 11, 1724, Miscellaneous Records (1724–1725), 71, South Carolina Department of Archives and History; "Will of Colonel John Woodward," February 25, 1728, *Charleston County Wills* 2 (1727–1729): 67–69, South Carolina Department of Archives and History; Property Grants, 39: 14, South Carolina Department of Archives and History; A. S. Salley, ed., *Journal of the Commons House of Assembly of South Carolina, June 2, 1724–June 16, 1724* (Columbia: General Assembly, 1944), 37.

30. Salley, ed., *Journal of the Commons House of Assembly, June 2, 1724–June 16, 1724,* 37.

31. Easterby, ed., *Journal of the Commons House of Assembly, 1741–1742,* 137.

32. Milling, *Red Carolinians,* 159.

33. British Public Record Office Transcripts, 8: 63, South Carolina Department of Archives and History.

34. Milling, *Red Carolinians,* 160.

35. Salley, ed., *Journal of the Commons House of Assembly, November 1, 1725–April 30, 1726,* 56; *November 15, 1726–March 11, 1727,* 77.

36. South Carolina Commons House Journals, no. 7, part 2, January 3, 1727–September 30, 1727, 575, 583, 593, 595, 596–602, South Carolina Department of Archives and History.

37. Crane, *Southern Frontier,* 249; Sirmans, *Colonial South Carolina,* 157; Wallace, *History of South Carolina,* 1: 303; "Inventory of the Estate of John Palmer," appraised March 25, 1745, Miscellaneous Records (1732–1746), 155; "Will of John Palmer," December 13, 1744, *Charleston County Wills* 5 (1740–1747): 358–60, South Carolina Department of Archives and History; *Biographical Directory of the South Carolina House,* 1: 58; 2: 500–1; Ivers, "Scouting," 128.

38. Milling, *Red Carolinians,* 161.

39. South Carolina Commons House Journals, Sainsbury Copy, January 31, 1728–February 21, 1729, 478, 537, South Carolina Department of Archives and History; Crane, *Southern Frontier,* 250.

40. Milling, *Red Carolinians,* 161.

41. Crane, *Southern Frontier,* 251; Sirmans, *Colonial South Carolina,* 157.

42. Milling, *Red Carolinians,* 162.

43. Crane, *Southern Frontier,* 251; Sirmans, *Colonial South Carolina,* 157.

44. Brown, "Early Indian Trade," 123.

6

Settling the Indian Lands between
the Combahee and Savannah Rivers

Colonel John Palmer's raid on St. Augustine in 1728 finally ended the
Yemassee War. This event marked the permanent removal of the Indians from the
Beaufort District, the most important result of which was to open the mainland
swamps for white settlement and the cultivation of rice. Throughout the eighteenth century, this territory, which had been reserved for the Yemassee tribe by
the treaty of 1707, was referred to as Indian land. The three later parishes of the
Beaufort District were all formed from this land: Prince William Parish between
the Combahee and Coosawhatchie Rivers in 1745, St. Peter's Parish along the
Savannah River in 1747, and St. Luke's Parish between those two in 1767.

Political events following the end of the Yemassee War contributed to the
rapid development of the rice lands of Prince William Parish. The transition of
South Carolina from a proprietary to a royal colony occurred in 1729, and the
first royal governor, Robert Johnson, arrived in 1731. His first acts were of almost immediate benefit to the Beaufort District. The Quitrent Act of 1731 reopened the land office so that land could be legally granted to settlers for the first
time in a decade. And the first experiment of Governor Johnson's township plan
to settle European immigrants on the frontiers was the Swiss community of
Purrysburg on the Savannah River in 1734.[1] In addition, the establishment of
the new royal colony of Georgia at Savannah in 1733 provided more security
than the Beaufort District had ever known.

The result was the rapid movement in the 1730s of some of South Carolina's
wealthiest and most prominent planter families to the neck of land between the
Combahee and Coosawhatchie Rivers. With three large freshwater streams, which
lazily found their way to salt water—the Combahee, Pocotaligo, and
Coosawhatchie Rivers—this country was perfect for the cultivation of rice.

The method of rice production that these first planters brought with them
was the inland swamp method so prominent in early-eighteenth-century South

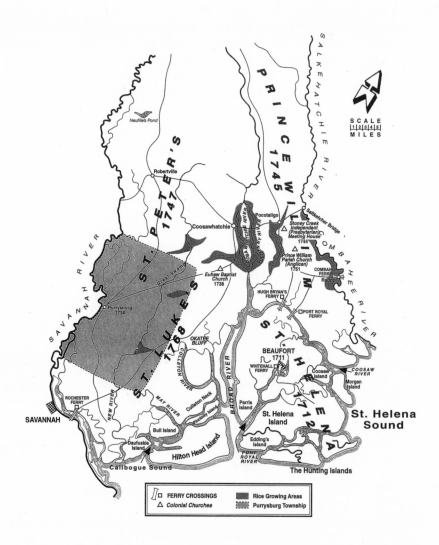

Colonial parishes of Beaufort District, 1769

Carolina. Three methods of rice cultivation were practiced in colonial South Carolina: upland or open field, inland swamp, and tidal culture. The earliest known method was the upland or open field method which did not need extensive irrigation. The inland swamp method followed shortly and was the typical form of South Carolina rice cultivation until after the Revolution. The tidal culture system was introduced by a few of the wealthier planters around Georgetown after the middle of the eighteenth century, but it did not become predominant in Prince William Parish until the 1790s.[2]

The inland swamp rice plantation required considerable preparation of the land and, therefore, a substantial labor force. First, a suitable swamp or wetland had to be located. Then its downstream end had to be dammed and the numerous cypress, gum, and tupelo trees had to be cut. Usually the felled trees were used to construct the dam. A "trunk," or sluice gate, was then built into the dam. The trunk allowed the cleared field to be drained. Normally, inland swamp fields had no way of controlling the supply of fresh water, so the planter was dependent on the vagaries of weather. These inland swamp fields were usually not more than thirty or forty acres in size due to the constraints of topography. Rice was planted between April 1 and May 20. It was harvested from the first week of September to the second week of October.[3] Port Royal pioneer Thomas Nairne claimed in 1710 that these fields would produce "seldom less than thirty bushels or more than sixty" per acre. This appears to have remained fairly constant throughout the eighteenth century, for in 1795 the duc de La Rochefoucauld reported, on his visit to the lowcountry, rice production of twenty to forty bushels per acre per year.[4]

Almost all the clearing, construction, preparation, planting, weeding, and harvesting of rice on an inland swamp plantation was done by hand. Thus, a large slave labor force, and consequently a large capital investment, was an absolute requisite for the lowcountry rice planter. The beginning of large-scale rice production in Prince William Parish in the 1730s was, therefore, the cause for bringing thousands of African slaves into the region south of the Combahee River. The 1730s also saw the Beaufort District transformed from a predominantly white and Indian population to a predominantly black one.

Some of the most prominent families in colonial South Carolina developed rice plantations in Prince William Parish in the 1730s. They brought with them money and slaves, so Prince William Parish "never had a log cabin period." First among the planter families were the Bellingers and the Bulls. Other prominent families, mostly from the Ashley River area, soon followed.[5]

The interest of the Bellinger family was extended south of the Combahee River by virtue of the first grant given to Landgrave Edmund Bellinger for the twelve-thousand-acre Tomotley Barony on May 7, 1698. This was the only proprietary barony in Prince William Parish, a restriction imposed by the Yemassee treaty of 1707. On the death of the first Landgrave Edmund Bellinger in 1705, this barony passed to the second Landgrave Edmund Bellinger and his two sisters: Lucia and Elizabeth. Lucia Bellinger married Burnaby Bull and Elizabeth Bellinger married Colonel John Palmer. While Edmund Bellinger remained a resident of St. Andrew's Parish, both Bull and Palmer were veteran Indian fighters and pioneers of the Beaufort District. During the 1730s, the Bellinger family connection to Prince William Parish was extended by Andrew DeVeaux II's marriage to Colonel John Palmer's daughter, Hannah. Burnaby Bull, John Palmer, and Andrew DeVeaux all established rice plantations along the Coosawhatchie River on lands that were part of the original Tomotley Barony.

Ultimately more important to Prince William Parish was the Bull family. The Bull brothers, William, Burnaby, and John, all began gradually to shift their principal planting interests to Prince William Parish in the 1730s. Both Burnaby and John Bull were residents of Colleton County at the time of the Yemassee uprising, and both were veterans of the Indian wars. Burnaby Bull was a militia captain under Colonel John Barnwell on the Tuscarora expedition of 1711, and John Bull was a militia captain during the Yemassee War. Captain John Bull's first wife was one of the many victims of the Yemassee massacre of 1715. Each of these brothers acquired large holdings in Prince William Parish during the 1730s. Burnaby Bull remained a resident of St. Paul's Parish until the 1740s while developing his rice plantations in Prince William Parish. When he died of apoplexy in 1754, he owned 2,679 acres in Prince William Parish, worked by fifty-nine slaves. He was buried in the graveyard of the Prince William Parish Church.[6] Captain John Bull also remained a resident of St. Paul's Parish until the 1740s when he moved his country seat to his plantation on the north shore of the Coosaw River in Prince William Parish. When he died in 1767 he left 2,694 acres and a large number of slaves in Prince William Parish as well as property in Colleton County. Captain John Bull is also buried in the graveyard of the Prince William Parish Church.

The Bull family greatly increased its influence in Prince William Parish by the investment of William Bull I. In 1732, William Bull purchased six thousand acres from Thomas Lowndes. In the 1730s, he developed this property into the five-thousand-acre Sheldon Plantation and the thousand-acre Newbury Plantation. William Bull had been a militia colonel during the Yemassee War, and he was married to Mary Quintyne, stepdaughter of Thomas Nairne, a pioneer Indian trader and settler of the Beaufort District. William Bull I was one of the most influential political figures in colonial South Carolina, serving for many years on the Royal Council and from 1737 to 1743 as acting governor of the province. His was one of the most difficult and successful administrations in colonial South Carolina. Though William Bull's principal seat was his father's Ashley River plantation, Ashley Hall, by the time of his death in 1755, William Bull had moved most of his planting interests and the majority of his large slave force to Prince William Parish. At the time of his death, William Bull had 107 of his 138 slaves at Sheldon Plantation. Like his brothers, William Bull is buried at the Prince William Parish Church.[7]

The movement of the Bellingers and the Bulls to Prince William Parish was followed by a parade of some of the wealthiest planters and merchants in South Carolina. Joseph Blake, whose principal seat was at Newington Plantation on the Ashley River, developed two plantations on the Combahee River in Prince William Parish.[8] He was the son of Governor Joseph Blake and one of the wealthiest men in South Carolina. By the time of his death in 1751, Joseph Blake had 114 slaves, 189 cattle, 21 horses, and numerous buildings and equipment on his two Combahee River rice plantations. Though it was only a portion of his estate, Joseph Blake's Prince William property was worth 20,157 pounds currency. His son, William Blake, further developed these properties, which came to be called Bonny Hall Plantation.[9] Major Walter Izard, another veteran of the Yemassee War, also made major investments in Prince William Parish during the 1730s and 1740s. At his death in 1750, Walter Izard had 88 slaves, a large herd of cattle and hogs, and ample tools and buildings on his Combahee River rice plantation. Though he had nearly 30,000 pounds currency invested in Prince William Parish, it represented barely one-third of Walter Izard's South Carolina property, and his principal country seat remained the Dorchester Plantation on the Ashley River.

The two most prominent investors in Prince William Parish from the merchant and professional community in Charleston were Thomas Jenys, a merchant, and James Michie, a lawyer. By the time of his death in 1745, Thomas Jenys had invested thirteen thousand pounds currency in Prince William Parish. On his Coosawhatchie River plantation, Jenys had sixty slaves, one hundred cattle, one hundred hogs, and all necessary tools and buildings. Most of Jeny's wealth was tied up in his Charleston mercantile business but his interest in the Beaufort District prompted him to loan considerable sums to the local planters of Prince William and St. Helena Parish. Among his papers were loans to Richard Capers, Jonathan Norton, Andrew DeVeaux, William Palmer, and Stephen Bull.[10]

Perhaps the best example of an early Prince William rice plantation is that of Charleston lawyer James Michie. Michie was an active colonial politician and speaker of the Commons House of Assembly from 1752 to 1754. He died in 1760, and the inventory of his estate is particularly detailed and revealing because it was conducted after the rice harvest had been gathered but before it had been sent to market. James Michie operated three rice plantations on the Combahee River in Prince William Parish. Two of these plantations, Richfield and Mount Alexander, he owned, and a third adjoining plantation he leased from Mr. Young. At these three plantations, he had ninety-five slaves: fifty-four at Richfield, twenty-two at Mount Alexander, and nineteen on the leased land. At each plantation he raised some livestock but only in small herds, suggesting they were provisions for his own slave workforce. At each plantation he grew corn, peas, and potatoes also for his own slave communities. There were no household furniture or personal effects listed for any of his plantations. Clearly James Michie, like many of the larger Prince William investors, was an absentee owner. Nevertheless, he invested thirty-two thousand pounds currency in Prince William Parish. This represented slightly less than half of his moveable estate. He also owned a town house in Charleston and a country seat at St. James in Goose Creek.[11]

In 1760, these three plantations produced a rice crop worth fifty-nine hundred pounds currency. Richfield Plantation produced three hundred barrels of rice, Mount Alexander produced two hundred barrels, and the leased land produced ninety barrels. In 1760, the labor force produced an average of six barrels of rice per slave. Using the 1760 crop as a basis, it would have taken James Michie slightly more than five years to recover his initial capital investment. In ten years he would have doubled his money on income alone, not counting the appreciation of land and slaves. If James Michie's experience was typical, it indicates that rice planting in Prince William Parish was not the source of overnight fortunes, but even by modern business standards, it was a solid investment.

The movement of these large rice planters to Prince William Parish in the 1730s and 1740s encouraged smaller planters and merchants to follow. Two small commercial centers grew in Prince William Parish: one at Radnor where the Combahee ferry crossed into Prince William Parish from Colleton County and the other at Coosawhatchie where the King's Highway crossed that river into what was to become St. Luke's Parish.

The town of Radnor was carved out of William Bull's Newbury Plantation and laid out as early as 1734.[12] This was at the landing of the Combahee ferry, which was established in 1715. In 1741, a bridge replaced the ferry, but by 1754 the bridge had fallen into the river and was replaced by a rope ferry which served as the principal crossing of the lower Combahee for the rest of the colonial era. Radnor was established as a market town by an Act of the Commons House of Assembly on March 11, 1737.[13] The project was never a commercial success, and William Bull was still left holding almost all the town lots at the time of his death in 1755. By 1754, Colonel John Mullryne of Beaufort had built a store, lodging house, and public house at Radnor. This was the only colonial enterprise in the town. It was housed in a two-story frame building with a one-story veranda across its forty-foot front. In the 1750s, this establishment was managed by Katherine Weyerhuysen.[14]

Coosawhatchie was never surveyed or officially created as a town during the colonial period. During the 1740s, an enterprising Swiss merchant from Purrysburg, Henry DeSaussure, opened a store and lodging house at the foot of the bridge which crossed the Coosawhatchie River. This was also at the head of navigation of that small stream which winds out to Port Royal Sound. Henry

DeSaussure was the founder of one of South Carolina's most prominent families in the revolutionary and antebellum eras. Coosawhatchie, which was in the geographic center of the Beaufort District, grew into an important crossroad for the southern parishes and eventually became the county seat for fifty-one years following the American Revolution.

Also during the 1740s, two churches were established in Prince William Parish. On May 20, 1743, a group of local families of non-Anglican beliefs formed the Stoney Creek congregation and called Reverend William Hutson, a convert of Reverend George Whitefield, to be their pastor. In 1744, they built the Stoney Creek meeting house beside the King's Highway on the banks of the Pocotaligo River. The local planters who organized this church were Hugh Bryan, Jonathan Bryan, William Gilbert, Robert Ogle, James Rowland, Joseph Bryan, and Stephen Bull Jr. (son of Burnaby Bull and son-in-law of Joseph Bryan). William Hutson served until 1756 when he became pastor of the Circular Church in Charleston. The Stoney Creek Church was reorganized in 1772, and all voting members were required to be landholders and slaveholders. At that time the church purchased a number of slaves, managed by John Cuthbert, to hire out to produce income for the organization. On March 17, 1785, the Stoney Creek congregation was incorporated as the Independent Presbyterian Church of Prince William Parish.[15]

This movement of the 1730s and 1740s prompted the formation of the Prince William Parish in 1745. On May 29, 1736, the Commons House of Assembly passed an act for establishing an Anglican Chapel of Ease on Huspa Neck between the Combahee and Pocotaligo Rivers. The commissioners were Stephen Bull, Joseph Izard, John Mullryne, Hugh Bryan, and Jonathan Bryan. The Anglican Chapel was never constructed until after the Commons House of Assembly had formally established Prince William Parish on May 25, 1745. The parish was named in honor of the son of King George II, William, duke of Cumberland, known as the victor over Bonnie Prince Charlie at Culloden in 1745. Thus, Prince William Parish was a bastion of Hanoverian influence in South Carolina.

In 1747, Elizabeth Bellinger, widow of the second Landgrave Edmund Bellinger, gave fifty acres of the Tomotley Barony for the purpose of erecting the Anglican parish church. It was located right next to William Bull's Sheldon Plantation settlement. Trustees for building the church were William Bull, Stephen Bull, Robert Troup, John Green, and James DeVeaux. In 1751, the cornerstone of the Prince William Parish Church was laid, and the structure began largely at the expense of the Bull family.[16] In 1752, the Commons House of Assembly allocated six hundred pounds currency towards the construction of the church, and by 1757 the church interior was completed and the first services were conducted.[17] The man most responsible for building the Prince William Parish Church was William Bull I, who did not live to see it completed. He was buried in the place of highest honor—inside the church before the altar. Prince William Parish Church was a grand edifice symbolic of the wealth that was being produced from the rivers and swamps which surrounded it. When it was completed, contemporary observers called the Prince William Parish Church the "finest country church in America."[18]

Indeed, recent scholarship has revealed that Prince William Parish Church was the first temple-form neoclassical building in America, and as such, it was the prototype of the Greek Revival architecture so characteristic of the antebellum south. The church was built from, or adapted from, the work of English architect James Gibb's unused plans for St. Mary-le-Strand Church in London. The plans were probably brought to South Carolina by William Bull II, who had many mutual acquaintances with the architect during the years of Bull's education in Europe.[19] It is ironic to note that the first American building built in this architectural style, which later came to symbolize American democracy, was directed, sponsored, and paid for by the most thoroughgoing family of Hanoverian Royalists in South Carolina history.

PURRYSBURG

Next to the founding of the town of Beaufort in 1711, the most significant single event in the settling of the Beaufort District was the establishment of Purrysburg on the Savannah River in 1734. Not only was Purrysburg the largest immigration of Europeans directly to the Beaufort District, but it was also the origin of most of the French- and German-speaking families in the southeastern corner of South Carolina.[20]

The story of the Purrysburg settlement began in Neufchatel, Switzerland, with one of the state's most adventurous and colorful characters, Jean Pierre Purry. Purry, a wine merchant, was born in Neufchatel in 1675. By 1713, he had left Europe to seek his fortune in Dutch East Indies and traveled as far as South Australia in search of new lands to colonize. By 1717, he was back in Europe where he presented a plan to the directors of the Dutch East India Company for a Swiss settlement in Australia. In 1718, he published a pamphlet in Amsterdam which advanced the theory that the best places on the globe for human habitation were at thirty-three degrees north and south latitude. It was this theory which brought Jean Pierre Purry to the banks of the Savannah River in 1731.

Rebuffed by Dutch colonial officials, Purry approached English colonial officials with a similar scheme. In 1724, he wrote a memorial to the duke of Newcastle proposing a Swiss settlement in America near thirty-three degrees north latitude. In his memorial, Purry suggested that the settlement be called "Georgia" or "Georgina" in honor of England's new Hanoverian king, George I. The Lords Proprietors of Carolina, anxious to better settle and defend the southern frontier during the devastating and ongoing Yemassee War, initially agreed to transport Purry's Swiss immigrants to America at the Proprietors' expense.

Purry, in 1726, advertised in the Swiss Cantons for volunteers to immigrate to America, and a case of "Carolina fever" swept the mountain communities. Two hundred people gathered in Geneva and one hundred more in Neufchatel. But the proprietors reneged on their promise of transportation, Purry's Swiss creditors backed out, and the Swiss immigrants were left penniless, hungry, and angry.[21] Purry was nothing if not persistent, and, in 1729, the Lords Proprietors finally relinquished control of the South Carolina colony to the crown. This greatly improved the political and financial opportunities for Purry's scheme. Purry's plan fit perfectly into the highest priority instructions from the king's ministers to the first royal governor of South Carolina, Robert Johnson. One of the principal reasons for the crown's interest in acquiring South Carolina was to defend British imperial interests in America and particularly to counter the entrenched Spanish in Florida and the encircling French in Louisiana. Johnson was instructed to establish "townships" on the South Carolina frontier and settle them with European protestants.[22] Governor Johnson's "Township Plan" grew not only out of Purry's memorial to the duke of Newcastle, but also out of the "Barnwell Plan" of 1721.[23]

Thus, Purry's scheme for a Swiss settlement was revived in 1730, and by 1731 Purry was in South Carolina. He was led across the lowcountry to the banks of the Savannah River by Captain Rowland Evans of the Carolina Rangers, a militia unit which guarded the southern frontier with mounted patrols that rode between McPherson's Cowpen at Yemassee and the ranger fort at Palachacola Bluff on the Savannah River. The place that Evans and Purry chose for the Swiss township was called "Great Yemassee Bluff" on the South Carolina side of the river between Savannah and Palachacola. The name chosen for the new town was Purrysburg.

In 1732, an advance party of settlers cleared the site and laid out the lots in the new town. Two years later the bulk of the new Swiss settlers arrived in Purrysburg. By 1736, there were 100 houses and as many as 450 settlers in the new town.[24] The town of Purrysburg was well situated for the defense of the South Carolina lowcountry, but not well situated for either subsistence or commercial agriculture. The settlers suffered from heat, disease, and lack of viable agricultural ground. Over the next several years, numerous complaints reached the colonial authorities regarding the unhealthy site, the lack of adequate support from the colonial government, and numerous legal conflicts regarding overlapping or worthless land grants.[25] Over the next decade, many of the settlers sought better lives in Georgia, where the new town of Savannah (1733) and the Salzberger settlement at Ebenezer (1736) had recently been established.

In 1736, Jean Pierre Purry died, leaving the struggling Swiss immigrants to fend for themselves. Along with his wife, Lucrece de Chaillet, he left two sons, neither of whom remained in Purrysburg. His son, David, remained in Europe, where he became a prominent banker and benefactor in Lisbon, Portugal. A statue of David Purry remains in the public square of the family's hometown of Neufchatel.

Charles Purry, the elder son, left Purrysburg to become a prominent Bay Street merchant in Beaufort. He also started a store at Okatee Bluff in the 1740s. Okatee Bluff was the closest tidewater landing to Purrysburg township and provided direct access from the mainland to the inland passage through the sea islands to Beaufort and Charleston. Okatee Bluff acted as the "back door" to the Purrysburg settlement, and several mercantile establishments were located there in the colonial period. During the 1750s, Charles Purry's Okatee store was managed by another Huguenot associated with the Purrysburg settlement, André Verdier. In 1754, Charles Purry was poisoned by one of his trusted household slaves. It was the most famous slave murder case in colonial Beaufort and sent shudders through the lowcountry planter community. The slave perpetrator was tried, executed, and gibbeted on Bay Street in 1754. Charles Purry left only one daughter, Eleanor, who married John Bull of Prince William Parish. No children survived John and Eleanor Bull, and the Purry family in America died out.[26]

The Purrysburg settlement did not thrive. It never developed a strong agricultural base and only survived because it was the principal crossing of the Savannah River on the King's Highway from Charleston to Savannah. In 1747, Purrysburg became the seat of St. Peter's Parish along the Savannah River, and Reverend Henry Chiffelle was sent by the Society for the Propagation of the Gospel in Foreign Parts to organize the Anglican Church there. Though Reverend Chiffelle struggled for many years, neither the town nor the established church prospered. Henry Chiffelle's son, Philotheos, moved off to Charleston and became a successful merchant.

While old Purrysburg did not prosper, the descendants of the Swiss pioneers who settled there became some of the most productive and influential citizens in the old Beaufort District. They formed the core of the Huguenot influence in that region. Among the French-Swiss names from Purrysburg were DeSaussure, Huguenin, Jeanneret, Robert, Verdier, Borquine, deBeaufain, Mongin, LaFitte, Pelot, and Bugnion.[27] Among the German-Swiss settlers at

Purrysburg were Mengersdorff, Holzendorf, Mayerhoffer, Winkler, Strobhar, and Zubly.[28] Approximately two-thirds of the Purrysburg settlers were French speaking and one-fourth were German speaking.[29] In addition, twenty-five families originated from Salzburg, Austria, and forty families were Protestant refugees from the Italian Piedmont. The best-known name among the Piedmontese was Jean Louis Poyas.

Most of the Purrysburg immigrants moved away from the township to seek their fortunes in more productive places. Hector Berenger de Beaufain moved to Charleston and served for twenty-four years as collector of customs (1742–1766). The Mongin family moved to Daufuskie Island where, in the nineteenth century, they became successful sea island cotton planters. Mongin Creek on the west side of Daufuskie Island bordered their plantation lands. Reverend Francis Pelot moved to the eastern border of the township and founded the Euhaws Baptist Church at the crossroads there in 1738. This was the "mother church" of the Baptist movement in the Beaufort District and the center of the antebellum village of Grahamville. The Huguenin family moved to Coosawhatchie and became the largest rice-planting family on the Coosawhatchie River. Henri DeSaussure moved to the strategic crossroads of Coosawhatchie and began that families' fortune with a small country store.[30]

Though the dream of Jean Pierre Purry failed, the result was, nonetheless, an infusion into the Beaufort District of a large number of the most talented, enterprising, and productive families in the long history of the South Carolina lowcountry.

FERRIES, ROADS, AND BRIDGES

This settlement of the "Indian land" and the Purrysburg immigration necessitated the establishment of a transportation infrastructure to serve the southern parishes. While the numerous tidal estuaries and larger rivers served as convenient transportation for bulk products, these same estuaries, with strong currents and an eight-foot range of tide, were often a hinderance to day-to-day travel.[31] Thus ferries, roads, and bridges were established during the colonial era which determined the principal routes of travel to this day.

The constant parade of Indian traders, cattlemen, planters, and gangs of slaves caused the ancient Indian paths to widen into highways and the old Indian fording places to become established causeways, ferries, and bridges. Even before the Yemassee War broke out, the first public road was cut in the southern parishes. Between 1711 and 1714, the road from the Combahee River crossing to the mainland opposite Port Royal Island was carved from the forest. At the same time a road was cut from the north end of Port Royal Island to the old fort and new town of Beaufort at the south end.[32] In 1715, the principal crossing connecting this road to St. Bartholomew's parish (Colleton County) was established by the Commons House of Assembly as the first operating ferry in the southern parishes. The act of 1715 specified its purpose of "mending and keeping in repair the causeway (and ferry) over the marshes of the Combahee." The ferry operation was vested in Joseph Bryan, the father of Hugh and Jonathan Bryan. He was permitted to charge a surplus fee to travelers because the cost of maintaining this vital facility was "likely to prove very bothersome to the adjacent inhabitants who are, for the most part, of small means and few in number."[33]

After the Combahee ferry, the next most important crossing was that connecting the mainland of Prince William parish with Port Royal Island across the Whalebranch River. In 1733, a public ferry was established at this location and vested in Col. Samuel Prioleau, whose plantation occupied the island side of the crossing. This was the "Port Royal Ferry" which remained Beaufort's principal connection to the mainland for the next two centuries. In 1733, Prioleau was required to maintain "a good and sufficient boat, two horses and men" at all times. For ferriage across this difficult piece of water, Prioleau was authorized to charge seven and one-half shillings for a man, ten shillings for a man and horse, two shillings per head for small livestock, and ten shillings per head for cattle.[34]

In 1737, a second ferry was added barely a mile to the west of the Port Royal ferry which connected Port Royal Island with Huspa Neck. This ferry was vested in Hugh Bryan whose Cedar Grove plantation occupied the mainland landing. The road leading from Bryan's ferry toward the west joined the main road from Charles Town to Savannah at Pocotaligo, the site of the old Yemassee town. This remains one of the principal crossroads of the district to this day. As was usual for all these ferries, ministers, government messengers, and all those travelling to attend militia musters were exempt from ferry charges. Church attendance was encouraged by allowing ferriage on Sundays free of charge. In addition, the ferry master had to forfeit to a traveller the sum of twenty shillings for a delay of one hour and forty shillings for every hour thereafter.[35]

By 1741, traffic across the Combahee ferry was heavy enough to justify the expense of replacing the ferry with a bridge. Half the cost was to be borne by the provincial government while the other half was to be raised by levying a tax on all male inhabitants and all male slaves in St. Helena parish. By 1754, even the important Combahee crossing had become too great a burden for the planters. The bridge had not been maintained and had "gone to decay, so that it is become dangerous to pass over." Temporary measures were enacted, but by 1766 the bridge had completely collapsed, and the inhabitants reverted to the use of a short ferry operated by the local magnate, Stephen Bull of Sheldon. Bull laid out his town of Radnor at the landing of the Combahee ferry. As was usual, the ferry was operated for the profit of the owner, but rates were fixed and conditions were regulated by the provincial government. This particular crossing was short and rates were not high: fifteen pence for one man, thirty pence for a man and a horse, seven and one-half pence per head for small livestock. Ministers, government messengers, and free Indians were exempted from payment. The operator was charged with maintaining a stout boat, a loading ramp, a dependable rope and capstan, a canoe for attending the ferry, and a shelter for travellers on the end of the Combahee causeway. With a permanent shelter for travellers and a rope-drawn ferry operated by capstans, this was undoubtedly the most elaborate and most used facility in the southern district.[36] By 1751, traffic across the Port Royal ferry had increased enough to justify a third ferry franchise vested in John Green. The advantage of two ferries at the same crossing was that Prioleau could maintain the facility on Port Royal Island and accommodate travellers heading north while Green could maintain the mainland facility and meet travellers heading south. Apparently this arrangement was satisfactory for it was continued in 1762 with George Roupell operating the island landing and Joshua Morgan operating the mainland side. At that time the rates were slightly reduced from the level established in 1733. A man and a horse were now charged seven shillings instead of the previous ten, though rates for livestock remained the same. During most of the colonial period, then, three ferries were operating across the same river within a mile of each other. This somewhat complicated arrangement indicates the difficulty the colonial settlers had in employing the swift tides of the sea islands.[37]

Some less essential crossings operated without government regulations until the complications became too great. One such was the ferry from Whitehall Point on Lady's Island to the town of Beaufort. It was officially vested in William Harvey in 1767. In his petition to the Commons House of Assembly, Harvey reported that he was "possessed of land on each side of the river ... where a ferry is now kept." What he desired was relief from the "many disputes and inconveniences that arise from want of a law to fix ... rates and other regulations." The subsequent act allowed Harvey to charge seven and one-half shillings for transporting a man and his horse to town.[38]

Another crossing was that from St. Helena Island to Lady's Island. In 1744 the inhabitants of St. Helena Island complained of the difficulty of regular communications with the town of Beaufort and requested the assistance of the provincial government in overcoming that difficulty.

The petitioners reported that they had begun work on a causeway across the creek separating the two islands, but they were prevented from continuing the work because "they were mostly new settlers and their circumstances (would) not permit them to do more." The Commons House felt the petitioners' arguments were well founded and authorized Richard Capers, John Cowan, and Jonathan Norton to collect a tax on all males, black and white, between the ages of sixteen and sixty.[39] This bridge, however, was either never completed or promptly collapsed. No futher mention of it is made, and in 1765 Miles Brewton and David Blake petitioned for regulations regarding the ferry they had "long since kept up and maintained" for the benefit of the public. According to the petition, their property lay across the "only accustomed road from . . . many parts of this province to St. Helena Island." Once again they wished to be relieved of the "many disputes and inconveniences" that resulted from a lack of legal regulation. The Assembly granted their request, and the rates were fixed. A man and a horse were charged seven and one-half shillings for the crossing.[40]

Purrysburg became the regular crossing of the Savannah River after the settlement of Savannah in 1733 and Purrysburg in 1734. A road was cut through the pine barrens from Purrysburg to Pocotaligo between 1733 and 1740. The most important crossing on this road was the fording place of the Coosawhatchie River. This was the head of navigation for the "Port Royal Broad" River now known as the Broad River. A bridge was built at Coosawhatchie during the 1750s. This soon became one of the busiest crossroads in the southern parishes and an active commercial center.

By the late colonial era, the Purrysburg ferry had become the most expensive crossing in the Beaufort District. The rates of twenty-five shillings for a single man, thirty-two shillings for a horse, and six pounds for a loaded wagon established in 1778 may reflect both wartime inflation and the desires of the Revolutionary leaders of South Carolina to discourage trade with the Georgians who were at the time more sympathetic to the British cause.

The roads connecting these public river crossings were established in the normal manner, the initial cost being raised by taxing all male inhabitants of the area between the ages of sixteen and sixty as stipulated in the act of 1721. The local road commissioners were empowered to collect the tax and to demand the labor of the local planters, or their slaves, in maintaining the roads. The road from the Combahee River to Beaufort was cut between 1711 and 1714. The road from the Combahee ferry and the Port Royal ferry to Purrysburg was authorized in 1733, but three years later it had "not yet been effected being far too great an extent and undertaking for so few commissioners to direct and supervise.[41] In spite of some delays, public roads connected the major points of the southern district through the colonial period. As M. Eugene Sirmans remarks, "In spite of its drawbacks, the road system was successful and South Carolina enjoyed one of the best networks of internal roads in colonial America."[42]

NOTES

1. M. Eugene Sirmans, *Colonial South Carolina: A Political History, 1663–1763* (Chapel Hill: University of North Carolina Press, 1966), 34–42.

2. "Will of Joseph Blake," December 18, 1750, *Charleston County Wills* 6 (1747–1752): 534–36; "Inventory of Joseph Blake," appraised October 30, 1751, Charleston Inventories, R (1751–1753): 112, South Carolina Department of Archives and History; *Biographical Directory of the South Carolina House,* 2: 80–83; Converse D. Clowse, *Economic Beginnings in Colonial South Carolina, 1670–1730* (Columbia: University of South Carolina Press, 1971), 126; Lewis Cecil Gray, *History of Agriculture in the Southern United States to 1860,* 2 vols. (Gloucester: Peter Smith, 1958) 1: 278.

3. Duncan Clinch Heyward, *Seed from Madagascar* (1937; rpt., Columbia: University of South Carolina Press, 1993), 12–13.

4. Gray, *History of Agriculture,* 2: 284.

5. John R. Todd and Francis M. Hutson, *Prince William Parish and Plantations* (Richmond: Garrett and Massie, 1935), 32.

6. *Biographical Directory of the South Carolina House,* 2: 112–13.

7. Todd and Hutson, *Prince William Parish,* 61.

8. *Biographical Directory of the South Carolina House,* 2: 81–82.

9. Heyward, *Seed from Madagascar,* 11–16; Clowse, *Economic Beginnings,* 127; Gray, *History of Agriculture,* 1: 279–80.

10. "Wills of Thomas Jenys," November 27, 1745, *Charleston County Wills* 5; "Inventory of Thomas Jenys," appraised January 2, 1746, Inventories, MM (1746–1747): 140–62, South Carolina Department of Archives and History; Sirmans, *Colonial South Carolina,* 238.

11. Sirmans, *Colonial South Carolina,* 247; Jack P. Greene, *Quest for Power: The Lower Houses of Assembly in the Southern Royal Colonies, 1689–1776* (Chapel Hill: University of North Carolina Press, 1963), 460, 482.

12. H. A. M. Smith, *The Historical Writings of Henry A. M. Smith,* 3 vols. (Spartanburg, S. C.: Reprint Co., 1988), vol. 2, *Cities and Towns of Early South Carolina,* 151–54.

13. Thomas Cooper and David J. McCord, eds., *The Statutes at Large of South Carolina,* 10 vols. (Columbia: A. S. Johnston, 1836–1841), 9: 37, 116, 173.

14. *South Carolina Gazette,* July 11, 1754.

15. Todd and Hutson, *Prince William Parish,* 85–87.

16. Todd and Hutson, *Prince William Parish,* 32–71.

17. South Carolina Commons House Journals, no. 31, part 2, November 2, 1756–July 6, 1757, 53, 94; no. 27, November 14, 1751–October 7, 1752, 222–23, 326–27, South Carolina Department of Archives and History.

18. Frederick Dalcho, *An Historical Account of the Protestant Episcopal Church in South-Carolina from the First Settlement of the Province. . .* (Charleston: E. Thayer, 1820), 379.

19. Jane Frederick, "An Investigation of the Origins of Prince William Parish Church" (manuscript). The authors are indebted to Beaufort architect and student of South Carolina history Jane Frederick for sharing her original research on this topic. See also Roger G. Kennedy, *Greek Revival America* (New York: Stuart, Tabori and Chang, 1989), 329.

20. A considerable amount of published material exists on the Swiss settlement at Purrysburg. Early works are Henry A. M. Smith, "Purrysburg," *South Carolina Historical Magazine* 10 (October 1909): 187–219; Verner W. Crane, *The Southern Frontier, 1670–1732* (Durham: Duke University Press, 1928), 281–87; Robert L. Meriwether, *The Expansion of South Carolina, 1729–1865* (Kingsport, Tenn.: Southern Publishers, 1940), particularly 34–41. Newer scholarship, including the important article by Arlin C. Migliazzo, "A Tarnished Legacy Revisited: Jean Pierre Purry and the Settlement of the Southern Frontier, 1718–1736" [*South Carolina Historical Magazine* 92 (October 1991): 232–52], has been a major basis of this section. Very useful for those researching the German origins in the Purrysburg settlement is George Fenwicke Jones, "Compilation of Lists of German-speaking Settlers of Purrysburg," *South Carolina Historical Magazine* 92 (October 1991): 253–68.

21. The best description of these negotiations is in Crane, *Southern Frontier*, 284–87.

22. On proprietary and royal motives for encouraging Purry, see Migliazzo, "A Tarnished Legacy Revisited," 235–37.

23. For more on the "Barnwell Plan," see Stephen B. Barnwell, *The Story of an American Family* (Marquette, Mich.: Privately printed, 1969), 14–16.

24. Meriwether, *Expansion of South Carolina*, 35.

25. Migliazzo, "A Tarnished Legacy Revisited," 250–51; Smith, "Purrysburg," 131; Meriwether, *Expansion of South Carolina*, 36.

26. *Biographical Directory of the South Carolina House*, 2: 114–15.

27. List compiled from Smith, "Purrysburg," 136–50.

28. List compiled from Jones, "Compilation of Lists," 258–68.

29. Meriwether, *Expansion of South Carolina*, 35.

30. Several published genealogies and local histories trace the progress of many of these families in the Beaufort District. Among them are Coy K. Johnston, *Two Centuries of Lawtonville Baptists, 1775–1975* (Columbia: State Printing Co., 1974); Grace Fox Perry, *Moving Finger of Jasper* (Ridgeland, S.C.: Confederate Centennial Committee, 1947); Annie Elizabeth Miller, *Our Family Circle: Being a Reunion of Our House of Langrave Thomas Smith, House of Robert, House of Bostick, House of Lawton, House of Grimball, House of Erwin, House of Stafford, House of Maner, including Screvens, Jaudons, Rhodes, Daniels, Willinghams, Baynards, Polhills, Goldwires, and Caters* (Hilton Head: Lawton and Allied Families Association, 1987); Asselia Strobhar Lichliter, *Pioneering with the Beville and Related Families in South Carolina, Georgia and Florida: Their Lives, Times, and Descendants* (Washington, D.C.: Privately printed, 1982). Many descendants of these Purrysburg pioneers appear in Chalmers Davidson, *The Last Foray: The South Carolina Planters in 1860, A Sociological Study* (Columbia: University of South Carolina Press, 1971).

31. See Charles F. Kovacik and Lawrence S. Rowland, "Images of Colonial Port Royal, South Carolina," *Annals of the American Association of Geographers*, 83 (September 1973), 331–340.

32. Cooper and McCord, eds., *Statutes of South Carolina*, 9:14–17, 34.

33. Cooper and McCord, eds., *Statutes of South Carolina*, 9:37.

34. Cooper and McCord, eds., *Statutes of South Carolina*, 9:80–82.

35. Cooper and McCord, eds., *Statutes of South Carolina,* 9:80–82, 102–103.

36. Cooper and McCord, eds., *Statutes of South Carolina,* 9:116, 173, 216–218.

37. Cooper and McCord, eds., *Statutes of South Carolina,* 9:205.

38. Cooper and McCord, eds., *Statutes of South Carolina,* 9:219–220; March 12, 1768, South Carolina Commons House Journals, no. 37, part 1, p. 300, South Carolina Department of Archives and History.

39. J. H. Easterby, ed., *The Colonial Records of South Carolina: Journal of the Commons House of Assembly, 1744–1745* (Columbia: South Carolina Archives Dept., 1955), 222–223; Cooper and McCord, eds., *Statutes of South Carolina,* 9:138.

40. A. S. Salley, ed., *Journal of the Commons Houses of Assembly of South Carolina* (Columbia: Historical Commission of South Carolina, 1949), 94; Cooper and McCord, eds., *Statutes of South Carolina,* 9:207–209.

41. Cooper and McCord, eds., *Statutes of South Carolina,* 9:14–17, 34, 49–57, 80–82, 92–93, 262–263.

42. M. Eugene Sirmans, *Colonial South Carolina: A Political History* (Chapel Hill: University of North Carolina Press, 1966), 251.

7

Africans and Evangelists

EARLY SLAVERY

The settlement of the Prince William rice plantations necessitated the first large influx of African immigrants into the Beaufort District. Only a few African slaves had been employed on the southern frontier prior to the Yemassee War. Of those, more than half were killed or carried off to St. Augustine during the uprising.[1] The Yemassee raids, which continued sporadically until Palmer's Raid in 1728, carried away more slaves and discouraged planters from investing in what was considered an expensive and highly mobile form of property. St. Helena minister Reverend Lewis Jones reported 224 slaves in the whole parish in 1725 and only 170 in 1726.[2] Not until the frontier was pushed further south by the settlement of Savannah and Purrysburg, and not until the labor-intensive business of rice cultivation had begun in earnest, were African slaves employed on a large scale in the Beaufort District.

The period between 1720 and 1740 was the longest period of unrestricted slave importation in South Carolina history. Nearly forty thousand new Africans reached the colony, and it can be assumed that most slaves brought to the Beaufort District in these years were new arrivals. They came from many tribes and regions and were mingled in the Beaufort District with blacks of different languages and cultural traditions. Among them were people from Calabar, Gambia, Guinea, and Senegal, as well as other regions of West Africa. Probably the largest single group came from the Congo/Angola region of Africa.[3] Together, they were hurled into an alien land only recently wrested violently from its native inhabitants. They were dragged into the swamps of the Beaufort District to fell trees, clear fields, and begin the cultivation of rice, a process with which many were already familiar from West Africa. In addition to these hardships, the African immigrants soon learned that the ruling whites were warring among themselves, and the strange land to which they had been involuntarily brought was in a constant state of military alert. Next to control of the land and its native population, control of the African slaves was the most important source of friction between the English in South Carolina and Georgia and the Spanish in Florida. The new slaves of the Beaufort District soon learned to exploit that rivalry to their own advantage. The early history of the blacks in the Beaufort District was one of almost constant slave runaways and disturbances highlighted by the Stono Rebellion in neighboring St. Paul's Parish in 1739.

During the 1730s, the new slaves brought to the Beaufort District were well aware of the existence of a refuge for slaves at St. Augustine. Runaway slaves had first reached the Florida capital in 1687 and were sufficiently sophisticated, even at that early date, to seek instruction in the Roman Catholic faith. These first fugitive slaves had fled as a result of the Spanish invasion which destroyed Stuart Town on Port Royal Island in 1686.[4] In 1693, the fugitives were granted legal status as free men on the condition that they convert to Catholicism and remain in Florida to work on the fortress San Marcos.[5] This Spanish policy, expanded during the 1730s, was one of the most serious matters of contention between South Carolina and Florida throughout the colonial era. Its effect on the Beaufort District was not only to provide an opportunity for the restless population of newly arrived Africans but also to make the southern parishes the common route for runaway slaves from across the colony. These runaways, frequently harbored by plantation slaves, were a disruptive influence in the early colonial era.

Before the Yemassee War, South Carolina had been aided in controlling its slave population by its alliance with the southern Indians. After the Yemassee War, those Indians were no longer useful as slave catchers. In 1715, ninety-eight slaves from St. Helena Parish ended up in St. Augustine, more than half the total slave population of the parish at that time. During the later stages of the Yemassee War, Yemassee Indians and fugitive slaves cooperated in raiding plantations in the Beaufort District, encouraged by the generous Spanish bounty of one hundred pieces-of-eight for every live black delivered to St. Augustine.[6] In 1720, a major plot was discovered, the first known slave conspiracy in South Carolina, the purpose of which was to destroy Charleston and escape to St. Augustine with the help of a Creek Indian guide. The conspirators were too few to attack the capital so they fled through the depopulated pine barrens of the Beaufort District to the Savannah River seeking aid from the Indians at "Savanna Town." The Indians declined to help, and the desperate band of runaways was captured by the rangers from the Pallachicola garrison. The consequences of their conspiracy were harsh. Some were burned alive and others were hanged.[7]

During the 1730s, Florida authorities defined their policy toward runaway slaves. In 1733, Governor Antonio Benavides received in St. Augustine the royal "cedula" of King Philip V of Spain declaring that any fugitive slaves from South Carolina who adopted Roman Catholicism and served four years as state slaves in St. Augustine would be given their freedom. Governor Manuel de Montiano issued a widely circulated proclamation to this effect in 1738. Also in 1738, a special settlement for runaway slaves was established just north of St. Augustine called Gracia Real de Santa Teresa de Mosa. It was known to the English as Fort

Moosa and was the site of the most bitter defeat of the English forces during General Oglethorpe's siege of St. Augustine in 1740. Many of the fugitive slaves distinguished themselves fighting for the Spanish at the Battle of Fort Moosa.

Word of the Spanish policy toward fugitives and of the free black community at Fort Moosa spread through the lowcountry parishes by official and unofficial means. In 1733, Abraham de Broc, a French Catholic thought to be a spy for the Spanish, escaped from the Charleston jail with an English renegade named Edward Gilbert. The two miscreants "took shelter in the vast woods to the southward, where they continued committing disorders . . . killing the horses and cattle of the distant planters." South Carolina authorities feared they would reach St. Augustine and "entice Spanish Indians to join them." The "two spies" were captured by General Oglethorpe's patrols as they were going from Georgia to St. Augustine in a stolen canoe.[8] In November 1738, more than sixty slaves belonging to Captain Caleb Davis and others on Port Royal Island fled to St. Augustine. This band of runaways escaped by stealing several boats and rowing down the inland passage in full view of the town of Beaufort and past the silent guns of Fort Frederick. It was this large group of fugitives that became the nucleus of the black settlement at Fort Moosa.[9] In 1738, four or five slaves belonging to Captain James McPherson of Prince William Parish escaped to St. Augustine. These fugitives "were cattle hunters and knew the woods." In making their escape they had stolen several horses and some weapons and wounded McPherson's son. This band took the overland route and successfully evaded the Georgia patrols, though one man was killed by Indian pursuers. When they finally arrived in St. Augustine they were received with great honor, and their leader was "given a commission and a coat faced with velvet."[10]

The first slaves sold in the town of Beaufort were a large group of Angolans imported on a Savannah merchant vessel in 1736. They were owned by Jean Pierre Purry and his partner, a merchant named David Montagut. Most of these slaves were sold to Beaufort District planters, but three years later many had still not been sold. In 1739, Purry and Montagut advertised the remaining Angolan slaves as "seasoned to this country" but they may not have been seasoned at all. In 1738, three "Angola men" escaped from Benjamin Godin's plantation on the Edisto River and, while crossing the Savannah River, were joined by three other Angolans from the Montagut Plantation near Purrysburg.[11]

During the spring of 1739, with war plans brewing on the southern frontier, there was a marked increase in runaways headed through the Beaufort District to Florida. In January 1739, Lieutenant Governor William Bull, whose own slaves in Prince William Parish were in jeopardy, warned the Commons House of Assembly that the "desertion of our slaves is a matter of such importance . . . that the most effectual means ought to be used to discourage and prevent it."[12]

St. Helena Parish Church, Beaufort, originally built from 1724 to 1726 (photo by Robert W. Jenkins).

A portion of the tabby walls of Fort Frederick, built from 1726 to 1740 on Port Royal Island (photo by Robert W. Jenkins).

Tabby ruins of the Chapel of Ease, St. Helena Island. The chapel was constructed about 1748 and burned down in 1886 (photo by Robert W. Jenkins).

Prince William Parish Church, constructed in 1751, was the first temple-form Greek Revival building in America. It was burned by Tories in 1779 and by the Union Army in 1865 (photo by Robert W. Jenkins).

The Purrysburg Cross, erected by the Huguenot Society of South Carolina at the site of the original settlement in 1734 (photo by Robert W. Jenkins).

The landing at Great Yemassee Bluff on the Savannah River, site of the Swiss settlement of 1734 (photo by Robert W. Jenkins).

There were two common routes of these runaways through the Beaufort District. One route passed through the pine barrens on the mainland where they could make good time across high ground and, by travelling at night and hiding during the day, avoid the ranger patrols. The two crossing places on the Savannah River north of Savannah, Purrysburg and Pallachicola, were the most likely places to escape and also the most likely places to be apprehended. The other common escape route was the maze of waterways which wind through the sea islands of the South Carolina and Georgia coasts. There is evidence that some of the inaccessible and uninhabited barrier islands may have been used as safe havens by fugitives headed south. In 1735, Flanders, a runaway from Edisto Island, was discovered after a two-month stay on "Cochran's Island" in Port Royal Sound.[13] At least two fugitive slaves were captured at different times on Otter Island in St. Helena Sound, the same island where refugee slaves were abandoned by the retreating British army during the Revolutionary War.[14]

Spanish complicity in these disturbances was well known. The most colorful and famous of the Spanish agents, Colonel Don Miguel Wall, was actually a South Carolina renegade named John Savy. He had been a captive during the Yemassee War and a lieutenant in Palmer's Raid of 1728. In 1737, he visited the Spanish court to try to convince them of the vulnerability of South Carolina and Georgia to a strong Spanish attack. He was suspected of stirring up lowcountry slaves for two years from 1736 to 1738.[15] Another Spanish agent was Captain Piedro, whose 1739 mission to the sea islands was thought to be the cause of the infamous Stono Rebellion.[16]

The Stono Rebellion of September 1739 was the first open slave revolt in South Carolina history. As many as one hundred slaves led by a man named Jemmy stole weapons from Hutchinson's store in St. Paul's Parish and headed toward the Beaufort District and the Florida sanctuary to the south. They killed twenty whites and narrowly missed killing Lieutenant Governor Bull, who was returning to Charleston from his Sheldon plantation. Bull was able to escape, alert the militia, and trap the fugitives at Parker's Ferry on the Edisto. Most of the slaves were killed or captured after a hard fight. For weeks following the Stono Rebellion, an intensive hunt netted other runaways in the southern parishes, many of whom were executed on the spot. The Purrysburg militia and the Pallachicola garrison in particular were put on alert to prevent fugitives from crossing the Savannah River.[17]

The provincial government took steps to prevent this flight to the southward. In 1734, slaves were forbidden to own horses or canoes to discourage escape by land or water.[18] The Stono Rebellion resulted in the harsh Negro Act of 1740, which was the basis of South Carolina's slave code. These acts, and numerous police measures, failed to deter runaways from the Beaufort District fleeing toward Florida.[19] In 1745, three slaves escaped by canoe from Port Royal Island.[20] In 1746, a "strong, sturdy fellow named Matthew" escaped from Colonel Joseph Flowers at Beaufort and remained at large for months "lurking in and about some of the islands near the mouth of the Savannah River."[21] In 1748, two Angola men named Moses and Sampson escaped and "were supposed to be gone by canoe to the southward."[22] In 1749, three men, two women, and two children ran away from John Stanyarne's Port Royal plantation. They were captured at St. Simon's Island, Georgia. In October 1749, twenty-one blacks at Beaufort stole a boat from Captain James MacKay and sailed to St. Augustine. The planters continued to complain that the Spanish were still encouraging desertions and that most of the runaways were being "harbored to the southward."[23]

The combination of restless, newly arrived Africans and a Catholic sanctuary in Florida made control of the growing slave population in the Beaufort District a difficult and dangerous proposition in the early eighteenth century. Many of these slaves came from Angola, where they were familiar with the Portuguese and were sometimes baptized into the Roman Catholic faith before being sent to America.[24] The Angolans may have been particularly motivated to seek out the Spanish in Florida. These factors combined with the almost constant warfare and intrigue between the English and Spanish in America made early slave and plantation life in the Beaufort District very unstable.

GREAT AWAKENING AMONG BLACKS AND WHITES

Into the turbulent world of the early-eighteenth-century Beaufort District marched a number of famous and highly effective Christian evangelists. The middle years of the eighteenth century were known as the "Great Awakening" in Colonial America. This general revival is thought to be the origin of America's unique forms of Protestant enthusiasm. Both of the most famous evangelists of the Great Awakening in America, John Wesley and George Whitefield, visited the Beaufort District. George Whitefield, in particular, had a telling and lasting effect on both the white planters and black slaves of the area.

Almost since the first arrival of blacks in South Carolina, sincere efforts were made to convert them to Christianity. The efforts of several Anglican missionaries sent out by the Society for the Propagation of the Gospel in Foreign Parts were earnest, but not effective. Planters were skeptical of christianizing their slaves, believing that they might then demand freedom. Thomas Nairne of Port Royal specifically criticized Reverend Samuel Thomas, in 1705, for opening his mission among the plantation slaves of Goose Creek and ignoring the Yemassee Indians of the Beaufort District.[25] The founder of St. Helena's Church, Reverend Lewis Jones, in 1726, noted the complete failure of the mission to the slaves of St. Helena Parish, a circumstance he blamed on "the frequent alarm of the Spaniards and Indians in this place."[26]

When the Great Awakening touched South Carolina, the Beaufort District was fertile ground. Nowhere in the colony did the evangelical movement have a greater effect than in the southern parishes. The first to arrive was John Wesley. On December 7, 1737, he visited Beaufort, where he was a guest of Reverend Lewis Jones. At Beaufort, he was entertained by Colonel Nathaniel Barnwell, who gave Wesley "a lively idea of old English hospitality."[27] Wesley's work in nearby Savannah was well known in Beaufort. He had established missions at Ebenezer, Skidaway, and Thunderbolt and probably already had followers at Purrysburg, Daufuskie, and Hilton Head. Wesley's visit to Beaufort, however, was on the occasion of his fleeing an embarrassing lawsuit in Georgia. Wesley had become romantically involved with the daughter of Thomas Causton. When she married another man, Wesley spitefully refused her communion. A lawsuit ensued, and Wesley fled to South Carolina. The episode undermined Wesley's influence in Georgia and limited the impact of his ministry in South Carolina. He returned to England to gain lasting fame as the founder of Methodism.[28]

The most effective evangelical minister of the Great Awakening in America was Reverend George Whitefield. Whitefield had already established himself as an inspirational orator in England when he sailed for America in 1737 to continue the ministry begun by John Wesley in Savannah, even though Wesley had advised him to turn back. From his first arrival in Georgia in 1738 until his death in Newburyport, Massachusetts, in 1770, Whitefield traveled throughout the colonies and established himself as the most influential evangelist in early American history. Because of the opposition of the Anglican establishment in South Carolina, led by Commissary Alexander Garden, Whitefield's influence in South Carolina was limited. Among the settlers of the Beaufort District, however, he had enormous influence.[29]

Whitefield was the guide and mentor of the Euhaws Baptist Church at Coosawhatchie and the Stoney Creek Independent Presbyterian Church at Pocotaligo. While the St. Helena Church remained part of the Anglican establishment, its leading vestryman during the colonial era, Colonel Nathaniel Barnwell, was one of Whitefield's converts and sent his four sons to be educated at the Bethesda School in Savannah. These men were the ancestors of the most prominent family in antebellum Beaufort.

Whitefield's first contacts with the inhabitants of the Beaufort District came in 1740. In August, Whitefield was visited in Savannah by some of the most prominent men in the Beaufort District—Hugh Bryan, Jonathan Bryan, Nathaniel Barnwell, Reverend Lewis Jones, and Reverend William Tilly. During this visit, Nathaniel Barnwell experienced a personal awakening. While Whitefield was praying during the service, Barnwell "dropped down as though shot with a gun." The next day, Jonathan Bryan and Nathaniel Barnwell came to Whitefield to make personal confessions of sin. While Jonathan Bryan spoke, "Mr. Barnwell lay on a bed groaning in bitterness of soul, under a sense of guilt." Whitefield instructed them on the "nature of the new birth and the necessity of a saving closure with Christ." The Bryan brothers and Barnwell returned to South Carolina to spread Whitefield's enthusiasm. Another very influential convert among this group was Reverend William Tilly, pastor of the newly formed Euhaws Baptist congregation near Coosawhatchie. The Euhaws Baptist Church was the "mother church" of the many influential Baptist churches that grew up in the Beaufort District in the post-Revolutionary era.

The Euhaws Baptist congregation had been assembled during the 1730s by families that moved from Edisto Island to Port Royal, Hilton Head, and the Euhaws section of St. Helena Parish. The most prominent members of this group were Ephraim Mikell, his uncle Joseph Sealy, and the Parmenter family of Hilton Head and Daufuskie. The land at Coosawhatchie on which the first meetinghouse was built was donated by Francis Pelot, a Swiss immigrant from Purrysburg.[30]

George Whitefield maintained a long, if intermittent, relationship with the Euhaws Baptist Church, both during the ministry of William Tilly and that of his successor, Francis Pelot. After William Tilly died in 1744, Reverend Francis Pelot moved to Coosawhatchie from Purrysburg, where he had been one of the first settlers in 1734. Pelot was the leader of this scattered Baptist congregation from 1746 until his death in 1774. Whitefield often performed services at the Euhaws Church, and his influence caused a growth in the congregation during the 1740s and 1750s. The new meetinghouse, constructed in 1751, was consecrated by Whitefield on March 5, 1752. Whitefield's last service at the Euhaws Baptist Church was the marriage of Joseph Sealy Jr. to Joanna Staples in 1754.[31]

In 1743, some of the most prominent of George Whitefield's converts broke away from St. Helena's Church and formed the Stoney Creek Independent Presbyterian Church. They called as their first minister the Reverend William Hutson of New York. Hutson was already a convert of Whitefield's. He served the Stoney Creek Church from 1744 to 1756 when he became the influential minister of the Independent Church of Charleston. Whitefield's most famous converts, Hugh and Jonathan Bryan, were the leaders of this congregation.[32] Also among the founders of the Stoney Creek Church were Joseph Bryan, his son-in-law Stephen Bull, James DeVeaux, and Robert Ogle.[33]

It was the Bryan brothers, Hugh and Jonathan, who brought the most notoriety to the evangelical movement in South Carolina. They were responsible for initiating the evangelical mission to the growing slave population of the Beaufort District. The conversion of the slaves to Christianity was one of the most important events in South Carolina history, and the particular form of evangelical Christianity practiced by many black Americans to this day may have begun with George Whitefield, the Great Awakening, and the Bryan brothers of the Beaufort District. At the time, however, the mission to the slaves was very unpopular with the political and social power structure as well as the Anglican establishment, in South Carolina. Ultimately, it was the excesses and antics of Hugh Bryan that brought discredit on the evangelical movement, delayed the mission to the slaves, and confirmed the Anglican opposition to the Great Awakening.[34]

Hugh Bryan was the scion of one of the first families of the Beaufort District, a major land and slave owner, vestryman of St. Helena Parish, and representative to the provincial Commons House of Assembly. As a youth during the Yemassee War, he had been captured by the Indians and held for many months, his life being spared by the intercession of the Huspa king. Hugh Bryan's early conversion to evangelical Christianity was influenced by his wife, Katherine Barnwell, daughter of "Tuscarora Jack." The journal of his religious experience and that of Mary Hutson, wife of Reverend William Hutson, was later published in London under the title of *Living Christianity Delineated in the Diaries and Letters of Two Eminently Pious Persons Lately Deceased with Preface by Reverend Mr. John Condor and Reverend Mr. Thomas Gibbons.*[35]

In addition to his own personal conversion, Hugh Bryan undertook to follow the dictates of George Whitefield in similarly converting his black slaves. Whitefield had criticized planters in South Carolina for not doing more to bring Christianity to the slaves and had also criticized the Anglican approach of trying to educate the slaves before introducing them to the gospel, "for there is a vast difference between civilizing and Christianizing the Negro." Whitefield thought the slaves deserved the same "new birth in Christ" that he brought to the white settlers.[36] Hugh Bryan, accordingly, began enthusiastically to preach to his slaves and those of neighboring plantations. The slaves were told to seek Christ as their true master "to which they replied in the height of joy and transport, Christ was a very good master if he would get them a holy day, they would seek him every day."[37] These enthusiastic gatherings frightened the local authorities, and reports reached the Commons House of Assembly of "frequent and great assemblies of Negroes in the parish of St. Helena."[38] Hugh Bryan was named as the instigator of these slave meetings. To make matters worse, Bryan published a letter in the *South Carolina Gazette* on the occasion of the Charleston fire of 1740, blaming the fire, the Stono Rebellion, the recent failure of English forces at St. Augustine, and several other disasters on the wrath of God as retribution for the many sins of the colony.[39] Hugh Bryan's personal behavior then attracted attention and ridicule. He seemed to have lost touch with reality after the death of his wife, Katherine, in 1740. Bryan began to have visions and wandered into the woods for several days to record the prophesies that God sent him. One of his prophesies was of another slave rebellion. He also predicted that he would divide the waters of the Whale Branch River with a wand and would shortly thereafter be called to his maker. Eliza Lucas wryly recorded his failure, "the water continued as it was and himself a living fallacy of his own predictions. . . . [He] was convinced that he was guided not by the infallible spirit but by that of delusion." Thereafter, Bryan ceased his bizarre activities.[40]

The stridency of Bryan's attack on South Carolina society angered the provincial authorities, the most powerful of whom was Bryan's neighbor in Prince William Parish, Lieutenant Governor William Bull. And the timing of these events could not have been worse. England was at war with Spain and South Carolina's slave population was a particular target of the Spanish in Florida. The residents of the coast were being harassed by Spanish privateers, and the failure of Oglethorpe's siege of St. Augustine, as well as the Stono Rebellion, was fresh on the minds of South Carolinians. To those in authority, Bryan's behavior and public statements were seditious not religious. Bryan was arrested and forced to explain his behavior before a committee of the Commons House of Assembly. He formally apologized to the speaker of the house. This episode was widely publicized in the colony, and the ridicule and general opprobrium to which Hugh Bryan was subjected undermined the influence of the Great Awakening in South Carolina.

The evangelical movement, however, had a lingering effect. Hugh and Jonathan Bryan continued to preach to the slaves on their own plantations, albeit more quietly. As they prospered, their plantations became examples of peaceful Christian slave communities. In October 1742, Johann Martin Bolzius visited Jonathan Bryan's plantation near Pocotaligo and found "the most beautiful order in housekeeping and among the Negroes, of whom several were honestly converted to God. They love their master and mistress so well that they do not desire freedom and show great loyalty in their work." According to Bolzius, the neighboring planters complained that Bryan's slaves "do nothing but pray and sing and thereby neglect their work." But Bolzius observed that the industry of Bryan's slaves and the success of their master belied those complaints.[41] The Bryan plantations continued to be centers for the Christian instruction of slaves, and when Jonathan Bryan moved to Georgia in 1752, he took with him the evangelical mission that George Whitefield and Hugh Bryan had introduced to him. This culminated after the Revolution in the establishment of the Bryan Baptist Church in Savannah under the leadership of Jonathan Bryan's slave, Andrew Bryan, one of the first great black preachers in America.[42]

The evangelical preachers succeeded with the slave population of the Beaufort District, much to the frustration of sincere Anglican missionaries who had preceded them. Reverend Lewis Jones of St. Helena Church in Beaufort summed up the different approaches of the two Christian traditions in trying to reach the slaves. While the Anglican missionaries believed in careful instruction, the evangelical preachers "taught enthusiasm rather than religion"; they pretended "to see visions and receive revelations from Heaven and to be converted by an Instantaneous Impulse of the spirit."[43]

NOTES

1. John Donald Duncan, *Servitude and Slavery in Colonial South Carolina, 1670–1776* (Ann Arbor: University Microfilms, 1980), 646.

2. Duncan, *Servitude and Slavery,* 320.

3. Daniel C. Littlefield, *Rice and Slaves: Ethnicity and the Slave Trade in Colonial South Carolina* (Baton Rouge: Lousiana State University Press, 1981), 111; Jane Landers, "Gracia Real de Santa Teresa de Mose: A Free Black Town in Spanish Florida," *American Historical Review* 95(February–June, 1990): 27; Peter H. Wood, *Black Majority: Negroes in Colonial South Carolina from 1670 through the Stono Rebellion* (New York: Knopf, 1974), 302.

4. John J. TePaske, "The Fugitive Slave," in Samuel Proctor, ed., *Eighteenth-Century Florida and Its Borderlands* (Gainesville: University Presses of Florida, 1975), 1–12.

5. J. G. Dunlop, "William Dunlop," *South Carolina Historical Magazine,* 34 (1935): 1–30.

6. Duncan, *Servitude and Slavery,* 646.

7. Peter H. Wood, *Black Majority,* 298, 304–6.

8. *South Carolina Gazette,* March 10, 1783; March 31, 1783.

9. J. H. Easterby, ed., *Journal of the Commons House of Assembly, 1741–1742* (Columbia: Historical Commission of South Carolina, 1953), 595; TePaske, "Fugitive Slave," 6–8; Wood, *Black Majority,* 306; Duncan, *Servitude and Slavery,* 661.

10. Duncan, *Servitude and Slavery,* 662–63.

11. *South Carolina Gazette,* March 17, 1739.

12. *South Carolina Gazette,* January 25, 1739.

13. *South Carolina Gazette,* May 3, 1735.

14. Easterby, ed., *Journal of the Commons House of Assembly, 1741–1742,* 150, 595; David Ramsay, *History of South Carolina from Its Earliest Settlement in 1670 to the Year 1808* (Newberry, S.C.: N. J. Duffie, 1858), 179.

15. *South Carolina Gazette,* March 5, 1737; John Tate Lanning, *The Diplomatic History of Georgia* (Chapel Hill: University of North Carolina Press, 1936), 57–66; Lanning, "Don Miguel Wall and the Spanish Attempt against the Existence of Carolina and Georgia," *North Carolina Historical Review* 10 (July 1933): 186–213.

16. Wood, *Black Majority,* 132; *South Carolina Gazette,* January 26, 1740.

17. Wood, *Black Majority,* 318–19; John K. Thornton, "African Dimensions of the Stono Rebellion: Notes and Comments," *American Historical Review* 96 (1996): 1101–1113.

18. *South Carolina Gazette,* May 4, 1734.

19. M. Eugene Sirmans, *Colonial South Carolina: A Political History, 1663–1763* (Chapel Hill: University of North Carolina Press, 1966), 210; Wood, *Black Majority,* 324.

20. *South Carolina Gazette,* February 4, 1745.

21. *South Carolina Gazette,* February 6, 1746.

22. *South Carolina Gazette,* April 27, 1748.

23. *South Carolina Gazette,* October 30, 1749.

24. Duncan, *Servitude and Slavery,* 301; Littlefield, *Rice and Slaves,* 41, 160.

25. Duncan, *Servitude and Slavery,* 291–95.

26. Duncan, *Servitude and Slavery,* 320–21.

27. Donald G. Matthews, *Religion in the Old South* (Chicago: University of Chicago Press, 1977), 13.

28. "An Extract of the Rev. Mr. John Wesley's Journal from His Embarking for Georgia to His Return to London," in Trevor R. Reese, ed., *Our First Visit to America: Early Reports from Georgia* (Savannah: Beehive Press, 1974), 239.

29. Matthews, *Religion in the Old South,* 14.

30. George Whitefield, "A Journal of a Voyage from London to Savannah, Georgia," in Reese, ed., *Our First Visit to America,* 309–11.

31. Leah Townsend, *South Carolina Baptists, 1670–1805* (Baltimore: Genealogical Publishing, 1974), 36–39.

32. R. W. Hutson, ed., "Register Kept by Rev. Willilam Hutson of Stoney Creek Independent Congregational Church and (Circular) Congregational Church in Charleston, 1743–1760," *South Carolina Historical Magazine* 38 (January 1937): 21–36.

33. John R. Todd and Francis M. Hutson, *Prince William Parish and Plantations* (Richmond: Garrett and Massie, 1935), 85–87.

34. Alan Gallay, *The Formation of a Planter Elite: Jonathan Bryan and the Southern Colonial Frontier* (Athens: University of Georgia Press, 1989), 30–54.

35. Harvey H. Jackson, "Hugh Bryan and Great Awakening in South Carolina," *William and Mary Quarterly* 43 (October 1986): 594–614.

36. Duncan, *Servitude and Slavery,* 327–28.

37. Duncan, *Servitude and Slavery,* 332.

38. Easterby, ed., *Journal of the Commons House of Assembly, 1741–1742,* 461–62.

39. *South Carolina Gazette,* January 15, 1741.

40. Stephen B. Barnwell, *The Story of an American Family* (Marquette, Mich.: Privately printed, 1969), 26–27; Sirmans, *Colonial South Carolina,* 231–32; Elise Pinckney, ed., *The Letterbook of Eliza Lucas Pinckney* (Chapel Hill: University of North Carolina Press, 1972), 29–30; John J. TePaske, *The Governorship of Spanish Florida, 1700–1763* (Durham: Duke University Press, 1964), 148.

41. George Fenwicke Jones, "John Martin Bolzius' Trip to Charleston, October 1742," *South Carolina Historical Magazine* 82 (1981): 87–110.

42. Gallay, *Formation of a Planter Elite,* 393.

43. Gallay, *Formation of a Planter Elite,* 387.

8

Beaufort and the Caribbean Cockpit

DEFENSE OF THE SEA ISLANDS, 1728–1740

With the close of the Yemassee War the concern of the people of the Beaufort District shifted from fear of attack by the Indians from the landward side to fear of invasion by a European rival from the seaward side. The highly praised harbor of Port Royal became not so much an economic asset as a likely target. During the 1730s, the Port Royal frontier was no longer the southernmost English settlement in North America. The English colony of Georgia was established at Yamacraw Bluff on the Savannah River in 1733, and Governor Johnson's township plan bore fruit in the Beaufort District that same year by the settlement of a few hundred Swiss dissenters at Purrysburg on the South Carolina side of the Savannah River. The Georgia colony provided a buffer between Port Royal and St. Augustine against attacks up the inland passage, and the Purrysburg Township provided some security against Indian threats from the interior. But Port Royal Sound remained the single most accessible harbor on the southern coast. Throughout the colonial period, though, it was never adequately defended.

During the later stages of the Yemassee War, half of the garrison of Fort King George had been removed to Port Royal, and in 1726 plans were made for a permanent fort at Beaufort. The vulnerability of Port Royal Sound to attacks by sea was well recognized at that time and was used to justify the construction of Fort Frederick on Port Royal Island. The Commons House Committee reported in 1727 that "in case of war . . . the enemy will be encouraged to invade our southward parts." The sea islands were "more exposed and . . . the harbor of Port Royal [was] capable of receiving many large ships of war."[1]

With the successful conclusion of Palmer's Raid in 1728 and the temporary end of the colonial wars, construction on Fort Frederick progressed slowly. Five years later, the barracks were not yet erected and the bastion was made of temporary earth and timber construction. In 1731, Governor Robert Johnson pointed out that it would be "much more serviceable with oyster shell and lyme than with earth and timber," but the money provided by the Commons House of Assembly fell short of that required for more permanent construction. The Commons House of Assembly also proved tardy in providing the necessary wages for the garrison, which worked "great hardship" on the soldiers and contributed to bad morale.[2]

Before a permanent structure could be completed, however, the Georgia settlers had arrived, and it was suggested that the fort and barracks at Port Royal would "not be so useful as at first imagined." Governor Johnson asked that it be completed anyway, and in 1733 Beaufort merchant and planter John Delabere was given a contract to complete Fort Frederick "as far as he can but not to exceed 2,000 pounds currency." In 1735, the committee reported that the "fort is indeed complete and the wall is five feet high and five feet thick at the top." Fort Frederick never provided much security, however, and would have been powerless in opposing a strong naval force. By 1740, it had fallen into disrepair, and during the 1740s and 1750s it was seldom used.[3]

It was the settlement of Savannah which provided the greatest measure of security for the Port Royal area. Indeed, many Port Royal planters were deeply involved in the military colonization of Georgia. Most prominent among these were Hugh Bryan, who as a boy had been kidnapped and held as a captive slave for more than a year by the Huspa king of the Yemassee; his younger brother, Jonathan Bryan, who was later to become one of the most prominent and controversial citizens of Georgia; Colonel Nathaniel Barnwell, eldest son of "Tuscarora Jack"; and Captain James McPherson, one of the first settlers of the backcountry of the Beaufort District.[4]

When Oglethorpe was proceeding with his colonists from Charleston to Yamacraw Bluff, Captain Jonathan Bryan of the South Carolina scout boat and Captain James McPherson of the Carolina Rangers were glad to "attend the new settlers" and provide for their safe passage to the site of Savannah. As the Georgia colony became established, the bulk of the responsibility for defense of the southern frontier was turned over to Georgia authorities. In 1734, Captain Joseph Parmenter of the South Carolina scouts was relieved of his duty at Fort King George and all of his powder and shot was turned over to the Georgians. The South Carolina scouts operated in Georgia waters through the early 1730s and, under the command of General Oglethorpe, helped construct the fort and town of Frederica on St. Simons Island in 1736.[5] In that year, Oglethorpe took a party by the inland passage as far south as the St. Johns River to determine exactly where Spanish occupation ended and Georgia claims could begin. Port Royal planters Jonathan Bryan and Nathaniel Barnwell accompanied Oglethorpe as veteran advisors.[6] In 1737, the South Carolina authorities decided the further military support of Georgia was unnecessary and terminated the finances for support of the scout boat and its crew in Georgia waters. Oglethorpe immediately enlisted the entire crew and bought the scout boat, naming it "Carolina." Thereafter, Georgians were the principal guardians of the inland passage.[7]

Backcountry defense of Port Royal was provided by the Palachacola Fort established on the Savannah River in 1723 and by Saltcatcher's Fort, established in 1727 at the confluence of the Salkehatchie and Combahee Rivers near the present town of Yemassee and near the site of Governor Craven's victory over the Yemassee in June 1715. These forts had been established during the later stages of the Yemassee War, and a mounted company of Carolina Rangers patrolled between the two. In 1734, Captain James McPherson, who had established a plantation and cowpen and moved his family to the Saltcatcher's Fort during the 1720s, was ordered south to establish a similar frontier fort in Georgia to protect Savannah. This was Fort Argyle on the Ogeechee River. James McPherson, like Jonathan Bryan and Nathaniel Barnwell, became a close associate and advisor to General Oglethorpe.[8]

Not just protecting but also provisioning the Georgia settlers was an interest of the Port Royal planters. When the Georgia colony was bolstered by the settlement of several hundred German Salzburgers at Ebenezer on the Savannah River, it was Hugh Bryan, by then one of the largest cattle ranchers and planters in the Port Royal area, who willingly provided the struggling community with provisions. In turn he was perhaps influenced by their religious zeal.[9] And in 1736, Captain James McPherson arrived at the Darien settlement with a herd of cattle which he had brought "all the way overland" from South Carolina. This first overland cattle drive "caused joy" among the Georgia settlements "to find the communication for cattle by land opened."[10]

The establishment of the Georgia colony, however, did little to allay the fears of a naval assault on Port Royal Sound, which thrust like a maritime salient into the heart of the Beaufort District. In 1733, Captain Nathaniel Coverly of the Rhode Island sloop *Batchelor* reported that in Havana "three 60-gun ships of war were then fitting out to destroy Port Royal, South Carolina." He claimed to have prevented this threat from materializing by falsely informing the Spanish that the bar at Port Royal was so dangerous that their ships were not likely to return. With this misinformation, the Spanish canceled the expedition and sailed instead for Spain.[11] Early in 1737, an English ship stranded in St. Helena Sound by fog was mistaken for a Spanish naval assault by the planters on Edisto Island.[12] Later in 1737, the Commons House of Assembly heard the report of Captain Watson of the sloop *Rebecca and Mary* that "a large ship and sloop" were cruising off the bar at St. Augustine with the possible intention of attacking Port Royal. Colonel Thomas Hext ordered a hundred men stationed at Beaufort on the assumption that Port Royal Sound was the intended Spanish target.[13]

Steps were taken to prepare for an attack on Port Royal in the 1730s. At least one South Carolina scout boat remained stationed near Beaufort until 1764. In 1737, Colonel Nathaniel Barnwell convinced the Commons House of Assembly to provide funds for a series of lookout posts along the southern coast.

Lookouts were to be posted at the Stono Inlet, the South Edisto Inlet on the north edge of St. Helena Sound, and on St. Phillip's Island (Bay Point) on the north edge of Port Royal Sound. In addition, the scout boat commanded by Captain John Cowan was to be stationed at the mouth of Port Royal Sound rather than at Beaufort.

In 1738, Colonel Nathaniel Barnwell and Captain Hugh Bryan wrote a letter to the Commons House of Assembly suggesting another plan for the protection of their neighbors in the Port Royal area. They proposed to build a fort on the mainland "to which people from the islands may flee in case of attack by sea." Bryan and Barnwell apparently had in mind a spot on Hugh Bryan's property on Huspa Neck. Lieutenant Governor William Bull, however, suggested that the proposed fort be built at the Port Royal ferry.[14] The fort was never built, but the plan reveals the shifting fears of the Port Royal inhabitants. Instead of seeking refuge among the sea islands from attacks by the Indians as they had during the Yemassee War, they were now seeking refuge on the "Indian land" (mainland) from attacks by Spanish, and later French, naval forces. The sea islands had changed from a place of refuge to a place of vulnerability.

Later in 1738, a Commons House committee on the defense of Port Royal made a comprehensive three-part recommendation. The first was to settle a group of Notchee Indians on Polawanna Island to be used for scout and ranger duty. Polawanna Island, between St. Helena and Datha Islands, was the state's first Indian reservation, established in 1712. But the last remnants of the indigenous Cusabo tribe had long since disappeared, and the island had reverted to the provincial treasury for public use. The second recommendation was to provide Colonel Barnwell with 250 pounds currency to construct a fortified barracks at Cochran's Point on the north end of Port Royal Island as a refuge for the inhabitants. The third recommendation was to place two lookout posts of seven men each on St. Phillip's Island on Port Royal Sound and at Callibogy Point at the south end of Hilton Head Island. These posts were to be provided with good boats and oars and one cannon each. Only the third recommendation was implemented.[15]

In 1738, Reverend Lewis Jones, Rector of St. Helena Church, wrote that fear of attack by Spaniards was a common topic of conversation in the community. For the first time in fourteen years on the Port Royal frontier, he asked to be transferred from "this dangerous situation."[16]

SEA ISLANDS DURING THE WAR OF JENKINS'S EAR

War clouds had been building over the southern frontier throughout the 1730s. The Spanish continued to try to convince the English to evacuate Georgia, and Don Antonio de Arredondo, in his meeting with Governor Oglethorpe at Frederica in 1736, claimed all the Beaufort District of South Carolina as well. Oglethorpe, in turn, claimed all the land to the St. Johns River in Florida by right of occupation.[17] Yemassee Indians committed murders in Georgia, and Creek Indians raided Florida in the same year.[18] In 1738, the Spanish began building a fort at the mouth of the St. Johns River to counter the English.[19] When Captain Robert Jenkins presented to a horrified Parliament in London the severed ear he had lost to the St. Augustine "Guarda Costa," Captain Emiliano Fandino, the English declared war on Spain.[20] The War of Jenkins's Ear (1739–1742), as it has become known to history, was particularly disruptive to the southern coast in general and to the Port Royal area in particular. When the Commons House of Assembly convened in 1739, they began to debate the best way to assist in the defense of Georgia.[21] Not all South Carolina politicians were enthusiastic supporters of the Georgia governor. In 1737, it was rumored in Charleston that Oglethorpe was to be commissioned captain general of both provinces and that South Carolina would have no governor, only a lieutenant governor to report to him.[22] Though this did not transpire, some South Carolinians remained suspicious of Oglethorpe's ambitions. The leading planters of the Port Royal area, recognizing their community of interest with the defense of Georgia, and several of them being personally close to Oglethorpe, did not wait for the conclusion of the debates. They reported that because the Commons House was not in session when word of war was received, they had taken it upon themselves to equip and deploy a scout boat for their own protection. Nathaniel Barnwell, Hugh Bryan, Thomas Wigg, James Cochran, William Hazzard, and Jonathan Bryan stated that because Port Royal was "much exposed to the incursions of the Spaniards" they had hired a scout boat to cruise southward "as the most expeditious method to prevent being surprised and also to deter slaves . . . from attempting to desert this government to the Castle of St. Augustine." It was two years before they were reimbursed for their expense.[23]

In 1740, the Commons House recommended yet another plan for the defense of Port Royal. They reported that the best way to repel a Spanish attack "on our sea coasts with their row galleys is to oppose them with boats capable of resisting those galleys." They proposed to build two "half-galleys" capable of holding forty or fifty men with a 9-pounder and several "swivel guns, oars and all other necessaries." One boat would be stationed at Port Royal and the other at the South Edisto Inlet on St. Helena Sound.[24] These were the *Beaufort Galley* and the *Charles-town Galley*, launched early in 1742.[25]

In 1737, Governor Oglethorpe had been appointed by the crown as overall military commander on the southern frontier. When the war broke out, he received orders from the duke of Newcastle to take whatever action he could to harass and contain the Spanish in Florida. Oglethorpe, therefore, sent word to the South Carolina government requesting their aid in an expedition against St. Augustine. The South Carolina authorities set about to assist Oglethorpe, and the men of the Port Royal area played a major role in the expedition. Two hundred men were raised "to the southward" to join the expedition, and Oglethorpe suggested to Lieutenant Governor William Bull that "if the Carolina people will pay them, I believe they may raise fifty very good men at Purrysburg."[26] Of the first thirty-one "gentleman volunteers" to respond to the call, sixteen were from St. Helena and neighboring St. Bartholemew Parish.[27] Colonel Nathaniel Barnwell of Beaufort served as Oglethorpe's aide-de-camp. Colonel John Palmer commanded a detachment of militia and rangers from the southern parishes. Captain Stephen Bull, Lieutenant Jonathan Bryan, Lieutenant Henry DeSaussure, Lieutenant Joseph Parmenter, and Lieutenant Philip Delegal, all from the Port Royal area, commanded units at the siege of St. Augustine in 1740.[28]

The siege of St. Augustine did not go well. The English army languished on the beaches opposite the Castillo San Marcos from May until July 1740. The HMS *Flamborough* and the rest of the naval squadron withdrew in July to avoid the summer hurricanes, and the army abandoned the siege. Oglethorpe accused the four hundred South Carolina troops of ensuring the failure by arriving late and leaving early. The South Carolinians countered by accusing Oglethorpe of failing to exercise proper judgement and blamed the failure on him. Many of the South Carolina volunteers went home in disgust. Nathaniel Barnwell remained Oglethorpe's aide-de-camp until the end of the campaign. The failure of the expedition caused a burst of controversy in the Commons House, in which the testimony of Jonathan Bryan and Nathaniel Barnwell played a large part.[29]

During the Commons House investigation following the siege of St. Augustine, the South Carolina officers severely criticized Oglethorpe. His deployment of troops was improper, he failed to act against obvious Spanish weaknesses, and he discriminated against the South Carolina volunteers in provisioning and quartering troops. Colonel Nathaniel Barnwell testified that the siege should have been conducted from the mainland side and that both he and Colonel John Palmer advised him so. But Oglethorpe stationed his troops on the beach because he feared they would be discouraged if they lost sight of the men-of-war. In his deposition, Lieutenant Jonathan Bryan accused Oglethorpe of personal misconduct when, after Bryan had captured some runaway slaves belonging to South Carolinians, Oglethorpe claimed them for himself.[30]

But the incident which seems to have touched off the controversy was the death of the state's intrepid Indian fighter, Colonel John Palmer, at the Battle of Fort Moosa. Palmer and the South Carolina scouts, in company with some highland rangers and regulars from the Forty-second Regiment of Foot under Captain Hugh MacKay, had been given the dangerous assignment of securing a mainland salient for English forces and preventing Spanish foragers from leaving St. Augustine from the north and west.[31] They made their camp at Santa Teresa de Mosa, or Fort Moosa, north of St. Augustine—the settlement that had been specifically established for fugitive slaves from South Carolina. There was confusion of command at the English camp between Colonel Palmer and Captain MacKay. Palmer, the frontier veteran, tried to warn MacKay of the danger of an Indian-style surprise attack, but he paid no heed. When a force of Spanish regulars, fugitive slaves, and Yemassee Indians assaulted Fort Moosa in the predawn darkness of June 15, they caught the English force literally napping. Colonel John Palmer and seventy-eight men died defending the exposed position with no support from Oglethorpe's troops on the beaches.[32] News of Palmer's death prompted an angry letter from Lieutenant Governor William Bull to General Oglethorpe to the effect that the South Carolinians expected some success for so costly a sacrifice. It might have been pointed out that Palmer had achieved greater success in 1728 without the loss of a single man. When the siege was abandoned, though, the controversy began. The testimony of the Beaufort men all revolved around the incident at Fort Moosa which had ended the life of Port Royal's last hero of the Yemassee War.[33] On the other side, twenty black fugitives from South Carolina were singled out by the Spanish for special recognition for their valor at the Battle of Fort Moosa.[34]

The result of the expedition of 1740, as many South Carolinians feared, was to encourage a counterstroke by the Spanish. For two years, Spanish "guarda costas" and privateers harassed the sea islands and Spanish Indians raided English settlements.[35] In June 1742, reports reached Charleston of a powerful squadron from Havana off the Georgia coast.[36] The Beaufort militia went on alert. "At Port Royal . . . all the militia was in arms and prepared for a vigorous defense in case of attack."[37] The *Beaufort Galley*, launched early that year, was dispatched with the HMS *Flamborough* to assist the Georgians.[38]

News of the Spanish invasion fleet in Georgia occasioned a panic among inhabitants of the sea islands. Reverend Lewis Jones of St. Helena Church wrote that fear of a Spanish invasion had caused "most of the families in this place to fly for refuge to Charleston and other parts of this province." He feared that the area would be subjected to depopulation and "universal ruin" because of its "being very much exposed and unguarded." Lewis Jones resided in Beaufort, and his correspondence reveals the nervousness of the inhabitants who had "lived in fear and danger many years from the Spaniards and Indians."[39]

South Carolina authorities were well aware of the vulnerability of the coast, and of Port Royal Sound in particular, to naval assault. In 1742, Lieutenant Governor William Bull wrote to the duke of Newcastle about the "defenseless condition of Port Royal and parts adjacent." Intelligence had revealed the details of the Spanish plan. The governor of Cuba was to dispatch a strong fleet from Havana to enter Port Royal Sound and capture Port Royal Island. While they worked to fortify this foothold, the Spanish would encourage the slave population of the lowcountry to desert their masters and gain refuge on Port Royal Island. The report admitted that the Spanish strategy was sound and, if properly executed, was likely to succeed. One difficulty was that militia of the southern parishes could not concentrate a large enough force to defend Port Royal Island. Some of them "must be left in time of alarm in their several districts to guard against any insurrection by their slaves."[40] The same report described specifically the weakness of the area around Port Royal Sound. "In respect to Port Royal . . . it is an island surrounded by deep rivers and channels and having about forty families on it and a small fort and town, in its present condition not able to make much resistance." In addition, communication with the mainland was slow, and Lieutenant Governor Bull's concluding lament was that Port Royal Island was "as difficult for us to defend as it is easy for the enemy to be masters."[41]

Miraculously, General Oglethorpe and the Georgians repulsed a vastly superior force of Spanish troops at the Battle of Bloody Marsh on St. Simon's Island on July 7, 1742. Only a few Carolina Rangers arrived in time to help Oglethorpe. The HMS *Flamborough* and the *Beaufort Galley* arrived off St. Simon's Island just in time to see the Spanish sails slipping over the horizon. The escape of the Spanish fleet was ominous news for Port Royal.[42] In August, it was rumored that "they will soon pay another visit . . . to Port Royal which place it was their orders to attack whether they succeed or not" in Georgia.[43]

The Spanish fleet, though, did not return. Oglethorpe's victory at the Battle of Bloody Marsh provided considerable relief for the inhabitants of the Port Royal area and apparently vindicated Oglethorpe in the eyes of some South Carolinians. The planters of Port Royal were so thankful that they felt obliged to send Oglethorpe a message of gratitude for saving them from their "inveterate and barbarous enemy, the Spaniards." They knew that if Georgia had fallen, the Spanish would soon have overrun their lands and "filled our habitations with blood and slaughter." The inhabitants of the sea islands also realized that in matters of military security, their fortunes were more closely linked with those of the Georgians than with their fellow South Carolinians in Charleston. They pointed out that by keeping his boats stationed off the Georgia coast, Oglethorpe had "secured our trade and fortunes in safety more than all the ships of war that were ever stationed in Charleston." Nathaniel Barnwell, Jonathan Bryan, and William Palmer, son of Colonel John Palmer, all of whom had criticized Oglethorpe in 1740, signed a petition which acknowledged the common interest between Port Royal and Georgia on matters of defense and revealed the resentment toward the Charleston leadership for their disinclination to take decisive steps for the protection of Port Royal.[44]

SMUGGLING, PRIVATEERS, AND MARITIME COMMERCE, 1739–1763

In its first thirty years, the town of Beaufort never lived up to its original promise of becoming an active commercial center. The Yemassee War cut off the Indian trade which was the basis of the early settlement at Beaufort. With the removal of the Indians from the region, that branch of commerce was never recovered. The Yemassee War also depopulated the sea islands and retarded the development of the town. The original act establishing the town had stipulated that grantees were required to build on their lots within six years. The Yemassee War halted this development, and progress was slow even after the Indian raids subsided. In 1728, the St. Helena vestry ordered the wardens to examine the original act and sought the opinion of the local delegates to the Commons House of Assembly in pursuing the prosecution of defaulters. No action was taken by the colonial legislature, and the matter was ignored for many years. Not until 1740 did the Commons House of Assembly pass "An Act for Better Settling the Town of Beaufort." This act stipulated that anyone owning a lot on the river was required to build within three years or be fined ten pounds currency per year thereafter. Those owning back lots were given four years to build. This act of 1740 replaced the original act, which "had never really answered the good design for which it was made." It was hoped that the act would help revive Beaufort as a commercial center.

Three new streets were laid out toward the west after the 1740 act. They were named after prominent members of the British Board of Trade: the duke of Newcastle, Lord Harrington, and Colonel Martin Bladen. The legislative committee which drafted this act included the two absentee representatives for St. Helena Parish, Samuel Prioleau and William Pinckney. The two local representatives, Colonel Nathaniel Barnwell and Major Ephraim Mikell, were not available for political work. Both were serving with General Oglethorpe at the siege of St. Augustine.[45]

The Battle of Bloody Marsh was not the end of the conflict between the English and Spanish on the southern coast. Throughout the 1740s and into the 1750s, a parade of Spanish, and later French, privateers ravaged South Carolina commerce and terrorized the sea island planters. Port Royal and St. Helena Sounds in the Beaufort District were the most accessible and least defended harbors in South Carolina, so it was natural that Spanish and French privateers would frequently use these sounds as safe havens. Much of the action in this intermittent naval war took place off the shore and in the bays and harbors of the southern coast. The naval warfare of the 1740s was a specific threat to the sea island settlers, and it prevented for more than a decade any attempt by Beaufort merchants to realize the highly advertised commercial potential of Port Royal Sound.

Because of the constant alarm on the southern coast, maritime commerce at Port Royal was nearly nonexistent. In 1735, for instance, only two ships left Charleston bound for Port Royal while ten ships left for the newly established rice port of Georgetown to the north.[46] And most of what trade existed in Beaufort was with the hated Spaniards in St. Augustine.[47] Captain William Lyford, as one of colonial South Carolina's most intrepid seamen, began his career as the master of the coasting schooner *Port Royal,* which hauled supplies between Charleston, Beaufort, and St. Augustine. Beaufort's most prominent sea captain in the 1730s was Caleb Davis, who was master of the same schooner for a time, but later acquired his own ship, *Virgin's Adventure.* Captain Davis and the *Virgin's Adventure* traded between Beaufort and St. Augustine from 1733 to 1737. The nature of this trade was highly suspect by the Charleston authorities. Davis was a regular violator of the customs regulations; in fact, he was a famous smuggler. His regular communication with St. Augustine was a conduit for information in the runaway slave "grapevine," and it was black seamen aboard the *Virgin's Adventure* who first brought news of the Spanish king's proclamation of sanctuary for South Carolina slaves. As relations with St. Augustine deteriorated, Caleb Davis's cozy trade with the Spanish was finally halted. In 1737, he was arrested for supplying provisions to the garrison at St. Augustine. After promising to stop, he slipped away at night, confirming the accusations in Charleston that he was motivated only by "sordid principles of self-interest."[48]

With the outbreak of the War of Jenkins's Ear in 1739, Spanish privateers infested the coast, and maritime commerce from Port Royal virtually ceased. In September 1739, King George II issued the "Letters of Marque and Reprizal" to counter the Spanish privateers. Also announced was news of numerous naval engagements throughout the West Indies and off the Georgia coast. The naval war soon arrived on the South Carolina coast. In April 1740, a sloop commanded by Captain Stewart was wrecked on Bay Point, Port Royal Sound, after being hunted by a Spanish privateer. In October, Major Heron, aboard a small schooner, was chased for nine hours by a "large Spanish privateer off St. Helena Sound." The long boat from the privateer closed on the schooner, but withdrew under fire from the South Carolina crew and ran into the shoals of St. Helena Sound. Major Heron reported the Spanish privateer was anchored unmolested off Coffin's Point on St. Helena Island.[49]

In 1741, after the siege of St. Augustine, the naval war intensified. Reports from Havana and St. Augustine described seven heavily armed Spanish privateers operating in South Carolina waters. Together, these ships mounted 60 guns and carried 640 men, more than a match for the combined naval forces of South Carolina and Georgia.[50] One of these vessels which was often seen operating in the waters of St. Helena and Port Royal Sounds was described as a "Bermuda built, about 70 tons, having 90 men, 6 carriage guns and 12 swivel guns, very sharp built, mast rakes much aft, 2 windows only in her stern, her quarters painted green, mouldings yellow and sides black. She is a prime sailor." This was the *Invincible Shepherdess,* commanded by the most effective and famous of the Spanish privateer captains, Don Francisco Loranzo of Havana and St. Augustine.[51]

These privateers fitted out in St. Augustine in the summer of 1741 and took their prizes back to the Florida capital for sale or refitting.[52] In March 1742, a Spanish privateer sloop anchored in the Edisto Inlet for two days, and the next month came word of a running sea battle in St. Helena Sound. The New York brigantine *Elizabeth,* with only eleven crew aboard bound from Jamaica to Charleston, was attacked by a black Spanish privateer sloop of ten guns and sixty men. Despite the odds against him, Captain Thomas Perdue held off the Spanish for three hours before they quit the fight and sailed off shore. Captain Perdue owed his good luck to his small crew who "behaved with extraordinary courage." This battle was in full sight and sound of the planters on both St. Helena and Edisto Islands.[53]

In May 1742, a "fine new schooner," just built in Beaufort and owned by Ephriam Mikell, sailed from Port Royal with one hundred barrels of rice and was almost immediately taken by a Spanish privateer.[54] In June 1742, two schooners from Port Royal were chased by a privateer off Edisto Island but made it safely to Charleston.[55]

South Carolina, or at least Charleston, was not defenseless in the face of this threat. There was a Royal Navy presence in Charleston Harbor: the HMS *Phoenix,* commanded by Captain Fanshaw. South Carolinians had little confidence in the Royal Navy, however. When the HMS *Phoenix* finally left port in 1741 to search out the enemy, the *South Carolina Gazette* reported with obvious sarcasm that Captain Fanshaw "met with his usual success" and encountered no Spaniards.[56] And in July 1741, the *Gazette* commented with mordant humor, "surely our coast will be sufficiently guarded by *Spanish* privateers."[57] What did prove effective were South Carolina privateers, or privateers from northern colonies, who were paid five pounds sterling bounty for each Spanish prisoner delivered to Charleston. In July 1741, Captain John Rouse, aboard the sloop *Speedwell,* captured a Spanish privateer with nineteen crewmen three days north of St. Augustine.[58]

The greatest success for South Carolina, however, was the capture of the Spanish Captain Don Francisco Loranzo in November 1741. Loranzo and his "famous black sloop," *Invincible Shepherdess,* was defeated and captured by the Rhode Island privateer *Revenge.* In three cruises over eighteen months, Don Francisco had taken fifty-four prizes off the South Carolina and Georgia coast. He had always been kind to his English captives and was described as "a man of great clemency and humanity" as well as skill and courage. His arrival in Charleston on November 25, 1741, with a wound in his arm from the sea battle, drew a large crowd of grudging admirers.[59]

Slowly, measures were taken to protect the exposed harbors of Port Royal and St. Helena. Early in 1742, the two coastal defense ships, the *Beaufort Galley* and the *Charles-town Galley,* were fitted out in Charleston with six light cannons and twelve swivel guns each. They were designed for a crew of fifty. With shallow draught, removable masts, and oars for propulsion, they were specifically adapted for cruising among the sea islands. They were, however, little use at sea.[60] The *Beaufort Galley* had assisted the Georgians at the Battle of Bloody Marsh in July 1742, and Lieutenant Governor Bull suggested in September that both galleys be stationed at Port Royal to protect that harbor. In October, both ships arrived in Beaufort "to the great satisfaction of the people residing in the southward parts of the province." The fleet was commanded by Captain William Lyford.[61]

The year 1743 brought a temporary end to the naval war, and in July, William Lyford sailed with the *Beaufort Galley* to Florida with a flag of truce and a shipload of Spanish captives to be exchanged for the English prisoners in St. Augustine. There he was "handsomely received" and the truce was cemented. During that year the naval defenses at Port Royal were improved by the arrival of the HMS *Loo* and the HMS *Spy.* The four ships operated from Port Royal for the rest of the year. The peace, however, was short lived. In 1744, European diplomacy dissolved into the War of Spanish Succession (1744–1748), which was called King George's War in America. The principal enemy was France, but in the naval war on the southern coast, the French were aided and abetted by the Spanish in St. Augustine.[62]

Hostilities began inauspiciously for the English. The HMS *Loo* left Port Royal for a cruise to the West Indies in January 1744. In March, word reached Charleston that the HMS *Loo* had been sunk off Cuba and much of the crew imprisoned in Havana.[63] In April 1745, the fifteen-ton schooner *St. Joseph,* the first ship to be recorded in the ship register as built at Port Royal, was captured by the French ship *Torrent* and a Spanish privateer commanded by the notorious captain Don Julian de Vega of St. Augustine. The *St. Joseph,* owned by Edward Wigg and William Hazzard of Beaufort, was held in St. Augustine for two months along with its master, Edward Morris, and a passenger, Mr. Benjamin Lloyd, a prominent South Carolina merchant. In late May, the *St. Joseph* and its crew were returned under a flag of truce. Early in 1746, a schooner bound from

Charleston to Port Royal was chased into the Stono Inlet, where the lookout fired the watch cannon into the privateer's long boat and destroyed it.[64]

In 1746, the English began to fight back. Captain William Lyford, formerly of the Port Royal station and "a man of known courage and experience," had gone to the Bahamas where Governor John Tinker outfitted a small fleet of privateers under Lyford's command.[65] In June 1746, Lyford returned to Nassau with a major prize: the two-hundred-ton Spanish treasure ship *Nuestra Senora de la Luz* with four hundred chests of silver. In April, the HMS *Tartar* from Charleston captured the notorious privateer Don Julian de Vega with his 16-gun ship and 160-person crew. Don Julian was known as the scourge of the coast and "a man of spirit."[66]

Despite these successes and the regular presence of the *Beaufort Galley* at Port Royal, Spanish and French privateers continued to harass the coast. In March 1747, the sloop *Wanton* was lost on the banks of St. Helena Sound after encountering a Spanish privateer. And in September 1747, a large French privateer sloop chased a schooner bound from Antigua to Charleston across the Port Royal bar. In October, Captain Campbell's schooner, previously captured near Port Royal, was recaptured by a Georgia privateer out of Frederica.[67]

In the spring of 1748, the sea island planters were again put on alert. A renegade Irishman named Collings had escaped the Charleston jail by burning it down and had fled to St. Augustine through the Beaufort District. He had been a "pilot and decoy" for the infamous French privateer, Captain Bernard. Bernard and Collings, operating from St. Augustine, had taken sixteen ships off the South Carolina coast. With Collings's escape it was now rumored that he would return with Captain Bernard and a fleet of small craft to land among the sea islands to "steal slaves and burn the plantations on the sea coast."[68]

The constant harassment of the sea islands by Spanish and French privateers in the 1740s brought new cries from Beaufort District planters and new plans for the defense of Port Royal harbor. In 1748, the "gentlemen and landowners" of St. Helena and Prince William Parishes once again requested more troops and more ships for their protection.[69] The feeling of isolation and insecurity of the sea island settlers during the colonial wars of the 1730s and 1740s is best summed up by a petition of St. Helena Island planters in 1744 requesting the assistance of the Commons House of Assembly in constructing a bridge across the tidal creek which separates Lady's Island from St. Helena Island, "The petitioners habitations lying on the sea coast of this province were exposed very much to the sudden attempts of our enemies, especially cruising along shore in their privateers, who might land their boats and cut off many families before any assistance would come from neighboring companies (of militia), for want of communication between Lady's Island and St. Helena . . . a bridge between them would be of great advantage against the attempts of a foreign enemy."[70]

In 1745, Governor James Glen wrote to the duke of Newcastle recommending his solution for the protection of Port Royal Sound. He pointed out that the harbor at Port Royal was easily capable of receiving fifty- or sixty-gun ships or larger. Because the sound was surrounded by many islands and tidal creeks, and communication with the mainland was difficult, it was almost impossible to protect the harbor from the landward side. Glen, therefore, suggested that "two forty gun ships-of-war stationed there would prove a great security to the whole province, it would draw people there to settle . . . and thus strengthen the frontier."[71]

The Royal Navy responded to this request. In October 1747, the forty-gun frigate HMS *Adventure* arrived at Port Royal, albeit dismasted by a recent hurricane at sea. The commanding officer of the HMS *Adventure* was Captain Joseph Hamar. He was well acquainted with South Carolina, having previously commanded the HMS *Flamborough* at the Battle of Bloody Marsh. Captain Hamar settled in for a long stay and set about the business of repairing his crippled vessel. Once in port, he had the usual problems of sailors jumping ship. Captain Hamar warned the local population not to harbor deserters who may seek to "be employed on shore, in the woods or in boats up the river." By the spring of 1748, HMS *Adventure* was refitted and ready for sea, but desertions had depleted Captain Hamar's crew to the point that he advertised to pay some local men for a three-month cruise and then a return trip to Port Royal.[72]

During the summer of 1748, the twenty-gun brig HMS *Rye* joined the HMS *Adventure* at Port Royal, and in August both ships bore out of Port Royal Sound in pursuit of eight Spanish vessels off the coast. The foray was successful as the two Royal Navy ships captured an armed Spanish coasting vessel with eight men aboard and retook a schooner which had been captured by a Spanish privateer the previous year. During the fall of 1748, the HMS *Rye* was careened at Port Royal, probably against the high bluff on the west side of the bay at Beaufort. Nearly one-third of Captain Wray's crew from the HMS *Rye* deserted on this occasion. Rear Admiral Watson, in command of the Royal Navy on station in southern waters, sent orders for Captain Hamar to try to replace them with local men knowledgeable about South Carolina and Georgia coastal waters to act as pilots for the HMS *Adventure* and the HMS *Rye* operating out of Port Royal.[73]

In 1748, King George's War was ended by the Treaty of Aix-la-Chapelle, and the naval war on the southern coast wound down. The presence of the Royal Naval Squadron at Port Royal made a large impact on the town of Beaufort. Not only did it provide security and encourage commerce, but the crews of the HMS *Adventure* and the HMS *Rye* added significantly to the population and activity of the small town. Cash from the Royal Navy payroll found its way into the few inns, public houses, and dry-goods stores in the village. Artisans were employed repairing and refitting the ships, and lucrative contracts for naval stores were awarded to local planters. Many of the sailors were released, or jumped ship, to become permanent residents of the Beaufort District. This was the first major stimulus to the commerce of the town since the end of the Indian wars. Two streets, Hamar and Adventure, were laid out to the west of town, being named for the HMS *Adventure* and its captain, Joseph Hamar.

With the end of King George's War, an attempt was made again to bring maritime commerce into the harbor at Port Royal. In 1748, an act was passed by the Commons House to authorize Nathaniel Barnwell, Thomas Wigg, John Barnwell, Charles Purry, and John Smith to collect a local tax to employ a pilot for the harbor. By 1750, enough tax had been collected in St. Helena and Prince William Parishes to hire a harbor pilot and build a pilot boat to serve Beaufort. Prince William planters objected to the tax, but the pilot boat was built anyway; throughout the rest of the colonial period, Port Royal harbor was served by able pilots. In addition, the construction of a lighthouse on Tybee Island, Georgia, in 1738 guided the way to the approaches at Port Royal Sound as well as the Savannah River. Ships headed for Savannah frequently hove down in Port Royal Sound, particularly in storms. For the rest of the colonial period the two ports grew together.[74]

 During the 1750s, most of the maritime commerce at Port Royal was in coastal trade between Charleston; Beaufort; Savannah; Sunbury, Georgia; and occasionally St. Augustine. But during these years also, Beaufort began to develop a special commercial relationship with the West Indies. In December 1752, of the five ships entering or leaving Port Royal for overseas voyages, four were in the West Indian trade and one was from London. On December 1, the sloop *Two Brothers* arrived at Port Royal from St. Eustatia, and the next day the schooner *Beaufort* arrived from Antigua. On December 3, the sloop *Early Horn* left Port Royal for St. Kitts, and on December 8, the schooner *Lucretia* left for St. Croix.[75] Throughout the 1750s, the trade between Port Royal and the West Indies remained brisk. The schooner *Beaufort* made regular runs to Antigua and St. Kitts under several masters, and in 1755 the schooner *Beaufort Packet* began trading between Charleston, Beaufort, and Barbados. Other vessels like the schooner *Betsy* sailed between Port Royal and St. Eustatia, and the sloop *Beaver* traded between Nassau and Port Royal.[76]

The products of this West Indian trade from the sea islands were derived from the rice and cattle industries. Rice from the new Prince William plantations and beef from the large herds of cattle on the sea islands provided sources of starch and protein for the large slave communities of the West Indian sugar plantations. The beef was pickled in brine and shipped in barrels. In addition, the hides were rendered on many sea island plantation tanneries and sent to the Caribbean, where such products, and the livestock themselves, were rare. A small industry grew around this trade when Beaufort merchant Colonel Joseph Edward Flowers opened a slave-operated shoe factory on Bay Street in the 1750s. In exchange for rice, beef, leather, and shoes, the return voyages brought rum, molasses and, perhaps, some slaves.[77]

The most active of the South Carolina sea captains in the West Indian trade in the 1750s was Captain William Lyford, who had begun his maritime career at Port Royal and, no doubt, was responsible for establishing some of the commercial connections between Port Royal, the Bahama Islands, and the West Indian Islands. In the early 1750s, William Lyford commanded the schooner *Mary* between South Carolina, Curaçao, Jamaica, and other Caribbean ports. By 1756, Lyford had a larger ship, the brigantine *Darling,* operating between South Carolina, Antigua, and Jamaica. In 1759, another South Carolina sea captain, Samuel Grove, began in the West Indian trade by commanding the brigantine *Caroline* between Charleston and Antigua. By the late 1760s, Samuel Grove had settled his family in Beaufort and had become the most successful and prominent ship captain in the community. He remained active in the West Indian trade, particularly with Jamaica.[78] These early maritime connections probably encouraged the movement of West Indies merchants to Beaufort in the 1750s and 1760s. Most prominent of these were John Grayson, who had moved to Beaufort from Montserrat by 1758, and Peter Lavein, who had moved to Beaufort from St. Croix by 1767.[79]

Other Beaufort sea captains in the 1750s were Alexander McGillivray, who was born in St. Helena Parish in 1738 but later moved to Skidaway Island, Georgia; and Captain James Talbert, who remained in coastal trade with a schooner built in Port Royal, the *Indian Land,* throughout the late 1750s and 1760s. Talbert also later settled in Georgia.[80]

The peacetime of the early 1750s, however, did not mean that the coast was entirely rid of freebooters. In 1754, the pirate Don Fernando appeared off Port Royal. His large, fast Spanish schooner disrupted shipping from Port Royal and renewed the traditional fears of the sea island planters. In October 1754, Captain Seymour barely escaped the pirates, arriving at Port Royal from St. Croix after a two-day chase. That same month, Captain McClellan's schooner *Jenny* was seized off Hilton Head. Don Fernando was reported cruising two miles off Port Royal harbor, and the local citizens feared that his powerful ship would be "too much for any small force that may be sent after him." Don Fernando, however, was an outlaw pirate, unlike previous Spanish privateers, and Florida authorities were as anxious to halt his activities as South Carolina authorities. Late in October, word came that Don Fernando had been arrested and imprisoned in St. Augustine.[81]

In 1756, European rivalry degenerated into the Seven Year's War (1756–1763) between England and France. Colonial rivalry in North America became the French and Indian War in which Spain was an ally of France. This brought renewed fears of naval attack on Port Royal and slave insurrections in the southern parishes. It also began feverish preparations to protect the exposed southern coast. Two new galleys were commissioned: one to be "stationed at Port Royal, to cruise frequently for intelligence" and the other at Charleston "to be always ready for sea on any sudden appearance of privateers on this coast." In addition, privateers were commissioned in both Georgia and South Carolina to counter the expected raids from the south.[82]

In July 1757, William Lyford arrived from the West Indies reporting numerous engagements between English and French naval forces. In August 1758, word came of a running sea battle between the Georgia privateer sloop *Tryal* and a fast French privateer off Tybee Island. Captain Robinson of the *Tryal* was killed, but the Georgia sloop escaped. Reports from Georgia related that "the French privateer had some Carolina runaways on board who were to serve as pilots on a design of plundering some of the plantations near Port Royal of their Negroes." Thus, the old fears of the sea island planters were renewed and complaints about defense were repeated. "Georgia has made its effort and now it must be our turn," commented the *South Carolina Gazette*.[83]

In September 1758, an English privateer from Liverpool, the *Cate,* remained briefly at Port Royal providing some security, but it was soon gone. It was recognized that the only permanent relief from privateer raids was to eliminate their base of support at St. Augustine. The South Carolinians proposed to blockade St. Augustine and cut off its supplies "on account of the dangerous consequences to the trade of the whole continent from that port becoming an asylum and rendezvous of French privateers."[84]

Throughout the war the privateer raids on the South Carolina coast and the major naval battles in the West Indies had slowed shipping at Port Royal. Near the end of the war, in the spring of 1763, the last of the Spanish privateers interrupted South Carolina commerce. Don Martin de Hamassa, in the privateer sloop *Santa Maria,* out of St. Augustine, took five ships off the coast, including the brigantine *Neptune* off Port Royal. He also landed on North Island, Winyah Bay, and plundered a plantation near Edisto. Late in January, Don Martin captured the schooner *Mary* off the South Edisto Inlet and sunk it in St. Helena Sound. In February, Captain Thomas Tucker's schooner, *Tybee,* was captured between St. Helena and Hilton Head and taken to St. Augustine by Don Martin. The schooner *Tybee* was a familiar sight at Port Royal since it was regularly engaged in the coastal trade by Beaufort merchant John Gordon. Captain Tucker had previously been suspected of conspiring to trade with the enemy at

St. Augustine, but this event cleared him of suspicion.[85] This was the last significant naval action among the sea islands of the Beaufort District during the colonial era.

The end of the French and Indian War also brought to Beaufort the last, and
perhaps most famous, of the colonial sea captains of Port Royal: Captain John
Joyner. Joyner's first command as a young sailor was the provincial scout boat
stationed at Port Royal in 1763. Shortly after the Treaty of Paris ended the Seven
Year's War, Captain Joyner led a small party from Port Royal down the inland
passage to survey Spanish lands and installations on the St. Johns River.[86] Soon,
East Florida would become the newest English colony.

BUILDING OF FORT LYTTELTON

During the French and Indian War, the Commons House of Assembly began to marshal the resources to build a third and more permanent fort at Beaufort for the defense of Port Royal. It was reported in 1752 that Fort
Frederick—long since abandoned by its garrison, which, under Lieutenant Philip
Delegal, had moved to Frederica, Georgia, in 1737—had fallen into disrepair
and was "in ruinous condition."[87] No action was taken to repair the old fort,
though the stout tabby walls remain in place to this day. With the outbreak of
war in 1756, the local citizens petitioned for a new and larger fort.[88] This was the
beginning of Fort Lyttelton, the largest fort built in the Beaufort District before
the Civil War.

Fort Lyttelton, named for South Carolina Royal Governor William Henry
Lyttelton, was built on the end of Spanish Point with its principal battery facing
northward across a deep bend of the Beaufort River. It was shaped like a triangle
and was more than 350 feet on a side. The walls were of tabby with earth piled
on the outside. Within the walls were officers' quarters, barracks, a well, a kitchen,
and a powder magazine.[89]

Near the end of 1758, the *South Carolina Gazette* reported, "We here from
Port Royal, that the works erecting for the defense of that place go on well and
that many gentlemen there talk of forming themselves into an artillery company." This was also the genesis of the Beaufort Volunteer Artillery, which was to
be an institutional feature of the Beaufort community until the Civil War.[90]

Work progressed slowly, and when the local militia mustered at Fort Lyttelton
in preparation for the Cherokee expedition of 1760, the fort was only partially
completed.[91] In April 1762, Colonel Thomas Middleton reported the fort only
two-thirds complete and asked the Commons House for five thousand pounds
currency to finish it.[92] In May 1762, an officer and detachment of the Independent Regiment was sent to garrison the fort.[93] Two years later, in October 1764,
Colonel Middleton reported to Lieutenant Governor William Bull II that the

gun platform at Fort Lyttelton was finally ready for its cannon, and they should be sent along with their carriages and supplies.[94] The war, however, was over by then, so only seven of the eighteen cannons were mounted. The rest were stored out of the weather. Only a skeleton crew maintained the fort through the peaceful years of the 1760s.[95] But the large imposing battery opposite the town of Beaufort must have been a reassuring sight to local residents, who by 1763 had struggled through half a century of continuous colonial warfare.

NOTES

1. A. S. Salley, ed., *Journal of the Commons House of Assembly, November 15, 1726–March 11, 1727,* 77; South Carolina Commons House Journals, Sainsbury Copy, January 21, 1731–September 22, 1733, 814, 851, 879, 880, South Carolina Department of Archives and History.

2. Salley, ed., *Journal of the Commons House,* 77.

3. South Carolina Commons House Journals, Sainsbury Copy, January 21, 1731–September 22, 1733, 960–61, 966, 986; South Carolina Commons House Journals, no. 9, part 1, November 6, 1734–January 29, 1736, 44, South Carolina Department of Archives and History.

4. Larry E. Ivers, *British Drums on the Southern Frontier: The Military Colonization of Georgia, 1733–1749* (Chapel Hill: University of North Carolina Press, 1974); Harvey H. Jackson, "Hugh Bryan and Great Awakening in South Carolina," *William and Mary Quarterly* 43 (October 1986): 594–614.

5. South Carolina Commons House Journals, Sainsbury Copy, January 21, 1731–September 22, 1733, 894, South Carolina Department of Archives and History. Capt. John McPherson held grants in both St. Paul's and Prince William Parishes.

6. *South Carolina Gazette,* May 1, 1736.

7. South Carolina Commons House Journals, no. 8, February 7, 1734–May 31, 1734, 69, South Carolina Department of Archives and History.

8. Ivers, *British Drums,* 11.

9. Jackson, "Hugh Bryan," 154.

10. *South Carolina Gazette,* October 9, 1736.

11. Larry E. Ivers, "Scouting the Inland Passage," *South Carolina Historical Magazine* 73 (July 1972): 121.

12. *South Carolina Gazette,* February 26, 1737.

13. Governor Robert Johnson to Lords of Trade, April 10, 1733, British Public Record Office Transcripts, 16: 149, South Carolina Department of Archives and History; J. H. Easterby, ed., *Journal of the Commons House of Assembly, 1736–1739,* 353, 371.

14. Easterby, ed., *Journal of the Commons House of Assembly, 1736–1739,* 577.

15. Easterby, ed., *Journal of the Commons House of Assembly, 1736–1739,* 582.

16. Lewis Jones to Dr. Bearcroft, July 17, 1738, SPG Papers (microfilm), South Carolina Department of Archives and History.

17. *South Carolina Gazette,* September 18, 1736; October 9, 1736.

18. *South Carolina Gazette,* January 5, 1736; June 26, 1736.

19. *South Carolina Gazette,* August 24, 1738.

20. Easterby, ed., *Journal of the Commons House of Assembly,* 1741–1742, 195–98; Edward Lawson, "What Ever Happened to the Man Who Cut Off Jenkins' Ear?," *Florida Historical Quarterly* 37 (1958): 33–41.

21. Lewis Jones to Dr. Bearcroft, July 17, 1738, Society for the Propagation of the Gospel in Foreign Parts, Papers (microfilm), South Carolina Department of Archives and History.

22. *South Carolina Gazette,* June 11, 1737.

23. Easterby, ed., *Journal of the Commons House of Assembly, 1739–1741,* 210–11, 541.

24. Easterby, ed., *Journal of the Commons House of Assembly, 1739–1741,* 385–86; *1741–1742,* 273.

25. Rusty Fleetwood, *Tidecraft: An Introductory Look at the Boats of Lower South Carolina, Georgia, and Northeastern Florida, 1650–1950* (Savannah: Coastal Heritage Society, 1982), 56.

26. Easterby, ed., *Journal of the Commons House of Assembly, 1739–1741,* 160, 271; *1741–1742,* 567; David Duncan Wallace, *History of South Carolina,* 4 volumes (New York: American Historical Society, 1934), 1: 238–39.

27. *South Carolina Gazette,* May 3, 1740.

28. Easterby, ed., *Journal of the Commons House of Assembly, 1741–1742,* 97, 98, 101, 104, 107, 108, 182, 183, 210.

29. Easterby, ed. *Journal of the Commons House of Assembly, 1741–1742,* 78, 247; Edward McCrady, *The History of South Carolina under the Royal Government, 1719–1776* (1899; rpt., New York: Russell & Russell, 1969), 193–229; M. Eugene Sirmans, *Colonial South Carolina: A Political History, 1663–1763* (Chapel Hill: University of North Carolina Press, 1966), 210–12; Wallace, *History of South Carolina,* 1:438–40.

30. Easterby, ed., *Journal of the Commons House of Assembly, 1741–1742,* 189–91, 210.

31. Ivers, *British Drums,* 113–24.

32. Easterby, ed., *Journal of the Commons House of Assembly, 1741–1742,* 189–91, 210.

33. Easterby, ed. *Journal of the Commons House of Assembly, 1741–1742,* 195–98, 210.

34. John J. TePaske, *The Governorship of Spanish Florida, 1700–1763* (Durham: Duke University Press, 1964), 8.

35. *South Carolina Gazette,* April 2, 1741.

36. *South Carolina Gazette,* June 21, 1742; June 28, 1742.

37. *South Carolina Gazette,* July 5, 1742.

38. *South Carolina Gazette,* July 12, 1742; July 19, 1742.

39. Lords of Trade to Privy Council, Dec. 2, 1742; British Public Record Office Transcripts, 20:604, South Carolina Department of Archives and History.

40. Easterby, ed., *Journal of the Commons House of Assembly, 1741–1742,* 195–98, 210; Lawson, "What Ever Happened?," 33–41.

41. Jones to Dr. Bearcroft, August 4, 1742, SPG Papers (microfilm), South Carolina Department of Archives and History.

42. Ivers, *British Drums,* 151–73.

43. *South Carolina Gazette,* August 2, 1742.

44. Petition from the Planters of the Port Royal Area to General Oglethorpe, August

24, 1743, British Public Records Office Transcripts, 21: 166–68, South Carolina Department of Archives and History.

45. Easterby, ed., *Journal of the Commons House of Assembly, 1739–1741*, 146, 341–44; Thomas Cooper and David J. McCord, eds., *The Statutes at Large of South Carolina*, 10 vols. (Columbia: A. S. Johnston, 1836–1841), 3: 575–77; A. S. Salley, ed., *Minutes of the Vestry of St. Helena's Parish, South Carolina, 1726–1812* (Columbia: Historical Commission of South Carolina, 1919), 18.

46. *South Carolina Gazette*, November 8, 1735.

47. *South Carolina Gazette*, March 31, 1733.

48. Joyce E. Harman, *Trade and Privateering in Spanish Florida, 1732–1763* (St. Augustine: St. Augustine Historical Society, 1969), 131.

49. *South Carolina Gazette*, September 8, 1739.

50. *South Carolina Gazette*, September 21, 1741.

51. *South Carolina Gazette*, September 26, 1741; November 28, 1741.

52. *South Carolina Gazette*, June 4, 1741; June 18, 1741.

53. *South Carolina Gazette*, April 3, 1742.

54. *South Carolina Gazette*, May 29, 1742.

55. *South Carolina Gazette*, June 21, 1742.

56. *South Carolina Gazette*, July 16, 1741.

57. *South Carolina Gazette*, July 30, 1741.

58. *South Carolina Gazette*, July 16, 1741.

59. *South Carolina Gazette*, November 28, 1741.

60. *South Carolina Gazette*, October 17, 1741; Fleetwood, *Tidecraft*, 56.

61. *South Carolina Gazette*, September 20, 1742; September 27, 1742; October 4, 1742.

62. *South Carolina Gazette*, July 4, 1743; August 1, 1743; October 3, 1743; October 24, 1743.

63. *South Carolina Gazette*, January 16, 1744; March 5, 1744.

64. *South Carolina Gazette*, April 15, 1745; February 17, 1746; R. Nicholas Olsberg, ed., "Ship Registers in the South Carolina Archives, 1734–1780," *South Carolina Historical Magazine* 74 (October 1973): 263.

65. *South Carolina Gazette*, March 10, 1746; May 5, 1746.

66. *South Carolina Gazette*, April 28, 1746.

67. *South Carolina Gazette*, June 30, 1746; March 2, 1747; September 14, 1747; October 26, 1747.

68. *South Carolina Gazette*, April 4, 1748.

69. Petition of the Planters of St. Helena and Prince William Parish to the South Carolina Council, March 5, 1748, British Public Record Office Transcripts, 23: 88, South Carolina Department of Archives and History. In contrast to Port Royal Sound, the inhospitable coast of North Carolina served as a barrier to maritime invasion. See Gary S. Dunbar, *Historical Geography of the North Carolina Outer Banks* (Baton Rouge: Louisiana State University Press, 1958), 21–22.

70. Easterby, ed., *Journal of the Commons House of Assembly, 1744–1745*, 46–47.

71. Glen to Newcastle, May 28, 1745, British Public Record Office Transcripts, 22: 103, South Carolina Department of Archives and History.

72. *South Carolina Gazette,* October 27, 1747; November 23, 1747; May ll, 1748.

73. *South Carolina Gazette,* August 15, 1748; August 17, 1748; September 26, 1748; October 3, 1748; Mabel Webber, ed., "Journal of Robert Pringle, 1746–1747," *South Carolina Historical Magazine* 26 (April 1925): 105.

74. *South Carolina Gazette,* October 1, 1750; August 27, 1763; March 17, 1764.

75. *South Carolina Gazette,* January 1, 1753; January 29, 1753.

76. *South Carolina Gazette,* January 22, 1754; February 5, 1754; May 29, 1754; September 12, 1754; May 29, 1755.

77. *Charleston Inventories,* January 15, 1755, 279.

78. *South Carolina Gazette,* February 6, 1755; May 22, 1755; May 21, 1759; Salley, ed., *Minutes of the Vestry,* 142–45.

79. Marvin D. Bass, ed., "Autobiography of William J. Grayson," Ph.D. diss., University of South Carolina, 1933, 2; Beaufort County Public Library, typescript; William B. Clark, ed., *Naval Documents of the American Revolution,* 8 vols. (Washington, D.C.: U.S. Government Printing Office, 1964–1981), 3: 1056, 1069; Harold C. Syrett, ed., *The Papers of Alexander Hamilton,* 27 vols. (New York: Columbia University Press, 1961–1979), 3: 235; Salley, ed., *Minutes of the Vestry,* 139–42, 144.

80. *South Carolina Gazette,* May 29, 1755; May 26, 1759; June 2, 1759; June 26, 1760.

81. *South Carolina Gazette,* October 3, 1754; October 10, 1754; October 31, 1754.

82. *South Carolina Gazette,* December 23, 1756; June 23, 1757.

83. *South Carolina Gazette,* August 4, 1758.

84. *South Carolina Gazette,* September 1, 1758.

85. *South Carolina Gazette,* January 8, 1763; January 22, 1763; February 12, 1763.

86. *South Carolina Gazette,* June 16, 1763.

87. South Carolina Commons House Journals, no. 27, part 1, 140, South Carolina Department of Archives and History.

88. South Carolina Commons House Journals, no. 31, part 2 (November 2, 1756–July 6, 1757), 53, South Carolina Department of Archives and History.

89. Larry E. Ivers, *Colonial Forts of South Carolina, 1670–1775* (Columbia: University of South Carolina Press, 1970), 61–62.

90. *South Carolina Gazette,* September 8, 1758.

91. *South Carolina Gazette,* September 22, 1759.

92. South Carolina Commons House Journals, no. 35 (Februuary 6, 1762–September 12, 1762), 76, 80–81, South Carolina Department of Archives and History.

93. *South Carolina Gazette,* May 1, 1762.

94. South Carolina Commons House Journals, no. 36 (January 29, 1763–October 6, 1764), 269, South Carolina Department of Archives and History.

95. South Carolina Commons House Journals, no. 37, part 1 (October 28, 1765–May 28, 1767), 378; no. 38, part 1 (March 14–November 7, 1769), 150, South Carolina Department of Archives and History.

9

Indigo Culture, 1750–1775

Though rice was the predominant crop in colonial South Carolina, and was primarily responsible for the settlement of Prince William Parish, it had little effect on St. Helena, the oldest and most heavily populated parish in the Beaufort District. The families who had earlier claimed the attractive lands among the sea islands had to wait nearly half a century for the introduction of an export crop suited to their sandy soil and maritime climate.

The introduction of indigo to the South Carolina lowcountry in the 1740s provided the cash crop for which the sea island planters were searching. Indigo was the principal blue dye used by European textile manufacturers. It was grown in many parts of the world, but most notably by French colonials in Haiti and by Spanish colonials in Guatemala.[1] Though indigo had been originally contemplated as one of the products of the South Carolina colony, early attempts to grow it had failed due to hard frosts, the Yemassee War, and more advanced competition from the French West Indies and Spanish Central America.[2] During the 1740s, several circumstances combined to encourage the reintroduction of indigo to South Carolina. First, the colonial wars of 1739 to 1748 cut off the French and Spanish sources of indigo dye for British textile manufacturers. Second, the continuous naval war between Charleston and St. Augustine disrupted trade, greatly increased freight and insurance rates, and thereby caused a major depression in the rice industry. South Carolina planters then began seriously searching for a less bulky export product than rice. In fact, processed indigo was worth nearly ten times as much per weight as rice. And third were the efforts of a few visionary and enterprising local planters. Traditional credit for the reintroduction of indigo goes to Eliza Lucas Pinckney, whose successful experiments with seed sent from her father in Monserrat, between 1741 and 1744, led to the distribution of seed to her neighbors along the Stono River and Wappoo Creek: John Bee, James Stobo, Robert Sams, Isaac Hayne, and her future husband, Charles Pinckney. Seldom mentioned, but crucial to the success of indigo in South Carolina, was the talent of another neighbor, Andre DeVeaux, whose knowledge of French West Indian processing techniques freely contributed to Eliza Lucas's experiments. DeVeaux's contribution was the real key to the commercial viability of indigo in South Carolina. Andre DeVeaux's son, Andrew DeVeaux II, married Hannah Palmer, daughter of Colonel John Palmer, and moved to the Beaufort District in the late 1740s. The DeVeauxs became one of the most influential planter families in Prince William and St. Helena Parishes. Also crucial to the success of indigo were the promotional and political efforts in London of the energetic agent for South Carolina, James Crokatt. His efforts led to the British Imperial Indigo Bounty of 1748, a British government subsidy to encourage the colonial production of indigo which lasted until the Revolutionary War, and proved an enormous stimulus to the indigo industry among the sea islands.[3]

All these factors made indigo a successful crop in South Carolina, and within a few years it was second only to rice as an export product. Indigo was perfectly suited to the sea islands. It grows well in sandy soil and is adversely affected by frost, so the milder maritime climate of the islands was an additional advantage. It is not known when the first commercial indigo was grown in the Beaufort District, but there is no evidence that it was grown much before the mid-1700s. In 1744, the *South Carolina Gazette* published a long letter from Thomas Stoakes, a planter at Ashley Ferry, explaining the culture and process of indigo. In 1745, Andre DeVeaux offered indigo seed for sale at his Ashley River plantation with the promise that, "I will teach the making of it gratis to all those that buy seed." When DeVeaux advertised to sell the same plantation two years later, he had planted twenty-five acres of indigo and constructed permanent brick indigo vats. Nevertheless, there is no indication that Beaufort District planters had caught on to indigo before 1750, and export statistics from Charleston show only modest quantities of indigo exported prior to 1754.[4]

In 1755, however, the *South Carolina Gazette* reported 23,000 pounds of indigo shipped from Georgetown and Beaufort, in addition to 177,000 pounds shipped from Charleston. And in 1755, the first advertisement for a Port Royal area plantation appeared which specifically mentioned indigo. James Watson's three-hundred-acre plantation on Battery Creek, three miles from Beaufort, was promoted as "exceedingly good for indigo . . . has a small pasture with a good dwelling house on it." Obviously the Beaufort planters had begun to produce indigo a few years before.[5]

From that time through the Revolutionary War, indigo was the dominant feature of the agricultural economy of the sea islands. In 1755, Edward Wigg's plantation on Port Royal Island was sold with crops of corn and indigo as well as a dwelling house, slaves, cattle, horses, tools, and a canoe.[6] In 1757, Alexander Fraser's three hundred acres on the Coosaw River near the Port Royal ferry were said to be typical of the sea islands, "extraordinary good for indigo with some middling rice land."[7] By 1760, John Chapman of Port Royal Island could adver-

Colonial crop distribution, 1760s

tise a fully developed indigo plantation. His five-hundred-acre plantation was six miles from Beaufort by road and eight miles by water. It contained a "dwelling house, barn and outhouses. Good dam of water convenient for making indigo. One set of vats, a lime vat and a good pump."[8] This description also reveals the effect of a profitable cash crop on the land. In fifty years of ownership, John Chapman had cleared barely 20 percent of the land, but, because of indigo, he cleared nearly 10 percent of the tract in the single year of 1759 and could claim "40 acres cleared last year and only one year planted."

The cultivation and processing of indigo among the sea islands of St. Helena Parish was similar to other parts of the province. The land was cleared of trees, and planting often began around the stumps which were left to rot. Cleared and "grubbed" land was, of course, preferable. In 1761, George Cuthbert moved to Savannah and advertised his 350-acre St. Helena Island indigo plantation, with a small dwelling house on a navigable creek, outbuildings and two sets of cypress indigo vats. He noted particularly that much of the land "has been grubbed, the logs burnt, ploughed and planted."[9] The ground was prepared for planting in December and it was hoped that winter frosts would help retard the growth of weeds. The seeds, which were often imported from the West Indies, were planted in early April. Each plant bed was made with a hoe, approximately eighteen inches apart. The seeds were planted about two inches deep. Within two weeks the plants would begin to appear. The beds had to be constantly maintained for the next three months to prevent weeds from choking out the plants. When the leaves of the plants were full, usually in July, the first cutting began. Two and sometimes three cuttings were accomplished by the end of September. The indigo plants were processed in three shallow vats arranged in line so that one vat could be drained into the next. Among the sea islands, these vats were commonly made of rot-resistant cypress boards. Some plantations closer to Charleston constructed indigo vats of brick when that material was more available. The indigo leaves were allowed to steep in the first vat until the water had absorbed the blue dye from the leaves and stems. Then the water was drained off into the second vat where it was violently agitated by beaters at either end. The blue residue, like silt, was then allowed to settle in the bottom of the vat, and the water was carefully drawn off into the third vat. The residue in the bottom of the second vat was the marketable indigo dye. It was collected in cloth or "oznaburg" sacks and allowed to drip. Next, the dye was placed in shallow pans to dry further. Then it was cut into small cubes, placed in casks, and shipped to market. The processing usually continued through the fall months. Indigo, like rice, was a labor intensive activity. It did not, however, require as much land preparation as rice.[10]

The decade of the 1750s showed great promise and activity among the sea islands due to the rise of indigo. Land which had lain unused or little used for years was now cleared and planted. New planters moved to St. Helena Parish, and old families made new and ambitious purchases in anticipation of profits from indigo. In 1752, Colonel Nathaniel Barnwell purchased one-half of Parris Island from John Delebere and Jane Parris Delebere, heirs of former provincial treasurer Alexander Parris.[11] With his neighbors, Colonel Thomas Wigg and William Elliott, he finally forged a profitable enterprise from the famous old island which had frustrated French, Spanish, and English colonials for two hundred years. Also in the 1750s, Colonel John Stuart, the South Carolina Indian agent, and his brother, Beaufort merchant Francis Stuart, transformed 1,800 acres on the islands across from Parris Island, known today as Cat, Cane, and Gibbes Islands, into the most profitable indigo plantation in South Carolina on the eve of the Revolution.[12]

In 1753, Peter Perry purchased 473 acres of land on St. Helena Island from William Chapman for 1,892 pounds currency. Chapman had done little with the land since it had been granted to him before the Yemassee War. In the next twelve years, Perry transformed the property on the banks of Chowan Creek into a completely developed and prosperous indigo plantation called Orange Grove. By 1765, he had forty-six slaves, thirty-seven cattle, numerous hogs, and a set of cypress indigo vats. After Perry's death in 1765, Orange Grove Plantation was acquired by John Evans, who became the largest indigo planter on St. Helena Island.[13]

A closer look at Colonel Nathaniel Barnwell of Port Royal Island and John Evans of St. Helena Island will illustrate the development of sea island indigo plantations during the colonial period. Colonel Nathaniel Barnwell (1705–1775) was the eldest son of Colonel John Barnwell, the man most responsible for founding Beaufort. "Tuscarora Jack" Barnwell left his six daughters and two sons a considerable legacy of frontier land, but at his death he was not a wealthy man. The foundation of the family fortune was left to the venerable and persevering Colonel Nathaniel Barnwell (1705–1775), whose life spanned the entire colonial history of Beaufort. Nathaniel Barnwell inherited 1,400 acres on Port Royal. In 1752, Barnwell purchased the 1,520-acre Delebere tract on Parris Island. These two large plantations made him the most productive indigo planter in the Beaufort District.[14]

Nathaniel Barnwell was a colonel in the militia, member of the Commons House of Assembly, justice of the peace, and vestryman of St. Helena Church for most of his career. But he was less politically active than his father, and the family was never as influential during the colonial period as many of the Charleston-based families. Barnwell's principal accomplishment was to build a respectable fortune based on indigo. It was this fortune which allowed his sons, John and Robert Barnwell, to forge Beaufort's most powerful political faction in the era of the American Revolution. It was this wealth which also allowed his two daughters, Ann and Mary, to make very fortunate marriages. Ann married Colonel Thomas Middleton and Mary married William Elliott. When Barnwell died in 1775, his surviving children divided an estate which included eighty-nine slaves, more than 3,000 acres of land in the sea islands, and two substantial town houses in Beaufort. Barnwell's moveable estate included 147 head of livestock and was valued at 50,841 pounds currency. Among his possessions were six sets of "indigo vats and pumps," more than any planter in the Port Royal area.[15]

John Evans Jr. of St. Helena Island (1748–1775) was the son of John and Elizabeth Evans and the grandson of George Evans who had immigrated to Charleston from the West Indies in 1703. His father's move to St. Helena Island during the 1730s was probably encouraged by his brother-in-law, Colonel Thomas Wigg. John Evans inherited considerable land and slaves from his father and in 1766 married Sarah Fripp, thus extending his connection to the first families of the Beaufort District. By the time of his death in Philadelphia in 1775, Evans had become the largest indigo planter and the wealthiest man on St. Helena Island with a total estate valued at 42,244 pounds currency. He owned two developed indigo plantations and one undeveloped barrier island which he used for livestock and hunting. All three properties totaled more than 2,000 acres. He also owned ninety-seven slaves, the largest slave workforce on St. Helena Island. At his "home plantation," which his father developed during the 1750s, Evans had fifty-two slaves, four horses, fifty cattle, nineteen sheep, thirty-three hogs, a crop of corn, a crop of peas, two sets of cypress indigo vats and pumps, and a newly processed crop of indigo worth three thousand pounds currency. He also had all the necessary items of country life on the sea islands: "plantation tools, surveying compass and instruments, pocket pistols, silver, china, books, a flute, a violin, a spyglass and a fine rowboat with rigging."

Evans's second indigo plantation was Orange Grove, which he acquired from the estate of Peter Perry. On this 473-acre plantation in 1775, Evans had 38 slaves, 102 cattle, 79 sheep, a crop of potatoes, 2 sets of indigo vats, and a processed crop of indigo worth two thousand pounds currency. Evans's third property was his undeveloped barrier island called simply "the Hunting Island." On the island, Evans kept seven slaves, thirty-seven cattle, a stock of hogs, two guns, plain utensils, and no planting tools. Obviously, this island was used only for hunting and livestock range. When he died in 1775, Evans was survived by his wife and his young daughter, Elizabeth. In 1782, Elizabeth Evans married Captain Joseph Jenkins of Edisto Island.[16]

Nathaniel Barnwell and John Evans, however, were not typical sea island indigo planters. They were among the wealthiest men in the Beaufort District, and indigo had its greatest impact on the average planters of the sea islands. Perhaps the most striking feature of the agricultural economy of the colonial sea islands is its middle-class aspect. Most historians divide the colonial planters of South Carolina into three classes. The upper class of planters normally owned several plantations, a large number of slaves, and one or more town houses. They left the direction of their plantations to managers and overseers. In the Beaufort District, this class was characterized by the absentee rice planters of Prince William Parish, the younger branches of prominent families such as the Bulls, Blakes, and Middletons, and occasionally local families such as the Barnwells and Heywards. The poorest class of settlers were the township farmers, who were recent immigrants, owned only a few acres and no slaves, and as often as not, had the poorest land for planting. In the Beaufort District, the largest body of this class were the Purrysburgers of St. Peter's Parish.[17]

The largest class of planters among the sea islands were what historian Eugene Sirmans described as the "poorer lowcountry planters." They represented the middle class of colonial South Carolina and made up the bulk of the white families of the sea islands. These planters owned a few slaves, lived on their own farms, and directed their plantations personally. Because most of these families were not prominent, records regarding their lives, aspirations and failures, personal and familial relations, and daily operations of their plantations are scarce. They can be identified, however, through the militia lists, which were the closest thing to a census in colonial South Carolina. Through the existing inventories of their estates, taken after their deaths, we can establish their material success and glimpse their way of life. An analysis of a representative section of the population of St. Helena Parish for the two decades prior to the American Revolution will illustrate the average planter of the sea islands.

The militia muster of 1756 for the Beaufort District on the eve of the French and Indian War was as complete a census as any in the colonial era. Records on the families listed in 1756 reveals the following: of the fifty-eight men of the Port Royal Company for whom official records remain, forty-two owned less than 1,000 acres and sixteen owned more than 1,000 acres. Of the thirty-nine men of the St. Helena Company for whom official records remain, thirty owned less than 1,000 acres while only nine owned more than 1,000 acres. What is remarkable is that only two men in the St. Helena Company, Richard Capers and John Evans, owned more than 2,000 acres of land. The men of the Port Royal militia for whom no information was found may have been artisans and laborers in the town of Beaufort. Those in the St. Helena Company were probably plantation managers, overseers, and free white laborers.[18]

There is some difficulty arriving at an accurate average figure for the amount of land held, the value of that land and the number of slaves per planter family. The sample may not be complete, and nearly half the men listed left no official records in South Carolina. The planters who did leave official records were probably richer, thus the averages obtained are probably inflated. In spite of this inherent statistical bias, the figures present a strikingly middle-class portrait of the average sea island planter.

The average amount of land held per planter in St. Helena Parish was 574 acres. In the period from 1750 to 1775, the average value of that land was approximately three-fourths of a pound currency per acre. Great variations in land value occurred throughout the period and land value was generally determined by its stage of development. In the early years, however, a good deal of land sold for approximately one pound currency per acre, while on the eve of the Revolution much sea island property was fetching four to five pounds currency per acre. Information on slaveholdings is somewhat more clear cut. The estate inventories for the period 1750 to 1775 indicate that the average planter owned fifteen slaves, of which slightly less than 40 percent were adult males. A few families owned more than fifty slaves, but the vast majority of planters owned less than the average.

Two of the twenty-five larger landowners, who owned more than 1,000 acres, represent the more modest type of lowcountry planter. Thomas Searson of the Euhaws neighborhood had, by the eve of the Revolution, acquired 1,094 acres in three separate tracts. Two tracts of 800 and 194 acres were located south of the Broad River in what was later to become St. Luke's Parish, and the third tract consisted of 100 acres of rice land on the Coosawhatchie River. His estate was inventoried in 1777, and the total value of his moveable goods was estimated to be the modest sum of 3,992 pounds currency. Of this total, his eight slaves comprised 2,500 pounds currency. Not a single one of his eight slaves was an adult male, indicating limited workforce. Instead, there were three boys, two women, and three children. In addition to his eight slaves, Searson owned five horses, twenty-eight cattle, eighteen sheep, and nine hogs. He had a complete assortment of plantation tools, including a set of indigo vats. The furnishings listed reflect a modest abode, but do include the comfort of a feather bed.[19]

John Chaplin of St. Helena Island presents a similar portrait of the average sea island planter. In the late 1760s, he owned 1,700 acres of land on St. Helena and Hilton Head Islands. The appraisal of his estate in 1776 valued it at 3,030 pounds currency, of which 1,950 pounds currency was invested in seven slaves. Of the seven slaves, only two were adult men, again indicating a limited workforce. Chaplin possessed the necessary plantation tools, and indigo vats, as well as modest household furnishings. A small stock of cattle and hogs provided sustenance, and three volumes of *Arabian Nights* provided amusement. Although he owned a spyglass, fishing net, and hand lines, no boat was listed.[20]

One of the earliest and most numerous of the local families were the Parmenters. Joseph and Thomas Parmenter had immigrated to South Carolina with their father, Philemon Parmenter, in 1683. Between 1697 and 1704, both brothers acquired land among the sea islands.[21] Lieutenant Thomas Parmenter was killed by the Yemassee Indians in 1716, but his brother, Joseph, also a veteran of the Yemassee War and later a scoutboat commander, survived the war. In 1733, Joseph Parmenter owned a lot in Beaufort and nine hundred acres on Port Royal

Island. The family fortunes did not prosper, however, probably because of the disruptions of war, the lack of an early cash crop, and the numerous offspring which subdivided the land. By the 1760s, most of the later generations had moved away from town to the outlying islands. In 1764, Joseph Parmenter of Hilton Head died, and his moveable possessions were valued at 3,767 pounds currency, including fifteen slaves worth 3,250 pounds currency. Of these fifteen slaves, only three were men, while there were five women and seven children. Among his other possessions were three beehives, some fishing gear, and fishing nets. In 1768, Joseph Parmenter Jr. died, leaving personal property worth 4,460 pounds currency. The bulk of this value was his twenty-one slaves. Oddly, only two of the twenty-one slaves were men while the rest were women and children. The next year Thomas Parmenter died on his plantation on Daufuskie Island. He left personal property worth only 1,260 pounds currency, including five slaves, furniture, tools, weapons, a stock of hogs, and a set of indigo vats. When John Parmenter of Hilton Head died in 1776, his moveable goods were valued at 4,766 pounds currency, but of that total an even 4,000 pounds currency was invested in ten slaves, of whom four were adult males. His other goods included tools, utensils, furniture, ten cattle, and indigo vats.[22] The Parmenter family was probably representative of the majority of the sea island planters.

On St. Helena Island the situation was similar. Captain John Fendin, in his will of October 22, 1758, divided several plantations totaling 1,154 acres on St. Helena and Lady's Island among his four sons: John, Jacob, Isaac, and Abraham. The greatest part, 398 acres, went to his eldest son, John Fendin Jr. When he died in 1766, John's total moveable estate was only 1,339 pounds currency. Once again, most of that wealth was in slaves, of whom he had three men and one woman. His other possessions included fishing gear, tools, furniture, and "a lot of books." John's brother, Abraham, died the next year, and all his moveable possessions only totaled 1,021 pounds currency. He owned four slaves, but only one was a field hand. He also owned four horses, twenty-eight cattle, essential tools, and modest furnishings. Like the Parmenters across Port Royal Sound, the Fendin family of St. Helena Island exemplified the static fortunes of some of the earliest settlers of the sea islands.[23]

The Reynolds family also represented the typical middle-class planter of St. Helena Island. The Reynolds owned five hundred acres on the barrier island known as Reynolds Hunting Island. To the south of it was Fripp's Hunting Island, then Mazyck's Hunting Island, then Capers Hunting Island, then Jenkins's Hunting Island—all forming the chain of barrier islands between St. Helena and Port Royal Sounds. The agricultural value of these low sandy islands in the colonial period was negligible. They were used for hunting and stock. Normally only a few black cattle hunters inhabited the islands. The Reynolds family also owned

812 acres on St. Helena Island. Judging from the inventories of two members of the second generation of Reynolds, little was made of any of this land. In 1756, the total value of William Reynolds's estate was only 943 pounds currency, of which 780 pounds currency was invested in seven slaves. Twelve years later, Richard had prospered little more than William. His moveable estate was appraised at 1,540 pounds currency. Seven slaves made up 1,250 pounds currency, and the rest was furniture, tools, two horses, and a set of indigo vats.[24]

Thus, the portrait of the average sea island planter was distinctly work-a-day. Though there were a few families who had the wealth to afford sumptuous homes and a labor force sufficient to provide them considerable leisure time, the average planter probably spent most of his working hours in the fields with his slaves and, more likely than not, performed a good deal of the skilled labor himself. The average planter of the colonial sea islands was his own plantation manager. The wealthy few could afford to live apart from their legions of black workers; the majority of the sea island planters could not. The planter families of Barnwell, Elliott, Heyward, and Wigg all built substantial town houses along with Beaufort merchants Francis Stuart, Charles Purry, and Jean DelaGay before the Revolution; the Parmenters, Fendins, and Reynolds did not. For the wealthy few, trips to Charleston or Savannah were not uncommon; for the average planter, a trip to nearby Beaufort was often a hardship.

The average sea island planter was neither rich nor poor by the standards of the time. Almost all the sea island planters owned sufficient land to support their families. Almost all these planters also owned some slaves, usually between five and fifteen. Though much of the land lay undeveloped, it proved useful for grazing the stocks of cattle, hogs, and sheep which were present on nearly every plantation. In addition, the spread of indigo in the 1750s and 1760s provided a money crop perfectly suited to the sea island geography and afforded most of the middle-class planters of the Port Royal area a modest income. Among the items listed in the estate inventories of the sea island planters in the two decades prior to the Revolution, only cattle and slaves are mentioned more than indigo vats as major items of personal property.

The average amount of indigo that could be worked by a single slave in a season has been estimated to be about two acres. Even if we include mature women in the workforce, the average sea island planter could rarely muster more than fifteen laborers. Thus, a generous estimate of the amount of acreage that most planters could cultivate by their own resources would be thirty acres. One acre of indigo was estimated in 1761 to produce "not above thirty pounds of good indigo." In the period between 1747 and 1776, one pound of indigo sold for between twenty-five and thirty-five shillings per pound. Deducting the 6 percent cost of marketing, we arrive at an average annual income of 1,150 to

1,480 pounds currency from indigo.[25] Though many planters supplemented their income by the sale of livestock, timber, and a variety of other goods, the primary cash crop of the colonial sea islands was indigo. Under those circumstances the primary hindrance to the acquisition of more wealth was an inadequate labor force. It is quite understandable that the sea island planters should have reinvested much of their income in additional slaves.

The life of the average sea island planter was given considerable security by the large amount of easily obtainable natural food which surrounded him. The numerous tidal creeks and expansive salt marshes produced a bounty of marine and estuarine life. Large crabs could be plucked from the streams with a dip net, and many oyster beds were exposed to easy access at low tide. Large numbers of shrimp could be caught with the use of a small seine or a "casting net." In addition, there were, according to one contemporary account, several types of edible fish, including mullet, whiting, blackfish, rockfish, porgys, trout, bream, and many others. Sturgeon, also mentioned in this account, is still occasionally caught in the freshwater reaches of the Combahee River for the marketing of its caviar. The numerous references to fishing gear, seine nets, and casting nets among the inventories of the period give testimony to the prevalence of this activity.

The natural products of the land were also useful. The Spanish moss, which festoons the great oaks and adds so much to the characteristic grace of the lowcountry, was used to make saddles and mattresses and was a major form of winter forage for livestock. The palmetto trees, so numerous among the sea islands, were impervious to "sea worms" and made "good posts in salt water to secure dams and other structures." Wax was made from the myrtle bushes, and salt was derived from the "barilla grass." The expansive live oak produced lumber "fit for ships knees and beams" and was hard enough to use for mill wheels and other machines. Acorns from the oak trees served as excellent feed for the hogs. Even the otherwise useless salt marsh provided grazing for cattle, though the consumption of spartina grass was thought to make a cow's milk "disagreeable."[26]

The average sea island family of the colonial period was not wealthy. Because of ample lands, mild climate, and bountiful sea, however, their lives were comfortable. With the arrival of indigo, these planters had hope of a more prosperous future.

NOTES

1. H. Roy Merrens, ed., *The Colonial South Carolina Scene* (Columbia: University of South Carolina Press, 1977), 145–49; Lewis Cecil Gray, *History of Agriculture in the Southern United States to 1860* (Gloucester: Peter Smith, 1958), 1: 290–95.

2. Gray, *History of Agriculture,* 1: 292; John J. Winberry, "Reputation of Carolina Indigo," *South Carolina Historical Magazine* 80 (July 1979): 242–50.

3. David L. Coon, "Eliza Lucas Pinckney and the Reintroduction of Indigo Culture in South Carolina," *Journal of Southern History* 42 (February 1976): 64, 66–70; Arthur Hirsch, "French Influence on American Agriculture in the Colonial Period with Special Reference to Southern Provinces," *Agricultural History* 4 (1930): 9; Terry Sharrar, "Indigo in Carolina, 1670–1796," *South Carolina Historical Magazine* 72 (April 1971): 94–103; George C. Rogers Jr., *The History of Georgetown County, South Carolina* (Columbia: University of South Carolina Press, 1970), 52; Gray, *History of Agriculture,* 1: 294.

4. *South Carolina Gazette,* October 22, 1744; December 16, 1745; February 9, 1747; Winberry, "Indigo," 93.

5. *South Carolina Gazette,* August 21, 1755.

6. *South Carolina Gazette,* October 9, 1755.

7. *South Carolina Gazette,* January 20, 1757.

8. *South Carolina Gazette,* January 19, 1760; December 26, 1761.

9. *South Carolina Gazette,* August 8, 1761.

10. Chapman James Milling, ed., *Colonial South Carolina: Two Contemporary Descriptions by Governor James Glen and Dr. George Milligan-Johnson* (Columbia: University of South Carolina Press, 1951), 203–6; Gray, *History of Agriculture,* 1: 295–97; Rogers, *Georgetown County,* 89–90; Guion Griffis Johnson, *Social History of Sea Islands* (Chapel Hill: University of North Carolina Press, 1930), 18–23; "Will of John Barnwell," June 16, 1724, *Charleston County Wills* 1 (1722–1724): 94–97; "Inventory of John Barnwell," appraised June 11, 1724, Miscellaneous Records (1724–1725), 71, South Carolina Department of Archives and History.

11. Stephen B. Barnwell, *The Story of an American Family* (Marquette, Mich.: Privately printed, 1969), 21–22.

12. John Richard Alden, *John Stuart and the Southern Colonial Frontier: A Study of Indian Relations, War, Trade, and Land Problems in the Southern Wilderness, 1754–1775* (Ann Arbor: University of Michigan Press, 1944), 163–64, 170–71, 174–75; Wilbur Henry Siebert, *Loyalists in East Florida, 1774–1785,* 2 vols. (Deland: Florida State Historical Society, 1929), 1: 27, 2: 322; A. S. Salley, ed., *Minutes of the Vestry of St. Helena's Parish, South Carolina, 1726–1812* (Columbia: Historical Commission of South Carolina, 1919), 53, 59–64, 87–128, 135–39, 145, 148, 152, 158; *Biographical Directory of the South Carolina House,* 2: 661–63; "Claim of Sarah Stuart," Loyalist Transcripts, 56: 245, South Carolina Department of Archives and History.

13. Barnwell and Webber, eds., "St. Helena Parish Register," *South Carolina Historical Magazine* 23 (January–October 1922): 60–61; "Inventory of the Estate of Peter Perry," November 14, 1765, *Charleston Inventories* 10: 189–91, South Carolina Department of Archives and History.

14. Milling, *Colonial South Carolina,* 203–6; Gray, *History of Agriculture,* 1: 295–97; Rogers, *Georgetown County,* 89–90; Johnson, *Social History of Sea Islands,* 18–23; "Will of John Barnwell," June 16, 1724, *Charleston County Wills* 1 (1722–1724): 94–97, South Carolina Department of Archives and History; "Inventory of John Barnwell," appraised June 11, 1724, Miscellaneous Records (1724–1725), 71, South Carolina Department of Archives and History.

15. "Will of Nathaniel Barnwell," September 9, 1770, *Charleston County Wills* 17 (1773–1775): 650, South Carolina Department of Archives and History; "Inventory of Nathaniel Barnwell," appraised January 7, 1778, Inventories, CC (1776–1778): 308, South Carolina Department of Archives and History.

16. "Inventory of the Estate of John Evans," January 26, 1778, *Charleston Inventories* (1774–1786): 64, South Carolina Department of Archives and History; "Will of John Evans," 1 October 1774, *Charleston County Wills* 16 (1774–1779): 208.

17. Barnwell, *Story of an American Family,* 23–26, 30, 52.

18. M. Eugene Sirmans, *Colonial South Carolina: A Political History, 1663–1763* (Chapel Hill: University of North Carolina Press, 1966), 227; Robert M. Weir, ed., "Muster Rolls of the South Carolina Granville and Colleton County Regiments of Militia, 1756," *South Carolina Historical Magazine* 70 (October 1969): 226–27. Manuscript sources used for compiling data on land ownership, land value, and slaveholdings are as follows: Land ownership was derived from Proprietary Land Grants, Royal Land Grants, and Memorials; land values for the period from 1750 to 1775 were derived from Charleston County Deeds; and information on slaveholdings for the period from 1750 to 1775 was derived from Charleston County Inventories. All sources are available at South Carolina Department of Archives and History.

19. Royal Grants, 33: 362; 25: 160; Memorial Books, 10 (1771–1773): 322, 12 (1774–1775): 410; 14 (1774–1775): 12, South Carolina Department of Archives and History; "Inventory of Thomas Searson," appraised August 12, 1777, Inventories, CC (1776–1778): 256–57, South Carolina Department of Archives and History; Memorial Book, 8 (1765–1769): 313, South Carolina Department of Archives and History.

20. "Inventory of John Chaplin," appraised October 3, 1776, Inventories, CC (1776–1778): 110–12, South Carolina Department of Archives and History; Proprietary Grants, 34: 210, South Carolina Department of Archives and History; Memorial Book, 5 (1733–1742): 64, 72, South Carolina Department of Archives and History.

21. A. S. Salley, ed., *Warrants for Land in South Carolina, 1672–1711* (Columbia: University of South Carolina Press, 1973), 369, 575, 589, 617, 622.

22. "Inventory of Joseph Parmenter," appraised March 26, 1764, Inventories, W (1763–1767): 123, South Carolina Department of Archives and History; "Inventory of Joseph Parmenter, Jr.," appraised May 9, 1769, Inventories, Y (1769–1771): 133, South Carolina Department of Archives and History; "Inventory of Thomas Parmenter," appraised September 22, 1769, Inventories, Y (1769–1771): 203, South Carolina Department of Archives and History; "Inventory of John Parmenter," appraised September 7, 1776, Inventories, CC (1776–1778): 34, South Carolina Department of Archives and History.

23. Memorial Book, 7 (1752–1763): 129, South Carolina Department of Archives and History; "Inventory of Peter Perry," appraised November 14, 1765, Inventories, X (1765–1769): 189–91, South Carolina Department of Archives and History; "Will of John Fendin," October 5, 1758, *Charleston County Wills* 8 (1757–1763): 308, South Carolina Department of Archives and History; "Inventory of John Fendin," appraised September 5, 1766, Inventories, X (1765–1769): 57, South Carolina Department of Archives and History; "Inventory of Abraham Fendin," appraised January 14, 1767, Inventories, X (1765–1769): 138–39, South Carolina Department of Archives and History.

24. Memorial Book, 5 (1733–1742): 114, South Carolina Department of Archives and History; "Inventory of William Reynolds," appraised December 16, 1756, Inventories, S (1756–1758): 29, South Carolina Department of Archives and History; "Inventory of Richard Reynolds," appraised January 27, 1768, Inventories, X (1765–1769): 262, South Carolina Department of Archives and History.

25. Dwight Honeycutt, "The Economics of the Indigo Industry in South Carolina," M.A. thesis, University of South Carolina, 1948, 21, 31; Gray, *History of Agriculture*, 1: 294, 297; Milling, *Colonial South Carolina*, 17; Merrens, *Colonial South Carolina Scene*, 160–63.

26. "Memoranda of C. C. Pinckney, 1818–1819," in Ulrich B. Phillips, ed., *Plantation and Frontier Documents, 1649–1863*, 2 vols. (Cleveland: Arthur Clark, 1909), 1: 203–6; Milling, *Colonial South Carolina*, 133; John Gerar William De Brahm, *Report of the General Survey in the Southern District of North America*, ed. Louis J. DeVorsey (Columbia: University of South Carolina Press, 1971), 69–70.

10

Beaufort Economy
on the Eve of the Revolution

The years before the American Revolution were years of unusual optimism and rapid economic expansion in the Beaufort District. The spread of indigo through the sea islands in the 1750s and the end of the colonial wars by the Treaty of Paris in 1763 brought more prosperity and security than the southern parishes had ever known. The decade of the 1760s provided good years for rice exports, and the plantation economy of the Combahee, Tullifinny, and Coosawhatchie Rivers of Prince William Parish spread to the banks of the Savannah River in St. Peter's Parish. The expanding agricultural base of the Beaufort District and the cessation of the naval wars among the sea islands after 1763 encouraged the movement of new and large mercantile firms to the port of Beaufort. These merchants, with connections in Great Britain and the West Indies, brought orders for large ships to be constructed of live oak, cypress, and pine still plentiful in the southern parishes. The burgeoning economy of the 1760s was accompanied by rising political aspirations, and some local planters and merchants thought the capital of the province might be moved to Beaufort in 1772.

The mood of optimism among the southern parishes was reflected in the enthusiastic celebrations accompanying news of the coronation of King George III in 1760. In February 1761, the local militia turned out in arms and paraded from Beaufort to the still uncompleted bastion of Fort Lyttelton on Spanish Point. The guns of the fort fired in salute, and that evening there was an "elegant entertainment at Mr. Green's and many loyal toasts were drank on the occasion." During the evening there were crackling "illuminations" and many "bonfires."[1] Two years later, Governor Boone received notification of the preliminary articles of peace ending the French and Indian War in America. Among the articles, to the enormous relief of the planters and merchants near Port Royal Sound, was the provision requiring the Spanish evacuation of St. Augustine and the British occupation of Florida.[2] The Treaty of Paris of 1763 marked the end of almost a century of endemic colonial warfare between South Carolina and Florida; warfare that led to the conquest of Port Royal by the Spanish in 1686, the massacre by Yemassee Indians in 1715, the evacuation of the sea islands in expec-

.tation of a Spanish invasion in 1742, the establishment of an "underground railway" for South Carolina slaves through the Beaufort District to Florida, and
almost twenty years of intermittent piracy and privateering among the sea islands. Given the dangers that the Beaufort settlers had to bear in the early colonial period, it is not surprising that great optimism would accompany the successful
resolution of those troubles in 1763.

There are strong indications that the growth of the Beaufort District in the
1760s and 1770s was more rapid than any other settled area of the province. The
growing population and expanding economy was reflected not only in population estimates but also in the tax receipts of the provincial treasury. For reasons
already discussed, the population grew rather slowly in the early colonial period,
but in the decade of the 1760s, the population more than doubled. One study
estimates the population of the southern parishes at approximately one thousand
in 1720; sixteen hundred in 1740; eighteen hundred in 1760; and nearly four
thousand in 1770. Much of this influx was filling up the unsettled areas of the
mainland parishes. The creation of Prince William Parish (1745), St. Peter's Parish (1747), and St. Luke's Parish (1767) from the mainland portions of old St.
Helena Parish reflects the growth in those neighborhoods.[3] In 1762, St. Helena
Island petitioned the South Carolina Commons House of Assembly for permission to be formed into a separate parish mainly because of the inconvenience of
travel across two islands and two ferries to Beaufort. The committee which studied the request reported that, while the population of St. Helena Island had
largely stabilized, the mainland was growing rapidly. They reported that "the
whole tax of that island (St. Helena Island) will not pay the charge of a minister,
as they apprehend there is not land enough to contain more inhabitants than are
already settled there; that the Euhaws (mainland south of Broad River) being as
yet part of the same parish (St. Helena) and greatly increasing the number of its
inhabitants, it may be expected it will soon become another parish." The "Euhaws"
became part of St. Luke's Parish in 1767, while St. Helena Island was never
formed into a separate parish; their church, constructed in 1748, remained a
"chapel of ease" with no permanent minister.[4]

This population growth was accompanied by an expanding tax base. The
general tax receipts and payments from 1761 to 1768 among the records of the
public treasurer provide an excellent guide to the relative growth of the South
Carolina parishes. These taxes were collected on several forms of wealth including land, town lots, slaves, and money loaned at interest. The earliest return
submitted in 1761 listed St. Helena Parish a lowly number ten out of the eighteen parishes that year. Charleston was far in the lead, with St. John's Berkeley
near Charleston and Prince George Winyah surrounding Georgetown ranking
second and third in relative wealth. In 1762, St. Helena Parish moved to a more
respectable fifth place, and by 1765, St. Helena had become the third wealthiest

parish in the province. By that year, Prince George Parish had overtaken St. John's Berkeley as the second largest in aggregate wealth. In 1767, both St. Helena and Prince George were reduced in size and wealth by the creation of St. Luke's Parish from the southwest portion of St. Helena and All Saints' Parish from the northeast portion of Prince George. If we combine the returns of these parishes, St. Luke's with St. Helena and All Saints' with Prince George, for the years 1768 and 1769, we find the same relative standing prevailed with the Beaufort area growing somewhat faster than the Georgetown area.[5] These returns also indicate, through the specific tax on town lots, that the town of Beaufort, though seventeen years older, never approached Georgetown in size or substance during the colonial period. Both communities remained small compared to Charleston.

The growth and optimism of the 1760s caused a substantial increase in the real wealth of the Beaufort District. The major bases of wealth for most of the lowcountry inhabitants were land and slaves, and the value of these two forms of property rose steadily during the 1760s. The increase in the value of slaves for the period is clearly reflected in the estate inventories. In 1756, the average value of the slaves of William Reynolds was 110 pounds currency, and three years later the average value of a slave of his neighbor on St. Helena Island, Benjamin Cowan, was valued at 200 pounds currency. By the middle of the 1760s, the average value of slaves in the area—as reflected in the inventories of Joseph Parmenter of Hilton Head in 1764, Ralph Toomer of the Euhaws and John Fendin of St. Helena Island in 1766, and William Harvey of Beaufort in 1768—had risen to 230 pounds currency. At the end of the decade, the average value of the slaves of William Bell of Beaufort and Nathanial Adams of Hilton Head was 275 pounds currency. Also at the end of the decade, the average value of slaves, as reflected in the estate of John Parmenter of Hilton Head and John Chaplin of St. Helena, was 340 pounds currency. There was, of course, a wide variation in the value of individual slaves. Jack "the Taylor," a skilled slave of John Rattray of Charleston and Prince William Parish, was valued at just over five hundred pounds currency as early as 1761.[6] Generally, the value of slaves in the southern parishes more than doubled in the 1760s and 1770s.

The value of land also generally increased. Variations in land value, however, were great. The records of transactions gave no indication as to what buildings had been built or how much land was cleared and planted. Obviously the stage of development had much to do with the price. Two examples involving the same pieces of property at different times will illustrate the rising land values across the Beaufort District during this period. In 1758, John Kinnard Delebere sold two small islands called Horse Island and Sheep Island to Drury Dunn of Virginia for 850 pounds currency. The two islands totaled 239 acres and were located on the edge of Port Royal Sound between Parris Island and Port Royal Island. Their names describe the predominant function of each island in the early colonial period. By 1773, John Barnwell, whose father Colonel Nathaniel Barnwell owned the adjoining property on Parris Island, had acquired the islands and was able to sell them to Jacob Deveaux of Savannah for thirteen hundred pounds currency. Town lots also rose in value. In 1758, Thomas Green sold lot number 141 in Beaufort to shoemaker George Bland for fifty-five pounds currency. Bland must have improved the property because, in 1775, he was able to sell it to shopkeeper Elizabeth Read for three hundred pounds currency. This rising value of land and slaves is indicative of the buoyant economy of pre-Revolutionary Beaufort.[7] This alone could be reason for increased optimism and economic activity, but other factors of the 1760s created unique inducements to the burgeoning growth of the Beaufort District.

In addition to indigo which had brought prosperity to the sea island planters in the 1750s, rice cultivation spread through the Beaufort District to the southern boundary of the province at the Savannah River. From its beginning in Prince William Parish, rice cultivation spread across the Coosawhatchie River to Bee's Creek, Great Swamp, May River, and New River. This region was formed into St. Luke's Parish in 1767. The first major rice planter in St. Luke's Parish was Colonel Daniel Heyward who settled his Old House Plantation on the west shore of the Broad River in 1741. By his death in 1777, Daniel Heyward had become one of the wealthiest men in South Carolina. He and his wife, Jane Gignilliat, had numerous descendants who formed one of the most influential family groups in South Carolina history.[8] Many families followed the Heywards to St. Luke's Parish, among them were the Draytons, Middletons, Proctors, Porchers, and Duponts. Several of the early Purrysburg families also became rice planters in this neighborhood. Among them were the DeSaussures, Roberts, Bourquins, Huguenins, and Mongins.[9]

Eventually the spread of rice planting reached the Savannah River, which was destined to become the most productive rice-growing area in the Beaufort District during the nineteenth century. The major event in the spread of rice cultivation on the lower Savannah River was the end of Georgia's prohibition on slavery in 1751. Jonathan Bryan of Prince William Parish led a parade of South Carolina planters to the south side of the Savannah River when he developed his five-hundred-acre Walnut Hill Plantation just east of Savannah. Bryan moved sixty-six slaves to Georgia in 1752 and soon became one of the most prominent citizens of that province.[10] Following Bryan were Miles Brewton of Charleston and William Williamson of St. Paul's Parish.[11]

Hutchinson Island opposite Savannah was developed for rice by Colonel John Mullryne; merchant John Gordon of Beaufort; and Gordon's partner, Grey Elliott, of Sunbury, Georgia. By 1762, the thirteen-hundred-acre island in the Savannah River had eight hundred acres of rice land, a fifty-acre dammed field, an eighty-acre cleared field, a "barn 68' x 39', and overseers house 36' x 18' with a brick chimney and two good floors, eight Negro houses, and a rice machine."[12]

Among the most enterprising of the early Savannah River rice planters were Charles and Cornelius Dupont, who had developed large and successful rice plantations in St. Peter's Parish by the eve of the Revolution. Charles Dupont had 1,400 acres of rice land with "a new dwelling house and 60 valuable slaves" in 1774, and when Cornelius Dupont decided to move to Georgia the same year, he advertised his "pleasant, healthy, valuable and well-settled plantation in St. Peter's where he now resides." Cornelius Dupont had 835 acres of rice, corn, and indigo land with "a two story dwelling house 44' x 22' with a piazza: good new barn, 40' x 30', new eight horse stable and other out-buildings." By the eve of the Revolution, these plantations had reached at least ten miles upriver from Savannah. In 1774, Daniel, Henry, and Thomas DeSaussure and their brother-in-law, William Kelsal, advertised their rice land in St. Peter's Parish as "15 miles from Savannah with high knolls for building a good landing with deep water."[13]

The largest rice planters on the lower Savannah were Charles and Jermyn Wright. They were the sons of South Carolina Chief Justice Robert Wright and the brothers of Georgia's royal governor, Sir James Wright. Charles and Jermyn were the pioneers of tidal culture rice on the Savannah River. Tidal culture rice production was soon to eclipse the inland swamp method, which had predominated through most of the colonial era. The beginning of this new method of rice cultivation is marked by the construction of the Rochester Causeway. Beginning from Tunbridge Neck, the southernmost extremity of mainland South Carolina, the Wright brothers began to construct a long ditch and embankment from the mainland of the South Carolina shore to the edge of the Savannah River channel opposite Jonathan Bryan's Walnut Hill Plantation. This ditch and embankment was just over three miles long. A huge expense of money, time, and labor, it served a dual purpose. First, it provided a barrier to the salt water which flowed up the estuary behind Daufuskie Island, now known as the Wright River, and allowed the diversion of fresh water from the Savannah River to the fields behind the embankment. Secondly, a road was built on top of the embankment, and a ferry was established connecting the new road with Bryan's plantation in Georgia, adjacent to the city of Savannah. This was the Rochester Ferry, established in 1762 and licensed to Charles and Jermyn Wright. It became the principal crossing of the lower Savannah River for the next century. In the antebellum years, it was commonly known as the Union Causeway and Screven's Ferry.[14]

Charles and Jermyn Wright were more ambitious than careful. During the 1760s they fell into financial difficulty, and in 1767 they advertised 4,890 acres on the lower Savannah River for sale. The most valuable tracts were purchased in May 1768 by Henry Laurens for 8,160 pounds currency. What Laurens found at his new Wright's Savannah Plantation was that for all their energy, the Wrights had been able to put only a small portion of their land into rice production. Less than two hundred acres of the two-thousand-acre tract that Laurens purchased were under cultivation, but considerable construction of buildings, dams, fences, and roads had occurred. Laurens was clearly excited about the potential of this plantation. In April 1768, he wrote to Richard Oswald: "I have lately begun to settle another plantation on the northern verge of the Savannah River almost opposite the town of Savannah within two days ride or one days sail of Charleston, which everybody tells me may be made one of the most valuable in the province according to its contents of 2000 acres."[15]

From 1768 until the Revolutionary War, Henry Laurens made continual progress in developing the first large tidal culture rice plantation on the South Carolina shore of the Savannah River. Laurens developed the rice fields from the mainland of Tunbridge Neck out toward the Savannah River. By 1772, he had 102 slaves and 250 acres under regular cultivation. The slaves were working tasks of approximately 100 feet square, laid out in the symmetrical pattern characteristic of tidal culture rice plantations. In that year, the plantation harvested 252 barrels, or approximately 150,000 pounds, of rice. A new water-powered rice mill was constructed at the plantation in 1772, probably the first on the South Carolina side of the river. By 1773, a canal was completed from the mainland to the Savannah River that provided water transportation for rice barges and small crafts. And new slaves from the Guinea Coast and Mandingo Country of West Africa were added to the workforce. In 1774, the plantation produced 330 barrels or about 190,000 pounds of finished rice.[16]

This movement of planters and settlers into St. Luke's and St. Peter's Parishes in the 1750s and 1760s naturally drew the southern parishes into the economic orbit of the burgeoning port of Savannah. The rapid growth of Savannah in the 1760s had a direct impact on much of the Beaufort District. At communities such as Purrysburg on the South Carolina side of the Savannah River, the ordinary medium of exchange was Georgia currency. Many planters in St. Peter's and St. Luke's Parishes had town houses or other property in Savannah. When Adrian Meyer and John Linder were charged with collecting taxes for St. Peter's Parish in 1767, they could not do so without publishing a strong warning in the *Georgia Gazette* threatening to bring legal action against all those residents of Georgia who owned property in the parish. And when Purrysburg's most prominent colonial merchant, John Lewis Bourquin, died in 1774, his funeral was held among his friends and business associates in Savannah.[17]

The reasons for the connection between St. Peter's Parish and Savannah are apparent. Not only did the physical proximity promote close ties, but the Savannah River acted as a natural artery for trade. If the strong ebb and flood of the tidal rivers among the sea islands made travel difficult in the Port Royal area, the gentle drift of the Savannah River toward the sea naturally drew the communities along its bank into the economic sphere of the Georgia seaport. Savannah was the natural entrepot for the southern parishes of South Carolina just as it was for the northern parishes of Georgia. The expansion of Savannah's economic influence into the southern parishes of South Carolina was considered unwelcome competition by some Charleston merchants and political leaders.[18] Mention of this competition always brought swift action from the Charleston-dominated Commons House—whether it was for roads from the backcountry of Prince William Parish or, as in a revealing petition in 1762, for more money to support a harbor pilot at Port Royal. The lack of a regular harbor pilot, the petition noted, "has occasioned several vessels to go to the Georgia port that would if they could come to Beaufort." They complained that "the resort of vessels to Savannah is occasioned with many public disadvantages." It has created in Savannah "a demand for our commodities and . . . affords a great plenty of West India and other produce which entices people from most parts of this parish and many from Prince William for want of a market nearer home . . . to traffic and barter their crops at that place."[19]

The maritime connection between Savannah and Port Royal harbor also drew the two communities together. Prominent Beaufort sea captains such as William Lyford and Thomas Tucker moved between the two harbors regularly. For a time, Lyford functioned as harbor pilot for both ports, operating from Cockspur Island in the mouth of the Savannah River. Captain David Cutler Braddock, Lyford's son-in-law, served for several years as Savannah's harbor pilot, operating from Bloody Point on Daufuskie Island.[20] The *Georgia Gazette* reveals the constant connection between Savannah and Port Royal. Because of the size of the harbor at Port Royal, ships bound for Savannah often put in there first. More often, ships bound for Beaufort, especially those coming from the West Indies, would make first landfall at Tybee Island and proceed from there to Port Royal Sound.[21] Geography contributes to this connection since the entrance to Port Royal Sound heads almost due south while the channel emerging from the Savannah River heads nearly due east. These two lines converge approximately twelve nautical miles offshore, and from that point the most visible promontory (often the only visible land on this low lying coast) was Tybee Island. In fact, Tybee Island is the most seaward land mass visible anywhere south of Port Royal Sound. The lighthouse built on Tybee Island in 1738, and precariously maintained throughout the colonial period, functioned for Port Royal Sound as well as the Savannah River entrance.

Several mercantile firms had connections in both Beaufort and Savannah before the Revolution. James Edward Powell operated in Beaufort in the 1750s before becoming a prominent merchant in Savannah in the 1760s. The firm of Kelsal and Darling was managed in Beaufort by William Kelsal and in Savannah by Andrew Darling. Kelsal was the brother of prominent Georgia merchant and planter Colonel Roger Kelsal, originally from St. Helena Parish.

The most active mercantile connection between Beaufort and Georgia in the 1750s was the firm of Elliott and Gordon, which was operated in Beaufort by John Gordon and in Sunbury, Georgia, by Grey Elliott.[22] By 1760, Elliott became the deputy auditor for Georgia; the firm was dissolved; and Gordon advertised his "very convenient dwelling house with kitchen, stable, stores and etc., on the Bay in Beaufort."[23] Gordon then moved to Charleston. In 1764, he purchased vast tracts of land from evacuating Spaniards in Florida. These titles were never settled before Gordon's death in England in 1778. Gordon's vast commercial network in South Carolina, Georgia, and Florida formed the basis of the largest mercantile firm on the southern frontier in the 1790s: the partnership of Panton, Leslie, and Forbes.[24]

The economy of the Beaufort District in the late colonial era was also greatly enhanced by the shipbuilding industry. The late eighteenth century was the end of centuries of evolution in the construction of wooden ships propelled by sails. European shipbuilders scoured the world for the right combination of timber resources near deepwater locations to construct oceangoing vessels. By the 1760s, they had discovered the sea islands of the Beaufort District.

The first genuine oceangoing vessel built in colonial Beaufort was the fifteen-ton schooner *St. Joseph,* built in 1740 for Edward Wigg and William Hazzard. For the next twenty years, a few small vessels were built near Beaufort while the shipbuilding industry was growing rapidly in Charleston and Georgetown.[25] Between 1740 and 1760. sixteen small coasting vessels, mostly schooners that averaged eighteen tons, were built in the Beaufort area. A few of these ships were built for local planters to carry produce to market and provisions back to the plantation. One such vessel, the forty-ton schooner *Mary Ann,* built for John Bull in 1745, was the largest vessel built at Beaufort before 1763. At that time, the Bulls were the only local planter family wealthy enough to have ships built for them in the district. All the other vessels were owned by Beaufort merchants such as Edward Wigg, Robert Williams, and James Edward Powell; by local mariners such as William Lyford and Joshua Morgan; or by Beaufort shipwrights such as Thomas Crotty.[26] Though some of these vessels may have ventured as far as the West Indies, it is more likely that they were limited to the coastal trade between Charleston, Beaufort, and Savannah. In 1735, the average size of vessels trading between Charleston and the Caribbean was slightly over thirty tons, nearly twice the size of the average vessel built in Beaufort before 1763.

Between 1763 and the Revolution, however, the shipbuilding industry in the Beaufort District grew rapidly. The area around Port Royal Sound, in fact, became the principal shipbuilding center in the southern colonies in the thirteen years before the Revolutionary War.[27] The sea islands around Port Royal Sound contained many natural advantages for the construction of large wooden ships. The existence of many deep creeks and their proximity to the largest harbor in the province were obvious advantages. The most extreme tide in the southern colonies, averaging between seven and eight feet, and reaching over nine feet on a "spring tide," was a decided advantage to the colonial shipwright. In addition, the timber resources were particularly good. The graceful live oak, numerous among the sea islands, by virtue of its great strength and unusual density, was perfect for knees, beams, ribs, frames, and other points of stress on a ship's hull.

In 1771, the *South Carolina and the American General Gazette* proudly claimed that South Carolina live oak was gaining a transatlantic reputation. The many orders which had recently come in from England for large ships to be built in the province were evidence of the "goodness of vessels built here and the superior quality of our live oak timber to any wood in America for shipbuilding."[28] This was no idle boast. One historian of American shipbuilding stated of live oak, "this was a luxury timber. It far surpassed white oak in durability being rated at from 40 to 50 years when properly seasoned."[29] In 1771, famous British shipwright Roger Fisher noted the extremely high quality of South Carolina live oak aboard the *Fair American* and wrote to the admiralty recommending it as "the greatest utility to Great Britain's Navy."[30]

The method of constructing wooden ships in the eighteenth century was time-consuming and, by modern standards, very wasteful of material.[31] The first step was the conception and design. From the design of the vessel, a model was built to scale with all the pieces of the hull in miniature. Next, templates were made of paper or cloth which were the actual size of the structural pieces of the hull. These templates were taken into the woods and laid against the trees to find just the right size, shape, and natural curve. The unusual density of live oak prevented it from being warped into shape by the traditional method of steaming. Thus, the lines of the pieces had to follow the natural grain of the wood. This was one of the characteristics of live oak that made it the strongest shipbuilding material. But this building method was also terribly wasteful. Sometimes an entire tree was cut down to acquire one specific structural piece. Since a live oak tree requires more than a century to reach maturity and many of the trees used were four or five centuries old, this was not an easily replaceable resource. Rapid exhaustion of live oak resources may explain why the major shipbuilding center in the southern colonies moved from Charleston and Georgetown in the early eighteenth century to Beaufort on the eve of the Revolution.[32]

Between the Treaty of Paris and the Revolutionary War, the shipbuilding industry in the Beaufort District boomed. In fact, pre-Revolutionary shipbuilding was the largest industrial activity in proportion to the overall economy in the entire history of the community prior to the Civil War. In the decade between 1764 and 1774, no less than thirty ships were built on the sea islands.[33] In 1765, the *South Carolina Gazette* listed ten shipbuilders operating in the Beaufort area with fourteen ships under construction or contract. The average size of the thirty vessels launched in those years was over 70 tons.[34] Many were over 100 tons and built as transatlantic merchant ships. In 1772, the average size of vessels trading between Great Britain and South Carolina was 135 tons, and the average size of vessels employed in the West Indian trade was 45 tons.[35]

In the decade before the Revolution, most of the large ships built in South Carolina were built near Beaufort. Between 1765 and 1775, 2,714 tons of shipping were launched into the rivers and bays around Port Royal Sound. The size of the ten major ships built at Port Royal between 1765 and 1775 averaged nearly 200 tons.[36] The 240-ton, three-masted ship *Rose Island* was launched at Beaufort on May 26, 1766. It had a ninety-six-foot keel, 31.5-foot beam, and could carry eighteen hundred barrels of rice. The *South Carolina Gazette* boasted that "she is esteemed to be as good a ship as has ever been built in America." Its owner and master was Beaufort sea captain, Samuel Grove.[37] The largest ships built in the Beaufort District were as follows:

Date	Ship	Tonnage	Builder	Owner
1766	*Rose Island*	240		Samuel Grove
1766	*St. Helena*	170		Francis Stuart
1766	*Udny*	240		Thomas Middleton
1768	*Peggy*	100		Thomas Rutledge
1771	*Pallas*	200		Roger Smith, Thomas Laughton Smith, James Laurens, John Edwards, Peter Bacot & John McNutt (London)
1773	*Countess of Dumfries*	120		Master R. Eason, McDouall, Brown, Read (Saltcoats), Hamilton (Greencock)
1773	*Atlantic*	260	James Black	Richard Maitland, John Maitland & Alexander Rose
1774	*Georgetown*	100	James Black	James Bonneau
1774	*Ashley-Cooper*	200	James Black	Jos. Nicholson, Wm. Maskall (London)
1775	*Live-Oak*	200	Enoch Laurens John Russell	"some gentlemen of Glascow"[38]

All of these large vessels were employed in the transatlantic or West Indian trade. In addition to the large ships, at least twenty smaller vessels were constructed near Beaufort in the same period. They were employed in the coastal trade and were owned by local merchants and planters. Like similar vessels built earlier in the colonial era, these vessels averaged approximately 20 tons in size. One ship not listed in the South Carolina Ship's Register was by far the largest ship built in colonial South Carolina. Built on Hilton Head Island by shipwright Robert Watts of Savannah in 1773, it displaced 420 tons and was employed in the Jamaican sugar trade.[39] The shipbuilding industry at Beaufort also attracted ships to Port Royal Sound for repair. In 1767, the large New York brigantine *King George* put in to Port Royal to refit for a voyage to the logwood coast of Honduras. And in 1769, the HMS *Fowey*, on station off Georgia, put in at Port Royal for repairs after encountering a storm at sea.[40]

The industry employed a small class of shipbuilders such as Thomas Crotty, John Emrie, Robert Watts, and James Black, who in turn employed shipwrights, ship carpenters, blacksmiths, and loggers. The shipbuilding industry also required the acquisition of important skills by the plantation slaves of the sea islands. These slaves were trained as carpenters, sawyers, boatswains, caulkers, riggers, blacksmiths, and many other skilled occupations associated with the industry. These skills increased the value of the slaves not only to their owners but also to themselves. In the settlement of the estate of Beaufort merchant and shipowner Francis Stuart, the most prized of his sixty slaves were the "sawyers, coopers, boat-negroes and caulkers."[41]

Evidence indicates that the nature of colonial shipbuilding in the Beaufort area was highly itinerant. The only established shipbuilding yard was perhaps the area of the "Old Point" acquired by James Black from the estate of Thomas Middleton and known for years as "Black's Point." Usually large ships were built at remote locations where a favorable combination of accessible timber supplies and easy deepwater access existed. Some favorite locations were Spanish Point near Beaufort, Bloody Point on Daufuskie Island, Skull Creek on Hilton Head Island, and Factory Creek on Lady's Island. These temporary shipyards never became the nucleus for permanent settlements. Probably the shipbuilding crew established a temporary camp which disappeared as soon as the ship was launched. Nevertheless, for a few years at the end of the colonial era, the sea islands around Beaufort supported an active and prosperous industry whose product gained an international reputation. For local blacks it required skills previously unknown and previously unnecessary. And for local citizens it must have been delightful entertainment to watch the launching of such handsome crafts as the *Atlantic*, the *Pallas*, or the *Countess of Dumfries*. It was a source of considerable local pride to know that nowhere in America were ships of higher quality built.

The shipbuilding industry, the spread of indigo, and the growth of rice production in the Beaufort District combined to increase maritime activity at Port Royal in the 1760s. Colonial warfare and privateering restricted maritime traffic at Port Royal before the Treaty of Paris in 1763, but thereafter, ships began to regularly visit the port of Beaufort. Most of this maritime traffic was coastwise between Beaufort, Charleston, and Savannah, but several ships traded with the West Indies, and a few went directly from Port Royal to England. Between 1765 and 1770, the *South Carolina Gazette* reported that thirty vessels cleared Charleston to and from Beaufort, six ships came to Beaufort from the West Indies, and three went directly from Port Royal to England. One Spanish vessel came to Port Royal from Campeche in 1770 seeking provisions to relieve a severe famine in eastern Mexico. While most of the produce from the Beaufort District continued to be transported via the inland passage to Charleston or down the Savannah River to the Georgia port in "piraguas," the nascent maritime trade at Port Royal was at least a hopeful sign. The high point of Beaufort's new maritime activity came in March 1770, when the ship *Minerva,* under Captain Hugh Rose, sailed for London from Port Royal Sound with 70,000 pounds of locally produced indigo. The *South Carolina Gazette* reported that this valuable cargo "made her the richest vessel that ever sailed from an out-port of this province."[42]

The maritime traffic from Beaufort was, however, not without its hazards. The lack of a regular harbor pilot for Port Royal, a frequent political complaint of the Beaufort community, and no pilot at all for dangerous St. Helena Sound contributed to several shipwrecks. In February 1770, the sloop *Betty* was "beat to pieces on the 'bird cage,' (now called Egg Bank), in St. Helena Sound" and, in November 1770, Benjamin Huger's schooner, the *Betsy,* bound from Jamaica with a cargo of rum and sugar for Savannah, was wrecked on "one of the Hunting Islands."[43] Two noted acts of piracy in the late colonial period renewed the old fears among the sea islands. In June 1768, three young sailors, two slaves and a young white boy, stole a forty-five-ton Port Royal-built schooner belonging to local merchant William Kelsal. It contained six hundred bushels of corn "in ears," some peas, potatoes, live hogs, and "indigo vats belonging to Mr. William DeVeaux."[44] No notice indicated that the ship was ever recovered. In March 1770, Colonel Joseph Glover's forty-four-ton schooner, *Two Josephs,* its cargo of 167 barrels of rice, and its slave crew was pirated by three white men: Thomas Dannails, Joseph Jordan, and Edmund James. Four months later the schooner was discovered off Dominica in the West Indies, and the three pirates were returned in chains to Charleston.[45]

The burgeoning economy of the Beaufort District on the eve of the Revolution attracted new merchants and new money to the town of Beaufort. Most of the local merchants who had dominated Beaufort's commerce during the

1740s and 1750s were gone by the 1760s. Colonel Joseph Edward Flowers, Beaufort's principal producer of shoes and leather goods, husband of Mary Woodward and son-in-law of Colonel John Woodward, died in 1756, leaving the administration of his handsome but somewhat incumbered estate to his largest creditor, Stephen Bull Jr.[46] In 1754, Charles Purry, son of Jean Pierre Purry, was murdered in Beaufort by his slaves. His business was continued by Huguenot immigrant and Beaufort merchant John DelaGaye in behalf of Charles's minor daughter, Eleanor Purry. Eleanor Purry later married John Bull. Andrew Verdier, another Huguenot immigrant, began his career managing Purry's store and plantation at Okatee Landing in St. Luke's Parish.[47] John Gordon became rich from his Beaufort and Georgia trade, and in 1760 he and his family left Beaufort for England. In that year, he sold his "dwelling house with kitchen, stable and storehouses, on the Bay in Beaufort," along with his six-hundred-acre indigo and corn plantation located two miles from town.[48] Gordon returned to Charleston before the Revolution and became a major speculator in East Florida lands. Tory sympathies forced him from South Carolina during the war, and he died in Westminster in 1778.[49] His large and complicated estate included 994 acres in the Beaufort District. Colonel John Mullryne, one of Beaufort's most prominent citizens during the 1740s and 1750s, moved from Beaufort to Savannah in 1764. He sold his store at the Combahee ferry and left his Beaufort property in the hands of his son-in-law, William Elliott.

Of the prominent local merchants, only Francis Stuart remained in business in Beaufort throughout the transition from the early 1750s to the late 1760s. Stuart came to South Carolina because he was the younger brother of Colonel John Stuart, superintendent for Indian affairs for the Southern Department of North America and one of the most important royal officials in the American colonies. Francis Stuart came to Beaufort to manage the Beaufort branch of his brother's mercantile firm of Stuart and Reid.[50] In 1752, he married Ann Reeve, daughter of Dr. Ambrose Reeve and granddaughter of Colonel "Tuscarora Jack" Barnwell.[51] Stuart prospered in Beaufort despite the collapse of his brother's firm in Charleston in 1754. Francis Stuart developed his mercantile business in Beaufort and his indigo plantation on Lady's Island, owned jointly with his brother, so well that by his death in 1766, he had become one of Beaufort's richest men. He was a merchant, planter, shipbuilder, and shipowner. He was also, as were most merchants of that time, a banker. When his estate was inventoried in 1767, his property included a complete stock of mercantile goods at his store; fifty-three slaves, numerous livestock, and indigo vats at his plantation; the valuable ship, *St. Helena,* at sea; and a new schooner "on the stocks," all totaling 39,729 pounds currency. Perhaps more important, among his papers were found notes totaling

149,900 pounds currency to 432 planters and merchants in the Beaufort area.[52] Years later, his younger brother and estate administrator, Henry Stuart, was still trying to collect these debts.[53]

The growing economy of the 1760s and the void left by the departure of most of the local merchants of the 1750s presented opportunities for other merchants to move to Beaufort. What characterized the new mercantile firms of the 1760s was first their size; they were much larger. Additionally, they tended to have financial connections with major Charleston firms. The most important of the new mercantile partnerships to move to Beaufort was that of Middleton, Liston, and Hope. The principal partner in this firm was Colonel Thomas Middleton, who moved to Beaufort in 1761 after his marriage to Ann Barnwell, eldest daughter of Colonel Nathaniel Barnwell. Colonel Thomas Middleton was one of South Carolina's most influential citizens, and his personal and financial commitment to the Beaufort community is indicative of the expanding economy of the southern parishes on the eve of the Revolution. Colonel Thomas Middleton was the son of Governor Arthur Middleton and uncle of Arthur Middleton, signer of the Declaration of Independence. With family connections as influential as anyone in the province, he served regularly in the Commons House of Assembly for St. James, Goose Creek, St. Bartholomews, Prince William, and St. Michael's Parishes. He was also colonel of the provincial regiment of militia and in that capacity was commander of the South Carolina provincial troops on the Cherokee campaign of 1760 to 1761. His disagreement with Colonel James Grant, commander of the British regulars, became an open confrontation in the Charleston newspaper, with most South Carolinians supporting Middleton. This confrontation led to a duel which James Grant won, sparing Middleton's life. Thomas Middleton thus moved to Beaufort under a bit of a cloud. Nevertheless, he served regularly on the St. Helena vestry and made many public contributions locally, notably seeing to the completion of Fort Lyttelton.[54]

With his large financial resources and broad business connections, Thomas Middleton's partnership of Middleton, Liston, and Hope altered the mercantile community in Beaufort. The partnership invested heavily in the shipping and shipbuilding industry. The firm owned the 230-ton ship *Udny,* which regularly traded between Charleston and London; the 180-ton ship *Middleton;* the 110-ton brig *Beaufort;* and the 40-ton sloop *Delight.*[55] The large ship, *Udny,* was built at Beaufort. Middleton, Liston, and Hope was also the only Beaufort mercantile firm of the colonial era to engage in slave trade. In 1765, the firm advertised the first load of slaves to be shipped directly to Beaufort from Africa since the 1730s. These were Angolan slaves similar to those imported by Swiss merchants David Montagut and Jean Pierre Purry in 1736. The *South Carolina Gazette* noted the "150 very healthy and likely Angola Negroes just arrived on the ship *Essex* . . . to be sold at the town of Beaufort." Three years later, another load of one hundred Angolans was advertised by Middleton, Liston, and Hope.[56]

The principal local merchants, Francis Stuart and Jean DelaGaye, were both hard pressed to match this big-money competition, and both advertised heavily in the *South Carolina Gazette*. In 1762, Stuart built a new store next door to DelaGaye and advertised "cloth, clothes, glassware, tools, furniture, guns, knives, swords, tea, pepper, ginger, olive oil, spices, gunpowder, liquor, rum, coffee" and many other items for sale.[57] DelaGaye, in turn, advertised cloth, nails, paint, and "European goods suitable for the season ... to sell cheap in Beaufort," all recently imported from London and Bristol.[58] And, as if to keep pace with Middleton, Liston, and Hope, Stuart also had the 170-ton ship *St. Helena* built for him in 1766.

Both Middleton and Stuart died in 1766. This left a huge vacuum in the business community, rather like the collapse of two major banks. When Middleton died, he owed 329,000 pounds currency to a string of creditors all the way to London. His huge estate—which included four ships, three plantations, a large town house in Beaufort, and 189 slaves—was tied up for years.[59]

Middleton, Liston, and Hope ceased to function. The shipyard on the point was sold to shipwright James Black. The largest plantation, Laurel Bay, was sold to Stephen Bull of Sheldon. Thomas Rutledge of Charleston inherited lot number 3, the store, warehouse, and wharf on the bay at Beaufort. As with the estate of Stuart, the most prized of Middleton's 189 slaves were the many ship carpenters employed at his shipyard.

Stuart also left many creditors, among them Henry Laurens of Charleston, who had difficulty collecting from the estate.[60] In 1767, Henry Stuart and Lewis Reeve had to plead with and threaten the local planters who owed money to the estate of Francis Stuart. They noted that "It would be unreasonable for them to expect the same indulgence from administrators that they might from the deceased when alive."[61]

Thomas Rutledge continued to operate a mercantile business on the bay at Beaufort until the Revolution, but not on nearly so large a scale as Thomas Middleton. Henry Stuart and William Shaw formed a partnership to continue the trade of Francis Stuart. In 1769, Shaw "drowned while bathing himself in the river," and Stuart turned over this mercantile business to Robert Porteous while he worked to untangle the estate of his brother Francis.

In 1766, a new partnership with Charleston and West Indian connections with strong financial backing opened up in Beaufort. Captain Samuel Grove, one of the most experienced shipmasters in Charleston who was long associated with the West Indian trade, opened a store on the bay in Beaufort to be run by Peter Lavein.[62] Grove had owned a store on Tradd Street since the 1750s where he sold a variety of West Indian goods such as rum, sugar, chocolate, coffee, tea, and wine which he imported aboard his schooner, *Hannah and Betsy.*[63] In 1766, Grove opened his store in Beaufort, and by 1768 he had moved there. His partner Lavein moved to Beaufort from St. Croix in 1766.[64] He was the son and heir of John Lavein, a wealthy Danish Jew and the most prominent merchant of St. Croix. When he moved to Beaufort, Peter Lavein adopted Christianity, and both he and Samuel Grove served on the St. Helena Parish vestry before the Revolution.[65] Lavein's mother had abandoned him as a child and eloped with Colonel James Hamilton of Nevis. There, she gave birth to her illegitimate second son, Alexander Hamilton, one of the moving spirits of the Revolution and the new American government. Apprenticed to Lavein at the Beaufort store was Grove's stepson, John Kean, who was to become Beaufort's first congressman and an influential citizen of the new United States.[66] In 1766, Grove took command of the 240-ton *Rose Island*. Thereafter, he traded between Charleston and London. He maintained his family and residence in Beaufort and left his store to be run by Peter Lavein.

In 1769, Jean DelaGaye, the last of the local merchants of the 1750s, left Beaufort and sailed with his family for Europe. He left his business in the hands of another Huguenot merchant, Daniel DeSaussure.[67] In 1772, DeSaussure bought out DelaGaye's share of the business and DelaGaye retired in comfort to his ancestral home at Nimes in southern France.[68] DeSaussure was the eldest son of Henry DeSaussure, a modest storekeeper and rice planter at Coosawhatchie. Daniel inherited these businesses from his father. The growth of the region in the 1760s and the increased traffic on the Charleston-Savannah Highway had made him prosperous by the end of that decade. In 1769, DeSaussure moved to Beaufort. Through his wife, Mary Bower Williamson, and his sister, Elizabeth Kelsal, wife of St. Helena merchant and planter, William Kelsal, he had connections from the sea islands to the backcountry of the Beaufort District.[69] As early as 1770, DeSaussure and DelaGaye became associated with George and Josiah Smith of Charleston, and in 1774, the firm DeSaussure, Poyas, and Company was formed with DeSaussure, James Poyas, Josiah Smith, and Edward Darrell as partners. This business connection survived the Revolution to become the largest mercantile business in South Carolina in the 1790s under the name of Smiths, DeSaussure, and Darrell. DeSaussure resided in Beaufort before the war and employed John Mark Verdier to run his Beaufort store. Verdier's father, Andrew Verdier, another Huguenot immigrant, had been the manager of Charles Purry's store at Okatee in the 1750s. John Mark Verdier became Beaufort's most prominent merchant after the Revolution because of his early and loyal association with Daniel DeSaussure.

The busy commercial life at Beaufort on the eve of the American Revolution was both a hope and a fear to the local population. Large new investments, new stores, more maritime traffic, and a new and famous shipbuilding industry all inspired hope and optimism. But local indigo and rice planters soon fell into unpleasant debt to the large merchants. And local merchants, no doubt, resented the heavy competition of big money from Charleston. The balance of power in the local society and government seemed to tip toward the merchants, and in 1768, for the first time in the colonial period, the majority of the St. Helena vestry were merchants, not planters.[70]

Surely there were those who resented this new influx of wealth and power into their quiet and tightly controlled community. And the skeptics seemed correct when Middleton, Liston, and Hope went bankrupt and Henry Stuart had to struggle for years just to keep his brother's business afloat. But new and progressive merchants moved into the void. On the eve of the Revolution—with merchants such as Daniel DeSaussure, Thomas Rutledge, and Peter Lavein; ship captains and shipbuilders such as Samuel Grove and James Black; and a solid economic base in indigo, rice, and shipbuilding—the commerce of Beaufort was continuing its healthy expansion.

NOTES

1. *South Carolina Gazette,* February 28, 1761.
2. *South Carolina Gazette,* February 28, 1761.
3. Records of the Public Treasurer of South Carolina, 1725–1776, General Tax Receipts and Payments, 1761–1769, 145, 164, South Carolina Department of Archives and History. These returns also indicate, through the specific tax on town lots, that the town of Beaufort never approached Georgetown in size or substance during the colonial period. Herman R. Friis, *A Series of Population Maps of the Colonies and the United States, 1625–1790* (New York: American Geographical Society, 1940), 12–13; Friis estimates the population of the Port Royal area at approximately one thousand in 1720, sixteen hundred in 1740, eighteen hundred in 1760, and nearly four thousand by 1770.
4. South Carolina Commons House Journals, no. 35 (February 6–September 12, 1762): 68.
5. Newton Jones, *Guide to the Records of the Public Treasurer of South Carolina, 1725–1776* (Columbia: South Carolina Department of Archives and History, 1969), 5. Records of the Public Treasurer of South Carolina, 1725–1776, General Tax Receipts and Payments, 1761–1769, 39, 54, 90, South Carolina Department of Archives and History.
6. "Inventory of the Estate of William Reynolds," appraised December 16, 1756, Inventories, S (1756–1758): 29, South Carolina Department of Archives and History; "Inventory of the Estate of Benjamin Cowan," appraised May 9, 1759, Inventories, I (1758–1761): 195, South Carolina Department of Archives and History; "Inventory of the Estate of Joseph Parmenter," appraised March 26, 1764, Inventories, W (1763–1767): 123, South Carolina Department of Archives and History; "Inventory of the Estate of Ralph Toomer," appraised September 5, 1766, Inventories, X (1765–1769): 118, South Carolina Department of Archives and History; "Inventory of the Estate of John Fendin," appraised September 7, 1766, Inventories, X (1765–1769): 57, South Carolina Department of Archives and History; "Inventory of the Estate of William Harvey," appraised January 19, 1769, Inventories, X (1765–1769): 268–69, South Carolina Department of Archives and His-

tory; "Inventory of the Estate of William Bell," appraised January 12, 1769, Inventories, X (1765–1769): 407, South Carolina Department of Archives and History; "Inventory of the Estate of Nathaniel Adams," appraised March 21, 1769, Inventories, X (1765–1769): 439, South Carolina Department of Archives and History; "Inventory of the Estate of John Parmenter," appraised September 7, 1776, Inventories, CC (1776–1778): 34, South Carolina Department of Archives and History; "Inventory of the Estate of John Chaplin," appraised October 3, 1776, Inventories, CC (1776–1778): 110–12, South Carolina Department of Archives and History; "Inventory of the Estate of John Rattray," appraised December 30, 1761, Inventories, IV (1761–1763): 99–102, South Carolina Department of Archives and History.

7. Charleston Deeds, E4 (1773), 219; F4 (1773–1774), 443; I4 (1774) 1; TT (1758–1759), 210; T4 (1775–1778), 552, South Carolina Department of Archives and History.

8. Duncan Clinch Heyward, *Seed from Madagascar* (1937; rpt. Columbia: University of South Carolina Press, 1993), 45–52.

9. Henry A. M. Smith, "Purrysburg," *South Carolina Historical Magazine* 10 (October 1909), 187–219.

10. Harvey H. Jackson, "The Carolina Connection: Jonathan Bryan, His Brothers and the Founding of Georgia," *Georgia Historical Quarterly* 68 (Summer 1984): 147–72.

11. Mary Granger, ed., *Savannah River Plantations* (Savannah: Georgia Historical Society, 1947), 9, 45.

12. *South Carolina Gazette,* March 20, 1762.

13. *South Carolina Gazette,* July 29, 1774; August 19, 1774; September 16, 1774.

14. M. Eugene Sirmans, *Colonial South Carolina: A Political History, 1663–1763* (Chapel Hill: University of North Carolina Press, 1966), 181–82; *Colonial Plats,* 3: 190, 191; 6: 176; 7: 153, 176, 331; Agnes Baldwin, "Savannah River Property Map," May 24, 1977, South Carolina Historical Society.

15. George C. Rogers Jr., et al., eds., *The Papers of Henry Laurens,* 14 volumes to date (Columbia: University of South Carolina Press, 1968–1994), 4 (1763–1765): 54N; 5 (1765–1768): 58, 64–66, 169, 663–69; 6 (1768–1769): 610.

16. Rogers et al., eds., *Papers of Henry Laurens,* 7 (1769–1771): 209; 8 (1771–1773): 89N, 287–91, 505, 554, 634; 9 (1773–1774): 46, 108–9, 190, 333–34, 384.

17. Charleston Deeds, B3 (1764), 332, South Carolina Department of Archives and History; *Georgia Gazette,* May 31, 1769; October 14, 1767; August 24, 1768; *South Carolina Gazette,* December 23, 1774.

18. South Carolina Commons House Journals, no. 38, part 3 (January 15, 1771–November 5, 1771), 477, 504, South Carolina Department of Archives and History.

19. South Carolina Commons House Journals, no. 35 (February 6, 1762–September 12, 1762), 45–46, 52, 58, 68, 75, 78, 83, 104–5, 117, South Carolina Department of Archives and History.

20. Rusty Fleetwood, *Tidecraft: An Introductory Look at the Boats of Lower South Carolina, Georgia, and Northeastern Florida, 1650–1950* (Savannah: Coastal Heritage Society, 1982), 52–56.

21. *Georgia Gazette,* March 22, 1764; August 2, 1764; May 10, 1764; February 28, 1765; April 25, 1765; August 22, 1765; October 3, 1765; September 3, 1766; June 10, 1767; February 3, 1768; September 14, 1768; May 31, 1769; April 4, 1770; December 28, 1774;

August 28, 1775; *Royal Georgia Gazette,* January 18, 1781; March 15, 1781; Mar. 22, 1781.

22. *Georgia Gazette,* October 21, 1767; February 24, 1768; "Will of Peter Lavein," July 7, 1781, *Charleston County Wills* 19 (1780–1783): 193–95, South Carolina Department of Archives and History.

23. *South Carolina Gazette,* January 19, 1760; March 15, 1760; July 19, 1760.

24. "Will of John Gordon," proved in England, March 31, 1778, *Charleston County Wills* 9 (1760–1767): 223.

25. Ship Register, 1 (1734–1765): 304, South Carolina Department of Archives and History; Fleetwood, *Tidecraft,* 44.

26. Ship Register, 1 (1734–1765): 66, 146, 304, 313, South Carolina Department of Archives and History.

27. Leila Sellers, *Charleston Business on the Eve of the American Revolution* (Chapel Hill: University of North Carolina Press, 1934), 62; Sellers's definition of a "square-rigged vessel" is ambiguous, but in the parlance of the time such a category would include brigs, briganteens, snows, and ships. Sellers's assumption that a square-rigged vessel was an ocean-going ship is accurate as the overwhelming majority of coastal traders and plantation craft were either sloops or schooners. See also James F. Shepherd and Gary M. Walton, *Shipping, Maritime Trade and the Economic Development of Colonial North America* (Cambridge: Cambridge University Press, 1972), 195–98; Joseph A. Goldenberg, *Shipbuilding in Colonial America* (Charlottesville: University of Virginia Press, 1976), 241–42.

28. *South Carolina and American General Gazette,* August 8, 1771.

29. Frederick Gardiner Fassett, *The Shipbuilding Business in the United States of America,* 2 vols. (New York: Society of Naval Architects and Marine Engineers, 1948), 1: 14–61.

30. Fleetwood, *Tidecraft,* 66.

31. Virginia S. Wood, *Live Oaking: Southern Timbers for Tallships* (Boston: Northeastern University Press, 1981), 7–43.

32. Shepherd and Walton, *Shipping, Maritime Trade,* 242–45; G. P. B. Naish, "Ships and Shipbuilding," in *A History of Technology,* ed. Charles Singer et al., 5 volumes (Oxford: Clarendon Press, 1954–58), 3: 486–93; Christopher Lloyd and J. Douglas-Henry, *Ships and Seamen from Vikings to the Present Day* (London: Weidenfeld and Nicolson, 1961), 121; George C. Rogers Jr., *The History of Georgetown County, South Carolina* (Columbia: University of South Carolina Press, 1970), 46–47.

33. Bureau of the Census, *Historical Statistics of the United States* (Washington, D. C.: United States Government Printing Office, 1960), 760.

34. *South Carolina Gazette,* September 28, 1765; Fleetwood, *Tidecraft,* 65.

35. Bureau of the Census, *Historical Statistics of the United States,* 760.

36. R. Nicholas Olsberg, "Ship Registers in the South Carolina Archives," *South Carolina Historical Magazine* 74 (1973): 189–299; Ship Register, 2 (1766–1780): 156, 180, 204, South Carolina Department of Archives and History.

37. *South Carolina Gazette,* June 9, 1766.

38. Compiled from Olsburg, "Ship Registers," 189–299; *South Carolina Gazette* and *South Carolina Gazette and Country Journal.*

39. *South Carolina Gazette and Country Journal,* February 16, 1773; *South Carolina Gazette,* February 15, 1773.

40. *South Carolina Gazette,* January 5, 1767; May 4, 1769.

41. *South Carolina Gazette,* April 18, 1768.

42. *South Carolina Gazette,* April 5, 1770.

43. *South Carolina Gazette,* January 23, 1770; February 15, 1770.

44. *South Carolina Gazette and Country Journal,* June 28, 1768.

45. *South Carolina Gazette,* March 29, 1770; August 9, 1770.

46. *Charleston Inventories* S (1756–1758): 104–15; "Will of Joseph Flowers," January 14, 1757, *Charleston County Wills* 8 (1757–1760): 17–18.

47. "St. Helena Parish Register," *South Carolina Historical Magazine* 23 (1922): 146; *Charleston Inventories* R (1753–1756): 279; *Biographical Directory of the South Carolina House,* 2: 114–15.

48. *South Carolina Gazette,* March 15, 1760.

49. Robert M. Weir, *Colonial South Carolina* (Millwood, N.Y.: KTO Press, 1983), 304.

50. John Richard Alden, *John Stuart and the Southern Colonial Frontier: A Study of Indian Relations, War, Trade, and Land Problems in the Southern Wilderness, 1754–1775* (Ann Arbor: University of Michigan Press, 1944).

51. Stephen B. Barnwell, *The Story of an American Family* (Marquette, Mich.: Privately printed, 1969), 23.

52. *Charleston Inventories* X (1766–1768): 101–14.

53. *South Carolina Gazette,* January 4, 1770.

54. *Biographical Directory of the South Carolina House,* 2: 460–62.

55. *South Carolina Gazette,* January 26, 1767.

56. *South Carolina Gazette,* April 13, 1765; April 13, 1768.

57. *South Carolina Gazette,* February 27, 1762.

58. *South Carolina Gazette,* July 19, 1760.

59. *Biographical Directory of the South Carolina House,* 2: 461.

60. Rogers et al., eds., *Papers of Henry Laurens,* 4: 256–57, 576–77; 5: 322–28, 548.

61. *South Carolina Gazette,* January 5, 1767.

62. *South Carolina Gazette,* September 8, 1766.

63. *South Carolina Gazette,* June 2, 1754; October 2, 1758; January 19, 1760; September 6, 1760; December 6, 1760; December 30, 1760.

64. A. S. Salley, ed., *Minutes of the Vestry of St. Helena's Parish, South Carolina, 1726–1812* (Columbia: Historical Commission of South Carolina, 1919), 142.

65. Salley, ed., *Minutes of the Vestry,* 139–47, 155, 160–61.

66. Steven G. Baker, *A Partial Biography of John Kean, South Carolinian* (Elizabeth, N.J.: Privately printed for Mrs. John Kean, 1971), 5–19.

67. *South Carolina Gazette,* April 27, 1769.

68. Letter, January 1, 1770, DeSaussure Papers, South Carolina Historical Society; *Charleston Deeds* E4 (1778): 299.

69. "Will of Henry DeSaussure," August 10, 1761, DeSaussure Papers, South Carolina Historical Society.

70. Salley, ed., *Minutes of the Vestry,* 142.

11

Beaufort Assembly of 1772

Just as the economy and population of the Beaufort District were rapidly expanding in the pre-Revolutionary years, the political relationship with Great Britain was rapidly deteriorating. In 1772, Beaufort became the scene of one of the most significant political contests between the royal governor and the elected representatives of the people of South Carolina.

Between 1766 and 1773, the administration of the royal government of South Carolina was shared by Governor Lord Charles Greville Montagu and Lieutenant Governor William Bull Jr. of Ashley Hall. During their joint administration, the battle lines between the King's party and the opposition party were drawn over issues such as the Stamp Act, the Townshend Acts, and the Non-Importation Association. But, perhaps no issue worked to create an impasse between the Commons House of Assembly, the governor, and council more than the Wilkes Fund Controversy. From the end of 1769, the Commons House had asserted its sole right to allocate public funds by refusing to pass any money bill unless the governor and council acceded to the allocation of fifteen hundred pounds sterling for the defense of British radical publisher John Wilkes. The royal governor and the king's supporters stubbornly refused to acknowledge such a pointed insult and for six years tried numerous maneuvers to break the impasse. In 1772, Governor Montagu devised the "constitutional operation" of moving the place of assembly from Charleston to Beaufort.[1]

To some Beaufortonians and many Charlestonians, this was not an aberrant incident. They thought at the time there was a real chance of moving the capital to Beaufort. The principal impetus for the Beaufort Assembly of 1772 was, of course, the constitutional struggle between the royal governor and the Commons House. But other factors were also at work. One was the issue of a governor's mansion. Throughout the colonial period, no permanent residence had been constructed for the royal governors. By the 1760s, South Carolina had become one of the richest colonies in the worldwide British empire, and fine homes had been built by South Carolina planters throughout the lowcountry. It was probably not unreasonable to expect that appropriate quarters be constructed for royal governors from the public revenue of so wealthy a province. But, by the mid-1760s, the constitutional struggles had begun, and the South Carolina gentry in the Commons House balked at spending their tax revenue for the aggrandizement of their political opposition. When Lord Charles Greville Montagu returned to South Carolina in 1771, he had to resort to barracks quarters in Fort Johnson, two miles across Charleston harbor from the capital. As if to draw attention to this inconvenience, Montagu ordered the guns of Fort Johnson and the Charleston Battery to fire in salute as his long boat crossed the harbor. This elicited ridicule from the *South Carolina Gazette* and an official complaint in the Commons House against the waste of gunpowder.[2] This issue poisoned the political atmosphere that year and contributed to Montagu's decision to move the assembly to Beaufort.

Some Beaufort men, it turns out, had offered to build a mansion at their own expense if "they had any reason to believe the assembly would be continued there." As Montagu pointed out in his explanatory letter to Lord Hillsborough, "Tis in the interest of the Beaufort gentlemen to ingratiate themselves to the government, as they know their harbor and bar exceed any in this province, hoping by such a behavior, that the seat of government might be fixed in their town."[3] Exactly who these "Beaufort gentlemen" were and where they proposed to build a governor's mansion is not known. It should be noted that two of the most imposing structures of colonial and antebellum Beaufort were either just completed or under construction in 1772. One was the William Elliott House, today known as the Anchorage on Bay Street. This three-story tabby building was constructed just prior to the Revolution as the town residence of one of Beaufort's wealthiest colonial planters, William Elliott. The other structure was the four-story "double house" built by Colonel Nathaniel Barnwell on the site of the present Beaufort County Courthouse and known to generations of Beaufortonians as the Barnwell Castle. This building was also begun just before the Revolution. It was often used for public functions in the antebellum years; for several years after the Civil War, it was the Beaufort County Courthouse. It was destroyed by fire in 1881.[4] Both William Elliott and Nathaniel Barnwell were prominent local boosters and might have been inclined to have their new houses become the governor's mansion if Beaufort could become the capital. Though the sons of both men became supporters of the patriot cause, the political leanings of the elder Barnwell and Elliott are not known. Colonel Nathaniel Barnwell died the year the Revolution began, and William Elliott died in Charleston in 1778 before active hostilities forced the unhappy decision.[5] Whatever the realities, some Beaufort men, probably of the older generation who were riding the crest of the economic boom of the 1760s and 1770s, thought the provincial capital might actually be moved to Beaufort if they established a cordial relationship with the royal administration.

Stephen Elliott House, Beaufort, built ca. 1760, as it appeared during the Civil War (Beaufort County Public Library Collection).

Smith–Gordon House, Beaufort, built ca. 1770. This property belonged to the colonial merchant John Gordon and was the antebellum home of the Fuller family. The house is shown as it appeared during the Civil War (Beaufort County Public Library Collection).

William Elliott House, Beaufort, built by William Elliott I about 1770. The house is shown as it appeared during the Civil War (Beaufort County Public Library Collection).

Barnwell Castle, Beaufort, was built by Colonel Nathaniel Barnwell about 1770. It was used as the Beaufort County Courthouse from 1868 to 1881, when it was destroyed by fire (Beaufort County Public Library Collection).

The grave of Thomas Heyward Jr., St. Luke's Parish. Heyward was the Beaufort District's signer of the Declaration of Independence (photo by Robert W. Jenkins).

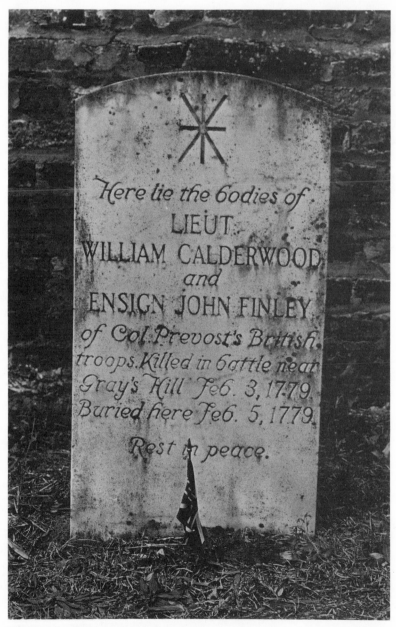

The grave at St. Helena Church graveyard of two British officers killed at the Battle of Port Royal Island, February 3, 1779 (photo by Robert W. Jenkins).

This was not the first time such a constitutional operation had been suggested to intimidate local political forces in Charleston. Early in the proprietary period, the electorate from populous Berkeley County (Charleston) had suggested that assembly seats be apportioned according to population, thus allotting more members to Berkeley County than to newly settled Colleton County. The Lords Proprietors opposed this suggestion and on March 16, 1685, instructed Governor Joseph West to hold to the original ten seats for each county. If the Charleston men persisted in their opposition then Governor West was to inquire if "ye inhabitants of Berkeley County think it equal to have all ye twenty members chosen at a town at Port Royal?"[6] This implicit threat may explain some of the hostility in Charleston toward Lord Cardross's Stuart Town settlement at Port Royal in 1686. Thus, even before Beaufort was founded, it was suggested as an alternate capital.

By moving the assembly to Beaufort, Governor Montagu had hoped to achieve one of two possible political advantages. The first was that the Charleston men "most violent in opposition" to the royal administration would be prevented from attending an assembly in Beaufort or would not be able to attend for long because "by the nature of their private affairs, they cannot be often absent from Charleston, or for any length of time." Governor Montagu further explained his tactics to Lord Hillsborough. He expected the opposition members to attend the first session out of pure anger, but he intended to fatigue the opposition by frequent and inconvenient prorogations. "They might attend at first, out of their natural spirit, yet frequent prorogations and for a short time, must be insuperable bars to their giving such an attendance at Beaufort as could for any length of time obstruct a Tax Bill." The other possible benefit to the royal administration was the formation of a loyal party among Beaufort men. As Montagu explained, "For the members for the Beaufort part of the province, residing there, would be always on the spot at the different meetings of the Assembly, ready to seize an opportunity, in the absence of the violent party, either to exclude them, by a vote of non-attendance, or to dispatch the business out of hand, before they could arrive at Beaufort."[7]

Montagu was frustrated on both accounts. Nearly all the Charleston members made the long trek to Beaufort. On October 8, 1772, one of the most august assemblies of men in the town's long history gathered in Beaufort. Christopher Gadsden, Charles Cotesworth Pinckney, John Rutledge, William Moultrie, and Thomas Heyward Jr. were all in attendance. In fact, the opposition party was so offended by Montagu's highhanded use of the royal prerogative that more members attended the opening session of the Commons House of Assembly in Beaufort than had ever attended an opening session in Charleston.[8] In addition, Montagu was unable to effect his plan of fatiguing the Charleston delegation. Between the time Montagu had officially called for new elections for an assembly to meet in Beaufort and the opening session of the Beaufort Assembly in October, he had received additional instructions from Lord Hillsborough suggesting a more conciliatory approach to the provincial party.[9] Thus, before the Beaufort Assembly even convened, Montagu realized his constitutional operation had been a blunder. By the time most of the Charleston members angrily gathered at the newly constructed Beaufort District Court House on the town square, Montagu had already decided to attempt no public business in Beaufort. After a short speech, he prorogued the assembly to reconvene in Charleston.

The response of the Commons House of Assembly to Governor Montagu on the subject of the aborted Beaufort Assembly contained some of the sharpest language exchanged between the governor and the Commons House in the pre-Revolutionary period. Members, through the Grievance Committee, labeled Montagu's operation the most "extraordinary use of the prerogative." The governor replied curtly that "I need not say anything more than that I exercised the Royal power in such a way as I thought was best for the public benefit." The Grievance Committee responded that "His Excellency's proceedings seem to be founded upon his ill-will to the body of free men of this province" and that calling the assembly to meet in Beaufort and then proroguing it within three days was "adding insult to injury and plainly manifested his contempt of the people's representatives." The recommendation of the Grievance Committee was that the Committee of Correspondence immediately send to the South Carolina colonial agent in London the strongest possible objection to Montagu's "oppressive measures" and that he be directed to ask the king to remove Montagu from service in South Carolina.[10]

The idea that the governor might be able to influence the formation of a party of loyal Beaufort men was also frustrated. While there may have been a group of influential Beaufortonians seeking an accommodation with the royal administration, they were not elected to the Commons House. Thomas Evance, a Charleston merchant and member of the opposition party, was chosen to represent Prince William Parish, and John Bull, a local planter, declined to serve for St. Peter's Parish. The most interesting delegation was that from St. Helena Parish. Both John Barnwell Jr., twenty-four years old, and Thomas Heyward Jr., twenty-six years old, began their long and distinguished public careers in the Beaufort Assembly of 1772. They were to become the two most steadfast and influential supporters of the patriot cause during the Revolution in the Beaufort District. Barnwell was also first chosen for the St. Helena vestry at Easter 1772 and may have been the John Barnwell who delivered the welcoming address to Governor Montagu on his arrival in Beaufort in October 1772.[11] How he felt about the issue of moving the assembly to Beaufort is not known. As a youthful representative of the sea island gentry, he may have initially been influenced by the opinions of his elders, particularly his father, the venerable Colonel Nathaniel

Barnwell, in believing that Beaufort could become the capital.[12] If that was the case, he was quickly impressed by the power of the Charleston elite and the political isolation of the elder generation of sea island planters. He was also impressed by the inconsistent and unpredictable nature of royal administration in South Carolina. He soon became a staunch patriot both in the council chamber and on the battlefield.

The beginning of Heyward's career at the Beaufort Assembly of 1772 is even more significant. Heyward was the eldest son of Daniel Heyward, probably the richest planter in the Beaufort District on the eve of the Revolution.[13] Daniel Heyward had settled his Old House Plantation in St. Luke's Parish in 1741 and over the next thirty years had acquired 17,000 acres, mostly south of the Broad River, to become the principal landowner in the southern parishes. When Heyward was married for the third time, to Elizabeth Simons in 1771, the *South Carolina Gazette* claimed he was "the greatest planter in this province." Though, like most of the planters from the Beaufort District, he had never been politically active, he sent his eldest son, Thomas, to Great Britain to be educated as a lawyer. Like most of his contemporaries, Heyward probably held conservative views regarding the American Revolution, but his death in 1777, two years after Nathaniel Barnwell and one year before William Elliott, occurred before active hostilities in South Carolina forced a decision. Heyward referred to the Revolutionary upheaval in his will as "the present commotions."[14]

Like Barnwell, Thomas Heyward may have been initially influenced by his father's political views, but by 1772, he had been widely traveled, well educated, and exposed to the arrogance that characterized the attitude of the British ruling class toward American colonials. He had just returned from England in 1771 where he had studied law at the Middle Temple in 1765. He was admitted to the Charleston Bar in 1771 and was practicing there in 1772 when he was elected to represent his home parish of St. Helena in both the Thirtieth and Thirty-first Royal Assemblies. Heyward was older, more experienced, and more exposed to both the anger of the Charleston opposition and the ineptness of the royal administration than was Barnwell. Heyward came to the Beaufort Assembly as a staunch supporter of the provincial party and almost immediately assumed an active role in the opposition. He was placed on the two most important committees of the Beaufort Assembly: the Grievance Committee, which vociferously objected to Montagu's removal of the assembly to Beaufort, and the Committee of Correspondence, which communicated the intense displeasure of the Commons House members to their agent in London and formally asked for Montagu's removal.[15]

Heyward became an active member of the Revolutionary Party in South Carolina and, in 1776, was chosen to replace Christopher Gadsden as one of the South Carolina delegates to the Second Continental Congress. In Philadelphia in July, he fixed his place in history as one of the four South Carolinians who signed the Declaration of Independence. It is not coincidental that one of the principal grievances of the twenty-seven listed in the Declaration of Independence referred directly to the Beaufort Assembly of 1772. Thomas Jefferson wrote in 1776 that the fourth of the "causes which impel" the American Colonies to declare their independence was the unusual exercise of the royal prerogative by calling "together legislative bodies at places unusual, uncomfortable and distant from the repository of the public record for the sole purpose of fatiguing them into compliance with his measures."

The Beaufort Assembly of 1772 was the high point of political life in colonial Beaufort. But it was a disaster for Governor Montagu and a disappointment for those Port Royal planters like Nathaniel Barnwell, William Elliott, and John Barnwell Sr. and merchants such as Henry Stuart and his powerful brother, Colonel John Stuart. As historian Jack P. Greene pointed out in *The Nature of Colony Constitutions* (1970), "Montagu could scarcely have made a more serious blunder." This action, as much as any other in the crucial period before the Revolution, seemed to point out to the people of Charleston the hostility of the imperial authorities toward their interests. And those hopeful Beaufortonians seem to have been used as pawns for the governor's constitutional operation. The issue remained to poison relations between the royal and provincial parties. The idea that the capital might be moved to Beaufort seemed to linger until the Revolution. In 1774, an English traveler remarked that because Charleston was "first peopled and more in the center of the province than Beaufort, it now most probably will continue as the capital in the future, which was rather dubious a few years back." And in the same year Christopher Gadsden wrote to Samuel Adams in Boston that the royal authorities in South Carolina were still using the threat of moving the capital to intimidate the Charleston radicals. Ever since the Beaufort Assembly, "it has been . . . strongly insinuated . . . that if we are not quiet we may expect the seat of government to be moved thither."[16] Clearly the Beaufort Assembly of 1772 was one of the causes of the Revolutionary movement in South Carolina.

NOTES

1. Jack P. Greene, "Bridge to Revolution: The Wilkes Fund Controversy in South Carolina, 1769–1775," *Journal of Southern History* 29 (1963): 399–422; A. S. Salley, ed., *Records in the British Public Records Office Relating to South Carolina,* 5 vols. (Columbia: Historical Commission of South Carolina, 1928–1947), 2: 32; Alan Watson, "Beaufort Removal and the Revolutionary Impulse in South Carolina," *South Carolina Historical Magazine* 84 (July 1983): 121–35.

2. Robert M. Weir, "Beaufort: The Almost Capitol," *Sandlapper Magazine* (September 1976): 43, 44.

3. British Public Record Office Transcripts, 33: 173–80, South Carolina Department of Archives and History.

4. John Milner and Associates, *The Beaufort Preservation Manual* (Westchester, Pa.: John Milner and Associates, 1979), 5.

5. *Biographical Directory of the South Carolina House,* 2: 57, 231.

6. A. S. Salley, ed., *Records in the British Public Records Office,* 2: 32.

7. British Public Record Office Transcripts, 33:175–76, South Carolina Department of Archives and History.

8. Watson, "Beaufort Removal and the Revolutionary Impulse," 130.

9. Robert M. Weir, *Colonial South Carolina* (Millwood, N.Y.: KTO Press, 1983), 308.

10. South Carolina Commons House Journals, no. 39, October 8, 1772–August 30, 1775, 7, 9, 11, 12, 20–21, South Carolina Department of Archives and History.

11. A. S. Salley, ed., *Minutes of the Vestry of St. Helena's Parish, South Carolina, 1726–1812* (Columbia: Historical Commission of South Carolina, 1919), 149; Weir, "Beaufort," 44.

12. Stephen B. Barnwell, *The Story of an American Family* (Marquette, Mich.: Privately printed, 1969), 29.

13. "Will of Daniel Heyward," *Charleston Wills* 17 (1774–1779): 690–96.

14. Duncan Clinch Heyward, *Seed from Madagascar* (1937; rpt. Columbia: University of South Carolina Press, 1993), 45–53.

15. *Biographical Directory of the South Carolina House,* 2: 323–24.

16. Jack P. Greene, *The Nature of Colony Constitutions: Two Pamphlets on the Wilkes Fund Controversy in South Carolina by Sir Egerton Leigh and Arthur Lee* (Columbia: University of South Carolina Press, 1970), 24–26; "Charleston, South Carolina, in 1774, as Described by an English Traveler," *Historical Magazine* 9 (1865): 345; Richard Walsh, ed., *The Writings of Christopher Gadsden, 1746–1805* (Columbia: University of South Carolina Press, 1966), 95–96; Watson, "Beaufort Removal and the Revolutionary Impulse," 136.

12

American Revolution
in the Beaufort District, 1775–1778

THE REVOLUTIONARY PARTY

As the royal administration in South Carolina gradually unraveled, the opposition party throughout the province began to form extralegal bodies which eventually became the organs of the first effective government of the independent state of South Carolina. This process of forging a working organization from demonstrations and mob actions took place largely in late 1774 and early 1775. Of critical importance to the success of the Revolution in South Carolina was the formation of dependable and influential groups in the outlying regions of the province. In the Beaufort District, the rudiments of an opposition party had begun with the Beaufort Assembly of 1772. In late 1774 and early 1775, the organization and composition of the Revolutionary Party in the Beaufort District took shape.

As if to inaugurate the new provincial organization, a great celebration was held in Charleston on November 7, 1774. This was not merely a demonstration by the active and partisan group of Charleston workers and "mechanics." The sympathetic *South Carolina Gazette* crowed that the event was "attended by thousands of the best ladies and gentlemen. There was no opposition." Effigies of the devil, the pope, and the king's prime minister, Lord North, were paraded through the streets where "they were seen to bow to those who had helped them" before being burned.[1] Clearly popular sentiment in Charleston was united in opposition to the royal administration. Whether or not this sentiment was as strong in the outlying regions of the province was the most critical question in the early stages of the Revolution in South Carolina.

In order to solidify the colony, an extralegal Provincial Congress was called to meet in Charleston on January 11, 1775. Elections were held in each parish and throughout the backcountry on December 19, 1774, to choose delegates to this convention. Most of the men selected from the southern parishes had never served in the Commons House. Colonel Stephen Bull of Sheldon, who had served in the Commons House, was the commander of the militia of the Beaufort District and was the only man selected to represent all three parishes. He sat as a delegate for St. Peter's Parish in the First Provincial Congress. Bull was the natural leader of the Revolutionary Party in this district.

Other members from the southern parishes were John Barnwell Jr., Captain John Joyner, Daniel DeSaussure, Thomas Rutledge, and Daniel Heyward Jr. for St. Helena Parish; Colonel Benjamin Garden, Isaac MacPherson, John Bull, Isaac Motte, and John Ward for Prince William Parish; and William Williamson, Thomas Middleton, Cornelius Dupont, Gideon Dupont, and Philotheos Chiffelle for St. Peter's Parish. Conspicuously missing from this delegation were the principal leaders of the older generation in the Beaufort District, Colonel Nathaniel Barnwell, his brother, John Barnwell Sr., Colonel Daniel Heyward, and William Elliott.[2]

Of the seventeen men who served for the Beaufort District in the First Provincial Congress, nine remained loyal to the patriot cause, and some, such as John Barnwell, Daniel DeSaussure, and Isaac Motte, became prominent leaders of the new state. Four died of natural causes during the war: Daniel Heyward Jr., Thomas Rutledge, Thomas Middleton, and John Ward. Two of the delegates, Colonel Benjamin Garden and Gideon Dupont, switched sides and cooperated with the occupying British army after 1780. And the two half-brothers, Stephen and William Bull, were soon more involved with family affairs than with politics. Both initially supported the patriot cause, but Stephen Bull of Sheldon performed no active civil or military service after the fall of Charleston in 1780 and remained in exile in Virginia; William, on a promise to his uncle, Lieutenant Governor William Bull, refused to take up arms against the British. Both men maneuvered for control of their uncle's vast estate, which eventually passed to William in 1791. The most ardent revolutionary from the Beaufort District, Thomas Heyward Jr., served in the First Provincial Congress for the Charleston parishes of St. Philip and St. Michael.[3]

The most controversial issue of the First Provincial Congress related directly to the Beaufort District. The chief purpose of the Provincial Congress was to enforce the agreements of the First Continental Congress, which had met in Philadelphia in September and October 1774. The delegates of the thirteen colonies had agreed to a strict embargo on all trade with Great Britain. The South Carolina delegation (Henry Middleton, Christopher Gadsden, Thomas Lynch, and John and Edward Rutledge, none from the Beaufort District) had lobbied successfully to exempt rice from the embargo because of the economic hardship it would create in South Carolina. Indigo, however, was not exempted, and the sea islands around Beaufort were the principal indigo-producing region of the colony on the eve of the Revolution. When the First Provincial Congress convened in Charleston in January 1775, they found that the delegates were "very divided on the issue of excepting rice."[4] In order to achieve regional support for the embargo, the Provincial Congress devised a complicated plan to set aside one-third of the rice crop to compensate the indigo and other planters for their losses. The First Provincial Congress then set about to appoint local committees to enforce the regulations of the Provincial Congress. They also appointed an executive Council of Safety to direct the work of the local committees. The local committees for the Beaufort District were the same men who were delegates to the First Provincial Congress, as well as some significant additional men in each parish. Added to the local committee in St. Helena Parish were William Reynolds, Joseph Jenkins, and William Waite of St. Helena Island; James Doharty of Hilton Head; Francis Martinangle of Daufuskie Island; and Tunes Tebout, a blacksmith recently moved to Beaufort. These members must have been considered the most sympathetic and trustworthy of the Revolutionary leadership among the sea islands. The additional members gave the Revolutionary Party contacts on each of the major islands of the parish.[5] Tunes Tebout had strong connections with the most radical faction of the Charleston mob. He was the business partner of William Johnson, a leader of the Liberty Tree Party and a close political ally of fiery Christopher Gadsden. With almost no local connections in the southern parishes before or after the war, Tebout was nevertheless appointed sheriff of the Beaufort District by the new state government in 1776. Of the men on the local committee for St. Helena Parish, only one, Francis Martinangle of Daufuskie, later became a Tory.

The most important addition to the local committee for Prince William Parish was William Harden, a backcountry planter who was to become a militia colonel, a member of Francis Marion's famous brigade, and the most effective partisan commander in the Beaufort District late in the war. He was added to the Prince William Parish committee to extend the influence of the Revolutionary Party to the backcountry neighborhoods of the Beaufort District. Added to the local committee for St. Peter's Parish to keep watch on the border were Purrysburg merchant John Lewis Bourquin and Savannah River planters John Chisolm and Adrian Mayer.[6]

The work of these local committees was directed by the Council of Safety in Charleston, and the critical task of extending the revolutionary message to the outlying provinces was entrusted to its "committee of intelligence." Beaufort patriot Thomas Heyward Jr. was appointed to the executive council by the First Provincial Congress and became a member of the crucial "committee of intelligence."

"DROWSY SENTINELS"

The last meeting of the moribund Commons House occurred on August 28, 1775, and Lord William Campbell, the last British governor, sought refuge on the royal navy ship HMS *Tamar* in Charleston harbor on September 15. Thereafter, the Second Provincial Congress and its successor, the General Assembly of the state of South Carolina, ruled through their executive committee, the Council of Safety. The immediate problems concerning the Council of Safety in the Beaufort District were those of militia discipline and smuggling.[7]

Militia discipline was a problem common enough to all areas of South Carolina, and the Beaufort District was not exempt. When the initial call for the militia muster was made in 1775, the patriotic sentiments of the local population were apparently not strong enough to cause them to flock to the new colors. Many demanded cash for their services.[8] The Council of Safety was skeptical of this expensive form of recruitment and strongly suggested that it not be made a precedent. They pointed out to Colonel Bull, "You are too well acquainted with public business to need information that if the militia are to be courted to their duty by promises of ready money before services performed . . . we should certainly run into a confusion of accounts." The militia was no more enthusiastic a month later when the council admitted in a letter to Bull that "we have not yet thought of any other means for compelling militia men, whether rich or poor, to do their duty than . . . the militia law which we are persuaded you will cause to be carried into execution with rigor or with political tenderness as each case may require." Such reliance on the leadership qualities of the local militia commanders in the Beaufort District proved to be a nettlesome problem for state authorities later in the Revolutionary War.[9]

The other serious problem for patriot forces in the Beaufort District in late 1775 and early 1776 was enforcing the trade embargo with Great Britain. The restrictions of the Continental Association, as it was called, were a particular hardship on the sea islands. This was the principal indigo-producing area of the province, and indigo was the most important export from the port of Beaufort. Not only were the sea island planters unable to sell their crop, but many prominent Beaufort merchants were virtually shut down. The favoritism shown toward the rice planters and Charleston merchants by the Continental and Provincial Congresses also must have rankled many in the Beaufort area. It is not surprising that attempts were made to evade the trade restrictions of the Continental Association. The geographic proximity to Savannah, the close association of many Beaufort merchants with the Georgia port, the virtual impossibility of patrolling the many tidal estuaries without adequate naval support, and a basic distrust of their less-enthusiastic Georgia brethren created considerable concern among the leaders in Charleston for controlling smuggling on the southern coast.[10]

On December 6, 1775, in order to halt the illicit trade from the sea islands, the Council of Safety instructed their local committee at Beaufort to "use every means in your power to effectively prevent the loading of vessels in . . . your district with rice, indigo or other produce of this colony" in order to prevent its being shipped out of the colony and eventually benefitting the enemy. This task proved to be too much for the local committee owing to the abundance of "inlets and private landings" and the maze of waterways in the area.[11]

The avenue for this illegal trade was provided by the "seeming apostasy of Georgia, and the ingenuity of some of our associates in finding a law to cloak their transgressions." While the Council of Safety was not empowered to take action against Georgia, they could control the activities of their own province—especially that of the Beaufort District. The council, therefore, approved a plan for "posting a few men on Hilton Head Island" to prevent the passage of boats through Skull Creek to Georgia. The council also ordered the committee for St. Helena Parish to seize the brig *Beaufort*, suspected of smuggling South Carolina products to Georgia.[12] The *Beaufort* was detained on the Savannah River from January until March 1776, when it slipped past Cockspur Island into Tybee Roads under the protecting guns of the HMS *Scarborough,* along with the large Port Royal-built brigantine *Live Oak*. In late 1776, the *Beaufort* was regularly smuggling goods to St. Augustine for Tory merchant William Panton of Florida, a close associate of Charleston merchant John Gordon, formerly from Beaufort. In December 1776, General Lachlan McIntosh seized the *Beaufort* on the Ogeechee River. Eventually the brig was returned to South Carolina and in 1779 was refitted for service in the South Carolina Navy. The brig served with D'Estaing's fleet at the siege of Savannah in 1779.[13]

The 260-ton brigantine *Live Oak* had barely been launched when the Revolution started. It was built at Hilton Head by Enoch Laurens and shipbuilder John Russell. After its escape from the Savannah River, it made for Jamaica, where it picked up a cargo of rum and sugar. On return to Glasgow, the ship was captured at sea by Captain James Wallace of the Rhode Island privateer *Diamond.* While returning to Newport with the *Diamond,* the *Live Oak* ran on the rocks in Narragansett Bay. The fine ship was lost, but its valuable cargo of rum and 260 hogshead of sugar was salvaged by Rhode Island patriots.[14]

The HMS *Scarborough* remained in Tybee Roads during the spring of 1776, clearly visible from Daufuskie and Hilton Head. It escorted sixteen merchant ships out of the Savannah River by March, many of them loaded with valuable cargoes of indigo and rice from South Carolina. Marines from HMS *Scarborough* occupied Tybee Island, which became a refuge for Georgia Tories and the temporary headquarters of Colonel John Stuart. This activity made a mockery of the continental embargo and frustrated the South Carolina Council of Safety. It also explained the orders of the council to move Colonel Stephen Bull's Beaufort District militia to Savannah in March 1776.[15]

The Beaufort merchant most successful at evading the limitations on exports was Peter Lavien. On the eve of the Revolution, Lavien was Beaufort's largest indigo shipper. On January 30, 1776, Lavien appealed to the Council of Safety to release the brigantine *William* then in Savannah River with 122 casks of indigo and 100 barrels of rice on board. The Council of Safety refused and ordered the cargo detained at Beaufort. On February 1, 1776, Quinton Pooler, a Savannah merchant, claimed the cargo belonged to him, and the captain of the *William* produced authorization for departure from the Georgia Council of Safety. The vessel sailed, and a frustrated Henry Laurens warned the Georgia council that they should "obey the laws of Congress." In spite of the proper authorization from Georgia, the South Carolina Council of Safety still believed that the cargo of the *William* belonged to Peter Lavien, who had acquired it from sea island indigo planters in the Beaufort District. That Peter Lavien's son-in-law, John Charles Lucena, was a Savannah merchant with connections to Quinton Pooler lends credence to the suspicions of the council. These episodes reveal that Savannah was the pipeline for Beaufort's smuggling trade early in the Revolution. The close connection of many Beaufort merchants and planters with Savannah and the "seeming apostasy of Georgia" helped give Beaufort a Tory reputation.[16]

Underlying these particular problems, and certainly contributing to them, was the fact that the local committee at Beaufort had displayed considerable reluctance to punish "disaffected and contumacious persons." This is not surprising. The leadership at Beaufort embraced a wide range of opinion. Colonel Nathaniel Barnwell, leader of the older generation, had died in 1775 and his contemporaries Daniel Heyward, William Elliott, and John Barnwell Sr. showed no enthusiasm for the Revolution. Even for those who were staunch supporters of independence, the task of imposing unpleasant and costly restrictions on their friends and neighbors was odious. The Beaufort committee, therefore, applied to the Council of Safety in Charleston, requesting that the council bear the responsibilities for the committee's local actions. The council interpreted this as a sign of weakness. The reluctance of the Beaufort committee to exercise their new authority over those "who would oppose the public measures whenever they dare" was thought to be "in a high degree culpable." Henry Laurens, president of the council, admonished that "men so timid and overcautious are perhaps more injurious to the public welfare than the few disaffected; the latter are known and by proper means may be deprived of the power to hurt." On the other hand, wrote Laurens, "we may unfortunately confide in the former, and believe ourselves secure, while they, like drowsy sentinels, suffer the enemy to pass and insult us." It was fortunate for the cause of independence in South Carolina that the British waited three years before testing the resistance of the "drowsy sentinels" of the Beaufort District.[17]

GUNPOWDER SEIZURES AND JOHN STUART

As the royal government in South Carolina was collapsing and the Council of Safety in Charleston was trying to wrest control of the province, word reached South Carolina of the opening of hostilities at Lexington and Concord.[18] Rumors circulated throughout the province suggesting possible action against South Carolina, and the local committees were directed to attend to militia discipline and secure arms and ammunition. The available resources of public gunpowder became objects of concern. The Council of Safety seized 3,000 pounds of gunpowder in Charleston, and in September 1775 Captain Thomas Heyward Jr. led the patriot company which crossed Charleston harbor in a rainstorm to occupy strategic Fort Johnson and commandeer its artillery.

The most feared and most likely threat to South Carolina was that royal authorities would use their contacts to incite the Cherokee and Creek Indians to lay waste to the frontier settlements. The Council of Safety learned in June 1775 that two large shipments of powder were being sent to Savannah, still controlled by Governor Wright's royal administration, and to the British garrison at St. Augustine. It was suspected that this powder was destined for the Indians, and the council promptly dispatched two expeditions to intercept the ships at sea.

The first expedition, in June of 1775, was led by Captain John Barnwell Jr. of the Beaufort militia and Captain John Joyner, the Port Royal harbor pilot. With forty men in two barges, they lay in wait at Bloody Point, Daufuskie Island, where they could command the Savannah River entrance from the South Carolina side. Governor Wright of Georgia learned of their presence and dispatched an armed schooner to Tybee Island to counter the Beaufort vessels and escort the powdership to Savannah. The forces of Barnwell and Joyner, however, had encouraged the previously weak opposition party in Georgia. Joseph Habersham now assumed the leadership of the patriot cause in Georgia and with the help of John Joyner secured an armed ship in the Savannah River. Habersham, Captain Brown, and a body of Georgia patriots bore down on the British schooner at Tybee Island and chased it out to sea. Just as the British armed schooner sailed off, the London packet ship *Little Carpenter,* under the command of Captain Maitland, arrived off Tybee Island with 16,000 pounds of gunpowder. Sensing trouble, Maitland tacked about and tried to escape to the open ocean. The powder ship was overtaken and captured by Habersham's ship from Savannah and Barnwell and Joyner's two barges from Beaufort.[19] The powder was divided between the patriot forces of the two colonies. Colonel Stephen Bull, in command of the militia forces of the Beaufort District, stored a good deal of the powder in the Prince William Parish Church next to his own Sheldon plantation. Five thousand pounds of the prize was shipped directly to Philadelphia at the request of the Continental Congress to eventually find its way to the artillery of Washington's army currently besieging Boston.[20]

The second expedition, in July 1775, was commanded by Captain Clement Lempriere of Mount Pleasant, one of South Carolina's most experienced seamen. The armed sloop *Commerce* left Port Royal for St. Augustine sometime after July 28, intent on intercepting the second shipment of powder destined for royal forces. On August 8, he captured the brigantine *Betsy* off the St. Augustine bar with 11,000 pounds of gunpowder. The sloop *Commerce* made for Port Royal, where Bull mustered the Beaufort militia to secure the valuable prize. Some of the powder was left with Bull while most was transported via the inland passage to Charleston. These two loads of gunpowder brought from Beaufort were nearly ten times the amount previously stored in Charleston for the defense of the colony. Securing the powder was a great victory for the patriot forces. Allowing it to fall into the hands of the royal forces in Savannah and St. Augustine, or into the hands of their Indian allies, would have been a great threat.[21]

The man most responsible for the alliance of the southern Indians with the royal forces was the superintendent of Indian affairs for the Southern Department, Colonel John Stuart of Charleston. Stuart had strong ties with the Beaufort District. His brother Francis had founded Beaufort's most successful colonial mercantile firm before his death in 1766. The firm passed to another brother, Henry, who was one of Beaufort's most prominent citizens on the eve of the Revolution.

In addition, Colonel John Stuart's most valuable single plantation in South Carolina was his eighteen-hundred-acre indigo plantation which occupied the southern end of Lady's Island and adjoining Maple Cane Island. Stuart's mercantile partner in Beaufort, Charles Shaw, also a prominent Beaufort citizen, was the manager of the Lady's Island property.[22]

During 1775, Stuart was considered by the patriot party to be the most dangerous royal official in the province. He was the archenemy of fiery revolutionary William Henry Drayton and consequently was the principal object of much of the public animus directed at the royal administration by the radical "Liberty Boys." When rumors reached Charleston of possible Indian attacks against South Carolina in May 1775, Stuart fled to his Lady's Island plantation. There, the Council of Safety dispatched Captain John Barnwell and Captain John Joyner to arrest him. Governor Wright of Georgia, through Stuart's contacts in Beaufort, warned him of the plot. Stuart fled by boat to Tybee Island, where he made contact with Georgia officials, attempting to assure them that he had no plans to incite the Indians. Reports of these conversations reached Charleston from Joseph Habersham via Philotheous Chiffelle of Purrysburg, member of the Provincial Congress and leader of the patriot party in St. Peter's Parish. Colonel John Stuart then left Georgia for St. Augustine and eventually ended up in Pensacola, where, during the Revolution, he was able to keep the Creek and Cherokee nations loyal to the king. Stuart died in Pensacola in 1779.[23]

Stuart's property in the Beaufort District was seized in 1776; perhaps the first loyalist property in South Carolina thus confiscated. The following year, both Henry Stuart and Charles Shaw left Beaufort, following John Stuart into exile in Florida.[24]

STEPHEN BULL AND THE CAMPAIGN IN GEORGIA

Preparations for the defense of South Carolina occupied most of the activities during 1776. British naval forces from east Florida and the HMS *Scarborough* at Tybee Island caused alarms on the coast. The Provincial Congress ordered the removal of all cattle, hogs, and other stock from "the Hunting Islands" to prevent their seizure by royal forces. Lookouts were posted at Bay Point on Port Royal Sound and at Coffin Point on St. Helena Sound. In March 1776, British forces moved far up the Savannah River to seize several embargoed ships and landed troops on Hutchinson Island. Shots were exchanged with the beleaguered patriot forces in Savannah.[25]

At this point, the South Carolina Council of Safety decided to seize the momentum in Georgia and secure their southern border. They ordered the nearest militia unit to cross the Savannah and march to the Georgia capital to bolster the patriot cause. The chief patriot of Georgia at that time was Jonathan Bryan, formerly of Beaufort, who had for some years been feuding with Governor Wright. Colonel Bull's move to Savannah was decisive. The Tories were isolated, arrested, or forced out of Savannah and the morale of the patriots was bolstered, though powerful Tory elements remained in Georgia throughout the Revolution. The sentiment in Beaufort regarding this move seems to have been ambivalent. Of the 222 men who accompanied Bull, only 95 were from the Beaufort District while there were 127 volunteers from distant Charleston. And of the various detachments from the southern parishes, the largest was the 37–member "Euhaws Volunteers," neighbors of the Heyward family. Only 16 men served from Beaufort.[26]

The securing of Savannah was only partly successful for Georgia. Royal marines remained on Tybee Island, and British and Tory forces from East Florida ranged with impunity throughout much of South Georgia. Loyalist forces took slaves from South Carolina plantations along the Savannah River and deposited them on Tybee Island. This raised fears of slave insurrections along the coast. Colonel Bull went so far as to suggest employing some friendly Creek Indians to raid Tybee Island and massacre the runaway slaves as a precaution.

During the spring of 1776 there were real fears of a major naval assault on Charleston, Savannah, or Beaufort. Henry Laurens wrote to Archibald Bullock in March 1776, "while we are busily employed guarding Savannah, it behooves us to look well to Beaufort—the loss of that place together with the acquisition of the harbor by our enemy would be a fatal blow to both our colonies."[27]

The expected naval assault came at Charleston, not Port Royal, in June of 1776. At the Battle of Sullivan's Island, brave patriot gunners behind palmetto-log bulwarks repulsed a far superior naval force and beat back a landing party to prevent the royal navy from entering Charleston harbor. It was a great victory for the American forces, and it secured relative peace for South Carolina until 1779.

Beaufort's Revolutionary leadership played no great role in the victory. Captain John Barnwell Jr. had resigned his commission in the Continental Army six months earlier in order to serve with Colonel Bull in Savannah. Captain Thomas Heyward Jr. of the Charleston Artillery would normally have been on duty somewhere around the harbor, but he had been selected by the Second Provincial Congress to replace Christopher Gadsden as one of the South Carolina delegates to the Second Continental Congress. In Philadelphia in July, Thomas Heyward Jr. signed the Declaration of Independence. The best-known hero of the Battle for Sullivan's Island, Sergeant William Jasper, was, however, a native of the Beaufort District. A previously unknown farmer of the backcountry along the Savannah River, Sergeant Jasper distinguished himself at Fort Moultrie by ignoring a hail of musket and artillery fire to replace the fallen flag on the top of the bastion. His bravery became part of the popular literature of the Revolution, and his name is commemorated in one of the three modern counties of the old Beaufort District.

With the repulse of the British fleet at Sullivan's Island in 1776, the major theater of the Revolutionary War shifted to the northern colonies. Most of 1777 and 1778 were quiet on the southern front. British forces, however, remained ensconced in the powerful Spanish-built fortress at St. Augustine and East Florida Tories raided with impunity throughout south Georgia. These skirmishes on the Georgia-Florida border drew little attention among American leaders preoccupied with major events in the north, but they worried the patriots in Charleston and terrified those in Savannah. One of the principal Tory instigators on the border was Colonel Roger Kelsal, formerly from Beaufort, whose Indian trading station on the St. Mary's River became the fortified British post known as Fort Tonyn.[28]

When Henry Laurens arrived in Congress in the summer of 1777, he set about to secure the southern border and calm the nerves of the patriots in South Carolina and Georgia. He convinced Congress to authorize money for an expedition of Continental forces, Georgia militia, and South Carolina militia to capture St. Augustine. Confusion of leadership and hot weather delayed the expedition until 1778. When the American forces headed south in the late spring of 1778, the command was divided between Continental commander General Robert Howe and Georgia Governor Houstoun. Many of the South Carolina militia forces on this expedition were from the Beaufort District under the command of Colonel Andrew Williamson and Colonel Stephen Bull of Sheldon. John, Robert, and Edward Barnwell were officers in Colonel Bull's regiment and probably joined the expedition. Beaufortonians knew that in military matters, their fate rested with that of Georgia. The campaign of 1778 was a costly failure. They never engaged the British forces, and the elusive East Florida Rangers under Colonel Thomas Brown harassed their line of march. The expedition collapsed before reaching the St. Johns River due to disunity between the Continental and state forces, desertions, and low morale.[29] The British remained strongly fortified in St. Augustine and began immediately planning a counteroffensive.

The British response was not long in coming. In the fall of 1778, a strong force of British Regulars, Tory militia, and mixed naval forces, under the command of Brigadier General Augustine Prevost, moved against Georgia. They moved up the coast from St. Mary's in three columns. Colonel Thomas Brown and his East Florida Rangers moved through the pine forests of the mainland on the westward flank. The main body of Regulars moved up the inland passage behind the Georgia sea islands aboard a flotilla of piraguas and armed barges. And at sea a naval squadron of nine ships and 167 guns, led by Commodore Hyde Parker aboard the 44-gun HMS *Phoenix,* protected the seaward flank. In November 1778, the town of Midway, south of Savannah, was burned by British troops, and the port of Sunbury was evacuated. By December 29, British forces were before Savannah.[30]

Among the preliminaries to the campaign against Georgia was the harassment of the South Carolina sea islands by Tory privateers from St. Augustine. On October 23, the schooner *Betsy* was taken by the Florida privateer, Captain McFarland, off Tybee Island. Captain Gillingham of the *Betsy* escaped to the South Carolina shore in his longboat. By early December 1778, it was reported in Charleston that St. Augustine privateers "sailed with impunity, making many captures and even operating out of four of our inlets." Three sailors from a privateer were captured on Edisto Island, and a privateer schooner was driven out of St. Helena Sound by the Edisto militia. The South Carolina brig *Notre Dame* and two privateers, the *Sally* and the *Family Trader,* were sent out from Charleston to protect the southern coast. They did not succeed.[31]

The week before the British attacked Savannah, a low, Virginia-built privateer schooner attacked the large brig *Fair American* off St. Helena Sound. The privateer was driven off and escaped into the shallow waters of St. Helena Sound, but the *South Carolina Gazette* remarked that they must be "a daring crew to take on a ship the size of the *Fair American.*" Another St. Augustine privateer, the *Shark,* of only five tons, was operating among the sea islands. The *Shark,* with three swivel guns and twenty men, was perfect for the shallow estuaries of the Beaufort District.[32]

Prevost attacked Savannah on December 29, and on December 30 an express rider from St. Peter's Parish arrived in Charleston with the news that a "heavy cannonade" had begun against Savannah at 6 A.M. The Georgia capital fell the same day. Royal forces were soon entrenched in Savannah, and, as the year 1779 began, the Beaufort District was in peril.

NOTES

1. *South Carolina Gazette,* November 21, 1774.

2. *Biographical Directory of the South Carolina House,* 1 : 154–56; *South Carolina Gazette,* December 26, 1774; January 23, 1775.

3. *Biographical Directory of the South Carolina House,* 2: 3.

4. *South Carolina Gazette,* January 23, 1775.

5. *South Carolina Gazette,* January 30, 1775.

6. *Biographical Directory of the South Carolina House,* 8: 383; W. Edwin Hemphill, Wylma Anne Wates, and R. Nicholas Olsberg, eds., *Journals of the General Assembly and House of Representatives, 1776–1780* (Columbia: University of South Carolina Press, 1970), 11.

7. South Carolina Commons House Journals, no. 39, February 17, 1773, September 15, 1775, 314, South Carolina Department of Archives and History; Edward McCrady, *The History of South Carolina in the Revolution, 1775–1780* (1901; rpt., New York: Russell and Russell, 1969), 66.

8. William B. Clark, ed., *Naval Documents of the American Revolution* (Washington, D.C.: U.S. Government Printing Office, 1964), 3: 1056, 1069, 1092; Allen D. Candler, ed., *The Revolutionary Records of the State of Georgia,* 3 vols. (Atlanta: Franklin-Turner, 1908), 2: 126.

9. Henry Laurens to Bull, December 23, 1775, January 10, 1776, George C. Rogers Jr. et al., eds. *The Papers of Henry Laurens,* 14 vols. to date (Columbia: University of South Carolina Press, 1968–1994), 10 (1774–1776): 582–89; 11 (1776–1777): 18–20.

10. Henry Laurens to Commissioners for Repairs to Fort Lyttelton, December 6, 1775, Rogers et al., eds., *Papers of Henry Laurens,* 10 (1774–1776): 540–41.

11. Henry Laurens to Committee in Beaufort, December 6, 1775, *Collections of South Carolina Historical Society,* 5 vols. (Charleston: South Carolina Historical Society, 1857–1897), 3: 61–62.

12. Henry Laurens to Bull, December 29, 1775, Rogers et al., eds., *Papers of Henry Laurens,* 10 (1774–1776): 597–98.

13. Clark, *Naval Documents,* 4: 1113–14; Candler, *Revolutionary Records,* 1: 216–17; Heyward C. Stuckey, "The South Carolina Navy and the American Revolution," M.A. thesis, University of South Carolina, 1972, 106–9. There were three ships named *Beaufort* which served the South Carolina Navy during the war: the brig described here, a sloop commissioned in 1777, and a galley built in 1779.

14. Clark, *Naval Documents,* 7: 73, 139, 644–45.

15. *South Carolina and American General Gazette,* March 8, 1776; April 3, 1776; Stephen B. Barnwell, *The Story of an American Family* (Marquette, Mich.: Privately printed, 1969), 32; Kenneth Coleman, *The American Revolution in Georgia, 1763–1789* (Athens: University of Georgia Press, 1958), 69.

16. Clark, ed., *Naval Documents,* 3: 1056, 1069, 1092; Candler, *Revolutionary Records,* 2: 126.

17. Henry Laurens to Bull, December 18, 1775; December 23, 1775; January 10, 1776, Rogers et al. eds., *Papers of Henry Laurens,* 10 (1774–1776): 569–72.

18. *South Carolina and American General Gazette,* May 12, 1775.

19. Joseph Johnson, *Traditions and Reminiscences of the American Revolution in the South* (1851; rpt., Spartanburg: Reprint Co., 1972), 63; *South Carolina and American General Gazette,* September 22, 1775.

20. *South Carolina and American General Gazette,* July 21, 1775.

21. McCrady, *South Carolina in the Revolution,* 21–22; Johnson, *Traditions and Reminiscences,* 56–58; *Biographical Directory of the South Carolina House,* 2: 401.

22. John Richard Alden, *John Stuart and the Southern Colonial Frontier: A Study of Indian Relations, War, Trade, and Land Problems in the Southern Wilderness, 1754–1775* (Ann Arbor: University of Michigan Press, 1944), 163–64, 170–71, 174–75; Wilbur Henry Siebert, *Loyalists in East Florida, 1774–1785,* 2 vols. (Deland: Florida State Historical Society, 1929), 1: 27; 2: 322; A. S. Salley, ed., *Minutes of the Vestry of St. Helena's Parish, South Carolina, 1726–1812* (Columbia: Historical Commission of South Carolina, 1919), 53, 59–64, 87–128, 135–39, 145, 146, 148, 152, 158; *Biographical Directory of the South Carolina House,* 2:, 661–63; "Claim of Sarah Stuart," *Loyalists Transcripts,* 56: 245, South Carolina Department of Archives and History.

23. Johnson, *Traditions and Reminiscences,* 107; *Biographical Directory of the South Carolina House,* 3: 663.

24. Hemphill, Wates, and Olsberg, eds., *Journals of General Assembly and House,* 91–99; Salley, ed., *Minutes of the Vestry,* 144, 145; Alden, *John Stuart,* 174–75; "Claims of Charles Shaw," *Loyalists Transcripts,* 55: 266–67; Siebert, *Loyalists,* 322.

25. Hemphill, Wates, and Olsberg, eds., *Journals of General Assembly and House,* 129, 171, 172.

26. John Drayton, *Memoirs of the American Revolution in South Carolina* (1821; rpt., New York: Arno, 1969), 212–34; Barnwell, *Story of an American Family,* 31–32; Coleman, *American Revolution in Georgia,* 69–70.

27. Clark, ed., *Naval Documents,* 4: 166.

28. John Barnwell and Mabel Webber, eds., "Register of St. Helena Church," *South Carolina Historical Magazine* 23 (July 1922): 127.

29. Coleman, *American Revolution in Georgia,* 105; Barnwell, *Story of an American Family,* 32.

30. *South Carolina and American General Gazette,* January 13, 1779; Coleman, *American Revolution in Georgia,* 119.

31. *South Carolina Gazette,* November 4, 1778.

32. *South Carolina Gazette,* December 30, 1778.

13

American Revolution
in the Beaufort District, 1779–1783

BATTLE OF PORT ROYAL ISLAND, 1779

With Savannah secured, General Augustine Prevost began to plan the invasion of South Carolina, and American forces in the state took steps to defend the southern parishes. Among the British units stationed at Savannah in January 1779 were the Seventy-first Highland Infantry under Colonel John Maitland, a detachment of Hessians, a detachment of De Lancy's New York Volunteers, Colonel Thomas Brown's East Florida Rangers, and an assortment of South Carolina and Georgia Loyalists and Creek Indians. Prevost was provided with some naval support consisting of the twenty-four-gun ship-of-the-line HMS *Vigilant;* the armed brig *Keppel;* and the armed sloop *Greenwich.*[1]

With the fall of Savannah in December 1778, George Washington had sent south Major General Benjamin Lincoln of Massachusetts to assume overall command of the southern forces from Robert Howe. He rushed twenty-five hundred Continental and South Carolina militia forces to the Beaufort District and encamped them at Purrysburg. From there they could move to oppose any crossing of the Savannah River by British forces. Lincoln's army at Purrysburg was supported by fifteen hundred men under General Ashe at Brier's Creek on the Georgia side of the Savannah and eight hundred men under General John Rutherford halfway between Augusta and Purrysburg. In addition, there were twelve hundred militia under Andrew Pickens near Augusta. Thus, the total American force available to oppose a British invasion of South Carolina was about six thousand men. Port Royal Island was protected by Fort Lyttelton on Spanish Point opposite Beaufort. It had twenty-one cannons and a small garrison of Continental troops under the command of Captain Richard De Treville.

The early weeks of 1779 were spent with both armies jockeying for position along the banks of the Savannah River. Late in January 1779, General Prevost countered Lincoln's move to Purrysburg with an amphibious assault on Port Royal Island. The British movement through the sea islands was almost unopposed, and Port Royal Sound again proved undefendable against naval forces. This move led to the Battle of Port Royal Island, the opening foray of the first British invasion of South Carolina.

On January 29, 1779, the British man-of-war HMS *Vigilant* was towed through Skull Creek behind Hilton Head Island. Aboard this small flotilla were two hundred British regular infantry of the Sixtieth and Sixteenth Regiments under Major William Gardner.[2] The HMS *Vigilant* was a large ship deemed unseaworthy by the royal navy and dismasted for use as a floating battery. It was, however, particularly effective among the sea islands of Georgia and South Carolina. Without sails, the HMS *Vigilant* had to be towed by men in longboats. On this expedition, the ship was accompanied by several privateer craft. To make this passage with a large ship, the British forces would have to have had expert knowledge of the tidal creeks behind Hilton Head Island. This knowledge was probably provided by Andrew DeVeaux IV, who had defected to the British after the fall of Savannah and on whose plantation at Laurel Bay Major Gardner was to make his landing on February 2.[3] According to reports reaching Charleston, the British and Tory flotilla passing Hilton Head Island "has burnt every house in their way as well as taken off a number of Negroes."[4] At this juncture, poor communications between the American army on the mainland and the small garrison of artillerymen at Fort Lyttelton hampered American efforts to oppose the naval attack.

Reports reached Charleston in the last two days of January that Port Royal Island had fallen to the British. General Stephen Bull withdrew his command from the encampment at Purrysburg to the post at Port Royal Ferry. American opinion about British intentions was divided. Colonel Charles Cotesworth Pinckney in Charleston thought the British would seize Port Royal Island and use it as a base to attack Charleston. A committee of both houses of the assembly asked for three thousand troops to defend the capital. General Lincoln and others, however, believed the move against Beaufort to be only a diversion designed to draw the America forces from Purrysburg.[5] Captain DeTreville at Fort Lyttelton was not privy to these communications between the American commands at Charleston and Purrysburg. He knew only that a well-armed British flotilla was in Port Royal Sound, that no word of reinforcements from the mainland had arrived, and that he was outstaffed and outgunned. On January 31, DeTreville ordered the cannons of Fort Lyttelton spiked and the bastion blown up to prevent its being used by the enemy.[6] The remnants of the tabby walls can still be seen along the banks of the Beaufort River beneath the earthworks of Fort Marion.

General William Moultrie arrived at the Port Royal ferry on January 31 to take command of American forces and prevent the destruction of Fort Lyttelton.

He was too late, "that business being done in too-great a hurry and the people moved off: it is lucky the militia from (Charles) town are come up as they have put spirits into those who hurried away so fast." Captain Thomas Heyward Jr. was in command of the Charleston Artillery detachment which had rushed to the defense of Beaufort. In defense of Captain DeTreville, he had no knowledge of Moultrie's arrival and under the circumstances made the only prudent military decision. DeTreville served the patriot cause loyally through the rest of the Revolution.

On February 1, 1779, General Moultrie moved three hundred South Carolina militia and a few Continentals across the Port Royal ferry and into Beaufort. On February 2, he detached Colonel Barnard Beekman of the Continentals and Captain Thomas Heyward Jr. of the Charleston Artillery to "the Cedar Causeway" north of Beaufort to protect the rear of the town. That night, or early the next morning, Major Gardner and his redcoats landed at Laurel Bay. British troops, not knowing of Moultrie's forces in Beaufort, rushed a detachment to George Roupel's plantation at the Port Royal ferry. There they discovered an American post on the opposite bank of the Whale Branch River and learned that a large body of Americans were already on Port Royal Island. Major Gardner turned his forces toward the town to meet the Americans.[7]

On the morning of February 3, dispatch riders informed Moultrie of the British landing. He roused his forces and marched them out of town to meet the British, picking up the detachments of Colonel Beekman and Captain Heyward at the Cedar Causeway on the way. The two forces met about halfway between the town and the ferry along the main road just west of the present U.S. Marine Corps Air Station.

When the two small armies encountered one another, the situation common to much of the fighting during the American Revolution was reversed. The British occupied a position along a tree line facing an open field to the south. The road ran through the center of the field toward the tree line, and the American forces formed in the open field about two hundred yards from the enemy, safely out of range of musket fire. In Moultrie's own words:

> I halted about two hundred yards distant from the enemy and drew up the troops to the right and left of the road with two field pieces (6 pounders) in the center and one small piece (2 pounder) on the right in the woods; on the enemies near approach, I ordered Captain Thomas Heyward to begin with the two field pieces and I advanced my right and left wings nearer the swamp and then the firing became pretty general. This action was reversed from the usual way of fighting between British and Americans; they taking the bushes and we taking the open ground. After some

little time, finding our men too much exposed to the enemy's fire, I ordered them to take to the trees; about three quarters of an hour after the action began I heard a general cry go through the line "no more cartridges" . . . upon this I ordered the field pieces to be drawn off very slowly; and the right and left wings to keep pace with the artillery to cover their flanks, which was done in tolerable good order for undisciplined troops; the enemy had beat their retreat before we began to move, but we had little or no ammunition and could not of consequence pursue.[8]

This action took place about 4:00 P.M. on February 3. The British had advanced on the American formation with fixed bayonets, but effective fire from the line and from the two field pieces of the Charleston Artillery had halted their advance and forced them to retreat. It was unusual for the American militia to defeat British Regulars on an open field, and Moultrie was proud of his small command. Moultrie remarked, "I had in action only nine Continental troops: Captain DeTreville, two officers and six privates, with one brass two pounder, and only fifteen rounds. I must . . . say they behaved well."[9]

As the British were retreating toward their flotilla at Laurel Bay, the intrepid action of Captain John Barnwell of the Beaufort militia and a few light horses nearly turned the defeat into a rout.[10] By riding around the enemy formation and capturing stragglers, Barnwell made the impression of hot pursuit and nearly panicked Major Gardner's command. Barnwell captured twenty-six men including Captain Bruere, son of the governor of Bermuda; with only a few men, he could not hold them all, and Bruere escaped.[11] Barnwell was given a field promotion to major after this action.

American forces lost seven men, including Lieutenant Benjamin Wilkins of the Charleston Artillery. Captain Thomas Heyward Jr. was one of those slightly wounded. British losses were seven men killed and seven men captured, though deserters from the British force reported that the American fire was so effective that nearly half of Major Gardner's forces had been hit. Two of the British dead were Lieutenant William Calderwood and Ensign John Finlay, whose bodies were discovered on the field the next day by John Barnwell. Barnwell had the bodies removed to the St. Helena Church yard and decently interred, saying, "we have shown the British we not only can best them in battle but that we can give them a Christian burial."[12]

It was a proud moment for the South Carolina militia, and glowing reports of the victory appeared in the Charleston papers for a month following. The *South Carolina Gazette* noted that, "If the people of this state will now exert themselves, there may soon be another Burgoyne in the southern quarter of America."[13] In Savannah, the reports were, of course, different. According to the

Royal Georgia Gazette, the British casualties were only thirty, "notwithstanding the exaggerated accounts lately propagated by some people." The South Carolina militia "made some stand, but being attacked by our forces, though much inferior in number, they were put to flight, and afterwards, suffered our men to retreat to their boats without ever firing a gun."[14]

Except for a temporary morale boost for the Americans, the Battle of Port Royal Island had little practical effect. The principal object of the British assault, Fort Lyttelton, had already been destroyed. "Would you believe it?," wrote Moultrie, "The enemy had not more than 300 men when our people took fright, spiked up the guns, blew up the fort and ran away." Had General Moultrie or Colonel Bull been swifter in sharing their intelligence with Captain De Treville, they could have avoided that consequence.

In addition to the loss of Fort Lyttelton, the sea islands suffered other losses. The privateers that accompanied the HMS *Vigilant* burned all the plantations along Skull Creek on Hilton Head and Pinckney Islands. They also sailed into St. Helena Sound and attacked Edisto Island, causing the death of James Murray, a member of the General Assembly, when the Edisto militia cannon exploded. Upon landing on Port Royal Island, the British "ravaged wherever they could without danger and burnt the house at Laurel Bay and every other building on that and several other plantations."[15] The plantation home at Laurel Bay was owned by Colonel Stephen Bull and was formerly the property of Colonel Thomas Middleton. The burning of Laurel Bay might have been the work of Andrew DeVeaux, who led the British expedition to the landing. A long running feud between the DeVeauxs, the Bulls, and the Barnwells developed during the Revolution. The Prince William Parish Church at Sheldon was a casualty of that feud.

The destruction of Fort Lyttelton was important to General Augustine Prevost's planned invasion of South Carolina. Not only did it house twenty-one cannons and valuable ammunition, but also it would have provided a constant threat to Prevost's right flank on his overland approach to Charleston. As it turned out, the Americans had to abandon any serious effort to defend Port Royal Island. It could not be held without substantial naval support.[16] In addition, the loss of Fort Lyttelton left open the inland passage, the route by which Prevost made his retreat five months later.

The sea islands were now entirely unprotected. In March, the *Gazette* lamented that, "Our coast still swarms with privateers of our enemy." Early in April, a privateer raided Port Royal and took forty-seven slaves from Benjamin Guerard's plantation on the Broad River. At the same time, the Euhaws militia under Lieutenant Heape fell in with a privateer landing party and drove them off. One of the captured crewmen reported five privateers fitting out in Georgia to attack the Beaufort District, two to go up the May River and two to go up the Broad River. Their pilot was a "traitor and guide who lives on Stoll's Island."[17] Despite the victory at the Battle of Port Royal Island, the sea islands of the Beaufort District still lay open to attack from the sea, and the British had no trouble finding local citizens to assist them.

PREVOST'S INVASION

While lowcountry leaders were still basking in the glow of Moultrie's mixed victory at Port Royal, American arms suffered a disaster on the Savannah River. On March 3, a strong force of nine hundred British regulars from the Seventy-first and Sixtieth regiments surrounded and destroyed fifteen hundred American militia and the remnants of the Georgia Continentals under Brigadier General John Ashe at Brier's Creek on the Georgia side of the Savannah River. Only 450 men of Ashe's forces escaped to join Lincoln's army in South Carolina. More than two-thirds were killed, captured, or deserted.[18] This victory cleared the British advance toward Augusta, where backcountry loyalists had "flocked to the colors." The South Carolina backcountry was now in peril, and Colonel Archibald Campbell estimated that three to four thousand British forces "at this juncture would terminate the fate of the neighboring province."[19]

On April 20, General Lincoln moved the bulk of his forces from Purrysburg toward Augusta. He took with him three thousand, men leaving only twelve hundred, mostly South Carolina militia, under General Moultrie in the Beaufort District. Moultrie's command itself was scattered. Moultrie was at Black Swamp with half the militia forces while Lieutenant Colonel Alexander McIntosh of the 2nd South Carolina Continental Regiment remained at Purrysburg. The militia, however, proved unreliable. As early as February 9, the Charleston Artillery, which had proved decisive at the Battle of Port Royal Island, had expressed displeasure with an order to advance from Sheldon to Purrysburg and informed General Lincoln that they had to return to Charleston by March 1. In addition, General Lincoln had to reprimand Colonel Stephen Bull of the Beaufort Militia for allowing his command to leave "almost unguarded, a small pass from Matthew's Bluff upwards."[20]

General Augustine Prevost recognized the weakness of the American forces in the Beaufort District. On the night of April 28, Prevost and the greater part of the British forces in Georgia crossed the Savannah River "at a spot so difficult as to completely surprise the enemy." Lieutenant Colonel McIntosh retreated from Purrysburg on April 29 in the face of three hundred British Regulars. Moultrie abandoned his camp at Black Swamp and joined McIntosh's forces at Coosawhatchie.[21]

It had been a dry spring in 1779 which allowed many fording places along the banks of the Coosawhatchie River. Moultrie decided to make his stand on higher ground and, on May 1, moved his army to a sharp rise in the terrain a few miles away called Tullifinny Hill. He left a small command of one hundred men at the Coosawhatchie Bridge. On word that the British were approaching the area, Moultrie sent a strong force of 350 men to protect the retreat of the detachment there. Lieutenant Colonel John Laurens volunteered for the duty and General Moultrie readily agreed, considering himself lucky to have a brave and experienced Continental officer, former aide-de-camp to George Washington, and son of South Carolina's most prominent patriot, Henry Laurens, to assist him. In Laurens's command at Coosawhatchie were Major John Barnwell Jr. and Captain William Hazzard Wigg along with a cavalry detachment from the Beaufort District.[22]

The ensuing battle of Coosawhatchie was a setback for American forces in the lowcountry and a disaster for the patriot cause in the Beaufort District. Rather than retreat as ordered, Laurens decided to oppose Prevost's crossing of the Coosawhatchie. He placed most of his forces at the west end of the bridge, thus jeopardizing their avenue of retreat. The houses on the hill were quickly occupied by British forces, and their fire covered the exposed American position. Sensing an opportunity to eliminate nearly one-fourth of Moultrie's lowcountry forces, the British pressed hard. After the loss of several men and an incapacitating wound to Laurens, Captain Thomas Shubrick, second in command, ordered a hasty retreat. Most of the party made it safely back to Moultrie's position at Tullifinny Hill, and Laurens himself was carried from the field by a small group of Beaufort horsemen led by Captain William Hazzard Wigg.[23]

With this defeat, Moultrie was determined to withdraw from the Beaufort District. Judging the enemy to be "vastly superior" to his own forces, Moultrie abandoned his camp at Tullifinny, crossed the Combahee River at the Salkehatchie Bridge, and made camp at the Salkehatchie Chapel in Colleton County, virtually upon the site of Craven's decisive victory over the Yemassee Indians sixty-four years before.

The effect of the defeat at Coosawhatchie on May 3 and the retreat of the American forces from the Beaufort District completely discouraged the local militia. General Moultrie reported from Ashepoo on May 5 that most of the Beaufort and Colleton Regiments had deserted his command. With sympathy for their plight, Moultrie noted that they left "to take care of their families and property which is a very natural consequence."

Moultrie retreated rapidly through the lowcountry felling trees and destroying bridges to slow the British pursuit. Repeated messages to General Lincoln for aid were not answered. Moultrie estimated that his dwindling command was opposing more than three thousand British troops. On May 6, he retreated to Jacksonborough, and by May 8, he had reached Charleston. The lowcountry was in enemy hands.[24]

The British advance through the southern parishes was particularly destructive. Prevost's regulars of the Seventy-first and Sixtieth Regiments were accompanied by a large body of Tory militia and swarming bands of Indians. To make matters worse, hundreds, and perhaps thousands, of lowcountry slaves were induced to leave their plantations with false promises of freedom and seek protection from the British. If General Prevost ever had any intention of disciplining his motley auxiliaries, he soon lost control. The *South Carolina Gazette* described these auxiliaries as "a large body of the most infamous banditi and horse thieves . . . under the direction of Colonel McGirt; a corps of Indians with Negro and white savages dressed like them and about fifteen hundred of the most savage disaffected poor people seduced from the back settlements of South Carolina and N.C."[25]

General Stephen Bull's niece, Maria Lucia, wrote of her flight from Sheldon. She and her aunt, Ann Barnwell Bull, along with several relatives, hid in their home at Sheldon as a "parcel of Indians came bolting into the house." They looted the house of its finery and broke down the bedroom doors looking for more. Maria Lucia, her aunt, Mrs. Bellinger, and her other relatives were saved by the intervention of one of the British colonels who secured their safe passage, but could not stop the plunder.[26] The auxiliaries burned Captain Hardstone's Savannah River plantation, burned two Heyward plantations in St. Luke's Parish, wrecked the DeSaussure buildings at Coosawhatchie, and looted everything near Sheldon. The *South Carolina Gazette* called it not a campaign, but wanton destruction: "Stripping women, children and Negroes . . . cutting up feather beds . . . robbing all the plate . . . dashing household furniture, killing livestock, burning houses and carrying off some thousands of Negroes and horses."[27] The most infamous destruction was, of course, the burning of the Prince William Parish Church, a fine edifice to the Anglican establishment, often described as the "finest country church in America." It was also a monument to the wealth and power of the Bull family who contributed the land and largely paid for the church's construction. Andrew DeVeaux and a small band of Tories from Beaufort were credited with burning the church in what DeVeaux later admitted began as a "frolicsome episode."[28]

When Moultrie arrived in Charleston he had barely six hundred men with him. Among these were Captain Robert Barnwell, commanding the remnants of the Beaufort Militia, and Major John Barnwell in command of twenty horsemen, the only cavalry remaining in Moultrie's army. Fully half the militia had abandoned the American army on the retreat. Prevost followed closely on Moultrie's heels and early in May prepared to assault the capital. The siege was lifted when General Lincoln returned from Augusta with four thousand troops and threatened to cut off Prevost's retreat. The now superior American forces denied Prevost the mainland route by which he had advanced, and the British were forced to withdraw via the difficult sea island route. Prevost did not have enough boats to carry his army and their unruly auxiliaries through the inland passage so he had to move from island to island securing each water passage as he went. Prevost first camped on Johns Island and fortified the Stono crossing leading to it. There he remained through most of May and June.[29]

At this juncture the Americans decided to attack the British earthwork at Stono. Shortly before the Battle at Stono Ferry on June 20, the Beaufort Militia under Captain Robert Barnwell was attached to a larger local company commanded by Captain John Matthews, later to be governor of South Carolina. These local militia took up a forward post at Matthew's own plantation on the Stono River to keep an eye on British movements. Barnwell and the Beaufort Militia took a position on Fenwick's neighboring plantation, and the American officers accepted a dinner invitation from Fenwick believing him to be a friend. After learning the strength of the American force Fenwick went directly to the British commander. The British surrounded and captured Matthew's company and demanded the surrender of Barnwell's small command. When Barnwell was refused terms, he ordered his men to make a stand. Faced with determined opposition, a British sergeant in command then offered "honorable quarter," whereupon Robert Barnwell and his men laid down their arms. Having disarmed the Americans, the British treacherously fell upon them with bayonets, killing or wounding almost every man in the militia. Captain Barnwell received seventeen wounds and was left for dead. He was found on the field the next day by his cousins, the Gibbes, who lived nearby. Barnwell was nursed back to health by Mary Anna Gibbes. Among those killed was James Black, one of Beaufort's most successful prewar shipbuilders, who had courageously tried to warn his companions of the British approach while standing guard, but was quickly subdued and bayoneted to death.[30]

The American attack at Stono on June 20 was the largest single battle of Prevost's campaign of 1779. General Lincoln attacked the British bastion commanded by Lieutenant Colonel Maitland. Maitland's position was rendered hazardous by the removal of most of the boats which had formed his bridge of retreat to Johns Island. Nevertheless, the British were able to drive off a spirited American assault. Casualties were heavy with the British losing 129 men and the Americans losing 150.[31]

The tactical effect of this encounter was negligible. The British had already decided to abandon Johns Island and retire down the coast to Beaufort. By this time, the British invasion force in South Carolina had logistical problems. Prevost's correspondence with Sir Henry Clinton revealed a chronic shortage of supplies, and his troops had not been paid in months. In addition, Prevost was badly in need of naval support, which he repeatedly urged Clinton to provide.[32] Governor Patrick Tonyn of east Florida was supposed to keep Prevost's army in Georgia supplied, but their correspondence revealed considerable disagreement as to the amount and nature of those supplies. Governor Tonyn reported to Sir Henry Clinton that Prevost had been well supplied at the start of the campaign, and "if they suffer from any want of provisions, it is owing to their own omissions." Prevost also had some discipline problems within his army, although he was naturally silent on the subject in his correspondence. Tonyn again became the conduit for critical reports. In June, he wrote to Clinton, "It is reported that great discontent prevails among the officers of that army and a relaxation of discipline."[33]

In any case, Prevost had dangerously extended his lines of communication. By the middle of July, he was almost three months away from his closest base of support at Savannah. He was deep in enemy (though not always hostile) territory and faced an American army vastly superior in number to his own. Beset by all these problems, Prevost began his retreat through the sea islands to Beaufort. There he could occupy an easily defensible position on Port Royal Island and obtain supplies from Savannah while still maintaining a salient position in South Carolina. He had reported in June his decision "to quarter the troops on Beaufort and the other islands where they will have comfortable quarters and easy access to Carolina and Georgia."[34]

The retreat of the British army through the sea islands was the most remarkable military maneuver of the campaign. Prevost had to transport his army, including cavalry and artillery, across four large tidal rivers in addition to the broad and treacherous St. Helena Sound. The retreat began immediately after the Battle of Stono Ferry and was not completed until the last of Prevost's troops arrived in Beaufort on July 8: a period of seventeen days to cover a distance of scarcely forty miles. The army had to cross the North Edisto River to Edisto Island and the South Edisto River to Otter Island. From there they traversed the broad St. Helena Sound. Half of the forces went directly across the sound to Coffin Point to secure St. Helena Island. The other half proceeded up the Coosaw River to Sam's Point and thence across Lady's Island to the Whitehall Ferry. There they crossed the Beaufort River and occupied the town. As Prevost reported, "from the difficulty of passing a sound eight miles over through strong tides and shoals and two ferries, our rear did not arrive until the eighth."[35]

Other problems hampered the British retreat. While retreating through the islands, the soldiers and their auxiliaries had continued to plunder the neighboring plantations, and the weight of the booty slowed their movement. In addition, thousands of runaway slaves had attached themselves to the British army in hopes of freedom. Contemporary historian David Ramsay estimated that

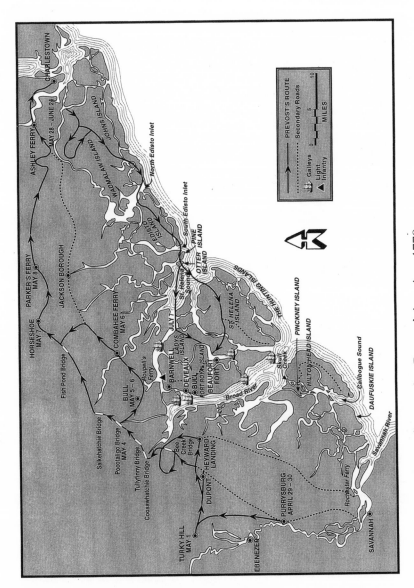

Route of British general Augustine Prevost's invasion, 1779

lowcountry planters lost four thousand slaves to Prevost's invasion and that many of these were carried to Georgia and East Florida and sold to West Indian planters as contraband. While many of these slaves had tried to help the British by providing local information and acting as guides, when the army began its retreat, their large numbers became a burden and a hazard.[36] They were abandoned on Otter Island in St. Helena Sound where many perished from starvation and disease. As Ramsay remembered it:

> They had been so thoroughly impressed with the expectation of the severest treatment, even certain death from their owners, in case of their returning home, that in order to get off with the retreating army they would sometimes fasten themselves to the sides of the boats. To prevent this, the fingers of some were chopped off. Those who got off with the army were collected on Otter Island, where camp fever continued to rage . . . hundreds of them expired. Their dead bodies as they lay exposed in the woods were devoured by beasts and birds and to this day (1785) the island is strewn with their bones.[37]

Thus, the retreat revealed the sad lot of the slaves who found an opportunity for freedom in the turmoil of war only to have the opportunity cut short.

General Prevost found Beaufort and the area around it much to his liking. Besides having easy access to Savannah, the sea islands were considered the most salubrious part of the lowcountry. Prevost decided to "leave Lieutenant Colonel Maitland and the light infantry for the defense of Beaufort and the other islands." Prevost reported that at Beaufort "the people have almost all submitted, and there is a good chance of keeping part of the army in tolerable health, these islands being reckoned the Montpelier of this country."[38]

At Beaufort, Prevost was met by HMS *Vigilant,* the dismasted warship which had been used at the Battle of Port Royal Island in February. The HMS *Vigilant* was of little use as a naval ship, but it did provide twenty-four cannon with which to defend the town. From July to September 1779, the ship was anchored in the Bay at Beaufort with its cannons ready to defend or destroy the town as necessary. Early in September, an American report revealed the ingenuity of the British in making use of their dwindling resources. Many of the guns were removed from the HMS *Vigilant* and placed in earthen bastions at key locations around Port Royal Island. At least two 24-pounders were placed at Sam's Point to guard the Coosaw River. Two more were placed at Roupel's plantation on the island side of the Port Royal ferry. In addition, several of the guns were removed and placed in flat-bottom barges which were designed to carry fifty men and a cannon. These proved to be ideal craft for guarding the inland passage and harassing the American posts on the mainland.[39]

While the British occupied Beaufort and the sea islands during the summer and fall of 1779, General Lincoln established a strong post with his headquarters at Sheldon. There he could keep an eye on both of the British garrisons at Beaufort and Savannah. In contrast to the British reports of the docility of the sea island residents, the American commanders at Sheldon were regularly aggravated by the local inhabitants. In August, Colonel Barnard Beekman complained of the unauthorized dispersal of some of the Beaufort District militia under Colonel Benjamin Garden's command. He reported that at the post which Garden's troops had abandoned, "boats pass and repass between that part of the main and Port Royal." Beekman would not trust the local militia to reconnoiter British positions on Port Royal Island, but dispatched instead "some men of the (continental) artillery in whom I placed confidence."[40] By the end of August, the British had become so confident that they were "able to pass . . . with their boats in daytime" at the Port Royal Ferry, and the American detachment had to "bear with their insults" because they were "powerless to oppose them."

Beekman was not timid in placing the blame where he thought it belonged. He complained of the "vicinity of the enemy and the number of landing places on the main it affords on each side of the ferry which remain unguarded." He complained also that the "majority of the people living at or near those places are wives and families of disaffected husbands and brothers, some of them with the enemy at Port Royal." These people he accused of passing intelligence to the British at night, making the American position hazardous. According to Beekman, the difficulty of geography and the hostility of the local population rendered the situation of the American post at the Port Royal Ferry "critical."[41]

American troops on the mainland also encountered difficulty in procuring supplies from the local residents. Colonel Daniel Horry reported from Sheldon that "we meet with very great difficulty in procuring forage . . . the people say they will be a good deal distressed to spare any from the plantations."[42] Whether this represented the disaffection of the local residents or a real shortage of supplies is difficult to determine, but procurement was a problem for all American commanders in the area. Later in 1779, Colonel Francis Marion, in command of the post at Sheldon, reported that he caught some local inhabitants driving off their cattle and sheep to prevent seizure. At the same time, he was advised by Colonel Benjamin Garden of the local militia not to "attempt to seize any cattle near the Broad River as it might occasion lawsuits."[43]

While the Americans were having their problems at Sheldon, the British were comfortably ensconced in Beaufort. During the summer of 1779, there were nine hundred British and Hessian troops on Port Royal Island under the command of Lieutenant Colonel John Maitland. The HMS *Vigilant* at Beaufort was joined by the HMS *Vindictive* and HMS *Scourge* to protect Port Royal Sound.[44] General Prevost himself preferred Beaufort to Savannah. The milder maritime climate was easier on his ever-increasing attacks of gout.[45] In early September, this pleasant arrangement for the occupying army was rudely interrupted. The advanced squadrons of the Count D'Estaing's powerful French West Indian fleet were sighted off Tybee Island, and reports reached Prevost of American maneuvers south and west of Savannah.[46] Preliminary movements for the siege of Savannah had begun.

SIEGE OF SAVANNAH, 1779

The arrival of Count D'Estaing's French West Indian fleet was so sudden that it surprised not only the British posts at Beaufort and Savannah, but also the American commander, General Lincoln. Count D'Estaing had carried out several successful operations against the British in the West Indies and wished to add another laurel to the expedition with a quick victory on the American mainland. He responded to a request directly from Governor John Rutledge of South Carolina through the French consul in Charleston to join with General Lincoln in an allied assault on Savannah.

General Prevost at Savannah hurried his troops into action by throwing up earthworks around the city and calling in his outlying forces. The most important detachment was that at Beaufort: eight hundred men of the experienced Seventy-first Highland and Sixtieth Royal American Regiments under Lieutenant Colonel John Maitland. Prevost ordered their immediate withdrawal from Beaufort aboard their available naval forces: HMS *Vigilant,* three galleys, and three armed barges. The water route to Savannah, however, was blocked. The French fleet of twenty-two ships-of-the-line and eight frigates commanded Tybee roads and all available seaward approaches to Savannah. The American army advancing from Sheldon was denied the overland route.

Maitland had to move fast. He called in his lookouts from Coffin Point and Ashdale and abandoned the shore-mounted cannons guarding the Coosaw River at Sams Point. Between September 13 and 15, Maitland and his troops hauled HMS *Vigilant* down the Beaufort River and into Port Royal Sound. There they joined the two galleys which had been anchored in Archer's Creek and the Whalebranch River. The flotilla move slowly through Skull Creek past Hilton Head and Pinckney Islands and then across Callibogue Sound to Daufuskie Island. The French ships-of-the-line, with 1,472 cannons, dominated Tybee Roads. Several smaller French frigates had moved upriver, two of them fast aground on the banks off Turtle Island, almost within musket shot of Bloody Point.

The HMS *Vigilant,* the large galleys, and the armed flats could not move past Daufuskie Island without being intercepted by French naval forces. Maitland, therefore, threw up hasty fortifications at Bloody Point and secured the ships in the Cooper River. He then commandeered as many canoes and piraguas as he could in the vicinity. With the help of a local slave expert in the marshes and waters of the lower Savannah River, the British troops were able to move up the Wright River unnoticed and cross over the Savannah River at high tide via a hidden channel. Maitland arrived in Savannah with the Seventy-first and Sixtieth Regiments on September 16 "to the great joy of the inhabitants."[47]

Deliberations on the surrender of Savannah to the French and Americans were well under way when the Beaufort detachment arrived. According to Alexander Garden, Colonel Maitland strode boldly into the council chamber, struck the hilt of his Scottish broadsword on the table and declared, "The man who utters a syllable recommending surrender, makes me his decided enemy; it is necessary that either he or I should fall." The British command, bolstered by the arrival of the Seventy-first Highlanders and Sixtieth Royal Americans from Beaufort and heartened by the determined character of John Maitland, decided to fight.[48]

The subsequent siege and assault of Savannah was a costly failure for the French and Americans. After a lengthy bombardment, Count D'Estaing became impatient and concerned for his fleet during hurricane season on the southern coast. On October 9 a hastily conceived assault of French and American troops against the fortifications south of Savannah was repulsed with great loss of life. Nearly thirteen hundred French and American troops were killed, among them Sergeant William Jasper, the hero of Fort Moultrie, and Count Pulaski, the gallant Polish cavalry commander. Count D'Estaing himself was seriously wounded. The British had far fewer casualties, but among them was Lieutenant Colonel John Maitland, for whom the following epitaph was published in the *Royal Georgia Gazette:*

> When Gallic perfidy and rebel pride
> Presumed the British Lion to subside
> With rapid wing, but not before untried
> From Beaufort's banks the gallant Maitland flew.
> In time to save he reached Savannah's coast.
> The force of France and perjured foes defied.
> Repelled, dispersed the formidable host
> Preserved a country, blessed the day, and died.[49]

The failure at Savannah was a costly blow to the morale of the patriot forces in South Carolina. Count D'Estaing's fleet soon left for France, and the coast was again open to naval attack. In November, the *Rutledge* and the *Myrtle* were driven ashore at the mouth of the Savannah River, and some of the crew escaped to Hilton Head. The *South Carolina Gazette* in Charleston again complained of privateers harassing the sea islands.[50] The people of the Beaufort District, not yet recovered from the punishing campaign of Prevost in the spring and Maitland's summer occupation of Beaufort, now found themselves caught in a vise between American forces in Charleston and British forces in Savannah. Many wavered in their loyalty.

When Maitland evacuated the British forces from the sea islands, Colonel Barnard Beekman of the Continental artillery at Sheldon noted how quickly the inhabitants changed their sympathies. In September, Beekman sent Captain John Jenkins to St. Helena Island to reconnoitre the situation. He reported, "Now that none of our external enemies were left on the island . . . many of the inhabitants wish to have it in their power to extend themselves in our favor."[51]

The winter of 1779 to 1780 provided a few months respite on the southern frontier. The Americans maintained a strong post at Sheldon commanded by Lieutenant Colonel Francis Marion of the Continental Army, soon to become South Carolina's premier hero of the Revolution: the partisan guerrilla known as the "Swamp Fox." While stationed at Sheldon, Marion developed a healthy distrust of the local inhabitants. He had difficulty obtaining supplies and found the local militia unreliable. "I assure you," he wrote to General Lincoln, "the militia here are not of the least service." The situation deteriorated in the spring of 1780. The new commander of the post at Sheldon, Colonel Daniel Horry, as much as accused the Beaufort militia of treachery. He reported to Lincoln, "The militia at Port Royal are bad people, they have quitted [sic] their post and . . . none of them will come off (the island)" to join the American forces on the mainland.[52] Both Francis Marion and Daniel Horry sensed that even before the fall of Charleston many of the people of the Beaufort District had already abandoned the American cause.

FALL OF CHARLESTON

The failure of the American and French assault of Savannah gave the British forces a secure base from which to once again attack South Carolina. The return of Count D'Estaing's fleet to France made it possible for the British commander in North America, Sir Henry Clinton, to attack Charleston.[53] During the spring of 1780, preparations began in earnest for the conquest of South Carolina, and the Beaufort District was faced with imminent occupation and destruction. Clinton sailed from New York at the end of 1779 with eighty-five hundred troops and a strong fleet of five ships-of-the-line and nine frigates under the command of Admiral Mariot Arbuthnot. The fleet anchored in Tybee Roads, and the troops disembarked on Tybee Island in January 1780. From Tybee they dominated not only the Savannah River but also Daufuskie and Hilton Head Islands.[54]

On the voyage south, several transport vessels accompanying the fleet were sunk in a storm off Cape Hatteras. Most of the artillery and all the horses for

Clinton's cavalry were lost. In order to remount his cavalry regiment, Lieutenant Colonel Banastre Tarleton commandeered boats from the British quartermaster at Tybee and transported his entire command to Port Royal Island in February 1780. There he collected "from friends or enemies, by money or by force, all the horses belonging to the islands in that neighborhood." Banastre Tarleton later became infamous for leading his "bloody legion" on destructive forays through-out South Carolina.[55] Tarleton immortalized his archenemy and nemesis, General Francis Marion, with the nickname "Swamp Fox." The most famous horse on Port Royal Island, however, escaped Tarleton's grasp. It was at this time that Major William Hazzard Wigg of Beaufort evaded Tarleton's legion by swimming the Broad River with his famous charger, Independence, who had been born on July 4, 1776.[56]

In February, Clinton landed forces on Johns Island and began to secure the inland passage in preparation for the siege of Charleston. Tarleton's legion re-mained on Port Royal Island until Brigadier General James Patterson with fif-teen hundred men of the Georgia garrison crossed the Savannah River at Two Sisters Ferry into the Beaufort District in mid-March. On his advance toward the Combahee River "through swamps and difficult passes," Patterson had "fre-quent skirmishes with the militia of the country." The flanks of his column were protected by two corps of rangers commanded by Major Cochrane and Major Patrick Ferguson. Ferguson was the inventor of the first useful breech-loading weapon, which proved effective at the Battle of Brandywine in Pennsylvania. He was killed while in command of the British forces at King's Mountain later in the year. Near Garden's Corners, they were joined by Tarleton's mounted legion, which had crossed the Port Royal ferry. Together these forces crossed the Combahee River into Colleton County and surprised the American forward post near Jacksonborough. By March 25, Patterson and Tarleton had joined with Clinton's forces at Rantowle's bridge.[57] The southern parishes were again se-curely behind British lines, and the siege of Charleston was about to commence.

The sudden arrival of the British forces from the southern parishes sur-prised the Americans and, by securing the Ashley Ferry and Charleston Neck, sealed the fate of the capital. General Lincoln surrendered the city to Sir Henry Clinton on May 12, 1780. The surrender of Charleston was the worst single defeat suffered by Americans in the Revolutionary War. With no avenue of es-cape, virtually the entire American army in the South, more than six thousand men, was lost along with most of the political leadership of the Revolution in South Carolina.[58] While most of the garrison was paroled, much of the civil and military leadership was imprisoned aboard British ships in the harbor. The Beau-fort Patriots were all aboard the *Pack-Horse*. John, Robert, and Edward Barnwell; Henry W. DeSaussure; William Elliott Jr.; Benjamin Guerard; Thomas Grayson; James Heyward; John Kean; and William Hazzard Wigg all suffered the indignities and dangers of incarceration aboard the prison ship for more than a year. The most important Patriot leaders in the state, however, were removed from South Carolina to the ancient dungeons of the Castillo San Marcos in St. Augustine. In this distinguished company were Thomas Heyward Jr. and Daniel DeSaussure. Both men were later exchanged in Philadelphia.[59]

The fall of Charleston was the lowest point of the Revolutionary War in South Carolina. The state was soon overrun by British and Tory forces, and American resistance was sporadic and disorganized. In these dark days, only the most determined and ingenious of the South Carolina Patriots—Francis Marion, Thomas Sumter, and Andrew Pickens—continued to elude and resist Lord Cornwallis's army.

The correspondence between Beaufort Patriot Daniel DeSaussure and his uncle Cesar DeSaussure in Switzerland during the Revolution reveals the steadfastness of some of the Beaufort Patriots to the cause of liberty. Cesar wrote to his nephew in Philadelphia in 1781 reflecting the sad news from America. The firm of DeSaussure and Poyas had all of its Charleston property confiscated by the British, the Beaufort store had been seized and turned over to Tory merchant Zephaniah Kingsley, and the original DeSaussure family property at Coosawhatchie had been destroyed by Prevost's army in 1779. DeSaussure's partner, James Poyas, had lost three brothers and his young daughter during the war. Daniel DeSaussure's only son was a prisoner aboard the *Pack-Horse,* and his wife, Mary McPherson, had been forced to beg relief from the British occupiers to get herself and her three young daughters to Philadelphia to reunite the family. "Mon Dieu," wrote Cesar DeSaussure, "Voila les fruits de la guerre." Despite these crushing personal hardships, Daniel DeSaussure wrote to Switzerland of the great victory at Yorktown and the buoyant mood of the South Carolinians in Philadelphia, to which his uncle replied "that's what you said after Saratoga." Cesar could not comprehend his American nephew's optimism. "All these losses and you are happy?" he wrote, "You are a fanatic American."[60]

FORT BALFOUR AND WILLIAM HARDEN

With the fall of Charleston in May and the disastrous defeat of the Continental Army under General Horatio Gates at Camden on August 16, 1780, the new British commander, Lord Cornwallis, proceeded northward accompanied by the bulk of the king's army. South Carolina was secured by a string of posts from Georgetown to Augusta. The key to the British occupation of the backcountry was the heavily fortified post at Ninety-Six. Between these posts, communications and supply lines were maintained by the cavalry of Lieutenant Colonel Banastre Tarleton's British Legion.[61] Behind this extended line, strong garrisons were left in Charleston and Savannah. The Beaufort District was in the heart of this occupied territory. In order to maintain control of the Beaufort District and protect communications on the King's Highway between Savannah and Charleston, an earth and palisade fort was built on high ground between the Coosawhatchie and Pocotaligo Bridges: the strategic crossroads of the southern parishes. This fort was named for the commander of the British garrison at Charleston during the fall of 1780, Lieutenant Colonel Nisbet Balfour, one of the most disliked British officers in South Carolina.[62]

Fort Balfour was garrisoned by the Granville County Loyalist regiment commanded by Colonel Nicholas Lechmere, son-in-law of John Barnwell Sr. Second in command was Lieutenant Colonel William Kelsal of St. Helena Island. Major Andrew DeVeaux IV, Colonel Lechmere's nephew, served in the garrison. Occasionally this regiment was joined by units from Colleton County commanded by Colonel Fenwick. The Beaufort District remained in peaceful occupation throughout the fall and winter months of 1780 and 1781.

With the fall of Charleston, several American partisan commanders began to organize scattered resistance fighters into effective guerrilla bands in the South Carolina backcountry. Andrew Pickens in the piedmont, Thomas Sumter in the midlands, and Francis Marion in the lowcountry led these small forces. Among those officers who escaped the surrender of Charleston to join Francis Marion on the Pee Dee River was William Harden of Prince William Parish. Harden had been a captain in the colonial Granville County militia under Stephen Bull. In 1776, he was made captain of the Beaufort artillery company and commanded Fort Lyttelton until April 1777. Harden was promoted to colonel in the South Carolina Militia and, in 1781, began to plan a campaign to disrupt the British occupation of the Beaufort District with Marion.[63]

By March 21, 1781, Harden had been detached from Marion's brigade with a force of more than one hundred men. He crossed the Edisto River at Givhan's Ferry and established a post at Godfrey's Savannah near the Ashepoo River, severing communications between Charleston and Fort Balfour.[64] There he reported to Marion on April 7 that he had stopped several supply vessels on the Combahee River and that he had been able to keep the road "from Purrysburg to Pon Pon clear." Harden had hoped to join with one or two hundred more volunteers from the Edisto region but their colonel, Isaac Hayne, balked at breaking his parole, and Harden had to proceed alone with his small force.

Harden's rangers skirmished with a force of 160 regulars near Parker's Ferry and then retreated southward. On April 7, a detachment of Harden's men under Major Cooper captured Barton's Post in Colleton County, with a Tory captain and six men, after a sharp fight. That night they crossed the Salkehatchie Bridge into the Beaufort District. The garrison at Fort Balfour sent Colonel Fenwick and a corps of mounted dragoons up the Pocotaligo Road to stop Harden's approach. On April 8, Harden laid an ambush along the road for the Tory party. When Harden's partisans opened fire, the Tory horsemen charged their position and sent them scattering through the woods. One of Harden's men was killed, seven were wounded, and two were taken prisoner. Thinking himself safe, Fenwick failed to pursue his advantage and retired to Fort Balfour.[65]

Colonel Harden was able to regroup his small command and, on the night of April 13, his men were positioned within sight of Fort Balfour. Harden sent ten of his best men to draw out the garrison. Just at that moment, however, the two senior Tory commanders, Colonel Fenwick and Colonel Lechmere, were visiting the wounded at Van Bibber's Tavern across the bridge on the east side of the Pocotaligo River. Harden's men surprised them and took them prisoner along with seven soldiers of the garrison. On April 14, Harden then sent word to Lieutenant Colonel Kelsal and Major Andrew DeVeaux, both old acquaintances from the Beaufort area, that they could either surrender the fort or expect no quarter. Harden kept many of his men with the supply wagons in the woods to make it appear as if he had a large force in reserve, which of course, he did not. Paul Hamilton, one of Harden's cavalry, later to be governor of South Carolina and U.S. secretary of the navy, accompanied Colonel Harden's brother to parlay with Lieutenant Colonel Kelsal's second in command, Major Andrew DeVeaux. At first DeVeaux refused to surrender, but Hamilton and some of the American party exchanged nods and signals with numerous friends recognized among the garrison. Hamilton reported some confusion in the fort, and finally Kelsal and DeVeaux surrendered. Ninety-two Tory soldiers marched out and laid down their arms. Harden's small army marched in and found Fort Balfour well stocked with arms, provisions, and a six-pound field piece. The ruse had worked.[66] Word reached Harden that day that a force of 170 British regulars of the Seventy-first Regiment was on the march from Charleston to relieve Fort Balfour. Harden spent the night and the next day destroying the palisade, barracks, and storehouses at the fort. Then he paroled his Tory prisoners and disappeared into the Coosawhatchie Swamp.

Harden's campaign of April 1781, like Marion's, was a bold stroke. In one week he had broken behind the British lines, disrupted their main line of communication to the south; destroyed the principal post in the Beaufort District; and killed, wounded, or captured as many of the British forces as he had in his own small command. After destroying Fort Balfour, Harden moved toward Augusta in order to join forces with General Andrew Pickens. The British commander at Augusta, Tory colonel Thomas Browne of the infamous East Florida Rangers, led a strong force across the Savannah River to destroy Harden's army. They met at Wiggin's Hill in Barnwell County. Despite the initial advantage of surprise, Harden's forces were routed and eighteen of his men, nearly 20 percent of his forces, were killed or captured. Harden then fled to an island hidden in the Coosawhatchie Swamp. There he tended the wounded and sent out small parties to reconnoiter the enemy. For months, though, they were too weak to risk another foray.

By the end of July 1781, both Marion and Sumter had inflicted severe damage behind British lines, General Nathanael Greene's Continental Army was beginning to take command of the South Carolina backcountry, and Lord Cornwallis's British army was well along on its fateful march to Yorktown. Harden then emerged from his Coosawhatchie Swamp hideout to form a juncture with lowcountry partisans at Horse Shoe Savannah on the Edisto River. There he met Colonel Isaac Hayne and began the chain of events which led to Hayne's capture at Parker's Ferry and execution in Charleston on August 4, 1781. Colonel William Harden's letter was the first word that General Greene received of that famous event.[67]

Harden then kept his mounted patrols beyond the Edisto River. Early in August he was attacked near the forks of the Edisto River by Tory Captain Connaway from Orangeburg, and eighteen of his men were killed. When he moved further into the lowcountry, Harden found a strong detachment of four hundred Tories from Charleston pressing through the country to finish off his battered force. Harden sent an urgent request for assistance to Francis Marion, who responded with a daring enterprise that helped make him one of America's greatest Revolutionary heroes. He sent a decoying force against the British post at Monck's Corner while he led two hundred picked horsemen on a hundred-mile dash around Charleston and across the Edisto River. Marion's and Harden's forces ambushed the British and Tory detachment under Major Thomas Fraser on the causeway at Parker's Ferry. Thinking he was opposing only Harden's small band, Fraser pressed his men down the causeway into a murderous crossfire from the Edisto Swamp. Marion retreated before he could count the casualties, but the Americans reported men and horses lying in heaps along the causeway. Marion returned north of Charleston, leaving Harden again to watch and elude the superior British and Tory forces between Savannah and Charleston.[68]

August 1, 1781, also saw the return to South Carolina of Governor John Rutledge, the nominal commander-in-chief of the scattered partisan units in the state. Establishing himself near General Greene's Continental Army, Rutledge set about with great energy during the fall of 1781 to re-establish civil government in South Carolina and reorganize the state militia. Among the directives for reorganizing the militia forces in September 1781 was the creation of a new brigade to cover the territory between Savannah and Charleston. Rutledge considered this region too remote to be effectively commanded by Brigadier General Francis Marion, Colonel Harden's immediate superior. When the new brigade was formed, Harden had every right to expect a promotion to brigadier general and command of the region he had operated in for most of the year. Instead he was passed over in favor of John Barnwell of Beaufort, who had outranked Harden at the time of the fall of Charleston and who was considered by Rutledge and General Greene as more capable of bringing organization and discipline to the violent and sometimes lawless partisan bands. In November 1781, Harden resigned in disgust.[69]

Whatever the merits of controlling the partisans and re-establishing civil order, the actions of Governor Rutledge and the attitude of General Greene in the fall of 1781 offended most of the militia volunteers, including Marion, and caused the resignation of the popular General Thomas Sumter, "the Gamecock," as well as Colonel Harden. South Carolina lost the services of the Beaufort District's only effective guerrilla commander.

Rutledge's appointment of Barnwell over Harden was a mistake. The troops who had been serving under Harden refused the orders of the new commander. Faced with a virtual mutiny, Barnwell resigned. During 1782, the defense of the Beaufort District depended on detachments of Greene's Continental Army camped at Round-O on the Edisto River and on scattered bands of local volunteers. Two years later, Barnwell wrote to Governor Benjamin Guerard accusing the men of the militia of "personal prejudice" against him and "an invincible aversion to duty." Alexander Garden remarked, "I have always considered it a misfortune that his strictness in command rendered him so unpopular with his brigade." Barnwell's method of discipline was "too suddenly applied and too imperious."[70]

More may have been at stake here than personality or style. Most of the men of Harden's tough and courageous band were backcountry farmers disinclined to any form of regimentation. Other than Paul Hamilton, few sons of the coastal planters served among them. And Hamilton, though loyal, was critical of Harden and referred to him as "an indifferent commander."[71] The men harbored political and social resentments which preceded the Revolution. The controversies surrounding the Circuit Court Act of 1769 and the location of the Beaufort District Court House in Beaufort in 1772, highlighted the prewar differences between the mainland farmers and the sea island planters. The appointment of Barnwell as brigade commander for the Beaufort District was no doubt seen as an attempt to re-establish the prewar political supremacy of the coastal planters. Harden and his men naturally resented both the personal affront and its political implications.

JACKSONBOROUGH ASSEMBLY

When British forces evacuated Beaufort in November 1781, it was Captain Robert Barnwell of the Beaufort militia who accepted the surrender.[72] But all was not well in the district. The British were still encamped in nearby Savannah, and many prominent citizens of the Beaufort District had so committed themselves to the British cause that they could not now abandon it. A period of guerrilla raids, murders, and retaliations plagued the district until the bitter end of the Revolutionary War.

The first General Assembly following the fall of Charleston was held in Jacksonborough on the Edisto River in St. Bartholomew's Parish on January 18, 1782. The Jacksonborough Assembly has been a source of controversy for two hundred years. The members were chosen in the fall of 1781 at the height of the destruction and hatred engendered by three years of damaging campaigns and humiliating occupation. When the representatives gathered on the banks of the Edisto River they were not in a compromising mood. Their vindictive actions against their Loyalist neighbors perhaps forced the violent reactions of some Tory partisans late in the war.

The Jacksonborough Assembly was barely able to form a quorum when it gathered for business. After Christopher Gadsden declined to serve as governor, the members elected John Matthews and set about to pass laws to reorganize the fiscal chaos of the state and raise funds for the maintenance of the Continental Army. Then they punished the Loyalists. The famous Act of 1782 confiscated the property of active Tories and partially confiscated the estates of many others who sought the protection of the British army or failed to aid the American cause. These Loyalists were banished from the state, but their families were allowed to petition for temporary support and were allowed to petition for return. In addition to real estate, the principal property confiscated was slaves. Four hundred and forty slaves were to be designated for the logistical and camp service of the Continental Army at Round-O, and most of the rest were to be used as bounty payments for the Continental enlistees.[73] This act included not only active Tories but many citizens who were simply caught by the shifting tide of war. Many patriotic citizens of the areas around Charleston and Beaufort, long occupied by the British army, spoke eloquently against the injustice of this act and in defense of their less stalwart neighbors. Gadsden was the most famous of these. General John Barnwell of Beaufort was one of the most eloquent. As a senator in 1780, Barnwell had urged a conciliatory attitude to those militiamen from Beaufort who had abandoned the field in the face of Prevost's invasion of 1779. After a shouting match with Thomas Ferguson, Barnwell remonstrated his angry colleagues, saying, "The danger which drove the unfortunates, in whose behalf I would plead for mercy, has never been brought to your own doors. Remember, when it does reach you, that you swerve not from your duty nor forget the opinions you now support. From you, Gentlemen, I shall on every future occasion, look for unshaken firmness and exemplary intrepidity."[74] At the close of the Revolution and in the years after the war, Barnwell continued to support a liberal attitude toward most of those sea island planters who had been accused of Loyalism.

Barnwell, however, was not elected as either a senator or a representative from any of the southern parishes to the Jacksonborough Assembly. It was the only session of the General Assembly between 1775 and 1788 that he did not serve in some capacity, despite being the man charged by Governor Rutledge to issue the writs of election for the sea islands in 1781.[75] William Harden was elected senator for Prince William Parish along with Major William Davis, Dr. Aaron Gillet, Thomas Hutson, John McPherson, Captain Andrew Postell, and James Smith as representatives. St. Peter's Parish elected Cornelius DuPont as senator and Thomas Cater, Charles DuPont, James Moore, William Stafford, and Colonel James Thompson as representatives. St. Helena Parish elected Benjamin Guerard as senator and Pierce Butler, Jacob Guerard, Thomas Heyward, John Kean, and Charles C. Pinckney as representatives.[76] The delegation from St. Helena Parish was extremely interesting. Not one of that delegation, with the possible exception of Kean, had his principal property interests on Port Royal or St. Helena Island. All of these men were from the Euhaws section of St. Helena Parish, which had been St. Luke's Parish until the royal disallowance of the act establishing that separate district in 1772 and was soon to become St. Luke's Parish again and remain so until after the Civil War. St. Luke's Parish, or the Euhaws district, was the original home of both Thomas Heyward Jr. and Daniel DeSaussure, the most ardently patriotic neighborhood in the Beaufort District.

The other piece of legislation passed by the Jacksonborough Assembly of significance to the Beaufort District was the moving of the Beaufort District Courthouse to Coosawhatchie on the mainland.[77] This placed the judicial capital in the geographic center of the district at the headwaters of Port Royal Sound and at the strategic crossroads of the southern parishes. This move resolved the longstanding complaints of the mainland planters about the inaccessibility of the courthouse on Port Royal Island. It was also a political stroke by the mainland farmers, no doubt led by Colonel Harden of Prince William Parish, against the entrenched interests of the original sea island planters, whose principal spokesperson, General John Barnwell, was conspicuously absent.

SKIRMISHES AND REPRISALS

In January 1782, General Washington sent General Anthony Wayne to Georgia to assume command of Continental forces there and drive the British from Savannah. General Barnwell was ordered by Nathanael Greene to mobilize the Beaufort Brigade of militia and assist Wayne in liberating Georgia. The Beaufort Brigade, however, refused to serve under Barnwell, and the only assistance Wayne received from the Beaufort District was a few volunteers. Though General Wayne did not have enough troops to attack the British garrison of one thousand men at Savannah, he was able to control the hinterland and cut off the outlying posts, particularly at Ebenezer on the Savannah River opposite Purrysburg, where many of the Hessian troops serving for the British were induced to desert to the Americans. By midsummer, the British command at New York had decided to abandon Savannah and concentrate its forces in Charleston and St. Augustine. By July 11, British forces had evacuated Savannah; by July 21, they had disembarked from Tybee Island; and by July 31, Colonel Thomas Browne and his East Florida Rangers, the last of the Tory resistance, finally crossed the St. Mary's River on their overland trek to St. Augustine.[78]

British forces were then concentrated in Charleston, where they were closely guarded by General Greene's army headquartered on the Sanders's plantation at Round-O. The Beaufort District, without British or Continental occupying troops to maintain order and with no functioning militia to enforce the restoration of civil government, became the scene of numerous acts of plunder, murder, and revenge between Patriot and Tory partisans. Dr. Joseph Johnson recalled that "The southern part of South Carolina had . . . many records of vindictive murders, committed in the name of patriotism and . . . supposed by their deluded perpetrators to be justifiable."[79]

Late in the war, Tory partisans from the Beaufort District tended to gather on Daufuskie Island, where they were protected from partisan bands on the mainland and were within comfortable distance of the British garrisons at Savannah and Tybee Island. Neighboring Hilton Head Island became a patriot stronghold probably because of the destruction and plunder caused there by Gardner's and Prevost's incursions of 1779. The patriots on Hilton Head harassed the Tories on Daufuskie Island, which they nicknamed "Little Bermuda" because of its staunch loyalism. Late in 1781, the British were provoked into retaliating.[80] About the time Beaufort was being evacuated in November 1781, British Major Maxwell and Tory Captain Philip Martinangele of Daufuskie Island led a raiding party to Hilton Head which burned several homes and laid an ambush for the patriots at "Two Oaks plantation near the head of Broad Creek." Charles Davant, son of a prominent family of patriots on Hilton Head Island, was killed. This raid was avenged by Captain John Leacraft and the Hilton Head company of patriots known as the "Bloody Legion." In late December they crossed to Daufuskie Island and surprised Martinangele at his home. While two patriots held his wife, a third shot and killed him.[81]

These ambushes instigated the incident in 1782 which cost the life of one of the earliest and staunchest patriot commanders in the Beaufort District. Captain James Doharty, who lived on Bear Island adjoining the mainland opposite Pinckney Island (probably Buckingham Landing), had been a member of the first local Committee of Correspondence for the Revolutionary Party in the Beaufort District and was the commander of the perilous post at Fort Lyttelton from March to June of 1779. He eluded the British army in 1780 and served with William Harden's partisans in 1781. Doharty's neighbor, Richard Pendarvis, was a resolute Tory, and a "bitter and deadly hatred arose between them." Doharty received warning that Pendarvis and a gang of Tories was proceeding to murder him. With Doharty were his nephews: Captain John Leacraft of Hilton Head; his fourteen-year-old brother, William Leacraft; and Thomas Talbird of Hilton Head, whose plantation on Broad Creek was likely one of those recently destroyed by Maxwell and Martinangele. Pendarvis arrived at Doharty's home just as they were leaving. Doharty yelled to his nephews to run and was then shot down. As he lay wounded, a second volley killed him. William Leacraft was captured and tortured, but refused to disclose the whereabouts of John Leacraft and Thomas Talbird. He was later released. Doharty was buried with honors at Whale Branch on Port Royal Island. Later that year, as Pendarvis was evacuating his plantation to move with the other Tories to St. Augustine, he and his Tory associate, Patterson, were both killed by Captain John Leacraft.[82]

In February 1782, General John Barnwell was order by General Anthony Wayne to move the Beaufort regiment against a large quantity of rice stored on Hutchinson Island opposite Savannah to prevent its being used by the British. Barnwell gathered several boats at Beaufort for the purpose, but before he could embark the boats were destroyed by Major Andrew DeVeaux, who had appeared before the town with a Tory naval force. Barnwell's brother, Colonel Edward Barnwell, did lead elements of the Beaufort District militia against Hutchinson Island, but their plan was betrayed to the British, and a sharp exchange of fire killed five or six militiamen and forced Edward Barnwell to retreat.[83]

Major DeVeaux became the leading Tory partisan in the lowcountry at the close of the Revolution. He had served the occupying British army in a number of valuable capacities, principally as a pilot and guide among the sea islands and, though only twenty-four years old, as a major with command of the "Royal foresters," as the Granville County Loyalist Regiment of Militia was known. During 1782, his knowledge of the inland passages of the sea islands made him particularly useful to the British on their foraging expeditions to supply the garrison and Tory refugees in Charleston. DeVeaux had in 1779 destroyed General Stephen Bull's Sheldon plantation and burned the Prince William Parish Church in order to confirm his band of Tories in their allegiance. His cousin, Robert Barnwell, once captured DeVeaux in 1780 before the fall of Charleston, but DeVeaux talked Barnwell into giving him a parole, whereupon DeVeaux forced four blacks to row him across Charleston harbor to the British army on James Island. Thereafter, DeVeaux particularly harassed Barnwell, engendering the special hatred of Robert, who swore to kill him if he returned to South Carolina after the war.[84]

At the end of February 1782, DeVeaux and his Tory followers set out from the Stono River aboard two galleys, the *Scourge* and the *Adder,* and one sloop.

This flotilla anchored at Beaufort on March 4 with the twofold purpose of gathering provisions for the British and recapturing Loyalist property on Port Royal, Lady's Island, and St. Helena Island. DeVeaux and his Tory force effectively occupied Beaufort for the next three weeks and prevented General Barnwell from being of any help to General Anthony Wayne in Georgia. While in Beaufort, DeVeaux recaptured a British schooner and attempted to carry off an American vessel hidden in Caper's Creek. During this effort they were fired on by some patriot militiamen on St. Helena Island. Three militiamen were wounded, but DeVeaux was unable to carry off his prize. It was probably on this expedition that DeVeaux carried from the plantation of James Reynolds on St. Helena Island sixty-one slaves, which he eventually took to East Florida and then to the Bahama Islands. One of these slaves, a cooper named Carolina, was later freed by a British court in Nassau for his service to the king's forces.[85]

In order to prevent the British and Tory forces from plundering the plantations of the Beaufort and Colleton Districts, General Nathanael Greene dispatched General Mordecai Gist with a unit of Continental cavalry under Colonel George Baylor and a unit of Continental light infantry under Lieutenant Colonel John Laurens. When Gist's corps reached the Combahee Ferry, they found a strong force of three hundred British regulars and two hundred Tory partisans with eighteen vessels, including the armed galleys *Balfour* and *Shark*, already on the Combahee River. Gist sent a detachment across the Combahee Ferry to drive off the plunderers on the Beaufort side of the river. Then he sent Laurens down the Chehaw Neck to Tar Bluff at the mouth of the Combahee River. The British vessels had to pass under this commanding bluff before escaping into St. Helena Sound and returning to Charleston. At Tar Bluff, Laurens threw up a hasty earthwork and staffed it with his small force of fifty men and one howitzer. The American artillery men were so effective with the howitzer that the British flotilla was stopped. Major Brereton then landed a party of 130 to 140 men to dislodge the Americans from their strategic position. Laurens fell back, but unwisely decided to engage the much larger British force before General Gist's reinforcements could reach him. Laurens and several of his command were killed, and the British force escaped.

Rather than return to Charleston, however, Major Brereton and his flotilla went up St. Helena Sound and into the Coosaw River. General Gist crossed into the Beaufort District on September 2 and established an artillery post at the Port Royal Ferry. The American artillery drove off the British galleys, one of which, the *Balfour*, was abandoned by the British and captured by the Americans with its cargo of provisions and two nine-pound cannons.[86] This was the last major action of the Revolutionary War in the Beaufort District. Sporadic fighting occurred between Patriots and Tories, particularly around the Salkehatchie Swamp in the extreme northern corner of the Beaufort District. Here Tory parties led by Captains Oldfield, Jones, and Chesire continued to pillage the region during the spring and into the fall of 1782. Occasional skirmishes continued around Charleston, but by December 14, 1782, the British garrison had evacuated Charleston and the Revolutionary War in South Carolina was over.

THE FATE OF PROMINENT TORIES

The American Revolution forced the departure from the Beaufort District of some of the most prominent merchants and landowners in the southern corner of the state. Royal officials Lieutenant Governor William Bull and Colonel John Stuart had two of the most valuable indigo plantations on the sea islands around Beaufort, but both were seized. Merchants Henry Stuart and Charles Shaw, both associated with Colonel John Stuart, were also forced out. Neither Peter Lavien nor Zephaniah Kingsley ever returned to their thriving Bay Street mercantile establishments. St. Helena planter and Beaufort merchant William Bellinger Kelsal followed his arch-Tory brother, Colonel Roger Kelsal, to the Bahama Islands. Dr. James Fraser of Port Royal Island lost his professional practice and considerable property before returning thirteen years later. And the saga of Beaufort's most famous Tories, Andrew DeVeaux Sr. and Andrew DeVeaux Jr., is one of the most fascinating stories of the Revolution.

When Lieutenant Governor William Bull Jr. left the province in 1777, he left behind some of the most valuable property in the district. He had 3,871 acres in the southern parishes with the largest, and most valuable, tract being the thirty-three-hundred-acre Frogmore Plantation stretching across the center of St. Helena Island. Bull was one of the wealthiest men in America at the time of his departure, and his estate in South Carolina alone was valued at 51,554 pounds sterling or approximately 360,000 pounds in South Carolina currency. He also had estates in Georgia and Jamaica. The disposition of this estate became a matter of controversy for years after the Revolution and cast some doubt on the character and motivation of the point man for the Revolution in the Beaufort District, William Bull's nephew, General Stephen Bull of Sheldon.[87]

Upon leaving the province in 1777, William Bull had, through his lawyers in Charleston, agreed to a "confidential conveyance" of his vast estate to someone he could trust completely "for the purpose of saving it from the gulf of the province treasury." A price of twenty-three thousand pounds sterling was agreed on, approximately half the value of the estate. Stephen Bull was captured and paroled by the British upon the fall of Charleston in 1780 and performed no further military duties for the state. He and his family lived in exile in Virginia and Maryland until the war was over, and his old command was given to General John Barnwell. After the Revolution, Stephen Bull was reported to have used his influence in the South Carolina Senate to "uniformly oppose any motion for his uncle's return to his native country." William Bull's attorney, Robert Williams, testified that Stephen Bull's entire conduct was "actuated by self-interested views" and that his behavior was "extremely dishonorable."[88]

This was not the first trouble with Stephen Bull's personality. Captain John Joyner, who had captured the gunpowder off Tybee in 1775 with John Barnwell, reported Bull's hoarding of the powder at Sheldon to the Council of Safety. When the council confronted Bull, he attacked Joyner, calling him "a man of no influence."[89]

In 1776, General Charles Lee ordered some Continental forces under Colonel Isaac Huger to Fort Lyttelton to guard Port Royal against possible naval attack. Thinking himself superseded in command of the district, Bull wrote to his friends on the council that he considered the order "insulting to his rank." The council then required General Lee to give "formal evidence" of the necessity of the order. Lee was naturally irritated by this political interference. He told the council he thought his "word would have been sufficient to justify a military order."[90] Stephen Bull's haughty character may have explained the particular animosity toward him exhibited by Andrew DeVeaux Jr. and his gang of Beaufort Tories.

Stephen Bull's attempt to gain control of his uncle's vast estate in South Carolina failed. In his will of 1791, William Bull divided his estate among his other nieces and nephews. Stephen's half-brother, William Bull, who took no part in the Revolution at his uncle's request, inherited the principal estate of Ashley Hall. William Bull's wife's niece, Catherine Beale Stapleton, inherited the valuable Frogmore Plantation on St. Helena Island.

After Colonel John Stuart escaped from Lady's Island in 1775, he made his way to Florida. His wife, Sarah, followed him later that year. Stuart died in Pensacola in 1779, and his large estate in South Carolina, which had been seized in 1775, was confiscated by the Act of 1782. Sarah Stuart returned to London after the Revolution and on behalf of her son, Lieutenant John Stuart of the Third Foot Guards, and her daughter, Christiana Stuart Fenwicke of South Carolina, submitted a claim for 17,765 pounds sterling or approximately 124,355 pounds South Carolina currency. The most valuable Stuart property in South Carolina was the eighteen-hundred-acre "settled indigo plantation" on Lady's Island and adjoining Maple Cane Island.[91] This plantation was worked by 175 slaves and, in 1777, produced a crop of 3,800 pounds of processed indigo. The manager of this large and productive plantation was Charles Shaw. Shaw had followed his brother William Shaw, the mercantile partner of Henry Stuart, to Beaufort in the 1760s. William Shaw accidentally drowned while swimming in the Beaufort River in 1769, and Charles Shaw assumed many of his brother's responsibilities.[92] He became prominent in Beaufort before the war, serving several times as church warden at St. Helena. Early in the Revolution, Shaw was imprisoned for smuggling supplies to the British troops in East Florida, and in 1777 he was banished from South Carolina for refusing to take the oath of allegiance.[93] Shaw made his way to Pensacola where he assisted Colonel John Stuart in his efforts to maintain the Indians' loyalty to the crown. After John Stuart's death in 1779, Shaw served the British in various capacities during the occupation of Charleston and went to England after the evacuation.

Henry Stuart also followed Colonel John Stuart into exile. Henry Stuart had come to Beaufort in 1766 in order to manage the large mercantile establishment of Francis Stuart after his death in that year. The family business, at the corner of Bay and Carteret Streets, was beset by many problems: large debts to John Stuart and other Charleston merchants, heavy competition from the new Beaufort merchants, "some disagreement" with the large Middleton establishment next door, and the untimely death of his partner, William Shaw, in 1769.[94] Nevertheless, the firm grew on the rising prosperity of indigo production until the Revolution interrupted their trade. Henry Stuart followed his brother John to Florida in 1777, and the family store was confiscated in 1782. Henry Stuart served the British in Florida and South Carolina and died in London after the Revolution. His nephew, Dr. James Stuart, son of Francis Stuart and Ann Reeve, took the American side in the war.[95]

One of the most intriguing of the Beaufort Tories was merchant Peter Lavien. Lavien moved to Beaufort in 1765 from the island of St. Croix in the West Indies, where his father had been the wealthiest merchant in Christiansted. In Beaufort, Lavien formed a partnership with Charleston merchant and West Indies sea captain Samuel Grove. The firm prospered, and, at the beginning of the Revolution, Lavien and Grove were considered the largest indigo shippers in the Beaufort District. Lavien became prominent in Beaufort and was selected for the vestry of St. Helena Parish despite the fact that his father, John Lavien, was one of the most prominent Jewish merchants and planters in the Danish West Indies. The Revolution disrupted the firm's trade and Lavien's partner died at sea in 1775. Lavien then became Beaufort's most prominent smuggler early in the Revolutionary War. Family and business connections, and political hostility, forced Lavien to move to Savannah in 1777. There he lived with his daughter, Joanna, and his son-in-law, John Charles Lucena, until his death in 1781. Lavien had left his Beaufort property in the hands of his former partner's stepson, John Kean, who was a consistent patriot and a member of Beaufort's local committee. Lavien's will divided his large estate between the Lucenas of Savannah and John Kean of Beaufort. The Lucenas remained loyal to the crown, and most of their Georgia property was confiscated; Kean served as deputy paymaster of the South Carolina militia, along with John Mark Verdier. Both served under Daniel DeSaussure, who was paymaster general of the South Carolina Militia.[96]

Lavien's estate was large enough to arrange an appointment for John Charles Lucena at the Portuguese Consulate in London after the Revolution and help launch John Kean's career as a nationally prominent politician in the 1780s and 1790s. Kean was Beaufort's first congressman (1784–1787). While in Philadelphia, he married wealthy Susan Livingston of New York. Lavien's will also left a considerable bequest to his illegitimate half-brother, Alexander Hamilton of New York, a famous patriot and one of the founders of the new nation.

The largest merchant in Beaufort during the British occupation was Zephaniah Kingsley. Kingsley was a merchant in Charleston before the Revolution, but had never cooperated with the Non-Intercourse Association. Kingsley acquired two plantations in the Beaufort District before the war and moved to Beaufort as a merchant in 1780. He acquired the Bay Street store of Daniel DeSaussure, then imprisoned in St. Augustine. This establishment had been built on the corner of Bay and Scott Streets by longtime Beaufort merchant Jean DeLaGaye, who sold it to Daniel DeSaussure in 1772. On the property were two houses facing Bay Street, one a dwelling house and the other a dry-goods store. In the back were a kitchen, dairy, wash house, smokehouse, coach house, and stable "all built of tabby." Across Bay Street by the Beaufort River was a storehouse capable of holding one hundred barrels of rice. This property was confiscated by the Act of 1782, and Kingsley was banished from South Carolina.[97] In 1783, John Mark Verdier bought the property and reopened it after the war as the Beaufort branch of the large Charleston firm of Smiths, DeSaussure, and Darrell.[98] About 1800, he demolished Jean DeLaGaye's original house and rebuilt the federal-style home now housing the museum of the Historic Beaufort Foundation. Kingsley left South Carolina for St. John's, Nova Scotia, and then acquired lands and established a plantation on Fort George Island in East Florida. In the early nineteenth century, his son and namesake became notorious for marrying one of his slaves and publishing articles recommending the mixing of the races.[99]

William Bellinger Kelsal was another prominent sea island planter and merchant who was forced to leave Beaufort because of political hostility. Kelsal was a planter and merchant on St. Helena Island before the Revolution. He was an officer in the St. Helena Company of Militia and a warden of St. Helena Church. In 1772, he married Elizabeth DeSaussure, sister of Daniel DeSaussure.[100] During the Revolution, he served in the Tory Militia of the Beaufort District and negotiated the peaceful surrender of Fort Balfour to William Harden. Kelsal was not banished by the Act of 1782, but in 1783 he was singled out by the grand jury of the Beaufort District for his "infamous and violent practices to the good citizens of the District during the late war."[101] In 1788, Kelsal left Beaufort with his entire family aboard the schooner *Eliza* and sailed for the plantation of his brother, Colonel Roger Kelsal, on Little Exuma in the Bahama Islands.

The brothers were the sons of John Kelsal and Mary Bellinger and grand-sons of Landgrave Edmund Bellinger. Roger Kelsal had moved from Beaufort to Georgia in the 1760s and became a successful merchant in Sunbury and St. Mary's. He was a Tory and colonel of the Sunbury Regiment of Loyalist Militia. Banished from Georgia, he established a plantation on Little Exuma in 1784.[102] Colonel Roger Kelsal may have been the first successful planter of long-staple, black seed cotton on the Bahama Islands and as such the forerunner of the cotton revolution in North America. He died in England in 1788 still "cursing the Revolution." William Kelsal operated the Little Exuma cotton plantation until his death in 1791. In his will, Kelsal listed his brother-in-law, Daniel DeSaussure, as executor of his Charleston property and DeSaussure's junior partner, John Mark Verdier, as executor of his Beaufort property.[103]

Another prominent Beaufort Tory was Dr. James Fraser. He was one of the few medical doctors in the Beaufort District before the war and was elected warden and vestryman of St. Helena Church from 1773 to 1777.[104] In 1776, he was selected for the local committee of safety. At the outbreak of hostilities, Fraser administered to the local militia despite "being suspected of Toryism." Fraser never took the oath of allegiance but was not banished because he was the only medical doctor in the community. With the arrival of British forces in 1779, Fraser gladly offered his services and was employed in several capacities by the occupation forces until they evacuated Charleston in 1782. He went to St. John's, Nova Scotia, and from there migrated to England. He lost considerable property including a 350-acre indigo plantation on Port Royal Island by the Act of 1782.[105] In 1798, Fraser was allowed to return to Beaufort largely due to a petition signed by most of the leading planter families of St. Helena Island.[106]

No story of the American Revolution in the Beaufort District is more romantic and exciting than that of Major Andrew DeVeaux Jr. (1758–1812). DeVeaux's father, Andrew DeVeaux Sr., was born in 1735 in Prince William Parish.[107] He was the grandson of both Yemassee Indian fighter Colonel John Palmer, who was killed at the siege of St. Augustine in 1740, and the indigo innovator, Andrew DeVeaux of St. Paul's Parish. In 1757, Andrew Sr. married Catherine Barnwell, daughter of John Barnwell Sr. and granddaughter of "Tuscarora Jack." Their eldest son, Andrew DeVeaux Jr., was born April 30, 1758. The DeVeaux family of colonial Beaufort was related to most of the important families of the colonial sea islands. Andrew Jr.'s sisters married into the Lechmere, Ashe, and Seabrook families, and his cousins were Barnwells, Heywards, and Bulls. Andrew Sr. was a prosperous and successful planter on Port Royal Island before the Revolution. He owned 4,725 acres in the Beaufort District, including rice plantations on the Coosawhatchie and Tullifinny Rivers and a large livestock ranch on Port Royal Island. In the 1760s, Andrew Sr. built a large town house in Beaufort with four floors, twelve rooms, and eight fireplaces.[108] Here he raised his large family of four boys and four girls. Andrew Sr. had been one of the commissioners of the courthouse in Beaufort in 1769 and as such was probably one of the "influential gentlemen" from Beaufort who encouraged Lord Montagu's Assembly of 1772. Early in the Revolution, Andrew Sr.'s loyalist leanings were well known in Beaufort, and he was subjected to some abuse by the patriot supporters. His son, being a spirited teenager at the time, leapt to his father's defense and gathered about him a gang of "inconsiderate and frolicsome young men and embarrassed the proceedings of the Whigs whenever the opportunity occurred."[109] When the British forces arrived in 1779, Andrew DeVeaux Sr. tried to remain neutral, but his son and his Tory followers eagerly aided the invaders. Andrew Jr. proved useful to the British occupiers and rose to the rank of major in the Tory militia at the age of twenty-three. When the British evacuated Beaufort in November 1781, Andrew Sr. left for Charleston because of warnings that "his life was threatened by some personal enemies among the Americans." His estate was confiscated in 1782, and his son led the Tory expedition to Beaufort in March to carry off as much property as they could before it was seized by the Americans. Both father and son left Charleston in December 1782 for exile to St. Augustine.[110]

In St. Augustine in the spring of 1783, Andrew Jr. began to plan his most daring and famous expedition. He had first suggested going overland to capture Pensacola but this was discouraged by British authorities. Then he turned his attention to the Bahama Islands. Nassau had been captured from the British in 1782 by a combined Spanish and American naval force which included Commodore Alexander Gillon commanding the frigate *South Carolina.* Many of the British subjects had fled to Great Abaco Island. In the spring of 1783, DeVeaux, now a twenty-five-year-old lieutenant colonel, hatched a plan to recapture the islands for the British.[111]

In March 1783, DeVeaux assembled the seventy men who had served with him in South Carolina and outfitted six ships at his own expense. Two of the ships were the *Perseverance,* with twenty-six guns, and the *Whitby Warrior,* with sixteen guns. DeVeaux also enlisted some local volunteers, including a number of Seminole Indians, to round out his crew. He talked Colonel Browne, commander of the British garrison at St. Augustine, into giving him three hundred regular British army uniforms. Late in March, DeVeaux's flotilla left Florida and rendezvoused at Hole-in-the-Wall on Great Abaco Island. There DeVeaux gathered about 150 volunteers and a number of Bahamian fishing craft from the English population of the island. With this small fleet he sailed for Nassau. By dressing his volunteers as British Regulars and blocking Nassau Harbor with his fishing vessels, DeVeaux forced the surrender of six hundred Spanish troops and seventy cannons. Don Antonio, the Spanish governor, was imprisoned, and DeVeaux of Beaufort was made the de facto governor of the Bahamas from April to September 1783.[112]

This daring expedition opened the way for the British government to reward their southern Loyalist followers with land grants among the islands to make up for property confiscated in South Carolina and Georgia. One of the major grantees was Andrew Sr., who received 2,160 acres on Cat Island, Little Island Cay, Hyburn Cay, and a lot in Nassau. Andrew Sr. transported the slaves he had salvaged from South Carolina to his principal plantation of 1,380 acres on San Salvador (Cat Island), where he developed a thriving enterprise of long-staple cotton production. He gained a reputation as one of the Bahamas' "best planters and a model of industry and efficiency." Settling with him on San Salvador were two of his younger sons and three daughters. Andrew Sr. died in San Salvador on Christmas Eve, 1814, surrounded by his many children and grandchildren.[113] His eldest son, however, was far too restless for the sedentary life of a farmer. After capturing the Bahama Islands, Andrew Jr. traveled to London to submit his Loyalist claim to the British government. Fortified with the written support of Lord Cornwallis and a petition of gratitude from the citizens of the Bahamas, he garnered only 450 pounds sterling. Andrew Jr. was given one-half pay as an active lieutenant colonel in the British army and dazzled British society with his feats of horsemanship.[114] He traveled frequently between England and the Bahama Islands, where he was wounded in a duel with John Stiles in 1789. In 1797, he went to New York and there married wealthy heiress Anna Maria Verplanck. DeVeaux then settled with his wife and two daughters at Red Hook in Dutchess County, New York. A restless spirit plagued him, however, and he frequently fell into debt. In 1805, he asked his brother-in-law Philip Verplanck to help discharge his debts, describing himself as an "extravagant dog." In 1811, he advertised his Red Hook estate for sale along with its house with a ninety-foot brick front and a bas relief on the fireplace representing the fortifications at Nassau. On July 4, 1812, he fell from a piazza in New York City, struck his head on the stone walk below, and died of lockjaw seven days later.[115]

NOTES

1. Col. Archibald Campbell to Sir Henry Clinton, January 16, 1779 and March 9, 1779, Carleton Papers, microfilm at South Carolina Department of Archives and History; David Duncan Wallace, *The History of South Carolina*, 4 vols. (New York: American Historical Society, 1934), 2: 184; John Richard Alden, *The South in the Revolution, 1763–1783* (Baton Rouge: Louisiana State University Press, 1957), 235; Wilbur Henry Siebert, *Loyalists in East Florida, 1774–1785*, 2 vols. (Deland: Florida State Historical Society, 1929), 1: 71–80.

2. *South Carolina and American General Gazette*, February 3, 1779.

3. "Loyalist Claims," 57: 32–47, South Carolina Department of Archives and History.

4. *South Carolina and American General Gazette,* February 3, 1779.

5. William Moultrie, *Memoirs of the American Revolution,* 2 vols. (1802; rpt., 2 vols. in one, New York: New York Times, 1968), 1: 286–89.

6. Moultrie, *Memoirs,* 1: 290.

7. Moultrie, *Memoirs,* 1: 296.

8. Moultrie, *Memoirs,* 1: 292–93.

9. Moultrie, *Memoirs,* 1: 294.

10. Moultrie, *Memoirs,* 1: 294.

11. *South Carolina and American General Gazette,* March 10, 1779.

12. Stephen B. Barnwell, *The Story of an American Family* (Marquette, Mich.: Privately printed, 1969), 33.

13. *South Carolina and American General Gazette,* February 4, 1779; March 10, 1779.

14. *Royal Georgia Gazette,* February 11, 1779.

15. *South Carolina Gazette,* February 3, 1779; February 24, 1779.

16. Moultrie, *Memoirs,* 1: 305.

17. *South Carolina Gazette,* March 10, 1779; April 14, 1779.

18. Edward McCrady, *The History of South Carolina in the Revolution, 1775–1780* (1901; rpt., New York: Russell and Russell, 1969), 344; Henry Lumpkin, *Savannah to Yorktown: The American Revolution in the South* (Columbia: University of South Carolina Press, 1981), 30.

19. Campbell to Clinton, March 9, 1779, Carleton Papers, South Carolina Department of Archives and History.

20. Bull to Moultrie, February 12, 1779, *Memoirs,* 1: 313; Lincoln to Bull, March 9, 1779, Lincoln Papers, microfilm at South Carolina Department of Archives and History.

21. Gen. Augustine Prevost to Clinton, April 29, 1779, Carleton Papers, South Carolina Department of Archives and History.

22. McCrady, *South Carolina in the Revolution,* 352; Moultrie, *Memoirs,* 1: 402.

23. Wallace, *History of South Carolina,* 2: 188; Moultrie, *Memoirs,* 1: 393, 403.

24. Moultrie, *Memoirs,* 1: 405.

25. *South Carolina Gazette,* July 9, 1779.

26. Katherine M. Jones, ed., *Port Royal Under Six Flags* (Indianapolis: Bobbs-Merrill, 1960), 129–30.

27. *South Carolina Gazette,* July 9, 1779.

28. Lydia Austin Parrish, "Records of Some Southern Loyalists" (manuscript), Georgia Historical Society, 219–20; Joseph Johnson, *Traditions and Reminiscences of the American Revolution in the South* (1851; rpt., Spartanburg: Reprint Co., 1972), 176

29. Prevost to Clinton, May 21, 1779, Carleton Papers, South Carolina Department of Archives and History; McCrady, *South Carolina in the Revolution,* 359; Wallace, *History of South Carolina,* 2: 192.

30. Barnwell, *Story of an American Family,* 33; Joseph Johnson, *Traditions and Reminiscences,* 184–85; McCrady, *South Carolina in the Revolution,* 397.

31. McCrady, *South Carolina in the Revolution,* 388–92; Moultrie, *Memoirs,* 1: 491–93; Wallace, *History of South Carolina,* 2: 193.

32. Prevost to Clinton, June 10, 1779, Carleton Papers, South Carolina Department of Archives and History.

33. Gov. Patrick Tonyn to Clinton, May 1, 1779; June 13, 1779, Carleton Papers, South Carolina Department of Archives and History.

34. Prevost to Clinton, June 15, 1779, Carleton Papers, South Carolina Department of Archives and History.

35. Prevost to Clinton, July 14, 1779, Carleton Papers, South Carolina Department of Archives and History.

36. McCrady, *South Carolina in the Revolution,* 393.

37. David Ramsay, *History of South Carolina from Its Earliest Settlement in 1670 to the Year 1808* (Newberry, S.C.: N. J. Duffie, 1858), 179.

38. Prevost to Clinton, July 14, 1779, Carleton Papers, South Carolina Department of Archives and History.

39. Col. Barnard Beekman to Lincoln, September 1, 1779, Lincoln Papers, South Carolina Department of Archives and History.

40. Beekman to Lincoln, August 5, 1779, Lincoln Papers, South Carolina Department of Archives and History.

41. Beekman to Lincoln, August 19, 1779, Lincoln Papers, South Carolina Department of Archives and History.

42. Col. Daniel Horry to Lincoln, July 1, 1779, Lincoln Papers, South Carolina Department of Archives and History.

43. Col. Francis Marion to Lincoln, December 23, 1779, Lincoln Papers, South Carolina Department of Archives and History.

44. *South Carolina Gazette,* August 11, 1779.

45. Prevost to Clinton, July 30, 1779, Carleton Papers, South Carolina Department of Archives and History.

46. *South Carolina Gazette,* September 15, 1779; Alden, *South in the American Revolution,* 236; McCrady, *South Carolina in the Revolution,* 400.

47. Franklin Hough, ed., *Siege of Savannah* (1866; rpt., Spartanburg: Reprint Co., 1975), 31.

48. Alexander Garden, *Anecdotes of the Revolutionary War* (1822; rpt., Spartanburg: Reprint Co., 1972); Hough, ed., *Siege of Savannah,* 63–64.

49. Hough, ed., *Siege of Savannah,* 114.

50. *South Carolina Gazette,* December 1, 1779.

51. Alden, *South in the American Revolution,* 237.

52. Beekman to Lincoln, September 1, 1779, Lincoln Papers, South Carolina Department of Archives and History.

53. Alden, *South in the American Revolution,* 239.

54. McCrady, *South Carolina in the Revolution,* 430; Bernhard Alexander Uhlendorff, ed., *Siege of Charleston* (Ann Arbor: University of Michigan Press, 1968), 179.

55. Banastre Tarleton, *A History of the Campaigns of 1780 and 1781 in the Southern Provinces of North America* (1787; rpt., Spartanburg: Reprint Co., 1967), 7.

56. Barnwell, *Story of an American Family,* 35.

57. Tarleton, *Campaigns of 1780 and 1781,* 7.

58. Lumpkin, *Savannah to Yorktown,* 41–50.

59. Garden, *Anecdotes of the Revolutionary War,* 165–66.

60. DeSaussure Papers, South Carolina Historical Society.

61. Tarleton, *Campaigns of 1780 and 1781,* 86.

62. John Todd and Francis M. Hutson, *Prince William Parish and Plantations* (Richmond: Garrett and Massie, 1935), 55; McCrady, *South Carolina in the Revolution,* 715.

63. *Biographical Directory of the South Carolina House,* 3: 314–15.

64. McCrady, *South Carolina in the Revolution,* 129–36.

65. Robert Wilson Gibbes, *Documentary History of the American Revolution,* 3 vols. (1853–1857; rpt., Spartanburg: Reprint Co., 1972), 3: 50.

66. Jones, ed., *Port Royal Under Six Flags,* 136.

67. McCrady, *South Carolina in the Revolution,* 318; Gibbes, *Documentary History,* 3: 125.

68. McCrady, *South Carolina in the Revolution,* 434–39.

69. McCrady, *South Carolina in the Revolution,* 509–16.

70. "Letters of John Rutledge," *South Carolina Historical Magazine* 18 (1917): 66; Barnwell, *Story of an American Family,* 41; Garden, *Anecdotes of the Revolutionary War,* 51.

71. Jones, ed., *Port Royal Under Six Flags,* 134.

72. Barnwell, *Story of an American Family,* 36.

73. McCrady, *South Carolina in the Revolution,* 570–88.

74. Garden, *Ancedotes of the Revolutionary War,* 48–51.

75. *Biographical Directory of the South Carolina House,* 3: 53–55.

76. *Biographical Directory of the South Carolina House,* 1: 187–91.

77. Theodora J. Thompson, ed., *Journals of the House of Representatives, 1783–1784* (Columbia: University of South Carolina Press, 1977), 74–75.

78. Kenneth Coleman, *The American Revolution in Georgia, 1763–1789* (Athens: University of Georgia Press, 1958), 141–45.

79. Johnson, *Traditions and Reminiscences,* 444.

80. Robert E. H. Peeples, *Tales of Antebellum Hilton Head Island Families* (Hilton Head: Hilton Head Island Historical Society, 1970), 7.

81. Terry W. Lipscomb, "South Carolina Revolutionary Battles, Part Nine" (manuscript), South Carolina Department of Archives and History; *Royal Georgia Gazette,* January 30, 1782; William Elliott, "Chas. Davant," *Magnolia,* 2: 382, South Caroliniana Library.

82. Johnson, *Traditions and Reminiscences,* 445.

83. McCrady, *South Carolina in the Revolution,* 610–11.

84. Johnson, *Traditions and Reminiscenses,* 174–82.

85. Parrish, "Southern Loyalists," 222; Lipscomb, "South Carolina Revolutionary Battles," 2.

86. Lipscomb, "South Carolina Revolutionary Battles," 14–16.

87. "Claim of William Bull," Loyalist Transcripts, 57 (March 12, 1784): 160–214, South Carolina Department of Archives and History.

88. *Biographical Directory of the South Carolina House,* 2: 118–20, 122–25.

89. "Papers of the First Council of Safety of the Revolutionary Party in South Carolina, June–November 1775," *South Carolina Historical Magazine* 1 (1900): 73, 74, 127, 303, 308; Bull to Laurens, August 19, 1775, *South Carolina Historical Magazine* 1 (1900): 305–7.

90. Gen. Charles Lee to Col. Isaac Huger, July 23, 1776, Charles Lee Letterbook, South Caroliniana Library.

91. "Claim of Sarah Stuart," Loyalist Transcripts, 56: 234, South Carolina Department of Archives and History.

92. *South Carolina Gazette,* August 10, 1769.

93. A. S. Salley, ed., *Minutes of the Vestry of St. Helena's Parish, South Carolina, 1726–1812* (Columbia: Historical Commission of South Carolina, 1919), 144, 145; John Richard Alden, *John Stuart and the Southern Colonial Frontier: A Study of Indian Relations, War, Trade, and Land Problems in the Southern Wilderness* (Ann Arbor: University of Michigan Press, 1944), 174–75; "Claim of Charles Shaw," Loyalist Transcripts, 55: 266–67, South Carolina Department of Archives and History; Wilbur Henry Siebert, *Loyalists in East Florida, 1774–1785,* 2 vols. (Deland: Florida State Historical Society, 1929), 1: 322.

94. Johnson, *Traditions and Reminiscences,* 109.

95. Barnwell, *Story of an American Family,* 23, 139–40.

96. William B. Clark, ed., *Naval Documents of the American Revolution* (Washington, D.C.: U.S. Government Printing Office, 1964), 3: 1056, 1069, 1092; Allen D. Candler, ed., *The Revolutionary Records of Georgia,* 3 vols. (Atlanta: Franklin-Turner, 1908), 2: 126; 3: 60–62; Harold C. Syrett, ed., *The Papers of Alexander Hamilton,* 27 vols. (New York: Columbia University Press, 1961–1975), 3: 235; "Will of Peter Lavien," July 7, 1781, *Charleston County Wills,* 19 (1780–1783): 193–95, South Carolina Department of Archives and History.

97. "Claim of Zephaniah Kingsley," Loyalist Transcripts, 52, South Carolina Department of Archives and History.

98. "Petition of John Mark Verdier," November 28, 1806; General Assembly Papers, 1806, South Carolina Department of Archives and History.

99. Charles E. Bennett, *Twelve on the River St. Johns* (Jacksonville: University of North Florida Press, 1989), 89–113.

100. Barnwell and Webber, eds., "St. Helena Parish Register," *South Carolina Historical Magazine* 23 (1922): 127.

101. Jerome Nadelhaft, *Disorders of War: The Revolution in South Carolina* (Orono: University of Maine at Orono Press, 1981), 80.

102. Parrish, "Southern Loyalists," 367–69, Georgia Historical Society.

103. Candler, *Revolutionary Records,* 3: 447; Robert M. Weir, ed., "Muster Rolls of the Colleton and Granville Militia, 1757," *South Carolina Historical Magazine* 70 (1969): 229; Salley, ed., *Minutes of the Vestry,* 138, 152; Ulrich B. Phillips, ed., *Plantation and Frontier Documents 1649–1863,* 2 vols. (Cleveland: Arthur Clark, 1909), 1: 266–71; Lewis Cecil Gray, *History of Agriculture in the Southern United States to 1860* (Gloucester, Mass.: Peter Smith, 1958), 2: 676; Barnwell and Webber, eds., "St. Helena Parish Register," 127.

104. Salley, *Minutes of the Vestry,* 152, 159, 160, 162.

105. "Claim of Dr. James Fraser," Loyalist Transcripts, 56: 268–80, South Carolina Department of Archives and History.

106. "Petition of Dr. James Fraser," December 9, 1797, General Assembly Papers, South Carolina Department of Archives and History.

107. Barnwell and Webber, eds., "St. Helena Parish Register," 59.

108. "Claim of Col. Andrew DeVeaux," Loyalist Transcripts, 57: 32–47, South Carolina Department of Archives and History.
109. Johnson, *Traditions and Reminiscences,* 175.
110. "Petition of Andrew DeVeaux, Sr.," February 5, 1783, General Assembly Papers, 1783, South Carolina Department of Archives and History.
111. Johnson, *Traditions and Reminiscences,* 180–81.
112. Parrish, "Southern Loyalists," 223–25.
113. Parrish, "Southern Loyalists," 213–17.
114. "Claim of Andrew DeVeaux, Jr.," Loyalist Transcripts, 57: 40–47, South Carolina Department of Archives and History; Johnson, *Traditions and Reminiscences,* 180–81; Siebert, *Loyalists in East Florida,* 145–47.
115. Parrish, "Southern Loyalists," 233.

14

Beaufort District and the New Nation

LOCAL GOVERNMENT

The Beaufort District was devastated by the Revolutionary War. Most of the major plantations on Hilton Head Island and the mainland of St. Luke's and Prince William Parishes were partially or wholly destroyed. Thousands of slaves had been carried off by Major Andrew DeVeaux and other Tory and British raiders. Thousands more had run away seeking the protection of the British army. Many perished in the turmoil. The contending armies and partisan bands had decimated the livestock herds, and in the lower part of the Beaufort District the cattle industry never recovered. Colonel Banastre Tarleton had stolen all the horses from Port Royal Island to mount his cavalry legion in 1780, and over the next two and a half years the equine stock of the district was almost entirely stolen. Rev. Archibald Simpson of the old Stoney Creek Independent Meeting House on the Pocotaligo River could not get his former parishioners to return to church. "No one comes to see me," he lamented, "for none have horses."

Simpson summarized the postwar condition of the Beaufort District in 1783 as follows:

> All was desolation. . . . Every field, every plantation shows marks of ruin and devastation. . . . No garden, no enclosure, no mulberry, no fruit trees, nothing but wild fennel, bushes, underwood, briars to be seen . . . a very ruinous habitation.
>
> Every person, every family in both parishes [Prince William and St. Luke's] and through all this district of the county appears to be in the same situation. . . . Every person keeps close to his own plantation. Robberies and murders are often committed on the public roads. The people that remain are peeled, pillaged and plundered. Poverty and want appear on every countenance. A dark melancholy gloom appears everywhere and the morals of the people are almost entirely extirpated. A general discontent, dissatisfaction and distrust of their present rulers and of one another prevails throughout the country. In Charleston, they appear more happy.[1]

In order to rebuild to prewar prosperity, the new leaders had to reconstitute the institutions of a civil society and reimpose civil order. Out of the vortex of the Revolution were forged the institutions which were to form the structure of local government through the antebellum era. Nowhere in the state was this task more difficult than in the Beaufort District. An entire generation had grown up between 1775 and 1783, and many knew only the uncertainty, violence, and terror of a long war that in the Beaufort District, as Dr. Joseph Johnson recalled, took a particularly vengeful turn.

The murders referred to by Reverend Simpson are a case in point. In 1783, a gang of villains led by young James Booth roamed the forests of the mainland of the Beaufort District robbing and murdering at will. On February 19, 1783, the Booth gang robbed and murdered Dr. Orr while he was making his neighborhood visits. A few months later they murdered Dr. Brown of Virginia, who had come south seeking the killers of Dr. Orr. Both of these prominent and useful citizens had been "shot, scalped and otherwise most barbarously used" by Booth's gang of brigands. The South Carolina Privy Council offered "450 Mexican dollars" as a bounty for the arrest of Booth, and Governor Houston of Georgia asked that Booth be extradited to that state for crimes committed south of the Savannah River. By the fall of 1783, Booth had been captured by Sheriff Daniel Stevens and incarcerated in Beaufort, the only jail in the district.

Booth, it turned out, was barely twenty years old when he was arrested. When the war began he was an orphan of twelve. His only family was an older brother who was murdered by Tories as young Booth looked on. With nowhere to turn, he joined Colonel William Harden's army and spent much of his formative years plundering Loyalists and foraging the Coosawhatchie Swamp simply to survive. The war produced many like Booth, and a Beaufort District jury in 1784 convicted and sentenced him to death. Because of the extenuating circumstances of his life, the jury recommended a pardon. The case reached the Privy Council, which voted four to one to have Booth executed. Finally, Governor Benjamin Guerard pardoned Booth and banished him to Georgia to face equally serious charges.[2]

Another example of the breakdown of civil order caused by the Revolution in the Beaufort District was the community of runaway slaves that lived in the vast Savannah River swamps of upper St. Peter's Parish for four years following the war. This group of irregulars had run away to join the British army, but had been left behind after the evacuations of Savannah and Charleston. They called themselves the "King of England's Soldiers" and established a fortified encampment on an island in the Savannah River swamp.[3] Their stronghold was half a mile long and 400 feet deep with twenty-one houses and fields of corn, potatoes, and melons. The whole encampment was surrounded by a four-foot breastwork of log and cane pilings. At night, they issued out of the swamp to raid the plantations of St. Peter's Parish.

This remnant of the Revolutionary War remained unchecked on the frontier of the Beaufort district until 1786. They were "too numerous to be quelled" by the local militia. In May 1786, a combined force of militia and Catawba Indians led by Captain Richard Hutson of Charleston finally defeated them and destroyed their swamp fastness. Many escaped, however, and a second militia expedition had to be sent to St. Peter's Parish in 1787.[4]

These violent episodes prompted a harsh response from the new state government. From 1778 to 1808, the chief law enforcement officer in the judicial districts of South Carolina, the sheriff, was elected by the General Assembly. The assembly's selection in 1783 of the first postwar sheriff of the Beaufort District revealed the high priority the legislature placed on re-establishing order. They chose the toughest and most relentless of the partisan commanders of the Beaufort District, Captain John Leacraft of Hilton Head. The whole district knew him to be a man capable of using any force necessary in the administration of justice. As leader of the "Bloody Legion," it was Leacraft who personally meted out revenge on the Tories for the ambush murders of Charles Davant and James Doharty.[5] When a slave conspiracy at Purrysburg was revealed in 1792, it was dealt with ferociously. The instigators were hanged and decapitated. Their severed heads were placed atop poles on the mile markers between Purrysburg and Coosawhatchie as a gruesome reminder.

Given these disrupting events, the most pressing issue for the leaders of the new state was the re-establishment of the court system and the reimposition of civil order on the troubled frontier. The Circuit Court Act of 1769 had established the first courthouse and jail in the southern parishes at Beaufort before the Revolution. But a major political controversy unique to the Beaufort District interfered with the functioning of the court after the Revolution. The geography of the district had divided the population into islanders and mainlanders. The older, more established, and wealthier of the resident families lived on the sea islands, while much of the mainland remained a yeoman frontier throughout the eighteenth century. The mainlanders had long complained about the inaccessibility of the court at Beaufort. A petition in 1787 stated that the court at Beaufort on Port Royal Island was "surrounded by broad and dangerous waters accessible but at certain times by boat . . . and by no means central to the district."[6]

In addition to the separation of the islands from the mainland, the entire district was sliced into equal halves by the deepest sound and widest tidal estuary on the coast. A petition from the citizens of St. Luke's Parish in 1784 commented that the Beaufort District was "divided by the Broad River into two divisions equal or nearly so in numbers of inhabitants." The petition further noted that the Broad River is "by far the broadest and most dangerous river in the state, a river which may be crossed by small rowing boat only in the most moderate weather and in blowing weather is impassable even to the largest canoes." The only other way to Beaufort was via the Port Royal Ferry, "which from its natural situation is one of the most delaying and troublesome in this country." The trip to Beaufort and back took "not less than four tides" and consequently was "dangerous, uncertain, long, fatiguing and expensive."[7]

The mainlanders wanted to shut down the original court in Beaufort and re-establish it at the crossroads of Coosawhatchie in the geographic center of the district. This little village, which had grown up around Henry and Daniel DeSaussure's store in the 1760s, was located where the King's Highway from Charleston to Savannah crossed the Coosawhatchie River. It was also the head of tidal navigation for the Broad River and the border between Prince William and St. Luke's Parishes. It was a location, as noted in the petition of 1787, "where boats from the islands . . . may attend as well as mainlanders."

During the war, the radical Jacksonborough Assembly of 1782 had acceded to the demand of Colonel William Harden, leader of the Beaufort District delegation and wartime hero of the yeoman farmers of the mainland, to move the court from old Beaufort, considered by the radical faction a stronghold of Tory nabobs and their defenders, to Coosawhatchie on the mainland.[8] But during the early 1780s, the court was not moved, and its location was a major local complaint of the populist faction against the planters of the islands. The issue divided the district geographically, sociologically, and politically and hindered attempts to establish law and order.

The courthouse issue continued to fester until 1787 when a very pointed and revealing series of petitions finally prodded the legislature to act. The most important petition, from Prince William and St. Luke's residents, strenuously objected to being required to work on a causeway to Port Royal Island. The task, which had been rejected as impractical in the colonial era, was far beyond the reduced means of the citizens in 1787. Before the Revolution, "the inhabitants of this District were more capable of compleating a work of this kind being then more free of debt and far richer than they are at present." Additionally, the causeway would only benefit the one-fourth of the population that lived on the sea islands while doing harm to the rest of the population that lived on the mainland. Lastly, the project was ill-conceived and impractical because "being exposed to Wind and Tide, must of course, daily wash away."

The whole causeway project had begun as a means to justify keeping the court in Beaufort, a location so inconvenient as to "prevent many notorious offenders to this state being carried and confined there for further prosecution, on account of the difficulty in crossing the ferry and the expense of carrying them so great a distance." Thus, they requested in strong language that the court and jail be moved from Beaufort to Coosawhatchie.[9] The act was finally passed by both houses of the legislature on February 29, 1788, and Coosawhatchie became the judicial seat of the Beaufort District.[10]

The principal local court was the Court of Common Pleas and General Sessions established by the Act of 1769. This court was conducted in the spring and fall by a circuit judge chosen by the legislature and tried criminal and civil cases in the district. The chief local law enforcement officer was the sheriff, a position established by the wartime Constitution of 1778. From 1778 to 1808, the sheriff was elected by the legislature. From 1808 to 1822, the sheriff was elected annually by the people, and after 1822 the sheriff was elected by the people to a four-year term.

Other officers of the court were the clerk of court who managed its daily business and the district coroner. The clerk of court was established by the Constitution of 1778 to be elected by the legislature, but after 1815 this officer, like the sheriff, was elected by the people to a four-year term. A host of other court officers were appointed by the legislature. The ordinary was a court officer who performed the modern function of a probate judge. Colonel William Harden was the first postwar ordinary for the Beaufort District.[11] There was also a register of mesne conveyance and a commissioner of locations to manage land transactions and state grants in the district.[12] A separate equity court was established in South Carolina to handle property disputes, but it met only once a year, and, until 1810, the equity court for the Beaufort and Colleton Districts was held in Charleston. After 1810, there was an equity court at Coosawhatchie.[13] For a brief time there was a separate county court in the Beaufort District located in what is today Hampton County. The Act of 1785 reorganized the counties of the state and carved "Lincoln County" out of the northern part of the Beaufort District. A separate court was established in that rural neighborhood so its citizens would not have to travel to Beaufort. When the district court was moved to Coosawhatchie in 1788, the Lincoln County Court was closed at the request of its citizens.[14]

The turmoil of the 1780s and the sectional controversies within the Beaufort District had a lasting political effect. Into the early nineteenth century, elections in the legislature for local court offices frequently pitted a candidate from the sea islands against a candidate from the mainland. In 1802, James DeVeaux of St. Helena Parish bested John Hay of St. Peter's Parish for sheriff of the Beaufort District. The vote in the legislature was close: fifty-five to forty-six. In 1810, William Joyner of St. Helena Parish was chosen as the first local commissioner of equity over Thomas Screven of St. Luke's Parish by a joint house vote of ninety-one to sixty-five.[15] The favoritism shown by the legislature to the coastal planters probably explains why, shortly after the Compromise of

1808 reapportioned the legislature to finally give the majority of the seats to the upcountry, the local court offices of sheriff, clerk-of-court, coroner, commissioner of locations, register of mesne conveyance, and ordinary were then filled by local popular elections.

The Beaufort District capital at Coosawhatchie never did grow into a real town, though President Washington passed through in May 1791 on his way to the nearby plantation of Judge Thomas Heyward Jr. In 1802, John Davis, an English tutor at the Drayton family plantation near Coosawhatchie, described the village as "consisting of a blacksmith's shop, a courthouse, and a jail. A small river rolls its stagnant water near the place, on whose dismal banks are to be found many vestiges of the Indians that once inhabited them."[16]

Despite the unappealing nature of the lowcountry swamplands to some travelers, the village of Coosawhatchie was conveniently located for the surrounding planters and farmers of the district, and, as their fortunes began to improve, so did their ambitions for their judicial capital. During the 1790s, rice production began to recover, and new fortunes were made as cotton replaced indigo among the sea islands. This brought increased legal activity to the court at Coosawhatchie. By 1810, the local court of equity had moved to Coosawhatchie, and some of South Carolina's most distinguished lawyers began their practices in the district. James Louis Petigru, Daniel Huger, William Lowndes, James Hamilton Jr., Robert W. Barnwell, Robert Barnwell Rhett, and Richard Fuller all practiced law for a time at the Coosawhatchie court.[17] As a result, a movement to construct a new courthouse was begun in 1816. By the end of 1817, the Senate had set aside twelve thousand dollars for a new structure.[18] The new courthouse, designed by noted architect William Jay, was erected in 1819. The Coosawhatchie Court was two stories high, forty feet in width, and fifty feet in length with a glazed pantile roof. The stairs were located inside the front portico, and the second floor courtroom could be shut off when not in use. This courthouse lasted until 1836 when the judicial capital was moved; six miles north to the higher, healthier pineland village of Gillisonville.[19]

The removal of the Beaufort District Court to Coosawhatchie prompted the older sea island community to recover a measure of local control by establishing a municipal government at Beaufort. During the colonial period there had been no town government at Beaufort. The parish of St. Helena had performed the local functions for the sea islands, and the establishment of the colonial court at Beaufort in 1769 had caused a flurry of local political activity. After losing the court in 1788, the old town set about establishing the institutions that would allow the local planters to control their own neighborhood. Accordingly, the town of Beaufort was incorporated on December 17, 1803. The municipal government was to consist of an intendant and six wardens to be elected by "all

free white inhabitants of the . . . town." The intendant and wardens were designated the town council of Beaufort. The town council was to regulate the harbor
streets, lanes, public buildings, workhouses, markets, wharves, public houses,
and cart and horse traffic. They were also responsible for the care of the poor,
regulation of "seamen and negroes," and preservation of "peace order and good
government within" the town limits. The town council also licensed taverns and
billiard halls.[20]

On April 2, 1804, the first municipal elections were held. Colonel Robert
Barnwell was elected as Beaufort's first intendant. The original town council
consisted of Major Samuel Lawrence, John Rhodes, Barnwell DeVeaux, R. B.
Screven, James Stuart, and John Mark Verdier.[21] The town council employed a
sheriff to maintain order until 1823 when they were empowered to establish a
police patrol. The first sheriff of Beaufort was William Joyner. The town council
busied itself maintaining order, settling disputes over road rights-of-way, collecting taxes and license fees, and dispensing charity to paupers and transients. The
daily work of the town was managed by William Joyner whose title was changed
in 1818 to clerk of the council.[22]

During the early years of the town the principal matters occupying the
town council were the establishment and extension of public streets, the maintenance of law and order, and the dispensation of charity to the poor. A controversy over town streets preceded the incorporation of Beaufort and contributed
to the need for local government. In 1795, some citizens, led by Edward Barnwell,
petitioned the legislature, objecting to private occupation and construction on
the ends of the streets at the waterfront. The petition noted that the original
town plat showed the public rights-of-way "laid out into the rivers." On December 21, 1798, the state legislature passed an "Act to Prevent Stopping Certain Streets," which opened the streets to the water. One of Beaufort's principal
mariners, Captain Francis Saltus, who was just completing his large new mercantile establishment on Bay Street, petitioned for compensation and permission to build a sea wall to protect his property. In 1801, the legislature, unhappy
at being harassed by local controversy, established the commissioners of streets
in Beaufort to handle the problem. This body was the precedent of the town
council and two of its first four members, Colonel Robert Barnwell and Major
Samuel Lawrence, were later elected to lead the town government. As late as
1821, the town council was still trying to open West Street "to the river" and
remove a derelict building which was a fire hazard and nuisance, "being
inhabited frequently by low white people and Negroes who . . . disturb the
peace."[23]

The town extended its original boundaries and laid out new streets during
the first decade of the nineteenth century. The colonial town had extended from

East Street to Hamar Street along the bay and from Bay Street to Duke Street away from the bay. To the east of town was a small creek and marsh which separated "Black's Island" or "Black's Point" from Beaufort. Between 1801 and 1809, this marsh was crossed by causeways, and streets were laid out on the area known today simply as the Point. These new streets were named for heroes of the Revolution such as Hancock, Hamilton, Laurens, and Pinckney. One street was named for Isaac Hayne but was renamed Federal Street during the Civil War. In addition to the Point, new streets were laid out to the north of town during these years. These new streets were named Washington, Greene, and Congress, also celebratory of the Revolution. The northern limit of antebellum Beaufort was Boundary Street. These town limits were established by statute in 1809, and it was well into the twentieth century before Beaufort was again expanded.[24]

One of the preoccupations of the local planters was order and security. Harassed by colonial wars, ruined by the Revolution, and surrounded by ever-increasing numbers of potentially hostile slaves, the sea island planters hoped to create a citadel of security at Beaufort. Responding to federal and state militia laws in 1798, they replaced the colonial courthouse with the arsenal. Two local militia companies, one artillery and one infantry, were attached to this facility. Inside the arsenal were stored "400 stands of arms," twelve cannons, and considerable amounts of powder and shot. This installation, originally a source of pride and security, had, by 1819, become a source of concern. A petition to the legislature complained that "no collection of arms in the state is so much exposed" because most planters leave town in the winter and the blacks outnumber the whites nine to one. The Denmark Vesey conspiracy of 1822 in Charleston heightened anxieties in the lowcountry, and by 1824 Beaufort had established a regular police patrol, part of whose stated purpose was to protect the arsenal in case of a slave uprising.[25] The old arsenal was, throughout the antebellum period, the symbol of security that the town of Beaufort provided for the planter class of the sea islands. It was the "citadel" of antebellum Beaufort.

No slave uprisings occurred, and Beaufort remained a peaceful village throughout the antebellum period. Nevertheless, the old jail, located on the northeast corner of Craven and Carteret Streets, remained regularly in use for drunks, vagrants, and local blacks guilty of "riotous conduct." In 1816, the town council employed local carpenter John Oldings to repair the jail and ensure its structural soundness and continued utility. Finally, in 1840, the old jail was deeded over to the town. It remained in use until the Civil War.[26]

The town council also spent time and money administering to the poor and distressed travelers who occasionally appeared in Beaufort. In 1816, the council formed a separate organization, the Committee for Paupers and Transients, headed by John Verdier Jr., to tend to this business. This committee replaced the old commissioners of the poor for Port Royal Island, established by the legislature in 1791, and caused some confusion on St. Helena and Lady's Islands, where both the town council and the commissioners of the poor were collecting the poor tax. Ultimately, the town council of Beaufort functioned only for Port Royal Island.[27]

As long as Beaufort remained an isolated sea island community, this public business was never too burdensome. But in 1821, steam paddlewheelers began making regular runs along the inland passage from Charleston, through Beaufort to Savannah, and up the river to Augusta. Beaufort then began to regularly play host to "sick seamen and passengers," and the costs to the town council soon outran their small revenues. They sought help from the state, and in 1822 the town spent $277.34 while the state contributed $222.66 to bring the fund to an even $500. By 1824, the state and town governments were spending $600 per year for blankets, food, lodging, medical expenses, and occasionally a coffin for the transient poor. Only poor women appeared to have regularly received direct assistance. In 1824, three local women received regular direct payments. All other payments were to storekeepers, doctors, and boardinghouse operators. The most famous of these distressed transients was Mason Weems of Virginia, an itinerant bookseller who fell ill on the steamboat from Savannah to Charleston and was left at Beaufort, where he died in 1824. He was the famous "Parson Weems" who wrote the first popular biographies of George Washington and Francis Marion and originated the legend of the cherry tree. Mason Weems was first buried in St. Helena Churchyard and later removed to Dumfries, Virginia.[28]

Throughout the antebellum era, the town council of Beaufort busied itself with the public business of the sea island community. But not everyone in town was happy with the municipal government. As Beaufort grew, a small class of tradesmen, artisans, and laborers mingled in town with the planters, lawyers, and doctors. The working classes never participated in the municipal government and resented paying taxes to an institution they saw as exclusively managed by and for the benefit of rich planters and their families. When the original Act of Incorporation came up for renewal in 1816, these people petitioned the legislature to disestablish the town government. This group tended to gather at the Bay Street tavern operated by John Cross, and it was probably there that Thomas Gardner, James Keely, James Clark, and thirty-one of their friends signed a petition to the legislature opposing the town council. The boldest signature on the petition was that of John Cross. The group claimed "that no utility tending to the general good has ever hitherto been derived from a charter of incorporation in this town." In fact, all the council did was levy taxes for the purpose of spending them. They wanted to end the municipal government "to avert further impending evils." This petition was vigorously and swiftly opposed by a larger and far more powerful group of planters and property owners. They highlighted the "growing population, the increase in trade and the great resort of Negroes . . . demanding active and vigilant magistrates." They claimed that those opposing the town government "desire to profit from illicit traffic and unlawful practices and are averse to any government in the town." The petition was signed by fifty-five of the leading citizens led by outgoing intendant William Robertson and incoming intendant Robert Means. All the wealthiest families, including the Barnwells, Elliotts, Cuthberts, Fripps, Graysons, Habershams, Fullers, and Verdiers, signed the petition.[29] Not only was the town council reincorporated in 1816, but the legislature also allowed the establishment of a court of wardens, or small claims court, and a court recorder for the town of Beaufort, further separating the Beaufort and Coosawhatchie centers of government.

The institutions of local government, established between 1788 and 1820, were to serve the Beaufort District throughout the antebellum era. In 1805, the *Charleston Courier* published the following description of the town: it had 656 white inhabitants, 944 black inhabitants, and 186 students residing in the town. There were in the town 120 dwelling houses, 13 stores, 9 workshops, 4 schools, a college, a jail, an arsenal, a lodging house, and 3 churches—an Episcopal, a Baptist, and an Independent (Presbyterian). The population, institutions, and functions of the town achieved unusual stability by the 1820s. As William J. Grayson commented years later, "The little town has not increased as American towns are accustomed to do. It is remarkable for the conservative property of standing still. Its population is no greater now than it was fifty years ago and its condition as to all material advantages remains very much the same."[30]

THE FEDERALIST FACTION

One of the principal political results of the Revolutionary War in the Beaufort District and the civil disorder which characterized the 1780s was the formation of a powerful faction of federalist politicians with great influence in early state and national politics. During the Revolutionary War, before political factionalism was defined and while the new nation was governed by the Articles of Confederation (1777–1789), the Beaufort District sent two delegates to the Continental Congress: Thomas Heyward Jr. (1776–1778), the signer of the Declaration of Independence, and Richard Hutson (1778–1779), signer of the Articles of Confederation. Both of these men were strong supporters of the South Carolina Federalist faction during the 1780s and 1790s, and both voted to ratify the U.S. Constitution in the Ratifying Convention in 1788.[31]

The first postwar delegate to the Confederation Congress from the southern parishes was John Bull, who served in Philadelphia from 1784 to 1787. Bull was the son of Stephen Bull and Elizabeth Bryan of Prince William Parish. He was, along with his cousin, General Stephen Bull of Sheldon, one of the only members of the Beaufort District's most powerful colonial family who supported the American cause during the Revolution. John Bull had married Eleanor Purry, the only daughter of Beaufort merchant Charles Purry and the only descendant in America of the famous Swiss colonizer Jean Pierre Purry. Though the party factions were still indistinct when Bull served in the Confederation Congress, he later identified with the Federalist Party and was an elector for President John Adams in 1796.[32] John Bull was the last of his distinguished family to achieve high political office in South Carolina. His sons predeceased him, John in 1798 and Stephen before 1802. His own death in 1802, and that of Eleanor Purry Bull a few years before, mark the end of the political influence of the Bull family in the Beaufort District, as well as the end of the famous Purry family in South Carolina. It was one of the many historic changes wrought by the Revolutionary era in the district.

The next delegate from Beaufort to the Confederation Congress was a young man who saw many opportunities in the turbulent era of the American Revolution, and he seized every one with gusto. If John Bull was the last of the old colonial aristocracy from the Beaufort District, then John Kean was the first of a new breed of energetic and ambitious national politicians. John Kean (1756–1795) was born in Charleston and raised in Beaufort by his mother, Jane Grove, and his stepfather, Captain Samuel Grove. He was the executor of Grove's very substantial estate. As a young man, Kean was apprenticed to Grove's partner, Peter Lavien, to learn business and bookkeeping. He evidently learned well. When the Revolutionary War arrived in South Carolina, Kean served the American cause as deputy paymaster of the South Carolina Militia. The paymaster of the state militia under whom Kean served was Beaufort merchant and patriot leader Daniel DeSaussure. After the Revolution, DeSaussure helped form the largest mercantile firm in South Carolina, the firm of Smiths, DeSaussure, and Darrell. DeSaussure's son, Henry William DeSaussure, remained in Philadelphia after the war and, in 1795, was appointed first director of the U.S. Mint by President Washington. These connections were to serve Kean well when he arrived in Philadelphia.

The other connection which served Kean well was through Peter Lavien. Lavien had amassed a sizeable fortune in South Carolina before the Revolution. He died in occupied Savannah in 1780, his daughter and son-in-law returned to Europe, and Kean became the agent for Lavien's estate in America. Lavien's connection to Alexander Hamilton of New York brought Kean into contact with the great financial genius of the new nation and one of the founders of the Federalist Party. Kean saw opportunity in Philadelphia and used these contacts to secure several important appointments from President Washington in the new national government. He was one of the commissioners to audit the accounts of the Revolutionary Army and later was appointed cashier (chief operating officer) of the first Bank of the United States in Philadelphia. He held this position until his death in 1795.

His most important contact in Philadelphia, however, was with Susan Livingston of New York, whom he married in 1786. The Livingstons were New York's most prominent family of patriot leaders, and Susan's uncle was Robert R. Livingston, the signer of the Declaration of Independence. After his marriage, Kean sold his South Carolina and Georgia properties and remained in Philadelphia. Their descendants formed the New Jersey dynasty of Republican politicians that included Senator John Kean, Congressmen Hamilton Fish Kean, John Winthrop Kean, and Governor Thomas Kean.[33]

The last delegate to the Confederation Congress from the Beaufort District was Colonel Robert Gibbes Barnwell, one of Beaufort's Revolutionary War heroes. He was elected to serve in Congress in 1788 and 1789, but that congressional session was held in New York, and Barnwell declined to attend. Like many generations of Barnwells before and after, Barnwell preferred to stay close to his sea island home rather than seek the limelight of national politics. His older brother, General John Barnwell, was elected to Congress for the fourth session (1795–1797) but also declined to serve, preferring to remain in South Carolina. These two brothers, Revolutionary veterans and natural leaders of the sea island planters, became the core of the Federalist faction of the Beaufort District.[34]

The Barnwell faction was the Federalist faction synonymous with Beaufort District politics during the 1790s. The Rutledge-Pinckney faction was the most influential of the Federalist factions in South Carolina because its leaders stood closest to George Washington. Smiths, DeSaussure, and Darrell was the second most important faction because it drew its strength from its standing in the Anglo-Carolina mercantile community. Once Alexander Hamilton gained the ascendancy in Washington's administration, it may have been the most influential. The partners in this firm were the leading native-born merchants in Charleston, with strong roots in the Beaufort community. The DeSaussure family had come out of the Purrysburg settlement, and later generations had managed stores at Coosawhatchie and Beaufort.

The faction of the wealthy Huger family in Georgetown District and the Barnwell faction in Beaufort District were of lesser importance although each had a regional influence that could not be overlooked. Together the four factions stood by Washington and Hamilton and contributed many valuable officeholders to the new national government.[35]

These Federalist factions had supported the movement for a new Constitution. The delegation to Philadelphia was led by John Rutledge and Charles

Cotesworth Pinckney, supported by their slightly less important colleagues, Pierce Butler and Charles Pinckney III. Once the new Constitution had been ratified, Butler and Charles Pinckney III began to move away from the Federalist Party and toward the Republican or Jeffersonian Party. Their careers demand close scrutiny because in 1800 they helped Jefferson to his victory over the party of Washington and Adams. From the vantage point of Beaufort politics, Butler's drift across the political spectrum was crucial. Between 1788 and 1792, Butler transferred his planting operations out of South Carolina and into Georgia.

On January 19, 1788, the legislature voted to call a convention to consider the ratification of the Constitution. St. Helena Parish voted six to zero in favor with Robert Barnwell leading the way. Prince William voted three to two with Pierce Butler in the majority. St. Peter's voted four to zero against calling the convention. St. Helena and the lower portions of St. Peter's and Prince William were in favor with the interior portions of those two lowcountry parishes, and St. Peter's against. This reveals that St. Helena parish was the center of Federalist strength throughout the decade.[36]

Robert Barnwell was the spokesman for the Beaufort District supporters of ratification. When Rawlins Lowndes argued that too much had been given away to the Northern interests, Barnwell reminded his listeners that the Eastern states had been "the first in the field." When the South was overrun they had come to its aid. "He saw not a man who did not know that the shackles of the south were broken asunder by the arms of the north." This was a tribute to General Nathanael Greene of Rhode Island and to the troops of the Southern Continental Army in the last year of the war. Barnwell admitted that the South had to give up something in return for this aid. American vessels should be given a preference in the carrying trade. Barnwell, however, saw a reduction in freight rates which would come in time. He was pleased that the question of the foreign slave trade would not be discussed for twenty-one years. It was to the interest of the eastern states to have the South export. He believed that even in 1807 the northern interests would not object to the continuation of the slave trade. "I am of the opinion, that, without we ourselves put a stop to them, the traffic for negroes will continue forever."[37]

As happened so often in elections to membership in called conventions, many wealthy and influential planters who did not want to waste their time in day-to-day legislation would come forward and serve in conventions. St. Helena was represented in the Ratification Convention by John and Robert Barnwell, John Joyner, John Kean, William Hazzard Wigg, William Elliott, and James Stuart. The delegation voted seven to zero in favor of ratification. Prince William had seven votes in favor and none against: Thomas Hutson, John McPherson, James Maine, John A. Cuthbert, John Lightwood, John Simmons, and Stephen Deveaux.

Only in St. Peter's was there any opposition: John Fenwick, Joachin Hartstone, Seth Stafford, and the Reverend Henry Holcombe were in favor; John Chisholm and John Lewis Bourquin Jr. were against; and William Stafford was absent. The largest slaveholders, the wealthiest men, were in favor.[38]

Once the Constitution was ratified by a number of states sufficient to put the new government in operation, the South Carolina legislature had to create the machinery for holding the first federal elections in South Carolina, which it did in November 1788. On November 4, 1788, a Congressional election district which combined Beaufort and Orangeburg districts was formed. The *South Carolina Gazette,* November 8, 1788, stated that John Bull of Oaketee, John Barnwell, Aedanus Burke, and John Kean would run for Congress. Burke won, showing the importance of the Orangeburg addition to this lowcountry election district. Burke, as a circuit court judge, had gotten to know the interior regions of the state in a way in which the others had not. December 1, 1788, the *South Carolina Gazette* stated that Robert Barnwell carried the election in Prince William Parish. Orangeburg, representing the interior portion of the state, would be a determining area in the elections for this Congressional District during the first decade of the new nation.

Pierce Butler was the only person in nomination for a seat in the U.S. Senate who got a majority on the first vote in the House and Senate. He and Ralph Izard were the first two senators to represent South Carolina in the new Congress. Butler, Sumter, Gillon, and Burke were appointed to offices which removed them from the state legislature. John Cutting wrote John Rutledge Jr. on February 21, 1789: "These gentlemen and a few others you know are the leaders of that fierce column of rural representation which when influenced by any popular passion rushes to whatsoever may be the object of the hour with an irresistible impetuosity."[39]

In the 1790 census, there were twenty-three slaveholders in the Beaufort District who owned more than one hundred slaves. The list was headed by Frederick Whitsall, who held 607.[40] This is misleading in that Whitsall was the manager for all of the Blake family properties in the Beaufort District. Daniel Blake died in 1792, and his younger brother, William, died in 1803. They had extensive properties along the Combahee and Pocotaligo Rivers. Their descendants lived in England after the Revolution.[41] It was the death of Mrs. Daniel Blake in 1792 that brought on the fierce debate between Pierce Butler and the Rutledge-Pinckney connection. Pierce Butler's feelings were fully expressed in a letter that he wrote to Mrs. Graeme on August 21, 1792: "Mrs. Blake's will, or rather Mr. E. Rutledge's diction, is not highly affrontive to me." It was an attempt to divide the daughters from their father. "The wording of the will is a base assassinating attempt to lessen me in the eyes of my Fellow Citizens." "The parties knew it wou'd be recorded, & handed to posterity." Pierce Butler wrote to John McPherson on November 6, 1792, "that he had received a letter from the managers of Prince William informing me I have been elected one of their representatives." Butler sent his thanks to McPherson for his "long, steady, & warm friendship for me." The first, second and third Congresses have gone too far in some measures, tending to establish "an aristocracy as detestable as that of Venice." Butler states that one must elect good republicans as Charleston will elect an aristocrat "for if Mr. [William] Smith is a republican, I don't know what republicanism is." Since Barnwell has declined standing, the inhabitants will support Gillon. "Gillon is a republican in principle." But Gillon is not much known to the freeholders on the Savannah River or about Prince William, "so do support him. He doesn't want McPherson's support for himself, but would like to know who is for me and who is against."[42]

Next was Thomas Heyward, who owned 440 slaves, followed by Stephen Bull with 233, John Rutledge with 217, and John Bull with 181. Much further down the list were Major P. Butler with 112 (Butler had already removed many of his slaves to Georgia), William Wigg with 103, and John McPherson with 103. The major slaveholders must be considered leaders in the Federalist bloc.

The Federalist faction dominated the Beaufort District's delegation to the state legislature during the 1790s. John Barnwell, Thomas Talbird, and Robert Barnwell sat in the state senate in the 1790s for St. Helena Parish. John Bull of Okatee and Samuel Maner sat for St. Peter's. Daniel Stevens, James Garvey (who married the sister of John Bull of Granville District), Micah Jenkins, William Hazzard, and James Postell sat for St. Luke's. Prince William was represented by John McPherson, who sat from December 11, 1792 until his death on August 24, 1806, first as representative and then as senator. General Stephen Bull had been elected but had refused to attend.[44]

Another part of the power structure which must be analyzed are those men who held commissions in the new state militia. In 1792, the U.S. Congress passed a law which described the way in which the militia should be organized in each state. Each state then had to enact legislation to implement the federal law, which South Carolina did on May 10, 1794. By this law the state was divided into two divisions. Andrew Pickens was commander of the upper division, and Charles Cotesworth Pinckney was commander of the lower division. By this time, Pinckney was ensconced on Pinckney Island, a central point in the southeastern parishes. The lower division was divided into five brigades, with a brigadier general in command of each. The Fifth Brigade, which covered Beaufort, Colleton, and Orangeburg districts, was commanded by Brigadier General John Barnwell. Of the five regiments in the Fifth Brigade, the Twentieth Regiment coincided with Prince William Parish and was commanded by Colonel

John McPherson. The Seventh Brigade covered Charleston District and was commanded by Brigadier General William Washington. The Thirtieth Regiment was commanded by Colonel Arnoldus Vanderhorst.[45]

Pinckney was sent as minister to France in 1797. When he returned in early 1799, he became ranking general in the U.S. forces after Washington and Hamilton. In 1799 and 1800, he was the most powerful military figure in the southeastern part of the United States. During the crisis over the quasi war with France, he took an active role in organizing the defenses of the new nation. He was therefore at the top of the military pyramid in the Beaufort region.

The Federalists in the Beaufort District had certainly gained the ascendancy when the XYZ Affair broke in May 1798. Ralph Izard wrote Jacob Read from Charleston on May 9, 1798: "You will have learnt from Mr. DeSaussure every thing respecting the doings of our Town meetings, as they would be called in New England. I am not in general fond of such meetings, they seldom do good, and are often productive of mischief. I regret however extremely, that my ill health did not permit me to attend this last meeting. A considerable degree of unanimity appeared at it, and I flatter myself that some good may be derived from it."[46]

On May 19, 1798, there was a meeting held in St. Luke's Parish to show support for the government, constitution, and independence of the United States. Daniel Stevens of Charleston, the supervisor of the customs in the state, was called to the chair and made a speech on the dispatches recently received. Stevens, George Hipp, and William McKimmey were appointed to a committee to prepare an address to the president and both branches of the national legislature. A subscription was taken for the defense "of the harbours and inlets of the parish of St. Lukes." Stevens's address and Adams's reply were printed in the *South Carolina Gazette* on July 19, 1798. There had also been a meeting in Beaufort at St. Helena Church on July 4, 1798, with General John Barnwell as chair. Barnwell condemned the French republic "in their treatment of the distinguished characters who have been sent them as the messengers of peace." A committee was appointed to collect funds for the defense of the "sea coast and rivers of the district of Beaufort."[48]

Henry William DeSaussure wrote Senator Jacob Read on July 14, 1798: "a high national spirit has arisen, to vindicate our country—the Beaufort people have entered into very spirited resolutions, and have subscribed, each man, equal to one years tax, in order to provide gallies and other means of defence—they have written to the Sect. at war, and I would be glad if you would support their representations."[49]

The *South Carolina Gazette* on April 4, 1799, noted the appointment of William Macpherson to be brigadier general in the army of the United States.

John Barnwell had been created a brigadier general by Governor John Rutledge at the end of the Revolution. Barnwell succeeded Charles Cotesworth Pinckney as major general of the lower division of the state militia when Pinckney was promoted to the Federal Army. He served in that position until his death in 1800.[50]

Colonel John McPherson succeeded Barnwell as the new brigadier general. In May 1798, Barnwell reviewed at Tulifinney Hill the Beaufort District Regiment of Granville County commanded by McPherson when there appeared upward of four hundred men in arms, among which were two well-uniformed companies of artillery and light infantry and an additional number of well-mounted cavalry under the command of Major James Elliott McPherson.[51]

The power and importance of the Beaufort leaders is nowhere better illustrated than in the lineup of Federal electors in 1796. The Republican electors should also be listed in contrast for nothing better shows the split with the Rutledge–Pinckney faction:

Republican electors for Jefferson	Federalist electors for Adams
Edward Rutledge	Arnoldus Vanderhorst
Andrew Pickens	H. W. DeSaussure
John Mathews	Robert Barnwell
Thomas Taylor	William Washington
Arthur Simkins	David Ramsay
John Rutledge Jr.	General John Barnwell
John Chesnut	Nathaniel Russell
William Thomas	John Bull of Okatee

John Barnwell, Robert Barnwell, and John Bull were all from the Beaufort District, and H. W. DeSaussure was only one generation removed. The Rutledges would have hoped that Thomas Pinckney would have become vice president in 1796. The name of Pinckney was put forward without his agreement. Jefferson, however, won. This was the point at which John Rutledge Jr. began his drift towards the Federalist Party. Charles Pinckney had become governor in December 1796. Edward Rutledge became governor in December 1798.[52]

An important vote in the state senate on December 16, 1794, on the question of reapportionment reveals the tensions that divided these two important groups. In that year a Republican-inspired petition was presented to the Senate which asked for apportionment according to population. General Charles Cotesworth Pinckney, Henry Laurens Jr., Dr. (Charles) Drayton, General William Washington, General John Barnwell, Colonel John McPherson of Prince William Parish, John Bull of St. Peter's Parish, and Colonel (William) Thomson were among the seventeen who voted aye against sixteen nays on the insertion of the following words: "That the object of society is to promote public happiness, by securing the liberty and property of the individuals who compose it, however variant their interests may be—That with this avowed intention, and after full discussion, the representation was formed by solemn compact; and that the liberty and property of every citizen of this state, has hitherto been secured by it; that while we are thus in the full enjoyment of this happiness, it would be unwise to risque it by granting the prayer of the petitions." The arguments of Henry William DeSaussure were the most telling in the debate over reapportionment.[53]

In the watershed election of 1800, Thomas Jefferson and Aaron Burr defeated Federalist candidates John Adams and Thomas Pinckney. This was the beginning of the Jeffersonian Republican dominance in national politics and the beginning of the end of the power of the Federalists. Electors for the two parties in South Carolina were:

Electors for Jefferson	*Electors for Adams*
John Hunter	William Washington
Paul Hamilton	John Ward
Robert Anderson	Thomas Roper
Theodore Gaillard	James Postell
Arthur Simkins	John Blassingame
Wade Hampton	William McPherson
Andrew Love	William Falconer
Joseph Blyth	Henry Dana Ward[54]

An analysis of these two groups vividly shows what had happened to the Federalist strength in the state and thus in the old Beaufort District also. Only William Washington as a man of outstanding leadership potential stands forth in 1800 as compared to the Federalist Electors in 1796. Major Thomas Roper of St. Philips Parish is a minor Charleston figure. John Ward was admitted to the bar in Charleston in 1787. James Postell (1745–1824) was elected sheriff of Beaufort District on February 19, 1791. On November 23, 1797, he was elected senator from St. Luke's Parish and served until 1804. Postell had been a lieutenant colonel under Marion during the Revolution. John Blassingame was from Union, and William McPherson was from Prince William Parish. William Falconer was an attorney who arrived in Charleston about 1785 and resided in Society Hill in Chesterfield District. Henry Dana Ward, from Connecticut, was admitted to the bar in 1795 and lived in the Orangeburg District. The loss of the leadership of the older generation can be also seen by noting the deaths of the generals at the end of the century. General Stephen Bull of Sheldon died in 1795, General John Barnwell died in September 1800, and John Bull of Okatee died in August 1802.

John McPherson was lost at sea in the wreck of the *Rose in Bloom* in August 1806. When one considers that General William Moultrie and Christopher Gadsden died in 1805 in Charleston, one can understand the devastating effects these deaths had upon the continuation of the Federalist Party.

The one person who seemed destined to inherit the mantle of the Federalist leadership was John Rutledge Jr. as a continuation of the Rutledge-Pinckney faction. John Rutledge Sr. died in 1800, and his brother, Edward Rutledge, died in office as governor on January 23, 1800. John Drayton, the first lieutenant governor to become a governor, was an able man, but not a commanding figure. The leader of the South Carolina Federalists became General Charles Cotesworth Pinckney, who ran for president in 1804 and 1808. Pinckney was very influential in the Beaufort District and spent most of his later years on his favorite sea island plantation, Pinckney Island behind Hilton Head, but he apparently lacked a significant popular following in the rest of the state.[55]

In 1796, John Rutledge Jr. (1766–1819) was elected to Congress from the Beaufort District. He was a strong Federalist and the last of his party to represent the Beaufort District in Congress. Rutledge was the son of John Rutledge and Elizabeth Grimke. From his famous father he inherited immense wealth and thoroughly aristocratic leanings. He was elected to the state legislature from the Beaufort District because his principal plantation property was Poplar Grove, the very profitable Savannah River rice plantation in St. Peter's Parish on which he employed 312 slaves at the time of his death. While Rutledge had all the ingredients necessary for political success in South Carolina, his political career and personal life were marked by scandal.

When Rutledge entered state politics in 1796, he was an anti-Federalist and an unsuccessful Jefferson elector. But by the time he entered Congress in its fifth session (1797–1799), he had shifted his allegiance. He became a thorough Federalist and remained so until he left Congress in 1803. His political timing was poor. Even then the Federalists were on the decline, and the Jeffersonian Republicans were rising to political dominance. Rutledge further alienated Thomas Jefferson during his presidency when he was implicated in the Geffrey Letters scandal of 1801. These letters, revealing political corruption in Rhode Island where Rutledge spent every summer, turned out to be fraudulent. Nicholas Geffrey denied authorship, and the Jeffersonian Republicans accused the Federalists of trying to embarrass the new president. When the evidence began to point to Rutledge, he refused to seek re-election and left Congress.

Rutledge's personal life was also beset by controversy. He had made a politically and financially advantageous marriage to Sarah Motte Smith in 1791. In fact, Poplar Grove was a wedding gift from Smith's family to the young couple. Though the marriage produced six children, it ended in scandal. In 1804, in Charleston, Rutledge discovered his wife in an illicit rendezvous with Dr. Horatio

Senter of Newport, Rhode Island. The ensuing "affair of honor" resulted in a duel in Savannah in which Dr. Senter was killed. The marriage did not survive this public scandal. In 1809, the couple legally separated and never lived together again. Rutledge died in Philadelphia in 1819. During his later years in Charleston, he made an enormous contribution to the state by helping to found the *Charleston Courier,* one of the great newspapers of the old South and the mouthpiece of the Federalist faction in South Carolina. Significantly, in the late antebellum period, the *Charleston Courier* became the outlet for the unionist and anti-secessionist political factions in the state.[42]

On July 4, 1803, Robert Barnwell delivered before the Philomathean Society and Inhabitants of Beaufort an oration by one of the society's members. The object of this society was to nurture public speaking. This was a good Federalist view of public events at this time in Beaufort. Barnwell contrasts the "debility of the 1780s with the strength of the new system in the 1790s. He painted a gruesome picture of the French Revolution and then praised Washington's role as a neutral in 1793. Perhaps it was good that Washington has departed "for already has the pestiferous breath of calumny cast a shade upon the bright characters of your friends and advisers; and already has a new order of things trampled under foot the favorite objects of your administration." Britain alone stood opposed to Napoleon, and Napoleon was after Louisiana. Barnwell questioned whether the United States should prepare its defenses and whether the exemption from taxes could be the criterion of national happiness: "the value of liberty to be calculated by the rules of arithmetic."

Barnwell spoke of the heroes—Screven, Roberts, and Laurens—but bewailed the rise of party. We should use this day "to allay the venom of that party poison which rankles in the bosom of our country" and noted that "republicanism cannot long exist devoid of virtue." He addressed the women "to implant in the youthful bosoms of your sons the principles of liberty."[57]

On December 2, 1805, Robert Barnwell was elected president of the South Carolina Senate and presided for the remainder of the Sixteenth General Assembly. He then retired from statewide politics. His death in Beaufort on October 24, 1814, marked the end of the once powerful Federalist faction in the Beaufort District.[58]

NOTES

1. Katherine M. Jones, ed., *Port Royal Under Six Flags* (Indianapolis: Bobbs-Merrill, 1960), 138–39. In 1783 Charleston Town was incorporated by state law and the name officially changed to "Charleston."

2. Adele Edwards, ed., *Journals of the Privy Council, 1783–1789* (Columbia: University of South Carolina Press, 1971), 5, 137, 150, 154; Jerome Nadelhaft, *Disorders of War: The Revolution in South Carolina* (Orono: University of Maine at Orono Press, 1981), 128, 132.

3. Location of the actual encampment is unknown, but it was somewhere between Two Sisters Ferry and Matthew's Bluff in upper St. Peter's Parish.

4. Edwards, ed., *Journals of the Privy Council*, 186, 203–4; Nadelhaft, *Disorders of War*, 132; William Bacom Stevens, *A History of Georgia from Its First Discovery by Europeans to the Adoption of the Present Consitution in MDCCXCVIII*, 2 vols. (1847; rpt., Savannah: Beehive Press, 1972), 2: 376–78.

5. Theodora J. Thompson, ed., *Journals of the House of Representatives, 1783–1784* (Columbia: University of South Carolina Press, 1977), 97.

6. "Petition on Location of Beaufort District Court," General Assembly Papers, February 8, 1787, South Carolina Department of Archives and History.

7. "Petition From St. Helena South of the Broad River," General Assembly Papers, March 1, 1784, South Carolina Department of Archives and History.

8. Thompson, ed., *Journals of the House of Representatives*, 74, 75.

9. Michael E. Stevens, ed., *Journals of the House of Representatives, 1787–1788* (Columbia: University of South Carolina Press, 1981), 57–58.

10. Thomas Cooper and David J. McCord, eds., *The Statutes at Large of South Carolina*, 10 vols. (Columbia: A. S. Johnston, 1836–1841), 5: 76.

11. Thompson, ed., *Journals of the House of Representatives*, 118.

12. George C. Rogers Jr., *The History of Georgetown County, South Carolina* (Columbia: University of South Carolina Press, 1970), 203–5.

13. "Petition to Move Equity Court to Coosawhatchie," November 29, 1810, General Assembly Papers, South Carolina Department of Archives and History.

14. "Petition From Lincoln Co.," n.d. 1788, General Assembly Papers, South Carolina Department of Archives and History.

15. "Report on Votes for Sheriff," n.d. 1802, and "Report on Equity Court Election," n.d., General Assembly Papers, South Carolina Department of Archives and History.

16. John Davis, *Travels of John Davis in the United States of America, 1798 to 1802* (Boston: Privately printed, 1910).

17. *Biographical Directory of the South Carolina House*, 4: 292–94, 359–61.

18. "Report on Courthouse at Coosawhatchie," December 2, 1816 and December 10, 1817, General Assembly Papers, South Carolina Department of Archives and History.

19. Gene Waddell and R. W. Liscombe, *Robert Mills's Court Houses and Jails* (Easley, S.C.: Southern Historical Press, 1981), 32, and figures 2 and 3.

20. Cooper and McCord, eds., *Statutes of South Carolina*, 8: 218–21.

21. *Charleston Courier*, April 17, 1804, 2–3.

22. Cooper and McCord, eds., *Statutes of South Carolina*, 8: 330; "Wm. Joyner's Account Book" (manuscript), September 7, 1818, South Caroliniana Library.

23. "Petitions of Inhabitants of Beaufort on Streets," December 17, 1795; "Petition of John Rhodes on Streets," 27 November 1800; "Petitions on Beaufort Streets," August 3, 1821, General Assembly Papers, South Carolina Department of Archives and History; A. S. Salley, ed., *Minutes of the Vestry of St. Helena's Parish, South Carolina, 1726–1812* (Columbia: Historical Commission of South Carolina, 1919), 225, 227, 228.

24. Cooper and McCord, eds., *Statutes of South Carolina*, 8: 252.

25. "Petition for Guard at Arsenal," n.d. 1819; "Petition From Beaufort Town Council," November 26, 1824, General Assembly Papers, South Carolina Department of Archives and History.

26. "An Act to Grant the Gaol in Beaufort to the Town Council," 18 December 1840, General Assembly Papers, South Carolina Department of Archives and History; "Wm. Joyner's Account Book," September 17, 1816 and November 11, 1816, South Caroliniana Library.

27. "Wm. Joyner's Account Book," August 23, 1816, South Caroliniana Library; "Petition From St. Helena and Lady's Island," November 29, 1810, General Assembly Papers, South Carolina Department of Archives and History.

28. "Mason Locke Weems," *Dictionary of American Biography,* 10: 604–5; "Petition on Transient Poor From Beaufort," August 3, 1821; "Report on Transient Poor Account," November 15, 1824, General Assembly Papers, South Carolina Department of Archives and History.

29. "Petition of the Wardens and Inhabitants of Beaufort," November 12, 1816, and "Petition Against Incorporating Beaufort," November 13, 1816, General Assembly Papers, South Carolina Department of Archives and History.

30. *Charleston Courier,* January 4, 1805, 3; Marvin D. Bass, ed., "Autobiography of William J. Grayson," Ph.D. diss., University of South Carolina, 1933, 4–5.

31. *Biographical Directory of the American Congress, 1774–1961* (Washington, D.C.: U.S. Government Printing Office, 1961), 1049, 1101, 1102.

32. *Biographical Directory of the South Carolina Senate,* 1: 229.

33. "Will of Samuel Grove," June 5, 1776, *Charleston County Wills,* 18 (1776–1784): 60–62; *Biographical Directory of the American Congress,* 1145; Steven G. Baker, *A Partial Biography of John Kean, South Carolinian* (Elizabeth, N.J.: Privately printed for Mrs. John Kean, 1971), 42–88.

34. *Biographical Directory of the South Carolina Senate,* 1: 99; *Biographical Directory of the South Carolina House,* 2: 52–54.

35. George C. Rogers Jr., *Evolution of a Federalist: William Loughton Smith of Charleston (1758–1812)* (Columbia: University of South Carolina Press, 1962), 191–92, 205, 227, 277, 363.

36. Jonathan Elliot, ed., *Debates on the Adoption of the Federal Constitution,* 5 vols. (Salem, N.H.: Ayer, 1987), 4: 339–40.

37. Elliot, ed., *Debates,* 4: 291–97.

38. Elliot, ed., *Debates,* 4: 333.

39. John Brown Cutting to John Rutledge Jr., February 21, 1789, John Rutledge Jr. Papers, SHC.

40. *Heads of Families, 1790 Census, South Carolina,* 10–13.

41. "Blake of South Carolina," *South Carolina Historical Magazine* 1 (April 1909): 153–62.

42. Pierce Butler to Mrs. Graeme, August 21, 1792; Butler to John McPherson, November 6, 1792, Pierce Butler Letterbook, South Caroliniana Library.

43. *Heads of Families, 1790 Census, South Carolina,* 10–13.

44. *Biographical Directory of the South Carolina House,* 4: 500–2.

45. Jean Martin Flynn, "South Carolina's Compliance with the Militia Act of 1792," *South Carolina Historical Magazine* 69 (1968): 26–43.

46. Ralph Izard to Jacob Read, May 9, 1798, Izard Papers, South Caroliniana Library.

47. *Carolina Gazette,* May 31, 1798.

48. *Carolina Gazette,* July 17, 1798.

49. Henry William DeSaussure to Jacob Read, July 14, 1798, miscellaneous mss., New York Public Library.

50. "Notes and Queries," *South Carolina Historical Magazine* 2 (April 1901): 155.

51. Barnwell of South Carolina," *South Carolina Historical Magazine* 2 (January 1901): 55, 91–92.

52. Rogers, *Evolution of a Federalist,* 351–52.

53. Speech delivered in the South Carolina Senate, December 16, 1794.

54. Rogers, *Evolution of a Federalist,* 293, 351.

55. Rogers, *Evolution of a Federalist,* 352–55.

56. Robert K. Ratzloff, "Biography of John Rutledge, Jr.," Ph.D. diss., University of Kansas, 1975.

57. Robert Barnwell, *An Oration, delivered before the Philomathean Society and Inhabitants of Beaufort, South Carolina, on Monday, July 4, 1803* (Charleston, 1803).

58. *Biographical Directory of the South Carolina Senate,* 1: 99–100.

15

Introduction of Sea Island Cotton
to the Beaufort District, 1790–1829

SEA ISLAND COTTON

The story of sea island cotton is the beginning of the story of antebellum Beaufort. The story of upland cotton is the beginning of the story of the antebellum South. These important stories emerged in the late 1780s and early 1790s out of the small southeastern corner of South Carolina. Sea island cotton became the principal crop on the sea islands south of Charleston. Sea island cotton was to divide the four southeastern parishes. Prince William and St. Peter's were the great rice-producing parishes while St. Helena and St. Luke's were the sea island cotton parishes. All of this was clear to the perceptive observer by 1790.

The story of cotton is first of all a story of seeds. "Cotton is a vegetable fiber attached to the seeds of various species of the genus Gossypium."[1] The species, *Gossypium Barbadense,* was the long-staple, silky-fibered, smooth-seeded cotton which became known as the sea island cotton. There were experiments with the culture of cotton from the first settlement at Jamestown. Green seed cotton, the lint of which adheres tenaciously to the seed, had been widely grown in the backcountry before the Revolution. Yet it was strange that when the South Carolina Agricultural Society (founded in 1785) began its search for new staples for the South Carolina economy it did not spend much time considering cotton. By what path did cotton come to South Carolina? The introduction of sea island cotton is largely a story that involves the West Indies, Florida, Georgia, and South Carolina. Something was happening from the Mosquito Inlet in Florida to James and Johns Island at the southern threshold of Charleston.

There are four accounts which, placed together, provide the larger story. Dr. Andrew Turnbull's New Smyrna settlement in East Florida deserves more consideration than it has formerly been given. Dr. Turnbull received a large grant of land in 1763 at Mosquito Inlet. He had married Maria Garcia in Smyrna, Asia Minor, where their eldest son Nicholas had been born in 1754. They arrived with immigrants from the eastern Mediterranean and obviously brought cotton seeds with them.[2] John Earle of Skidaway Island in Georgia was an over-seer in East Florida prior to 1771.[3] Nicholas Turnbull later wrote that Earle, while in the employ of his father in Florida, communicated to him the results of his five-year experiment in growing cotton. Nicholas Turnbull began planting cotton in Georgia in 1787 at a plantation near the Rochester Ferry. This was long-staple cotton for export.[4] In October 1824, the *Savannah Republican* re-ported that Turnbull had died "at his plantation, Deptford Hill, 3 miles from Savannah, a native of Smyrna, aged about seventy years, during forty of which he has maintained an unblemished reputation in this country. Mr. Turnbull, it is believed, was the first planter who cultivated upon a scale for exportation the article of cotton, now the greatest staple of our state."[5]

A parallel story is that of the family of Francis Levett Sr. who had lived at Leghorn in Italy before immigrating to join his brother-in-law, Governor Patrick Tonyn of East Florida. Francis Levett Jr. received seeds in Georgia in 1786. In 1791, a Savannah firm shipped 10,000 pounds of his cotton to London to the firm of Simpson and Davidson.[6]

The second story is of the movement of South Carolinians from the neigh-borhood of Beaufort to Georgia, many of whom would afterward produce this new crop on the islands. Captain Philip Delegal, who had fought with Oglethorpe in 1742 at the Battle of Bloody Marsh on St. Simons Island and had secured by grant lots 175 and 177 in Beaufort on April 13, 1747, was planting short-staple cotton "on a small island near Savannah" in the early 1760s.[7] Henry Laurens, who was extending his planting interest into Georgia in the 1760s, wrote in 1767: "I never saw anything grow more luxuriantly than Cotton does upon Broughton Island." Laurens spoke of acquiring seeds from the island of Grenada in the West Indies.[8]

The career lines of Kinsey Burden Sr. and Kinsey Burden Jr. focus upon the most successful of all the sea island planters. According to the son, Kinsey Bur-den Sr. had planted cotton on Burden's Island, a part of Johns Island in St. Paul's Parish, Colleton County, in 1778 and 1779. That early effort was stimulated by a need to produce cloth locally to clothe the slaves during the American Revo-lution. His wife had tried to carry on after the war and failed. By 1793, James King, who had married Mrs. Burden's daughter, was selling cotton for export to the firm of Teasdale and Kiddell, the only purchasers of cotton at that time in the Charleston market. On May 22, 1843, Kinsey Burden Jr. wrote W. B. Seabrook that his father had used a roller gin in preparing his sea island cotton for the market.[9]

But none of these early experiments represents the main thread of the story which concerns the Loyalists, who, having left South Carolina and Georgia at the end of the Revolution for East Florida, fled from St. Augustine to the Bahamas in 1783, 1784, and 1785. The South Carolina family of DeVeaux was at the heart of this movement. Andre DeVeaux, the immigrant, had helped Eliza Lucas develop the culture of indigo near Wappoo Cut on the Stono River. He died in 1784. His son, Andrew II, married Hannah Palmer, the daughter of Captain John Palmer, the Indian fighter. Their son, Andrew III, married Catherine Barnwell and as a Loyalist took the path to St. Augustine and then to the Bahama Islands. The principal figure in this part of the family history was Andrew IV (1758–1812), who, as we have already seen, led the British to Port Royal Island in 1779 and was responsible for the burning of Sheldon Church and General Stephen Bull's home. Andrew IV led an expedition in 1783 from St. Augustine to take the Bahama Islands from the Spaniards. His small expedition captured New Providence, and when the British had to leave East Florida after the Peace of Paris, many of the Loyalists took their slaves and moved to the islands of the archipelago. The British Board of Trade, in order to assist these planters, had long-staple cotton seeds sent from the island of Anguilla in the West Indies. Many land grants were made from 1784 to 1789 to the Loyalists in the Bahama Islands. Boom times ensued in these islands.[10]

In 1783, there were 1,722 whites and 2,336 blacks in the Bahama Islands; by 1789, these numbers had increased to 3,300 whites and approximately 8,000 blacks. By the end of 1785, long-staple cotton was being produced in exportable quantities: 2,476 acres produced 124 tons for export in 1785; 3,050 acres produced 150 tons in 1786; and 4,500 acres produced 219 tons in 1787, which in that year was valued at 27,393 pounds sterling.[11] In October 1787, Lord Dunmore, who had been the last royal governor of Virginia, had arrived in the Bahamas to become the royal governor of this newly important British colony. As many of the Loyalists were of Scottish descent, this was an admirable choice for leadership of the colony. The cotton boom, however, was not to last, as the lands in the Bahama Islands were sandy and wore out quickly. By the end of the 1790s, a survey of conditions indicated that much soil was being blown away. The planters were forced to look elsewhere for land. They could move once again either further into the West Indies or back to the lands that they had left.[12]

These Loyalists all had friends and relatives on the mainland in South Carolina and Georgia. Even if they did not go back themselves with their slaves, they could pass on seeds and know-how to their friends at home. The introduction of this knowledge and technology (e.g., the roller gin) into the area was the driving force behind the new boom on the sea islands. These forces came about at just the right time as the sea island indigo planters were looking for a new staple. The cultivation of indigo had gone into a rapid decline with the end of the Revolution when the subsidy of the British Parliament for indigo was eliminated.[13]

An important document has survived that measures the decline of indigo. It is the "Merchant's Account Book, 1785–1791," which was kept in the Beaufort store of John Mark Verdier. In 1785, the store bought 6,751 pounds sterling of indigo; in 1786, 5,787 pounds sterling; and in 1788, 3,389 pounds sterling.[14]

By the opening of the decade of the 1790s, the shift from indigo to sea island cotton had taken place, and a new era was opening up. Wealth was at hand. In the 1790s, there was a new crop, perhaps the premier crop in the whole history of the United States. By the 1850s, politicians would talk about King Cotton. But perceptive planters could see in 1790 that if you could move this crop from the sea islands to the vast rich lands of the interior there would be an unparalleled bonanza. The capital amassed from these exports could be used as the foundation for the new American economy. At the end of Whitemarsh B. Seabrook's *Memoir on the Sea Island Cotton Plant* there is a list of exports from America to Liverpool. The Charleston firm at the center of this export trade was that of John and Isaac Teasdale.[15]

William Elliott II, at his Myrtle Bank plantation on the northern tip of Hilton Head Island, was first in the Beaufort District to plant sea island cotton. This became the foundation of one of antebellum Beaufort's wealthiest families. According to his son, William Elliott III, the year was 1790.[16] Close behind him were General John Barnwell and his brothers. These were all sons of Colonel Nathaniel Barnwell (1705–1775) and thus grandsons of "Tuscarora Jack." They were Nathaniel Barnwell Jr. (1746–1798), General John Barnwell (1748–1800), Edward Barnwell (1757–1808), and Colonel Robert Barnwell (1761–1814).

The new wealth produced by the introduction of sea island cotton was the foundation of the Elliott and Barnwell families' fortunes. It was also the basis of the political influence of the Beaufort community in South Carolina's Federalist Party in the early nation. The Barnwells were to sea island cotton what the Heywards were to rice. Of course, the Barnwells had been indigo planters on the islands while the Heywards had been rice planters on the mainland. Thus the first cotton boom represented a shift of power back from the mainland to the sea islands.

The Duc de la Rochefoucauld visited Beaufort in 1796 and pinned down the transition to cotton with these words: "The Island of Port Royal occupied today by sixty or seventy planters was, as late as four years ago, entirely devoted to the growing of indigo. At that time, poor results . . . difficulties in processing and low prices . . . forced people to try to convert to cotton, begun two years earlier in Georgia." By 1796, indigo had thus been "totally abandoned on Beaufort Island (Port Royal Island) and on the neighboring islands . . . where it is being replaced by cotton."[17]

A quick and efficient method of separating the fibers from the seeds had to be found. The solution would be a gin (the word derives from *engine*) which would make the separation possible. The Eve family of South Carolina and the Bahama Islands was responsible for the invention of the roller gin, which squeezed the seeds from the fiber. Kinsey Burden's father had used a roller gin in South Carolina in 1778. And Eli Whitney had invented the saw-toothed gin in 1793. This revolutionary development occurred at Mulberry Grove Plantation on the Savannah River, directly across from the Beaufort District.[18]

These dual developments in agronomy and technology led to the explosive growth in the production and export of sea island cotton from South Carolina. In the period from October 1, 1789, to September 30, 1790, 9,840 pounds of sea island cotton were exported from South Carolina. In the period from October 1, 1800, to September 30, 1801, 8,301,907 pounds were exported. The crop of 1804 was more than eight times that of 1794. Between 1790 and 1800, the price of cotton was averaging about thirty-five cents a pound at the ports. An even greater bonanza occurred in the last four years prior to 1820, when prices reached 63.2 cents per pound in 1818.[5]

Throughout the antebellum era the sea island cotton product of specific plantations was often known by the name of the planter that produced it, much as wine has generally been known by the name of the vineyard that produced the grapes. The rapid development of the sea island plantations of the Beaufort District, based on the promise of rising profits from the production of cotton, can be illustrated by the development of two of South Carolina's premier cotton plantations: Coffin Point Plantation and Frogmore Plantation on St. Helena Island. In the antebellum era, St. Helena Island became one of the premier locations in South Carolina for the cultivation of sea island cotton.

Coffin Point Plantation was settled by Ebenezer Coffin, a New Englander who moved to St. Helena Island during the 1790s at the beginning of the sea island cotton boom. Coffin Point is the northernmost point of St. Helena Island, overlooking St. Helena Sound and the Atlantic Ocean beyond. Ebenezer Coffin began clearing the fields for cotton and erecting the structures for the plantation settlement in the spring of 1800. The dwelling house (which stands today), the cotton house, and the kitchen house were all built that year. Three thousand shingles, twelve hundred feet of board siding, five hundred feet of floor boards, and four thousand bricks went into the main house. The house was forty feet by twenty feet, raised well off the ground. When the structure was complete, Coffin ordered boards, rafters, scantling, and "six columns" to complete the "piazza" overlooking St. Helena Sound. The cotton house, forty-eight feet by sixteen feet, and the kitchen were also completed in 1800. The next year, Coffin erected a number of "Negro houses" that formed the slave street at Coffin Point. He employed five carpenters at two dollars per day to construct these cottages. By 1803, the whole plantation community was complete.

Over the next decade, Coffin continued to clear and plant the cotton ground. By 1813, Coffin Point Plantation was already a large plantation with ninety-six slaves, fifty-two of whom were "working" hands. They worked 232 acres of "cotton ground" and another 124 acres of corn and potato fields. Ebenezer Coffin died in 1816 and left Coffin Point Plantation to his son, Thomas A. Coffin. Thomas Coffin was born in Charleston in 1795 and graduated from Harvard in 1815. Throughout the antebellum era, he expanded and improved his cotton land and added to his slave labor force. In 1829, Coffin married Harriet Butler McPherson, daughter of James Elliott McPherson of Brewton Hall Plantation in Prince William Parish. McPherson was one of the wealthiest men in the Beaufort District, and the marriage, which lasted twenty-three years, brought additional wealth and social connections. With summer homes in Charleston and Newport, Rhode Island, as well as his Coffin Point Plantation, Coffin was the epitome of a sea island cotton nabob. By 1850, he had become one of the largest cotton producers in the Beaufort District and the largest slaveholder on St. Helena Island. In 1850, he owned 2,911 acres, with 1,811 acres in prime cotton fields, and 301 slaves.[20]

The largest plantation on St. Helena Island in the colonial and antebellum era was Frogmore Plantation. The plantation was part of the vast estate of Lieutenant Governor William Bull II, who died in 1791. Originally granted to his father, William Bull I, in 1731, Frogmore Plantation comprised 3,300 acres that stretched across the middle of St. Helena Island from Seaside Road on the east side of the island to the headwaters of Chowan Creek on the west side. The northwest corner of the tract was the natural crossroads of St. Helena Island with roads leading west to Beaufort, south to Land's End on Port Royal Sound, and east to Coffin Point on St. Helena Sound. It was known in the antebellum era as "Frogmore Corner." The main settlement of Frogmore Plantation was on Seaside Road. Before the revolution, some of this tract had been cleared and planted with indigo. William Bull's loyalist claim estimated the property and slaves to be worth fifty-seven hundred pounds sterling, one of his most valuable properties in South Carolina. When Bull died as a Tory refugee in England in 1791, Frogmore Plantation passed to his niece, Hannah Beale Stapleton, wife of Colonel John Stapleton of the British army. The Stapletons never returned to America, and in the forty-five years that they owned Frogmore, they never set foot on the plantation.

In 1800, there were seventy-eight slaves living on Frogmore, the largest slave community on St. Helena Island at the turn of the century. In addition to Abram, the driver, there were three carpenters, two sawyers, one cooper, and forty-one adult men and women available as fieldhands. Other special occupations were those of Dye, the nurse-midwife; Lilly, the cook; and Lame Dick, the "basket maker and fisherman." Old Dorothy, Rose, Nanny, Sylvia, and Judy spent their days minding the twenty-four children and tending to the cotton house. With a large labor force and ample land, Frogmore Plantation was ideally situated to capitalize on the first sea island cotton boom.

A succession of plantation managers were given free housing and servants, as well as ample food from the plantation, and were paid an annual salary of two hundred dollars. These managers rapidly expanded the Frogmore operation between 1800 and 1816. Between 1800 and 1810, the slave population grew 42 percent with the addition of new slaves imported directly from Africa. By 1810, Abram the driver had retired and passed the responsibility of field management on to his son, Bern. With several different plantation managers in sixteen years, continuity and efficiency in the plantation operation was provided by both of these drivers.

This effort brought great rewards to the owners. Between October 1815 and February 1816, Frogmore's manager, William Bell, sold 133 bales of sea island cotton on the Charleston market. At prevailing prices, the 1815 crop would have earned $20,162 for the Stapletons, a princely sum in those years. By 1818, the slave population had grown to 139, and the primary plantation settlement on Seaside Road consisted of the main house occupied by the overseer, a barn, a provisioning house, a cotton house, a ginning shed, and "18 negro houses" on the "street." In 1836, prompted by the emancipation of slaves in the British empire in 1833 and the prohibition against British citizens owning slaves, Colonel John Stapleton sold most of the original Frogmore lands and all the slaves to U.S. Congressman William J. Grayson for eighty-eight thousand dollars.[21]

The first sea island cotton boom caused similar expansion and capital accumulation throughout the sea islands. The wealth amassed by the sea island cotton planters between 1790 and 1825 made them among the richest families in early America. For the rest of the antebellum era they rivaled the rice princes of the mainland for social status and political influence in the Old South. The wealth produced by sea island cotton also made the old town of Beaufort the social and cultural capital of the sea islands and one of the wealthiest towns in antebellum America.

EDUCATION AND CULTURAL INSTITUTIONS

The Beaufort District at the turn of the nineteenth century, buoyed by the introduction of sea island cotton, saw the establishment of the educational and cultural institutions that represented the rising aspirations of the planter community. In 1786, the St. Helena Society and Beaufort Society were formed for the purpose of developing schools on St. Helena and Port Royal Islands.[22] With depressed postwar conditions, they were initially unsuccessful. But in 1795, the two societies merged for the more ambitious purpose of founding a college at Beaufort. Beaufort College was to become one of the most distinguished preparatory academies in the American South.

On November 23, 1795, a joint petition of the St. Helena Society, the Beaufort Society, and the Beaufort District Society asked the legislature for permission to be incorporated for the purpose of "promoting the education of youth." Together they had two thousand pounds sterling, and they had "resolved unanimously that the erection and endowment of a college would not only be the most likely means of carrying their intentions into effect, but would be a valuable asset to the state." They asked the legislature to apply the funds raised from the sale of confiscated estates in the Beaufort District toward their purpose. They intended to locate the college in Beaufort because the climate was morally and physically salubrious. The town boasted "a large share of health enjoyed there and a desirable absence of the usual materials for dissipation which large towns and cities so amply and so fately [sic] furnish." They hoped the new college would provide "a liberal education for the opulent . . . all branches of useful knowledge to those in middling circumstances . . . and at the same time present the pleasing prospect of bestowing a competent education on the poor."[23]

On December 19, 1795, the legislature incorporated the trustees of the Beaufort College and gave them the power to use the proceeds of confiscated estate sales to support the college. The trustees were empowered to "confer such degree or degrees in the liberal arts or sciences . . . as are usually conferred in other colleges in Europe and America."[24] The original trustees of Beaufort College were the town's most eminent citizens: General John Barnwell (president), Colonel Robert Barnwell, Major William Hazzard Wigg, William Elliott II, Stephen Elliott, Reverend Henry Holcombe, Dr. Thomas Fuller, General John McPherson, General John A. Cuthbert, John Jenkins Sr., William Fripp, John Bull, and John Mark Verdier. Almost immediately the trustees were embroiled in controversy. A petition from a group of mainland farmers objected to the use of funds from confiscated estates because of conflicting claims to that land. The legislature referred these conflicting claims to the courts and dedicated only the money from vacant town lots for the college.[25]

By 1803, the trustees had assembled sixty to seventy thousand dollars toward the building and operation of the college and had already begun the search for a president. Robert Barnwell wrote to Rufus King in New York in 1801 that the trustees hoped to find a man of "moderate and liberal sentiments both of Politiks and Religion." They hoped for a clergyman and were willing to pay him thirteen hundred dollars per year and ten dollars for each student in his charge.

This was a handsome salary at a time when large plantation managers were paid three to five hundred dollars per year. King referred the letter to Dr. Joseph Drury of Harrow, England, who called the opportunity "alluring."[26]

While the search for a president proceeded, the trustees forged ahead with the construction of the first college building, a large frame structure on the corner of Bay and Church Streets. The cornerstone was laid on November 16, 1802, and on January 18, 1804, Beaufort College opened. Though no president had been appointed, Reverend John Hedly was the first professor of languages.[27] Some of the other early faculty were Dr. James E. B. Finley, Reverend Martin Luther Hurlbut, Milton and Virgil Maxcy, and James L. Petigru. Of these men, only Petigru was a South Carolinian. Petigru, later one of South Carolina's pre-eminent lawyers and intellects, was the acting president from 1811 to 1812, when he was superseded by Reverend Martin Luther Hurlbut of Portland, Maine. Milton and Virgil Maxcy moved to Beaufort in 1804 to open a school for boys. Both also taught at Beaufort College. The Maxcy brothers had followed their oldest brother, Jonathan, to South Carolina. Jonathan Maxcy was the first president of the new South Carolina College founded in Columbia in 1801 and had previously been the second president of Rhode Island College (now Brown University). Virgil Maxcy later moved to Baltimore, but Milton Maxcy married local heiress Mary Bull, daughter of General Stephen Bull of Sheldon and widow of Nathaniel Barnwell II. Milton entered the law and became a prominent member of the Beaufort community. Dr. Finley also remained in Beaufort to pursue his active medical practice.

Despite an auspicious and well-funded beginning, the ambitions of the founders were soon tempered by reality. Enrollments did not meet expectations because of Beaufort's remote location and because many of the state's youth began attending the new South Carolina College. Beaufort College could not find or keep qualified instructors, and, as President Martin Hurlbut complained, the trustees seemed dilatory in their responsibilities to the college. This was not surprising, since the original trustees were very busy men with personal business and planting responsibilities as well as statewide political and military commitments. Eight of the original thirteen trustees served, at some time, in the state legislature. Three were generals in the state militia and one had been a U.S. congressman. In addition, Beaufort College never attracted the sons of West Indian cotton and sugar planters as they had hoped. The Napoleonic Wars disrupted the Caribbean, and, by the time the college opened in 1804, the original Bahamian cotton plantations, many founded by families with connections to the Beaufort District, were already in decline. As a consequence, Beaufort College settled into a lesser role as a college preparatory school for local families, and a feeder institution for the South Carolina College and established colleges in the north.[28]

Reverend Martin Hurlbut was replaced in 1814 by Reverend Martin Brantly and his assistant, William J. Grayson.[29] Grayson, like Petigru before him, was a South Carolinian who began his career at Beaufort College and went on to become one of the state's best-known intellects.

Though lowered from its original lofty pretensions, Beaufort College nonetheless became one of the most distinguished preparatory institutions in the South. With excellent young teachers from South Carolina as well as experienced northern educators, and one of the finest book collections in the southern states, the college produced a remarkable group of young men between 1804 and 1817. Educated there were, among others, statesman Robert W. Barnwell, author William Elliott III, minister and author Richard Fuller, and politician and publisher Robert Barnwell Rhett, the "Father of Secession."[30] Most of the students from Beaufort College went on to the South Carolina College, but many went on to distinguished academic careers in the north. Before the Civil War, no fewer than twenty-five men from the small town attended Harvard. Behind Harvard were Yale, Princeton, Columbia, and West Point. The most academically successful of these young men was Robert W. Barnwell, who was the acknowledged student leader of the Harvard class of 1821.[31]

Beaufort College suffered a major setback in 1817 when a serious epidemic of yellow fever swept the community. One-seventh of the town's population and a much higher percentage of the students died. Students commonly attended school during the spring and summer months (April through October) while their families were in Beaufort escaping the less healthy conditions of the plantations. The epidemic was thought to have been imported aboard a foreign vessel and spread among students mingling at the college. When the fever struck the town, many families fled to Bay Point to escape its ravages. The school was swiftly shut down and, because of the accumulated tragedies of 1817 and the fear that the college building was still infected, was not reopened for several years. The original college building was razed and the site abandoned.[32]

Closely associated with Beaufort College was another cultural institution of great pride to the local population. The Beaufort Library Society was incorporated on December 19, 1807.[33] Petitions to form such a society had begun as early as 1803, and, according to the petitions, a group led by Dr. James Finley, Stephen Elliott, Robert Barnwell, Milton Maxcy, and Robert Screven had been meeting in informal intellectual discussion groups for some years.[34] This was a distinguished group: Elliott was a state senator, Yale graduate, top candidate to be the second president of the South Carolina College, and "father of the free school system in South Carolina"; Maxcy and Finley were both teachers at the college. Barnwell was a former U.S. congressman and one of the state's most eloquent and formidable orators. Screven was a physician, graduate of Edinburgh University, and state legislator.[35] When the Beaufort Library Society was incorporated in 1807, Elliott was its first president and Maxcy was the secretary.

The Beaufort Library gathered one of the finest book collections in the South. By 1861, there were thirty-one hundred volumes of classic works: "A choice selection gathered in Europe by Hugh Swinton Legare."[36] The students at the college had the free run of this collection, and when the new college building was erected on Carteret Street in 1852, the Beaufort Library collection was housed in the mezzanine rotunda at the rear of the building. During the Civil War, this collection, as well as several private collections in town, were confiscated as contraband and shipped to New York for auction. The government sale in 1862 described "an immense collection of library books in all departments of literature, arts and sciences including very many important and scarce works." Some historians estimate as many as ten thousand volumes were shipped from Beaufort to New York for sale. The auction was abruptly halted by U.S. Secretary of Treasury Salmon P. Chase, whose timely comment was, "We do not wage war on libraries." The collection was sent to Washington and stored in the Smithsonian Institution where it was destroyed by fire in 1868.[37]

The women of the town, not to be outdone by the men, petitioned the legislature in 1815 to form the Ladies Benevolent Society of the Beaufort District "for the purpose of establishing a society for the relief of distressed and destitute female children." The women who originated this society were the social elite of the sea island planter community in the early antebellum era. They were led by Ann Barnwell and Margaret McKee, who were mentioned by William Elliott about 1839 as the last women in Beaufort eligible to receive pensions for a husband's service in the Revolutionary War. Others of the original group were Elizabeth Fuller, Mary Barnwell, Ann Cuthbert, Mary M. Stuart, Catherine Ann Campbell, Ann Stuart, Ann Brantly, Mary Means, Mary Fraser, Elizabeth Fripp, and Ann Farmer. The organization was incorporated on December 16, 1815. This society was reincorporated in 1831 and remained active throughout the antebellum era.[38] It remains active today and its minute books, almost continuous since 1815, are maintained in the archives of the Beaufort County Public Library.

The educational and cultural example of the Beaufort community spread throughout the district as numerous local schools were opened to serve the scattered rural communities of the mainland. The second oldest school in the Beaufort District was the Black Swamp Academy, founded in 1818 to educate the sons of the planter community of upper St. Peter's Parish. This remote corner of the Beaufort District along the Savannah River had been rising in prosperity and importance since the Revolution. The Black Swamp Academy was incorporated on December 18, 1818, and was located near the crossroads of Robertville. The school was run by Tristram Verstille and his wife, Charlotte. It was housed in a twenty-by-forty-foot building. In 1819, a proposal to begin a second school for young women failed to raise enough money, so in 1820, they also attended the Black Swamp Academy. Students who came from some distances were boarded at the home of Tristran and Charlotte Verstille. A significant reflection of the Savannah River community was the fact that the curriculum included not only standard grammar but also instruction in French and German—reflecting the heritage of the Swiss and Salzburger families that had settled that neighborhood two generations before.[39]

The Indian Land Library Society (no records of which now exist) was formed in 1817 near the district court at Coosawhatchie; the same community organized the Grahamville School Academy in 1830. An informal school was operating in the 1820s at Kirk's Bluff, a developing summer resort for the planters of Hilton Head and St. Luke's Parish that was later incorporated as the town of Bluffton.[40] This school was the beginning of the May River Academy.

The early years of the nineteenth century were characterized by economic expansion and optimism based largely on the growth of the cotton industry. During these years, South Carolina was the largest cotton-producing state in America, and, in 1816, the state was second only to New York in total value of its exports.[41] The Beaufort District was in the forefront of this cotton revolution, and many old families had made new fortunes in the first two decades of the nineteenth century. The cultural aspirations of the community were a reflection of the expectations of those years.

THE WAR OF 1812

Another event which influenced the economic growth of the sea islands during the years of the first cotton boom was the War of 1812. During this period, the old fears of naval attack against Port Royal Sound prompted appeals from local planters for more federal government protection against the powerful British navy. Even before hostilities were declared in 1812, requests to rebuild old Fort Lyttelton reached Washington. In 1807, William Elliott II wrote to the secretary of war seeking to rebuild the colonial fort on Spanish Point with palmetto logs and mount artillery pieces on the bastion. In 1808, Alexander McComb of the Army Corps of Engineers visited Beaufort and recommended the construction of a new battery on the site of old Fort Lyttelton. He recommended that the new fort be built of tabby construction because of its permanence and its local availability. The project was approved by the War Department along with the posting of an artillery garrison. The cost of the project was estimated to be $16,727.77. This was the beginning of Fort Marion.

Thomas Fuller House, Beaufort, built ca. 1786. Elizabeth Middleton Fuller raised nine children here (Beaufort County Public Library Collection).

Barnwell-Gough House in Beaufort, built ca. 1786. This three-story tabby house was built for Elizabeth Barnwell Gough, whose daughter, Marianna Gough Smith, raised the six Smith (Rhett) boys, including Robert Barnwell Rhett (Beaufort County Public Library Collection).

John Mark Verdier House in Beaufort, built ca. 1790, as it appeared during the Civil War (Beaufort County Public Library Collection).

Coffin Point Plantation House, St. Helena Island, built by Ebenezer Coffin in 1801 (photo by Robert W. Jenkins).

Mary Jenkins Place, St. Helena Island, built ca. 1800. A typical sea island cotton plantation with duplex slave cabin (to the left) (Reed Collection, Beaufort County Public Library).

Frogmore Plantation House, St. Helena Island, built ca. 1810, as seen from the marshes of Club Bridge Creek (photo by Robert W. Jenkins).

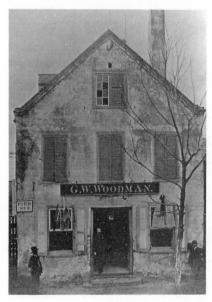

John Cross Tavern in Beaufort, built ca. 1800, as it appeared during the Civil War. G. W. Woodman was a wartime merchant who occupied the building (Historic Beaufort Foundation Collection).

Construction of Fort Marion was delayed until 1811. When hostilities with Great Britain commenced the following year, only the foundation had been completed, and Beaufort was defenseless. A committee of local planters led by Colonel Robert Barnwell petitioned President James Madison directly on May 9, 1812, to hasten the completion of Fort Marion. Governor Middleton proposed to bolster its garrison with a unit of state militia. Captain Prentiss Willard of the Corps of Engineers was sent to Beaufort to supervise construction, and by 1813 Fort Marion was nearly complete.

Fort Marion was a semicircular bastion built of heavy tabby and earth construction. It was designed to mount seven heavy guns on its platform. A barracks and powder magazine were also part of the installation. A detachment from the Eighth U.S. Infantry regiment was sent to garrison the fort in 1813. In 1814, the Fifth Brigade of the Twenty-second Regiment of South Carolina Militia was posted to Fort Marion.[42]

British naval forces did not directly attack Beaufort during the War of 1812, so the men at Fort Marion never saw military action. But two British armed brigs, the HMS *Mosell* and the HMS *Calabri,* blockaded Port Royal Sound, three miles downriver from Fort Marion, in August 1813. Sailors from the ships landed on St. Helena Island and Pinckney Island and carried off several slaves. They also burned a schooner owned by Charles Cotesworth Pinckney's sister. Within a week of their arrival, however, a "dreadfull hurricane" struck the sea islands. The naval flotilla was forced to put to sea into the teeth of the storm, and one of the British ships was lost.

Port Royal Sound suffered no further incursions, but events on the Georgia sea islands were well known in Beaufort. The war was ending when Admiral Sir George Cockburn occupied Cumberland and St. Simon's Islands and gave force to the Royal Navy orders of 1814 to offer freedom to any plantation slaves who sought British protection and allegiance. Nearly seven hundred slaves fled the Georgia sea islands and were later liberated in Halifax, Nova Scotia.[43] These events brought the specter of slave insurrection once again to the Beaufort District. The British naval campaign against slavery and the liberation of Haiti during the Napoleonic Wars were well known to South Carolina slaves and probably contributed to the Denmark Vesey conspiracy in Charleston in 1822.

Beaufort, however, was spared the worst ravages of war. The construction of Fort Marion and the posting of federal and state troops in Beaufort added significantly to the life and commerce of the town during the war years. America experienced a new burst of national pride in the years following the war, and the sea island planters prospered from the highest prices for sea island cotton during the antebellum era.

The hectic excitement of the cotton bonanza following the War of 1812 is best represented by the following letter written on February 15, 1819, by John Speakman and Co. of Savannah to their agents, cotton factors McConnell and Kennedy of Manchester, England, who were eager to purchase the best sea island cotton.

Gent:

Your very much esteemed letter of 30th December came to hand this morning and we pay particular attention to its contents.

We are particularly obliged to you for the list of Planters marks you have sent us, they will afford us a good criterion to go by, to suit you with cottons. Seabrooks are in Charleston held at 65 cents: Coffins are sold at 65. Butler ships his crop to Liverpool, to Harrisons and Latham — . . . Hanscombe sends to Charleston —Page has got his crop not yet at market, we have a preference of it—F. R. Matthews not yet at market, his plantation is St. Simons: Stapleton I believe ships: C. Jenkins goes to Charleston—Jacob Wood Vanderhorst sends to Charleston—R. Means has sold his crop in Charleston at 60 cents—Spalding, ships his crop from Darien— Habersham grows next field to Means, and 18 bags of his crop are now here which have been held at 60 cents and the actors will not take less: they are better put up than usual and are very excellent cottons, we shall try to buy them for you, but have no hopes of getting them under 60 cents—J. Johnson does not make mony on St. Catherine's, we have not been able to know yet, what he has, or means to do with them. . . . This evening we write to Charleston to make some enquiries about Seabrooks and to direct samples to be sent us: if we could get them at 60 or some little more we should be induced to buy some for you—on this subject we will write you more fully as soon as we hear from Charleston.[44]

The year 1819 may be marked as the watershed year for the Beaufort community. The pinnacle of pride and honor of the distinguished old sea island town was the visit of President James Monroe on May 6 to May 8 of that year. President Monroe's southern tour in 1819 was prompted by his desire to inspect the newly acquired territories of East and West Florida which had been ceded by Spain in the Adams-Onis Treaty of 1819. The removal of the Spanish presence was a great relief to southerners, harkening back to distant memories of colonial wars and more recent memories of the War of 1812.

Eighteen nineteen was also the year of the panic which collapsed credit and undermined the United States Bank. When the bank was reorganized it was, significantly, under the leadership of a South Carolinian, prudent, capable Langdon

Cheves. It was the year, as well, of the Missouri Compromise, which, as Charles Pinckney reminded South Carolinians, threatened the constitutional balance which had allowed southerners to be such ardent nationalists in the early nineteenth century. Eighteen nineteen was also the year when the first petition of sea island cotton planters objecting to the tariff policy of the federal government reached the U.S. Congress. These events were disturbing harbingers of the future, but none could predict the future in 1819. Many of the Beaufort planters who organized the reception for President Monroe in May and led the effusive Fourth of July celebration two months later were the same men who signed the first anti-tariff petition in 1819.

The president's party included Governor Geddes and Secretary of War John C. Calhoun, who came overland from Charleston and arrived at the Port Royal Ferry on the evening of May 5. The next day they crossed to Port Royal Island and rode the last six miles into Beaufort accompanied by most of the citizens of the town on horseback. There the president was provided quarters and officially welcomed by the chair for the occasion, Dr. Richard Screven, state senator for St. Luke's Parish. The president's speech to the citizens of Beaufort highlighted the mood of the community in 1819. The United States was a "spectacle of prosperity . . . a people in the full enjoyment of every right, and strangers to every kind of oppression; increasing harmony at home, increasing respect aboard: agriculture and commerce flourishing; our population increasing on principles which increase rather than diminish our national strength. These are blessings for which we ought to be profoundly grateful to the Supreme Author of all good." The next day, President Monroe inspected Fort Marion. In the afternoon, he met the citizens of the town of whom "all received his hand with most gratifying emotions, because all love him." That evening, he was given a banquet by the "citizens of the College, at which a number of patriotic toasts were drank." After dinner, the president "received an elegant assemblage of ladies in a most affable manner."

Early the next morning, after breakfast with Dr. Screven, the president's entourage departed from the bay at Beaufort aboard an "elegant 10-oared canoe" provided by the town. It was accompanied by the Charleston city barge and General Charles Cotesworth Pinckney's personal barge. The stately fleet proceeded from Beaufort to General Pinckney's favorite residence on Pinckney Island and then on to Savannah.[45]

Two months later, flushed with the compliments of "the Chief Magistrate of the Union" and full of patriotic pride, the town celebrated perhaps its most spectacular Fourth of July: "a truly great and bibulous celebration." Thirty-one toasts were offered to the Constitution, George Washington, the heroes of the War of 1812, the "fair sex," and many other worthy sentiments. Two of the final toasts reflected the changing tenor of 1819. Old Jacob Guerard, one of the last veterans of the Revolution, offered a toast to "the Union of the States, the Gordian Knot of our independence—may there never arise an Alexander to cut it asunder." Dr. Thomas Fuller offered the final toast to "the Honorable John C. Calhoun," soon to be the architect of southern rights.[46]

STEAMBOAT ERA

About the time of President Monroe's visit, the winds of social and economic change began to be felt among the sea islands. President Monroe visited the SS *Savannah,* commanded by Captain Moses Rogers, just before it sailed, May 22, 1819, from Savannah for Liverpool, the first steamship to cross the Atlantic. By 1816, the first effects of the early industrial revolution began to influence life and commerce in the Beaufort District. In that year, steam paddlewheelers made their first appearance on the Savannah River. Within three years, regular steamboat traffic connected Charleston, Savannah, and Augusta. Beaufort, Hilton Head, Purrysburg, and several other locations became regular stopping places for numerous steamboat lines that plied the inland passage and the Savannah River for the remainder of the antebellum period.

The first steamboat seen in the Beaufort District was the SS *Enterprise,* built in Savannah in 1816. The SS *Enterprise* was 90 feet long, 20 feet wide, and displaced 152 tons. Its intended purpose was to tow sailing merchant ships upriver from Tybee roads to Savannah. In April 1816, it made the first trip upstream to Augusta to the delight and amusement of the upcountry citizens. Thereafter, the Savannah River became its regular run, and the town of Purrysburg became one of its regular stops. In 1817 and 1818, five new steamboats were built in Charleston for the lucrative passenger and freight run from Charleston to Savannah to Augusta and back. These new vessels were named the SS *Georgia,* the SS *South Carolina,* the SS *Charleston,* the SS *Altamaha,* and the SS *Ockmulgee.* In 1819, the SS *Samuel Howard* and the SS *Columbia* were also launched in Charleston.

The first steamboat to appear in the town of Beaufort was the SS *Charleston,* commanded by Captain Rogers, which arrived from Charleston on December 13, 1817, after a passage of exactly twelve hours. It left Beaufort at 1:30 P.M. the next afternoon and arrived in Savannah ten hours later after being delayed by fog in Calibogue Sound for several hours.[47] The SS *Charleston* was commanded by Moses Rogers, who two years later became famous as the captain of the *Savannah* on the first transatlantic crossing under steam power.

After these first voyages, steam riverboats became the standard mode of passenger, freight, and mail transportation through the sea islands and on the Savannah River. Beaufort's old sailing masters, Captain Daniel Bythewood and Captain Francis Saltus, soon retired, but Saltus's son-in-law, Dr. Henry W. Lubbock, became the town's most prominent early steamboat captain. Regular steamboat connections to Savannah and Charleston improved in number and efficiency throughout the era. As a result, Beaufort and the sea islands became more dependent on the neighboring cities for the exchange of goods and information. The insular self-reliance which had characterized the sea islands in colonial times soon gave way to commercial and logistical interdependence characteristic of the emerging industrial societies.

The most famous passenger ever to arrive in Beaufort aboard a steamboat was the Marquis de Lafayette, the "hero of two worlds" and one of the last surviving compatriots of President George Washington. Lafayette's 1825 visit to Beaufort was aboard the elegant new steamboat SS *Henry Shultz,* commanded by Captain H. W. Lubbock. Beaufort District congressman James Hamilton Jr., whose father, Major James Hamilton, had also been one of Washington's aides-de-camp, attended General Lafayette. The whole day was declared a holiday as the town bustled in preparation for Lafayette's arrival. The Beaufort Volunteer Artillery turned out in their best dress uniforms for a parade in review, and the women of the town prepared for an elegant dress ball at Mrs. Elliott's house on Bay Street. The SS *Henry Shultz* was delayed by tide and weather and did not arrive until 11:00 P.M. Nevertheless, Beaufort Intendant William Elliott III greeted Lafayette at the steamboat landing, and an impressive candlelight procession along Bay Street was quickly improvised.[48] Like the visit of President Monroe in 1817, Lafayette's visit was one of the high points of antebellum Beaufort.

The six years between the 1819 visit of President Monroe, who arrived on horseback and departed by longboat, and the visit of the Marquis de Lafayette, who arrived and departed aboard a first-class steam paddlewheeler, marked a significant turning point in the town's history—the moment when Beaufort was first introduced to the profound changes that the Industrial Revolution was soon to bring to the rest of America. Those six years also mark the end of the first cotton boom among the sea islands of the Beaufort District. Between 1825 and 1827, the price of sea island cotton on the Charleston market dropped 57 percent, from fifty-four cents per pound in 1825 to twenty-one cents per pound in 1827. For the next twenty-five years, cotton prices never came close to the regularly high prices fetched by the luxurious fiber between 1800 and 1825. It was not until 1852 that the price of sea island cotton reached a level comparable to the prices of the first cotton boom. Consequently, cotton production stagnated, the black and white populations of St. Helena Parish stabilized, and new construction in the town of Beaufort came to a halt. The era of growth for Beaufort ended just as other parts of America began to explode with the economic opportunities of the industrial revolution.[49]

NOTES

1.   Lewis Cecil Gray, *History of Agriculture in the Southern United States to 1860,* 2 vols. (Gloucester, Mass.: Peter Smith, 1958), 2: 673.

2.   E. P. Panagopoulos, *New Smyrna, An Eighteenth Century Greek Odyssey* (Gainesville: University of Florida Press, 1966).

3.   John Gerar William De Brahm, *Report of the General Survey in the Southern District of North America,* ed. Louis J. DeVorsey (Columbia: University of South Carolina Press, 1971), 181.

4.   Gray, *History of Agriculture,* 2: 677.

5.   *Savannah Republican,* October 19, 1824; Mary Granger, ed., *Savannah River Plantations* (Savannah: Georgia Historical Society, 1947), 32–33.

6.   Gray, *History of Agriculture,* 2: 676.

7.   For a full treatment, see David R. Chesnutt, *South Carolina's Expansion into Colonial Georgia, 1720–1765* (New York: Garland, 1989).

8.   George C. Rogers Jr. et al., eds, *The Papers of Henry Laurens,* 14 volumes to date (Columbia: University of South Carolina Press, 1968–1994), 5 (1765–1768), 473.

9.   W. B. Seabrook, *A Memoir on the Sea Island Cotton Plant* (Charleston: Walker and Cogswell, 1844), 19.

10.   Michael Craton and Gail Saunders, *Islanders in the Stream: A History of the Bahamian People* (Athens: University of Georgia Press, 1992), 169–71.

11.   Craton and Saunders, *Islanders,* 196–232.

12.   Craton and Saunders, *Islanders,* 179–95.

13.   The black seeds were sent from Col. Roger Kelsal to his former partner James Spaulding and from John Tattnall to his cousin Governor Josiah Tattnall of Georgia.

14.   "Merchant's Account Book, 1785–1791" (manuscript), South Carolina Historical Society.

15.   Seabrook, *Memoir,* 187–89.

16.   Stephen B. Barnwell, *The Story of an American Family* (Marquette, Mich.: Privately printed, 1969), 39.

17.   Duc de la Rochefoucauld-Liancourt, "Voyage dans Etats-Unis d'Amérique, fait en 1795, 1796 et 1797," Beaufort County Public Library. This translated typescript was obtained for the Beaufort County Public Library by Gerhard Spieler from David and Millicent Brandenburg of American University, Washington, D.C. The typescript is not paginated.

18.   Gray, *History of Agriculture,* 2:681.

19.   Gray, *History of Agriculture,* 2:679–81.

20.   "Thomas A. Coffin Plantation Book" (manuscript), South Carolina Historical Society; J. H. Easterby, "Shipbuilding on St. Helena Island in 1816: A Diary of Ebenezer Coffin," *South Carolina Historical Magazine* 47 (April 1946): 117–20; 7th Census (1850), Beaufort District, Agricultural Schedule, South Carolina Department of Archives and History.

21.   "Will of Willliam Bull, Esq.," October 5, 1790; "List of Negroes Belonging to Mrs. Bull," November 28, 1800; "List of Negroes Belonging to Col. Stapleton on St. Helena

Island," March 15, 1810; "Frogmore Plantation Journal, 1813–1816," "Higham Smith to John Stapleton," January 14, 1837, John Stapleton Papers, 1790–1839, South Caroliniana Library.

22. Thomas Cooper and David J. McCord, eds., *The Statutes at Large of South Carolina*, 10 vols. (Columbia: A. S. Johnston, 1836–1841), 8: 135.

23. "Petition to Establish Beaufort College," November 23, 1795, General Assembly Papers, South Carolina Department of Archives and History. The same act vested vacant Georgetown lots and Prince George Winyah confiscated estates in Winyah Indigo Society.

24. Cooper and McCord, eds., *Statutes of South Carolina*, 8: 189–92.

25. "Petition Against Beaufort College," December 10, 1796; "Joint Committee Report on Beaufort College," December 17, 1803, General Assembly Papers, South Carolina Department of Archives and History.

26. David Ramsay, *History of South Carolina from Its Earliest Settlement in 1670 to the Year 1808* (Newberry, S.C.: N. J. Duffie, 1858), 2: 301; Robert Barnwell to Rufus King, August 25, 1801, Rufus King Papers, New-York Historical Society.

27. *Charleston City Gazette,* November 16, 1802, January 10, 1804; *Charleston Courier,* March 23, 1804.

28. Jeffrey N. Lash, "The Rev. Martin Luther Hurlbut: Yankee President of Beaufort College, 1812–1814," *South Carolina Historical Magazine* 85 (October 1984): 305–16.

29. Lash, "Martin Luther Hurlbut," 315.

30. Laura Amanda White, *Robert Barnwell Rhett: Father of Secession* (New York: Century, 1931), 5.

31. Barnwell, *Story of an American Family,* 64, 108.

32. Barnwell, *Story of an American Family,* 63.

33. Cooper and McCord, eds., *Statutes of South Carolina,* 8: 224–25.

34. "Petition for Beaufort Library Society," November 15, 1803; "Petition of President and Members of Beaufort Library Society," November 20, 1807, General Assembly Papers, South Carolina Department of Archives and History.

35. *Biographical Directory of the South Carolina House,* 4: 49, 183–85, 386–87, 509–10.

36. Barnwell, *Story of an American Family,* 63.

37. Government Auction Pamphlet, November 17, 1862 (New York: C. C. Shelley, Printer, 1862); Clyde Cantrell, "The Reading Habits of Antebellum Southerners," Ph.D. diss., University of Michigan, 1960, 295.

38. "Petition to Form the Beaufort Female Benevolent Society," November 29, 1815, General Assembly Papers, South Carolina Department of Archives and History; Cooper and McCord, eds., *Statutes of South Carolina,* 8: 274–374.

39. Cooper and McCord, eds., *Statutes of South Carolina,* 8: 299; E. L. Inabinet, "The Lawton Family of Robertville," paper delivered at Allendale, South Carolina, June 8, 1963, South Caroliniana Library.

40. Cooper and McCord., eds., *Statutes of South Carolina,* 8: 285–369.

41. David Duncan Wallace, *The History of South Carolina* (New York: The American Historical Soceity, Inc., 1934), 2:380.

42. Gerhard Spieler, Lawrence Rowland, Larry Lepionka, Emmet Bufkin, and Arthur Wade, "Fortifications in the Beaufort Area, 1700–1900," compiled for the 16th Annual

Military History Conference of the Council on America's Military Past, Charleston, S.C., 1982.

43. "Frogmore Plantation Journal, 1813–1816," Stapleton Papers, South Caroliniana Library; Malcolm Bell Jr., *Major Butler's Legacy: Five Generations of a Slaveholding Family* (Athens: University of Georgia Press, 1987), 170–72.

44. McConnell and Kennedy Papers, Lewis Library, University of Manchester, England. See also Charles Arthur Roberts, "The Sea Island Cotton Industry as Revealed in the McConnell-Kennedy Letters, 1819–1825," M.A. thesis, University of South Carolina, 1965.

45. *Carolina Gazette,* May 15, 1819; Katherine M. Jones, ed., *Port Royal Under Six Flags* (Indianapolis: Bobbs-Merrill, 1960), 154–57.

46. Jones, ed., *Port Royal Under Six Flags,* 518–60; Barnwell, *Story of an American Family,* 68.

47. Ruby A. Rahn, *River Highway for Trade: The Savannah* (Savannah: U.S. Army Corps of Engineers, 1968), 19, 22, Appendix B: 4; "Moses Rogers (1779–1821)," *Dictionary of American Biography,* 8:106–7.

48. Francis Richard Lubbock, *Six Decades in Texas: or Memoirs of Francis Richard Lubbock, Governor of Texas in Wartime: A Personal Experience in Business, War and Politics* (Austin: Ben C. Jones, 1900), 5–6. Henry Schultz, an early South Carolina entrepreneur, was the guiding force behind the establishment of Hamburg on the Savannah River near Augusta, which was intended as the railroad terminus of the Charleston to Hamburg Railroad, thus to be an inland metropolis.

49. Gray, *History of Agriculture,* 2: 1031, 1032.

16

Upper St. Peter's Parish
The Last Frontier of the Beaufort District

The last area of the Beaufort District to be settled was the upper portion of
St. Peter's Parish between the Savannah and Coosawhatchie Rivers. Most of this
region was high, dry ground west of the pine barrens. When first settled, it was
covered with mixed pine and deciduous forest. While not possessing the swamp
and tidal land desirable for rice production or the maritime climate necessary for
sea island cotton, this district remained a bit of an economic backwater during
the eighteenth century. By the eve of the Civil War, however, some of the frontier families who first settled the area had become among the wealthiest and
most prominent families in the Beaufort District.

Before 1760, the boundary of the frontier was loosely delineated by a line
from McPherson's Cowpen, near the present town of Yemassee, to the Pallachacola
Bluff on the Georgia side of the Savannah River near the present community of
Garnet in lower Hampton County. Two large cowpens were operated on this
frontier during the colonial era. About 1725, McPherson's Cowpen began as a
frontier fort and post for the mounted rangers and was commanded by Captain
James McPherson during the later stages of the Yemassee War. During the great
expansion of rice production in the 1730s, this frontier was largely ignored in
favor of the lowcountry river lands. Several Charleston area families extended
their operations into the St. Peter's rice rivers during these years. Among them
were Porchers, Fenwicks, Proctors, and Wrights. One large cowpen was developed on the Savannah River across from Pallachacola Bluff during the 1750s by
William Williamson, a wealthy planter from St. Paul's Parish. The McPherson
and Williamson cowpens became extensive frontier ranching operations before
the Revolution and began the tradition in upper St. Peter's Parish of providing
provisions for the heavily populated rice and indigo plantations of the coast.

During the 1760s, several families moved into upper St. Peter's Parish seeking more land and greater opportunity. Some families, like the Roberts, moved
upriver from the less productive land around Purrysburg. Others, such as the
Thompson and Deloach families, moved across the lowcountry from the Santee
River area. A few, like the Williamson and Lawton families, moved from St.

Paul's Parish and Edisto Island to upper St. Peter's Parish. One significant migration was led by William Stafford of New Hanover township, North Carolina, in 1765 or 1766. William Stafford was the fifth of that name in a family that had wandered from Virginia to eastern North Carolina in the early eighteenth century. Stafford's father died in 1765 and shortly thereafter Stafford led his family and many relatives through the pine forests of eastern North Carolina across the coastal plain of South Carolina to the edge of the Savannah river near Black Swamp. Included in this large migration were William Stafford; his younger brothers, Richard, Samuel, and Seth Stafford; his cousins, Thomas and Edward Stafford; and his in-laws, John Tison, and Samuel and William Maner. On wagons and carts they brought their wives, families, livestock, and moveable possessions. When they reached the high ground along the northern edge of the Savannah River swamp, "they pitched their tents" and began to build a new community.[1]

The Stafford, Maner, and Tison descendants married into the Robert, Lawton, Thompson, Jaudon, McKenzie, and Porcher families, forming a large and extended network of cousins in the parish. These families formed the economic, social, and political elite of St. Peter's Parish through the antebellum era.

Throughout the eighteenth century, upper St. Peter's Parish was a community of subsistence farmers and frontier livestock operations. The census of 1800 reveals that while 163 families in the parish owned at least one slave, 173 families still owned none. Thus, 51.4 percent of the families were nonslaveholders as of 1800. Because much of the slave population was concentrated along the rice rivers of lower St. Peter's Parish, the vast majority of the families of upper St. Peter's Parish had few if any slaves. Of the families that had settled that neighborhood before the Revolution, the following list reflects their economic status as of 1800:

Head of Household	Number of Slaves
Reuben Robert	18
Peter Robert	5
Thomas Robert	1
Estate of Colonel James Thomson	8
James Thomson Jr.	7
Richard Stafford	0
William H. Stafford	0
Mary Stafford	2
Aaron Tison	0
John Tison Sr.	8
John Tison Jr.	3
John Maner	8
Samuel Maner	40

There were three Deloach families (headed by William, David, and Jesse) listed in 1800, but none owned slaves at that time. The Lawton family was curiously overlooked by the census, but Joseph Lawton owned twenty slaves in St. Peter's Parish in 1790. Thus, upper St. Peter's Parish was still a log cabin frontier at the end of the eighteenth century. While some families had begun the process of upward mobility, most had not.[2]

This community became fertile ground for the evangelical preachers spawned by the Great Awakening, particularly of the Baptist faith. The Euhaws Baptist Church at Coosawhatchie, founded in 1737 and reconstituted in 1752 by George Whitefield, was the mother church of the region. The first known services in upper St. Peter's Parish were those held at Black Swamp on Christmas Day, 1762, by Reverend Francis Pelot, a Swiss immigrant and pastor of the Euhaws Church. He was followed by Oliver Hart from Pennsylvania, Edmund Botsford from England, James Smart from Virginia, and Evan Pugh from North Carolina. Their work resulted in the formation of the Beech Branch Baptist Church in 1759 and the Pipe Creek Baptist Church in 1775. Pipe Creek became the principal congregation of upper St. Peter's and was incorporated by the new state government in 1787 as the Pipe Creek Church of Regular Baptists.[3]

Through the eighteenth century, the political leadership of St. Peter's Parish remained in the hands of the rice planters of the lower parish. When elections were held to choose delegates to the Ratification Convention of the U.S. Constitution in 1788, St. Peter's Parish returned a delegation which fairly represented the interests of the area at that time. Two men were rice planters, John Fenwicke and Joachim Hartstone; one represented the old Purrysburg community, John Lewis Bourquin; and three represented the frontier farmers of upper St. Peter's Parish, John Chisolm, Seth Stafford, and Reverend Henry Holcombe.[4]

John Fenwicke was a younger son of one of colonial South Carolina's most prominent families. Shortly after the Revolution, he extended his planting operation from the traditional family-seat on James Island to his 640-acre rice plantation on the lower Savannah River. In 1790, he had eighteen slaves clearing the swamps for rice production. John Fenwicke was a natural Federalist by family connection and business interest and thus voted in favor of ratifying the Constitution in 1788. Probably because of his strong family connections to Charleston, he was continuously returned to represent St. Peter's Parish in the new South Carolina House of Representatives from 1783 until his death in 1793.[5]

Joachim Hartstone was a rice planter at Great Swamp in the Purrysburg township in lower St. Peter's Parish. His plantation of 1,600 acres, probably including a country store, was on the road from Purrysburg to the Coosawhatchie Bridge. It was one of the many plantations burned by Tory marauders during Prevost's invasion of 1779. Thus, Hartstone, like many of his neighbors, had to rebuild his fortunes after the war. As a delegate to the Ratification Convention, Hartstone voted in favor of ratification. He represented St. Peter's Parish in the South Carolina House of Representatives from 1785 to 1790 and served in local offices as road commissioner and tax collector. Hartstone was one of the wealthiest residents of St. Peter's Parish, with forty-seven slaves in 1790 and twenty-nine slaves in 1800. Hartstone died before 1810, and the name disappeared from St. Peter's Parish.[6]

John Lewis Bourquin Jr. was a merchant and planter in Purrysburg township. A descendant of one of the original Swiss settlers, Bourquin was the natural leader of the Purrysburg community. His father, Colonel John Lewis Bourquin, had been colonial justice of the peace for Purrysburg and commander of the Purrysburg militia company. John Bourquin Jr. inherited two stores, at Purrysburg and Okatee, and a substantial estate of twenty-six slaves from his father. Bourquin fairly represented the modest farmers who were his neighbors and customers in the Purrysburg community and was one of the few lowcountry delegates to vote against ratifying the U.S. Constitution.[7]

John Chisolm was a rice planter on the upper Coosawhatchie River where it formed the border between upper St. Peter's and upper Prince William Parish. He was one of the early settlers, having moved to the neighborhood before 1764. Eventually he acquired, through grants, 1,872 acres along the Coosawhatchie and Savannah Rivers. Though Chisolm remained a modest planter throughout his life (he had only six slaves by the census of 1790 and 1800), he laid the foundation for his son, John M. Chisolm, to become one of the substantial rice planters of the lower Savannah River in the antebellum era. In 1820, John Chisolm had 104 slaves in St. Peter's Parish and, by 1850, his estate possessed 126 slaves. As a delegate to the Ratifying Convention in 1788, John Chisolm represented the divided opinion of the small, frontier farmers of upper St. Peter's Parish. He, like John Bourquine, was one of the few lowcountry delegates to vote against ratifying the U.S. Constitution. John Chisolm represented St. Peter's Parish in the South Carolina House of Representatives from 1785 to 1791. He was also road commissioner and justice of the peace for St. Peter's and, in 1787, was "escheator" of confiscated property for the whole Beaufort District.[8]

Seth Stafford, one of the leaders of the migration from the New Hanover township of North Carolina to St. Peter's Parish in the 1760s, had acquired a modest farm along the Savannah River. He served in the patriot militia during the Revolution and was captain of this local militia after the war. By 1790, he was one of the larger slaveowners in upper St. Peter's Parish, with eighteen slaves. Stafford represented St. Peter's Parish in the South Carolina House of Representatives from 1789 to 1802. As a delegate to the Ratifying Convention in 1788, he voted in favor of ratifying the U.S. Constitution, possibly because his own neighborhood was beset by continuing disruption and civil disorder caused by a hostile community of runaway slaves in the Savannah River swamp. Stafford and his constituents wanted a government strong enough to pacify their neighborhood.[9]

The most interesting of the St. Peter's delegates to the Ratifying Convention was Reverend Henry Holcombe of the Pipe Creek Baptist Church. Henry Holcombe had been converted to evangelical Christianity in his native Prince Edward County, Virginia, and was called to St. Peter's Parish on the eve of the Revolution. He served as a captain in the patriot militia and was present at the siege of Ninety-Six in 1781. He returned to St. Peter's as pastor of the Pipe Creek Baptist Church, where he was living in 1788. Like his parishioner Seth Stafford, Henry Holcombe voted in favor of ratifying the U.S. Constitution perhaps because his neighborhood was one of the last in South Carolina to recover from the physical destruction and civil disorder caused by the Revolutionary War. Reverend Henry Holcombe served in no other political office. In 1790, he became the pastor of the Euhaws Baptist Church, and, in 1795, he and several of his members moved to Beaufort to organize the congregation that became the Baptist Church of Beaufort in 1804. Reverend Henry Holcombe then moved on to Savannah, where he became the founder of the Savannah River Baptist Association, which united Baptist churches on both sides of the river from Savannah to Augusta and included the first independent black Baptist Church in America: the Bryan Baptist Church of Savannah founded by Reverend Andrew Bryan in 1791. Holcombe was an imposing man, being well over six feet tall and in excess of three hundred pounds. He became one of the most famous evangelists of his day. Holcombe left Savannah in 1811 to become the pastor of the First Baptist Church of Philadelphia, where he died in 1824.[10]

Holcombe's representation at the Convention of 1788 and his later career as a nationally prominent Baptist evangelist highlighted the importance of church communities to the rural neighborhoods of upper St. Peter's Parish. In addition to Holcombe's Pipe Creek Church, the Beech Branch Baptist Church was formed as early as 1759 on the edge of the Coosawhatchie Swamp by Reverend James Smart. His descendant, Henry Smart, became one of the political leaders of St. Peter's Parish in the antebellum era, and the families that formed the Beech Branch community remained in the neighborhood for generations—including the Larissy, Bagley, Thomas, Collins, Johnston, Wood, and Davis families. This group came from the Orangeburg District, showing that settlement of upper St. Peter's Parish in the late colonial era was influenced by migration from the upcountry as well as the lowcountry.

In 1786, a Baptist Church was organized at Black Swamp by the Lawton, Grimball, Jaudon, Audibert, and Robert families. In 1800, a federal post office was established at Black Swamp. In 1812, the post office and church were moved to nearby Robertville.[11] Robertville was the closest thing to a town in upper St. Peter's Parish. It was located where the high road from the Barnwell District to Savannah, known as the Augusta Highway, intersected the road from the Coosawhatchie Bridge to Two Sisters Ferry on the Savannah River. It became the busiest crossroads in upper St. Peter's Parish. After the federal post office was moved from Black Swamp in 1812, the Old Black Swamp Baptist Church soon followed. A new church was built at Robertville for a cost of four thousand dollars. In 1819, Alexander J. Lawton and his brother, William Henry Lawton, opened a store at Robertville which became Alexander J. Lawton and Co., the principal mercantile establishment in the region. With Alexander Lawton's death in 1833, the store became a branch of J. B. Jaudon and Company of Savannah. By 1821, Robertville had six houses, the Baptist Church, two stores, a blacksmith shop, and the Black Swamp Academy, a boarding school operated by Tristram and Charlotte Verstille.[12]

The economy of upper St. Peter's Parish had remained that of livestock and subsistence farming throughout the eighteenth century. During the 1790s, the introduction of sea island cotton replaced indigo among the coastal plantations and many of the old families of St. Helena and St. Luke's Parishes grew rich in one generation. Additionally, the great rice plantations of the Combahee, Coosawhatchie, and Savannah Rivers grew steadily in the first decade of the nineteenth century. This rapid expansion, spurred mostly by the introduction of cotton, added to the slave population of the plantations in St. Helena, St. Luke's, Prince William, and lower St. Peter's Parish. This newfound prosperity, however, did not immediately benefit the small farmers of upper St. Peter's Parish. Lack of opportunity and the opening up of fertile new land in the Mississippi Territory led to a significant out-migration from upper St. Peter's Parish between 1806 and 1811.

In 1806, ninety-seven settlers from upper St. Peter's Parish, led by Robert Tanner and Reverend Moses Hadley of Pipe Creek Church, abandoned their farms, packed their belongings, gathered up their families, and set out in ox-driven wagons for Mississippi. When they reached the Tennessee River they boarded flatboats and floated down the river to the Ohio River, and then down the Mississippi River to Fort Adams. Near Fort Adams they founded the town of Woodyville, Mississippi. Many members of the Grimball and Robert families were part of this first Mississippi Migration.[13]

Two years later, Seth Stafford, the youngest brother of Colonel William Stafford who had moved from North Carolina in 1766, took his family as well as some Cheney, Robert, and Maner relatives on the long trek to Mississippi. Ten years later, in 1818, many of this group moved across the Mississippi River to Louisiana where William Fendon Cheney founded Cheneyville.

Black Swamp Methodist Church Cemetery, St. Peter's Parish, established ca. 1790 (photo by Robert W. Jenkins).

Woodstock Plantation House, St. Peter's Parish, built in 1823, the home of Judge Edmund Martin and Mary Anna Maner Martin (photo by Robert W. Jenkins).

Mistletoe Grove, St. Peter's Parish, ca. 1832, the home of Reuben Henry Tison (photo by Robert W. Jenkins).

Ingleside Plantation House, St. Peter's Parish, as it appeared ca. 1860. Ingleside, the home of Benjamin R. Bostick, was burned by Union troops in 1865 (photo courtesy of Thomas O. Lawton of Allendale, S.C.).

In 1811, a third group from St. Peter's Parish joined the Mississippi Migration. Led by Alexander Scott, John Stafford, and John Audibert, this group included Reverend Howell Wall of the Black Swamp (Robertville) Church, John Tison, David McKenzie, William H. Tuten, Namaan and Seth Smart, Robert Chisolm, Joseph Tanner, Benjamin T. D. Lawton, and Allen and Morris Sweat. Not all of these pioneers, however, found success in Mississippi. Benjamin and Joseph Lawton, Namaan and Seth Smart, and Allen and Morris Sweat all returned with their families to their ancestral homes in upper St. Peter's Parish.[14]

This westward migration from St. Peter's Parish spread to the older coastal parishes and influenced some of the most successful and dynamic young men of the district to seek their fortunes in the west. In 1818, Henry McNish of Coosawhatchie, one of the principal rice planters of St. Luke's Parish with ninety-two slaves in 1800, and a third-generation resident of the Beaufort District, was struck with "Alabama fever." By 1820, he had moved his large operation to the pleasant rolling country of the Chattahootchie Valley.[15] Francis Richard Lubbock's father was one of Beaufort's first steamboat captains, and his grandfather was Captain Francis Saltus, one of Beaufort's well-known eighteenth-century mariners. Lubbock was raised and educated in Beaufort in the 1820s but moved west with his brother Thomas in the 1830s to help found the republic of Texas. Lubbock became the wartime governor of Texas (1861–1865) and the town of Lubbock in Texas was named for him.[16] By 1840, James Hamilton Jr., the largest rice planter on the Savannah River at the time and former governor, U.S. congressman, and intendant of Charleston, left South Carolina for Texas and then settled in Alabama.[17]

This out-migration from St. Peter's Parish was significant. In 1800, the white population of the parish was 1,733. In 1810, it was 1,578 and, by 1820, it had dropped to 950, a decline of 45 percent. Most of the families that migrated westward were small farmers with few, if any, slaves. During the same years, the slave population grew, particularly on the rice plantations of lower St. Peter's Parish, from 2,669 in 1800 to 3,584 in 1810, and to 5,503 in 1820—a growth of 106 percent.

In spite of the transformation of St. Peter's Parish, the census of 1820 reveals the marginal nature of the families that remained in the neighborhood. Of the 434 heads of families resident in St. Peter's Parish in 1820, virtually half (49.6 percent) still owned no slaves, and the vast majority (72 percent) were marginal planters with no slaves or fewer than ten slaves. The following table shows the distribution of slave ownership (a fair measure of economic strength in antebellum South Carolina) in St. Peter's Parish in 1820:

215 families with 0 slaves
61 families with 1–5 slaves
37 families with 6–10 slaves
47 families with 11–20 slaves
45 families with 20–50 slaves
18 families with 51–100 slaves
10 families with 100+ slaves

The ten families who owned more than one hundred slaves are listed below with the type of plantation where the slaves were employed, its location, and the permanent residence of the plantation owner:

Name	No. Slaves	Type/Location	Permanent Residence
Estate of John Rutledge Jr.	315	Rice/Savannah River	Charleston
Henry Taylor	205	Rice/Savannah River	Savannah
Henry Cruger	144	Rice/Savannah River	Charleston
James Ancrum	140	Rice/Savannah River	Charleston
Estate of James E. McPherson	124	Rice/Savannah River	Prince William Parish, Charleston
John H. Roberts	123	Cotton, Corn, Potato/ Matthews Bluff	
Estate of William Maner	120	Cotton, Corn, Potato/ Pipe Creek	
Benjamin R. Bostick	117	Cotton, Corn, Potato/ Black Swamp	
Daniel B. Huger	116	Rice/Savannah River	Charleston
James Porcher	107	Rice/New River	St. Peter's Parish[18]

Six of these major St. Peter's Parish planters in 1820 were absentee owners, while only four were permanent residents. All but one, however, had permanent investments in St. Peter's Parish. Only James Ancrum did not stay long in St. Peter's Parish. Inasmuch as he was an in-law to John and Martha Blake, who had substantial holdings on the Savannah River, he was probably temporary manager of Blake family property.

Even the wealthier of the resident families of upper St. Peter's Parish lived plain and modest lives compared to the style of Charleston, Savannah, and Beaufort. In 1821, Charlotte Verstille, a New England schoolmistress who had moved to Robertville with her husband, Tristram Verstille, as headmaster and mistress of the Black Swamp Academy, described the homes of the more substantial planters of upper St. Peter's Parish:

These buildings can boast neither of a cellar nor an upper story—all the rooms being on the surface of the ground. Glass windows are quite a rare luxury, light being admitted by throwing open a wooden door swung on hinges where the windows should be. When found necessary to guard against the cold, the light is sure to be excluded. It is surprising how many comforts these people of wealth will voluntarily deny themselves . . . the grand staple here is bacon—bacon and collards . . . you will find it on every table in every season.[19]

One of the unique features of upper St. Peter's Parish in the antebellum Beaufort District was the existence of a sizeable community of free black farmers. While a small number of free black artisans contributed to the town life of Beaufort and Coosawhatchie, upper St. Peter's Parish was the only area with a substantial number of free black farm families. In 1800, there were 134 free blacks in St. Peter's Parish, some of whom evidently migrated westward because, in 1810, their numbers had dropped to 83, and, in 1820, there were 84. Two family groups of free black farmers were clearly identified in the census of 1820. They were the Jones and Hiott families, forming two extended-family farming communities of twenty-three people in 1820. By 1840, the census reveals clearly the names of thirty free black farming families containing 147 people. Their names and numbers are as follows:

Name	No. in Household	Occupation
James Becket	3	Agriculture
John Becket	8	Agriculture
B. Caen	1	Trade & Manufacturing
S. Carte	3	Agriculture
John Clevis	4	Agriculture
B. Cohen	5	Trade & Manufacturing
R. Francis	6	Agriculture
Nettle Gardner	4	Agriculture
Wm. Gordon	9	Agriculture
Wm. Gordon Sr.	5	Trade & Manufacturing
M. Howard	4	Agriculture
J. Jackson	2	Trade & Manufacturing
Daniel Jones	11	Trade & Manufacturing
D. Jones	4	Trade & Manufacturing
J. Jones	9	Agriculture
R. Jones	2	Trade & Manufacturing

Name	No. in Household	Occupation
Spicey Jones	5	Agriculture
Abraham Orr	6	Agriculture
Benjamin Orr	8	Agriculture
John Orr Sr.	7	Agriculture
J. Orr	5	Agriculture
John Orr	7	Agriculture
Martha Orr	3	Agriculture
Mary Orr	4	Agriculture
D. Peake	6	Agriculture
Bryan Russell	3	Agriculture
Charles Russell	5	Agriculture
David Russell	3	Agriculture
William Russell	2	Agriculture
Webster Teat (?)	3	Agriculture[20]

During the 1820s, the economy of upper St. Peter's Parish began to achieve the balance of production which distinguished this neighborhood from the single-crop plantations of the sea islands and rice rivers. Over the next forty years, the steady growth of this agricultural community produced great wealth and a fine pastoral lifestyle for the families that remained. What characterized the agricultural economy of upper St. Peter's Parish in the late antebellum era was the development of very large, multicrop farming operations. Building on the tradition of frontier self-sufficiency which their ancestors had left, these families added many profitable cash crops and invested in numerous nonagricultural enterprises.

The introduction of short-staple, green-seed cotton in the early nineteenth century provided a steady, though modest, source of cash for those families who had some slaves and could rise above subsistence farming. Upper St. Peter's Parish was the only area of the old Beaufort District where short-staple cotton was grown in any large quantities. While short-staple cotton was the most common throughout the South, the Beaufort District, particularly the islands of St. Helena and St. Luke's Parishes, was famous as the home of long-staple sea island cotton. The differences between the two crops were significant. Sea island cotton produced a long, luxurious, and cream-colored fiber, while common short-staple cotton produced a pure white, coarser, and shorter fiber. Sea island cotton, therefore, produced fine, silky textiles while common short-staple cotton produced hardy but coarser cloth. Consequently, the difference in the market price of the two types of cotton was large. Sea island cotton sold for two to four times the price of short-staple cotton. In 1810, sea island cotton fetched twenty-eight cents per pound while short-staple cotton brought fourteen cents per pound. In 1830, sea island cotton was worth twenty-five cents per pound on the Charleston market, while short-staple cotton sold for only 8.5 cents per pound. Thus, those planters fortunate enough to have been situated on the sandy soil and drier maritime climate of the sea islands could amass capital much faster than the mainland planters.[21] Quick fortunes, therefore, were made on the sea islands between 1795 and 1820, while the small planters of upper St. Peter's Parish had to be content with more modest and more gradual profits. Nonetheless, the addition of small amounts of cotton to the agricultural product of the mainland portions of the Beaufort District provided much needed cash for the farm families of upper St. Peter's Parish.

An example of how the modest planters of upper St. Peter's gradually accumulated wealth and laid the economic basis for the transformation of upper St. Peter's Parish into a plantation society was the farm of Jonathan Tison. Tison was a second generation descendent of the colonial migration from North Carolina. When the cotton revolution reached upper St. Peter's Parish at the turn of the nineteenth century, he was already a modest planter with eight slaves. Between 1800 and 1810, he employed some of his slaves experimenting with small crops of cotton. By 1805, he was selling a few bales of short-staple cotton on the Savannah market, probably transporting them by ox-cart to the Pallachacola landing on the Savannah River and shipping them downriver on a barge. Tison died before 1807, but his property was managed for his minor children and grandchildren by his daughter, Eliza Maner. In 1807, she sold eighteen bales of cotton from Jonathan Tison's estate for $726, averaging nine cents per pound. Her factor was Saul Solomon, a Jewish storekeeper at Black Swamp and Savannah and longtime resident of St. Peter's Parish. After she paid her account at Solomon's store ($245), the blacksmith ($37), and the schoolmaster at Black Swamp who was educating the children ($9), she bought two more slaves in order to grow more cotton. By 1808, the estate sold twelve bales for $357 and, in 1809, sold twenty-seven bales at eleven cents per pound for $964. In 1810, the estate sold twenty-four bales, or 9,600 pounds, of short-staple cotton for $943. This was good income for an otherwise self-sufficient farm, and with the cash, Eliza Tison Maner bought cattle, molasses, whiskey, and a slave boy. The slave cost $450, nearly half the income the estate earned from cotton. The investment in labor paid off. By 1815, the estate sold seventy-one bales (28,400 pounds) of short-staple cotton at an average of eleven cents per pound for a handsome cash income of $2,489. The following year was even better, with a cash income from cotton of $3,153. In 1816, Maner bought a ginning machine for the estate. Thus, between 1800 and 1815, Tison's modest farm had become a cotton plantation. In accordance with his will, Maner dutifully recorded the cost of educating one of the principal beneficiaries of the estate, young Reuben Tison. When he came of age he built upon the largess, and by the close of the antebellum era he was truly one of the great planters of St. Peter's Parish with 208 slaves in 1860.[22]

Many of the families who remained in upper St. Peter's Parish had similar experiences. Cotton, however, was not the only crop these emerging planters profited from. In fact, the lower Savannah River valley was not particularly choice cotton land. It is well known that short-staple cotton preferred the red clay soils above the fall line. Thus, communities like Hamburg (Aiken), Edgefield, and Abbeville in the upper Savannah River region became much larger cotton-growing areas than St. Peter's. But during the 1820s and 1830s, a new market emerged, providing provisioning crops for the large slave populations of the sea island cotton plantations and tidal culture rice plantations of the coast. The crops which flourished in upper St. Peter's Parish were corn and sweet potatoes. By 1850, sweet potatoes had outstripped cotton as the largest product of the major plantations of upper St. Peter's. Sweet potatoes loved the sandy uplands of the lower Savannah region and were a favorite staple of the slave communities of the coast. Sweet potatoes were generally nonperishable, keeping for a year in a cool atmosphere. They were stored in low sheds or simply covered with pine straw to keep them out of direct sun.[23] In addition to being a primary staple of the slave diet, they were used in the antebellum era to make bread and beer, and to feed the large livestock herds which were present on all the large multicrop plantations of upper St. Peter's.

The census of 1840 reveals the impact of this economic growth. While the number of heads of family remained relatively static (434 in 1820 and 420 in 1840), the percentage of nonslaveholders decreased substantially (from 49.6 percent to 39 percent) and the number of major slaveholding families more than doubled (to twenty-one) in two decades. The following profile of slave distribution shows not only the rising economic status of the community, but also the more even spread of wealth:

> 167 families with 0 slaves
> 60 families with 1–5 slaves
> 41 families with 6–10 slaves
> 49 families with 11–20 slaves
> 45 families with 21–50 slaves
> 32 families with 51–100 slaves
> 21 families with 100+ slaves

By 1840, the largest slaveowner in St. Peter's Parish was no longer a rice planter but one of the multicrop planters. Almost half of the largest planters in the parish were from the upper district. The following is a list of the ten largest slaveowners in St. Peter's Parish:

Name	No. Slaves	Type/Location	Permanent Residence
John Maner	317	Sweet Potato, Corn, Cotton/ Black Swamp	St. Peter's Parish
James Hamilton Jr.	321	Rice/Savannah River	Charleston
Benjamin R. Bostick	253	Sweet Potato, Corn, Cotton/ Black Swamp	St. Peter's Parish
A. T. Gregorie	214	Rice/New River, Coosawhatchie River	Prince William Parish
Langdon Cheves	180	Rice/Savannah River	Charleston/ Pendleton
Edmund Martin	147	Sweet Potato, Corn, Cotton/ Pipe Creek	St. Peter's Parish
Daniel E. Huger	143	Rice/Savannah River	Charleston
T. H. Lawton	135	Sweet Potato, Corn, Cotton/ Lawtonville	St. Peter's Parish
Dr. William McDaniel	125	Rice/Savannah River	Savannah
J. P. Williamson	123	Rice/Savannah River	Charleston/ Savannah[24]

The enterprising planters of upper St. Peter's Parish, however, did not confine their activities to agriculture. They branched out into commerce and industry. In 1819, Alexander and William Lawton opened their store in Robertville. In the 1820s, J. B. Jaudon and Company of Robertville had become a major cotton factor in Savannah. By the 1830s, the Lawton family had opened a cotton brokerage house in Charleston known as Taylor and Lawton that dealt with many Beaufort District cotton planters. James Speights built a lumber mill on the upper Salkehatchie River in 1840 and bought slaves from the nearby plantations to work the mill and "flat and raft" the lumber downstream.[25] In 1850, Colonel William Lawton went to inspect the new textile mill in Graniteville, one of South Carolina's few antebellum industrial operations, with an eye toward building one in St. Peter's Parish. He never built the cotton mill but, in 1852, bought a large steam engine for sixteen hundred dollars to run his grist and saw mill.[26] On the eve of the Civil War, railroads began to snake across the southern countryside. Colonel Alexander J. Lawton became one of the South's first railroad financiers by backing the Augusta and Waynesboro Railroad. He was appointed as the first director and president of the railroad in 1855. After the Civil War, this was one of several lines that became the Central of Georgia Railroad.[27]

By the end of the antebellum era, the principal families of upper St. Peter's Parish had achieved all the wealth, comfort, and status commonly associated with the elite southern gentry. They began to dominate the politics of St. Peter's Parish. An analysis of the St. Peter's representation in the South Carolina Senate

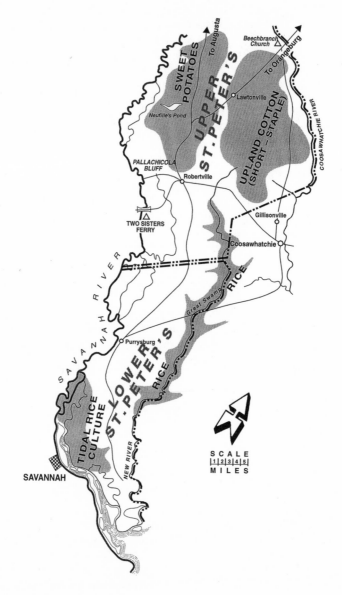

Crop distribution, St. Peter's Parish, 1850

reveals that between 1812 and 1863, virtually every senator from the parish was a member of, or related by marriage to, the Robert, Lawton, Maner, Bostick, Thompson, Johnston, Smart, or Martin family.[28]

They replaced the modest farmhouses of the early nineteenth century with fine plantation homes. Judge Edmund Martin built Woodstock at Pipe Creek about 1822. Joseph Maner Lawton built Cypress Vale near Lawtonville (now Estill) a few years later. In 1836, Benjamin Thompson began to construct Bonneywood on Big Pipe Creek. Family tradition holds that French artisans were brought over to finish the mantels, molding, and ornate ceilings for Thompson.[29]

The families began to form marriage alliances outside the parish, such as the 1859 union of Nancy Bostick and Dr. Henry DeSaussure of Charleston, with the social elite of Charleston and Savannah. And they began to send their children out of state to finish their education at such institutions as Brown, Princeton, Penn (Medical School), Harvard, and Colgate. Many of them became members of the learned professions.

Upper St. Peter's Parish was the last frontier of the Beaufort District. By the end of the antebellum era, the parish had created its own special society, helped launch the religious movement which dominated the South, and had become the breadbasket of the Beaufort District.

NOTES

1. George M. G. Stafford, *General Leroy Augustus Stafford: His Forebears and Descendants* (New Orleans: Pelican Publishers, 1943), 10–13.

2. 2nd Census (1800), Beaufort District Population Schedule, South Carolina Department of Archives and History. The largest slaveowner in St. Peter's Parish in 1800 was the estate of Lord William Campbell, the last royal governor of South Carolina on the lower Savannah River.

3. Coy K. Johnston, *Two Centuries of Lawtonville Baptists, 1775–1975* (Columbia: State Printing Co., 1974), 5–8; Thomas Cooper and David J. McCord, eds., *The Statutes at Large of South Carolina,* 10 vols. (Columbia: A. S. Johnston, 1836–1841), 8: 139.

4. *Journal of the Convention Which Ratified the Constitution of the U.S., May 23, 1788* (Atlanta: Foote & Davis Co. for the Historical Commission of South Carolina, 1928), 13–19.

5. M. Eugene Sirmans, *Colonial South Carolina: A Political History, 1663–1763* (Chapel Hill: University of North Carolina Press, 1966); *Biographical Directory of the South Carolina House,* 3: 230–31.

6. *Biographical Directory of the South Carolina House,* 3: 323; 1st (1790) and 2nd (1800) Census, Beaufort District Population Schedules, South Carolina Department of Archives and History; *Journal of the Convention Which Ratified the Constitution.*

7. *Biographical Directory of the South Carolina House,* 3: 81; 2nd Census (1800), Beaufort District Population Schedule, South Carolina Department of Archives and History.

8. *Biographical Directory of the South Carolina House,* 3: 142; 1st (1790), 2nd (1800), 3rd (1810), and 7th (1860) Census, Beaufort District Population Schedules, South Carolina Department of Archives and History.

9. *Biographical Directory of the South Carolina House,* 3: 684; 1st Census (1790), Beaufort District Population Schedule, South Carolina Department of Archives and History.

10. Johnston, *Two Centuries of Lawtonville Baptists,* 17–29.

11. Johnston, *Two Centuries of Lawtonville Baptists,* 17.

12. Johnston, *Two Centuries of Lawtonville Baptists,* 23; E. L. Inabinet, "The Lawton Family of Robertville, South Carolina," paper delivered at Allendale, South Carolina, June 8, 1963, South Caroliniana Library.

13. Johnston, *Two Centuries of Lawtonville Baptists,* 24.

14. Stafford, *General Leroy Augustus Stafford,* 11.

15. 2nd Census (1800), Beaufort District Population Schedule, South Carolina Department of Archives and History; "Register of St. Helena Parish," *South Carolina Historical Magazine* 68 (1969): 53.

16. Francis Richard Lubbock, *Six Decades in Texas: or Memoirs of Francis Richard Lubbock, Governor of Texas in Wartime: A Personal Experience in Business, War and Politics* (Austin: Ben C. Jones, 1900), 2–12.

17. Otis Clark Skipper, *J. D. B. DeBow: Magazinist of the Old South* (Athens: University of Georgia Press, 1958), 4–12.

18. 2nd (1800), 3rd (1810), and 4th Census (1820), Beaufort District Population Schedules, South Carolina Department of Archives and History.

19. James Kilgo, *Pipe Creek to Matthew's Bluff: A Short History of Groton Plantation* (Estill, S. C.: Privately printed for the Winthrop family, 1988), 47.

20. 5th Census (1840), Beaufort District Population Schedule, South Carolina Department of Archives and History.

21. Lewis Cecil Gray, *History of Agriculture in the Southern United States to 1860,* 2 vols. (Gloucester, Mass.: Peter Smith, 1958), 2: 1027–31.

22. "Account Book of Estate of Jonathan Tison," Lawton Papers, South Caroliniana Library.

23. Gray, *History of Agriculture,* 2:826. Storing potatoes under earth or straw was traditionally called "banking."

24. 5th Census (1840), Beaufort District Population Schedule, South Carolina Department of Archives and History.

25. Taylor and Lawton to A. J. Lawton, February 2, 1836; February 10, 1837, Lawton Papers, South Caroliniana Library; Inabinet, "Lawton Family," 5.

26. Inabinet, "Lawton Family," 7.

27. *Savannah Daily Morning News,* January 3, 1855, Georgia Historical Society.

28. *Biographical Directory of the South Carolina Senate,* 3: 1805–1888.

29. Kilgo, *Pipe Creek to Matthew's Bluff,* 48–61.

17

Savannah River Rice Plantations, 1820–1860

During the early nineteenth century, the Savannah River rice plantations of St. Peter's Parish did not develop rapidly. The best indication of the amount of agricultural development in St. Peter's Parish is the size of the slave force. Throughout the eighteenth century, St. Peter's had been the poorest and least developed of the four parishes of the Beaufort District.[1] In 1800, St. Peter's Parish was still the poorest, with 2,669 slaves, fewer than half the number in neighboring St. Luke's Parish. In 1810, St. Peter's Parish, although its slave population had doubled in the decade, still had the smallest slave labor force in the Beaufort District: 5,503 out of a total slave population of 27,349. This indicates modest capital investment and little development of the tidewater rice lands of the lower Savannah.[2]

Even the existing large plantations fell victim to absenteeism and mismanagement. In 1800, the heirs of Lord William Campbell, Louisa Izard Campbell Johnston, and William Conway Campbell were the largest slaveowners in St. Peter's Parish, with 107 slaves on their Smithfield and Inverary Plantations. But these were absentee owners, and the plantation was mismanaged. Louisa Izard Campbell was the wife of Sir Alexander Johnston, the chief justice of Ceylon. Her brother William Conway Campbell, who occasionally visited Savannah from his home in London, was mentally incompetent and legally declared a lunatic in 1819. Henry McNish reported finding "100 slaves and wretched fraud and mismanagement." The two plantations should have produced an income of two thousand pounds sterling per year, but instead yielded only five hundred pounds sterling per year.[3]

Despite such gloomy realities, a small number of prominent South Carolina rice planters saw the potential in the lower Savannah lands and began to make modest financial commitments in the area. In 1800, John Williamson had moved thirty-eight slaves to his plantation on the South Carolina side opposite Argyle Island, and John Rutledge Jr. had seventy slaves working his rice field across from the northern end of Hutchinson Island.[4] Between 1800 and 1810, three major lowcountry rice-planting families made investments in St. Peter's Parish. Daniel Blake moved fifty slaves to the Savannah River and developed a plantation adjacent to Rutledge's. About the same time, Daniel Heyward, son of Nathaniel Heyward of Colleton County, the state's premier rice planter, moved a large slave labor force to St. Peter's Parish and developed rice fields on the Savannah River. After his death, his plantation became the property of his widow, who married Nicholas Cruger of the prominent New York mercantile family. In 1810, Cruger listed eighty-eight slaves on his wife's Savannah River plantation. Another prominent rice planter, James Elliott McPherson of Prince William Parish, had sixty slaves working on the Savannah River by 1810.[5] Between 1810 and 1820, the Rutledge, Cruger, and McPherson plantations grew while the Blake and Campbell plantations did not. In 1820, the estate of Rutledge owned 160 slaves on the Savannah River while the Cruger Plantation had ninety-three slaves, and James Elliott McPherson had ninety slaves nearby. This period also saw numerous changes of ownership, indicating that some land speculation was taking place between 1800 and 1820.[6]

The great growth and development of the Savannah River rice lands, however, began during the 1820s. Several factors combined to create propitious circumstances for large-scale agricultural production in St. Peter's Parish. First, the technology for growing and processing rice on a tidal-culture plantation had matured at the same time that some of the older rice lands, notably around Charleston, had reached the limit of their expansion. In the early decades of the nineteenth century, considerable experimentation had revealed the most efficient method of controlling tidal flow, laying out fields and ditches, planting seeds, and then harvesting and milling the grain into a marketable product. At the same time that tidal-culture rice production was being refined, several longtime lowcountry rice-planting families were looking for new tidelands on which to employ their slaves, and some new investors from Georgia and South Carolina were seeking opportunities in rice production. Second, there were several years of exceptionally high prices for rice following the Napoleonic Wars, with the highest price in the antebellum era at 6.1 cents per pound in 1817.[7] Third, the decade of the 1820s was one of particular optimism and economic growth in the city of Savannah. Most of the central city of Savannah burned to the ground in January 1820, but the citizens rebuilt the commercial district of brick and stone. The optimism, boosterism, and schemes for internal improvement around Savannah in the 1820s seemed boundless. It was generally expected that Savannah would become the natural market for the export of produce from the entire southeast and would soon evolve into the "New York of the South."[8] This local enthusiasm naturally encouraged investment in the Savannah area.

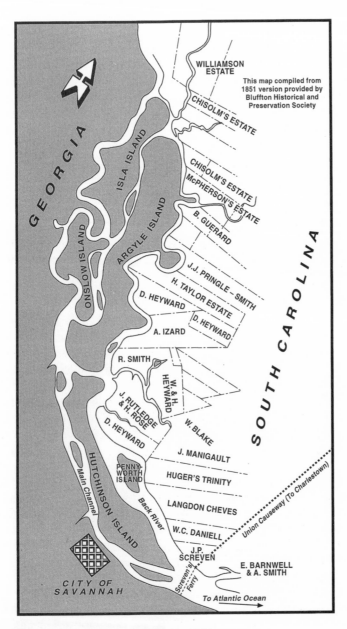

GEORGIA

ISLA ISLAND

ONSLOW ISLAND

ARGYLE ISLAND

WILLIAMSON ESTATE

This map compiled from 1851 version provided by Bluffton Historical and Preservation Society

CHISOLM'S ESTATE

CHISOLM'S ESTATE

McPHERSON'S ESTATE

B. GUERARD

J.J. PRINGLE - SMITH

H. TAYLOR ESTATE

D. HEYWARD

D. HEYWARD

A. IZARD

R. SMITH

W. & H. HEYWARD

J. RUTLEDGE & H. ROSE

D. HEYWARD

W. BLAKE

J. MANIGAULT

PENNYWORTH ISLAND

HUGER'S TRINITY

LANGDON CHEVES

W.C. DANIELL

J.P. SCREVEN

SOUTH CAROLINA

Union Causeway (To Charlestown)

HUTCHINSON ISLAND

Main Channel

Back River

E. BARNWELL & A. SMITH

Screven's Ferry

CITY OF SAVANNAH

To Atlantic Ocean

Savannah River rice plantations, 1850

Savannah in the late 1820s and early 1830s was abuzz with plans to enhance the city's status as the commercial center of the South. The local newspaper, the *Savannah Georgian,* noted the mood in America: "at the present moment we believe the subject of internal improvements has taken fast hold of the minds of our citizens." In January 1826, a charter was issued for a canal company to connect "the Atlantic Rivers with the rivers flowing to the Gulf of Mexico," to be called the Mexico-Atlantic Canal Company. The first leg of this network, the Savannah-Ogeechee Canal, was begun that month. Savannah was also the hub of the inland passage from South Carolina to Florida, where steamboat traffic was just beginning to have an impact. If these water passages were all connected, Savannah's trade would "increase tenfold, like New York." Some noted that Savannah was mortgaging its future for these expensive schemes: "Our present great exertions . . . depend on the future prosperity and increase of Savannah . . . far beyond the most sanguine dreams of those who went before us." Others pointed out that even if the projects failed, the public would gain from the expenditure, "because the expenditure of money on public works has an invigorating influence on industry and there will be just as much money in the state after as before."[9]

These internal improvement projects in Georgia drew attention in Charleston to the "fallen fortunes and declining prospects" of that city and spurred competing plans of internal improvement. In 1827, the *Savannah Georgian* first noted the proposal for "the construction of a railroad between Charleston and Augusta."[10] Savannah countered with a renewed effort to improve the river navigation to Augusta and a major project to deepen the channel from Savannah to the sea. The Savannah Harbor project began in 1826, with fifty thousand dollars of federal money obtained by Sen. John McPherson Berrien of Georgia, a Savannah River rice planter. The commissioner of the project was the mayor of Savannah, Dr. William Coffee Daniell. Daniell was also one of the major rice planters of St. Peter's Parish, and his Oglethorpe Plantation on the South Carolina shore was nearly opposite the site of the dredging operation. By 1828, the steamer *Metropolis* arrived in Savannah with a new steam-dredging machine for deepening the channel. In 1829, the dredging began. By 1830, the operation under Dr. Daniell's direction was clearly not succeeding. Questions arose about how Daniell had spent the money, and more money was requested from Congress. By 1831, the money was gone, but the obstructions in the channel remained, as did questions about Dr. Daniell's management.[11]

Other suggestions to improve Savannah's commerce followed. In 1831, a letter from "Questio" suggested placing a toll bridge across the Savannah River to attract the trade from lower South Carolina. People would be "incredulous to be told that there was almost as little intercourse with that section of South

Carolina as with us and North Carolina . . . the river with its swamps seems to interpose an impassable barrier. An attempt was made some years ago to remedy the evil by opening the Union Road. But owing to a long ferry and the price and difficulty of bringing carts across . . . it has entirely failed." The suggested path of the new road across Hutchinson Island would have also crossed the property of Judge Daniel Huger and Governor James Hamilton Jr.[12] This was truly a visionary suggestion inasmuch as the Eugene Talmadge Bridge connecting the two states at that location was not completed for more than a century. The suggestion may well have come from a South Carolina rice planter on the opposite bank. In 1833, suggestions were made for a railroad network connecting Savannah with Macon, Columbus, and eventually the Mississippi River.[13] These railroads were begun before the Civil War by Savannah businessmen who formed the Savannah, Albany and Gulf Railroad. The publicity and excitement surrounding these developments in Savannah attracted considerable interest in the rice lands across the river.

The men who developed the rice lands in St. Peter's Parish in the 1820s and early 1830s were among the wealthiest and most influential men in South Carolina and Georgia. Judge Daniel Huger moved fifty-three slaves to the Savannah River by 1820 to develop his plantation on the Savannah backriver opposite Hutchinson Island. By 1830, Huger had two hundred slaves on the river and owned more slaves than any other planter in St. Peter's Parish. Major John Screven of Savannah moved forty slaves across the river to develop rice fields adjacent to the Union Causeway. With control of this strategic real estate, he also gained control of the ferry across the river. Throughout the antebellum period, the principal crossing on the lower Savannah was known as Screven's Ferry. By 1830, he and his son, Dr. James Proctor Screven, had 115 slaves in St. Peter's Parish. Perhaps the key player in the rapid expansion of Savannah River rice lands in the 1820s was James Hamilton Jr., whose marriage to Elizabeth Heyward made him nephew-in-law to South Carolina's largest and richest rice planter, Nathaniel Heyward, and stepson-in-law to Savannah River investor Nicholas Cruger. Hamilton lived on Callawassie Island in St. Luke's Parish from 1815 to 1819 where he developed his wife's cotton and sugar plantation. He saw the possibilities for nearby St. Peter's rice lands and, in 1824, purchased Cruger's two Savannah River plantations. Hamilton's enthusiasm and wide contacts helped promote investment in St. Peter's Parish.[14]

Judge Daniel Huger (1779–1854) was the scion of one of the lowcountry's most experienced rice-planting families. He was an attorney and active politician most of his life, serving in the South Carolina legislature regularly from 1803 until 1819, when he was appointed associate judge of the Court of General Sessions and Common Pleas. He served in the South Carolina Senate from 1838 to 1841 and in the U.S. Senate from 1842 to 1845. Huger also had strong business and professional ties. He originally studied law in the office of Henry William DeSaussure and Timothy Ford in Charleston, and his first law partner was James Louis Petigru, who was the most prominent lawyer in the Beaufort District Court at Coosawhatchie in the early nineteenth century.[15]

Dr. James Proctor Screven (1799–1859) was the eldest son and heir of Major John Screven of Savannah. He was a graduate of the South Carolina College in 1817 and of the Medical College of the University of Pennsylvania in 1820. In 1826, he wed Hannah Georgia Bryan, granddaughter of pioneer rice planter, Jonathan Bryan. At the time of his father's illness and death in 1831, Screven abandoned his medical practice to devote his time to the management of his Savannah River rice plantation. He became one of the leading men of the city and an active politician. He was city alderman (1849–1854), Georgia state senator (1855–1856), and mayor of Savannah (1856–1857).[16] He was also one of the South's most enterprising businessmen. He was a banker and railroad builder as well as a rice planter. In the 1850s, he was president and principal promoter of the Savannah, Albany and Gulf Railroad.[17] By the time of his death in 1859, Screven was a millionaire. The basis of this great fortune was Screven's seven-hundred-acre river plantation in St. Peter's Parish. He reminded his wife in 1833 of the necessity of delaying his journey to join the family in Cecilton, Maryland, in order to attend to business on the river: "Recollect dear Georgia, that I am a planter and I cannot reap what I have not sown."[18]

James Hamilton Jr. (1789–1857) was the son of Major James Hamilton, "a favorite aide of General Washington's" in the Revolution, and the grandnephew of Thomas Lynch Jr., a signer of the Declaration of Independence and a relative of his mother. His mother's family, like the Hugers, Blakes, and Heywards, was among the oldest and most successful rice-planting families in the lowcountry. Hamilton was a veteran of the War of 1812, where he befriended two of the heroes of that war, Oliver Hazzard Perry and Steven Decatur. Returning to South Carolina, he became the law partner of Daniel Huger and James L. Petigru. In the 1820s, Hamilton was a political whirlwind. He was elected intendant of Charleston in 1822, where he successfully exposed the Denmark Vesey conspiracy and became the "most able and popular mayor ever chosen to the office." In 1823, he was elected to Congress from the Beaufort-Orangeburg District to replace his friend William Lowndes. In Congress in the 1820s, his aristocratic bearing and great oratory earned him the sobriquet "Chevalier Bayard of the South." In Washington, Hamilton was a major supporter of Andrew Jackson in his contests with John Quincy Adams for the presidency. In 1830, Hamilton returned to South Carolina, where he was elected governor until 1832.[19]

It was during this decade of political activity that Hamilton made major investments in St. Peter's Parish. As early as 1820, Hamilton communicated his interest in Georgia property to his agent in Savannah, Petit DeVillers.[20] DeVillers had just learned the rice trade from Savannah River planter, John G. Williamson, and probably helped convince Hamilton to buy Pennyworth Island in the Savannah backriver and Rice Hope Plantation on the South Carolina shore opposite Pennyworth Island from Nicholas Cruger in 1824. Rice Hope adjoined the plantation of Judge Huger. By 1829, the two plantations were fully operating, and Hamilton had DeVillers contract with Savannah bricklayers and carpenters to build a house for him on the shore. In 1830, Hamilton had 162 slaves working on Pennyworth Island and Rice Hope Plantation.[21] In 1844, Hamilton made another purchase further up the Savannah River when he bought the 120-acre Lucknow Plantation, on the South Carolina shore opposite Argyle Island, from Captain George Parsons Elliott of Beaufort for fifteen thousand dollars. By 1840, Hamilton owned the largest slave force in St. Peter's Parish, with 321 slaves working on his Savannah River rice plantations.[22]

The last member of the triumvirate of influential South Carolina planters who moved to the Savannah River by 1830 was Langdon Cheves I (1776–1857). Cheves was a lawyer, politician, and planter originally from the Pendleton District of South Carolina. He moved to Charleston in 1797 and became active in public life. Cheves served in the South Carolina legislature from 1802 to 1808. From 1808 to 1811, he was attorney general of South Carolina. In 1811, he was elected to Congress, where he became a friend and political ally of John C. Calhoun and Henry Clay. Cheves was elected speaker of the House of Representatives in 1814 and served until 1815. From 1816 to 1819, Cheves was an associate judge of the South Carolina Court of General Sessions and Common Pleas until he was succeeded by his friend and neighbor on the Savannah River, Daniel Huger. In 1819, Cheves became president of the Second U.S. Bank in Philadelphia and moved to Lancaster, Pennsylvania, where he resided until 1829. In 1829, Cheves returned to South Carolina and began to put together the pieces of what was to become the largest rice plantation on the lower Savannah: the 2,752-acre Delta Plantation.[23]

The principal transaction made by Cheves was the purchase of the Inverary Plantation from Dr. Charles W. Rogers. Rogers had bought the plantation from the estate of Lord William Campbell in 1823. He advertised it as having 473 acres of cultivated fields and 103 slaves in 1829. Cheves purchased the plantation and slaves intact in 1830 for $52,420, $40,400 of which was paid in Ohio, New York, and U.S. government securities. Cheves also bought the neighboring Smithfield Plantation from the estate of Edward Telfair of Savannah. The two plantations were combined to form the Delta Plantation with 1,132 acres of land. Later purchases of adjoining land brought the total to 2,752 acres.[24] The census of 1830 listed only seventy-nine slaves owned by Langdon Cheves in St. Peter's Parish, though his own records indicate that he bought 103 slaves from Dr. Charles Rogers that same year. Late in 1830, Cheves added to his labor force by the purchase of fifty-four slaves from Hugh Rose for $14,812. By 1840, Cheves had 180 slaves working in his rice fields on the Savannah River.[25]

Cheves's move to St. Peter's Parish was influenced by his friends, Daniel Huger and James Hamilton Jr.[26] Hamilton acted as Cheves's agent and attorney in the purchase of Inverary while Cheves was still in Pennsylvania. Early in 1830, the three men began a cooperative arrangement for the operation of the three adjoining properties. Hamilton wrote from Pennyworth Island to Cheves suggesting a meeting between himself, Cheves, and Huger on the Savannah River in May 1830, when they would all be inspecting their crops. He had some caution, but high expectations nevertheless, for the prospects of himself and his friends. "The mortality on the river . . . is a drawback to the otherwise certain profit of our fine and fertile lands which . . . all in all I think the best in the state."[27] For the next quarter century, the three powerful South Carolinians operated their St. Peter's rice plantations in concert.

Another important South Carolina rice-planting family followed Huger, Hamilton, and Cheves to the Savannah River in 1833. In that year, Charles Manigault bought the three-hundred-acre Gowrie Plantation and fifty slaves for forty thousand dollars. Gowrie Plantation had been developed during the 1820s by the Potter family of Charleston, Savannah, and Princeton, New Jersey. In addition to the slaves and 220 acres of developed rice fields, Gowrie contained a large water-powered rice-pounding mill which was widely used by planters on the Georgia and South Carolina sides of the river.[28]

Another prominent Georgian made major investments in St. Peter's in the 1820s, Dr. William Coffee Daniell (1793–1868). Daniell was born in Greene County, Georgia. He studied at the Medical College of the University of Pennsylvania and set up practice in Savannah in 1818. He gained fame as the author of the widely read medical treatise *Observations Upon the Autumnal Fevers of Savannah* and wealth by his marriage first to Martha Screven, and then after her death to her sister, Elizabeth Screven. These ladies were the daughters of Major John Screven and the sisters of Dr. James Proctor Screven. Marriage to them brought Daniell into the Proctor-Screven family circle and was the basis of his acquisition of the 700-acre Oglethorpe Plantation in St. Peter's Parish. Oglethorpe was between Screven's Ferry and Cheves's Delta Plantation. From these rice fields, Daniell "amassed a considerable fortune" before the Civil War. In 1830, he had 126 slaves at Oglethorpe Plantation and, by 1840, owned one of the largest labor forces in St. Peter's Parish, with 194 slaves. Daniell was also an active politician and one of the leading promoters of Savannah commerce. He was mayor of

Savannah from 1826 to 1828 and a major investor in the Savannah-Ogeechee Canal Company and the Mexico-Atlantic Company.[29]

During the 1830s, these St. Peter's Parish plantations produced regular and substantial income for their owners, allowing several to take prominent roles in the most serious constitutional crisis of the antebellum era: the Nullification Crisis of 1831 to 1833. In South Carolina, the leader of the radical Nullifiers was Governor James Hamilton Jr., while his two friends and neighbors on the Savannah River were South Carolina's leading moderates. Both Daniel Huger and Langdon Cheves bucked the popular tide in South Carolina.[30]

In Georgia, the popular forces considered Nullification absurd, but in the city of Savannah a clique of powerful merchants and planters formed a strong party for Nullification. They were led by Savannah River planter Dr. William Coffee Daniell, whose election to the Georgia Senate in 1833 was considered a victory in Charleston but a fluke by Georgia voters. Dr. Daniell's political career was ended with his defeat for Congress in 1834.[31] Thus, we have the irony of the five most prominent rice planters in St. Peter's Parish and their neighbors on the Savannah River taking contrary positions in two states on the most important constitutional crisis of the antebellum era. When the Nullification uproar was behind them, Hamilton, Huger, Cheves, Daniell, Screven, and their neighbors settled down to the business of planting.

The years between 1830 and the Civil War were years of great enterprise and production in the parish. The engines of the Industrial Revolution, which were generally thought to have bypassed the agricultural Old South, were very much in evidence on the lower Savannah. During the 1820s, the port city of Savannah became the hub for regular lines of paddlewheel steamships. These riverboats connected Charleston, Augusta, and the sea islands of South Carolina, Georgia, and north Florida with the Georgia port. By the 1850s, railroads were snaking westward from Savannah, and on April 20, 1860, the first through trip on the new Charleston and Savannah Railway was completed. On the eve of the Civil War, steam locomotives were beginning to replace paddlewheel riverboats. In May 1860, the *Daily Morning News* noted somewhat wistfully the retirement of Savannah River steamboat Captains J. P. Brooks and Frances Barden, who were "abandoning now a line of enterprise which has been closed by changes in the mode of transportation."[32]

The technology of the Industrial Revolution also increased the efficiency and productivity of the rice plantations of St. Peter's Parish. While the technique of tidal-culture rice was well refined by 1830, the introduction of new machines for processing the grain added to the speed and efficiency of rice production. In the spring of 1829, the first steam-powered rice-pounding mill was erected in Savannah by the firm of Hall, Shapter, and Tupper. It was driven by a twenty-horsepower engine and could clean twenty barrels of rice per day.[33] The planters on the South Carolina side soon followed. In 1831, a new steam-powered rice-threshing machine was demonstrated at Hamilton's Rice Hope Plantation, and all the great planters approved of its operation. Dr. William C. Daniell noted its chief potential as "a labor saving device . . . releasing slaves to improve land and increase yield per acre.[34] In 1833, Henry Taylor opened the first steam-powered rice mill on the South Carolina side at Laurel Hill Plantation and, by 1836, Hamilton had a steam rice mill on Pennyworth Island. Hamilton's mill was powered by four steamboilers thirty feet long and twenty-eight inches in diameter producing thirty horsepower. It was manufactured by the West Point Foundry of New York and cost Hamilton approximately five thousand dollars—manufactured, delivered, and assembled on Pennyworth.[35] By the middle of the next decade there were at least five steam rice mills operating on the South Carolina shore belching smoke from their tall iron stacks. In 1845, Langdon Cheves ordered the thirty-eight-foot mill stack at Delta Plantation built of brick rather than iron because, "It will last twenty years and is cheaper than iron."[36] Many of these brick mill stacks have lasted far longer than twenty years and can still be seen looming over the abandoned rice fields of the South Carolina and Georgia coast.

These mills were profitable operations for their owners. In 1847, Sen. John McPherson Berrien of Georgia had 166,352 pounds of rice processed at Blake's Mill on the South Carolina shore, for which the mill owners took 10 percent of the crop's value off the top.[37] This ten-percent cost of milling and storage proved to be significant income for the mill owners in bumper years and significant savings on their own crops in lean years. Hamilton was able for several years to reduce his heavy financial obligations to the Heywards, Hugers, and Cheves by milling the rice from their Savannah River plantations at his Pennyworth Island mill.[38] The new industrial technology was not without its risks, however. In 1852, Dr. William Coffee Daniell's steam rice mill at Oglethorpe Plantation exploded, killing the engineer and injuring five black assistants. In addition to the loss of life, the *Daily Morning News* reported, "All the rice in the vicinity was destroyed. The loss to Dr. Daniell will probably amount to between 5 and 10 thousand dollars."[39]

The most consistently successful of the Savannah River rice plantations during the thirty years prior to the Civil War was Cheves's Delta Plantation. In 1830, Cheves began his rice operation with seventy-nine slaves. In 1834, the 2,600-acre tract had 600 acres in cultivation and much more prime rice land to be developed. It was described then as the "best rice plantation in the state."[40] In the next twenty-five years, the land in cultivation nearly doubled. In 1840, Cheves had 180 slaves on the Savannah River. By 1850, he owned the largest labor force in St. Peter's Parish with 283 slaves. On the eve of the Civil War, Delta Plantation had 289 slaves working 1,100 acres of rice fields which produced 44,000 bushels, or approximately 1,056,000 pounds, of rice.[41] On the plantation was a steam rice mill, two steam-powered threshing machines, an overseer's house, an owner's house, and necessary outbuildings along the river. There were also two slave villages: one by the river and one with a slave hospital on the high pineland behind the rice fields. In 1845, the slave community at Delta Plantation consisted of 112 full hands, 8 male and 9 female half-hands, 3 drivers, 3 carpenters, 2 blacksmiths, a watchman, 2 trunkminders, 2 dikemen, 3 field cooks, 2 children's cooks, and a hospital nurse. At the residence there were 3 domestics: 1 in the garden, 1 in the cookhouse, and a trusted servant who had been dispatched to prepare the Cheves's summer residence in Pendleton. The natural increase of this slave community averaged five births per year for the decade ending in 1845. In addition to tending to the rice crop, these slaves grew provisions and raised livestock. A stock of cattle was added to Delta in 1846, and by 1847, hogs were introduced. These hogs were actually owned by some of the slaves. The shoats were sold to the plantation under contract.

The Cheves's plantation house on the Savannah River was a relatively modest story-and-a-half frame structure built well off the ground. It was used by the family only during the winter months, and then only occasionally. Other than managing the plantations, the principal activity while at Delta was hunting. Waterfowl were abundant among the rice fields, and deer and black bears inhabited the swamps behind the fields. For the children, the most memorable features of the dining room were the gun press and the large black bearskin hanging next to it.[42]

Delta Plantation set the style for the most successful planters on the Savannah River. The Hugers, next door at Clydesdale Plantation, and several generations of Hamiltons and Heywards next to them at Rice Hope and Laurel Hill, had similar operations. By the eve of the Civil War, there were more than two hundred slaves at both Clydesdale and Laurel Hill Plantations. The Georgia planters differed somewhat in that both Dr. James P. Screven and Dr. William C. Daniell lived in Savannah and could literally oversee their two large plantations in St. Peter's Parish from Factor's Walk in Savannah. They evidently visited their plantations more frequently and lived on them less. In 1850, Dr. James Proctor Screven was the largest rice producer in the Beaufort District with a bumper crop of 2,250,000 pounds worth $64,285. By 1860, he had 159 slaves on his plantation by the ferry, and his brother-in-law Dr. William C. Daniell had 107 slaves at his Oglethorpe Plantation next door.[43]

Rice planting, however, was an expensive business, and not all the Savannah River planters were successful. The most spectacular failure was James Hamilton Jr. He had begun his Pennyworth Island and Rice Hope operations through his Heyward and Cruger family connections. By 1840, he was by far the largest slaveholder in St. Peter's Parish with 321 slaves.[44] Hamilton was enthusiastic and energetic, but not very prudent. While the Cheveses, Hugers, and Heywards had resources with which to develop their Savannah River holdings, Hamilton expanded rapidly with borrowed money. Hamilton's numerous business and political adventures during the 1830s distracted him from the careful management of his Pennyworth and Rice Hope Plantations. Nevertheless, he reaped an annual income of between thirty and forty thousand dollars during these years.

During the 1830s, Hamilton became president of the Bank of Charleston and European financial emissary for the new Republic of Texas. His western land speculation and shifty European financial dealings finally landed him in court in 1841 with the James River and Kanawha Canal Company of Virginia, whose fifty thousand dollars he had misappropriated. Hamilton's Charleston creditors would not advance him more money, and, by 1842, he owed more than seven hundred thousand dollars, which even his productive Savannah River plantations could not repay. By 1844, Hamilton lost control of his St. Peter's Parish properties, and, in 1846, Rice Hope Plantation was sold at auction for forty thousand dollars. Through the help of his Heyward relatives, Hamilton's Savannah River properties were turned over to his sons, Lynch and Daniel, to manage for their mother's estate. By 1850, many of Hamilton's personal obligations had been satisfied by their labor.[45]

Despite the productivity of the Savannah River rice plantations of St. Peter's Parish in the years before the Civil War, there were consistent problems and frequent setbacks. The most consistent problem was the health of the slave labor force in a generally unhealthy environment. Dr. William Coffee Daniell had made himself an international expert in the chronic ill-health of the Savannah region with the publication in 1826 of his widely read treatise *Observations on the Autumnal Fevers of Savannah*. The city of Savannah had recognized the dangers of rice culture in the 1820s by passing "dry culture" ordinances prohibiting the flooding of rice fields within a mile of the city. Dr. Daniell and Dr. James P. Screven, both physicians, often treated their own labor force in St. Peter's Parish. Langdon Cheves's son became a physician, and the attic floor of the residence at Delta Plantation was entirely devoted to his medical workroom in the 1850s. Almost every plantation had a hospital and village on the high pine mainland in back of the rice fields to which slaves retreated in time of danger.

The Savannah River environment was considered very dangerous to whites, particularly in the summer. Cheves wrote to his son in 1843 not to stay too long on the river: "I have never allowed a white mechanic or other white workman to stay on the plantation after the 20th of May." He warned his son not to get fatigued or stay wet. "Every year," Cheves noted, "furnishes its victims."[46] Indeed, in 1838, Hamilton's eldest son died of fever at Pennyworth Island.[47]

While the black slave force was believed resistant to fevers, they succumbed to other diseases, causing tragedy for the villages and great loss to the planters. In 1834, Hamilton lost fifty prime slaves to whooping cough, a malady which continued to plague the Savannah River plantations for many years.[48] It was present at Delta Plantation in 1843, which caused Dr. Daniell to request that Cheves move his slave hospital away from Daniell's nearby slave village. Cheves then built Palmyra, on the mainland which he described "as healthy as Bluffton." In addition to whooping cough, cholera was common among the slave communities. Maintenance of slave health was a prime responsibility of the plantation manager, and Cheves's 1836 contract with George Lynes required that he "particularly attend to the negroes in sickness."[49]

The vagaries of weather often upset the productivity of the plantations as well. Periodic hurricanes drove salt water over the dikes from the east, and freshwater flooding from the west occasionally swept away whole crops. Savannah River plantations were particularly vulnerable to high water because they regularly stored the crops in the field during harvest. Cheves wrote, "I believe it is only on the Savannah River that rice is shocked in the field. The practice, I understand, grew out of large crops and comparatively few hands."[50]

In 1831, a "freshet" damaged the wharves in Savannah and flooded the rice plantations above Hutchinson Island. Some planters lost their entire crop.[51] In 1846, a severe storm caused flooding as far downriver as Delta Plantation, where it flooded the rice mill and destroyed some of the harvest stored there.[52] In 1852, a hurricane blew down mill stacks and damaged rice dikes along the river, and the accompanying heavy rains washed out bridges at Augusta. The descending flood swept over many of the Savannah River plantations "like a wave." The Daniell and Hamilton plantations were damaged by high tides and wind while the Williamson, Chisolm, King, and Manigault plantations upriver were completely overrun by flooding. The Savannah newspaper noted, "The extent of damage to the crop is impossible to estimate but known to be great."[53] Two years later another hurricane swept ashore. It was said to be "the most destructive storm since 1824." Three-quarters of the rice crop on the Savannah River was destroyed by high water.[54]

Another chronic problem in the management of the St. Peter's Parish rice plantations was absenteeism. Not one of the owners of the eighteen rice plantations on the South Carolina side of the Savannah River actually resided on his plantation, and many did not even visit their plantations for years at a time. Most of the owners such as Daniel Huger, Langdon Cheves, James Hamilton Jr., Daniel Heyward, Walter Blake, John Rutledge, Joseph Manigault, and J. J. Pringle Smith lived in Charleston. Others, like James P. Screven, William C. Daniell, Benjamin Guerard, and Archibald Smith, lived in Savannah. Two owners, Edward Barnwell and George Parsons Elliott, were from Beaufort, though Barnwell later became a prominent Charleston businessman and Elliott sold his plantation in 1844. The wealthier of these families spent considerable time away from the lowcountry in such places as Pendleton, South Carolina; Flat Rock, North Carolina; Lancaster,

Pennsylvania; and Cecilton, Maryland. By the 1850s, it had become fashionable for wealthy lowcountry planters to take their families on extended European tours.[55]

When the owners were in the lowcountry, they normally visited their Savannah River properties during November at the end of the rice harvest and during April at the early planting stage. During these visits, many planters stayed in Savannah and only visited their plantations during the day.[56] During these long absences and extensive travels, the plantation owners had to rely on their local agents, overseers, and drivers. Much correspondence was devoted to the problems of absentee ownership and local management. Cheves's advice to his son in 1843 was typical. Picking a manager, Cheves related, was "a very difficult subject. They tend not to be stable, and are resentful when released." Some managers, like Delta Plantation's Zantz, were good planters and technicians, but poor handlers of the slave workforce. Zantz produced a good crop, but because of inconsistent behavior to the blacks, "the negroes under him were almost rebellious." In other cases, the overseer might capably handle the blacks but produce a poor crop.[57] An overseer's annual salary on the river ranged between three hundred and one thousand dollars from 1833 to 1863, and there seemed to be plenty of men willing to work.[58] One problem unique to the Savannah River was that often even the overseer was absent from the plantation, preferring to live in Savannah and commute to work while leaving the leadership of the slave community to the black drivers, a difficult if not untenable position for the driver.[59] Cheves summed up the problem in 1844, "The long established practice of the river, a very bad one has been to leave the overseer altogether uncontrolled."[60]

Despite the problems of health, weather, and absenteeism, the St. Peter's Parish rice plantations were very productive throughout the 1840s. The peak year for rice production on the Savannah River was 1849. In that year, the Beaufort District grew 47,230,000 pounds of rice, most of which came from the Savannah River plantations of St. Peter's Parish. Throughout this period rice prices remained relatively stable, and, in 1849, the Beaufort District rice crop was worth $1,653,050. By 1850, St. Peter's Parish had become the largest slaveowning parish in the Beaufort District with 8,999 slaves.[61]

The following decade, however, was one of transition. The first was the passing of many of the great planters who had developed the tidewater plantations of St. Peter's Parish. Huger died in 1854, and his Clydesdale Plantation was divided among two sons and one son-in-law and renamed Trinity Plantation. In 1857, Cheves died at the age of eighty, shortly before the drowning of his long-time friend Hamilton in a steamship accident off Galveston, Texas. In 1854, Screven's eldest son was accidentally drowned in the Savannah River, and, five years later, Screven died in Savannah at the age of sixty.[62] In 1852 and again in

1854, hurricanes destroyed much of the rice crop and damaged dikes, canals, and buildings. Repair and rebuilding was costly for the dikes, ditches, and trunks that had been operating for twenty or thirty years. The slave labor force leveled off and, on some Savannah River plantations, declined sharply during the 1850s.

Also during the 1850s, several Savannah River planters began experimenting with alternative crops. In 1853, Colonel Green produced a bumper crop of wheat on former rice fields on Hutchinson Island, and in 1860, Charles Daniell, son of Dr. William C. Daniell, produced an excellent crop of wheat on the rice fields of his father's Oglethorpe Plantation. In 1860, a Mr. Clinch harvested eight hundred acres of grass on former rice fields on Hutchinson Island. The *Daily Morning News* commented, "A rice planter may smile at the thought of prostituting any of his rice land to growing grass, but an acre of grass will sell for more than an acre of rice."[63] If the heyday of rice on the Savannah River had not passed by 1860, the Civil War which followed surely ended it.

On the eve of the Civil War, Louis Manigault made a list of the tidewater plantations of the Savannah River with the number of acres planted and the expected average yield. Correlating this list with the St. Peter's Parish slave schedules and using an average figure for slave maintenance on the Savannah River, plus an average price per pound for rice sales that year, creates an agricultural and economic profile of the Savannah River rice plantations of St. Peter's Parish in 1860, as shown below.

Savannah River Rice Plantations of St. Peter's Parish, S.C., in 1860[64]

Name	Planted Acres	# of Slaves	Lbs. of Rice (Estimated)	Gross Crop Value (Est.)	Cost of Slave Maint.	10% Milling & Storage	Net Income (Estimated)	Market For Rice
James P. Screven	700	159	672,000	$21,504	$ 7,678	$2,150	$11,676	Savannah
Edward Barnwell and Archibald Smith	550	92	528,000	16,896	4,864	1,690	10,342	Savannah
Wm. C. Daniell	700	107	672,000	21,504	5,494	2,150	13,860	Savannah
Langdon Cheves	1,100	289	1,056,000	33,792	13,138	3,379	17,275	Savannah
Jos. Manigault	400	93	384,000	12,288	4,906	1,229	6,153	Charleston
Huger Family's "Trinity"	1,700	197	1,632,000	52,224	9,274	5,222	37,728	Charleston
Walter Blake	300	74	288,000	9,216	4,108	922	4,186	Savannah
John Rutledge and Hugh Rose	400	131	384,000	12,288	5,502	1,229	4,557	Charleston
James B. Heyward and Wm. H. Heyward	600	136	576,000	18,432	6,712	1,843	9,877	Charleston
Robt. Smith's Estate	400	109	384,000	12,288	5,518	1,229	5,481	Charleston
Allen Izard	1,200	263	1,152,000	36,864	12,046	3,686	21,132	Charleston
Daniel Heyward	1,100	242	1,056,000	33,792	11,164	3,379	19,249	Charleston
J.J. Pringle Smith	450	132	432,000	13,824	6,544	1,382	5,898	Charleston
Benj. Guerard	350	93	336,000	10,752	4,906	1,075	5,671	Savannah
Taylor Estate	600	104	576,000	18,434	5,368	1,843	11,221	Savannah
McPherson Estate	400	95	384,000	12,288	4,990	1,229	6,069	Charleston
Chisolm Estate	400	126	384,000	12,288	6,292	1,229	4,759	Charleston
Williamson Estate	450	145	432,000	13,824	7,090	1,382	5,352	Savannah

328   The History of Beaufort County

The Civil War was the beginning of the end of this tidewater rice enterprise. With the fall of Port Royal to the U.S. Navy in November 1861, large numbers of slaves ran away from lowcountry plantations to the Union occupying forces at Beaufort and Hilton Head. Still more disrupted the plantation routine by passing rumors, plotting, and "seeking to avoid work of any kind." Many Savannah River planters removed their slaves from their rice plantations to "places of safety in the interior of South Carolina and Georgia." Several plantations ceased production, and others cut back sharply with reduced gangs of slaves.[65] Production was thus inconsistent during the war, and foreign markets were cut off by the Union blockade.

NOTES

1. St. Helena (1712), Prince William (1745), St. Peter's (1748), and St. Luke's (1767) Parishes.

2. 2nd Census (1800), 3rd Census (1810), 4th Census (1820), Beaufort District Population Schedules, South Carolina Department of Archives and History.

3. Cheves, Chain of Title to Delta Plantation, Cheves-Middleton Papers, South Carolina Historical Society; 2nd Census (1800), Beaufort District Population Schedule, South Carolina Department of Archives and History.

4. 2nd Census (1800), Beaufort District Population Schedule, South Carolina Department of Archives and History. Both plantations are now part of the Savannah National Wildlife Refuge.

5. 2nd Census (1800) and 3rd Census (1810), Beaufort District Population Schedules, South Carolina Department of Archives and History.

6. 4th Census (1820), Beaufort District Population Schedule, South Carolina Department of Archives and History.

7. Lewis Cecil Gray, *History of Agriculture in the Southern United States to 1860,* 2 vols. (Gloucester, Mass.: Peter Smith, 1958), 2: 726–31, 1030; James M. Clifton, ed., *Life and Labor on Argyle Island: Letters and Documents of a Savannah River Rice Plantation, 1833–1867* (Savannah: Beehive Press, 1978), xix; Ulrich B. Phillips, *American Negro Slavery: A Survey of the Supply, Employment and Control of Negro Labor as Determined by the Plantation Regime* (1918; rpt. Gloucester, Mass.: Peter Smith, 1959), 254–58.

8. *Georgian,* September 14, 1833, Georgia Historical Society; Charles C. Jones Jr., *History of Savannah, Georgia, from Its Settlement to the Close of the Eighteenth Century* (Syracuse: D. Mason, 1890), 340.

9. *Savannah Georgian,* January 23, 1826; January 24, 1826; February 2, 1826; February 14, 1826; March 13, 1826; March 25, 1826, Georgia Historical Society.

10. *Savannah Georgian,* November 1, 1827; November 30, 1827; March 17, 1829; May 19, 1831, Georgia Historical Society.

11. *Savannah Georgian,* April 14, 1826; June 10, 1828; January 21, 1829; February 17, 1829; *Georgian,* November 19, 1830; June 3, 1831; September 27, 1831; October 22, 1831; November 1, 1831; December 31, 1831, Georgia Historical Society; Louis J. De Vorsey, *The Georgia-South Carolina Boundary Dispute: A Problem in Historical Geography*

(Athens: University of Georgia Press, 1982), 90–100; Mary Granger, ed., *Savannah River Plantations* (Savannah: Georgia Historical Society, 1947), 108–10. This article originally set out to discover the connection between this dredging operation and the development of the rice fields on the South Carolina shore. No direct connection could be found, but both William Coffee Daniell and his brother-in-law James Proctor Screven developed their successful rice plantations next to each other in St. Peter's Parish at this time. Both men were also major boosters of Savannah commerce and both were mayors of the city.

12. *Georgian,* May 19, 1831, Georgia Historical Society .

13. *Georgian,* August 31, 1833; September 14, 1833; September 5, 1883, Georgia Historical Society.

14. 4th Census (1820) and 5th Census (1830), Beaufort District Population Schedules, South Carolina Department of Archives and History; "Chart of Part of the Savannah River, 1833, by Lt. John MacKay," in De Vorsey, *Georgia-South Carolina Boundary Dispute,* 108–9. The backriver was the secondary channel of the Savannah River that ran behind Hutchinson Island and formed the boundary between South Carolina and Georgia. Virginia L. Glenn, "James Hamilton, Jr., of South Carolina: A Biography," Ph.D. diss., University of North Carolina, 1964, 62–63.

15. *Biographical Directory of the South Carolina House,* 4: 292–93.

16. Robert M. Myers, ed., *The Children of Pride: A True Story of Georgia and the Civil War* (New Haven: Yale University Press, 1972), 1672; William Hardin, "The Screven Family," *Georgia Historical Quarterly* 1 (1917): 166–67, 269–72; Henrietta Dozier, "Genealogy of the Screven Family" (typescript, 1935), Georgia Historical Society .

17. *Savannah Daily Morning News,* January 6, 1853; August 31, 1853; February 2, 1854; June 3, 1854; January 4, 1855; February 7, 1859, Georgia Historical Society.

18. Dr. James P. Screven to Georgia Bryan Screven, June 13, 1833, Forman-Bryan-Screven Papers, Georgia Historical Society .

19. Biography of James Hamilton Jr., by L. C., James Hamilton Jr. Papers, South Caroliniana Library; "James Hamilton, Jr.," *Biographical Directory of the American Congress, 1774–1961* (Washington, D.C.: U.S. Government Printing Office, 1961), 997. The "L. C." of the manuscript biography is clearly Hamilton's friend and neighbor on the Savannah River, Langdon Cheves I.

20. James Hamilton Jr. to Petit DeVilliers, January 24, 1820, James Hamilton Jr. Papers, South Caroliniana Library.

21. James Hamilton Jr. to Petit DeVilliers, March 21, 1829, James Hamilton Jr. Papers, South Caroliniana Library; 5th Census (1830), Beaufort District Population Schedule, South Carolina Department of Archives and History.

22. Clifton, ed., *Life and Labor on Argyle Island,* 12, 18, 23; 6th Census (1840), Beaufort District Population Schedule, South Carolina Department of Archives and History.

23. Archie Vernon Huff Jr., *Langdon Cheves of South Carolina* (Columbia: University of South Carolina Press, 1977), 17–146; *Biographical Directory of the South Carolina House,* 4: 111–14.

24. Notes of Langdon Cheves III, n.d., Langdon Cheves III Papers, South Carolina Historical Society; Cheves, Chain of Title to Delta, Cheves-Middleton Papers, South Carolina Historical Society; Closing Statement, Delta Plantation, Langdon Cheves to

Charles W. Rogers, May 5, 1830, Langdon Cheves I Papers, South Carolina Historical Society; Deposition of Anna West Rogers, January 6, 1831, Langdon Cheves I Papers, South Carolina Historical Society.

25. 5th Census (1830) and 6th Census (1840), Beaufort District Population Schedules, South Carolina Department of Archives and History; Langdon Cheves to Hugh Rose, November 27, 1830, Langdon Cheves I Papers, South Carolina Historical Society.

26. Huff, *Langdon Cheves,* 150.

27. Charles Rogers to James Hamilton Jr., March 1, 1830, Langdon Cheves I Papers, South Carolina Historical Society; James Hamilton Jr. to Langdon Cheves, April 4, 1830, Langdon Cheves I Papers, South Carolina Historical Society.

28. Clifton, ed., *Life and Labor on Argyle Island,* xx; Granger, ed., *Savannah River Plantations,* 226; *Savannah Georgian,* July 25, 1826, Georgia Historical Society. Argyle Island is in Georgia just a few yards across the backriver from St. Peter's Parish and is owned by a prominent South Carolinian. The complete records of Gowrie and Hermitage Plantations, kept by the Manigault family from 1833 to 1867, make this one of the best-known Savannah River plantations.

29. Myers, ed., *Children of Pride,* 1504; William Harden, "The Screven Family," *Georgia Historical Quarterly* 1 (1917): 271; Jones, *History of Savannah,* 438; 5th Census (1830) and 6th Census (1840), Beaufort District Population Schedules, South Carolina Department of Archives and History; *Savannah Georgian,* January 10, 1826; April 4, 1826; March 7, 1826; July 15, 1826; June 23, 1827; *Georgian,* October 17, 1830; November 18, 1830; February 27, 1832; June 22, 1832; January 3, 1833, Georgia Historical Society.

30. William W. Freehling, *Prelude to Civil War: The Nullification Controversy in South Carolina, 1816–1836* (New York: Harper and Row, 1966), 2–3, 145–52, 202–3, 217, 228, 242, 255, 261, 269; J. P. Ochenkowski, "The Origins of Nullification in South Carolina," *South Carolina Historical Magazine* 83 (April 1982): 121–53; *Biographical Directory of the South Carolina House,* 4: 111–14, 292–93; Langdon Cheves to David J. McCord, August 15, 1831, Langdon Cheves I Papers, South Carolina Historical Society.

31. *Georgian,* February 6, 1833; April 2, 1833; October 7, 1833; October 25, 1833; February 13, 1834; April 17, 1834; September 20, 1834, Georgia Historical Society.

32. Ruby A. Rahn, *River Highway for Trade: The Savannah* (Savannah: U.S. Army Corps of Engineers, 1968), 31–45; *Savannah Daily Morning News,* May 22, 1860; April 21, 1869, Georgia Historical Society.

33. *Savannah Georgian,* June 7, 1828; March 27, 1829, Georgia Historical Society.

34. *Georgian,* February 19, 1831, Georgia Historical Society.

35. James Hamilton Jr. to William Kemble, January 16, 1836, James Hamilton Jr. Papers, South Caroliniana Library.

36. Langdon Cheves to Langdon Cheves Jr., May 28, 1845, Langdon Cheves I Papers, South Carolina Historical Society.

37. Berrien's Account at Blake's Mill, January 22, 1847, John McPherson Berrien Papers, Georgia Historical Society.

38. James Hamilton Jr. to Langdon Cheves, Jan. 3, 1843, Langdon Cheves I Papers, South Carolina Historical Society.

39. *Savannah Daily Morning News,* January 30, 1852; January 31, 1852, Georgia Historical Society.

40. *Georgian,* November 26, 1834, Georgia Historical Society.

41. 5th Census (1830), 6th Census (1840), 7th Census (1850), and 8th Census (1860), Beaufort District Population Schedules, South Carolina Department of Archives and History; Louis Manigault, "Rice Lands Planted on the Savannah and Ogeechee Rivers," Manigault Papers, University of North Carolina, Chapel Hill, Southern Historical Collection. By 1860, Cheves's Delta Plantation had more cultivated acres and a larger slave force than all but three of the plantations on the Waccamaw River. For a comparison, see Charles W. Joyner, *Down by the Riverside: A South Carolina Slave Community* (Urbana: University of Illinois Press, 1984), 19–20.

42. Slave List, 1845; Langdon Cheves to Langdon Cheves Jr., July 14, 1846; March 11, 1847; Recollections of Langdon Cheves III, Winter of 1854, Langdon Cheves III Papers, South Carolina Historical Society. More on the internal slave economy is in Phillip D. Morgan, "Work and Culture: The Task System in the World of Lowcountry Blacks, 1700–1880," *William and Mary Quarterly* 39 (October 1982): 563–99.

43. Agricultural Census of 1850, Beaufort District; 8th Census (1860), Beaufort District Slave Schedule, South Carolina Department of Archives; Gray, *History of Agriculture,* 2: 1030.

44. 6th Census (1840), Beaufort District Population Schedule, South Carolina Department of Archives and History.

45. Glenn, "James Hamilton, Jr.," 62–63, 224, 342, 354, 360–63.

46. Langdon Cheves to Langdon Cheves Jr., April 6, 1843, Langdon Cheves I Papers, South Carolina Historical Society.

47. James Hamilton Jr. to Langdon Cheves, November 12, 1838, Langdon Cheves I Papers, South Carolina Historical Society.

48. Glenn, "James Hamilton, Jr.," 225.

49. Langdon Cheves to Langdon Cheves Jr., May 21, 1843; and July 26, 1844; Contract Between George Lynes and Langdon Cheves, November 21, 1836, Langdon Cheves I Papers, South Carolina Historical Society; Clifton, ed., *Life and Labor on Argyle Island,* xxxiv.

50. Langdon Cheves to Langdon Cheves Jr., August 3, 1844, Langdon Cheves I Papers, South Carolina Historical Society.

51. *Georgian,* September 6, 1831, Georgia Historical Society.

52. Langdon Cheves to Langdon Cheves Jr., October 13, 1846, Langdon Cheves I Papers, South Carolina Historical Society.

53. Clifton, ed., *Life and Labor on Argyle Island,* 99, 117–19; *Savannah Daily Morning News,* September 6, 1852, Georgia Historical Society.

54. *Savannah Daily Morning News,* September 9, 1854, Georgia Historical Society.

55. *Biographical Directory of the South Carolina House,* 4: 292–93; Huff, *Langdon Cheves,* 17–146; Glenn, "James Hamilton, Jr.," 62–72, 216–40; Stephen B. Barnwell, *The Story of an American Family* (Marquette, Mich.: Privately printed, 1969), 83, 94, 99; Clifton, ed., *Life and Labor on Argyle Island,* xxviii–xxx, 37–68.

56. James Hamilton Jr. to Langdon Cheves, November 12, 1838, and Daniel Huger to Langdon Cheves, April 12, 1839, Langdon Cheves I Papers, South Carolina Historical Society; Clifton, ed., *Life and Labor on Argyle Island,* 187–91.

57. Langdon Cheves to Langdon Cheves Jr., April 17, 1843, Langdon Cheves I Papers, South Carolina Historical Society; Clifton, ed., *Life and Labor on Argyle Island,* 11.

58. Clifton, ed., *Life and Labor on Argyle Island,* 1–2; Contract between George Lynes and Langdon Cheves, November 21, 1836, Langdon Cheves I Papers, South Carolina Historical Society; *Georgian,* December 5, 1833, Georgia Historical Society.

59. *Georgian,* January 17, 1831, Georgia Historical Society.

60. Langdon Cheves to Langdon Cheves Jr., September 27, 1844, Langdon Cheves I Papers, South Carolina Historical Society.

61. Sam B. Hilliard, "Tidewater Rice Plantation: An Ingenious Adaptation to Nature," *Geoscience and Man* 12 (1975): 62; Agricultural Census of 1850, Beaufort District; Gray, *History of Agriculture,* 2: 1030; 7th Census (1850), Beaufort District Slave Schedule.

62. *Biographical Directory of the South Carolina House,* 4: 111–14, 292–93; Emily Bellinger Reynolds and Joan Reynolds Faunt, comps., *Biographical Directory of the Senate of South Carolina, 1796–1964* (Columbia: South Carolina Archives Department, 1964), 229; *Savannah Daily Morning News,* June 2, 1854; May 18, 1860, Georgia Historical Society; Myers; *Children of Pride,* 1672–1673.

63. *Savannah Daily Morning News,* April 5, 1853; April 10, 1860; May 16, 1860, Georgia Historical Society.

64. Louis Manigault, "Rice Lands Planted on the Savannah and Ogeechee Rivers," Manigault Papers, University of North Carolina, Chapel Hill, Southern Historical Collection. Louis Manigault's estimate of crop yield at forty bushels per acre was very optimistic. His own Gowrie Plantation averaged only 29.5 bushels per acre for the six prior years, and his best crop was 36 bushels per acre. A 25 percent reduction in crop yield and gross value might be more realistic and would substantially lower the net income expected in 1860. The figure for slave maintenance on the Savannah River of forty-two dollars per year is derived from Clifton, ed., *Life and Labor on Argyle Island,* xxxvii, and Ralph B. Flanders, "Planters' Problems in Ante-Bellum Georgia," *Georgia Historical Quarterly* 14 (March 1930): 17–40. The price of rice at 3.2 cents per pound in 1860 is from Gray, *History of Agriculture,* 2: 1030. Slave figures are from the 8th Census (1860), Beaufort District Slave Schedule. The Taylor, McPherson, Chisolm, and Williamson estates were not listed under those names in 1860, so the slave population for those plantations is from the 7th Census (1850), Beaufort District Population Schedule, South Carolina Department of Archives and History. Another factor which could alter the crop yield assumptions is efficiency. Plantations with higher slave-to-acre ratios appear to be more costly, but may have been more efficient and have had a higher yield per acre. The large but thinly staffed Huger operation stands out. Cost of slave maintenance includes a one thousand dollar estimated overseer's salary.

65. Clifton, ed., *Life and Labor on Argyle Island,* 319–23.

18

Nullification Crisis and the Rise
of the Rhett Faction

As the prosperity of the first cotton boom began to subside during the 1820s, a crisis developed which was the pivotal political event of the antebellum era in the Beaufort District. This was the Nullification Crisis, which pitted the interests of South Carolina against those of the federal government. The tariff policy of the federal government taxed imported goods in order to protect domestic manufacturers. It also placed an ad valorem tax on exported cotton. The tariff was, thus, popular in the North but harmful to the South, whose commodities became relatively less valuable. South Carolina, therefore, challenged the right of Congress to pass laws harmful to the state's interest. This led to the political turning point of 1832. The political leaders of the Beaufort District played conspicuous and decisive roles in the Nullification Crisis. It was this event which launched the careers of the most famous and influential politicians that the old Beaufort District produced in the antebellum era: Robert Barnwell Rhett, Robert Woodward Barnwell, and William J. Grayson.

Just as the Nullification Crisis was a watershed in the political life of South Carolina, it also caused a fundamental shift in the political leadership of the Beaufort District. The district, particularly the sea islands of St. Helena Parish, had always had a reputation for staunch federalism. And even after the Federalist Party had long since been eclipsed in the old South by the Jefferson-Jackson Democratic Party, the political leadership of the southern parishes retained a strong, aristocratic echo of the old Federalists in the persons of William Lowndes (1782–1822), who represented the Beaufort and Colleton Districts in the U.S. Congress, and William Elliott (1788–1863), who represented St. Helena Parish in the South Carolina Senate from 1818 to 1821 and again in 1831.

Lowndes was the youngest son of Rawlins Lowndes, one of the political stalwarts of the American Revolution in South Carolina. William Lowndes was one of the most admired politicians in the state until his death in 1822. As a member of the South Carolina House of Representatives, he had been one of the authors of the constitutional amendment of 1808 which reapportioned representation in the South Carolina legislature and effectively ended the bitter sectional rivalries of the eighteenth century. As a U.S. representative from the Beaufort and Colleton Districts, he was always a strong supporter of the national governments led by Presidents Madison and Monroe. Lowndes supported the Tariff of 1816 against the interests of his planter constituents and helped craft the Missouri Compromise of 1820, which was the opening salvo of the U.S. Congress against the slaveholding South.

One of Lowndes's greatest admirers was William J. Grayson of Beaufort, who recalled a dinner with Lowndes and some prominent Beaufortonians at the home of Bay Street merchant Robert Porteous. Grayson, himself one of the state's premier intellects, engaged Lowndes in a discussion of classical literature and Latin hymns, whereupon Lowndes entertained the guests with a discourse on the subject "with a readiness, intelligence and interest that would not have been easily found with any other political leader of the day."

The pinnacle of Lowndes's public career came in 1821 when South Carolina nominated him for president over John C. Calhoun. To this signal honor, Lowndes replied in the aristocratic tradition of the old Federalists. The office of the president, he wrote, "is not, in my opinion, an office to be solicited or declined." The following year, Lowndes resigned from Congress due to failing health and died aboard ship on a passage to Europe. He was much lamented in South Carolina.[1]

Lowndes was replaced in Congress by James Hamilton Jr. (1786–1857), who began his career as a young lawyer at the Beaufort District Court at Coosawhatchie and married local heiress Elizabeth Matthews Heyward, daughter of Daniel Heyward of Pocotaligo and granddaughter of Thomas Heyward Jr. Hamilton represented the Beaufort/Colleton District in the U.S. Congress throughout the 1820s but returned to South Carolina in 1829 to become the organizing genius of the Nullification movement. The change in Congress from Lowndes to Hamilton represented the shift in the political leadership of the Beaufort District during the 1820s from strong nationalism to ardent states' rights.[2]

Another local political leader whose public career was transformed by the Nullification Crisis in South Carolina was William Elliott III (1788–1863). Elliott was the eldest son of sea island cotton pioneer William Elliott II, a leader of the Federalist faction of the Beaufort District during the 1790s. An acknowledged local leader and one of the wealthiest men in the Beaufort District, William III represented St. Helena Parish in the South Carolina Senate from 1818 to 1821. In 1822, he lost the election for U.S. Congress to Hamilton. He returned to the South Carolina Senate in 1831, only to resign his seat as a matter of principle because he disagreed with some of his constituents on the issue of Nullification. In 1832, he wrote a lengthy explanation to his constituents entitled "An Address to the People of St. Helena's Parish," criticizing them for their disunionist tendencies. He then retired permanently from local politics. A strong Unionist, Elliott could be considered the last echo of the old Federalist faction of St. Helena Parish.[3]

Even before Elliott returned to the South Carolina Senate, he was surrounded by Nullifiers. "Squire" William Pope of Hilton Head, one of the wealthiest and most influential of the sea island cotton planters and a leading Nullifier, represented St. Luke's Parish in the South Carolina Senate. William J. Grayson, though later a famous Unionist, was a leader in the States' Rights and Free Trade Party and an ardent Nullifier as state senator from St. Helena Parish between 1826 and 1831. And John Seth Maner, the longtime state senator for St. Peter's Parish and representative of the planters of the upper district, was also a supporter and signer of the Nullification Ordinance.[4]

By 1830, then, the Beaufort District had become strongly states' rightist and pro-Nullification. The younger generation had abandoned the federalism of their fathers. But the tariff policy as an economic issue and states' rights as a constitutional issue did not appear suddenly in the late 1820s. As early as 1790, the state's first senator from Beaufort, Major Pierce Butler, told the U.S. Congress that a protective tariff would cause "a dissolution of the Union, with regard to his state, as sure as God was in the firmament." And in 1819, sea island cotton planters sent a petition to Congress objecting to the Tariff of 1816. Even Elliott, in 1826, questioned the constitutionality of the Tariff of 1824 in private conversation with Congressman George McDuffie, though he never recommended Nullification as a solution.[5]

Several events of the late 1820s caused the popular storm of Nullification to break over South Carolina. First, in 1827, Robert J. Turnbull's riveting and compelling pamphlet *The Crisis,* which clearly explained to South Carolinians the constitutional arguments, political reasons, and economic justifications for aggressive states' rights action was published. James Hamilton Jr. said that "*The Crisis* was the first bugle call to the South." Turnbull was an "old Federalist" who was transformed by the Nullification issue into a leading states' righter. Second, the Tariff of Abominations was passed by the unpopular John Quincy Adams's administration, in May 1828, which enraged southerners generally and South Carolinians particularly. Third, the Colleton Address was delivered in June 1828 by state representative Robert Barnwell Rhett on the steps of the newly completed courthouse (designed by Robert Mills) in Walterboro. This speech called for immediate and unilateral state action against the laws of the U.S. Congress that were harmful to the interests of South Carolina, specifically the Tariff of Abominations.[6] These events galvanized the South Carolina electorate against the federal government, began the state's march on the road to secession, and launched the political career of the most influential politician Beaufort ever produced.

Robert Barnwell Rhett, the father of secession, was born in Beaufort on December 21, 1800, the fourth son of James Smith and Marianna Barnwell Gough. (In 1837, all six Smith brothers legally changed their name from Smith to Rhett to honor their maternal ancestor, Colonel William Rhett, whose name had died out in South Carolina.) Rhett was raised, along with his eleven siblings, in the large tabby home of his grandmother Elizabeth Barnwell Gough on Carteret Street in Beaufort. Rhett grew up among numerous Barnwell cousins in the prosperous capital of the South Carolina sea islands during the heady days of the first cotton boom. The Smith family, however, was not among the great planter families of the Beaufort District whose fortunes were rising rapidly during those years. They did not have the great wealth of their Barnwell, Elliott, and Heyward relatives. James Smith was a scholar but a poor rice planter. While he had graduated from the Middle Temple in London in 1781, he could not afford similar educational opportunities for his older sons. While the Barnwells, Elliotts, and Heywards finished their studies at Harvard, Yale, and Edinburgh, the Rhetts stayed home. Robert Rhett received all his schooling at the Beaufort College, where he was a student of James L. Petigru, later to be South Carolina's preeminent antebellum lawyer, who began his career as a teacher at the Beaufort College in 1811. As the state's leading Unionist, Petigru became a political adversary of his famous student. Despite their political differences, the two men remained close and admiring personal friends throughout their lives.

Rhett wore his South Carolina provincialism like a badge of honor, if not a chip on his shoulder. His daughter Elise revealed a private letter to Laura A. White, Rhett's biographer, that Rhett had written many years before stating, "I was born in this State . . . and never had seen any other than a Carolina sun rise or set, until after I was fifteen years old . . . and I have lived nowhere else" except in Washington as a congressman from the Beaufort/Colleton District. This parochial background was more representative of the majority of the planters of the Beaufort District and may have contributed to Rhett's consistent influence and support in the Beaufort District for over thirty years. Though Beaufort was certainly a wealthy district by national standards, only a small number of planters had the great wealth necessary to provide for northern schooling, European travel, and summer homes in the mountains. Rhett's provincialism was a political asset even in the wealthy district.

Rather than going north or to Europe for schooling, Rhett read the law in the office of Judge Thomas S. Grimke. He was admitted to the South Carolina Bar in 1822 and began his practice at the Beaufort District Court at Coosawhatchie. There he opened a lucrative law practice with his cousin and recent Harvard graduate, Robert W. Barnwell. Barnwell later abandoned the practice of law to pursue careers in planting, politics, and education. Rhett then moved to Walterboro, site of the Colleton District Court. It was at Walterboro that Rhett began the tumultuous and dynamic political career that was to earn him the sobriquet "father of secession."[7]

Rhett was a state representative from St. Bartholomew's Parish in 1828 when the ideas of states' rights and Nullification began to seize the imaginations of leading South Carolinians. On June 12, he suggested, in a fiery and well-received speech from the steps of the newly completed Colleton District Courthouse, that if South Carolina could not relieve itself of odious federal laws by unilateral state action, then it should leave the Union. Rhett knew his speech was inflammatory, but he invoked the brave memory of his lowcountry ancestors, and those of most of his planter constituents as well, by reminding them that South Carolina had never gained anything except by revolution, "The Spirit of '76 is not dead in Carolina."

The speech made Rhett an instant celebrity and the leader and spokesperson of the most radical faction in South Carolina politics known afterwards as the "Fire eaters." Rhett's call for immediate and unilateral state action was a sensation in newspapers across the state. In Charleston, the *Mercury* applauded the call for action while the *Courier*, the mouthpiece of Charleston's Unionist faction, urged caution. In the upcountry, the Greenville *Republican*, representing the only thoroughly Unionist area of South Carolina, raised the spectrum of sectional strife within the state: "if they [lowcountry aristocrats] succeed in separating South Carolina from the Union, we will separate from South Carolina." In Beaufort, Rhett's ideas were trumpeted to his admiring constituency by his brother-in-law, John A. Stuart, and William J. Grayson, then editors of the newly established *Beaufort Gazette*. The *Beaufort Gazette*, Beaufort's only antebellum newspaper, was to survive only as long as the Nullification Crisis lasted, from 1828 to 1833.[8] Stuart later went on to become editor of the Charleston *Mercury*, the most famous states' rights newspaper in the South. During the 1840s and 1850s, the *Mercury* was owned and controlled by members of the Rhett family.

What Rhett desired was for Governor John Taylor to call for an immediate special session of the South Carolina legislature to plan the state's resistance to federal laws, specifically the Tariff of Abomination. Governor Taylor declined to do so. South Carolina's most powerful politician, Vice President John C. Calhoun, sensed the popular uprising that Rhett had launched and joined the chorus for a statewide convention for the specific purpose of nullifying the tariff. This split the state between Unionists and Nullifiers, and several prominent Beaufort District planters rode the popular tide to fame and prominence.

James Hamilton Jr. had returned from Washington to tend his profitable Savannah River rice plantation. He became governor of the state when the crisis reached its peak and was the organizing genius of the Nullifier movement. Ironically, his neighbor on the Savannah River was Judge Daniel Elliott Huger, who was the state's leading Unionist during the struggle. In the height of legislative passions, in 1830, Huger actually challenged Rhett to a duel, which Rhett refused. Another prominent Savannah River rice planter, Langdon Cheves, was the first to chart a middle course of action between the Unionists and the Nullifiers, seeking the united resistance of all the southern states in a faction later known as the cooperationist party. While Hamilton, Huger, and Cheves were already prominent South Carolina statesmen, two other Beaufortonians emerged during the Nullification Crisis whose careers, like Rhett's, were to form a bridge in the Beaufort District from Nullification to secession: William Grayson and Robert W. Barnwell.

William J. Grayson (1788–1863) was the son of William John Grayson and Susannah Greene. Grayson began as a teacher at Beaufort College and in Savannah. He then read the law and was admitted to the South Carolina Bar in 1822. He established a practice at the Coosawhatchie Court the same year as Rhett. Grayson was heir to a sizeable estate in the Beaufort District and soon abandoned his legal practice for a career in planting, investment, and public service. He served in the South Carolina House from 1813 to 1825 and in the South Carolina Senate from 1826 to 1831. During the Nullification Crisis, Grayson became an ally of Rhett and a leader of the States' Rights and Free Trade Party. He was editor and cofounder, along with John A. Stuart, of the *Beaufort Gazette,* the Rhett faction mouthpiece in the Beaufort District.

Grayson rode the popular tide of Nullification into Congress, where he represented the Beaufort/Colleton District as a member of the new southern-dominated Whig Party from 1833 to 1837. In 1840, Grayson was given the important federal patronage post of collector for the port of Charleston by the Harrison-Tyler administration. He served in that post until 1853. During those years of federal service, Grayson moderated his view on states' rights and refused to adopt the increasingly secessionist views of the Rhett faction. By 1850, no doubt influenced by his old friend and college chum James L. Petigru, he had become a thorough Unionist and was out of step with the views of the majority of his constituents, neighbors, and friends.

During Grayson's years of public service, his principal financial support came from his Frogmore Plantation on St. Helena Island. In 1836, Grayson purchased the plantation and its slaves from the estate of Colonel John Stapleton and Catherine Beale Stapleton, the niece and heir of Lieutenant Colonel William Bull II. This was one of the largest sea island cotton plantations in the Beaufort District. It stretched across St. Helena Island from Seaside Road on the east to Frogmore Corner near the colonial Chapel of Ease on the west. In 1850, Grayson had 170 slaves on his plantation. By 1853, Grayson had sold his plantation and slaves to Thomas Aston Coffin of Coffin Point Plantation, who became the largest cotton planter in St. Helena Parish. Thereafter, Grayson devoted himself to literary pursuits.[9]

In his letters, Grayson reflected on the peculiar radicalism of his home district at the time of Nullification: "Beaufort, it is said, is willing to go the whole length of Governor Miller's (radical) course—ballot box, jury box, cartouch box." He also noted the particular perilousness of his sea island home should President Jackson make good his threat to use violence, "Strange too that Beaufort, the most exposed place in the State should be most eager to rush into danger. But many indigenous gentlemen of my acquaintance are seriously of the opinion that the same Yankees whom we now accuse as shameless robbers would desist from hurting us as soon as the Union is dissolved."[10] Grayson's comment was prophetic. Not only did President Jackson plan to enforce the federal tariff in 1833 by placing gunboats at Beaufort and Georgetown, but Beaufort was the first town in South Carolina to fall into Union hands when secession finally came in 1860.

In 1830, Grayson explained to his Beaufort constituents why he supported the radical Nullifiers. He stated that mere oppression can be borne patiently but the tariff was not only oppressive, it was also unconstitutional: "This it is that authorizes and requires you to act."[11]

The other famous Beaufort political leader who gained prominence during the Nullification Crisis was Robert Woodward Barnwell (1801–1882). By lineage and education, Barnwell was intended to be a leader of the sea island planter community. His father, Colonel Robert Barnwell, was a hero of the Revolution and leader of the Federalist faction in the early nation. His great grandfather was "Tuscarora Jack." Barnwell was born in Beaufort on August 10, 1801, and raised in the most prominent house in town, the Barnwell Castle at the top of Bay Street. He began his formal education at Beaufort College, where he was a schoolmate of Rhett and a student of James L. Petigru. He was sent to Charleston to live with Stephen Elliott and study at Reverend Martin Luther Hurlbut's classical academy. In 1817, he went north to finish his studies at Harvard. Barnwell was the academic and social leader of his class, was elected to Phi Beta Kappa, and became the valedictorian of the class of 1821. One of Barnwell's closest friends and admirers in that distinguished Harvard class was Ralph Waldo Emerson. The two remained close friends and correspondents throughout the vicissitudes of the Civil War era.

Barnwell returned to South Carolina and read the law in the offices of James Hamilton Jr. and James L. Petigru in Charleston. He was admitted to the South Carolina Bar in 1823 and began practice at the Beaufort District Court at Coosawhatchie in partnership with Robert Barnwell Rhett. In 1826, Barnwell was elected to the South Carolina House of Representatives from Prince William Parish, and in 1828, he was elected to represent the Beaufort/Colleton District in the U.S. Congress. He served two terms in Congress from 1829 to 1833. While in Congress, he was a protégé of his cousin, Senator Robert Y. Hayne, and Vice President John C. Calhoun. Thus, he was in Washington during the famous Webster-Hayne constitutional debates of 1830. Barnwell was a strong supporter of states' rights in the Congress and an active and prominent supporter of the Nullification Party in South Carolina. He was a representative from St. Helena Parish to the Nullification Convention and signed the Ordinance of 1832.[12]

The Nullification Controversy not only brought Rhett, Grayson, and Barnwell to prominence but it also began to separate their public careers. The Nullification issue split the South Carolina electorate. Nullifier and Unionist factions maneuvered and fought for three years for electoral advantage. Eventually the Nullifiers succeeded in getting the South Carolina legislature to call for a special state convention to deal with the constitutional issue of nullification, since special conventions had long been used in South Carolina to resolve constitutional differences. The U.S. Constitution was ratified by convention in 1788, and the South Carolina Constitution of 1790 was written by a special constitutional convention that year.

Because the convention had to be called by a two-thirds vote of the South Carolina legislature, the legislative election of 1832 was the deciding factor. This election was not just bitter but also violent. In Greenville, the Unionist leader, B. F. Perry, killed the Nullifier editor Turner Bynum in a duel. In Charleston, pitched battles were fought in the streets between gangs of thugs and sailors organized by the opposing sides. Ultimately the Nullifiers, who were brilliantly organized in almost every district by Governor James Hamilton Jr., swept the election and dominated the legislature. The South Carolina House and Senate voted to hold the Nullification Convention in November 1832. In the decisive election of 1832, the Beaufort District returned an 84 percent landslide for the Nullification Party. Barnwell was joined at the Nullification Convention by Dr. Thomas E. Screven and James Mongin Smith of St. Luke's Parish and Major John Seth Maner, who represented the mainland planters of St. Peter's Parish. All voted for nullification and signed the ordinance.[13]

At the Convention, Barnwell took a leading role. Many of the radical Nullifiers, with Rhett as their leader, hoped that the issue of nullification, and President Jackson's use of force in reaction to it, would actually compel the issue of secession and southern nationalism. When the convention reconvened in March 1833, Rhett declared in a speech, "Sir, if a Confederacy of the Southern States could now be obtained, should we not deem it a happy termination—of our long struggle for our rights against oppression?" But Rhett was ahead of South

Carolina leaders, let alone the rest of the South. Even Hamilton attacked Rhett's extreme view. And at this convention Barnwell established himself as a "moderate nullifier" and broke with Rhett's radical position. It was Barnwell who offered to the convention a compromise position on secession, suggesting that the Ordinance of Nullification contained only a threat of secession, rather than a declaration to secede, if President Jackson used federal military force to impose national laws in South Carolina.

The other issue which emanated from the Nullification Convention was the test oath issue which required all state officials and state militia personnel to take an oath of allegiance to the state. This was bitterly opposed by Unionists. Barnwell and other moderate nullifiers were willing to abandon the test oath entirely to placate the Unionists and reunify the state's leadership. Rhett was by then the South Carolina attorney general, who not only enforced the oath but also defended it in court. Barnwell was by nature and temperament a moderate man and, on the road to secession during the 1850s, became one of the leaders of South Carolina's conservative Cooperationist faction. Rhett, on the other hand, remained throughout his life an uncompromising purist on states' rights and the "greatest of all the fireaters."[14]

It was Rhett's view that prevailed among the majority of the planters of the Beaufort District. Following the Nullification Convention, Barnwell, like William Elliott before him, retired from active political life to become a "fireside politician only." Rhett went on as attorney general of South Carolina and then to thirteen years in the U.S. Congress as representative from the Beaufort/Colleton/Orangeburg District. In 1833, Dr. James Kirk of Bluffton, one of the great planters of St. Luke's Parish, reflected on the mood of his parish. In a letter to Henry Clay imploring him to compromise on the tariff issue before South Carolina exploded he stated, "I confidently believe that the 'Nullies'. . . would right or wrong shake off their oppressors at the sacrifice of the best blood of the country and that sooner or later the entire South would be at her side."[15]

But the radical view of Rhett and the South Carolina lowcountry did not extend far beyond its borders. In neighboring Savannah, an active party of Nullifiers was led by two Savannah River rice planters, Dr. William C. Daniell and Dr. James Proctor Screven. They were neighbors of Langdon Cheves and James Hamilton Jr. in St. Peter's Parish and had strong family connections in the Beaufort District. But the Nullifiers were ridiculed in the Savannah newspaper, and Savannah was isolated politically from the rest of Georgia, where President Jackson was wildly popular. "Savannah stands in solitude surrounded by her piney wood," stated a letter to the *Georgian*. When Daniell ran for Congress and Screven ran for the Georgia Senate as Nullifiers in 1834, they were both trounced by lesser-known opponents.[16]

As things turned out, the 1832 U.S. Congress, with William J. Grayson among them, was strongly against the high tariff of 1828, and a compromise was swiftly reached. South Carolina rescinded the Ordinance of Nullification, and Jackson did not have to make good on his threat of force. South Carolina calmed down, and only the Rhett faction and the radical Nullifiers regretted the peaceful solution. Many of them had genuinely hoped that nullification would lead to disunion. The Rhett faction not only stayed alive in South Carolina politics, it grew more powerful. In 1836, Rhett finished his term as attorney general, defeated William J. Grayson for the Beaufort/Colleton/Orangeburg congressional seat, and began his thirteen years in Congress. He became the closest political ally of John C. Calhoun, with whom he boarded while in Washington, and an important national figure during the Harrison, Tyler, and Polk administrations. The height of power for the Rhett faction came in the late 1830s. From 1838 to 1840, Robert Barnwell Rhett's brothers, James and Albert, were both in the South Carolina legislature while Rhett was in Congress. Rhett formed an alliance with Congressman Franklin Harper Elmore, a radical states' rights advocate and political power in South Carolina, whose younger brother was also in the South Carolina legislature. This Rhett-Elmore faction was the principal supporter of Calhoun and the most powerful political faction in South Carolina from 1838 to 1844. During those years, the Rhett family controlled the Charleston *Mercury,* first under John A. Stuart, Rhett's brother-in-law, and later under Rhett's son, R. B. Rhett Jr. The *Mercury* became the mouthpiece for the Rhett-Elmore faction.[17]

In 1838, Rhett offered a resolution in Congress to amend the Constitution in order to guarantee the rights of the southern states or dissolve the Union. Rhett's address and resolution was a national sensation. In South Carolina, the *Mercury* trumpeted the cause, and in Beaufort, Albert Rhett organized public meetings to call for a convention of the southern states to review the proposed resolution. But again, his call for action was premature. No district in South Carolina, except Beaufort, was ready for secession at that time.[18]

What was it that gave the Beaufort District its early and ardent attachment to radical states' rights and even secession? The answer was slavery. Behind all the constitutional rhetoric over nullification and states' rights was the deep and abiding fear that loss of local political control would eventually lead to the abolition of slavery—an unimaginable thought to the planter class of the Beaufort District. At the Nullification Convention of 1833, only Barnwell Rhett spoke out on the issue that more timid political leaders dared not whisper. The real issue of states' rights, Rhett declared, was not the tariff, internal improvements, or even President Jackson's Force Bill but was the South's peculiar institution. "A people owning slaves," he thundered, "are mad, or worse than mad, who do not hold their destinies in their own hands."[19] By giving bold and forthright expression to their deepest fears, Rhett endeared himself forever to the slaveowners of the Beaufort District and became the paramount political warrior of the planter class.

Several historical events that coincided with the Nullification controversy heightened the alarm of Beaufort District planters. In 1833, after decades of antislavery agitation led by Reverend William Wilberforce, slavery was abolished in the British empire. The West Indian sugar planters and Bahamian cotton planters, whose economic decline was already well advanced by 1833, were overwhelmed by a large number of freed slaves. The British example, and a triumphant visit to America by Wilberforce, inspired the formation of the American Anti-Slavery Society in 1833. Also in that year, William Lloyd Garrison began publishing the abolitionist newspaper the *Liberator* in Boston. Antislavery petitions began to reach Congress when William J. Grayson was representing the Beaufort District. The vituperative reaction of Grayson, otherwise a refined and reasonable man, reflects the particular sensitivity of his district to the abolitionist movement. "At last in 1834," Grayson wrote, "the abolition party reaches the degree of boldness and strength that enabled it to take the last steps and bring the two section of the country to arms and final separation." Grayson blamed former President John Quincy Adams since he was the political leader of the Abolitionists in Congress. To Grayson, "No man was more acrimonious, extreme or uncompromising" than John Quincy Adams. "With much learning and long experience, he had acquired neither taste nor tact."[20]

Ironically, the abolition of slavery in the British empire was the proximate cause of securing the personal fortunes of both Grayson and Rhett. Colonel John Stapleton and Katherine Beale Stapleton were British citizens and could not own slaves. During the 1830s, they sold their plantations and slaves in the South Carolina lowcountry. These were the last vestiges of the vast frontier empire of Lieutenant Governor William Bull II, whose heir was his niece, Katherine Stapleton. Frogmore Plantation, one of the premier sea island cotton plantations in the Beaufort District, was sold along with its slaves to Grayson in 1836. Blue House Plantation, a rice plantation on the Ashepoo River, and its slaves were sold to Rhett in the same year. James L. Petigru remarked, "Barnwell Smith [Rhett] has made a fortune by an advantageous purchase from Colonel Stapleton."[21]

Events in the British empire heightened the sense of isolation and anxiety of Beaufort District planters. In 1830, Robert W. Barnwell recognized the essence of the problem of unlimited federal authority over South Carolina. Without ever mentioning slavery or abolitionism, the meaning of his article in the *Mercury* was unmistakable. "There are some changes in the very forms of our Domestic policy, to which they (northern congressmen) could scarcely persuade us quietly to submit. And there are no changes however vital and subversive to our most absolute rights which fanaticism and misguided philanthropy would not attempt." During the 1830s, when Barnwell retired from Congress and served as president of the South Carolina College (1835–1841), his predictions about the abolitionists became a reality. During that time, he continued his correspondence with Rhett. By 1844, Barnwell's mood regarding the future of slavery and southern society was quite pessimistic. In a private letter from Beaufort to Rhett in Washington, he said:

> I believe that unless slavery is upheld as a political institution essential to the preservation of our civilization and therefore to be maintained and defended in the same high strain as liberty itself we must become a degraded people. . . .
>
> The greater part of slaveholders in other states are mere negro–drivers believing themselves wrong and only holding on to their negroes as something to make money out of. And we have retrograded and must soon fall into the same category.
>
> My friends here, Edmund [Rhett] also, think my views too gloomy.[22]

The same sense of gloom was evident in Bluffton planter James Kirk's private confession to his guest, James Edward Calhoun. Kirk remarked that "if he lives 10 or 15 years longer," his slaves will "gain ascendancy over him . . . they are gaining on him: confesses he whips half in a passion and half the time unjustly . . . [and] confesses scruples of conscience about slavery."[23]

It was this anxiety that fueled the political extremism of the Beaufort District. And this anxiety was greater for the middle–class planters and small slaveholders who formed the majority of planters in the Beaufort District than for the richer planters. Men like Nathaniel Heyward of Colleton and Henry A. Middleton of Prince William Parish, who owned literally thousands of slaves, had diversified their financial holdings, had other assets to support them, and had other places to live if abolition should prevail and Southern civilization should collapse. Even planters like Robert W. Barnwell, William Elliott, and Langdon Cheves, who had hundreds of slaves, had financial and educational resources which would at least allow them to survive. But the middle–class planters and small slaveowners like Thomas B. Chaplin of St. Helena, and the numerous mainland planters of upper St. Peter's and Prince William, had no other resources.[24] They were totally dependent on their small farms and few slaves. Should the South Carolina political leadership fail to protect the slave system, they would be trapped, like West Indian planters, in a world dominated by blacks. This threatened not only their material well-being but also, they believed, their personal safety. In their minds, the desperate stakes required vigilance and radical action.

But these planters were not "bad" people. And one of the responses to this anxiety was to reach an accommodation with their slaves: to allow them to build, within the confines of the plantation regime, their own societies, control their own pattern of work, and even develop their own distinctive religion. This was one of the reasons for the development of the uniquely independent slave communities of the Beaufort District.

NOTES

1. *Biographical Directory of the South Carolina House*, 4: 359–61; Stephen Meats and Edwin T. Arnold, eds., *The Writings of Benjamin F. Perry*, 3 vols. (Spartanburg: Reprint Co., 1980), 3: 52–62; Richard J. Calhoun, ed., *Witness to Sorrow: The Antebellum Autobiography of William J. Grayson* (Columbia: University of South Carolina Press, 1990), 90–91; William W. Freehling, *Prelude to the Civil War: The Nullification Controversy in South Carolina, 1816–1836* (New York: Harper and Row, 1965), 92–96.

2. Meats and Arnold, eds., *Writings of Benjanim F. Perry*, 2: 320–24; *Biographical Directory of the South Carolina Senate*, 1: 641–45; Freehling, *Prelude to Civil War*, 150–52.

3. *Biographical Directory of the South Carolina Senate*, 1: 470–71; Freehling, *Prelude to Civil War*, 174, 196; Stephen B. Barnwell, *The Story of an American Family* (Marquette, Mich.: Privately printed, 1969), 146–47.

4. *Biographical Directory of the South Carolina Senate*, 1: 599–601; 2: 1038–39, 1295–96.

5. Freehling, *Prelude to Civil War*, 94; Meats and Arnold, eds., *Writings of Benjamin F. Perry*, 1: 249.

6. Laura A. White, *Robert Barnwell Rhett: Father of Secession* (New York: Century, 1931), 14–15; Freehling, *Prelude to Civil War*, 126–28, 149.

7. "Rhett Family Genealogy" (manuscript), South Carolina Historical Society; White, *Robert Barnwell Rhett*, 4–6; Meats and Arnold, eds., *Writings of Benjamin F. Perry*, 240–45.

8. White, *Robert Barnwell Rhett*, 15, 24; Freehling, *Prelude to Civil War*, 149.

9. Calhoun, ed., *Witness to Sorrow*, 37–90; *Biographical Directory of the South Carolina Senate*, 1: 599–601; Stapleton Papers, South Caroliniana Library.

10. Calhoun, ed., *Witness to Sorrow*, 213; Gov. Stephen Miller (1828–1830) was a radical Camden states' righter and supporter of nullification.

11. Freehling, *Prelude to Civil War*, 198.

12. Barnwell, *Story of an American Family*, 108–11; *Biographical Directory of the South Carolina House*, 5: 12–15; Meats and Arnold, eds., *Writings of Benjamin F. Perry*, 2: 25–29.

13. Freehling, *Prelude to Civil War*, 253, 365; *Biographical Directory of the South Carolina Senate*, 2: 1037–38; *Biographical Directory of the South Carolina House*, 5: 239–40, 249–50.

14. Freehling, *Prelude to Civil War*, 148, 178, 262, 311.

15. Letter of James Kirk, March 14, 1833, Kirk Family Papers, South Carolina Historical Society.

16. *Georgian*, October 7, 1833; February 13, 1834; September 20, 1834.

17. White, *Robert Barnwell Rhett*, 35–44; *Biographical Directory of the American Congress, 1774–1961* (Washington, D.C.: U.S. Government Printing Office, 1961), 860.

18. White, *Robert Barnwell Rhett*, 39–40.

346 The History of Beaufort County

19. Freehling, *Prelude to Civil War,* 297.

20. Calhoun, ed., *Witness to Sorrow,* 154.

21. Stapleton Papers, South Caroliniana Library; White, *Robert Barnwell Rhett,* 32.

22. Freehling, *Prelude to Civil War,* 199; John Barnwell, "Hamlet to Hotspur: Letters of Robert Woodward Barnwell to Robert Barnwell Rhett," *South Carolina Historical Magazine* 77 (1976): 252.

23. Freehling, *Prelude to Civil War,* 68.

24. Theodore Rosengarten, *Tombee: Portrait of a Cotton Planter* (New York: Morrow, 1986); see especially chapters 5 and 7.

19

Beaufort District's
African American Communities

The formation of the slave communities of the antebellum Beaufort District was controlled by three major historical events: the introduction of sea island cotton in the 1790s, the "new importation" of Africans from 1804 to 1808, and the religious revival and plantation missions of the 1830s. Given the many problems of physical reconstruction, economic stagnation, and civil disorder following the Revolution, it was not surprising that the South Carolina legislature closed the slave trade in 1787. The legal immigration of Africans into South Carolina was prohibited for the next seventeen years.[1] While the slave importation was not stopped, it was significantly slowed by either the legal prohibition or the economic depression. From the beginning of the Revolution to the mid-1790s, there was no large infusion of new African immigrants into the state.

During the 1790s, long-staple cotton was introduced to the sea islands from the earlier plantations of the Bahama Islands. This new crop began a profound economic revolution in the Beaufort District and eventually across the entire South. The old indigo plantations were quickly converted to sea island cotton, and by 1795, when the Duc de la Rochefoucauld-Liancourt visited Beaufort, all the plantations on Port Royal Island had been converted to cotton. For the next thirty years, with the demand created by the Napoleonic Wars and the nascent industrial revolution, the cotton market continued to expand and prices remained high. Cotton produced more prosperity for the sea islands of the Beaufort District than they had ever known before or since. In these heady times, the only restriction on increasing the fortunes of lowcountry planters was lack of labor.

Thus, a clamor arose in South Carolina to reopen the slave trade to legal importation. Lowcountry planters, and increasingly upcountry farmers wishing to grow short-staple, green-seed cotton, were aware of the looming constitutional prohibition on slave importation and wished to increase their slaveholdings before the cessation cut the supply and increased the price. In 1803, Governor

James Richardson acknowledged that he could not effectively enforce South
Carolina's prohibition and that the demands of the new cotton economy had
compelled large-scale illegal importations. At the end of 1803, the South Carolina legislature reopened the slave trade into the state over the objections of the
scion of one of the oldest and largest slaveholding families in St. Helena Parish:
Colonel Robert Barnwell of Beaufort.[2]

The new profits from cotton and the reopening of the slave trade in South
Carolina set off a fever of speculative buying. Between 1803 and 1808, forty
thousand new African immigrants were transported to South Carolina; as many
as had been imported between 1720 and 1740, which had been the longest
period of unrestricted slave importation in South Carolina history. In addition to
the forty thousand slaves legally imported, perhaps half that number had been
illegally smuggled in between 1795 and 1804.[3] This influx of nearly sixty thousand new Africans was known to lowcountry planters as the "new stock of importations," as opposed to the "old stock of importations" referred to by Charles
Colcock Jones of Liberty County, Georgia.[4]

The new importation had a profound effect on the black population of the
Beaufort District. Particularly affected were the slaves on the newly prospering
sea island cotton plantations. Between 1800 and 1810, the slave population of St.
Helena Parish, which included almost all the sea island cotton lands in the Beaufort District, increased 86.5 percent. Significantly, the mainland parish of Prince
William, with its older established rice plantations, experienced a slight (1 percent) decline in their slave population between 1800 and 1810.[5] In other words,
nearly half the slave population of the sea islands of the Beaufort District, during
the antebellum era, were recent African immigrants of the new importation.

The effect of this new importation on the local plantation slave communities was fundamental. Some plantations were dominated by new Africans. In
1810, one of Beaufort's most prominent citizens, Major Samuel Lawrence, died,
leaving two newly developed sea island cotton plantations which were carefully
inventoried by William Joyner in 1815. Lawrence had two working cotton plantations: Red House on Port Royal Island and an unnamed plantation on St.
Helena and adjoining Toms Island. He also had a large residence in Beaufort.
The slaves on the two plantations were divided by family units. The place of
origin of each head of family was carefully noted. Sixty slaves at Red House
were divided into thirteen families, mostly headed by males. Of the thirteen
heads of families, eight were listed as "African" or "new Negro," three were
listed as originally part of the older estate of Richard Ellis (who was the father of
Lawrence's widow, Elizabeth Capers Ellis Lawrence), and two were listed as "country born." Thus, two-thirds of the heads of slave families on this plantation were
adult Africans of the new importation.

Lawrence's St. Helena Island cotton plantation was even more dominated by new African immigrants. The thirty-five slaves were divided into nine family groups. Seven of the nine heads of family were adult "Africans" and the driver of the St. Helena Island plantation was a fifty-year-old African named "Jack."[6] It may be that the majority of the slaves of the new sea island cotton plantations in the Beaufort District were first-generation Africans.

The implications of these facts are obvious. The prominent retention of African cultural and linguistic traditions among sea island blacks, so actively studied today, was not only because of their geographic isolation but also because of their more recent arrival compared to other locations. The children of this group would have been alive at the time of the Civil War. Thus, the antebellum slave culture of this area was strongly influenced, if not dominated, by first- and second-generation Africans.

Another effect of the new importation was revealed in the papers of the Frogmore Plantation, one of the oldest and largest plantation communities in St. Helena Parish. In 1800, there were 78 slaves, and in 1810, there were 111 slaves: an increase of 42 percent. Almost all of this increase was due to the new importation. In 1810, there were twenty-seven young men, all in their teens and twenties and all born in Africa. Many of these new arrivals were not part of any family group and in later years wandered off to find wives on neighboring plantations, a circumstance that plantation manager William Robertson could not prevent and soon stopped interfering with. These new arrivals formed a separate group at Frogmore Plantation and were relegated to a lower status. All the important jobs on the plantation (gunner, herder, fisherman, sawyer, and cook) went to seasoned South Carolina-born slaves while the newly arrived Africans were given the menial, less responsible, and less skilled tasks. The driver on Frogmore Plantation was a forty-six-year-old man named Bern, born at Frogmore, whose father, Abraham, had been the driver before him. Thus, a distinctive, even hereditary, hierarchy had developed within the slave community, and the new Africans were on the bottom rung.[7]

Plantation records of the Beaufort District did not reveal the precise cultural or tribal origins of these new slaves. The linguistic and cultural uniqueness which survived among the sea islands has long been referred to as "Gullah," and the origin of the term has been vigorously pursued and debated by historians, anthropologists, and linguists. A few tantalizing pieces of evidence may shed light on this mystery.

Of the forty thousand Africans legally imported into South Carolina from 1804 through 1807, South Carolina immigration records specify the African port of origin for 23,773 of them. Of those whose African port of origin is known, 14,217 originated from Angola, Congo, or "Congo and Angola." Thus, at least 59.8 percent of the new arrivals whose origin can be determined were natives of the Congo/Angola region of Africa.[8] Many of these settled on the new sea island cotton plantations of the Beaufort District.

Many historians have speculated that the origin of the term "Gullah" might have derived from Angola or "N'gulla" as it would have been phonetically represented. Indeed, on January 25, 1806, the *America* arrived in the Charleston harbor with a large cargo of 418 Africans. The port of origin of the *America* was listed as "Congo and Gulah." Significantly, while most of the slave merchants were in Charleston, the agent for this particular ship was Mein, MacKay, and Company in Savannah.[9] This may mean that these slaves were specifically intended for the emerging sea island cotton plantations of the Beaufort District as well as neighboring islands on the Georgia coast.

Clearly, these Africans swelled the slave population of the sea islands. If the majority of those people were from the Congo/Angola region, as the importation records indicated, then the term "N'gullah" or "Gullah" may have referred to any African of recent arrival. These new arrivals brought a new infusion of African tradition into the Beaufort district. African words, skills, dietary tastes, and religious beliefs were renewed and restored among the slave communities.

In some measure, this new importation was also dangerous. Earlier concerns about slave insurrection during the 1740s and again during the Revolutionary War were renewed. In 1809, a rumor swept the southern parishes of a general slave revolt. The plot was revealed, and ten or twelve conspirators were arrested, tried, convicted, and executed at the District Court in Coosawhatchie. Their heads were severed and placed on poles lining the road to Purrysburg as a gruesome deterrent.[10] It evidently did not work. Slave plots were discovered in Columbia in 1805, in nearby Ashepoo in 1816, and in Camden in June 1816 (generally regarded as a prelude to the famous Denmark Vesey Plot of 1822). When the Vesey conspiracy was revealed in Charleston, one of the ringleaders was an African "conjurer" or spiritual leader known as "Gullah Jack," who was responsible for leading the plantation slaves south of Charleston. "Gullah Jack" would only trust African slaves with the weapons that were secretly made and hidden in anticipation of a general revolt. For a time it was thought that the whole plot was hatched among the Gullah people in Beaufort. The intendant and town council met in secret session, and the night police patrol was doubled. The plot, however, was centered in Charleston, as later testimony revealed, and Beaufort remained quiet, though uneasy.[11]

The world the new Africans entered, however, was a vastly different one from that encountered by the older immigrants. The sea islands of the Beaufort District were no longer frontiers of a wild new continent but established agricultural communities. In some measure, the job of the original slaves was to help the whites conquer the wilderness. The job of the new Africans was to adjust to the regimen of established plantations. The sea island cotton planters quickly adopted the "task system" of labor management which they were well acquainted with from the neighboring rice plantations.[12] As the cotton plantation operations became larger, the task system of management became more useful. And as the sea island cotton planters became more prosperous, they began spending less time on their plantations and more time in their summer homes in Beaufort, Charleston, or Savannah. The task system allowed the planters the luxury of absenteeism. By the late antebellum period, it became customary for the large rice and cotton planters of the area to have several homes and travel freely.

The task system had originated as the principal method of labor management and organization on the colonial rice plantations and emerged in the antebellum era as the predominant form of labor management in the South Carolina lowcountry.[13] The task system involved assigning each individual slave a specific task for the day's work. Since most of the slaves daily work was in the field, the fields came to be divided into tasks measured on the ground to cover approximately a quarter acre. In the rice and cotton fields, tasks ranged from 105 feet to 150 feet per side. Each slave would be assigned his daily task based on his or her physical capacity and based on the rigor of the work being done. Each year slaves were classified by ability into full hands, half hands, or quarter hands. Full hands received full tasks and others proportionally less. Hoeing weeds in the cotton fields, which continued all summer, was relatively easy, so multiple tasks were often assigned each day. Picking cotton in the early fall was more laborious, so fewer tasks were assigned then. In addition, other types of plantation production were divided by tasks. Some common plantation tasks for full hands were as follows:

> Barrel making—three rice barrels per day for the cooper
> Setting fence—thirty-five to forty panels of split rail fence for four
>   hands
> Splitting rails—one hundred rails, 12 feet long
> Cutting wood—one cord of four-foot length
> Ginning cotton—20–30 pounds per day
> Sorting cotton—150–200 pounds per day
> Moting cotton—40 pounds per day
> Gathering marsh mud for fertilizer—three piled cart loads per day
> Digging rice ditches—600–700 cubic feet per day
> Forming new rice drains—210 linear feet per day
> Clearing old drains—six to ten quarters per day.[14]

Sam Polite was ninety-three years old when he was interviewed by the longtime librarian of the Beaufort Township Library, Miss Clotilde Martin, during the 1930s, but his recollection of the antebellum slave community of his youth was crystal clear. He was born on the St. Helena Island plantation of Marion Fripp, but as a youth he and his family were among thirty slaves moved to Prince William Parish on the mainland to start a new plantation for John Fripp. He described the task system from the viewpoint of a slave: "Every slave have task [quarter acre] to do; sometime one task, sometime two task and sometime three. You have for work till task through. When cotton done make, you have other task. Have to cut cord of marsh grass maybe. Task of marsh been eight feet long and four feet high. Then sometime you have to roll cord of mud in cowpen. Woman have to rake leaf from wood into cowpen. . . . When you knock off work you can work on your land."[15]

Each day the driver would assign tasks to the slaves and see that each was completed. Slaves who failed to complete their tasks due to recalcitrance or malingering were often subjected to corporal punishment or denial of favors and privileges. Administering corporal punishment, commonly with the lash, was also the duty of the driver, though the planter or overseer was always present at such events. The production of the plantation depended entirely on the loyalty, efficiency, and authority of the driver. The driver, along with the owner and overseer, was one of the principal characters in determining the personality of the individual plantation and the life of its slave community.

The driver, while a slave himself, was clearly of a different status. He was customarily provided with his own house slightly separate from the slave street. He was often socially separate as well. Bu Allah of Sapelo Island, Georgia, remained a Moslem while his charges were Baptists, and Limus, a driver of a St. Helena Island plantation, kept himself apart from his community and adopted the values and habits of his owners. When the northern missionaries met Limus in 1862, he had used his position of authority and privilege to make himself a wealthy man.[16] Despite their separation from the ordinary slave community, they were usually respected and often liked, as was the case with Robert, the long-time driver on Thomas B. Chaplin's Tombee Plantation.[17] A driver's job was a delicate balance. Too much discipline would demoralize the slave community; too much familiarity would reduce production.

Drivers were rarely responsible for more than one hundred slaves. Most plantations on St. Helena Island had only one driver, and none had more than two; but most plantations on St. Helena Island had fewer than one hundred slaves, and only one had more than three hundred slaves in 1850. On Langdon Cheves's Delta Plantation on the Savannah River, he had three drivers for 151 slaves.[18] The critical position of these drivers in the operation of the plantation and the dependence of the owners on them is reflected in the inscription on the tombstone of Miser, the chief driver of Daniel Heyward's Laurel Hill rice plantation on the Savannah River:

In Memory of
MISER
Who was a driver on this
Plantation for 30 years.
He was a faithful servant
A true Christian and
the noblest work of God
an honest man
This slab is placed over
his remains by his master
Daniel Heyward
in token of his love
and his esteem
He died in 1854[.][19]

Miser, Limus Robert, Israel, Moses, Cyrus, and the hundreds of other drivers were the most important slaves in the working lives of the slave communities of the Beaufort District. They were the managers of the task system and the controllers of the rhythm of work. The task system allowed the slaves the free time to form their own communities, develop and practice their own religion, devise their own amusements, provide extra sustenance and comforts for their own families, and even acquire wealth. The task system provided a measure of freedom for the slaves. By establishing standard daily work routines, a diligent slave could complete the master's work by midday and have the rest of the day to work for him- or herself. This allowed the development of a significant internal plantation economy managed by the slaves for their own sustenance and profit and rarely interfered with by a wise master. The concept of masters' time and slaves' time became fixed in the life and culture of the Beaufort District. Thousands of slaves cultivated crops, raised livestock and poultry, and acquired considerable property. This slave economy was encouraged by the planters. As Oliver Bostick of St. Peter's Parish pointed out, he "allowed his slaves to own and have their property and have little crops of their own for it encourages them to do well and be satisfied at home."

Average slave families cultivated four to five acres on their own time.[20] Their favorite crops were corn and sweet potatoes. Sweet potatoes, derived from the African staple, yams, were most efficient for small plots and became a common part of the slave diet. In fact, by midcentury a significant local commercial market developed in that commodity. In addition to planting, slaves raised their own livestock. Hogs owned by the slaves were common on most rice and cotton plantations. Slave-owned cattle were less common, and horses became the ultimate symbol of status within the slave communities. Regarding poultry, it was a lowcountry tradition that as chickens, ducks, turkeys, and geese roamed freely in the plantation communities, the ducks were reserved for the master's table, and the chickens were the property of the slaves. It was common for enterprising slaves to sell pork and fresh eggs to their masters for cash income. By the end of the antebellum era, slaves in the Beaufort District not only acquired the right to control their own time through the task system, but also the right to own significant accumulations of property and to pass it on to their heirs.[21]

During the years of the cotton boom in the Beaufort District from 1795 to 1820, the slave communities were still forming. The new Africans were still adjusting to, and in large measure creating, their new world. By the time Reverend George Moore visited the Beaufort District in 1832, the plantation task system had been well established for many years. Moore commented, "One fact I have often noticed is that not only on the cotton but also on the rice plantations those Negroes who are industrious can accomplish their task during the hoeing season by the middle of the day, and thus have the afternoon to themselves."[22]

The feature which seemed to crystalize the slave communities was the conversion of the new Africans to Christianity. The process of conversion, begun during the Great Awakening by George Whitefield and the Bryan brothers, was continued after the Revolution by the presence of the great Baptist evangelist Reverend Henry Holcombe, leader of the Baptist communities of St. Peter's Parish during the Revolution and founder of the first Baptist congregation in Beaufort in 1795.

The great revival of the antebellum era was begun by the visit of Presbyterian evangelist Reverend Daniel Baker to the Beaufort District in 1831. Reverend Baker initiated a revival in the Beaufort area and the surrounding sea islands that was a turning point in the history of the region. Reverend C. C. Pinckney recalled the notices of Reverend Baker's revival meeting being delivered to all the houses in town, including the home of the host of a local Whist Club noted for its hard drinking and social merriment. Eleven of the young men from the Whist Club decided to attend the revival meeting as a lark. So powerful was the message of Baker that before the evening was over, eight of them were "testifying to the power of Grace."[23]

Nearly a whole generation of wealthy and influential young planters and professional men were swept away by the religious fervor which began in 1831. Six men from one law firm abandoned their profession to take up the ministry in various denominations. The most important of these was Reverend Richard Fuller, one of the most celebrated Baptist ministers of the antebellum era and one of the founders of the Southern Baptist Convention (1845). From old St. Helena Church alone came no less than forty clerics of the Episcopal Church in a single generation, including Bishop Stephen Elliott, the first bishop of Georgia.[24]

The ecumenical evangelical revival of 1831 may have had its most profound impact on the black population. This revival corresponded with a growing enthusiasm among many planters for religious instruction of their slaves through plantation missions. The leading proponent of the plantation mission reform movement was Charles Colcock Jones of Midway, Georgia, known as the "Apostle to the Blacks," a man with strong family ties to the Beaufort District.[25]

The principle behind the plantation mission movement was that Christian instruction for the slaves would transform the plantations into harmonious and moral communities. Plantation missions not only made good Christian souls of the slaves but also justified the southern slave system on scriptural and religious grounds. It was fervently believed that proper Christian instruction would make the slaves better servants and the masters better people. The plantation mission movement was assiduously promoted by leaders and publications of every denomination. The Episcopal *Gospel Messenger* of Charleston continuously published articles on the plantation missions, and in 1834, the Presbyterian *Charleston Observer* published a series of biographies of servants from the scriptures to be used as lessons for the slaves. Leading sea island planters such as Charles Cotesworth Pinckney Jr. of Pinckney Island and Whitmarsh Seabrook of Edisto Island enthusiastically supported the plantation missions.[26] The culmination of this movement was the ministry of Beaufort's great Baptist pastor, Reverend Richard Fuller.[27]

One of the principal motivations for the plantation missions was the conversion of the Africans of the new importation. It is no coincidence that the plantation mission movement was centered in the coastal regions of South Carolina and Georgia, where the demographic impact of this importation was strongest. Many of the new Africans had no previous experience with Christianity, and, on plantations where the new Africans were dominant, proper Christian instruction from older South Carolina slaves was lacking. Some Africans retained their tribal beliefs and even the Islamic faith. Thomas Spaulding's enterprising African driver, Bu Allah of Sapelo Island, Georgia, remained a devout Moslem, raised a family of nineteen children, and was buried with his Koran and prayer rug.[28] "Old Friday," an African on Port Royal Island in 1843, remembered in his youth prostrating himself with the rising of the sun and the rising of the moon and praying to Allah. Several of the missionaries noted that "Old Friday" and many other Africans of the Beaufort area were affected by "Gree Gree worship" or old African beliefs. Methodist minister Reverend George Moore, founder of the plantation missions on the sea islands around Beaufort, noted that "One of our great enemies was superstition. Idolatry too, entered greatly into Negro worship."[29]

The plantation missions were to the antebellum Africans of the new importation what the Great Awakening was to the colonial slaves of the old importation. It was the time when European and American evangelical Christianity
fused with a variety of African beliefs to create the distinctive African American
Christianity so much a part of black communities in modern America.

In 1832, Reverend George Moore came to Beaufort from his plantation
mission on the Combahee River in order to enlarge the area of his mission
work. He brought with him a young protégé named John Coburn. Moore and
Coburn were Methodist ministers, but they noted with satisfaction that the way
for their work had been prepared by the Presbyterian evangelist, Reverend Daniel
Baker, who had begun the "revival among Baptists and Episcopalians in Beaufort" the year before. This was truly an ecumenical reform movement in which
all the congregations contributed to the noble work. Moore and Coburn preached
to slaves in "the Old Tabernacle Church belonging to the Baptists" and in the
Episcopal lecture room. The Baptist congregation of Beaufort already had a considerable body of South Carolina slaves who had been part of the church from its
earliest days under evangelist Henry Holcombe in the 1790s. Reverend Holcombe
was responsible for bringing thousands of slaves to the Baptist faith in St. Peter's,
St. Luke's, and St. Helena Parishes during the 1780s and 1790s. The Old Tabernacle Church had been established as a praise house for black members of the
Baptist congregation well before 1832. Ultimately, most of the slaves of the Beaufort District were to follow the Baptist rather than the Methodist persuasion.

The most important work of Moore and Coburn, however, was when they
left the town to establish missions on the island plantations. On Parris Island,
cotton planters Robert Means, Thomas Fuller, Stephen Elliott, William Eddings,
and Mrs. Mary Habersham allowed all the slaves on the island to gather for
religious services in a large frame building on Means's plantation. Moore and
Coburn then went to St. Helena Island, where they preached to the numerous
slaves of Colonel John Stapleton's Frogmore Plantation. As indicated in the
Stapleton correspondence, a large number of the slaves on Frogmore Plantation
were Africans of the new importation. Moore and Coburn also began a mission
at Dr. Scott's plantation on the west side of St. Helena Island.

Moore and Coburn then moved on to Datha Island, owned by Lewis Reeve
Sams and Dr. Berners Barnwell Sams. As a result of the mission of 1832, the
Sams brothers built a "comfortable house of worship" on Datha the following
year. The missionaries then moved on to Port Royal Island and established a
mission on Reverend William Hazzard Wigg Barnwell's Laurel Bay Plantation.
Moore noted that Reverend Barnwell began his religious career preaching to his
own slaves at sunrise on the plantation. A mission was begun at Edward Barnwell's
Myrtle Bush Plantation and across the creek at Thomas Cuthbert's Big Island
Plantation, now called Pleasant Point on Lady's Island. There, Cuthbert "built a

comfortable church" for the missionary work. Cuthbert was a generous and enthusiastic patron of the mission work allowing "his people to attend on week-days as well as Sundays." Moore and Coburn baptized thirty slaves on their first visit to Cuthbert's plantation.[30]

While Moore and Coburn were extending the missions around Beaufort, the Methodists sent Reverend Thomas Turpin to St. Luke's Parish to work the plantations of the Hilton Head, Daufuskie, and Bluffton areas. Of particular help and support to Turpin was William E. Baynard of Hilton Head, who used his influence with the local planters to open their slave communities to Turpin's ministry. While the plantation missions were established, they did not always succeed. The largest cotton planter on Hilton Head, William "Squire" Pope Sr., did not welcome the missionaries back. James Sealy of Bluffton also refused the missionaries return to his plantation, claiming that he could see little result. Both Pope and Sealy were leading Baptists, and Turpin noted that nearly all the slaves of the region were under the Baptist influence. Turpin felt the Baptists left the slaves too much to their own resources without pastors or proper Christian instruction. This allowed the slaves to continue some of their African practices under the umbrella of Baptist evangelical Christianity.[31] One of the reasons for the popularity of the Baptist denomination among lowcountry blacks was that it traditionally allowed them to form separate congregations and did not impose a strict orthodoxy.

Rebecca Grant was a young slave women raised on Port Royal Island. Her mother, Sarah, worked in Beaufort as a domestic servant, and Rebecca remembered the missionary lessons taught to her: "Used to have Sabbath school in the white people's house, on the porch on Sunday evening. The porch was big and they'd fill that porch. They never fail to give the chillun Sabbath school. Learn them the Sabbath catechism. And they was taught they must be faithful to the missus and marster's work like you would to your heavenly Father's work."[32]

The plantation missions were sustained by the planters themselves with occasional visits from itinerant missionaries. Many planters like Barnwell and Sams took it upon themselves to deliver the gospel lessons to their own slaves. The younger women of the planter families zealously undertook the responsibility of teaching the black children. Moore noted: "Frequently I found them under the shade of a spreading oak, with a group of little Negroes around them, instructing them in the catechism." During the 1830s, Reverend Thomas E. Ledbetter moved to Beaufort as pastor of the small Methodist congregation and as official host of the visiting missionaries. In 1843, Reverend A. M. Chreitzberg arrived to assist Ledbetter with the mission work. He lived with Ledbetter in his new town house on the old Point. Chreitzberg conducted mission revivals on Lady's, Parris, Daufuskie, and Port Royal Islands. He preached at the Smith, Barnwell, Cuthbert, and Elliott plantations, as well as many of their neighbors. Often he gave lessons to two or three hundred black children at one time. On Sundays he preached two, three, and four times per day at different plantations. The work was often exhausting and, on the rice plantations of the mainland, was also hazardous to the health of the missionaries.

But there were also considerable rewards. Chreitzberg recalled the many pleasant days at Captain John Joyner Smith's Old Fort Plantation overlooking the Beaufort River. The Smiths had built a comfortable mission church on their property which the black congregation took great "delight and pride in adorning . . . with such simple material as the forest gave them." They draped the support posts with garlands of woven Spanish moss "while graceful festoons of the same moss would hang in front with cords and tassels attached, the latter formed by the bur of the pine."

As pleasant as all this sounds from the view of the missionaries, the plantation missions were not universally popular with the slaves. Many slaves believed that the earnest Christian masters drove their slaves harder. Many others were accustomed to revelry and merrymaking on Sundays and did not appreciate having their one day of rest and relative freedom interfered with by a crowd of "windy do-gooders.""Now the card player and the horse racer won't be there to trouble you," one slave noted;"I would rather be with a card player or sportsman by half, than a Christian." One St. Helena Island slave named Sam, interviewed in 1863, said that the "Christian" masters were no better to their slaves than the irreligious ones."Dey's all mean alike," said Sam. But what of "Good Billy Fripp" of St. Helena Island? "Why do you call him Good Mr. Fripps?," the interviewer asked."Oh, dat no tell he good to wes, call him good 'cause he good Methodist man . . . he sing and pray loud on Sundays."[33] Thus, while Christianity was embraced enthusiastically by many slaves in the 1740s, 1790s, and 1830s, it was viewed with considerable irony, skepticism, and ambivalence by many others.

In addition, the Methodist mission ran afoul of some Gullah spiritual leaders who had maintained positions of authority within the slave communities and who saw their authority superseded by the missionaries. Also, some of the planters, who were largely Episcopalians and Baptists, became suspicious of the Methodists teaching of the slaves, on the one hand, and skeptical of the Methodists' more orthodox catechism, on the other. The Baptists had always allowed more emotional enthusiasm and were less insistent on formal teaching. Thus, within the Baptist fold, the slaves were allowed to develop their own congregations and, within reason, their own practices of Christian worship. The slaves were able to infuse their Baptist services with strong elements of African spirituality.

After the formation of the Southern Baptist Convention in 1845, Southern Baptist planters began to champion the plantation missions. Their meeting in Charleston that year heralded the return of the Baptist denomination to its position of prominence in the work of christianizing the slaves. The president of the

Southern Baptist Convention and one of the most powerful advocates of slave conversion was Reverend Richard Fuller of the Baptist Church of Beaufort. Fuller's skill, dedication, and sensitivity to the Gullah blacks he grew up with made him one of the few white men to be accepted as a true spiritual leader of the sea island blacks.[34]

Despite the influence of the Christian missions to the slaves in the eighteenth and nineteenth centuries, the slaves clung tenaciously to many African beliefs of diverse origin. By the late antebellum period, many of these African beliefs and practices had insinuated themselves into the predominant Christian faith of South Carolina. Margaret Washington Creel, in *A Peculiar People: Slave Religion and Community Culture Among the Gullahs,* expertly describes the origin and influence of these African links. She identifies two discernible threads of beliefs and practices among the Gullah people. One is the "Poro-Sande" belief whose origin is among several tribes, the Mende and Gola tribes prominent among them, of the Upper Guinea region of West Africa (modern Liberia and Sierra Leone). The other is the "Bakongo" culture of the Congo-Angola region.

The Poro-Sande belief held that the Poro-Sande spirit came from a supreme god and was reflected in bush, water, and ancestor spirits. Poro-Sande controlled the society, economy, and politics of the tribal peoples. Poro-Sande was enforced and perpetuated by a secret society whose council of elders could even depose a tribal chief. Poro-Sande beliefs easily adapted to other religions. The Vai people of the Guinea region of Africa were Moslems who continued their Poro-Sande beliefs and organizations. This old African tribal belief may have crossed the Atlantic and attached itself also to American Christianity.

The Bakongo belief of the Congo-Angola region also believed that nature was controlled by a supreme being. They had a strong belief in the continued influence of the spirit of the dead. To the people of that region the "Nganga," or medicine man, was the intermediary with the spirits. Bakongo spirits could be good or evil, and evil spirits could be called up by bad medicine, known as "kindoki." This Bakongo belief in spirits and the practice of medicine to influence them bears a strong resemblance to the beliefs and practices long observed among sea island blacks. Black Christian concepts of death and burial rites have long acknowledged a trinity of body, soul, and spirit. Body and soul corresponded to Christian belief, but the continuation of a present spirit was uniquely African. In antebellum times, the slave communities were influenced by "conjurers" who used charms and medicine to control the spirits. The most famous of these conjurers was "Gullah Jack," one of the ring leaders of the Denmark Vesey plot of 1822, whose medicine was so powerful as to prevent the testimony of many of the conspirators for fear of reprisal; he was executed on July 12, 1822.[35] In modern times, the Nganga or conjurer has been known as a "root doctor." Some of the most famous of America's modern root doctors have been located in the sea islands. Mr. Stephie "Dr. Buzzard" Robinson of St. Helena Island, who lived until the 1960s, was well known in the community and had clients across the eastern seaboard.[36]

It was from this fusion of work, religion, and cultural survivals that the largely independent plantation slave communities of the antebellum Beaufort District were formed. By the 1830s, the whole district had achieved a degree of economic and political stability it had not known before. For the rest of the antebellum era, the principal crops of the district remained rice, cotton, corn, potatoes, and livestock. No major new crops, markets, or work patterns were introduced. Almost all of the useful land was cleared and developed into farms and fields. The dynamic frontier had long since disappeared. The plantations of the district settled into a seemingly changeless and monotonous routine. Within those plantations, the slave communities arrived at a synthesis of work that was a compromise between what the planters and overseers wanted to produce and what the slave community was willing to tolerate. Within those slave communities they also achieved a synthesis of spiritual belief which combined Christian enthusiasm with African spiritualism. The religious beliefs and practices of the plantation slave communities were both the most important features of their communal lives and the principal instruments of their self-governance.

The antebellum Beaufort District contained several different types of plantations. The life of each plantation slave community was determined by the work required for the major crop, the geographical location of the particular plantation, the size of the plantation and its slave community, and, as previous studies have noted, the personality of the particular plantation. The personality of each plantation was controlled not only by its products, work, and geographical setting, but also by the habits and character of its leading figures: the owner, the overseer, the driver, and the slave community leaders.[37]

The slave communities ranged from the sea island cotton plantations of the coast to the upland provisioning plantations of upper St. Peter's Parish. The three major types of plantations were the long-staple cotton plantations of the larger sea islands, the rice plantations of the freshwater rivers, and the mixed-use provisioning plantations of the inland portion of the Beaufort District. Some islands such as Pinckney, Datha, Spring, Cat, and Callawassie were single units with one slave community. Other islands such as Parris, St. Helena, and Hilton Head contained several plantation units and several different slave communities. St. Helena Island had fifty-five different slave communities, Hilton Head had twenty-six different slave communities, and Parris Island had five different slave communities.[38] All of these slave communities shared the same geographical setting and maritime environment. Because they were all devoted to the production of sea island cotton, they also shared the same general pattern of work.

On the mainland the majority of the slaves lived along the edges of the freshwater rivers and swamps attached to plantations whose principal product was rice. The majority of the slave communities on the Combahee River, which was one of the principal rice-producing rivers in South Carolina, were on the higher, healthier Colleton County side, but a few existed in the Beaufort District. Slave communities existed along the Pocotaligo, Coosawhatchie, and New Rivers in Prince William and St. Luke's Parishes. The largest rice-producing region in the Beaufort District, and its largest slave communities, were along the lower reaches of the Savannah River in St. Peter's Parish. There were eighteen different slave communities on the South Carolina side of the lower Savannah River.[39]

In the upper part of St. Peter's Parish and the adjoining upland section of Prince William Parish there were a number of mixed-use plantations where the principal products of sweet potatoes, corn, and livestock were used to provide provisions for the thickly inhabited single-crop plantations of the sea islands and rice rivers. Because of the great disparity in the size of these upland plantations, from very large slave populations to very small, and because of the variety of activities required to produce the different crops, it is harder to characterize the slave communities in that region.

It is also important to note that, in addition to geographic variations and differences in crop production and work habits, each individual plantation had a personality which affected life in the slave community.[40] Many of the Beaufort District plantations were owned by absentee planters. The rice plantations of Prince William Parish found their owners in Charleston or, for at least half the year, in the pineland village of McPhersonville. The larger and more profitable plantations on the Savannah River were all absentee owners who lived in Charleston or Savannah and made only brief visits to the rice fields. In the late antebellum era, the majority of the sea island cotton planters lived most of the year in Beaufort and only went to their plantations during the Thanksgiving and Christmas seasons. In the absence of the owner, the slave community was influenced by the character of the overseer. Like the planters, some were harsh and others were lax; some were fair and others arbitrary. In any case, they rarely stayed long. The longest that the Stuart and Elliott plantations on Port Royal Island could hold an overseer was six years, and often they had to change overseers midyear.[41] Langdon Cheves on the Savannah River had to find a new overseer on average every two years. Thus, on absentee plantations, the personality of the plantation and life in the slave community could be frequently disrupted.

Many plantations in the Beaufort District were not large enough or profitable enough to support an absentee owner and an overseer. When John Fripp married, he was given five hundred acres and thirty slaves which he managed himself.

He kept his residence on the plantation until the Civil War. Likewise, Thomas B. Chaplin lived on Tombee Plantation and managed his thirty slaves without an overseer, a circumstance which separated him from the larger planters and which he always resented. But such circumstances were usually easier on the slave community. Chaplin had one driver for nine years and rarely whipped his slaves. On St. Helena Island, Thomas Coffin, Thomas B. Fripp, and Benjamin Chaplin were "well spoken of by their former slaves," while Gabriel Capers and Alviro Fripp were remembered as "devils in cruelty." "Proud Edgar" Fripp, who had a large plantation on St. Helena Island with 123 slaves, was known to whip a slave for not doffing his cap.[42] Fripp built an elaborate Victorian mansion in Beaufort in 1856, now called Tidalholm, and thereafter spent most of his time in town.

Life in the slave community was affected by the size, location, principal crop, and "personality" of the plantation. Larger slave communities were more likely to have absentee owners and the potential for frequent disruptive changes and harsher treatment. On Cheves's Delta Plantation, he fired his German overseer, Mr. Zantz, in 1843 because the slaves refused to work for him. Though Zantz was an excellent agronomist and brought in a large crop, Cheves released him because he was "without exception, the worst manager of Negroes I have known . . . the Negroes under him were almost rebellious."[43] The correspondence hints that Zantz, being unfamiliar with lowcountry tradition, may have tried to alter the tasks system in order to achieve greater efficiency.

The slave communities also asserted themselves in more subtle ways. Thomas B. Chaplin suspected his slaves of feigning illness or deliberately misunderstanding directions. In many ways, direct and indirect, the slaves might assert their desire to maintain the rhythm and habits of work to which they were accustomed.[44] The task system in the larger sense and the particular chores of the plantation in a smaller sense were not only systems and jobs imposed by the white power structure; to a considerable extent they depended also on those rhythms of work the slaves were willing to tolerate.

The plantation regimen did not permit the slaves to work for their own benefit, but the system of completing plantation chores by commonly accepted tasks allowed the slave to work for a commodity that mattered greatly to them: time for themselves. Under the task system slaves were punished only for not completing tasks. When they complete their chores quickly and efficiently, they earned more free time. Planters and overseers risked sullen resistance, disharmony, legal action, or open rebellion if they interfered with the slaves' time. And it was this time that allowed the slaves to create and maintain their own world within the plantation.

With their own time and enterprise, the slaves worked, learned skills, practiced various forms of amusement, and established elaborate and enduring religious practices. Slaves grew their own crops, raised their own poultry and livestock, and manufactured their own clothes and domestic items. Sam Polite recalls the work on their own time from his youth on St. Helena Island: "When you knock off work you can work on your own land. Maybe you might have two or three tasks of land round your cabin what marster give you for plant. You can have chicken, maybe hog. You can sell egg and chicken to store and marster will buy your hog. In that way slave can save money for buy thing like fish and whatever he want . . . sometime you can throw out net and catch shrimp. You can also catch possum and raccoon with your dog."[45] Commonly, the slaves planted potatoes and corn and sold the excess crops to the planter for provisions. They frequently supplemented their diets and entertained themselves hunting and fishing, though few slaves on the sea islands were trusted with boats.

Domestic skills were acquired by women during their free time. Rebecca Grant recalled learning to weave and dye cloth as a young girl in Beaufort and making clothes for herself in her own time. And Adeline Gray, who was a slave in St. Peter's Parish, learned how to process wild indigo into blue dye and make lye soap for her mistress and for the slave community.[46] Use of slave time for their own planting and craftmaking over many years allowed for the accumulation of wealth within the slave community. The property rights of slaves within the plantation community were almost universally recognized by owners and overseers. From this, a brisk market of barter and exchange developed within the plantation community. There was a substantial internal economy operating within the slave communities of the antebellum Beaufort District.[47]

In addition to work during slave time, the slaves practiced several forms of amusement. Fishing and crabbing in the creeks and marshes that bordered almost all the sea island plantations was a common leisure activity, and given the productivity of the estuarine environment, almost always rewarding. Slaves on the mainland hunted and fished in the freshwater swamps. Guns were not allowed, but dogs were; thus, treeing raccoons was a common pursuit.

A good deal of the slave's leisure activity was simple socializing. Most planters gave their slaves a daily ration of corn on the cob. The women customarily gathered under a tree on the slave street to husk and pound the corn together. Other slaves stopped by to participate and socialize, and this event often became an impromptu party.[48] On Saturday night, before the Sabbath, there was usually a party on the street. Singing, dancing, and storytelling were all communal forms of amusement on Saturday nights. The singing invariably was a joint performance with the rhythms and chants characteristic of the Gullah people evoking the unmistakable echo of Africa. The dancing was also their own. Rather than copying the formal dances of white society, the slave communities maintained their African heritage of dance. Dancing, unlike singing, was an individual expression. Beginning with swaying rhythmically and softly moving their feet, they often ended in wild gyrations.[49]

Another common form of amusement in the slave community was storytelling. Often, particular slaves became master storytellers, amusing their audiences with expressive language and almost musical intonation. These Gullah storytellers did more than amuse the community. They also kept alive the African language, customs, and beliefs within the slave community.[50]

The biggest party of the year was at Christmas when the planters usually gave the slaves three or four days off and permitted them to travel to other plantations or to nearby towns to socialize. St. Helena and Hilton Head slave communities socialized with each other. Beaufort filled up during the Christmas season with the slaves on Port Royal Island, and the rice communities of St. Peter's Parish cavorted across the river in Savannah.

The planters also dispensed gifts. In 1850, Reverend William Hazzard Wigg Barnwell dispensed the following gifts to approximately seventy slaves at his Cotton Hope Plantation on Port Royal Island: four gallons of molasses, three-quarters of a bushel of salt, fifty-six hands of tobacco and pipes, four dozen handkerchiefs, and sixteen caps. In 1854, he added to this Christmas largesse twenty-two pounds of coffee and two hundred pounds of flour.[51] On the Savannah River, Charles Manigault, who took particular pride in how his slaves dressed, bought a red flannel shirt and scotch-cap for each man and boy on his plantation.[52]

By far the most important part of life in the slave community was religion. By the late antebellum period, the work of the Baptist and Methodist missions had influenced virtually every slave community in the district. Because the Baptist denomination permitted the slaves to organize their own congregations, devise their own forms of worship, and adapt their old African spiritualism to the new Christian experience, it became the largest denomination among the slave communities. The center of the religious life was the "praise house." On larger plantations, the praise house was a separate building for religious activities. On smaller plantations, the cabin of the oldest person on the street was the site of regular worship. Slaves often met at the praise house two or three times per week. Some slaves also attended the larger white churches such as the Baptist Church of Beaufort, built in 1844, and the "Brick" Baptist Church, built on St. Helena Island in 1855. But the praise house was the real center of their religion.

The praise house meeting was conducted by an elder or "deacon" recognized by the whites as a leader in the community who was often used as an intermediary in community matters. In addition to the elder, there were spiritual fathers and mothers who formed the working committee of the praise house. As well as managing the praise house, these spiritual fathers and mothers were healers, seers, and spiritual guides. They were the successors to the Nganga of the Bakongo culture and the secret Poro-Sande councils of the upper Guinea coast. They were the people who kept the old African beliefs alive under the canopy of Christianity. They may also have been the real authorities within the slave community. At praise house meetings, they often served as ushers or "watchmen" at the door. Those who were being initiated into the religious community were called "seekers" and their process of initiation was called "seeking Jesus." Completing the initiation was called "catching sense."[53] The seeking process was so profoundly spiritual and so strongly influenced by the spiritual fathers and mothers as to represent not only the Christian experience of being "born again," but also the seeking of peace with the ever-present spirits of their ancestors, American and African.

The praise house meeting opened with a hymn or spiritual. The prayer session followed, with the deacon leading and the congregation responding. Often members of the congregation were invited to speak or exhort the others. Following the prayer, the deacon read a lesson from the Bible. After a concluding spiritual, the "shout" began. While the slaves always insisted that the shout was part of their Christian worship, white observers thought the shout was a separate ceremony of a different faith. Laura Towne, the founder of Penn School, thought it was "certainly the remains of some old idol worship." At the conclusion of the prayer meeting and the commencement of the shout, all the benches were put back against the wall and the congregation formed a ring on the floor. Accompanied by a separate choir, which sang and clapped in rhythm, the group began to dance in a circle first by walking, then by shuffling, and finally by stamping their way around the circle. Sometimes a shout would last well into the morning hours, exhausting the participants and keeping much of the slave community awake.[54] The praise house meetings were the clearest expression of the fusion of American Christian and African spiritual beliefs within the slave communities.

The slave communities of the Beaufort District were formed by the introduction of cotton, the new importation of slaves, the adoption of the task system of plantation management (and the concomitant emergence of the custom of slave time), and the spread of the missionary movement to the slave communities. The slaves endured insult, hardship, and abuse under the slave system. But, with perseverance, enterprise, and imagination, they seized their own time, preserved what they could of their African heritage, adopted what they wanted from white society, and forged the unique world of the Gullah.

NOTES

1. Elizabeth Donnan, ed., *Documents Illustrative of the History of the Slave Trade to America,* 4 vols. (1930–1935; rpts., New York: Octagon Books, 1965), 4: 494.

2. Donnan, ed., *Documents,* 4: 500.

3. Donnan, ed., *Documents,* 4: 501.

4. Albert J. Raboteau, *Slave Religion: An Invisible Institution in the Antebellum South* (New York: Oxford University Press, 1978), 47.

5. 2nd Census of the U.S. (1800), 3rd Census (1810), Beaufort District Population Schedules, South Carolina Department of Archives and History.

6. "William Joyner Account Book," South Caroliniana Library.

7. "List of Negroes on St. Helena Belonging to Mrs. Bull," November 28, 1800; "List of Negroes Belonging to Col. Stapleton on St. Helena," March 15, 1810, John Stapleton Papers, 1790–1839, South Caroliniana Library.

8. Donnan, ed., *Documents,* 4: 504–25; see also John C. Thornton, "African Dimensions of the Stono Rebellion: Notes and Comments," *American Historical Review* 95 (October 1990): 1101–3.

9. Donnan, ed., *Documents,* 4: 513.

10. Petitions, Legislative Papers, 1804, South Carolina Department of Archives and History.

11. Margaret Washington Creel, *A Peculiar People: Slave Religion and Community-Culture among the Gullahs* (New York: New York University Press, 1988) 127, 150–61; David Duncan Wallace, *The History of South Carolina,* 4 vols. (New York: American Historical Society, 1934), 2:383.

12. Philip D. Morgan, "Work and Culture: The Task System in the South Carolina Lowcountry," *William and Mary Quarterly* 39 (1982): 576.

13. Lewis Cecil Gray, *History of Agriculture in the Southern United States to 1860,* 2 vols. (Gloucester, Mass.: Peter Smith, 1958), 2: 552.

14. Gray, *History of Agriculture,* 2: 553, 554.

15. Belinda Hurmence, ed., *Before Freedom, When I Just Can Remember: Twenty-seven Oral Histories of Former South Carolina Slaves* (Winston-Salem: John F. Blair, 1989), 78.

16. Guion Griffis Johnson, *Social History of the Sea Islands* (Chapel Hill: University of North Carolina Press, 1930), 79.

17. Theodore Rosengarten, *Tombee: Portrait of a Cotton Planter* (New York: Morrow, 1986), 62–63, 717–18.

18. Slave List, 1845, Langdon Cheves to Langdon Cheves Jr., July 14, 1846, Langdon Cheves III Papers, South Carolina Historical Society.

19. Stone from Laurel Hill Plantation, now in possession of U.S. Savannah River Wildlife Preserve.

20. Morgan, "Work and Culture," 597.

21. Philip D. Morgan, "Ownership of Property by Slaves in the Mid-Nineteenth Century Low Country," *Journal of Southern History* 49 (August 1983): 416–17.

22. Katherine M. Jones, ed., *Port Royal Under Six Flags* (Indianapolis: Bobbs-Merrill, 1960), 166.

23. Stephen B. Barnwell, *The Story of an American Family* (Marquette, Mich.: Privately printed, 1969), 65.

24. *The History of the Parish Church of St. Helena, Beaufort, South Carolina . . . ,* compiled and written by the History Committee, St. Helena's Episcopal Church (Beaufort: Privately printed, 1991), 104–5.

25. Robert M. Myers, ed., *The Children of Pride: A True Story of Georgia and the Civil War* (New Haven: Yale University Press, 1972), 12.

26. Raboteau, *Slave Religion,* 154–55.

27. "Richard Fuller," *Dictionary of American Biography*, 4: 62.

28. Julia Floyd Smith, *Slavery and Rice Culture in Lowcountry Georgia, 1750–1860* (Knoxville: University of Tennessee Press, 1985), 171.

29. Jones, ed., *Port Royal Under Six Flags*, 167–71.

30. Jones, ed., *Port Royal Under Six Flags*, 164–66.

31. Creel, *A Peculiar People*, 180–81.

32. Hurmence, ed., *Before Freedom*, 61.

33. Raboteau, *Slave Religion*, 166–67.

34. Creel, *A Peculiar People*, 216, 222–23, 251.

35. Creel, *A Peculiar People*, 34, 44–49, 55–58, 153.

36. J. E. McTeer, *High Sheriff of the Lowcountry* (Beaufort: Beaufort Book Co., 1970); Isabelle Glen, *Life on St. Helena Island* (New York: Carlton Press, 1980), 56.

37. Rosengarten, *Tombee*, 55; John W. Blassingame, *The Slave Community: Plantation Life in the Antebellum South* (New York: Oxford University Press, 1972), 154; Charles W. Joyner, *Down by the Riverside: A South Carolina Slave Community* (Urbana: University of Illinois Press, 1984), 9–40.

38. Jones, ed., *Port Royal Under Six Flags*, 165; Rosengarten, *Tombee*, 324–25; Robert E. H. Peeples, *Tales of Antebellum Hilton Head Island Families* (Hilton Head: Hilton Head Island Historical Society, 1970), 8–9.

39. Lawrence S. Rowland, "Alone on the River: The Rise and Fall of the Savannah River Rice Plantations of St. Peter's Parish, South Carolina," *South Carolina Historical Magazine* 88 (July 1987): 121.

40. Blassingame, *Slave Community*, 154.

41. Johnson, *Social History of the Sea Islands*, 76.

42. Rosengarten, *Tombee*, 162–65.

43. Langdon Cheves to Langdon Cheves Jr., April 17, 1843, Langdon Cheves I Papers, South Carolina Historical Society.

44. Rosengarten, *Tombee*, 157–58.

45. Hurmence, ed., *Before Freedom*, 78.

46. Hurmence, ed., *Before Freedom*, 103; Mason Crum, *Gullah: Negro Life in the Carolina Sea Islands* (Durham: Duke University Press, 1940), 234.

47. Morgan, "Work and Culture," 590–95.

48. Crum, *Gullah*, 234.

49. Johnson, *Social History of the Sea Islands*, 143; Blassingame, *Slave Community*, 44.

50. Patricia Jones-Jackson, *When Roots Die* (Athens: University of Georgia Press, 1987), 37.

51. William Hazzard Wigg Barnwell Plantation Book, 1838–1857, South Carolina Historical Society.

52. Charles Manigault Letterbook, 1846–1848, South Carolina Historical Society.

53. Creel, *A Peculiar People*, 284–85.

54. Johnson, *Social History of the Sea Islands*, 148–50.

20

Beaufort District's Farmers
and Planters in 1850

By midcentury, the Beaufort District had become the cornucopia of the South Carolina lowcountry. The plantation regime had been stabilized for more than thirty years. Cotton and rice were, of course, the two principal crops, and the agricultural and labor management systems necessary for the production of these staples had been established for more than a generation. The rhythms of plantation activity had, in fact, become a way of life for both the white owners and the black slaves. The decade of the 1850s was the most prosperous in the long history of the Beaufort District. Cotton and rice prices remained high throughout the decade and many Beaufort District planters who had struggled financially during the 1830 and 1840s grew rich during this time. New homes were built in the summer resort villages of the district. Bluffton, McPhersonville, Gillisonville, and Lawtonville grew rapidly, and a large number of the mansions that grace Beaufort's National Landmark District today were constructed from the profits of the second cotton boom.

While cotton and rice were the best-known products of the district, in terms of sheer volume they were exceeded by the necessary provisioning crops of corn and sweet potatoes. While corn was ubiquitous on southern plantations and farms, sweet potatoes, derived from the African yam, was unique to the eastern Carolinas and Georgia.[1] The Beaufort District, with its excellent soil conditions for potatoes and its large African population, may have been the largest producer of sweet potatoes in the antebellum South. In addition, Beaufort District plantations all had large herds of livestock which provided meat, dairy products, and wool. In 1840, in fact, the Beaufort District had more cattle (41,000) than any district in the state.[2]

The first agricultural census of the United States was conducted in 1850, and it reveals the remarkably productive and balanced agricultural enterprise that characterized the Beaufort District in the late antebellum era. In 1850, the district produced 32,492,786 pounds of rice, 16,303 bales (or 6,521,200 pounds) of cotton, 411,483 bushels (or 20,574,150 pounds) of sweet potatoes, and 387,685 bushels (or 19,384,250 pounds) of corn. In gross terms, this was 16,246 tons of rice, 3,260 tons of cotton, 10,287 tons of sweet potatoes, and 9,792 tons of corn.[3] Based on average market prices, the rice crop was worth $1,104,754 and the cotton crop was worth $1,065,510 in 1850 dollars. All this was produced for the benefit of 5,946 planters and farmers by the labor of 30,279 African slaves.

THE GREAT PLANTERS

In 1850, there were 881 plantations in the four parishes of the district. The average number of slaves per plantation was 34.3. There were seventy-nine plantations with more than one hundred slaves (8.9 percent of the total). Of the 881 plantations, fifty-five were valued in excess of twenty thousand dollars (6.2 percent). Of equal importance to understanding the history of the Beaufort District were the much larger number of small planters. In 1850, 415 plantations were valued at less than fifteen hundred dollars (47 percent of the plantations).

There had always been geographical, economical, and social differences among the four parishes, and each parish had different neighborhoods with separate centers of activity. By 1850, St. Helena Parish had the smallest white population, 1,111; the second largest black population, 8,261 slaves; and 151 plantations of varying sizes. So, the average number of slaves per plantation was fifty-five. With the average value of an individual slave being approximately one thousand dollars, this would have made St. Helena Parish, by any measure, one of the wealthiest neighborhoods in America. In fact, 10 percent of the slaveowners in St. Helena Parish owned more than one hundred slaves, and 7.2 percent had real estate valued in excess of twenty thousand dollars. And there were few poor people among the white population. Only 11 percent of the St. Helena landowners had real estate valued at less than fifteen hundred dollars.

Because St. Helena Parish was comprised completely of sea islands surrounded by saltwater estuaries, its entire plantation regime was devoted to the production of sea island cotton. In 1850, St. Helena Parish produced 2,587 bales of cotton. At 400 pounds per bale that would amount to 1,034,800 pounds of cotton. The term "bale" is misleading because sea island cotton planters rarely pressed their fine, long-staple product into tight bales. Instead they packed and shipped their cotton in large, loose bags so as not to damage the silky fiber. In 1850, 1 pound of sea island cotton received 27.8 cents on the Charleston market. Thus, the total cotton crop for St. Helena Parish was worth $287,674.[4] The largest producers of sea island cotton in St. Helena Parish were William J. Grayson, Thomas A. Coffin, and Benjamin Chaplin Sr.

Largest Cotton Planters of St. Helena Parish, 1850

Name	No. of Slaves	No. of Acres	Location	Est. Income (in dollars)
William J. Grayson	170	1,700	St. Helena Island	19,126
Thomas A. Coffin	224	2,911	St. Helena Island	19,460
Benjamin Chaplin	272	1,373	St. Helena Island/ Port Royal Island	17,347

William J. Grayson (1788–1863), the largest producer of cotton in the parish, is well known to students of the history and literature of the South. His political and literary careers are covered in other chapters. Grayson owned property and slaves at different times across the lowcountry and earned his living mostly from his planting and business interests. His principal plantation was Frogmore Plantation on St. Helena Island, which he purchased from the Stapleton estate in 1836. In 1850, Grayson had 170 slaves on his plantation.[5] The 1,700-acre plantation had 900 improved acres and 800 unimproved acres. The property was valued at thirty thousand dollars. On the plantation were 11 horses, 6 mules, 40 milk cows, 12 working oxen, 141 cattle, 149 sheep, and 100 hogs valued at thirty-two hundred dollars. The plantation produced 1,700 bushels of corn (85,000 pounds), 200 bushels of peas and beans, 2,800 bushels of sweet potatoes (140,000 pounds), 750 pounds of butter, and 320 pounds of wool. The cotton crop was 172 bales, or bags, of 400 pounds each. At the prevailing price of 27.8 cents per pound, Grayson's income from the sale of the cotton was $19,126.

The next largest producer of sea island cotton in the parish was Thomas Aston Coffin. Coffin (1795–1863) was the son of New England sea captain Ebenezer Coffin, who purchased the northeast point of St. Helena Island during the 1790s. The land has been known as Coffin Point ever since, and in 1850 it made up the bulk of Coffin's 2,911 acres on St. Helena Island. Coffin Point Plantation had been developed by Captain Ebenezer Coffin at the turn of the nineteenth century during the first sea island cotton boom. The house that still stands there was built in 1800. By 1816, when Thomas Coffin began managing the plantation there were 357 acres of cleared ground and fifty-nine slaves.[6] By 1850, the plantation consisted of 2,281 acres, 1,181 acres of it cleared and developed for agriculture, with 224 slaves. Coffin also owned a smaller plantation of 630 acres and 77 slaves in the middle of St. Helena Island. Thus, his total holdings were 2,911 acres and 301 slaves. His land, slaves, livestock, tools, and buildings were worth nearly four hundred thousand dollars. Coffin was the largest slaveowner in the parish, and the fourth largest slaveholder in the district. Coffin Point Plantation contained 5 horses, 3 mules, 30 milk cows, 39 working

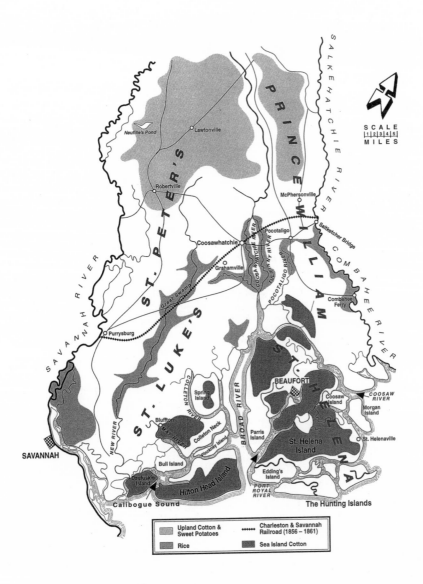

SCALE
1 2 3 4 5
MILES

S A L K E H A T C H I E   R I V E R

C O M B A H E E   R I V E R

P R I N C E   W I L L I A M

S T.   P E T E R' S

S T.   L U K E' S

S T.   H E L E N A

Neufille's Pond

Lawtonville

Robertville

McPhersonville

Saltketcher Bridge

Coosawhatchie

Pocotaligo

Grahamville

Combahee
Ferry

Purrysburg

SAVANNAH

Spring
Island

BEAUFORT

Coosaw
Island

COOSAW
RIVER

Morgan
Island

St. Helenaville

Bluffton

Colleton Neck

Parris
Island

St. Helena
Island

Bull Island

Edding's
Island

Daufuskie
Island

Hilton Head Island

PORT
ROYAL
RIVER

Calibogue Sound

The Hunting Islands

SAVANNAH RIVER

COOSAWHATCHIE RIVER

TULIFINNY RIVER

POCOTALIGO RIVER

Great Swamp

NEW RIVER

MAY RIVER

COLLETON RIVER

Mackey Island

BROAD RIVER

| | Upland Cotton & Sweet Potatoes | •••••• | Charleston & Savannah Railroad (1856 – 1861) |
| | Rice | | Sea Island Cotton |

Beaufort District, 1850

oxen, and 130 cattle, but no hogs or sheep. The plantation produced 2,000 bushels of corn (10,000 pounds), 200 bushels of oats, 1,200 pounds of rice, 200 bushels of peas and beans, 2,000 bushels of sweet potatoes (100,000 pounds), 300 pounds of butter, and 200 pounds of honey and beeswax. The sea island cotton crop was 165 bags, or 66,000 pounds. Together with another ten bags produced on the smaller plantation, Coffin's cotton crop was worth $19,460.

Benjamin Chaplin Sr. (1776–1851) was the third great sea island cotton planter in the parish. Like Coffin and Grayson, his life spanned the introduction and growth of sea island cotton in the Beaufort District. A descendant of one of the original St. Helena Island families, he married another descendant of colonial settlers, Elizabeth Jenkins, youngest child of Captain John Jenkins of the Revolutionary War. Chaplin was a careful agronomist and, as a result, a very successful planter. In 1829 and 1830, the *Southern Agriculturist* awarded Chaplin the St. Helena premium for corn with huge yields of 54 and 73 bushels per acre. This was a carefully tended experimental patch, however, as yields were typically less than 20 bushels per acre. Chaplin was the "Uncle Ben" often referred to, somewhat enviously, by his less successful nephew, Thomas B. Chaplin of Tombee Plantation.[7] In 1850, Benjamin Chaplin owned 1,373 acres, 930 acres of which were improved for agriculture. This land was worked by 272 slaves.[8] The plantation land was worth thirty thousand dollars and contained twelve horses, eight mules, thirty milk cows, ten working oxen, one hundred cattle, fifty sheep, and seventy-five hogs worth $2,860. Chaplin produced 1,200 bushels of corn (60,000 pounds), 200 bushels of peas and beans, 2,500 bushels of sweet potatoes (125,000 pounds), 350 pounds of butter, 100 pounds of wool, and 200 pounds of honey and beeswax. Chaplin's cotton production was 156 bags, or 64,400 pounds, worth $17,347.

Other large planters of St. Helena Parish were Dr. Thomas Fuller, the brother of the great Baptist minister Richard Fuller, with 1,000 acres and 145 slaves on Parris Island and 1,200 acres (600 acres improved) and 108 slaves on St. Helena Island. These plantations produced 112 bags of cotton (44,800 pounds) worth $12,454. Dr. Berners Barnwell Sams had 2,097 acres and 174 slaves on Datha and Lady's Islands which produced sixty-five bags (26,000 pounds) of cotton worth $7,228. His brother Lewis Reeve Sams had 1,467 acres and 166 slaves on adjoining property which produced seventy bags (28,000 pounds) of cotton worth $7,784. The Sams brothers were the sons of William Sams, who began to build that family's fortune on Datha Island in 1786, following the Revolution. By 1850, his two sons had amassed a fortune well in excess of four hundred thousand dollars.

Neighboring St. Luke's Parish was somewhat different from St. Helena's. First of all, it was larger. In 1850, St. Luke's Parish had 1,263 white inhabitants and 7,385 slaves. There were 188 plantation or farm units with an average of 39.2 slaves per plantation. St. Luke's Parish, like St. Helena, was a wealthy district. In fact, twenty-eight of the plantations in St. Luke's, or 12 percent of the owners, had more than one hundred slaves, and 7.4 percent had real estate valued in excess of twenty thousand dollars. But unlike St. Helena Parish, there were some small farmers in St. Luke's Parish: 38 percent of the planters had real estate valued at less than fifteen hundred dollars.

St. Luke's Parish was geographically divided into two distinct neighborhoods, the older, and generally wealthier, neighborhoods—the islands of St. Luke's, Hilton Head, Daufuskie, Pinckney, Spring, and Calliwassie—and the adjacent mainland neck around the village of Bluffton, which was the sea island cotton district. Further inland, along the Coosawhatchie and New Rivers (the Great Swamp), rice plantations dominated. The center of this neighborhood was the crossroads village of Coosawhatchie, which was the district courthouse and capital from 1789 to 1836. By the late antebellum era, Coosawhatchie was considered to be low, swampy, and unhealthy so the planters began to gather at Grahamville next to Ridgeland and at Gillisonville, which was the district court from 1836 to 1865. In addition to the rice planters of this neighborhood, there were also a number of smaller farmers with a few slaves and modest incomes. One of the chief institutions of this group was the Beaver Dam Baptist Church above Gillisonville, near the boundary with upper St. Peter's Parish, which was founded in 1834.[9]

Of the great planters of St. Luke's Parish in 1850, the largest cotton producers were George Edwards of Spring Island and James Kirk of Rose Hill. The largest rice producers were the heirs of John Heyward of White Hall and Alfred Huger and Charles C. DuPont.

Largest Cotton Planters of St. Luke's Parish, 1850

Name	No. of Slaves	No. of Acres	Location	Est. Income (in dollars)
George Edwards	253	5,500	Spring Island	16,680
James Kirk	253	3,000	Bluffton	13,344

George Edwards (1777–1859) of Spring Island was the second largest slaveholder in the parish with 253 slaves, and one of the wealthiest men in the district. Edwards acquired Spring Island through his marriage in 1801 to Elizabeth Barksdale.[10] She was the daughter of Thomas Barksdale and Ann Parmenter Bona, two of the first settlers of the sea islands. In 1850, Spring Island had a huge tabby mansion on the eastern shore and was composed of 1,000 improved acres and 4,500 unimproved acres valued at fifty thousand dollars. Edwards had a very large herd of livestock: 12 horses, 16 mules, 75 milk cows, 40 working oxen, 200 cattle, 70 sheep, and 103 hogs worth thirty-four hundred dollars. Spring Island produced 2,400 bushels of corn, 2,800 pounds of rice, 1,000 bushels of peas and beans, 1,000 bushels of sweet potatoes, 250 pounds of butter, and 150 bags of sea island cotton. The cotton crop was worth $16,680.[11]

James Kirk was the second largest cotton producer in the parish. He also had 253 slaves. Kirk's plantation consisted of 2,400 improved acres and 1,600 unimproved acres worth sixty thousand dollars. He owned 14 horses, 20 mules, 20 oxen, 100 cattle, 150 sheep, and 300 hogs. His dairy herd of 150 milk cows, and his production of 650 pounds of butter, was the largest in the district. His livestock were valued at $6,810. Kirk produced 4,700 bushels of corn, 300 bushels of oats, 23,000 pounds of rice, 200 bushels of peas and beans, and 500 bushels of sweet potatoes, and processed 120 bags of cotton worth $13,344. In addition to Edwards and Kirk, several different Pope and Baynard family plantations were major producers of sea island cotton in 1850.

Largest Rice Planters of St. Luke's Parish, 1850

Name	No. of Slaves	No. of Acres	Location	Est. Income (in dollars)
J. C. Heyward (estate)	100	3,000	White Hall	15,640
A. Alfred Huger	68	800	Coosawhatchie	14,892
C. C. DuPont	132	5,500	Hap Hazzard	12,512

The largest rice-producing plantation in St. Luke's Parish in 1850 was White Hall Plantation owned by the heirs of John Cuthbert Heyward, eldest son of Thomas Heyward and Ann Eliza Cuthbert, and grandson of Thomas Heyward Jr. Heyward's widow was operating White Hall Plantation that year with one hundred slaves. There were 800 acres of improved land and 2,200 acres of unimproved land valued at twenty thousand dollars. White Hall had 8 horses, 5 mules, 50 milk cows, 50 oxen, 40 cattle, and 120 sheep worth $2,750. The plantation produced 50 bushels of corn, 500 bushels of peas and beans, 2,000 bushels of sweet potatoes, and 320 pounds of butter. The principal cash crop was 460,000 pounds of rice worth $15,640. It is notable that while White Hall Plantation was the most productive rice plantation in the parish that year, it was much less productive than the newer tidal culture rice plantations of the lower Savannah and Combahee Rivers in neighboring parishes.

The second largest rice producer was A. Alfred Huger. Huger had an eight-hundred-acre rice plantation with 400 improved acres and sixty-eight slaves in 1850. He had ten horses, three mules, thirty milk cows, twenty-five working oxen, fifty cattle, twenty sheep, and forty hogs. The plantation produced 400 bushels of corn, 300 bushels of oats, 300 bushels of peas and beans, 700 bushels of sweet potatoes, and 150 pounds of butter. The plantation produced 438,000 pounds of rice worth $14,892. This was not among the largest plantations in the Beaufort District, but it was one of the most profitable. Eleven years later, Alfred Huger was a major in the new Confederate States Army and commanded an artillery battery at Fort Walker on that fateful day on Port Royal Sound.[12]

The third largest rice producer in 1850 was Charles Cater Dupont (1806–1872) of Hap Hazzard Plantation near Grahamville. Dupont was the great grandson of pioneer Huguenot rice planter Abraham Dupont, the grandson of revolutionary patriot Charles Dupont and the nephew of Henry McNish. Dupont had 132 slaves in 1850. The plantation had 2,000 improved acres and 3,500 unimproved acres worth twenty-two thousand dollars. Dupont also had 18 horses, 15 mules, 75 milk cows, 30 working oxen, 160 cattle, 75 sheep, and 200 hogs worth $4,983. Hap Hazzard produced 50 bushels of wheat, 350 bushels of corn, 30 bales of cotton, 1,000 bushels of peas and beans, 3,000 bushels of sweet potatoes, 500 pounds of butter, and 120 gallons of molasses. The principal crop was 368,000 pounds of rice worth $12,512. A secondary crop of short-staple cotton amounted to thirty bales worth $1,320 at eleven cents per bale. Cash income from the plantation was $13,832. Dupont's plantation, like Heyward's White Hall Plantation, was a prime example of a highly refined and still productive old colonial inland swamp rice plantation.

St. Peter's Parish by 1850 was the most populous parish in the Beaufort District. There were 1,889 white inhabitants, 8,999 slaves, and 272 plantation units—an average of thirty-three slaves per plantation. The unique circumstances of St. Peter's Parish, however, altered the meaning of this last figure. As explained in previous chapters, St. Peter's Parish had unique and distinctive neighborhoods with very different geographic and economic realities. Lower St. Peter's Parish, as described in chapter 23, was by far the most productive rice region in the Beaufort District and, for a few years, one of the most productive rice regions in North America. One of the descendants of the antebellum Savannah River rice planters, Daniel Elliott Huger Smith, described the lower Savannah River plantations as "a mine of gold for its owners and the state."[13] The lower Savannah River was a heavy concentration of wealth and slaves not typical of the rest of St. Peter's Parish. Nearly 30 percent of the slave population was concentrated on eighteen plantations on the lower Savannah River. If the plantations were removed from the calculation, the average number of slaves per plantation in St. Peter's Parish was twenty-five, a more representative figure.

The development of St. Peter's Parish from a frontier in the late eighteenth century to a settled farming community by the mid-nineteenth century is dealt with in chapter 17. By the census of 1850, St. Peter's Parish had become the largest producer of rice in the Beaufort District with 17,045,777 pounds, the largest producer of sweet potatoes with 6,253,850 pounds, and the largest volume producer of cotton, albeit short-staple upland cotton worth only half the value of sea island cotton, with 7,472 bales or 2,988,800 pounds. The total value of the parish's two principal cash crops, rice and short-staple cotton, was $908,324 in 1850.[14]

Largest Upland Cotton Planters of St. Peter's Parish, 1850

Name	No. of Slaves	No. of Acres	Location	Est. Income
Edmund Martin	249	8,000	Woodstock	$20,240
Benj. Bostick	215	19,000	Ingleside	27,709

The great planters of St. Peter's Parish were at that time virtually the same as those described in earlier chapters. The largest slaveowners were Langdon Cheves with 283 slaves on Delta Plantation on the Savannah River, Edmund Martin with 249 slaves on his eight-thousand-acre Woodstock Plantation in upper St. Peter's, the estate of Allan Izard with 242 slaves at Trinity Plantation on the Savannah River, and Benjamin R. Bostick with 215 slaves on his nineteen-thousand-acre Ingleside Plantation in upper St. Peter's. The most highly prized properties in the parish were the developed tidal culture rice lands on the Savannah River. The 600 developed acres of Izard's estate were valued at $150,000, and the 814 developed acres of Daniel Huger were valued at $100,000. The largest producer of rice in St. Peter's Parish was Dr. James Proctor Screven of Savannah with an 1850 crop of 2,250,000 pounds worth $76,500. The largest producers of short-staple cotton were Bostick with 500 bales and Martin with 460 bales. The largest producer of corn in the parish, and all of the Beaufort District, was Bostick. The largest producer of sweet potatoes in the parish and district was Martin. These two very large agricultural enterprises set the standard for that area.

Martin's Woodstock Plantation was located near the "old Augusta Road" through upper St. Peter's Parish along a side road leading down to Hudson's Ferry on the Savannah River. The plantation consisted of 8,000 acres, 1,800 acres of which was improved farm land. There he lived with his wife, Mary Anna Maner, their five children, and a slave community of 249 people.[15] There were fifteen horses, ten mules, one hundred milk cows, twenty oxen, two hundred cattle, three hundred sheep, and two hundred hogs worth thirty-five hundred dollars. Woodstock produced 10 bushels of rye, 2,500 bushels of corn, 1,200 pounds of rice, 300 bushels of wheat, 100 bushels of peas and beans, 300 pounds of butter, 200 gallons of molasses, and 7,000 bushels (150 tons) of sweet potatoes. Obviously this was ample produce to feed the plantation community and sell the rest on the market. His only cash crop was short-staple cotton, of which he produced 460 bales worth $20,240.

Bostick's Ingleside Plantation was located further down the Augusta Road on the edge of Black Swamp. The plantation consisted of 19,000 acres, 4,000 acres of which were developed fields. The land was valued at fifty-five thousand dollars. Bostick and his wife, Jane Aseneth Maner, raised twelve children on the plantation.[16] There were 215 people in the slave community. The plantation contained 17 horses, 24 mules, 126 milk cows, 250 cattle, 95 sheep, and 350 hogs worth forty-six hundred dollars. The produce grown was 25 bushels of wheat, 10 bushels of rye, 30,000 pounds of rice, 95 pounds of wool, 300 bushels of peas and beans, 500 pounds of butter, 6,000 bushels (150 tons) of sweet potatoes, 7,880 bushels (197 tons) of corn, and 500 bales of short-staple cotton. At prevailing market prices, the rice crop was worth $1,020, his corn crop was worth $4,689, and the cotton crop was worth $22,000.

Clearly these two plantations were virtually self-sufficient, so whatever crops went to market were nearly all profit. The volume of production of foodstuffs was more than adequate to feed the plantation community and maintain the livestock, therefore, Martin and Bostick must have been major suppliers of food produce for the Savannah markets. Woodstock and Ingleside were the two largest plantations in the upper parish, and they set the standard for the scores of smaller farms and more modest households that surrounded them.

Prince William Parish, like St. Peter's, had two distinctive geographic and economic neighborhoods. Lower Prince William Parish was comprised of freshwater swamps and tidal estuaries and was dominated by the great rice plantations of the Coosawhatchie, Tullifinney, and lower Combahee Rivers. The wealthiest plantations in the Beaufort District were in lower Prince William Parish. Upper Prince William Parish, however, was comprised of small plantations and modest homesteads strung out on the high ground between the Salkehatchie and Coosawhatchie swamps. In 1850, Prince William Parish had 1,683 white inhabitants and 5,634 slaves. There were 270 plantation units with an average number of slaves per plantation of 20.8.

The lower Combahee River, which drains the Salkehatchie River into St. Helena Sound, was one of the most productive rice-producing regions in South Carolina. Very large tidal culture rice plantations were developed on the lower Combahee principally by Nathaniel Heyward (1766–1851), whose ten plantations and more than one thousand slaves were the dominant economic engine of the southern parishes in the antebellum era. All of Nathaniel Heyward's rice enterprises, however, were located on the Colleton County side of the river in St. Bartholomew's Parish. He made his home at 118 East Bay Street in Charleston and at the Bluff Plantation, where he was buried in 1851. From the plantation he could survey the broad arc of the Combahee River and the vast acres of tidal culture rice fields that had made him one of the richest men in America.[17]

Heyward was the last surviving child of colonial rice pioneer Colonel Daniel Heyward of St. Luke's Parish and the youngest brother of Thomas Heyward Jr. While his own plantations were not in the Beaufort District, his economic influence was felt through the numerous Heyward family nieces, nephews, and grandchildren that he helped to support. While the rice plantations of Prince William Parish pale in significance compared to those of Heyward, three planters in particular deserve notice.

Largest Rice Planters of Prince William Parish, 1850

Name	No. of Slaves	No. of Acres	Location	Est. Income (in dollars)
H. A. Middleton (estate)	596	700?	Combahee River	95,608
Nathaniel Heyward	286	12,222	Combahee River	38,250
Daniel Heyward	129	1,700	Pocotaligo River	50,490

Henry Middleton's Hobonny and Nieuport Plantations, Nathaniel Heyward Jr.'s White Hall Plantation, and Daniel Heyward's Heyward Hall Plantation were all important rice producers. Middleton (1770–1846) was one of South Carolina's most prominent public figures. The son of Arthur Middleton, Henry Middleton was governor of South Carolina (1810–1812), U.S. congressman (1815–1819), and U.S. minister to Russia (1820–1830). While he resided at famous Middleton Place on the Ashley River, the bulk of his great wealth was concentrated in Prince William Parish. At the time of his death in 1846, Middleton had 224 slaves at Nieuport Plantation, 289 slaves at Hobonny Plantation, and 63 slaves at Old Combahee Plantation.[18] In 1850, these three plantations comprised 700 acres of improved land valued at seventy-seven thousand dollars. The proceeds of these plantations were divided among Middleton's eight surviving children. And the proceeds were considerable. The two larger plantations produced 1,507,000 pounds and 1,305,000 pounds of rice, respectively. The income from these two plantations would have been $95,608 in 1850.

Nathaniel Heyward Jr. (1816–1891) was the grandson of Nathaniel Heyward of Bluff Plantation. In 1850, Nathaniel Jr. possessed 1,303 slaves in St. Bartholomew's Parish and 286 slaves in Prince William Parish. This was all part of his huge White Hall Plantation which must have stretched across both sides of the Combahee River. The census lists 2,222 acres of improved rice fields and

10,000 acres of unimproved land. He owned no horses in Prince William, but had nine mules, twenty-five milk cows, ten working oxen, thirty-five cattle, one hundred sheep, and seventy hogs. The plantation at Prince William produced 2,000 bushels of corn, 300 bushels of oats, 300 pounds of wool, 50 bushels of peas and beans, no cotton, no butter, and no sweet potatoes. His Prince William Parish rice fields produced 1,125,000 pounds of rice worth $38,250.[19]

The other large rice producer was Daniel Heyward (1810–1888) of Heyward Hall Plantation on the Pocotaligo River. He was the grandson of Colonel Daniel Heyward of Old House Plantation and the son of William Heyward of Pocotaligo.[20] In 1850, Daniel Heyward had 129 slaves on 1,700 acres at Heyward Hall. Nine hundred acres were developed rice fields and 800 acres were unimproved. The land was worth one hundred thousand dollars. Livestock consisted of thirteen horses, thirteen milk cows, fifty mules, twenty-five working oxen, one hundred cattle, seventy-five sheep, and twenty hogs worth four thousand dollars. The produce included 2,700 bushels of corn, 1,000 bushels of oats, 150 pounds of wool, 1,500 bushels of peas and beans, 300 pounds of butter, no cotton, and no sweet potatoes. The rice crop consisted of 1,485,000 pounds worth $50,490. Heyward also had an additional one hundred slaves at his Laurel Hill Plantation on the Savannah River in St. Peter's Parish. They worked 500 acres and produced 36,000 pounds of rice worth $1,234 in 1850, a very poor year on an otherwise productive plantation. Heyward had a large investment in two steam rice mills: one at Heyward Hall which was valued at sixteen thousand dollars, and one at Laurel Hill on the Savannah River which was valued at ten thousand dollars. The rice mill at Heyward Hall was the only steam-powered rice mill in Prince William Parish.

Other great planters of Prince William Parish were Julius Gillison Huguenin of Point Comfort and Roseland Plantations on the Coosawhatchie River and Walter Blake of Bonny Hall Plantation on the Combahee River. Huguenin had 329 slaves working 3,900 acres on both sides of the Coosawhatchie River in Prince William and St. Luke's Parishes. Blake managed his father's huge estate of 610 slaves on Bonny Hall Plantation in Prince William Parish but lived in Charleston and at Hayfield Plantation near Flat Rock, North Carolina.[21]

VILLAGE LIFE

During the antebellum era, the wealthier planters of the Beaufort District spent less than half the year on their plantations. The great planters usually had town houses in Charleston or Savannah. Many, particularly the large rice planters, rarely visited their plantations at all. During the late antebellum era many of the richest lowcountry planters began to establish resort villages in the N.C. mountains. The most famous of these was Flat Rock, North Carolina, developed after 1831, where the large number of Heywards, Elliotts, Hamiltons, and Rutledges in the graveyard of the Episcopal Church of St. John in the Wilderness gave mute testimony to the summer migrations of the coastal planters. A large number of slightly less wealthy planters, who did not wish to keep up the expensive style of the cities and needed to be closer to their businesses, but did wish to escape the isolation and "country fever" of the plantation during the hot and unhealthy summer months, established several summer resort villages within the Beaufort District. These summer resort villages were where the planters mingled and socialized with their neighbors, established their churches, provided at least primary education for their children, and exchanged information on business and politics. These resort villages were the centers of white planter society just as the "street" was the center of the slave community.

It was customary for the planter families to leave the plantation during April after the crops had been planted so planters, overseers, and slaves could look forward to several months of routine crop maintenance. The planters would remain in the villages from April until just after the first frost in November. Then they would pack up and return to the plantation. As a consequence, Christmas season on the plantations was a great family reunion, featuring feasts for neighbors and friends. It was also the best holiday of the year for the slaves. Winter on the plantation was filled with recreational hunting and fishing for the planters and the busy tasks of preparing the harvested crops for market: winnowing and grinding rice and ginning and moting cotton. Another consequence of this routine for the planter families was that the school year for their children was reversed. Planter children went to school during the summer in the village and hunted, fished, and played for two months in winter on the plantation.

The antebellum resort villages of the Beaufort District were Beaufort and St. Helenaville in St. Helena Parish; Bluffton, Grahamville, and Gillisonville in St. Luke's Parish; Robertville and Lawtonville in St. Peter's Parish; and McPhersonville in Prince William Parish. Beaufort was the oldest and largest of the resort villages. It set the style not only for the smaller villages in the district, but also for much of the town life throughout the South. Beaufort was the ultimate example of an antebellum planter resort. In its early years, the town had some pretensions of becoming a seaport and busy center of commerce. And just before the Revolution, it did have a brief commercial and industrial boom based on indigo and wooden shipbuilding. But during the antebellum era, Beaufort became little more than a commercial outpost of Charleston and Savannah. The steamboats which plied the inland passage after 1819 regularly stopped in Beaufort, but only to load cotton for the city markets. The antebellum prosperity of Beaufort was dependant almost entirely on the price and produce of sea island cotton. That prosperity, however, was great, and Beaufort became one of the "wealthiest, most aristocratic and cultivated towns" in antebellum America. In 1844, the famous British geologist Sir Charles Lyell visited Beaufort and described it as a "picturesque town composed of assemblage of villas" each "shaded by a verandah surrounded by 4 beautiful live oaks and orange trees laden with fruit." George Stowits, a Civil War soldier from New York, waxed eloquent on the charms of Beaufort, "Words are feeble to describe this isle of the bay, this fairyland of the south with a gem of a town upon it."[22]

In this uniquely aesthetic setting, the sea island planters conducted business, raised and educated their children, and often engaged in social amusements. Because of the wealth of the town, Beaufort was an unusually social community. The Agricultural Society had dinners and sponsored debates. The Beaufort Volunteer Artillery held ceremonial musters and parades and sponsored the annual Fourth of July banquet at the Arsenal Hall. Joseph Barnwell recalled seeing Major John G. Barnwell, commander of the unit, preside over these festive events, calling the guests to order with a huge brass drum that sat beside his chair.[23]

One of the social highlights of the town in the 1850s was the visit of the naval sloop-of-war USS *Brooklyn,* commanded by Captain David Farragut, destined to become the first admiral in the U.S. Navy and a scourge of the Confederacy. The citizens put on a banquet and ball for the naval officers, and the next day were entertained aboard ship by Captain Farragut.[24]

Beaufort had five active congregations in the 1850s. The old Episcopal church, the large new Baptist church, a small Presbyterian church, and a small Methodist mission formed the Protestant congregations. In 1846 a Roman Catholic congregation was added when Irish boatbuilder Daniel O'Connell built St. Peter's Church on Carteret Street.

Much of Beaufort's social activity was purposeful. The ladies of the town formed the Ladies Benevolent Society of Beaufort in 1815, which engaged the most prominent women in charitable and social activities throughout the antebellum era. In 1837, Reverend Richard Fuller persuaded, or shamed, his sociable male neighbors into forming an equally purposeful Beaufort Male Benevolent Society.[25] Not all the social organizations, however, were so purposeful, and Beaufort men had long had a reputation for hard drinking and high living. In 1858, F. F. Sams, T. H. Spann, and Nathaniel Heyward, three of Beaufort's most privileged young men formed the Beaufort Billiard Club.[26] In addition to billiards, cockfighting and gambling were always popular in Beaufort. Richard Lubbock recalled that the most famous fighting cock in Beaufort, owned by a free black carpenter, was blown up in the explosion of the paddlewheeler *Henry Schulz* at Augusta. The blast threw the bird high in the air and ripped out all his fine feathers, but the bird survived to enjoy an honored retirement. Lubbock noted the belief held by Beaufortians that the "Gamecock is the bravest thing in the world."[27]

Beaufort became famous in the antebellum years as a center of education for the youth of the planter families. Children from across the lowcountry would stay with relatives or pay room and board with friends or acquaintances in order to attend one of Beaufort's several schools. Beaufort had a male seminary to educate young men, and at various times different private schools were conducted by lawyers in the town. In 1852, the Beaufort Female Seminary was chartered with Thomas Fuller, Lewis Reeve Sams, Jacob Guerard, Robert W. Barnwell, Stephen Elliott, Henry M. Stuart, Edmund Rhett, Henry M. Fuller, and Benjamin Johnson as trustees.[28] So successful was Beaufort's educational system that George Parsons Elliott could claim in 1857 that they could not find a single white man or woman native to St. Helena Parish who could not read or write; so literate was the population that 33,120 newspapers and 3,460 magazines were distributed through the Beaufort Post Office each year.[29]

The most famous of Beaufort's schools was, of course, Beaufort College chartered in 1795 and opened in 1803. The college closed in 1817 because it was thought to have been the source of the yellow fever epidemic. It opened again in 1820 and operated for the rest of the antebellum era. The college had a distinguished reputation throughout the South and sent its graduates on to degrees from Harvard, Yale, Princeton, Brown, and the South Carolina College, as well as schools in Europe. After 1841, the principal was John Fielding, an ex-Roman Catholic priest who caned the young men mercilessly. Dr. Hal Stuart recalled being unable to eat his breakfast for fear of the flogging he was sure to receive from Fielding. Joseph Barnwell remembered his texts at the college: *Walker's Dictionary,* Peter Parley's *History of the United States,* Comstock's *Philosophy,* Davis's *Arithmetic,* and classical works on Roman history and Greek mythology. Every Friday several students delivered public orations. In 1852, a new Greek Revival college building was built, designed by Major John Gibbes Barnwell II. The year before, Barnwell also designed and constructed the new arsenal building on Craven Street.[30]

These two public structures were the beginning of a great building boom in Beaufort during the 1850s. The rising prosperity of the planters, due to the second cotton boom, prompted many of the sea island cotton magnates to build a number of very large and sumptuous villas in Beaufort. The Castle was built by Dr. Joseph Johnson in 1850. Dr. Berners Barnwell Sams built his town house on the Green in 1852, and Edward Means built his fine Charleston-style brick house across the Green, in 1853. In 1856, Lewis Reeve Sams built his town house on Bay and New Streets, Colonel Paul Hamilton built the Oaks on the Green, and "Proud Edgar" Fripp built his Victorian mansion, Tidalholm, on the bend of the

Beaufort River at the eastern extremity of the town. This was a large number of major new construction projects for the town in just a few years and was indicative of the buoyant economy of the sea islands in the last decade before the Civil War.[31]

The two largest mercantile businesses on Bay Street on the eve of the Civil War were the store of William Morcock on the corner of Bay and West Streets and the cotton brokerage firm of Legare and Colcock. Morcock's business included a dry goods store, a steam-powered grist mill, and three cotton gins. At the wharf behind his store, he also managed the lucrative franchise for the White Hall Ferry to Lady's Island.[32] The partnership of Legare and Colcock brokered the sea island cotton, arranged for its shipment to Charleston aboard the steamers *Edisto* and *Cecile,* and provided dry goods on credit for the planters. William Henry Brisbane recalled that the local planters were so self-sufficient with their own fields, gardens, and orchards that there was no market for fresh fruit, vegetables, or meat in Beaufort.[33]

Beaufort had never had a bank on Bay Street before the 1850s. Prior to that time the merchants and cotton factors had acted as bankers by maintaining lines of credit and offering loans at interest to the planters. In 1852, the Beaufort Loan and Building Association was chartered by the South Carolina legislature. The directors of Beaufort's first bank were Edmund Rhett, Thomas O. Barnwell, John A. Johnson, A. McNeir Cunningham, William B. Means, E. J. Durban, David L. Thompson, and John M. Baker.

In the 1840s, another village began to develop on St. Helena Island exclusively for the planters of that prosperous island. It was called St. Helenaville and was located on a high bluff on the west bank of Village Creek overlooking the Morgan River and St. Helena Sound. Small frame summer homes began to spring up along the bluff where they could catch the sea breezes. There was also a pine forest on the high clay land at the north end of St. Helena Island. During the antebellum era the high pine forests were considered much more salubrious than the lower, sandier oak and palmetto lands. At St. Helenaville, a small clapboard chapel was built as an Episcopal church, and the minister, Reverend David McElheran and his wife, Ann, operated a school there and boarded some of the children at their home. The Popes, Jenkins, Fripps, Coffins, Chaplins, and other St. Helena Island cotton planters had summer cottages at St. Helenaville and sent their children to the McElherans for primary education. The village had the advantage of being close enough to attend to the plantation during the day and the family in the evening.[34] St. Helenaville no longer exists, though. The homes collapsed into the creek as a result of erosion and storm damage from the hurricane of 1893, but the bank and creek are still littered with foundation brick.

In St. Luke's Parish in the 1820s, many planter families from Hilton Head and the adjacent mainland plantations began building modest summer resort cottages along the spectacular forty-foot bluff with a commanding view of a beautiful bend of the May River. For many years this community was known simply as May River. Sometimes it was called Kirk's Bluff after the adjacent plantation of James Kirk Sr., one of the great cotton planters of the parish. A school was operating at Kirk's Bluff in 1825 known as the May River Academy. Later, this school was operated by Professor Hugh Train from Scotland. The South Carolina poet Henry Timrod taught there for a few years. The location had a local reputation for having a particularly healthy climate. In 1841, there were only a few summer homes there. By 1843, however, there was regular steamboat service to Bluffton from Savannah. In 1844, a meeting of the citizens proclaimed the community to be officially renamed Bluffton, which it has been called ever since. That same year, the citizens of St. Luke's Parish gathered under the spreading oak at the Verdier place to hear Dr. Daniel Heyward Hamilton of Bluffton and Robert Barnwell Rhett exhort the citizens to form a political movement for the secession of South Carolina from the union. By the 1850s, the Popes, Stoneys, Kirks, Verdiers, Heyward, Lynahs, Pritchards, Guerards, and other local planter families had summer homes at Bluffton. During the 1850s, the streets were laid out, and in 1852, the town was incorporated by act of the South Carolina legislature. In 1857, the Episcopal Church of the Cross was built to replace the earlier chapel. It was built in the Victorian gothic style popular at the time for a cost of five thousand dollars. The first rector was Reverend James Stoney. There was also a large Methodist Church in Bluffton. In 1863, much of the village and most of the antebellum summer homes were burned in a raid by Union troops from Hilton Head.[35]

The rice planters of upper St. Luke's Parish also created their own summer resort village in the center of their plantation neighborhood. Grahamville grew in a tall pine forest on the land of Captain John Graham. It was located at a crossroads where the highway from Coosawhatchie to Purrysburg crossed the road from Heyward's Bridge to Robertville. Not far from Grahamville was the site of the old Euhaws Baptist Church, which had served the region since 1752. During the antebellum years, the Baptists moved their church to Grahamville. In 1834, the Episcopal Church of the Holy Trinity was founded in Grahamville. Reverend Arthur Wigfall was the rector in the 1850s. A friendly rivalry developed between the two congregations of neighbors, friends, and relatives. Mrs. E. R. Schoolcraft, author of *The Black Gauntlet*, was raised as a Baptist in Grahamville and recalled being taught that the Baptists were closer to God because their prayers came from the heart and not from a book. As with all the planter villages, a school for the children was one of the primary functions of the community. The Grahamville School Academy was established in 1830 and functioned throughout the antebellum era. During the 1850s, Mr. Watson taught at the Boys Academy and Miss Dupont taught at the Girls Academy. Most of the large rice planters of the area—Screven, Bull, Heyward, Hazzard, Bolan, Howard, Huguenin, Strohbart, Dupont, Gregorie, Hasell, Glover, and others—had summer homes there. The most important event in the antebellum history of Grahamville was the completion of the Charleston and Savannah railroad in 1860. A station on the line was placed less than two miles from Grahamville at Gopher Hill. Much of Grahamville was destroyed by Union forces in 1865, and after the Civil War the present town of Ridgeland grew up around the railroad station.[36]

Also in St. Luke's Parish was Gillisonville. During the 1830s, many rice-planting families around Coosawhatchie began to build summer homes in the high pine forest between Coosawhatchie and Beaver Dam Creek. Cheneys, Davants, Fergusons, Tillinghasts, and other nearby planters built cottages among the pines. The village took the name of Derry Gillison, a Coosawhatchie shoe-maker and founder of a wealthy rice-planting family. In 1836, after years of complaints from lawyers about the unhealthy location of the Beaufort District Courthouse at Coosawhatchie, the district court was moved to Gillisonville, and a courthouse square was developed as the center of the village. A large and imposing Baptist church was built there in the 1840s, the successor to the Coosawhatchie Baptist Church. In 1852, the Episcopal Church of the Ascension was established at Gillisonville and, in 1860, Masonic Lodge Number 98 was chartered there. Lodge members included T. W. Gillison, J. B. Porcher, John Ferebee, T. E. Screven, T. S. Bolan, William Zealy, A. M. Speights, and Dedrich Peterman. Peterman had immigrated from Germany and, during the 1850s, built a large brick hotel and tavern on the east side of the courthouse square. Gillisonville was the site of the monthly district muster as well as regular court proceedings. Muster days were always good business days for the tavern. One traveler in 1860 noted that on muster day, "In the evening all the rowdies got tight, good deal of noise, a little fighting ... many left drunk on the field." All of Gillisonville, including the Beaufort District Court and its records since 1789, was burned by Union troops in 1865. Only the Baptist church was left standing.[37]

The planters of St. Peter's Parish developed two villages on the old Augusta Road in upper St. Peter's Parish. Robertville was the commercial crossroads of the early antebellum years described in chapter 16. By the late antebellum period, the social, religious, and education center of upper St. Peter's Parish had moved to Lawtonville. This village began to form when the congregation of the old Pipe Creek Baptist Church moved to Lawtonville in 1826, under the leadership of Reverend Winborn Lawton. In 1833, Lawtonville was established as a post office, and in the early 1840s, the Lawtonville Academy was founded possibly by George Rhodes, later a prominent planter and politician. In 1843, the Pipe Creek Baptist congregation built a new church building at Lawtonville. It was around these institutions that the village grew.[38] Lawtonville, however, could not accurately be termed a "resort village" since most of the planters in that area could not afford second homes and those that could already had plantation homes on high, healthy ground. Most of Lawtonville was burned by Union troops in 1865, and, after the Civil War, the completion of the railroad from Columbia to Savannah moved the center of the community to the present town of Estill.

The antebellum summer resort village for the planters of lower Prince William Parish was McPhersonville. This village was also built on high ground away from the rice fields in the midst of a tall pine forest. General John McPherson and Congressman James Elliott McPherson were among the first to recognize the health and comfort of the location and build resort homes there. The site was not far from the location of Captain James McPherson's original cowpen and ranger post of 1726. During the antebellum years, many Prince William Parish rice-planting families established summer homes in McPhersonville, among them the Draytons, McCleods, Mackeys, Brailsfords, Palmers, DeSaussures, Colcocks, Hutsons, and Gregories. In 1832, the old Stoney Creek Presbyterian congregation built a church at McPhersonville which stands today. This and the small Episcopal Chapel of Ease became the centers of village life. Charles DeSaussure, son of Dr. Louis McPherson DeSaussure, was born in McPhersonville in 1846 and recalled his youth in the village. All the families were simple and unpretentious but quite well-to-do. He described the summer homes as "low, broad, wide houses with large rooms and very broad piazzas, running almost entirely around the house and eaves extending about five feet beyond the edge of the piazza, forming what was called a 'sunshed.' These houses were neither lathed nor plastered nor finished inside with ceiling, but were whitewashed inside and out every spring. Those spacious houses had ordinary pine floors which were covered with fine china matting in white and red squares, checkerboard fashion." All these summer cottages had large yards outlined by a low fence. In McPhersonville the houses were irregularly spread around the pine forest at 100- to 400-yard intervals. The planters would leave in the morning by horse or buggy to tend to their plantations, and the families would regularly take carriage rides on the high road that split the village. There was no school at McPhersonville, and the children were tutored at home. When DeSaussure was eleven years old, his father sold the cottage in McPhersonville and bought a house in Beaufort so that the boy could go to school.[39]

Baptist Church of Beaufort, organized in 1804 and built in 1844. This photograph shows the church as it appeared in 1864 (courtesy of the Parris Island Museum Collection).

Henry Farmer House, Beaufort, built ca. 1810, was the home of the Reverend Richard Fuller from 1831 to 1847 (photo by Robert W. Jenkins).

Robert W. Barnwell House, Beaufort, built ca. 1810 (with an addition ca. 1855), as it appeared during the Civil War (Beaufort County Public Library Collection).

Episcopal Church of the Holy Trinity, Grahamville, St. Luke's Parish, built ca. 1856 (photo by Robert W. Jenkins).

Gillisonville Baptist Church, St. Luke's Parish, built in 1838 (photo by Robert W. Jenkins).

William Baynard Mausoleum, Zion Chapel of Ease Cemetery, Hilton Head Island, St. Luke's Parish. The mausoleum was built in 1846 (photo by Robert W. Jenkins).

Church of the Cross, Bluffton, St. Luke's Parish. The building was completed in 1857 (photo by Robert W. Jenkins).

St. Luke's Church, St. Luke's Parish, constructed ca. 1824. This church is often called Bull Hill Church because of its location at John Bull's plantation. Episcopal services were discontinued in 1857 when the Church of the Cross was completed. Since 1875 the building has served as a Methodist church (photo by Robert W. Jenkins).

Stoney Creek Presbyterian Chapel, built ca. 1833, McPhersonville, Prince William Parish (photo by Robert W. Jenkins).

Old Fort Plantation House, Port Royal Island, built ca. 1800, with an allée of magnolias. This plantation, owned by John Joyner Smith, is shown as it appeared during the Civil War (Reed Collection, Beaufort County Public Library).

A pole fence at Habersham Plantation, Port Royal Island, as it appeared during the Civil War (Reed Collection, Beaufort County Public Library).

Tabby ruins of Spring Island Plantation House, built ca. 1812 in St. Luke's Parish. Spring Island was the country seat of George Barksdale Edwards, the largest sea island cotton planter in the Beaufort District (photo by Robert W. Jenkins).

The Arsenal at Beaufort, built in 1795 and remodeled in 1851, as it appeared ca. 1898 (Beaufort County Public Library Collection).

Beaufort College, chartered in 1795 and built in 1852, as it appeared during the Civil War (Historic Beaufort Foundation Collection).

Beaufort Female Seminary, built ca. 1855, as it appeared during the Civil War (Beaufort County Public Library Collection).

COUNTRY PLANTERS

One characteristic of the antebellum Beaufort District not acknowledged by historians is the existence of a large number of small planters and yeoman farmers in the southern parishes. Without the economic resources to afford second homes in the resort villages, they spent their lives and raised their children on their small plantations and farms. They visited the villages only occasionally and conducted their business at the country stores. On Sundays, they attended the Baptist and Methodist country churches. These were the country planters of the district. The great planters almost always had real estate whose value exceeded twenty thousand dollars. Overall in the district, fifty-five of the 881 plantations, or 6.2 percent, were valued in excess of twenty thousand dollars in 1850. On the other end of the economic scale, 415 planters, or 47 percent of the planters, had plantations or farms valued at less than fifteen hundred dollars. While the average number of slaves per plantation was 34.3, these country planters often had fewer than ten slaves. Almost all the planters in the district, large or small, owned some slaves.

The country planters were fairly concentrated in the upper portions of St. Peter's and Prince William Parish. A breakdown of distribution of real estate value by parishes reveals the following:

No. of Plantations/Farm Units		No. less than $1,500	Percentage
St. Peter's	272	182	66
Prince William	270	144	53
St. Luke's	188	72	38
St. Helena	151	17	11[40]

This gives a different sociological character to those neighborhoods where the country planters were dominant. The census of 1850 also reveals much about the nature of their lives and circumstances.

Jacob Lightsey was a country planter in upper Prince William Parish near Broxton Ford where the Orangeburg Road crossed the Salkehatchie River. His plantation was 376 acres, only 100 acres of which was cleared for planting. There he lived with his family and twelve slaves. His real estate was worth $850, and his tools were valued at $170. His livestock consisted of five horses, seven dairy cows, fourteen cattle, fifteen sheep, and fifty hogs worth $460. From this small plantation he produced 600 bushels of corn, 50 bushels of oats, 675 pounds of rice, 25 pounds of wool, 100 bushels of peas and beans, 130 bushels of sweet potatoes, 10 pounds of honey and beeswax, and 7 bales of cotton. While this produce was ample to provide for his family and slaves, Lightsey's income from seven bales of cotton was $308, approximately equivalent to the salary of a plantation manager on a larger lowcountry plantation.

Many small country planters produced virtually no cash crops and operated mere subsistence farms. Four miles south of William McBride's store, the principal commercial establishment in upper Prince William Parish, next to the Hickory Hill Post Office, was the plantation of Abram Peeples. He owned 737 acres, only 50 acres of which was cleared for planting. Peeples owned three slaves. He had two horses, ten dairy cows, twenty-three cattle, forty sheep, and seventy-five hogs worth $575. This small plantation produced 9 bushels of wheat, 100 bushels of corn, 20 bushels of oats, 675 pounds of rice, 10 bushels of peas and beans, 200 pounds of wool, and 300 bushels of sweet potatoes. Peeples produced no cotton or other cash crops. This was virtually a subsistence farm for his family and three slaves.

Another country planter in upper Prince William Parish was James Deloach, whose three-hundred-acre plantation, valued at six hundred dollars, was two miles north of McBride's store and the Hickory Hill Post Office. Only 80 acres of James Deloach's plantation was cleared in 1850. He had five slaves to help him with the work. James Deloach owned two horses, five dairy cows, eight cattle, and fifty hogs worth $415. His plantation produced 15 bushels of wheat, 300 bushels of corn, 30 bushels of oats, 200 bushels of sweet potatoes, 30 pounds of butter, 20 pounds of molasses, 200 pounds of sugar cane, and 1,440 pounds of rice. Deloach produced no cotton on his plantation, and if he had marketed all the rice and sugar cane he produced, he would have earned only sixty dollars.[41]

Many similar examples can be drawn from upper St. Peter's Parish across the Coosawhatchie swamp. Washington Goettee was a small cotton planter with 200 acres of fields and fourteen slaves on the west side of the Coosawhatchie swamp near Goettee's Mill. With an additional 1,500 acres of undeveloped land, Goettee's plantation was valued at fifteen hundred dollars. His livestock consisted of five horses, ten dairy cows, thirty cattle, forty sheep, and fifty hogs worth $350. Goettee produced 400 bushels of corn, 40 bushels of oats, 230 pounds of rice, 40 pounds of wool, 200 bushels of sweet potatoes, and eighty dollars worth of slaughtered animals. His cash crop of six bales of cotton would have produced $264 worth of income in 1850.

An example of a small rice plantation in upper St. Peter's was that of Lawrence McKenzie. He owned 450 acres of land worth twelve hundred dollars. Nearly half the land was cleared and planted. McKenzie owned twenty-four slaves, who produced 200 bushels of corn, 10 bushels of oats, 10 bushels of peas and beans, 600 bushels of sweet potatoes, 40 pounds of butter, and fifty dollars worth of slaughtered animals. His principal crop was rice, of which he produced 16,000 pounds. If he sold it all he would have earned $54.40.

Country planters such as these were the vast majority in the upper part of the Beaufort District. Most had some slaves and still lived in the frontier log homes built by their fathers earlier in the century. One sign of rising prosperity was when they stockpiled enough boards from their own forests and their own labor to replace the original log homestead with a clapboard house, often turning the old structure into a barn. Some of these country planters could make enough money to buy their lumber from James Speight's sawmill on the Coosawhatchie River. Those with an eye to the future built their new homes with the abundant cypress from the Salkehatchie, Coosawhatchie, and Savannah River swamps.

The country planters of upper Prince William and upper St. Peter's Parishes created their own rural world. They socialized at McBride's store and the adjacent Hickory Hill Post Office next to the Coosawhatchie Swamp. They gathered for muster at the field next to Belger's Crossroads west of Mulligan's Ford. They bought their dry goods at Solomon's store on the old Augusta Road near Boggy Gut in St. Peter's Parish, at Huggin's store near Broxton Ford, or at Spear's store on the high road between Whippy Swamp and the Salkehatchie River. They ground their corn at Goettee's Mill west of the Coosawhatchie Swamp. They drank at Clifton's Tavern next to Alligator Branch or at Vasser's Tavern west of the Salkehatchie Swamp. They went to church at the Beech Branch, Lawtonville, Robertville, and Pipe Creek Baptist Churches in St. Peter's Parish; at the Beaver Dam Baptist Church in upper St. Luke's Parish; or at the Salkehatchie Presbyterian Church next to Vasser's Tavern or the Burnt Church two miles up the road in Prince William Parish.

The rising prosperity of the 1850s saw much of this rural life in transition. Some of these country planters could improve their circumstances with a single crop. R. B. Youmans of Prince William Parish produced twenty-seven bales of cotton, in addition to provisioning crops, with fourteen slaves on 200 cleared acres in 1850. His income was $1,188, enough to elevate him to more comfortable circumstances and, if he could sustain it, to a higher status in lowcountry society.

The country planters of the antebellum Beaufort District were squarely in the middle class by national and state standards. Their interests were tied almost exclusively to their land and their slaves. Unlike the great planters of the coast, they did not have town houses in Charleston or Savannah, or summer villas in Beaufort, Bluffton, McPhersonville, or Flat Rock, North Carolina. There was certainly no excess money for travel in the north or overseas. For these small planters, and a host of larger but "middling" sort of cotton planters on the coast, there was no escape from the torpor of summer, and no escape from the subtle suspicion and sullen resentment of the slaves that surrounded them all.

James Hamilton Jr., one of the great rice planters of the lower Savannah, was forced to spend the summer of 1817 on his wife's Calliwassie Island plantation. In his letters to her he referred to the "gloom of the plantation" in the summer. It was a psychological as well as a meteorological assessment. In 1861, J. J. Pringle-Smith, forced by circumstances to remain on his Beech Hill rice plantation after all the other planters had withdrawn to their town houses, lamented his being "alone . . . on the river."[42]

Hamilton and Smith were among the great planters who could usually escape the circumstances that made them uncomfortable and leave the unpleasantness to managers and overseers. The small and "middling" country planters did not have the resources to move about, and while their circumstances were comfortable and self-reliant, many felt trapped on their plantations. They were too rich in land and slaves to simply abandon their lives and head west as millions of Americans were doing in the 1850s. But they were too poor to hire managers and overseers and move into more polite urban society. In addition, most of the small planters did not have the education necessary to pursue business or professional careers and thus achieve the mobility of the upper class. In short, the economic realities of the antebellum Beaufort District glued these small planters to their land and slaves. It was all they had and all they knew.

The effects of these circumstances were both psychological and political. The psychological effect is excellently revealed in Theodore Rosengarten's *Tombee: Portrait of a Cotton Planter*. Thomas B. Chaplin was a descendant of one of St. Helena Island's pioneer families. The Chaplins prospered from the first cotton boom, and a large estate was divided among a numerous progeny. Some did well and some did not. Benjamin Chaplin, Thomas B. Chaplin's "Uncle Ben," became one of the great planters of the Beaufort District. And Thomas Chaplin started his planting career with high hopes and excellent family and social connections. But the economic troubles of the 1840s forced him to sell slaves and reduce his planting operation. Thereafter, beset by family health problems and financial troubles, he was never able to rise above a middling rank. In 1850, he had 406 acres and twenty-five slaves. Chaplin could not afford a plantation manager, had no town house of his own, and had little money for travel to Charleston or Savannah, let alone the North Carolina mountains or European capitals. When he escaped his plantation, it was because of the charity of his relatives, who had summer homes in Charleston, Beaufort, and St. Helenaville. In 1855 and 1856, he had to teach his children at home because he could not afford to board them in Beaufort, and he complained that the "regulations of schools are opposed to the diffusion of learning among those not rich." Chaplin often complained of friends and relatives richer than he, and, though the routine of the plantation went on year after year and his circumstances were not uncomfortable, he often saw himself as a failure. In 1851, he wrote, "I feel quite wretched today, nothing but trouble, trouble, trouble enough to break the spirit of any man. I feel very much like giving way altogether."[43]

Chaplin and all the other small planters of the Beaufort District were tied to their land and their slaves. Most were less resentful and less unhappy than Chaplin because most were surrounded by neighbors in similar circumstances rather than neighbors and relatives who were more fortunate. Almost all these small planters were self-sufficient in the basic necessities of life, and many were improving their opportunities every year during the 1850s. In short, they controlled their own worlds. As the Civil War approached, however, they saw national political events threatening their world. Swept along by the tide of events they could not control, they reacted to protect all that they had accumulated. And abolition was the specter they could not abide. With their fortunes fixed in the lowcountry, and lacking the liquidity to move and start over, they feared finding themselves in a world dominated by blacks, like the West Indian planters before them. Naturally they sought solace from political and religious leaders who shared their interest and offered them courage and comfort.

THE RAILROAD ERA

The Beaufort District was one of the richest agricultural areas of the South. And it was virtually all rural; only a few small villages interrupted the pastoral tapestry of fields, forests, islands, and swamps. Most of the commercial services traditionally provided by urban centers were found outside the Beaufort District in Charleston and Savannah. Among some of the large planters, there was hostility to the very idea of industrialization. The larger sea island cotton planters refused to use machines to gin their cotton, believing that the contraptions damaged the silky fiber. Instead they built long ginning houses and employed their ample labor force to remove each seed by hand and pack the cotton in loose bags. As a consequence the effects of the industrial revolution were slow in coming to the southern parishes. By the census of 1840, all the machinery in the Beaufort District was worth only $31,620.[44] The only significant mechanized operations in the district were the three steam-powered rice mills on the Savannah River, James Speight's sawmill on the Coosawhatchie Swamp, and at least one steam cotton gin in Beaufort. Only the steam paddlewheelers, which had plied the inland passage and the Savannah River since 1816, reminded these planters of the momentous changes that were affecting the rest of the country. The story was told about Nathaniel Heyward of Combahee that when he fell sick in 1846 his personal physician Dr. Ogier came from Charleston to carry him back to the city on a steam launch. The slaves who had never seen such a machine became frightened.[45] But in the last decade before the Civil War, the "gloomy iron idols" of industry, as Edmund Rhett of Beaufort called them, began to appear.

Several factors in the late antebellum era encouraged nascent industrial development. First, during the 1840s, the state government encouraged and finally assisted the construction of several railroads in South Carolina believing they would stimulate commerce and boost the flagging agricultural economy.[46] Secondly, during the 1850s, many of the great planters, reaping profits from the second cotton boom, sought to diversify their assets. Nathaniel Heyward financed the South Carolina Bank, James Hamilton Jr. organized the South Carolina Land Company to invest in Texas, Colonel William Lawton planned a textile mill for St. Peter's Parish, and the enterprising Dr. James Proctor Screven invested in the Merchant's and Planter's Bank and the Planter's Hotel in Savannah and became president of the Savannah, Albany and Gulf Railroad. In 1853, Edmund Martin, John G. Lawton, William J. Lawton, Benjamin Lawton, John Richardson, John R. Johnson, and Thomas Johnson put up thirty thousand dollars to form the Savannah River Steamboat Company.[47]

The real symbol of the early industrial revolution was the railroad. During the 1850s, two railroads were organized to run through the Beaufort District. On December 5, 1853, the state legislature authorized the incorporation of the Charleston and Savannah Railroad Company with initial capitalization of $1.5 million. Two weeks later, on December 20, 1853, the legislature authorized the incorporation of the Branchville and Savannah Railroad Company with an initial capitalization of $1 million. The Branchville and Savannah Railroad was never built. It was planned to run from Branchville west to Barnwell; down the east bank of the Savannah River through Pipe Creek, Lawtonville, Robertville, and Purrysburg; and then across the river to Savannah. Commissioners for the proposed railroad through the Beaufort District were all the leading planters along the route. Commissioners at Moore's Cross Roads (Pipe Creek) were B. W. Lawton, John M. Allen, and William M. Bostick; at Whippy Swamp were B. McBride, Thomas Willingham, and John J. Harrison; at Lawtonville were George Rhodes and Edmund Martin; at Robertville were J. Lartigue, Alexander J. Lawton, and Charles Jaudon; and at Purrysburg were John P. Raymond, John Meriff, and Joseph Hassell.

The Charleston and Savannah Railroad was built and began to operate on the very eve of the Civil War. The Charleston and Savannah Railroad was one of the great strategic prizes during the Civil War, and its influence after the war was to alter the geographical and commercial nature of the district. It was not open long enough before the war to have much impact, though. The building of the Charleston and Savannah Railroad was by far the largest single construction project and the largest industrial undertaking in the district. And the principal investors included many of the great planters. In 1856, the president of the railroad was Thomas Fenwick Drayton of Hilton Head, and the directors were W. Porcher Miles, William Kirkwood, William F. Colcock, Otis Mills, C. G. Memminger, L. T. Potter, J. B. Campbell, W. E. Martin, Edmund Rhett, and Henry Gourdin (from South Carolina) and William Hodgson and R. Bradley (from Savannah). On the eve of the Civil War, William Colcock of St. Luke's Parish was the new president.[48]

Slaves were employed across the Beaufort District, under contract with their owners, to lay the route and construct the causeways and trestles across the Combahee, Coosawhatchie, and Savannah River swamps. By 1858, the project was well under way. The Savannah newspapers reported that "the Savannah Railroad is at last in a way of speedy success." The trestles and causeways were then being graded, and the bridges across the Ashepoo and Edisto Rivers were under construction. By October 1859, the Savannah River was the last link in the "unbroken communication between Charleston and Savannah." The problem with bridging the Savannah River was that the bridge had to open to allow boat traffic. In November 1859, the SS *Headly* brought the great iron caissons from New Jersey to construct the last bridge. The bridge across the Savannah River was eleven hundred feet long and was located thirteen miles north of Savannah. By May 1860, the rails had reached the Savannah River, and, on April 21, 1860, the first through passengers on the Charleston and Savannah Railroad arrived in Savannah. They had had to travel the last ten miles by steamboat because the bridge was not completed for another year.[49] The completion of the Charleston and Savannah Railroad was the exclamation point to the enterprise of the antebellum Beaufort District.

NOTES

1. Lewis Cecil Gray, *History of Agriculture in the Southern United States to 1860*, 2 vols. (Gloucester, Mass.: Peter Smith, 1958), 2: 827–28.

2. Stephen B. Barnwell, *The Story of an American Family* (Marquette, Mich.: Privately printed, 1969), 59.

3. 7th Census (1850), Beaufort District Agriculture Schedule, South Carolina Department of Archives and History.

4. Except where otherwise noted, the following figures and statistics are from the 7th Census (1850), Beaufort District Agriculture Schedule, South Carolina Department of Archives and History, and the 7th Census (1850), Beaufort District Slave Schedule, South Carolina Department of Archives and History.

5. 7th Census (1850), Beaufort District Slave Schedule, South Carolina Department of Archives and History.

6. Thomas Aston Coffin Plantation Book, South Carolina Historical Society.

7. Theodore Rosengarten, *Tombee: Portrait of a Cotton Planter* (New York: Morrow, 1986), 116.

8. The Slave Schedule for 1850 lists two separate groups of slaves, one group of 133 slaves and another of 139 slaves, both owned by Benjamin Chaplin Sr.

9. Grace Fox Perry, *Moving Finger of Jasper* (Ridgeland, S.C.: Confederate Centennial Committee, 1947), 94.

10. Chalmers Davidson, *The Last Foray: The South Carolina Planters of 1860, A Sociological Study* (Columbia: University of South Carolina Press, 1971), 195.

11. All statistics for St. Luke's Parish are from *The Census of 1850 of St. Luke's Parish, Beaufort County* (Bluffton: Historic Preservation Society, 1984).

12. Barnwell, *Story of an American Family*, 189.

13. Davidson, *The Last Foray*, 149.

14. 7th Census (1850), Beaufort District Agriculture Schedule, St. Peter's Parish, South Carolina Department of Archives and History.

15. James Kilgo, *Pipe Creek to Matthew's Bluff: A Short History of Groton Plantation* (Estill, S.C.: Privately printed for the Winthrop Family, 1988), 63; *Biographical Directory of the South Carolina Senate*, 2: 1061.

16. Annie Elizabeth Miller, *Our Family Circle: Being a Reunion of Our House of Langrave Thomas Smith, House of Robert, House of Bostick, House of Lawton, House of Grimball, House of Erwin, House of Stafford, House of Maner, including Screvens, Jaudons, Rhodes, Daniels, Willinghams, Baynards, Polhills, Goldwires, and Caters* (Hilton Head: Lawton and Allied Families Association, 1987), 302.

17. Duncan Clinch Heyward, *Seed from Madagascar* (1937; rpt. ed. Columbia: University of South Carolina Press, 1993), 62–72; *Biographical Directory of the South Carolina House*, 3: 333–35.

18. *Biographical Directory of the South Carolina House*, 4: 394–96.

19. *Biographical Directory of the South Carolina Senate*, 1: 720–21; Davidson, *The Last Foray*, 210.

20. Barnwell, *Story of an American Family*, 143.

21. Davidson, *The Last Foray*, 210.

22. Barnwell, *Story of an American Family*, 58.

23. Barnwell, *Story of an American Family*, 62.

24. Miller, *Our Family Circle*, 359.

25. Thomas Cooper and David J. McCord, eds., *The Statutes at Large of South Carolina*, 10 vols. (Columbia: A. S. Johnston, 1836–1841), 8: 456.

26. *Acts of the General Assembly, 1850–1859* (Columbia: R. W. Gibbs, 1859), South Caroliniana Library, 705.

27. Francis Richard Lubbock, *Six Decades in Texas: or Memoirs of Francis Richard Lubbock, Governor of Texas in Wartime: A Personal Experience in Business, War and Politics* (Austin: Ben C. Jones, 1900), 7.

28. Cooper and McCord, eds., *Statutes of South Carolina*, 7: 194–95.

29. Guion Griffis Johnson, *Social History of the Sea Islands* (Chapel Hill: University of North Carolina Press, 1930), 115.

30. Barnwell, *Story of an American Family,* 63, 76.

31. *Historic Beaufort: A Guide to the Gracious Homes, Churches, and Other Points of Interest of Beaufort, South Carolina* (Beaufort: Historic Beaufort Foundation, 1977).

32. "Will of Susan Aggnew Morcock," December 9, 1861, Barnwell District Court.

33. Miller, *Our Family Circle,* 359.

34. Edith M. Dabbs, *Sea Island Diary: A History of St. Helena Island* (Spartanburg: Reprint Co., 1983), 98; Rosengarten, *Tombee,* 175.

35. *A Longer Short History of Bluffton, South Carolina, and Its Environs* (Hilton Head: Bluffton Historical Preservation Society, 1988), 8, 28; Mary P. Powell, *Over Home: The Heritage of Pinckneys of Pinckney Colony, Bluffton, South Carolina* (Columbia: R. L. Bryan, 1982), 146–47.

36. Cooper and McCord, eds., *Statutes at Large,* 8: 369; Perry, *Moving Finger of Jasper,* 32–42.

37. Perry, *Moving Finger of Jasper,* 28–29. Some controversy exists about the loss of the county records. The other version is that they were packed up by retreating Confederates and taken to Columbia, where they were burned in February 1865.

38. Coy K. Johnston, *Two Centuries of Lawtonville Baptists, 1775–1975* (Columbia: State Printing Co., 1974), 52–54.

39. Charles DeSaussure, "The Story of My Life Before the War Between the States," family manuscript provided by Charles A. DeSaussure of Gainesville, Ga.; Perry, *Moving Finger of Jasper,* 50–52.

40. Unless otherwise noted, all statistics are compiled from 7th Census of the United States (1850), Beaufort District Agriculture Schedule, South Carolina Department of Archives and History; and Slave Schedules, National Archives.

41. It should be noted that other members of the Peeples and Deloach families were much larger planters. Edward H. Peeples, for example, had eighty-six slaves in 1850.

42. Lawrence S. Rowland, "Alone on the River: The Savannah River Rice Plantations of St. Peter's Parish, South Carolina," *South Carolina Historical Magazine* 88 (July 1987): 121.

43. Rosengarten, *Tombee,* 514, 521, 652.

44. John R. Todd and Francis M. Hutson, *Prince William Parish and Plantations* (Richmond: Garrett and Massie, 1935), 37.

45. Heyward, *Seed from Madagascar,* 70.

46. Lacy K. Ford, *Origins of Southern Radicalism: The South Carolina Upcountry, 1800–1860* (New York: Oxford University Press, 1988), 219–43.

47. Cooper and McCord, eds., *Statutes at Large,* 7: 470.

48. *Savannah Daily Morning News,* January 19, 1856, Georgia Historical Society.

49. *Savannah Daily Morning News,* October 6, 1859; November 21, 1859; March 2, 1859; April 21, 1859, Georgia Historical Society.

21

The Mind
of Antebellum Beaufort

One of the most admirable results of the great wealth produced in the Beaufort District in the antebellum years was the flowering of an intellectual community of significant notice throughout the South. The old town of Beaufort was known not only as a place of significant educational institutions but also as the home of some of the best-known literary luminaries of the Old South. South Carolina historian Edward McCrady described antebellum Beaufort as "the wealthiest, most aristocratic and cultivated town of its size in America. A town which though small in number of inhabitants produced statesmen, scholars, sailors and divines whose name and fame are known throughout the country."[1]

The most significant institution in the cultural life of the sea islands was Beaufort College (1803–1861). Two of the early principals of the college were among South Carolina's premier nineteenth-century intellectuals and educators, James L. Petigru and Martin Luther Hurlbut. By the late antebellum period, South Carolina's best-known writer, William Gilmore Simms, rated Beaufort College as "highly creditable."[2] The college functioned as a preparatory school, and its graduates went on to attend the South Carolina College, Harvard, Yale, Princeton, and West Point. Twenty-five young men from Beaufort attended Harvard during the antebellum years. More young men from the Beaufort District attended the South Carolina College than from any district in the state except Charleston and Columbia. On the eve of the Civil War, when Northern colleges became less popular with Beaufort families, a number of young men chose to attend the University of Virginia. Between 1850 and 1860, twenty-one sons of Beaufort families attended that school. Almost all of these young men had been educated at Beaufort College.[3]

In addition to Beaufort College there were several other schools of note in the area. Milton Maxcy operated a classical school for young men; there were a number of primary schools that operated during the antebellum years; and the Beaufort Female Seminary provided education for the planters' daughters. As a consequence, antebellum Beaufort became, in addition to a planter's summer resort, a bit of a mecca for raising families and educating the youth of the region. Charles A. DeSaussure recalled moving from his boyhood home of McPhersonville in Prince William Parish to the town of Beaufort when he and his brother became teenagers so they could attend the Beaufort schools.[4] Likewise, Governor Francis Lubbock of Texas was educated at Beaufort College in the 1820s. Lubbock's father, Capt. Henry W. Lubbock, was briefly a practicing physician in Beaufort and was the captain and part-owner of the steam paddlewheeler *Commerce,* which made the first through passage from Charleston to Augusta. Francis Lubbock was raised at the home of his maternal grandmother, Mrs. Francis Saltus, and educated in several Beaufort schools. After a lifetime of adventure and achievement, Governor Lubbock recalled his boyhood in Beaufort as some of his happiest years: "through all these years, Beaufort has been one of the pleasures of my memory."[5]

Antebellum Beaufort often boasted that illiteracy was unknown among its white population and as a consequence there was great demand for books and magazines of all kinds. This led to the establishment of the Beaufort Library Society in 1807 and a collection of 3,100 volumes which was the "pride of the town." The collection contained a significant selection of European classics, a large collection of religious books, and numerous treatises on medicine, science, law, politics, and history.[6] In addition to books, newspapers and magazines were common in almost every home. George Parsons Elliott, one of Beaufort's many published authors, recalled that 33,120 newspapers and 3,406 periodicals passed through the Beaufort Post Office in a single year, surpassing by that measure the literary interest of any other town of its size in America.[7]

As a consequence of the high level of education, wealth, and literary interest in the town, it is not surprising that a number of the South's best-known literary figures would be attracted to Beaufort. James Louis Petigru, the central figure of Charleston's antebellum intellectual community, began his career as the principal of Beaufort College. Dr. John E. Holbrook, the author of the four-volume work *North American Herpetology* (1842) and the "foremost American zoologist of his time," was born in Beaufort.

Henry Timrod, South Carolina's most famous antebellum poet, was a teacher at Bluffton's May River Academy in the 1840s and a frequent visitor to Beaufort. Also a frequent visitor was J. D. B. DeBow, the founder of *DeBow's Review* of New Orleans, one of the Old South's most famous periodicals. Mason Weems, better known as "Parson Weems," the author of America's popular biographies of George Washington, Francis Marion, and others, died in Beaufort on one of his many trips as an itinerant bookseller.

The measure of antebellum Beaufort as an intellectual community, however, is not by who passed through, but by whom the town produced. Five literary figures of the Old South stand out among the many associated with Beaufort: Stephen Elliott (1771–1830), William J. Grayson (1788–1863), William Elliott III (1788–1863), Robert W. Barnwell (1801–1882), and Richard Fuller (1804–1876). Each one of these men was descended from the old colonial families of Beaufort. Each one received his formative education in Beaufort, and each one derived the basis of his wealth from property in the district. Each one also gained statewide and national notice for his intellectual achievements.[8]

These five men represent the intellectual life of antebellum Beaufort both because their fields of intellectual interest vary widely from botany to poetry to theology and because, as the antebellum era advanced toward its climactic destruction during the Civil War, their intellectual talents were more and more frequently employed in defense of those institutions which had nurtured, educated, and supported them. Whether through poetry, politics, or theology, they all became defenders of the Old South.

Stephen Elliott Sr., the only one of the five who did not live to see the end of the Old South, was one of the citizens most responsible for establishing the important cultural and educational institutions of antebellum Beaufort and of antebellum South Carolina. Stephen Elliott Sr. was born in Beaufort on November 11, 1771. He was the third child of William Elliott I and Mary Barnwell Elliott. His mother was the second daughter of Colonel Nathaniel Barnwell. Stephen Elliott's mother died when he was seven years old. Nevertheless, Elliott received the attention of a large, well-connected, and very wealthy family. As a boy he was tutored by Reverend Abiel Holmes and raised in the home of his older brother, William Elliott II. As a young man he was sent to New Haven, Connecticut, and given preparation for entrance into Yale College. He entered Yale in 1788 and was one of the outstanding students of his class. He graduated Phi Beta Kappa in 1791 and was chosen to deliver the English Oration. His title was "On the Supposed Degeneracy of Animated Nature."[9]

Elliott returned to South Carolina to manage his substantial plantation property. While living in Beaufort in 1796, he married Esther Habersham, granddaughter of Royal Governor James Habersham of Georgia. Over the next fifteen years, he was more active than any other Beaufort citizen in helping to establish the educational and cultural institutions of antebellum Beaufort. He was on the first board of trustees of Beaufort College in 1795 and was the principal organizer of the Beaufort Library Society in 1807. Hugh Swinton Legare was a protégé of Stephen Elliott. It was probably Elliott who engaged Legare to acquire the famous classical collection of the Beaufort Library while on a trip to Europe. Beaufort voters sent Elliott to the South Carolina House (1794–1799) and Senate (1808–1812). While serving as a state senator, Elliott was one of the leaders in passing the Free School Act of 1811 and was known as "the founder of the public school system" in South Carolina. In 1812, he authored the legislation establishing the Bank of the State of South Carolina and resigned from the Senate to become the bank's president, a position he held until his death. Elliott then sold his plantations and slaves in the Beaufort District and moved to Charleston.

While living in Beaufort, Elliott began the scholarly work which was to bring him national and international recognition. An avid interest in the natural world of the lowcountry and keen scientific discipline led Elliott to collect and catalogue botanical data for many years. This data was finally published as the two-volume *Botany of South Carolina and Georgia* (1821, 1824). It was to remain the standard work on the subject for a generation, and it established Elliott as one of the premier scholars in antebellum South Carolina. William J. Grayson described an encounter with Elliott at his home in Beaufort, more memorable than most of Grayson's formal education. "He pulled a flower to pieces for my special advantage and initiated me in the mysteries of petals, pistils and stamens. . . . He combined the manners of a refined gentleman with the most exact and comprehensive acquirements of natural philosophy." At his death, Elliott's private collection on natural history was one of the largest in the South. His estate contained a private library of twenty-five hundred volumes.[10]

After Elliott moved to Charleston, his effect on the cultural life of the state was even greater. In 1820 he was selected as president of the South Carolina College but refused the offer in order to continue managing the troubled state bank. Nevertheless, he served nine years (1820–1829) on the board of trustees of the state college. In 1824, Elliott was one of the principal organizers of the Medical College of South Carolina and became its first professor of natural history and botany. His scholarly achievements were recognized by honorary doctorates from Yale (1819), Harvard (1822), Columbia (1825), and the Medical College of South Carolina (1825).[11] In Elliott's address to the first graduating class of the Medical College of South Carolina in 1825, he expressed his lifelong commitment to higher education as one of the most important institutions of democracy in the new American nation. Public and private colleges in America, he believed, provided "opportunities by which even the poor and the humble might obtain instruction."[12]

Elliott was also the president of the Charleston Library Society, the founder of the Literary and Philosophical Society in 1813, and the founder and editor, along with Hugh Swinton Legare, of the *Southern Review* in 1828. Legare, who was one of South Carolina's most influential intellectuals, practically worshiped Elliott. On Elliott's death in 1830, Legare lamented that South Carolina would not produce such a man again.[13]

One of the products of the institutions which Elliott helped to found, and one of Elliott's protégés, was William J. Grayson (1788–1863). Like Elliott, Grayson was a man of widely varying interests. During his life, Grayson was a teacher, lawyer, politician, and poet; all the while receiving income from his sea island cotton plantations. Grayson was born in Beaufort in 1788, the son of William John Grayson and Susannah Greene. His grandfather, John Grayson, was a West Indian merchant from Montserrat, and his grandmother, Sarah Wigg Grayson, on whose Parris Island plantation William Grayson spent much of his childhood, was the daughter of Colonel Thomas Wigg, one of Beaufort's colonial pioneers. Just before Beaufort College opened, William Grayson, at the age of twelve, was sent north to a school in New Utrecht, Long Island. Grayson was entrusted to the care of Solomon Saltus, a New York ship chandler, whose brother, Captain Francis Saltus, was a prominent sailing master and cotton planter in Beaufort. While Grayson had happy childhood experiences in New York, he did not get much of an education. They had few books in the homes where he stayed, "Before I left home I loved reading. I had hung over a torch light in the chimney ... in the house of Mrs. Ann Joyner—widow of Captain John Joyner. . . . But on Long Island my mind was starved for want of food . . . at a period of life from twelve to fifteen, when the intellect hungers and thirsts after knowledge, I saw no books." After his schoolmaster on Long Island died, Grayson attended the Newark Academy in New Jersey, "a place of immense pretension and very small performance."

Grayson returned to Beaufort and was tutored in the classics by Milton Maxcy in preparation for entering the new South Carolina College in Columbia. He was somewhat critical of the academic level of the new state college and of the condition of the new capital of Columbia, which was little more than a frontier town when Grayson resided there (1807–1809). He did, however, have high regard for Dr. Jonathan Maxcy, the college's first president and brother of Milton Maxcy. The most enduring benefit of Grayson's college years was his lifelong friendship with James L. Petigru: "We were intimate companions, talked together with the ambition of undergraduates, read to each other Horace and Rabelais, Pope and Bacon and were admitted by all parties to be the best scholars of the class."[14] Grayson was forced by illness to leave the college before graduation, but received his diploma because of his superior academic record. Consequently, his friend Petigru became the valedictorian of the class of 1809.

Grayson returned to Beaufort to spend a few years as a "loiterer in the high ways and bye ways of life." He kept the company of the extravagant, hospitable, and poetry-loving Dr. Henry Farmer at his summer home in Beaufort and at his Combahee River plantation. But in January 1814, Grayson married Sarah Somersall of Charleston and was forced to seek employment. "Men who pursue knowledge for its own sake only and who are suddenly awakened to the necessity of seeking their own bread betake themselves commonly of one of two pursuits," Grayson noted wryly. "They become authors or schoolmasters."[15] Thus,

Grayson secured the position of assistant teacher at Beaufort College. Dr. William Brantly, the town's Baptist minister, was the principal of the college at the time. He was later to become president of the College of Charleston. Grayson taught for two years in Beaufort, one year at the Savannah Academy, and then back to Beaufort College in 1817. Among his teenage students in those years were Robert Barnwell Rhett, Robert W. Barnwell, Richard Fuller, and William F. Colcock. Grayson's return to Beaufort was just in time to witness the tragic yellow fever epidemic of that year. Of the 600 white inhabitants of Beaufort, 120 died, including Grayson's youngest daughter. The college was closed, and the large building built to house it was razed on suspicion that the epidemic had begun among the students. Grayson took his family north for an extended tour; the most memorable moment of which was his afternoon with former President John Adams at his home in Quincy, Massachusetts.[16]

On returning to South Carolina, Grayson began his career in law. He was admitted to the South Carolina Bar in 1822, and began his practice at the Beaufort District Court at Coosawhatchie. Within a few years, he abandoned the practice of law, for which he found himself temperamentally unsuited, and threw himself enthusiastically into politics. He was soon swept up in the passions of the Nullification Crisis and was one of the founders of the South Carolina States' Rights and Free Trade Party. It was during the Nullification Crisis that Grayson, along with John A. Stuart, founded Beaufort's first newspaper, the *Beaufort Gazette* (1828–1833). The paper was the political mouthpiece for the nullification faction in the Beaufort District and survived only as long as the crisis lasted. Afterward, Grayson went to Congress and Stuart went to Charleston to help start the Charleston *Mercury*.[17]

In 1836, Grayson made the most important business transaction of his life. He purchased the large and successful Frogmore Plantation with its large complement of slaves, from the estate of Colonel John Stapleton for eighty-eight thousand dollars. Grayson was given a mortgage for the purchase of the property, the annual payments on which were seventy-five hundred dollars per year. Robert Barnwell Rhett, who had defeated Grayson for Congress that year and who had previously purchased Stapleton's Blue House Plantation on the Ashepoo River, was the attorney for the transaction.[18] While these were huge sums in 1836, the purchase price for one of the largest sea island cotton plantations in South Carolina with well over one hundred slaves was a bargain. And the proceeds from Frogmore Plantation supported Grayson's comfortable life in Charleston for the next twenty years.

In 1841, Grayson was appointed collector for the port of Charleston, a federal patronage job he acquired from his friend President John Tyler. Thereafter, he immersed himself in the city life, reestablished his friendship with James

Petigru, and began the literary endeavors for which he is best known to history. In the 1840s and 1850s, Grayson published numerous literary reviews, political commentaries, a biography of Petigru (*James Louis Petigru: A Biographical Sketch,* 1866), and an unpublished biography of William Lowndes. Grayson contributed often to the *Southern Quarterly Review* and was one of the founders of *Russell's Magazine* (1856), the last literary periodical of the Old South. Novelist William Gilmore Simms, who was editor of the *Southern Quarterly Review,* described Grayson as "a very amiable and intelligent gentleman" and recommended him to J. D. B. DeBow of New Orleans as one of only a half-dozen literary authors left in South Carolina in 1858.[19]

What gained Grayson his national celebrity was his poetry. Mary Chesnut, who never met Grayson, knew him by his reputation as "the poet and friend of Mr. Petigru's."[20] By far the most famous and widely read of Grayson's poems was "The Hireling and the Slave" (1854), which favorably compared the conditions of the slaves in the rural South with the industrial laborers in the urban North and in Europe. Grayson summarized his defense of slavery, and the paternalistic view of the institution common among the sea island planters, as follows: "No want to goad, no faction to deplore, the slave escapes the perils of the poor."

Grayson's poem was wildly popular in the South during the highly charged ideological atmosphere of the 1850s. It remains an important literary monument of the Old South today because it was specifically written to counter the sensational propaganda of Harriet Beecher Stowe's *Uncle Tom's Cabin.* Like all of Beaufort's antebellum intellectuals, Grayson's admirable talent was enlisted in defense of the "peculiar institution."

According to the literary critics of the time, Grayson's best poetic work was not his most famous, but, rather his paean to American natural beauty called "Chicora." This is an epic legend of native American simplicity and natural beauty. That Grayson's powerful aesthetic sense was formed by his sea island homeland there can be no doubt. Through many adventures throughout the continent, his hero finally arrives at the Native American paradise:

> Those isles of the summer seas,
> Where stories say no winters come . . .
> In the blessed land, the spirits home;
> A richer verdure spreads the ground,
> The sky is of a softer blue,
> And scattered in profusion round
> Are flowers of every shape and hue,
> Their fragrance on unsated breeze
> Floats exquisite and evermore.

On purple vines and bending trees
Are various fruits, an endless store
Innumerable birds prolong,
With chattering joy their dainty cheer,
Of brighter plume and sweeter song
Than meet with mortal eye or ear.[21]

If Grayson's aesthetic sense was formed by his sea island home, William Elliott III made a national literary reputation for himself by simply describing what was commonplace amusement for antebellum sea island planters. Elliott was an exact contemporary of Grayson (1788–1863), but his youthful education was reversed. While Grayson went north for his secondary education and returned to South Carolina for his college years, Elliott remained in Beaufort for his secondary education as one of the first products of the new Beaufort College, which he attended from its opening in 1803 until 1806. Then he went north to receive his college education at Harvard (1806–1808), where he was elected to Phi Beta Kappa. Elliott was forced by illness to leave Harvard before he graduated, but in 1810, the college awarded him an honorary bachelor of arts degree as a consequence of his outstanding academic record.

Elliott was the son of William Elliott II and Phoebe Waight. Both of his parents were descendants of sea island pioneers, and Elliott's father was the first to plant sea island cotton in the Beaufort District. Elliott was, therefore, a man of immense wealth. Shortly before his death, Elliott's properties included twelve plantations in the lowcountry; homes in Beaufort, Adam's Run, and Flat Rock, North Carolina; and 217 slaves. Among his plantations was Myrtle Bank on Hilton Head Island, where his father had begun the sea island cotton revolution.

Elliott was, however, definitely not a man of leisure. He threw his great intellectual energies into his business of planting, wrote numerous articles for the *Southern Agriculturist,* and became famous in the South for his studies in scientific seed selection and his recommendations for the diversification of southern agriculture. He was the longtime president of the Beaufort Agricultural Society, vice president of the South Carolina Agricultural Society in 1839, and represented South Carolina at the Paris Exposition of 1855, where he worked to open a secondary market for sea island cotton in France. While in Paris, Elliott delivered a speech in French to the Imperial and Central Agricultural Society on the subject of cotton. He was one of the most successful cotton planters in America, and his top-of-the-line product, known as "Elliott Cream Cotton," often set the price for sea island cotton on the Charleston market.

Elliott also threw himself with equal ardor into his civic responsibilities. He was intendant of Beaufort (1819–1824), trustee of Beaufort College, state representative, and state senator for St. Helena Parish. His political career was cut short by his resolute opposition to the popular tide of Nullification in the Beaufort District. Rather than oppose the will of his constituents, he resigned from the South Carolina Senate in 1832.[22]

Thereafter, Elliott devoted himself to his plantations, his recreational pastimes, and his literary inclinations. In addition to his agricultural writings, Elliott often wrote pieces for the Charleston newspapers using the pen-names "Piscator" and "Venator." In 1850, he had a five-act drama published called "Fiesco: A Tragedy." In 1849, when William Gilmore Simms was trying to revive the *Southern Quarterly Review,* he pleaded with Elliott to become a regular contributor, appealing particularly to Elliott's southern patriotism in the ideological struggle with the North: "your name naturally suggests itself as . . . one whose writings would honor its pages. . . . I need not insist with you upon the importance of such an organ . . . for the mind and talent of the South—still less at this juncture need I remind you of the uses of such a work for the defense of our Institutions and the exhibition of our character. May I hope that you will not withhold yourself from the arena." While Elliott always opposed the secessionists in South Carolina, as did his friends Grayson and Petigru, he nevertheless staunchly defended slavery as "sanctioned by religion, conducive to good morals and useful, nay, indispensable."[23]

Elliott's most famous and lasting contribution to the antebellum literature of South Carolina was his *Carolina Sports by Land and Water,* published in Charleston in 1846. This book was a compilation of his contributions on lowcountry hunting and fishing to the Charleston newspapers over several years. This book was widely popular in its day and remains a classic for lowcountry hunters and fishers nearly a century and a half later. *Carolina Sports* went through two publications in America and one in England.

Elliott simply described, in a writing style that was "perfectly clear and extraordinarily animated," the actual pursuits of lowcountry planters in hunting for deer, wildcat, bear, partridge, dove, and turkey; and fishing for sheepshead, bass, and drum. Unquestionably the most famous episode was his essay on "devil fishing." This unusual and sensational sport of the sea island planters required a crew of men in a long boat to harpoon the giant manta ray, or devil fish, which spawn in Port Royal Sound in the early summer. The result of a successful strike with the harpoon was that the boat and crew would be towed on the South Carolina equivalent of the "Nantucket sleigh ride" until the great fish exhausted itself.

Like Grayson, Elliott's best work was reserved for affectionate descriptions of his lowcountry homeland. Describing a deerhunt at Chee-ha Plantation, he wrote: "It was a glorious winter's day—sharp but bracing. The sun looked forth with dazzling brightness, as he careened through a cloudless sky: and his rays came glancing back from many an ice covered lagoon that lay scattered over the face of the ground. The moan of an expiring north-wester was faintly heard from the tops of the magnificent forest pines."[24]

Neither Elliott nor Grayson, however, were as well known in their day nor as widely revered as the "oracle of Beaufort," Robert W. Barnwell (1801–1882). Barnwell's contemporary and political rival Benjamin F. Perry gave him the highest possible praise: "I have seen in my day and time a number of great men, but I never knew a more perfect one than Robert W. Barnwell."[25] Clement Eaton, in his survey of the intellectual life of the antebellum South, *The Mind of the Old South*, used Barnwell as the ultimate example of the aristocratic southern intellect. "With beautiful manners, a modest and unassuming personality, he possessed the poise and graces of an aristocrat of an old family."[26] And that is exactly what Barnwell was: the son of Revolutionary hero and Federalist congressman, Colonel Robert Barnwell, and the direct descendant of "Tuscarora Jack" who had founded the old village.

Barnwell was educated at Beaufort College, where he was a student of James Petigru. He then went to Charleston to study at Martin Luther Hurlbut's classical academy. While in Charleston he lived with, and was influenced by, his uncle, Stephen Elliott. In 1817, Barnwell entered Harvard, where he quickly rose to the top of his class. He was elected to Phi Beta Kappa in his junior year, was a member of the Porcellian Club, and was captain of the College Company. When he graduated from Harvard in 1821, Barnwell was valedictorian of his class.

Barnwell returned to South Carolina, read the law with James L. Petigru and James Hamilton Jr. in Charleston, and was admitted to the South Carolina Bar in 1823. He formed a partnership with Robert Barnwell Rhett at Coosawhatchie, and both men began the political careers which were to gain them national attention. These careers are described in chapter 18.[27]

Early in his career, Barnwell was recognized for his intellectual achievements. Benjamin F. Perry recalled in 1826 that Barnwell was noted in political circles as the "young member from Beaufort who graduated at Harvard College with the first honors of his class."[28] Following Barnwell's retirement from active politics in 1833, after two terms in Congress, his intellectual talents were recognized by the state when he was chosen to be president of the South Carolina College. Barnwell's tenure at the South Carolina College (1835–1841) was his greatest contribution to the intellectual life of antebellum South Carolina. He was selected not only as president, but also as professor of "political and moral philosophy." Barnwell proved to be an excellent professor and an outstanding college president. Maxmilian LaBorde noted that when Barnwell took over from the controversial Thomas Cooper, the college was nearly destitute, with only twenty students enrolled. Under Barnwell's leadership, "The college seemed to have revived as if by magic." By the time he left, enrollment had doubled four times, the confidence of the trustees had returned, and contributions from the legislature increased substantially. It was not an exaggeration to say that Barnwell saved the South Carolina College.

Barnwell's most lasting contribution to the college was the construction of the South Caroliniana Library, begun in 1838 and completed in 1840. It was the first freestanding college library in America. By 1850, the South Caroliniana Library housed 18,500 volumes, larger than the libraries of Columbia or Princeton and equal to Jefferson's University of Virginia. In 1841, Barnwell resigned the presidency due to failing health and returned to Beaufort. University historian Daniel C. Hollis regards Barnwell's administration as "one of the most successful in the history of the institution."[29]

After returning to Beaufort in 1841, Barnwell retired from active political participation but continued to support education in Beaufort and in the state. He continued to serve on the boards of trustees of Beaufort College and the South Carolina College. He was for many years the president of Beaufort College trustees, and it was under Barnwell's leadership that the new Beaufort College building was built on a block of Carteret Street in 1852.[30] Beaufort College's new building was built in the classical Greek Revival style, symbolic of the antebellum South. Interestingly, it was constructed almost exactly one hundred years after the construction of Prince William Parish Church, the building which began the Greek Revival style in the South. When the Beaufort College was constructed, it included a two-story mezzanine library in the rotunda at the rear of the building. This became the new home for the outstanding collection of the Beaufort Library Society begun by Stephen Elliott. Barnwell's impact on the intellectual life of antebellum Beaufort and antebellum South Carolina is symbolized by the buildings he built to house the libraries of the Beaufort community and the South Carolina College. It was during these years of semiretirement in Beaufort that Barnwell became the social and intellectual arbiter of the town. M. A. Fowles, who grew up and was educated in Beaufort during those years, recalled that few public or private decisions were made without first consulting "Cousin Robert."[31]

During the 1850s, as the crisis of secession in South Carolina grew, Barnwell was drawn out of retirement and into active service on behalf of the state and Confederate governments. Like all of Beaufort's intellectual leaders, Barnwell's talents were enlisted in the defense of southern institutions. Though Barnwell was a man of considerably more moderate political views than his famous cousin and former law partner, Robert Barnwell Rhett, when the final crisis of the Civil War occurred, Barnwell was in the forefront in the creation of the Confederate States of America. He led the South Carolina delegation to the Montgomery Convention in 1861, was the first president of the convention, signed the Confederate Constitution, and swung the election of the president of the Confederacy to Jefferson Davis. President Davis offered Barnwell the post of Confederate secretary of state. He declined but remained a member of the Confederate Senate in Richmond. One of Barnwell's closest friends and companions during the Civil War years was Mary Boykin Chesnut, whose pithy comments to her diary have so fascinated subsequent generations. Barnwell, then sixty years old, was evidently quite entranced by the vivacious and witty Chesnut, then thirty-eight years old. He escorted her to social events in Montgomery and Richmond and always asked to be seated next to her at the obligatory dinner parties. "Mr. Barnwell sat by me, as always," she noted in her diary in 1861.[32] Mary Chesnut was in awe of Robert Barnwell's powerful influence over all the Confederate leaders from South Carolina. "The Carolinians revere his goodness above all things," she observed. She attributed his influence to his years as president of the South Carolina College: "The younger men had been at the South Carolina College while Mr. Barnwell was President. Their love and respect for him is immeasurable. And he benignly received it smiling behind those spectacles."[33]

But Chesnut came to understand that respect was what Barnwell expected, and as the Confederacy began to falter and Colonel Chesnut's career began to stagnate, she found Barnwell's expectation of deference less attractive. Barnwell began to ridicule the braggadocio of the Confederate military leaders. On one embarrassing occasion in 1861, Barnwell used his superior intellect to goad General William "Shot Pouch" Walker of Georgia into losing his temper at the dinner table. Barnwell met the general's anger by repeating his "offensive little laugh" and all the while continuing "his fatuous smile."[34] Such intellectual amusements were no longer amusing when tens of thousands of young men were dying for an ideology that Barnwell had to defend only with his intellect. The societal conventions upon which Barnwell's social and intellectual elitism depended were crushed by the tragic weight of the Civil War.

In 1850, Barnwell was drawn back into the political arena, first as president of St. Helena Parish Southern Rights Association and then as the South Carolina representative to the Nashville Convention. In May 1850, Governor Whitmarsh Seabrook asked Barnwell to serve in the U.S. Senate to replace John C. Calhoun and Franklin Elmore who had both died in office that year. While in the Senate for nine months, Barnwell was plagued by the tedium of the discussion and "always escaped to the library." According to M.A. Fowles, it was Barnwell who suggested the arrangement of the library in the capitol building in alcoves in imitation of the library at the South Carolina College.[35] On June 27, 1850, Barnwell gave a speech before the Senate on the subject of the famous Compromise of 1850. His speech reveals the fundamental intellectual unity of the planter class of the Beaufort District. "He frankly admitted that there had been a time when the leading statesmen of the South regarded slavery as a social, moral and political evil. But driven by the attacks of the abolitionists, southerners had investigated the moral aspects of the subject; the result was they had found nothing in the Word of God condemning the institution and they now felt they could hold slaves in good conscience."[36]

The intellectual leader of antebellum Beaufort who contributed the most to the "good conscience" of the planter class of the Beaufort District regarding their slaves was Reverend Richard Fuller (1804–1876). Fuller was born in Beaufort as the ninth child of Thomas Fuller and Elizabeth Middleton Fuller. His grandmother was Anne Barnwell Middleton Bull, the eldest daughter of Colonel Nathaniel Barnwell, and his grandfather was Colonel Thomas Middleton. Fuller grew up in one of antebellum Beaufort's most remarkable families. Richard's mother, Elizabeth Fuller, was "a woman of superior mind and culture . . . a close and constant reader." Of her twelve children, Richard was the one who most resembled her in intellect, temperament, and appearance. Richard's father, Dr. Thomas Fuller, was a man of deep religious faith. He was one of Beaufort's earliest prominent converts to the Baptist denomination in 1804, when the Baptists were still a small and poor congregation. Subsequently, the Fuller family remained divided between the Baptist and Episcopal churches. Richard Fuller grew up in a large and prosperous household. Summers were spent at the family's large tabby mansion on Bay Street and winters were spent at the family's principal country seat at Sheldon. The most memorable feature of Sheldon Plantation was the avenue of giant magnolia trees planted in colonial times by the Bull family. By the antebellum era, these trees had reached across the road leading to the main house and formed a spectacular floral tunnel. One aspect of the household that affected Fuller's later life, and those of several of his brothers and sisters, was that their homes were always full of music. Fuller's mother and two sisters were accomplished pianists and singers, and his brother Henry was famous in Beaufort for "his magic flute" and guitar. Richard Fuller later published a book of hymns called *The Psalmist* that was widely used by Baptists in Europe and America.[37]

As well as literature and music, the Fuller sons also participated in the traditional field sports of the lowcountry planters. From his youth, Fuller was noted as an exceptional marksman. Throughout his life, when Fuller wished to escape his worldly toils, he escaped to the fields and forests of his childhood home.

As a youth, Fuller attended Beaufort College, where he was a student of Dr. William Brantley, the Baptist minister and principal of Beaufort College. At the age of sixteen, he was sent north to attend Harvard College. Despite his young age and an initial severe case of homesickness, he soon rose to the top of his class: "proof that his progress and scholarship in Beaufort must have been more than respectable." John Sibley, the librarian at Harvard, recalled years later that Fuller was "the best scholar in his class." His classmates remembered Fuller for his prodigious memory and his talent for flawless recitation. Charles Francis Adams, who was a class behind, recalled that Fuller "held a high position in his class." But his New England classmates also remembered that Fuller was a reserved, studious young man who did not run with the fast, fashionable crowd of southerners at Harvard. Before graduating, Fuller had to leave college due to illness, but in 1824, Harvard awarded him a degree anyway because of his stellar academic record.[38]

Fuller returned to Beaufort and prepared for the legal profession with Judge Clay in Savannah. He was admitted to the South Carolina Bar in 1825 and began his practice in Beaufort. Among his legal contemporaries were Robert W. Barnwell, Robert Barnwell Rhett, and Richard DeTreville, all of whom began their prominent political and professional careers in the Beaufort District in the 1820s. Fuller specialized in criminal law and excelled at his work because he was always "sharp, close and prepared."[39]

The turning point of Fuller's life came in 1831. First was his marriage to Charlotte Bull Stuart. Also in 1831, Fuller began the process of being "born again" in the Baptist faith. For many years, Fuller's spinster sister Harriet had been a dedicated member of the Beaufort Baptist Church. She was the principal teacher of the "colored Sunday School," which was part of the Baptist congregation. Her most ardent student was an old African woman named Aunt Judy. Harriet Fuller and Aunt Judy had both been trying to influence Fuller's conversion for several years. In 1831, Dr. Benjamin Screven, the Baptist minister, called Fuller to his deathbed and asked him to come to Jesus. Fuller cried at the encounter and was depressed for weeks afterward. Just around this time, the Presbyterian evangelist Reverend Daniel Baker came to Beaufort and commenced the "remarkable revival." Baker preached to "crowded aisles" in both the Baptist and Episcopal churches. Hundreds of Beaufortonians were reborn by the experience, and no one cared which church they joined: "Such was the feeling that all questions of holy places and holy orders were set aside for the time. The whole town was a holy place." Many young men in Beaufort left their professions and joined the ministry at that time, among them Reverend William Hazzard Wigg Barnwell, Reverend Charles Cotesworth Pinckney, and Bishop Stephen Elliott of Georgia. Of all of them, the most influential was Fuller.

Fuller recorded the date of his own religious conversion as October 26, 1831. When Reverend Baker came to call on him personally, he exclaimed, "Oh sir, I have oceans of joy." Later in life, Fuller recalled the lingering feeling of joy,

"Creation seemed full of God . . . for days I neither ate nor slept. I lived on the love of God . . . the name of Jesus spread a fragrance on everything." Shortly afterward, Fuller was baptized in the Beaufort River, and Harriet and Aunt Judy were "witnesses" to the event. Aunt Judy recalled the occasion, "the river looked bright that day . . . and the leaves on the trees on the shore were clapping their hands for joy."[40]

The following year, Fuller was ordained as a minister in the Baptist faith. He undertook his new calling with the same studiousness that he had previously undertaken in his college and professional work. Soon he had collected "a very valuable theological library."[41] It was almost inevitable that Fuller would be called to be pastor of the Baptist Church of Beaufort. For three years he poured his energy and prodigious intellect into building up the church. Fuller's ministry coincided with the plantation mission movement which was sweeping the South Carolina and Georgia lowcountry; it was the mission to the slaves which engaged Richard Fuller's religious passion. "I had resolved," Fuller noted, "when first called to the ministry to confine my labors wholly to our colored population."[42] It was this work which made Fuller the most influential intellect in antebellum Beaufort.

Fuller was a whirlwind of activity over the next three years. He conducted Sunday services and studied assiduously in preparation for his sermons. So popular was his preaching that many non-Baptists regularly attended Sunday services just to hear him speak. Each Wednesday evening he conducted lectures at the "Tabernacle" or black meeting hall on Craven Street. On Fridays, Fuller conducted prayer meetings, often going from house to house. Between these times he maintained a busy round of pastoral visits. But the work he thought most important was the establishment of "preaching stations" on the surrounding plantations where the slave communities could gather for worship and instruction. Many neighborhood planters were so inspired by Fuller's work that they clamored for more pastoral visits to their plantation communities. Fuller's inspiration and example caused the Baptist congregation to swell in numbers and enthusiasm. Most of the congregation was black, which was precisely Fuller's intention. "The great majority of the members were colored people of the town and adjoining plantations. . . . The middle classes of the white population and a few of the wealthier families constituted the rest."[43] Fuller's "preaching stations," the enthusiastic congregations of slaves that joined the Baptist faith, the slave Sunday schools operated by the wives and daughters of the planters, like sister Harriet, as well as the general impact of the plantation mission movement of the 1830s all led the sea island planters to convince themselves that the plantation system was genuinely contributing to the moral and education improvement of the slaves, as well as the wealth of the planters.

After three years of furious effort, Fuller was exhausted. In 1836, he toured Europe to recover his health. His most memorable visit was to the eternal city of Rome and the heart of western christendom. Despite his theological differences with the Roman Catholic Church, he was in awe of St. Peter's Cathedral. While standing in the tracks of St. Paul on the Appian Way, Fuller fell into a long period of silent contemplation.

Fuller returned to Beaufort and noticed that the roof of the old Baptist Church was sagging. The building was no longer able to hold the burgeoning congregation, so he turned his energy to the construction of a new sanctuary. Fuller, by then a very popular and well-known preacher, traveled to Savannah, Augusta, and other nearby towns giving speeches and raising money for the new building. The church was begun in 1843 and finished in 1844.[44] The Baptist Church of Beaufort remains today as an almost perfect example of the neoclassical, Greek Revival architecture so popular in the antebellum South and so symbolic of the Old South today. At the consecration of the new church, Fuller's old sponsors in the faith, sister Harriet and Aunt Judy, both wept for joy, and the town universally acknowledged that the new church was "in every respect superior to the old."[45] Fuller's church remains today as the finest example of antebellum architecture in Beaufort's National Landmark District and as a monument to his impact on the town.

During his ministry in Beaufort, Fuller established some of the ceremonies which became traditional celebrations for black and white Baptists in the community. Baptisms were always held in the Beaufort River at the foot of Charles Street. "With a noble river at the door of the sanctuary, the church of Beaufort had no need of a baptistry." Baptisms were always moments of high celebration. A solemn procession left the church, often dressed in white, and was always led by the "venerable colored sexton, Jacob Witter, with his staff." Baptisms were always held at high tide and Jacob Witter, wading into the river ahead of the procession, used his staff to sound the bottom for the perfect location for the sacrament of total immersion. These processions were always accompanied by singing and usually attracted large crowds of onlookers.[46] The other symbolic ceremony established during Fuller's ministry was called the "quarterly seasons." During these ceremonies, the black members of the congregation would assemble outside the church while the white members were seated in the pews. The black deacons of the church would then lead their members in procession through the front doors, up to the pulpit, and then down the center aisle to their seats in the gallery. As the procession progressed, the black members all "received hands" as they passed through the aisles in symbolic union of black and white Baptists. The quarterly seasons were always accompanied by hymns "sung by those thousands" and were always followed by great feasts where everyone was served together, "so the humblest Negro had his share of the feast where Richard Fuller presided." The best evidence of the impact of Fuller comes from the affectionate place he held in the memory of his own slaves. Jonas Singleton, in 1877 a prominent deacon of a Baptist church in Augusta, remembered Richard Fuller as "one of the best masters in the state and much loved by his slaves."[47]

Fuller's biographer and nephew, James Hazzard Cuthbert, identified him with the long line of great evangelists who influenced religious revivals in the old Beaufort District. From the early work of evangelizing the slaves by Hugh Bryan, through the establishment of the nascent Baptist movement by George Whitefield in the colonial period, to the founding of the Beaufort congregation by Reverend Henry Holcombe and the great revival of Reverend Daniel Baker in 1831, Fuller's ministry seemed to be the antebellum culmination of a century of evangelical labors in the Beaufort District.[48]

During the 1840s, Fuller began to establish himself as one of the intellectual leaders of the Baptist movement in the old South. A series of letters in the Charleston *Courier* exchanged with Roman Catholic Bishop John England were published as *Letters Concerning the Roman Chancery* (1840). In 1844, Fuller wrote a letter to the *Christian Reflector* of Philadelphia asserting that the institution of slavery was sanctioned by the Bible. This was quickly answered by Dr. Francis Wayland of Rhode Island, and the ensuing exchange of letters was published in 1845 as *Domestic Slavery Considered as a Scriptural Institution*.[49] It was this last work which established Fuller as one of the Old South's premier defenders of slavery and the man who did the most to establish the "good conscience" of the lowcountry planters regarding their slaves.

In this book, Fuller outlined his belief in the historical and scriptural justification of slavery. From the Old Testament, Fuller quoted the scriptures regarding bondsmen, "And ye shall take them as an inheritance for your children after you, to inherit them as a possession; they shall be your bondsmen forever." He pointed out that in the gospel and the epistles, slavery was acknowledged as a common condition of society and noted that, "Neither the Savior nor the Apostles commanded masters to emancipate their slaves."[50] The question of slavery, therefore, was a political and legal question, not a moral or religious one. The habit of the northern abolitionists of branding all slaveowners as sinful and claiming that slavery was "a heinous crime in the sight of God" was not only historically and scripturally incorrect, it was also a "monstrous and uncharitable" doctrine. Fuller invoked no less an authority than Reverend George Whitefield, who had begun the Great Awakening in America and who owned slaves in Georgia, by quoting his statement, "As to the lawfulness of owning slaves, I have no doubt." He concluded his argument by noting that, "Jesus and his Apostles found slavery existing as part of the social organization. Should they appear now, they would find this same institution."⁵¹ To the planters of the Beaufort District, Fuller's inspiration to convert and educate the slaves was the law, and his proof that slavery was justified by scripture was gospel.

In 1847, Fuller left Beaufort to become the pastor of the Seventh Baptist Church of Baltimore. Baltimore was one of young America's great metropolises in 1847. It had always been the principal seaport for the rich agricultural region of the Chesapeake Bay, and, beginning in the 1820s, it became America's first great railroad town. By the time Fuller arrived in the city, the Baltimore and Ohio Railroad had already reached through the Appalachian Mountains toward the Ohio River. In 1853, six years after Fuller's arrival, the historic linkage was made, and the port of Baltimore was connected by rail and steamboat to the heart of the North American continent. Maryland was still a slave state during Fuller's first residence, but less than 20 percent of Baltimore's households held slaves in the late antebellum period. Indeed, the industrial revolution was making powerful economic and social changes everywhere in the community.⁵² It was a sharp contrast with the almost idyllic agricultural complacency of Beaufort and the sea islands.

Fuller's reputation as a preacher and Baptist theologian spread to a national audience from Baltimore. In 1851, Fuller made a famous speech in Washington, D.C., to the annual meeting of the American Colonization Society. The president of the society was Senator Henry Clay of Kentucky, whose speech Fuller followed. In the audience was President Millard Fillmore. This speech was a significant expression of Fuller's anxiety over the issue of slavery, and as such it exemplifies the deepest concerns of the planter class of the Beaufort District in the years before the Civil War.

By 1851, the electorate of the Beaufort District had already decided to secede. They had only to wait for the rest of the state, as Robert Barnwell Rhett wished, or wait for the rest of the South, as Robert W. Barnwell wished. Fuller knew the mood of Beaufort and the mood of South Carolina, and he defended his homeland, "that chivalrous little state where I first drew breath, and which is only dearer to me because it is so much misunderstood and misrepresented." He justified the extremism of his planter friends as a natural reaction to the barrage of insults directed at them by northern abolitionists: "If Satan had had a choice of an agency, he could not have selected one more disastrous to the cause of truth and humanity. I am not surprised that the South is indignant. . . . How preposterous that such men [abolitionists] should undertake to counsel the Southern States upon the most difficult and delicate of all questions. . . . They have not counselled, they have only abused and libeled the South." But the South, Fuller admitted, had developed its own brand of irrationalism. In the South, "there is a morbid sensitiveness on the subject of slavery." No one would discuss the subject. But southerners had to admit the truth that "while slavery enriches the individual, it impoverishes and desolates the state, and fosters indolence and luxury." Fuller contended that deep in their hearts, southerners knew "that slavery is not a good thing, a thing to be perpetuated. I believe, Sir, there are few at the South who would hesitate about making this concession." He believed that slavery might be peacefully ended and the union preserved if extremists on both sides would make concessions, "if in one quarter fanaticism would cease to denounce every slaveholder as a monster of iniquity; and if in the other quarter, fanaticism would cease to advocate the perpetuation of slavery as a blessing."[53]

For a compromise to be reached, however, the deepest and most fundamental fears of the planter class must be relieved. The slaves were the capital base of the Beaufort District and the principal asset of almost every white family in the community. The planters must, therefore, be compensated for their losses as the British West Indian planters had been when their slaves were emancipated in 1833. Secondly, the planters feared losing control of society and having their real property and even their physical safety threatened by being abandoned in the midst of an overwhelming number of blacks. Beaufort planters could not even contemplate "the residence of such a vast number of Africans amongst us. Society would be subverted by the manumission of such a multitude belonging to another race." Such a situation was unthinkable to the planters and "most calamitous to both races." These were fears shared by both the great planters of the aristocracy and the middle-class country planters. The country planters had fewer resources to escape the collapse of their society, so their fear was more intense.

Colonization, Fuller said, was the answer. Congress should appropriate the money necessary to purchase the slaves and transport them back to their homeland. The cost would be great but the stakes were very high: "unless something is done, this Union cannot, I fear, be saved (which may Heaven avert!) from civil conflict." As Fuller concluded his speech, he pointed across the capital mall toward the half-finished Washington Monument and declared that if a compromise on slavery is not reached, that monument should be left unfinished as a "epitaph to the nation."[54]

Ten years later, Fuller's prophecy came to tragic fulfillment. No one knew better than Fuller the mind and heart of the planter classes of the Beaufort District. No one expressed more candidly, sincerely, or eloquently their most visceral and unspoken fears. But because he spoke candidly on the subject of slavery in 1851, he was almost not welcomed home. His honest and well-meaning message was lost in the clamor of the 1850s, and, within ten years, the civilization that raised Fuller had come to an end. His efforts to find a middle ground were not appreciated in the North either. At the beginning of the Civil War, the *New York Herald* labeled Fuller as "the most dangerous rebel in Maryland."[55]

Fuller did receive one moment of sublime reward for his lifelong efforts to help both his white and black neighbors. After the end of the Civil War, he returned to Beaufort with Secretary of the Treasury Salmon P. Chase to observe the work of the newly created Freedmen's Bureau. While the newly freed sea island blacks appreciated the secretary of the treasury's attention, they became ecstatic when they learned that the old pastor had returned. When word circulated to the surrounding plantations of Fuller's return, a huge crowd assembled in Beaufort, too large for any building in town. They assembled, as always on such occasions, under the ancient oaks. There Fuller delivered a sermon on the oneness of God's creation: that God had "made of one blood, all nations." He asserted the equality of all human souls in the eyes of God and how God had "created His image in ebony and ivory." As he concluded his sermon, the crowd surged forward to touch the old pastor. They pushed against him, touched his hands and called out "Lord bless ye."[56] The freedmen's recognition of Fuller's Christian sincerity, however right or wrong his opinions, was the greatest reward he ever received. Fuller was the conscience of antebellum Beaufort.

Even in the Beaufort District, where pro-slavery opinion was nearly unanimous among the planter class, there were still a few who were willing to abandon the South's peculiar "domestic institution." One of these, Reverend William Henry Brisbane, even became a prominent and politically active abolitionist. It is significant that this minority opinion was geographically concentrated in upper St. Peter's and Prince William Parishes. There had always been a passionate religious tradition among the families of those parishes, principally Baptist and Methodist. Added to this tradition, in the late antebellum era, were disturbing new thoughts on morality and society. Joseph A. Lawton attended Colgate College in upstate New York from 1832 to 1836 and for the first time encountered the hostility of northerners to slavery. Upstate New York was a hotbed of abolitionism, and Lawton was quite stunned to encounter rude behavior. "Some of them manifest a friendship for Southerners but most of them treat us quite rudely . . . they make uncharitable remarks about slavery and politics . . . do they think *me* guilty," Lawton lamented.[57] Consequently the only southerners at Colgate, Lawton, Talbird, Lathrop, and Duncan, stuck together and formed few lasting friendships in the North. These experiences spread quickly through the tight-knit community. That same year, Narcissa Lawton in Bluffton wrote to her cousin, A. J. Lawton in Robertville, that Joseph had sent home a "horrid account of the Yankees."[58] But the experience had an impact, and Lawton later expressed moral misgivings about slavery, sold his own slaves, and left the Pipe Creek Church for the Smyrna Church in the Barnwell District.

Other planters, without revealing their motivations, simply sold their slaves, took the money, and moved to areas where the moral contradictions did not exist. In 1857, T. F. Matthews sold "his settlement negroes," along with his plantation, in order to begin again in Iowa. John Lawton reported that "he is determined to go whether he sells or not."[59]

This was the only neighborhood of the Beaufort District to display any serious questioning of slavery in the antebellum era. No doubt some of the people retained memories of simpler times, and all the families certainly had stories of their pioneer ancestors who built the community largely by themselves. The whole of upper St. Peter's Parish was also proud of its historical place as one of the original centers of the Baptist evangelical revival in the late eighteenth century. Upper St. Peter's was one of the wellsprings of the Southern Baptist movement. Much of the zeal of the Baptist missionaries of the Savannah River Association was sustained by bringing thousands of their African brothers and sisters into the faith. The Methodists were equally energized by their mission to the slaves. It must have occurred to many of these sincere Christian planters, though none openly expressed it, that the next logical step after conversion was freedom. Perhaps that explains why upper St. Peter's Parish sustained the largest population of free blacks in the district.

Perhaps also it should come as no surprise that one of the most famous abolitionists in America was born and raised in upper St. Peter's Parish and was a central figure in the same family circle that built and ran the parish. In 1806, Reverend William Henry Brisbane was born in St. Peter's Parish, and in 1825 married his first cousin, Anna Lawton, daughter of Benjamin T. D. Lawton. Brisbane became a Baptist minister and served the Beech Branch and the Pipe Creek Churches. He was a very popular preacher in demand throughout the state. And he was a skilled writer who became in 1834 editor of *The Southern Baptist and General Intelligencer*. Brisbane was a wealthy man and a substantial slaveowner, which supported his writing, traveling, and speaking on behalf of the movement. When the subject of slavery was addressed, he expressed the standard biblical justification of slavery so eloquently expostulated by Reverend Richard Fuller of Beaufort, among others.[60] But in 1835, he read Dr. Francis Wayland, president of Brown University, whose book, *Elements of Moral Science,* changed his view of slavery. He became convinced that slavery was a sin. He was determined to free his own slaves, but sold them instead to his neighbor, Edward Peeples. His views were met with outrage. In 1838, he left South Carolina, fearing for his own safety. Though his slaves had initially requested to remain in St. Peter's Parish, the only land they knew, Brisbane's moral conviction compelled him to repurchase his slaves, transport them to Ohio, and set them free shortly after 1840.

Brisbane addressed the Female Anti-Slavery Society of Cincinnati in 1840 and thereafter was an active and effective spokesman of the abolitionist movement. In 1853, Brisbane moved to Wisconsin, but in 1865 he returned to his homeland as director of the U.S. Direct Tax Commission, which sold all the confiscated property on the sea islands.[61] He became, to the white population, the most hated man in the Beaufort District.

NOTES

1. Edward McCrady, *The History of South Carolina under the Proprietary Government, 1670–1719* (New York: Russell and Russell, 1901), 494.

2. Gilbert Voigt, "The Periclean Age of Beaufort," *South Carolina Historical Magazine* 58 (October 1957): 218–23.

3. Stephen B. Barnwell, *The Story of an American Family* (Marquette, Mich.: Privately printed, 1969), 64.

4. C. A. DeSaussure, "The Story of My Life Before the War Between the States," Memphis, 1927 (typescript provided by Charles A. DeSaussure, Gainesville, Ga.).

5. Francis Richard Lubbock, *Six Decades in Texas: or Memoirs of Francis Richard Lubbock, Governor of Texas in Wartime: A Personal Experience in Business, War and Politics* (Austin: Ben C. Jones, 1900), 1–6.

6. Voigt, "Periclean Age of Beaufort," 218–19.

7. Barnwell, *Story of an American Family,* 62–63.

8. Voigt, "Periclean Age of Beaufort," 223; significantly, all five of these Beaufortonians receive mention in *Appleton's Cyclopedia of American Biography,* ed. James Grant Wilson and John Fiske (New York: D. Appleton and Co., 1887), one of the standard American biographical reference works of the nineteenth century.

9. Barnwell, *Story of an American Family,* 50.

10. Richard J. Calhoun, ed., *Witness to Sorrow: The Autobiography of William J. Grayson* (Columbia: University of South Carolina Press, 1990), 86.

11. *Biographical Directory of the South Carolina Senate,* 1: 467–69.

12. Jane H. Pease and William H. Pease, "Intellectual Life in the 1830's: The Institutional Framework and the Charleston Style," in *Intellectual Life in Antebellum Charleston,* ed. Michael O'Brien and David Moltke-Hansen (Knoxville: University of Tennessee Press, 1986), 239.

13. David Moltke-Hansen, "The Expansion of Intellectual Life: A Prospectus," in *Intellectual Life in Antebellum Charleston,* ed. Michael O'Brien and David Moltke-Hansen (Knoxville: University of Tennessee Press, 1986), 130, 151.

14. Calhoun, ed., *Witness to Sorrow,* 76–83.

15. Calhoun, ed., *Witness to Sorrow,* 88, 92.

16. Calhoun, ed., *Witness to Sorrow,* 102–8.

17. Bailey, *Biographical Directory of South Carolina Senate,* 1: 599–601; Barnwell, *Story of an American Family,* 64.

18. Higham and Smith to John Stapleton, January 14, 1837, Stapleton Papers, South Caroliniana Library.

19. Mary C. Simms Oliphant, Alfred Taylor Odell, and T. C. Duncan Eaves, eds., *The Letters of William Gilmore Simms,* 6 vols. (Columbia: University of South Carolina Press, 1952–1982), 2: 498, 4: 129.

20. C. Vann Woodward, ed., *Mary Chesnut's Civil War* (New Haven: Yale University Press, 1981), 363.

21. Edwin A. Alderman and Joel Chandler Harris, eds., *Library of Southern Literature* (Atlanta: Martin and Hoyt, 1907–1913), 5: 2019.

22. Bailey, *Biographical Directory of South Carolina Senate*, 1: 470–72; Barnwell, *Story of an American Family*, 146–47; William Elliott, *Address to the People of St. Helena Parish* (Charleston: Charleston Press by William Estill, 1832), South Caroliniana Library.

23. Alderman and Harris, eds., *Library of Southern Literature* 4: 1569–71; Oliphant, Odell, and Eaves, eds., *Letters of William Gilmore Simms*, 2: 477; Barnwell, *Story of an American Family*, 147.

24. William Elliott, *Carolina Sports by Land and Water* (New York: Arno, 1967), 100.

25. Stephen Meats and Edwin T. Arnold, eds., *The Writings of Benjamin F. Perry*, 3 vols. (Spartanburg: Reprint Co., 1980), 2: 25.

26. Clement Eaton, *The Mind of the Old South* (Baton Rouge: Louisiana State University Press, 1967), 65.

27. Barnwell, *Story of an American Family*, 108–9.

28. Meats and Arnold, eds., *Writings of Benjamin F. Perry*, 2: 25.

29. Maximilian LaBorde, *History of the South Carolina College* (Columbia: Peter Glass, 1859), 236–43; Daniel W. Hollis, *University of South Carolina*, vol. 1, *South Carolina College* (Columbia: University of South Carolina Press, 1951), 127–41.

30. Barnwell, *Story of an American Family*, 111.

31. "M. A. Fowles Recollections" (manuscript), 54, South Carolina Historical Society.

32. Woodward, ed., *Mary Chesnut's Civil War*, 11, 124.

33. Woodward, ed., *Mary Chesnut's Civil War*, 54, 63.

34. Woodward, ed., *Mary Chesnut's Civil War*, 151–52.

35. "M. A. Fowles Recollections," 81.

36. Eaton, *Mind of the Old South*, 66–67.

37. J. H. Cuthbert, *The Life of Richard Fuller, D.D.* (New York: Sheldon, 1879), 21–28; Alderman and Harris, eds. *Library of Southern Literature*, 11: 156.

38. Alderman and Harris, eds., *Library of Southern Literature*, 11: 32–43.

39. Barnwell, *Story of an American Family*, 131–32; Cuthbert, *Life of Richard Fuller*, 49.

40. Cuthbert, *Life of Richard Fuller*, 63–74.

41. Cuthbert, *Life of Richard Fuller*, 75.

42. Cuthbert, *Life of Richard Fuller*, 103.

43. Cuthbert, *Life of Richard Fuller*, 77.

44. Cuthbert, *Life of Richard Fuller*, 97–102.

45. Cuthbert, *Life of Richard Fuller*, 102.

46. Cuthbert, *Life of Richard Fuller*, 71–76.

47. Cuthbert, *Life of Richard Fuller*, 105–6.

48. Cuthbert, *Life of Richard Fuller*, 121.

49. "Richard Fuller," *Dictionary of American Biography*, 4: 62–63; Richard Fuller and Francis Wayland, *Domestic Slavery Considered as a Scriptural Institution: In a Correspondence between Rev. Richard Fuller of Beaufort, South Carolina, and Rev. Francis Wayland of Providence, R.I.* (New York: Lewis Colby, 1845).

50. Fuller and Wayland, *Domestic Slavery,* 3–4.

51. Fuller and Wayland, *Domestic Slavery,* 127, 132, 200.

52. Gary Lawson Browne, *Baltimore in the New Nation* (Chapel Hill: University of North Carolina Press, 1980), 99, 165.

53. Richard Fuller, *Address before the American Colonization Society, delivered at Washington, D.C., January 21, 1851* (Baltimore: Office of the True Union, 1851), 6, 7, 10.

54. Fuller, "Address before the American Colonization Society," 10, 16.

55. Cuthbert, *Life of Richard Fuller,* 264.

56. Cuthbert, *Life of Richard Fuller,* 107–12.

57. Joseph A. Lawton to Winborn B. Lawton, July 25, 1835, Lawton Family Papers, South Caroliniana Library.

58. Narcissa Lawton to A. J. Lawton, August 1835, Lawton Family Papers, South Caroliniana Library.

59. John Lawton to Brother (Winborn?) Lawton, March 20, 1857, Lawton Family Papers, South Caroliniana Library.

60. Coy K. Johnston, *Two Centuries of Lawtonville Baptists, 1775–1975* (Columbia: State Printing Co., 1974), 59–65.

61. Anna Elizabeth Miller, ed., *Our Family Circle* (Hilton Head: Lawton and Allied Families Association, 1987), 358–59; Wallace Alcorn, "A Cavalry Chaplain's Farewell Sermon," *Military Chaplain* 61 (November–December 1988), 3; Willie Lee Rose, *Rehearsal for Reconstruction: The Port Royal Experiment* (Indianapolis: Bobbs-Merrill, 1964), 196, 202, 276–94; Theodore Rosengarten, *Tombee: Portrait of a Cotton Planter* (New York: Morrow, 1986), 263.

22

The Bluffton Movement
and the Road to Secession

The decade of the 1850s was a prosperous moment in the history of the Beaufort District. In fact, it was probably the most prosperous time in a history that was already 350 years old by the middle of the nineteenth century. Cotton prices were so strong that the decade could be called the second cotton boom of the antebellum era. New buildings were springing up in Beaufort, St. Helenaville, Bluffton, Lawtonville, Gillisonville, and McPhersonville—the summer villages of the planters. The Charleston and Savannah Railroad brought renewed enterprise and commerce to the old villages of Coosawhatchie and Grahamville, and whole new towns began to grow at the railroad stops of Gopher Hill (Ridgeland) and Hardeeville. Hardeeville soon replaced the old river town of Purrysburg nearby. But just as the 1850s began to produce wealth and opportunity for a new generation of planters, the dark cloud of secession began billowing over the South Carolina lowcountry.

The first organized political movement dedicated to the purpose of the independent secession of South Carolina from the Union began in the Beaufort District on July 31, 1844. The occasion was a dinner in Bluffton, the summer resort of the planters of lower St. Luke's Parish, in honor of Congressman Robert Barnwell Rhett. Rhett had spent most of the previous six years away from his home district, either in Washington during the congressional sessions or with his family in their new home in Charleston. He had, nevertheless, remained the popular champion of the lowcountry planters, and the Bluffton dinner was a homecoming of sorts. Most of the great planters of St. Luke's Parish, including "Squire" William Pope of Hilton Head, George Edwards of Spring Island, and James Kirk of Kirk's Bluff, were in attendance. A delegation of Beaufort planters crossed the Broad River for the occasion, led by Rhett's brother Edmund, the leader of the Rhett faction in St. Helena Parish. The welcoming speech was given by Dr. Daniel Heyward Hamilton of Bluffton, eldest surviving son of Governor James Hamilton Jr. and heir to much of the vast Heyward family holdings in the district. In deference to Rhett's support of temperance, the dinner was uncharacteristically free of alcohol. In eloquent oratory, Rhett exhorted the planters to stand by their principles and protect their mutual interests, "if you value your rights you must resist; submit not, discharge your duties faithfully to yourselves, your children, your country and your God, and we will ensure a glorious triumph."[1]

What Rhett was seeking to launch at Bluffton was a statewide political movement to call for an immediate state convention to nullify the Tariff of 1842, which had been raised again in violation of the Compromise of 1833, or for the immediate secession of South Carolina from the union. This was "independent state action" of the most radical sort. In the complicated political factionalism of antebellum politics in South Carolina, the greatest risk for Rhett was that this action was counter to the more moderate and pragmatic position of South Carolina's giant elder statesman, John C. Calhoun, with whom Rhett had been closely allied before 1844. Opposition to Calhoun had ended the political careers of some of South Carolina's most prominent political luminaries, such as Judge William Smith of York, the first states' righter; Senator William Preston of Columbia; and Governor James Hamilton Jr. of St. Peter's Parish, the architect of the Nullifiers' victory in 1832. Calhoun's main concerns in Washington in 1844 were to keep the northern and southern wings of the Democratic Party together, ensure the election of James Knox Polk to the presidency, and secure the annexation of Texas. The last thing Calhoun needed was a secessionist firestorm in his home state which might upset the delicate political balance. Rhett, however, saw the interests of South Carolina, and particularly his lowcountry planter constituents, subsumed in the process and struck out on his own. Rhett was never a man to worry about political risks when principles were involved. And besides, he knew very well the deep anxiety and daily frustration of his own planter constituents.

Animated dinners were held throughout the district, and the Blufftonites solidified their hold on the younger planters of the Beaufort/Colleton District. Ultimately, though, the Bluffton movement failed. Calhoun did not endorse the movement, and the rest of the state was not ready for so radical a course. A political coalition of opposition Whigs, old unionists, and Democratic Party leaders loyal to Calhoun accused Rhett of promoting "disunion," and his popular support was confined to his home district. The movement had gained many powerful adherents, however, including Governor James H. Hammond, Congressman George McDuffie, and Whitmarsh Seabrook of Edisto Island. Ultimately, it was Langdon Cheves of St. Peter's Parish, one of the most admired elder statesmen in South Carolina, who publicly outlined the tactic that was to galvanize the moderate members of the states' rights movement six years later. To counter the

Blufftonites' call for immediate separate state action, Cheves called on South Carolina political leaders to develop a program to prepare the other slaveholding states for united southern opposition to the federal government and the ultimate formation of a southern Confederacy. This was the beginning of the "Cooperationist" party, which was the moderate or conservative wing of the states' rights movement in South Carolina during the 1850s.[2] Though Rhett's call for separate state action was premature, it was a training ground for a new group of "fire eaters" and another step on the road to secession.

In 1844, Rhett's appeal was to a new generation of planters who had come of age since the Nullification Crisis. At the Bluffton speech, "he appealed to youth and they responded." In the newspapers this new group of youthful activists were dubbed the Bluffton Boys, and from then until the Civil War they formed the vanguard of the secessionist movement across the state. The leader of the "Bluffton Boys" in the Beaufort District in the 1840s, and Robert Barnwell Rhett's successor in Congress, was William Ferguson Colcock of Prince William Parish.

Colcock was born in Beaufort in 1804. His father was Judge Charles Jones Colcock of Charleston and Pocotaligo, and his mother was Mary Woodward Hutson. He was descended from Reverend William Hutson, the colonial founder of the Stoney Creek Church, and his grandfather was Thomas Hutson, Revolutionary War hero and one of the Beaufort District Federalists who voted to ratify the U.S. Constitution in 1788. Colcock attended schools in Beaufort a few years after R. B. Rhett and Barnwell. Later he moved to Charleston when Martin Hurlbut left the Beaufort College to open his classical school in that city. He was the valedictorian of the 1823 class at the South Carolina College and was admitted to the South Carolina Bar in 1825. He began his law practice at the Beaufort District Court at Coosawhatchie. During the 1820s, Colcock married Sarah Rebecca Huguenin, and after her death, in 1829, he married her sister, Emmeline Lucia Huguenin, his wife for the next thirty years. This marriage alliance is of great importance in understanding Colcock's leadership in the Beaufort District. First, it provided him a huge base of financial support. The Huguenin family was the largest rice-planting family on the Coosawhatchie River in the antebellum era and among the largest slaveowners in the Beaufort District. Secondly, the Huguenin's were descendants of the old Swiss families of Purrysburg and had family connections in St. Peter's Parish and business connections in Savannah. This complemented Colcock's own Hutson family connections in Charleston. His political alliance with the Rhett faction of Beaufort gave him strong support among the sea island cotton planters. Thus, he had supporters and connections across the district.

In 1834, he first served in the South Carolina Legislature as representative from Prince William Parish. In his second term he served for St. Luke's Parish but thereafter consistently served for Prince William. In 1841, Colcock was elected speaker of the South Carolina House and remained in that position until his election to Congress in 1848, succeeding Robert Barnwell Rhett. When the Bluffton movement began in 1844, Colcock was in a key position to help in the South Carolina legislature.[3]

The other leader of the Bluffton Boys in the Beaufort District was Edmund Rhett, the fifth brother of the Rhett family. Rhett was born in Beaufort in 1808. The second youngest son of the Rhett family, Edmund had educational advantages that the older sons did not. Rhett attended Philips Andover Academy in Massachusetts and then graduated Phi Beta Kappa from Yale College in 1830. He read the law with his older brother, Robert; was admitted to the South Carolina Bar in 1833; and opened his law practice at Ashepoo Ferry and in Beaufort. His principal residence was the fine home on the corner of Craven Street and Church Street overlooking the bay in Beaufort. Because of the prominence of the Rhett faction in the movement toward secession, and because Rhett's house was the unofficial headquarters of the radical fire eaters in Beaufort for the next sixteen years, the house is known to this day as the "Secession House."

Rhett was the leader of the secessionist faction in St. Helena Parish. He served in the South Carolina House from 1842 to 1844 and was the representative for St. Helena Parish when the Bluffton movement began. He was the longtime mayor of Beaufort in the 1850s when the town was experiencing an increase in new buildings resulting from the second cotton boom. Local residents considered that "he had done more good for the town than all the other inhabitants who had preceded him."[4]

The Rhett-Colcock faction of secessionists, however, did not completely control the Beaufort District. In St. Helena Parish, the pervasive influence of Barnwell led a conservative faction which, while equally ardent on states' rights and slavery, nevertheless regularly disapproved of the radical measures advocated by the Rhetts. In fact, in 1844, after the Bluffton movement broke like a storm over the state, Rhett was defeated for re-election by Benjamin Jenkins Johnson, a Beaufort attorney with family connections to the Jenkins family of St. Helena Island, one of the pioneer families of the sea island. Johnson represented St. Helena Parish in the South Carolina House and Senate for the next thirteen years. In a letter to Rhett after the election of 1844, Barnwell explained the local political situation in Beaufort. "Edmund's election was not the least bit dependant upon you, the fact is that his having succeeded before very much surprised me (and you know it was only by a majority of one or two votes) as soon as I heard that Ben Johnson intended to oppose him, I felt certain that Edmund would be defeated."[5]

Barnwell's letter also reveals that in Beaufort, the Rhett faction was seen as the aristocratic faction, not as the champions of the middle-class, country dwelling planters. This was in opposition to political conditions on the mainland, where the country planters rallied behind William F. Colcock's calls for radical action while many of the large absentee rice planters, Daniel Huger and Langdon Cheves on the Savannah River and Henry A. Middleton on the Combahee River, were more conservative. In addition, the years between 1820 and 1840 were important in improving the fortunes of most of the Rhett brothers. Robert Rhett was no longer the poor country lawyer of the 1820s. He had become rich, moved to a sumptuous home in Charleston, and spent much of his time in Washington. While he still eloquently represented the anxiety of the country planters, he was no longer of their social class. In 1842, Edmund made a fortunate marriage to Mary Williamson Stuart, another old Beaufort family. Edmund Rhett had a successful cotton plantation with eighty-six slaves in addition to his legal practice. The "Secession House" was one of the finest and most conspicuous homes in Beaufort. By any measure of the age, he was a rich man. As Beaufort's mayor, Edmund personally attended to the needs of the town's few indigent poor. He cultivated the role of paternalistic aristocrat, and the country planters rewarded him with defeat.

Robert Barnwell reflected on the inability of Beaufort's aristocratic planter class to be effective in democratic politics:"The fact is ... our social relations are in conflict with our political institutions, and I am cool enough to expect and democratic enough not merely to submit to but to acquiesce in the triumph of politics over taste." Early in his career, Barnwell had been advised by James L. Petigru, the great sage of Charleston, that if he desired political success he should not reside in Beaufort.[6] Petigru was right, and Barnwell was inactive in elective politics for seventeen years while residing comfortably in the old town. Barnwell's political inactivity may have been not so much personal reserve as political realism. In a town as small as Beaufort where people were well known to each other, pretenses to social exclusivity were sure to spell defeat at election time. Even though St. Helena Parish was one of the richest neighborhoods in America in the antebellum era, there were still class distinctions and personal animosities.

One of the best examples of the mood of these country planters in the late antebellum era is the diary left by Thomas B. Chaplin of St. Helena Island. A descendant of one of the pioneer families and relative of some of the richest cotton planters in the Beaufort District, particularly his uncle Benjamin Chaplin, Thomas Chaplin always struggled to make ends meet and never achieved the financial independence that would allow him to pursue social or political status. He often expressed envy of richer friends and neighbors and probably exercised that at the ballot box. Edmund Rhett, in fact, was attorney for his archenemy, J. L. Toomer. Chaplin's attorney was Richard DeTreville, longtime state senator for St. Helena Parish and a business rival of Robert Barnwell and Robert Rhett.[7]

But when the secession crisis arrived, the Beaufort planters put aside social resentments and personal rivalries and stood shoulder-to-shoulder in defense of slavery and their way of life, with Chaplin among them.

Regardless of class distinctions or social pretensions, rich urban planters and middle-class country planters in the Beaufort District shared the anxiety that not only the national government, but also much of Europe led by the British empire, was conspiring against their most fundamental political, economic, and personal interests. Slavery was under attack everywhere, and even the huge inexorable forces of the industrial revolution, which had made the cotton planters rich in the first place, seemed to be moving against the slave labor system. In August 1840, Edmund Rhett, then only thirty-two years old, had launched his own political career with a fiery speech to the Beaufort Agricultural Society in which he defended the South's plantation and slave system as morally superior to the industrial free-labor system that was rapidly developing in Europe and in the North. He described an industrial factory as "one vast Catholic workshop like unto a prison." He described the steam engine, the symbol of the early industrial revolution, as a "gloomy iron idol." Anticipating Karl Marx, Rhett described the new urban proletariat class as "the working man borne along in solemn procession by a fearful host styling themselves 'the armed phalanx of labour.'" William Elliott, perhaps the Beaufort District's most scientific planter, answered Rhett's rhetoric with a reasoned and informed rebuttal, but Elliott's appeals to reason were no match for Rhett's appeal to fear.[8]

Another key figure in the political life of the district was Beaufort attorney and longtime state senator Richard LaBoulardarie DeTreville. Richard DeTreville was born in Beaufort in 1801, son of Robert DeTreville and Sarah Ellis. DeTreville's mother was descended from one of the colonial pioneer families of Port Royal Island, and his grandfather was the garrison commander at Fort Lyttelton when the British landed on Port Royal Island in 1779. He was educated at James L. Petigru's law school in Charleston and graduated from West Point in 1823. Following family tradition, DeTreville was an artillery officer until he resigned his commission in 1825. He read the law and was admitted to the South Carolina Bar in 1825. He practiced law in Beaufort for the next forty-nine years until his death in 1874. DeTreville also had a law practice in Charleston. While not a large planter, DeTreville did acquire a plantation that had forty-six slaves by 1850. DeTreville was first elected to the South Carolina House from St. Helena Parish in 1830. From 1835 to 1853, he was the perennial state senator from St. Helena Parish. In 1848 and 1852, he ran for statewide office as attorney general but was twice defeated. In 1854, however, DeTreville was elected and served one term as lieutenant governor. It was the pinnacle of his political career. While ardent on states' rights and slavery, DeTreville held more moderate views than the Rhett faction. In 1844, he was a supporter of John C. Calhoun's cautious and politically expedient course and thereby a presidential elector for James Knox Polk. DeTreville had received his appointment to West Point in 1818 from Secretary of War John C. Calhoun, after an introduction from Henry W. DeSaussure. He was not one of the Bluffton Boys but the leader of the Calhoun faction in St. Helena parish. By 1850, he was vice president of the Southern Rights Association of Beaufort. DeTreville was a prominent cooperationist in the early 1850s and opposed the independent state action, or immediate secession of South Carolina, that the fire eaters promoted.[9]

DeTreville was not a friend of the Rhetts and Barnwells. In a private letter to Rhett in 1845, Barnwell urged the congressman to pay a substantial debt that was due in Charleston which Barnwell had cosigned for Rhett. The debt had been turned over to Richard DeTreville as attorney for the creditors. Barnwell warned Rhett,"It is certainly unsafe for either of us to be placed ... at the mercy of a man like DeTreville. For your sake, I trust that you will have the business removed from his control, before he is able to gratify his malice through the power of the court."[10] The Rhetts and Barnwells may not have liked DeTreville, but the majority of the country planters of St. Helena Parish did. It was an important commentary on the antebellum politics of the sea islands that those planters returned DeTreville to represent them in the South Carolina legislature for twenty-three years, not Rhett or Barnwell.

The years following the eruption of the Bluffton Movement were dominated by national political events. The annexation of Texas, the Mexican War, and the achievement of Manifest Destiny all put parochial interests on hold. But the southern planters simmered, and when Congressman David Wilmot of Pennsylvania nearly succeeded in attaching an antislavery proviso to the treaty annexing California and the southwest, they exploded again. Again it appeared that Congress was conspiring against their most fundamental interest, and this after so many sons of the South had died in the Mexican War. This led to John C. Calhoun's "Southern Address" of 1849, which was cosponsored by fifty congressmen from slaveholding states, including Robert Rhett. It was one of his last acts as congressman from the Beaufort/Colleton District. Rhett's last session was March 1849. He was replaced in Congress by his protégé, William Ferguson Colcock of Pocotaligo. Calhoun's address was the catalyst for the Nashville Convention of slaveholding states in June 1850. The Nashville Convention was the first united action of the southern states, and it precipitated another political crisis in South Carolina in which Beaufort District politicians again played leading roles.

The years 1850 to 1852 were watershed years in the secession movement in South Carolina and in the political careers of Beaufort's most prominent political sons. In March 1850, antebellum South Carolina's most talented and dominant political leader, John C. Calhoun, finally succumbed to pneumonia and heart disease. His loss was a blow to the state and the nation. It also opened avenues of advancement for ambitious younger politicians, both friends and foes of Calhoun. Within South Carolina, it was almost as if Calhoun's death took the lid off political activism. His influence had suppressed the radical secessionists, particularly the Bluffton Movement of 1844. With Calhoun gone, they precipitated a crisis which divided the state's political leadership between fire eaters and cooperationists.

When Calhoun died in March 1850, Frank Elmore, one of Rhett's early allies, was appointed to succeed him. Rhett, who had always coveted the Senate position, was lobbying for the appointment throughout the year. In May, Frank Elmore died, and Governor Whitmarsh Seabrook of Edisto Island, one of the Bluffton Boys of 1844, then appointed his friend Robert W. Barnwell of Beaufort, who served as U.S. senator from South Carolina from June 4, 1850, to December 8, 1850. It was the highest political position that Beaufort's intellectual leader ever held.

When Barnwell arrived in the Senate, his keen intellect and powerful oratory prompted Sen. Daniel Webster of Massachusetts to ask Sen. Andrew Pickens Butler if "South Carolina kept statesmen 'in petto' as the Pope keeps Cardinals to be used whenever the emergency arises?"[11] During the fall elections, Barnwell did not stand for re-election, and Rhett was elected to the Senate. He took his seat on January 6, 1851. It was the highest political position that Rhett ever held.

All this jockeying for position coincided with the excitement surrounding the Nashville Convention and the movement for southern nationalism. Rhett was passed over as an at-large delegate to the Nashville Convention. The state legislature chose instead Robert W. Barnwell, Langdon Cheves, and others whose moderation would not frighten the other southern delegates. Rhett was chosen as a delegate from the Colleton District, but, in accordance with the wishes of the South Carolina delegation to let other southern states play leading roles at the convention, Rhett was uncharacteristically quiet. The Nashville Convention formally communicated its opposition to the Compromise of 1850 which permitted California to enter the Union, but broke the 36 degree-30 minute provision of the earlier Missouri Compromise which had lasted for thirty years. The Nashville Convention, however, took no serious action against the national government, and Congress ignored their protests.

Rhett returned to South Carolina, and in a speech in Charleston declared the Nashville Convention to be "the beginning of a Revolution." To Rhett, this was not only the beginning of southern nationalism but also the beginning of disunion. As usual, Rhett's declaration, repeated to a large and friendly Georgia audience in Macon in August, was met with wild enthusiasm by the fire eaters and the Bluffton Boys and with consternation by the moderates. His enemies called him "traitor," and he wore the insult as a badge of honor.[12]

On July 24, 1850, Rhett was invited to a dinner in his honor hosted by the planters of St. Helena Island. The planters and their wives gathered at the summer village at St. Helenaville. Located on a high bluff with a spectacular view across Village Creek, Morgan River, and St. Helena Sound, the village was one of the most aesthetically pleasing spots on America's east coast. July 24 would have been predictably hot and humid, but the village was situated to gather the sea breeze which sweeps across St. Helena Sound on every summer evening.

A stand was erected for the guest of honor and welcoming committee. It had a canopy for shade and was festooned with evergreen branches. Pretenses to temperance that had characterized the Bluffton speech of 1844 were absent on St. Helena Island. Refreshments were offered and "freely partaken of by some." Rhett addressed the audience for nearly an hour in an "able and spirited manner." This was followed by dinner, champagne, and speeches by local politicians. State Representative Benjamin J. Johnson, Beaufort Mayor Edmund Rhett, and aspiring politician Joseph Daniel Pope all made "excellent speeches." At the conclusion of the festivities, the St. Helena planters presented Rhett with a silk banner embroidered with the words, "Oh, that we were all such Traitors."[13]

The subject of Rhett's speech was old hat to this crowd. What energized the evening, and others like it across South Carolina, was the confidence that the rest of the South was slowly but inevitably behind them. The southern rights movement had spawned a number of well-organized "Southern Rights Associations" throughout the South. These organizations were the grass roots of southern nationalism.

The key meeting of the Southern Rights movement in the Beaufort District was a meeting at the district courthouse in Gillisonville on November 11, 1850. Representatives from all four parishes in the Beaufort District attended. The *Charleston Courier* described the Southern Rights assembly at Gillisonville as "a very large meeting of the people." It may have been the most representative political assembly of the planter class in the long history of the district. All parishes were well represented, and all classes of planters were in attendance. The meeting was treated to a rousing speech by Congressman William Ferguson Colcock, who "councilled speedy action by the united South, if possible," and if not, "then he preferred separate state action." Colcock's speech was met with great enthusiasm and was "frequently interrupted by applause." The attendees then got down to the business of designing a constitution for the organization and writing a basic statement of principle as a preamble to the constitution. The conscious distribution of power in the Beaufort District Southern Rights Association was an expression of the democratic values of the secessionist parties. Alexander Moultrie of St. Luke's Parish was chosen to chair the meeting. The Committee of Twenty, which drafted the constitution and its preamble, represented not only each of the parishes but also genuinely reflected the economic and social interests of the various neighborhoods of the district. Edmund Rhett, John Barnwell, and Richard Reynolds represented the interests of the sea island cotton planters of St. Helena Parish. William Ferguson Hutson and Daniel Heyward represented the rice planters of lower Prince William Parish. Abram Ruth and J. A. E. Chovin represented the smaller planters of upper Prince William Parish. F. W. Fickling represented the sea island cotton planters of Hilton Head Island and lower St. Luke's Parish. Charles Dupont, Thomas Drayton, and John Ferrebee represented the rice planters of upper St. Luke's Parish. The lower St. Peter's rice planters were represented by Hardy Harrison and Daniel Heyward, who owned Laurel Hill Plantation on the lower Savannah River as well as his principal plantation in Prince William Parish. Upper St. Peter's Parish was represented by planter and entrepreneur Alexander J. Lawton and merchant, factor, and storekeeper Henry Solomons.

The constitution that this committee drafted called for a president and four vice presidents representing each of the parishes. Alexander Moultrie was confirmed as president of the association. His name and his successive marriage alliances with the Guerard, Howard, and Strobhar families gave him social and business connections throughout St. Luke's and St. Peter's Parishes. Among the vice presidents, John Seth Maner represented St. Peter's Parish, George Mackay represented Prince William Parish, Joseph J. Pope represented St. Helena Parish, and General John H. Howard represented St. Luke's Parish. R. H. Bacot of Prince William was the recording secretary and R. L. Tillinghast, the Grahamville schoolteacher, was the corresponding secretary. The executive committee of sixteen men was heavily weighted toward the country planters. James Lartigue, John Fitts, W. W. Hardee, Joseph Hazle, D. H. Ellis, James Gooding, and Robert Bowers were all rising country planters from Prince William and St. Peter's Parishes.

The preamble to the constitution of the Beaufort District Southern Rights Association was the most succinct expression of the political opinion of the planter class of the Beaufort District during the secession crisis. Its content revealed the intellectual influence of Beaufort Mayor Edmund Rhett, and its design was the training session for William Ferguson Hutson, who was to be the principal author of the South Carolina Ordinance of Secession ten years later. By November 1850, the electorate of the Beaufort District had already determined to leave the union one way or another and to use every means at their disposal to defend the "domestic institution" upon which their livelihoods and their communities' social order depended. Toward that end, the men gathered at Gillisonville and pledged: "all that we are, all that we have, all that we hope for." This statement was an expression of the predominant opinion not just of the wealthy and politically active planters of the Beaufort District, but also of the far more numerous country planters. It related their realization of the mortal ideological combat between slaveholders and abolitionists. It also repeated their belief in the social and even moral correctness of their "domestic institution." It also repeated their belief in the constitutional guarantees that supported slavery and their disappointment in the federal government's abandonment of those guarantees. It expressed their recognition of the hostility of a large body of the northern electorate to their interests, their values, and their society. And finally it asserted their willingness to risk everything to defend their way of life.

The full text of the Beaufort District Southern Rights Association statement of principle of November 11, 1850, is as follows:

We, the people of Beaufort District, in this our primary assembly, do declare: That we believe Abolitionism, in common with Socialism, Communism, and Agrarianism, is the natural fruit of a spirit of infidelity, rejecting the order of God's providence and the teachings of Revelation. That we regard domestic slavery as the great safeguard of political freedom. That without it Republic institutions have never long existed, and in the nature of things never can. That it is the only social arrangement capable of reconciling labor with capital, and protecting us from the inevitable tendencies of the free labor system towards the terrible alternatives of absolutism or barbarism. That it is our duty to maintain it at all hazards.

That a Government which threatens its security, or infringes the integrity of its safeguards, is not only useless but dangerous. That the Federal Union was based on a Constitution recognizing the securities and safeguards essential to its preservation.

That in rejecting the ultimatum of the Nashville Convention for dividing the acquired territory and inter-meddling with slavery in the District of Columbia, Congress has annulled the Constitution and virtually dissolved the Union.

That the indications of public opinion in the North exhibit no returning sense of justice, but only hostility to us and our institutions, and a determination to grant us neither justice or equality.

Therefore it is now the solemn duty of the Southern States to sever the formal tie that yet binds us to a Union already practically sundered, and to unite in a slaveholding Confederacy, maintaining as a fundamental principle, the perpetual recognition of that institution.

That it will be right and proper for such Confederacy to prevent all intercourse with the North except upon ample securities for non-interference with our domestic concerns, until a Southern Government is established which can enforce such regulations. We invite all Southerners to unite with us in a solemn pledge in abstain, as far as circumstances permit, from employing any person from a non-slaveholding State in any capacity whatever—to purchase no article grown or made, no book, paper, or other literary production, written, edited or printed in the enemy's country—not to travel therein, send our children there for education, nor in any way whatever, directly or indirectly, give them "aid and comfort."

At the same time we repudiate the idea of dictating to any who honestly differ from us as to these means. Nor do we intend by our actions to sanction the vicious principle of overbearing individual independence, or curtailing individual rights by the mass force of aggregated irresponsible and voluntary association.

In accordance with these views we earnestly recommend to our State Legislature speedy and prompt action for severing the political bonds which subject us to Northern vassalage, and to unite our Southern sisters in harmonious resistance to all attacks on our loved and cherished institutions.

Finally, by the recollection of a glorious history, by the memory of a gallant ancestry, by the love of posterity, by the hopes of human freedom, by the necessity of social order, by the blessings of civilization, by reverence for God and religion, by faith in His Wisdom and promises, his arrangements and designs, we call on every true hearted son of the South to come up to the help of our common country, in whose sacred cause "we pledge all that we are, all that we have, all that we hope for."[14]

This was the Beaufort District's declaration of independence from the Union.

The Southern Rights Association of St. Helena Parish was also formed in 1850. Nearly 120 planters joined the association and agreed to attend quarterly meetings. They formed an executive committee called the Committee of Safety in ominous memory of 1775. Its first chair was Edmund Rhett, and the resolution of the association was drafted by Sen. Richard DeTreville. Their alliance was significant. When the crisis over fundamental values arrived, they put aside former differences. DeTreville's resolution was drafted in such a way as not to be offensive to unionist and cooperationist members who formed a strong minority of the association. Beaufort's leading moderate, Robert Barnwell, was elected president. DeTreville's contribution to the association is intriguing and instructive. In 1850, he favored immediate secession, but within two years he changed his mind and "opposed separate secession for the state because he feared it would result in both failure and armed intervention and would impede future co-operation between the Southern states."[15] Perhaps his campaign for attorney general influenced his moderation in 1852. While the secessionists were the majority in his home district, they were still a minority in the rest of the state in 1852. De Treville was an experienced and informed state politician and may have made a tactical shift.

By late 1851, the St. Helena Southern Rights Association was itself breaking up. The majority of secessionists, led by Edmund Rhett and De Treville, had dominated the association, and those who favored waiting for the cooperation of other southern states were edged out. In September 1851, Barnwell, the leading proponent of cooperation, resigned as president of the association. At the fall meeting on October 13, thirty planters of moderate convictions, unionists, and cooperationists, tendered their resignation by letter.[16] Even in Beaufort, the home of secession, progress toward that goal was uneven and unsure.

In May 1851, a Convention of the Southern Rights Association of South Carolina met in Charleston. The city was filled by 431 angry young delegates from forty different associations from around the state. The secessionists were an overwhelming majority. It was this convention that divided the political leadership of the state into two opposing factions: the secessionists and the cooperationists. Congressman William F. Colcock, a secessionist leader at the convention, recalled that the question of separate state action versus cooperation "divided our citizens" at that time. The whole congressional delegation of the state addressed the Southern Rights Convention. William Colcock spoke in favor of separate state action while Senator Andrew Pickens Butler, Congressman James L. Orr, and former Senator Robert W. Barnwell spoke in opposition. Colcock recalled that the vast majority of delegates to the Charleston convention were in favor of separate state action, but when they "assembled in Constitutional Convention (1852) they thought this premature."[17]

The expression of the South Carolina electorate on the subject of secession versus cooperation came in the fall elections of 1851. As with the Nullification Crisis of 1832, the two factions campaigned vigorously across the state. When the election tally came in, the secessionists had suffered a resounding defeat. The cooperationists won majorities in six of the seven congressional districts. Only the Beaufort/Colleton/Orangeburg congressional district returned a secessionist majority. Barnwell pointed out that the cooperationists found themselves in an embarrassing position, nonetheless. While they had won the election in 1851, they still had a minority of seats in the state legislature and a minority of delegates to the state Constitutional Convention called for April 26, 1852.[18]

The state Constitutional Convention of 1852 was the culmination of the secession crisis that had begun two years before. The delegates had divided themselves into the radical secessionists and the moderate cooperationists. Without question, the leader of the radical secessionists in South Carolina was Beaufort's own Senator Robert Barnwell Rhett. Not only was Rhett the most prominent secessionist in South Carolina, he was also the most prominent secessionist in the nation.

Even in the Beaufort District, there were significant groups that opposed the radical position of the Rhett faction. In 1851, Colonel Alexander Lawton of St. Peter's Parish ran against Rhett as a delegate to the southern Congress, the successor to the Nashville Convention. Rhett won the election in the Beaufort District, but Lawton won the majority of votes in Robertville and the same number of votes in Purrysburg. Lawton ran because "he opposed the immediate secessionism of Rhett and the islanders."[19] Lawton represented the large planters of upper St. Peter's Parish whose rising prosperity in the late antebellum era; lesser dependence on single-crop, labor-oriented agricultural production; and old religious traditions separated them economically, culturally, and politically from the rice and cotton planters. Their community was more economically diverse and self-sufficient than the rice and cotton planters, and they shared with the upcountry farmers an aversion to the early radicalism of the Rhett faction.

The Constitutional Convention of 1852 is what Rhett called for in Bluffton in 1844. Of the cooperationists in 1852, two of their three leading champions were from the Beaufort District: Robert W. Barnwell of Beaufort and Langdon Cheves of St. Peter's Parish. This was probably the moment of greatest influence in the political life of the antebellum Beaufort District.

No one knew for sure how the delegates would vote when they assembled in Columbia in April. The secessionists had campaigned across South Carolina, trying to force candidates to pledge their intentions before the election, but the only district which adopted this hardline position was, once again, the Beaufort District. In the rest of the state the delegates were uncommitted to a specific course of action, and, by the time they met in convention, the popular mood had moderated. Congressman William F. Colcock recalled that between the Southern Rights Association Convention in 1851 and the state Constitutional Convention in 1852, many of the same men had changed their minds. The secessionists were disorganized, and leading cooperationists held key positions, such as Governor John Means as chair of the Convention and Langdon Cheves as chair of the powerful Committee of Twenty-one. Cheves was afraid of the unchecked authority of the convention, called it "an infernal machine" and wished to adjourn it before it could do harm. Many of those who originally favored secession now wished to work to unite the factions within the state. In a desperate attempt to keep the momentum for immediate secession alive, delegate Maxcy Gregg of Columbia proposed a motion to have Senator Robert Barnwell Rhett address the convention. This motion failed in the caucus of the secessionist faction, and Rhett was left isolated at the convention. A last-gasp amendment to the convention's resolutions was proposed by Edmund Rhett. He said the convention should nullify that provision of the U.S. Constitution which declared that "the citizens of each state shall be entitled to all the privileges and immunities of the citizens of the several states" and deny those rights to citizens of Vermont and

Massachusetts who had taken leading roles in the abolitionist struggle. This amendment was also soundly defeated.[20]

The failure of the Constitutional Convention of 1852 to adopt even partial attempts at active resistance to the federal government was a terrible blow to the secessionist movement in South Carolina and the Rhett faction in the Beaufort District. It was also the virtual end of the political career of Beaufort's firebrand "father of secession," Robert Barnwell Rhett.

As a matter of principle, Rhett resigned the senate seat he had sought all his political life on May 1, 1852. Richard DeTreville was defeated for attorney general that year, and Edmund Rhett hunkered down in the secessionist fortress of Beaufort. William F. Colcock left the U.S. Congress and took the federal patronage job of port collector for the port of Charleston offered to him by President Franklin Pierce, replacing William J. Grayson, who had held the post since 1841. As a Whig and a unionist, Grayson had long since ceased to be a factor in state politics, but he left office with a sense of bitter irony. "I went out of office with the rest of the Federal Officers in the State who had opposed Secession and were now obliged to make way for thorough going advocates of the opposite end."[21]

The most sensational effect was Rhett's resignation from the U.S. Senate. Governor John H. Means pleaded with Rhett to remain in the Senate, but on May 10, Rhett confirmed his decision with a letter to the governor which was published in newspapers across the state. "Sensible of the profound respect I owe the State as my sovereign, and deeply grateful for the many favors and honors she has conferred upon me; I bow to her declared will and make way for those who, with hearts less sad . . . can better sustain her in the course she has determined to pursue." It was the highest office Rhett ever achieved, and he abandoned its honors and perquisites without hesitation in order to remain true to the principles he had adopted twenty-four years before.[22]

This was the major turning point in South Carolina politics. The state decisively rejected the secessionist call. Only in the Beaufort/Colleton/Orangeburg District did the secessionists appeal to the majority of the electorate. Before 1852, the influence of the Rhett faction and Beaufort politicians on state politics had been enormous. After 1852, the influence of Beaufort politicians was marginal. Every congressman who represented the district between 1830 and 1852— Barnwell, Grayson, Rhett, and Colcock—had been born and educated in and maintained strong family ties to Beaufort. When Colcock left Congress to assume the post of port collector in Charleston, he was replaced in Congress not by a Beaufortonian, but by Laurence Massilon Keitt of Orangeburg.

Keitt was equally as ardent on states' rights, secession, and slavery as any Beaufortonian. In fact, he was one of South Carolina's strongest and most unrelenting voices in Congress from 1853 to 1860. He was active in the debates on the Kansas-Nebraska Bill and was deeply involved in congressional arguments over the admission of Kansas. He also participated in his friend Preston Brooks's caning of Sen. Charles Sumner of Massachusetts and was expelled from Congress as a result. Keitt was a natural orator. Talented, intelligent, and intense in his defense of southern institutions, the Washington press dubbed him the "Harry Hotspur of the South." Thus, he was representative of majority opinion in his congressional district and an able successor to Robert Barnwell Rhett. During the Civil War, Keitt raised the 20th Regiment of South Carolina Volunteers, defended Battery Wagner during the siege of Charleston, and died as a brigadier general of Confederate forces at the Battle of Cold Harbor, Virginia, in 1864. He not only spoke for but also fought and died for his convictions, a true hero of the Confederacy.[23]

The fact that Keitt was not from Beaufort, however, was significant to local politics. The census of 1840 and 1850 had changed the congressional district of Beaufort. The relatively stagnated population of the Beaufort District meant that the lowcountry parishes could no longer support a seat in Congress. They had to combine with the midland districts of Orangeburg and Barnwell to warrant a congressional voice. The majority of the voting population thus shifted to the inland districts, and the coastal parishes lost control of their seat. Lowndes, Hamilton, Barnwell, Grayson, Rhett, and Colcock had all descended from the pioneer planter families of the lowcountry, but Keitt descended from German immigrants that settled the Dutch Fork and Orange District in the late eighteenth century. His mother, Mary Wannamaker Keitt, was a member of one of the large planter families of St. Matthews near old Fort Motte. Thus, even before the Civil War began, the political ascendancy of the old Beaufort District in South Carolina politics had waned.

The planters of the Beaufort District and the other secessionists in South Carolina spent the years from 1852 to 1860 waiting for the rest of the state, and the rest of the South, to catch up with them. Issues such as the Kansas-Nebraska Act and "Bleeding Kansas," where pro-slavery gangs from Missouri and the South fought skirmishes against armed bands of free-soil immigrants known as "Jayhawkers," were followed assiduously in the South Carolina press. Small groups of young men raised money in South Carolina to go to Kansas to fight the first battles of the Civil War. One of these groups, dubbed the "South Carolina Bloodhounds" by their abolitionist enemies, insisted on riding beneath the palmetto flag. Their leader was Captain DeTreville which could have been either one of Richard DeTreville's two sons, Robert (1833–1869) or Richard (1834–1869). This was the unit that seized the Free State Hotel in Lawrence, Kansas, in the famous raid of May 20, 1856, and raised the palmetto flag over the town on orders of their captain. This was the event which began the "Bleeding Kansas"

War and prompted John Brown's retaliatory "Pottawatomie Massacre," launching Brown's reputation as the most violent abolitionist. Thus, even in far-off Kansas, the Beaufort District was in the forefront of the defense of slavery and the sensational events leading to the Civil War.[24]

The period between 1852 and 1860 was also a period of great prosperity especially for the cotton planters. Sea island cotton prices averaged nearly forty cents per pound from 1852 to 1860. That buoyed the spirits of the planters and kept them busy making and spending money. There was even a movement to reopen the African slave trade, as they had done during the first cotton boom in 1803. Radical secessionists supported the idea as a way to unite the South and hasten disunion. But many old Beaufortonians were skeptical and raised the time-honored specter of slave rebellion. William Henry Trescot, who was then assistant secretary of state in the Buchanan administration, had become a Beaufortonian by virtue of his marriage to Eliza Natalia Cuthbert and his consequent inheritance of Barnwell Island and its slaves. Trescot reminded South Carolinians that the 1820 Slave Trade Piracy Act, and the subsequent treaty with Britain to enforce the prohibition of the slave trade, had the concurrence of Secretary of War John C. Calhoun. Robert Barnwell Rhett noted in the *Mercury* that the slave-trade issue would only divide the South and hamper efforts to build southern nationalism.[25]

It was events in the North which eventually reawakened the South Carolina electorate to reissue the call for secession. Abolitionism had found an organized political home in the new Republican Party, and their success in northern elections aroused the old fears and anxieties of southern planters. Evidence began to mount regarding the hostility of the majority of northern citizens toward southern institutions—particularly slavery. The issue of slavery in the unorganized territory of the West was not only the subject of the famous Lincoln-Douglas debates in Illinois, it was also the issue that brought Rhett back into the limelight as the champion of secession in South Carolina.

When Rhett went back on the campaign trail to promote the cause to which he had devoted his political life, he began in the heart of his home district. His first public appearance in seven years was a Fourth of July oration at Grahamville in 1859. The crossroads village of Grahamville was the summer village of the planters of upper St. Luke's Parish. Colcocks, Heywards, Duponts, Huguenins, Gillisons, Bolens, Cuthberts, and others of the old planter families had cottages there. The village had two churches and a school, and nearby the construction of the Charleston and Savannah railroad was continuing apace. Rhett summoned his oratorical charisma to make a public appeal for united southern action to preserve western territory for the expansion of slavery and to throw off the yoke of northern domination. Rhett predicted to the St. Luke's planters that the election of 1860 would decide the fate of the nation. Rhett's ally, William L.

Yancey of Alabama, told a Columbia audience that if the Republican candidate won the election of 1860, the southern states should secede before the inauguration. Their statements were prophetic. Surrounded by the prosperity and enterprise of the Beaufort District, Rhett's appeal was enthusiastically and confidently received.[26]

Beaufort District planters again turned to the Rhett faction in anticipation of the expected crisis. Edmund Rhett was elected by St. Helena Parish to replace Ben Johnson in the South Carolina Senate in 1858 and continued there until his death in 1863. He was also sent by the parish as a delegate to the Democratic National Convention in Charleston in April 1860.[27]

As if to confirm the worst fears of the Beaufort District planters, on October 16, 1859, John Brown led a raid against the Harper's Ferry Federal Arsenal. His plan was to seize the store of weapons and call for the slaves of northern Virginia to flee their plantations and seek refuge at Harper's Ferry. There they would be provided with arms and ammunition with which to begin a general revolt of the slaves across the South. This bold, radical, and hostile act dramatized the hatred of northern abolitionists toward the planter regime. Newspapers across the South sensationalized the event, and the anxiety which Beaufort District planters had felt since the 1830s was fixed in the popular imagination of southern whites. Fear of slave revolt was something Beaufort District planters had known for five generations. The subject had long since disappeared from polite conversation: it was simply understood. As if to bring home the fear of slave rebellion, Keitt's own brother was murdered by his slaves in Florida in February 1860, and that district had been marked on a map of Florida among the papers recovered from John Brown's raid. Brown's raid on Harper's Ferry shocked the rest of the South, but it only confirmed the strident warnings of Rhett for the past thirty years and the calm prediction of Barnwell in 1830 that "there are no changes, however vital and subversive . . . which fanaticism and misguided philanthropy would not attempt."[28]

Despite the open cordiality which characterized the master-slave relations on many lowcountry plantations, and despite the pride that the country planters took in their intimate knowledge of the activities of the slave community and the slave families, in their hearts they knew that there was much they did not understand. Deep in the psyches of the country planters was the understanding that there was a realm of activity within the slave community that they were not privy to. This realization bred fear that was rarely expressed, and that fear bred political extremism.

In the spring of 1860, the Rhett faction reassembled to control the State Democratic Convention. Robert Rhett was chosen as a delegate from St. John's Colleton Parish, and his son, R. B. Rhett Jr., then editor of the *Mercury,* was chosen for Charleston. Edmund Rhett was chosen from St. Helena Parish. When the convention met, they chose Robert Rhett to lead their delegation to the meeting of southern states at Richmond, Virginia. Many South Carolina moderates objected vehemently to Rhett's leadership, but he stood his ground. By the middle of 1860, "there was no doubt that Rhett was once again a factor in South Carolina politics."[29]

In April 1860, the National Democratic Party met in Charleston. The northern and southern wings of the party could not reconcile their differences, and the party split. The northern Democrats nominated Sen. Stephen A. Douglas of Illinois for president, and the southern Democrats nominated John C. Breckenridge of Kentucky. The Republican Party united behind Abraham Lincoln. With the Democrats split, the real possibility existed in the summer of 1860 that the Republicans would be elected and the hated abolitionists would have influence in the highest councils of the federal government, just as Rhett and Yancey had predicted the year before. It was generally acknowledged in South Carolina, by secessionist fire eaters, moderate cooperationists, and even unionists, that a Republican victory in the presidential election of 1860 would precipitate disunion.

On October 8, 1860, South Carolina held a general election for the state legislature. It was the last popular expression of the electorate of South Carolina before the state left the union. The election was an overwhelming victory for the radical secessionists. When the new general assembly met in Columbia, they beat back a moderate attempt to adjourn and decided to call for a secession convention as soon as a Republican victory in the national election was confirmed. On November 7, 1860, word of Lincoln's election reached South Carolina. On November 13, a joint session of the South Carolina House and Senate met and called for a Convention of the People of South Carolina to be held on December 17, 1860, in Columbia.[30]

The Secession Convention had delegates from every electoral district in the state. The election for convention delegates was held on December 6. All the parishes of the Beaufort District sent representatives. Langdon Cheves Jr. of Delta Plantation on the Savannah River and George Rhodes of Lawtonville represented St. Peter's Parish. Cheves was the eldest son of Langdon Cheves Sr. who had died in 1854. Cheves was heir to one of the great fortunes of the Beaufort District. Three years later, he was killed as an artillery officer in the defense of Battery Wagner on Morris Island. Rhodes was part of the tightly connected group of large planters in upper St. Peter's Parish. He had been born on Calliwassie Island in 1802. In 1821, he married Thursa Elvina Robert, and after her death he married her sister, Eliza Jane Robert. Rhodes was a large planter and one of the founders of the planters' village center at Lawtonville. He was one of the original deacons of the Lawtonville Baptist Church.[31]

Richard James Davant and Ephraim Mikell Seabrook represented St. Luke's Parish. Davant was born on Hilton Head Island in 1805, but became a lawyer and conducted his practice at the district court at Coosawhatchie. He moved to Gillisonville when the new courthouse was built there in 1836. He was well known throughout the Beaufort District and had strong family ties to the great planters of upper St. Peter's Parish by his long marriage to Elvina Cheney. William Maner Bostick was Davant's son-in-law. Colonel Seabrook had his principal plantation on Sampson Island in the Colleton District. But he spent his summers in Bluffton with other members of the family, including Governor Whitmarsh Seabrook, who died at his Strawberry Hill Plantation in St. Luke's Parish in 1855. In 1860, Seabrook represented St. Luke's Parish at the Secession Convention.[32]

Prince William Parish was represented by Colonel John Edward Frampton of the Hermitage Plantation at Pocotaligo. He was the son of Theodora Pope Frampton and was born on St. Helena Island in 1810. He was one of the great rice planters of lower Prince William Parish. He had been a delegate to the Southern Rights Convention in 1852. William Ferguson Hutson also represented Prince William Parish. He was a first cousin of William Ferguson Colcock. His grandfather was Thomas Hutson of the Beaufort District Federalist faction. His father, Richard Woodward Hutson, was state representative from Prince William Parish, and William Ferguson Hutson occupied the same seat during the Civil War. His wife was Sophronia Lucia Palmer, the daughter of one of the pioneer planter families of Prince William Parish.

St. Helena Parish was represented by Joseph Daniel Pope of St. Helena Island and Robert W. Barnwell of Beaufort. Pope was the state representative from St. Helena Parish at the time of secession and later served as state senator during the Civil War. His father, Joseph James Pope, was a major sea island cotton planter and his mother, Sarah Jenkins Pope, descended from one of the pioneer families of St. Helena Island. Pope was a Beaufort attorney and law partner of Richard DeTreville.[33] St. Helena's other representative at the Secession Convention was one of the state's most honored elder statesmen and the sage of Beaufort. It was Barnwell's first public service since the crisis of 1852. He was soon to be thrust into the limelight as one of the principal leaders of the new Confederate States government. Robert Barnwell Rhett and Richard DeTreville were both delegates to the Secession Convention as well, but from the Charleston Parish of St. Philip's and St. Michael. Old Beaufort was powerfully represented at this defining moment of the state's history.

What strikes one about the delegation from the Beaufort District to the Secession Convention was its remarkable continuity. Virtually every man was descended from the pioneers of the southern parishes. Their ancestors had inaugurated the Indian trade, fought the Yemassee War, imported the first Africans, cleared the swamps, driven Spanish privateers from the shore, fought in the Revolution, ratified the Constitution, introduced cotton, and imported the last

Africans to America. This was their heritage and part of their psyches. Many of them still lived on the very land that had been carved from the wilderness by their ancestors, such as Barnwell's Woodward Plantation and Hutson's Cedar Grove Plantation. They were established, powerful, rich, and proud; perhaps more so than any group in any community in America at that moment. They took with them to the Secession Convention the collective fear of their planter constituents. They surely feared the consequences of their radical act, but they feared the consequences of not acting even more.

M. A. Fowles recalled that Barnwell, Maxcy Gregg, and Nathaniel Barnwell all stayed at Fowles's house in Columbia during the Secession Convention. He thought them to be "the most striking and most influential men at that remarkable convention." He recalled that the private conversations he overheard on those December evenings "marked an era in my life," as indeed they did for all Beaufortonians. Barnwell, always the cooperationist, worried that only Mississippi could be counted on to follow South Carolina out of the union. But neither Barnwell nor Gregg were considering whether secession was expedient, but only whether it was right: "Both were thinking of the rightfulness of secession rather than discussing its success." Maxcy Gregg particularly never admitted doubt, even in private conversation. And Barnwell's principal concern was for the slaves, most of whom were the innocent objects of abolitionist conspirators. Barnwell was concerned that whites might consider the slaves a dangerous class and exercise their fear against them. "Nothing," Barnwell noted, "is so cruel as fear."[34] Constitutional and political arguments aside, Barnwell understood the visceral fear that finally drove the country planters of his community over the precipice of secession.

The Secession Convention convened in Columbia on December 17. It soon adjourned due to a smallpox epidemic in the capitol and reconvened in Charleston. The convention reassembled in Institute Hall. David F. Jamison of Barnwell District was chosen president of the Convention. President Jamison appointed a committee of seven men to draft an Ordinance of Secession. Two of the seven members of this committee were Robert Barnwell Rhett and William Ferguson Hutson. Authorship of the actual ordinance has been disputed, but the most recent and thorough scholarship points to Hutson as the principal contributor.[35]

Charleston was agog with excitement. Crowds gathered in the streets and talked excitedly into the night. The newspapers published flurries of news. The Charleston Restaurant opposite the theater displayed a full-length transparency of Rhett, the father of secession. Finally on the morning of December 20, 1860, the Ordinance of Secession was prepared. One hundred and sixty-nine delegates met at St. Andrews Hall, and in the early afternoon the Ordinance of Secession was adopted by unanimous roll-call vote. Later that evening in the Institute Hall, every delegate affixed his signature to the parchment document that sealed the fate of South Carolina. No district in the state had contributed more to the secession movement than the Beaufort District. No district in America was to lose more as a result.

NOTES

1. Laura Amanda White, *Robert Barnwell Rhett: Father of Secession* (New York: Century, 1931), 70–74; "Toasts Prepared for an Oration by Squire William Pope," Pope Family Papers, South Carolina Historical Society.

2. Stephen Meats and Edwin T. Arnold, eds., *The Writings of Benjamin F. Perry*, 3 vols. (Spartanburg: Reprint Co., 1980), 3: 212; White, *Robert Barnwell Rhett*, 74–80.

3. "Autobiography of William Ferguson Colcock" (manuscript), 27–35, South Carolina Historical Society; Chalmers Davidson, *The Last Foray: The South Carolina Planters of 1860, A Sociological Study* (Columbia: University of South Carolina Press, 1971), 186.

4. Stephen B. Barnwell, *The Story of an American Family* (Marquette, Mich.: Privately printed, 1969), 172–74; *Biographical Directory of the South Carolina Senate*, 2: 1355–56.

5. John Barnwell, "Hamlet to Hotspur: Letters of Robert Woodward Barnwell to Robert Barnwell Rhett," *South Carolina Historical Magazine* 77 (October 1976): 253.

6. John Barnwell, "Hamlet to Hotspur," 255; Barnwell, *Story of an American Family*, 173; Bailey, *Biographical Directory of the South Carolina Senate*, 2: 1356–57.

7. Susan Walker, ed., "The Journal of Thomas B. Chaplin (1822–1890)," in Theodore Rosengarten, *Tombee: Portrait of a Cotton Planter* (New York: Morrow, 1986), 347–50.

8. Edmund Rhett, "Who is the Producer?," address delivered to the Beaufort Agricultural Society, August 1840, Wragg Papers, South Carolina Historical Society.

9. Clyde N. Wilson et al., eds., *The Papers of John C. Calhoun*, 22 vols. to date (Columbia: University of South Carolina Press, 1959–), 3: 706–7.

10. Barnwell, "Hamlet to Hotspur," 255.

11. *Biographical Directory of the American Congress*, 518, 860, 1512; Barnwell, *Story of an American Family*, 111; White, *Robert Barnwell Rhett*, 115.

12. White, *Robert Barnwell Rhett*, 99–110.

13. Walker, "Journal of Thomas B. Chaplin," 502; White, *Robert Barnwell Rhett*, 110.

14. *Charleston Courier*, November 16, 1850.

15. *Biographical Directory of the South Carolina Senate*, 1: 390.

16. Rosengarten, *Tombee*, 139–42.

17. "Autobiography of William Ferguson Colcock" (manuscript), 36, South Carolina Historical Society.

18. Philip M. Hamer, *The Secession Movement in South Carolina, 1847–1852* (New York: DaCapo Press, 1971), 123, 134; White, *Robert Barnwell Rhett*, 123; Richard J. Calhoun, ed., *Witness to Sorrow: The Antebellum Autobiography of William J. Grayson* (Columbia: University of South Carolina Press, 1990), 155.

19. E. L. Inabinet, "The Lawton Family of Robertville, South Carolina," paper delivered at Allendale, South Carolina, June 8, 1963, South Caroliniana Library.

20. "Autobiography of William Ferguson Colcock," 36; Hamer, *Secession Movement in South Carolina*, 139–41.

21. Calhoun, ed., *Witness to Sorrow*, 160.

22. White, *Robert Barnwell Rhett,* 132–33.

23. Harold S. Schultz, *Nationalism and Sectionalism in South Carolina, 1852–1860: A Study of the Movement for Southern Independence* (New York: DaCapo Press, 1969), 16–18; *Dictionary of American Biography,* 10: 294; *Biographical Directory of the American Congress* (Washington, D. C.: U.S. Government Printing Office, 1961), 1149.

24. Schultz, *Nationalism and Sectionalism in South Carolina,* 109; Samuel A. Johnson, *The Battle Cry of Freedom: The New England Immigrant Aid Society in the Kansas Crusade* (Lawrence: University of Kansas Press, 1984), 158–60, 181–84. At the time of the raid on Lawrence, Kansas, Richard DeTreville was the lieutenant governor of South Carolina.

25. Stephen Channing, *Crisis of Fear: Secession in South Carolina* (New York: Simon and Schuster, 1970), 150–52; Barnwell, *Story of an American Family,* 72.

26. Maxcy Gregg to Robert Barnwell Rhett, September 14, 1858, Robert Barnwell Rhett Papers, South Carolina Historical Society; White, *Robert Barnwell Rhett,* 154–55.

27. *Biographical Directory of the South Carolina Senate,* 2: 1355–56.

28. Channing, *Crisis of Fear,* 268; William W. Freehling, *Prelude to Civil War: The Nullification Controversy in South Carolina, 1816–1836* (New York: Harper and Row, 1966), 199.

29. White, *Robert Barnwell Rhett,* 165.

30. Charles H. Lesser, *Relic of the Lost Cause: The Story of South Carolina's Ordinance of Secession* (Columbia: South Carolina Department of Archives and History, 1990), 3; Channing, *Crisis of Fear.*

31. Coy K. Johnston, *Two Centuries of Lawtonville Baptists, 1795–1975* (Columbia: State Printing Co., 1974), 76–77.

32. *Biographical Directory of the South Carolina Senate,* 1: 362–63; Davidson, *The Last Foray,* 248.

33. Bailey, *Biographical Directory of the South Carolina Senate,* 2: 1291–92.

34. "M. A. Fowles Recollections" (manuscript), 56–57, South Carolina Historical Society.

35. The authors have relied on the scholarship and analysis of Lesser in his excellent study of the document in *Relic of the Lost Cause,* 6–7.

23

The Battle of Port Royal Sound

As South Carolina lurched toward secession in the 1850s, the citizens re-dedicated themselves to military preparedness. Beaufort and the sea islands had always remained slightly apart from the state militia organization. In 1852, the old arsenal in Beaufort was expanded to accommodate a garrison of 250 men and six guns. Since 1798, it had been the headquarters of the venerable Beaufort Volunteer Artillery. This organization had raised the money locally to rebuild the fortress and received no state support. In 1856, the Beaufort Volunteer Artillery was exempt from regimental militia musters because of the cost and difficulty of moving the heavy guns from the arsenal to the mainland muster ground. To ensure their readiness in case of emergency, and also to partially reimburse the Beaufort Volunteer Artillery for their expenses, the state authorized a stipend of $225 per year to see that each gun was regularly exercised and each gun crew trained. The following year the Beaufort Beat Company, an infantry and police unit, was also exempt from regimental review.[1]

In 1858, the militia of the sea island region was reorganized. A full battal-ion was formed from the previously independent companies of the Beaufort Volunteer Artillery, the Beaufort Beat Company, and the St. Helena Company of Mounted Rifleman. The battalion was commanded by a major who reported to the colonel commanding the Twelfth Regiment of the South Carolina Militia.[2]

Late in 1860, when secession was inevitable, the South Carolina legislature set itself to military matters. In November, they established a Board of Ordnance and authorized the employment of a military engineer "who shall, as soon as possible, make an examination of the coast of the state with a view to the defense of the same."[3] Three days before the Secession Ordinance was passed, on De-cember 20, 1860, the legislature passed "An Act to Provide Armed Military force," which organized the South Carolina Militia into a single division of state troops with upwards of four brigades and sixteen regiments. Artillery batteries were established at Georgetown, Charleston, and Beaufort.[4]

After secession, local militia units such as the Calhoun Guards, the Lexington Volunteer Rifles, the Hartsville Light Infantry, and the Rutledge Mounted Riflemen sprang up across the state. A Corps of Military Engineers was authorized to prepare the defenses of the state, and the students at the Citadel were formed into a separate unit called the Corps of State Cadets.[5]

The momentous events in the spring of 1861 were followed with interest and eagerness in Beaufort. The secession of the lower south in January, the formation of the Confederate government at the Montgomery Convention in February, and the ongoing siege and eventual bombardment of Fort Sumter on April 12, all featured prominent Beaufort citizens. Robert W. Barnwell was South Carolina's most respected representative at the Montgomery Convention, and the South Carolina delegation swung the selection of president of the Confederacy to Jefferson Davis. Barnwell was offered the position of secretary of state but declined.

When the war began in Charleston harbor, Beaufort's young men were prominent and active. Captain George B. Cuthbert was the commander of the Palmetto Guard and the Iron Battery on Cummings Point. He offered to Edmund Ruffin of Virginia the honor of firing the first and fateful shot. Lieutenant Alfred Rhett and Major John G. Barnwell were at Fort Moultrie. Lieutenant Edward H. Barnwell was on James Island, and Captain Stephen Elliott, commander of the Beaufort Volunteer Artillery, was on Cummings Point.[6]

The fall of Fort Sumter precipitated the blockade of southern ports by the U.S. Navy. The guns of Charleston harbor were barely cool before President Lincoln was poring over charts of the coast with his military advisors, looking for a likely location to serve as a base for the new South Atlantic Blockading Squadron. It was General Hiram Walbridge of New York who first pointed out to Lincoln the value and availability of Port Royal Sound.[7] During the summer of 1861, plans for an expedition against Port Royal began to take shape in Washington, New York, and Annapolis.

South Carolinians began to prepare for an assault on their coast. General P. G. T. Beauregard of the new Confederate States Army was given command of the provisional forces for the state of South Carolina and immediately established plans for coastal defense. In May, General Beauregard examined the whole coast accompanied by Lieutenant Colonel George Elliott of Beaufort and Elliott's brother-in-law, Cuban General Ambrosio Jose Gonzales. Shortly after his visit to Hilton Head Island on May 16, Beauregard ordered the construction of two forts to guard Port Royal Sound. Beauregard then went off to gain lasting fame as one of the heroes in the Battle of Manassas in July. When the log and earthen battery on Bay Point was completed later that summer, it was named in his honor.

The larger and more important installation on Hilton Head was built under the direction of Major Francis D. Lee of the Engineer Corps. It was called Fort Walker in honor of Confederate secretary of war, L. P. Walker. Ironically, the construction of Fort Walker was done mostly by slave labor. The work began in July, the hottest time of the year. To ease the burden of their labor, which was not ameliorated by the familiar respite of the plantation task system, the slaves sang a song that revealed their realization of impending events. In rhythmic repetition the verses went:

> No more peck of corn for me, no more, no more
> No more pint of salt
> No more drivers lash
> No more mistress call, no more, no more.[8]

By September, Fort Walker was ready for its armaments, which were supposed to have been seven ten-inch Columbiad rifled cannons, a truly formidable battery had they all been available. As it turned out, only one of the big guns was ever installed. They were replaced by nine old Navy 32-pounders, one rifled 24-pounder, and one eight-inch Columbiad. Brigadier General Thomas Fenwicke Drayton was put in command of Forts Walker and Beauregard and given the responsibility of protecting the sea islands. Drayton's own plantation home on Hilton Head, Fish Haul, was within walking distance of the fort. The garrison of Fort Walker itself was the Eleventh Regiment of South Carolina Volunteers, commanded by Colonel William C. Heyward. By October, reinforcements from Colonel DeSaussure's Fifteenth Regiment of South Carolina Volunteers swelled the Confederate forces on Hilton Head to 1,430 men.[9]

While the forts at Port Royal were under construction in the summer of 1861, the Blockade Board was holding secret meetings in Washington at the Smithsonian Institution Building. The Blockade Board had the daunting task of trying to determine how they could possibly establish an effective blockade of the entire three-thousand-mile coastline of the Confederate States. In order to accomplish their task, the U.S. Navy would have to establish coaling stations at strategic locations along the coast. The work of the Blockade Board was made much more urgent by the humiliating defeat of General Irvin McDowell's untrained Union forces by Generals Beauregard and Joseph E. Johnston at the first Battle of Manassas on July 21.

One of the most important members of the Blockade Board, and the senior officer in the U.S. Naval service at the time, was Captain Samuel Francis DuPont, nephew of Eleuthere Irenee DuPont de Nemours, founder of the gunpowder factory on the Brandywine River in Delaware. Captain DuPont, known as Frank to his family, was commissioned a midshipman in the U.S. Navy in 1815 and spent forty-five years in naval service, much of it at sea. During his long career, DuPont commanded ships and squadrons across the globe and had witnessed the revolution in naval tactics and strategy brought about by the transition from sail to steam power. At fifty-eight years of age, he had resigned himself to desk duty for the duration of the war, content to leave the rigor of sea duty to younger men. But when the army was routed at Manassas, he became anxious to go to sea. At the end of July, he wrote to his wife, Sophie: "I had been content to remain where the war found me and where I was doing quite as much good as I could blockading—probably a good deal more—but since the affair at Bull Run (Manassas) I have not been comfortable, and felt that every man who could be doing anything in addition . . . this hour of need required him to do so."

On August 5, DuPont received orders from secretary of the Navy, Gideon Welles, to prepare a naval expedition against the southern coast.[10] The officer chosen to command the army expeditionary force was General T. W. Sherman (not to be confused with General William Tecumseh Sherman). On August 2, General Sherman received his orders from the War Department.

General. You will proceed to New York immediately and organize, in connection with Captain DuPont of the Navy, an expedition of 12,000 men. Its destination you and the Navy commander will determine after you have sailed. You should sail at the earliest possible moment.
   Approved: A. Lincoln

President Lincoln emphasized the urgency of the expedition to Port Royal a month later with the following dispatch: "No misunderstanding . . . expedition not to be abandoned. Must move by first or early October. . . . Let all preparations go forward accordingly."[11]

DuPont was promoted to flag rank with the title of commodore, as there were not yet any admirals in the naval service, and his initial meeting in New York with General Sherman in early September was very successful. The two men immediately liked and respected one another. Commodore DuPont wrote to his wife, "I had a long visit this afternoon from General Sherman . . . he grows on you inasmuch as everything he says indicates a man of principle and I believe, a religious man. . . . He is also a thorough officer and understands what he is about and what is before him."[12]

Two minor naval victories in August and September, while the expeditionary force was being assembled, encouraged the Union planners. On August 29, the U.S. Navy seized Hatteras Inlet and could thereby command much of the North Carolina coast. In September, they occupied Ship Island on the Gulf

Coast without opposition. These two victories revealed the vulnerability of the Confederacy to naval operations, while the battle at Manassas had proven that a quick and decisive military victory was not possible. But neither Hatteras Inlet nor Ship Island had deep enough or protected enough harbors to serve as adequate coaling and provisioning stations for a blue water fleet. The expedition against Port Royal was crucial to the success of the blockade.[13]

General Sherman had hoped to have thirteen thousand troops assembled on Long Island by September 5 and was busily beating the drum in New England trying to enlist recruits. But problems of logistics and supply frustrated his expectations and slowed Lincoln's timetable.[14] Commodore DuPont was having his own problems assembling the fleet. He had to charter merchant ships to serve as troop transports and colliers. These had to be converted for naval service and equipped with defensive armament. He noted that trying to convert a merchant ship into a warship is like "altering a vest into a shirt." In the meantime, east-coast shipyards were hastening their production of "90-day gunboats."[15]

Early in October, General Sherman and Commodore DuPont were summoned to Washington for a meeting at Secretary of State William H. Seward's home. In attendance were Seward, General George B. McClellan, Navy Secretary Gideon Welles, Assistant Navy Secretary Gustavus Fox, several cabinet ministers, and President Lincoln. Lincoln was clearly agitated. Annoyed by the delays and anxious for a major victory, he ordered Welles to get the expedition underway within four days. On October 16, Commodore DuPont slipped out of the Verrazano Narrows aboard the steam frigate USS *Wabash* and led the naval squadron to Hampton Roads, Virginia, to rendezvous with the troop transports and supply ships.[16]

The fleet that put to sea from Hampton Roads on Tuesday, October 29, was the largest naval and amphibious expedition mounted by the U.S. Navy in the nineteenth century. There were 17 warships, 25 colliers, 33 transports, 12,000 infantry, 600 marines, and 157 big guns. DuPont and Sherman had been given three targets by the Blockade Board: Bull's Bay, South Carolina; Fernandina, Florida, and Port Royal, South Carolina. After they were at sea, they chose Port Royal. The voyage south was not smooth. Three days out, off treacherous Cape Hatteras, they were struck by a terrific gale which scattered the fleet. From the deck of the flagship, USS *Wabash,* the next morning Commodore DuPont could see only one sail on the horizon. As the fleet reassembled reports of damage and loss were brought in. The gunboat *Isaac Smith,* to save the ship, had jettisoned its valuable naval guns. The transport ship *Peerless* sank but managed to transfer its crew and passengers to the USS *Mohican.* The steamship *Governor* sank, but the nearby steam frigate USS *Sabine* saved all hands. Three cargo ships, one transport, and several men had been lost. Despite this setback, on Monday morning,

November 4, the USS *Wabash* and twenty-five ships anchored off Port Royal Sound.[17]

While southern military commanders always knew Port Royal was a prime target, it was not until November that they were certain where the mighty armada was headed. On November 2, while the fleet was still scattered off North Carolina, Governor Francis Pickens of South Carolina predicted they were headed for Port Royal and telegraphed a dispatch to Judah P. Benjamin, Confederate secretary of war, to request reinforcements. Judah P. Benjamin owned a house in Beaufort and knew quite well the vulnerability of that location. Benjamin ordered Brigadier General J. R. Anderson to send reinforcements when South Carolina was assaulted, and the point of attack was certain. The completion of the Charleston and Savannah Railroad through the Beaufort District in 1859 allowed the Confederate strategists to concentrate their forces in Savannah and Charleston and move large numbers of troops to any location in between in a matter of hours. Throughout the Civil War, that railroad was one of the great military prizes in the state and the principal instrument in the defense of the mainland. It was not much help, however, for the isolated sea islands. On November 4, Major General Alexander R. Lawton of St. Peter's Parish, in command of the defenses of Savannah, cabled to Benjamin: "The enemy fleet is concentrating between Savannah River and Port Royal. . . . Point of attack is still doubtful. . . . More than twenty vessels in sight."[18]

The next day the point of attack was known. Brigadier General Roswell Ripley at Coosawhatchie cabled to Major General Cooper in Charleston: "forty-one vessels reported off Beaufort. . . . Attack imminent. . . . Have requested General Lawton reinforce Hilton Head with from 500 to 1,000 men. . . . Have requested General Anderson send two regiments and a field battery." The same day Special Order Number 206 was dispatched from the secretary of war's office in Richmond: "Coasts of South Carolina, Georgia and East Florida are constituted a military department and General Robert E. Lee, CSA, assigned to command." Lee immediately set out by train from Virginia to South Carolina. He arrived the day after the battle.[19]

Aboard the USS *Wabash*, Commodore DuPont and General Sherman had determined by November 4 that Fort Walker on Hilton Head and Fort Beauregard on Bay Point would have to be destroyed by naval gunfire before any landing of the expeditionary force could be made. At 6:40 on November 5, Commodore DuPont sent a squadron of six vessels across the Port Royal bar in a reconnaissance in force. Captain John Rodgers aboard the USS *Ottawa* led the warships *Pembina, Seneca, Curlew, Penguin, Pawnee,* and the unarmed *Isaac Smith* into Port Royal Sound. Their task was to test the range and firepower of the Confederate forts and try to draw out the small fleet of Confederate gunboats commanded by

Commodore Josiah Tattnall of Savannah.

Tattnall's fleet was no match for the Union navy. His flagship was the armed riverboat *Savannah; Sampson, Resolute,* and *Lady Davis* were all converted tugs. Tattnall had attempted to hide his fleet from Union lookouts by anchoring up Skull Creek, but they noted that the Confederate ships fired their steam boilers with pitch pine, readily available across South Carolina and Georgia, instead of high-grade anthracite coal available in the north. The dense black smoke of the southern steamers was visible for miles over the low-lying islands.

Several long-range shots were exchanged between the fleet and the forts, but no hits were scored. Tattnall's fleet issued out from behind Hilton Head Island, but was soon chased back by Union gunners. Several paddlewheelers with onlookers and picnickers aboard hurried back to Savannah.[20] Captain Rodgers's reconnaissance had done its job, and confidence in the Union fleet was high.

On November 6, another naval skirmish occurred. Most of the fleet was held offshore by a strong westerly wind. Several ships, led by the USS *Seneca,* went again into Port Royal Sound, and Commodore Tattnall drove the *Savannah* out to meet them. Tattnall dipped his flag and withdrew up Skull Creek. Later in the day, Commodore DuPont tried to follow the other ships into the sound, but his large flagship, USS *Wabash,* grounded on the bar. DuPont was forced to reverse his engines to back the ship out of danger. The battle would have to wait another day.

Also on November 6, DuPont sent the shallow draft steamer *Vixen* into the sound to mark the channel and establish the course of the next day's battle.[21] In one of the ironies of the moment, the night before the battle a Union longboat laying buoys under cover of darkness encountered a Confederate longboat carrying messages from General Drayton at Fort Walker to Colonel R. G. M. Dunovant, commander at Fort Beauregard. In the smooth, deep water of Port Royal Sound, they hailed one another, rested on their oars, exchanged circumspect conversation, and passed by without hostility.

As the day of the battle approached, Beaufort and the sea islands were abuzz with rumors and activity. The women of the town had formed a Soldier's Relief Society. Mrs. W. A. Morcock, wife of the principal Bay Street merchant, was president, and Mrs. Thomas Fuller, Mrs. Edward Barnwell, Mrs. Thomas Wells, and Miss Elizabeth Barnwell served as officers. The parlor of Mrs. Stephen Elliott's home was converted to a cap factory, and up Bay Street at Barnwell Castle, the five daughters of Mrs. William Hazzard Wigg Barnwell were busy making bedding for the troops.

The Beaufort Volunteer Artillery moved from town during the spring of 1861 and reactivated Fort Marion on Spanish Point. They were reconstituted as

Company "D" and Company "A" of the Eleventh South Carolina Regiment and during the late summer were sent to Bay Point as part of the garrison of Fort Beauregard. The sand fort had a garrison of 640 men commanded by Colonel Dunovant, mostly from the Twelfth Regiment of South Carolina State Troops. The artillery-fire director was Captain Stephen Elliott of the Beaufort Volunteer Artillery. He was later promoted to brigadier general and gained lasting fame for his heroic and successful defense of Fort Sumter during the Union siege of Charleston from 1863 to 1864.

On Saturday, November 2, the citizens of Beaufort were informed that the fleet headed south might be headed for Port Royal. On Sunday, November 3, Dr. Joseph Walker, rector of St. Helena's Episcopal Church for thirty-seven years, asked the congregation to begin packing their belongings and to hold family prayers. On Monday, November 4, as the fleet anchored off Hilton Head, Brigadier General Roswell Ripley told the citizens that Port Royal was the target of attack and that they should evacuate Beaufort. All across town, trunks were packed, carts and horses were drawn up, and household servants began busily loading family possessions. For some slaves it was the last act they were to perform for their masters. Reverend Walker's niece Emily recalled her mother sending their trusted slave "Daddy Jimmy" to Retreat Plantation to get the family's longboat, *Santa Ana,* to town to evacuate them. The boat arrived at 9:00 at night. With a lantern rigged under a canopy, six burly slaves rowed Emily, her cousin Sarah Stuart with two infants, and her father up the Beaufort River past Brickyard Point and across the Coosaw River to the mainland. As they landed in the morning, they heard the boom of the big guns in Port Royal Sound.[22]

On St. Helena Island, the planters rode carriages and horses across the island to the home of Dr. Joseph Jenkins at Land's End. They gathered on the veranda with its broad view of Port Royal Sound to watch the duel of the great guns.[23] A sense of unreality was expressed by one Beaufort woman who, when asked if the Union fleet could enter Port Royal Sound answered, "Oh my no, Mr. Rhett is at Bay Point and he will simply not permit them to enter." Senator Edmund Rhett was then intendant of the town of Beaufort, the brother of Robert Barnwell Rhett, and one of the signers of the Ordinance of Secession.

But a formidable armada had descended, and Commodore DuPont had planned his strategy meticulously. The ships were to follow the USS *Wabash* in line-of-battle into the center of the sound and then bear to starboard, bringing Fort Beauregard within range of their guns. After passing Bay Point they would swing around to port, cross the sound, and bring their guns to bear on Fort Walker. They were to continue this two-mile-wide ellipse until the two forts were rendered incapable of returning fire. The brilliance of the maneuver was that each ship in DuPont's fleet would be under the guns of the forts for a few minutes at a time, while the fixed fortifications were continuously under fire from the naval guns.

The Battle of Port Royal Sound was one of the most important maritime engagements of the Civil War, which revolutionized naval warfare in the industrial age. Prior to that time, it had always been a rule of thumb among naval tacticians that one cannon on land, behind fixed fortifications, was worth four or five shipboard cannons, vulnerable to wind, tide, and pitching decks. Often sailing warships had to anchor in front of land emplacements to provide accurate firing platforms. This made them easy targets for land-based gunners. That had certainly been proven true at Sullivan's Island in 1776. But with the advent of steam power, naval vessels were no longer at the mercy of wind and tide. And November 7 was a perfect autumn day on Port Royal Sound: windless, cloudless, and glassy seas. Commodore DuPont was able to keep his ships slowly moving past the forts, allowing his gunners to find their range at each pass yet never presenting a fixed target for Confederate artillery. The thirty-nine guns of Fort Walker and Fort Beauregard, no matter how well-staffed, were never a match for the 157 guns of the fleet. Between the development of steam propulsion and the advent of airpower, naval gunnery was the premier weapon of war, and the Battle of Port Royal Sound was one of the events that proved it.

The morning of November 7, 1861, broke clear and calm over Port Royal Sound. At 8:00 A.M., the signal to weigh anchor and get underway was run up the mast of the USS *Wabash*. The steam frigates, *Wabash* and *Susquehanna*, led the deadly parade with Commodore DuPont prominent on the bridge of his flagship, bedecked in gold braid. It was the finest hour of his long and distinguished career. Following behind in line-of-battle came the sloops of war, *Mohican*, *Seminole*, and *Pawnee*, and behind them the gunboats *Pembina* and *Unadilla*. The sailing sloop-of-war *Vandalia* was towed by the steam gunboat *Isaac Smith*, which had lost its guns off Cape Hatteras. Forming a second, flanking, column were the gunboats *Bienville*, *Seneca*, *Penguin*, and *Augusta*.

General Drayton, astride his white horse atop a bluff on Hilton Head, and the St. Helena planters gathered on Dr. Jenkins's veranda at Land's End across the sound, knowing that the momentous battle was soon to commence. Drayton rushed to his post. Just after 9:00 A.M., the first shot was fired from Fort Walker and splashed ahead of the *Wabash*. This was followed by several shots from Fort Beauregard. A few minutes later the *Wabash* opened up against the shore batteries on Bay Point and against the Twelfth South Carolina Regiment bivouacked in the woods beyond. As the other vessels passed they also lobbed ranging shells and then opened up with broadsides. The smaller gunboats, equipped with eleven-inch swivel guns, were swift and accurate and moved closer to the shore. Shells burst in and around the battery. The Confederate fire from Fort Beauregard was quite accurate but had neither the range nor the volume to match the fleet. Before the *Wabash* had taken a quarter of a turn in Port Royal Sound, its guns were reloaded and trained on the small flotilla of Commodore Tattnall in the Broad River. After receiving broadsides from the *Wabash,* the *Susquehanna,* and the rest of the fleet, the Confederate Navy weighed anchor and retreated to the relative safety of Skull Creek. It was just past 10:00 A.M. At 10:40 A.M., the *Wabash, Susquehanna,* and *Bienville* were abeam of Fort Walker. The Union sloop-of-war USS *Pocahontas* had moved in behind Joyner Bank to take a position on the flank of Fort Walker. The captain of the *Pocahontas* was Commander Percival Drayton, younger brother of General Thomas Drayton, who knew that the lethal crossfire was directed against his brother. His resoluteness, bravery, and effectiveness aboard the *Pocahontas* at the Battle of Port Royal earned him the lasting respect of DuPont and a promotion to captain. He was later the commanding officer of the USS *Hartford,* Admiral David Farragut's flagship at the Battle of Mobile Bay, and the officer to whom the famous order, "Damn the torpedoes, full speed ahead!" was directed.

The *Wabash* then turned away from Fort Walker to complete another circle, clean and reload its cannons, and clear away wreckage from the Confederate shot. At 11:50, the *Wabash, Susquehanna,* and several smaller gunboats delivered another furious fusillade against Fort Walker. The reporter from the *New York Herald* counted forty shell bursts in one salvo in and above the fort. During the four-hour battle, the *Wabash* alone fired 888 rounds. By noon, the garrison of the forts and the crew of the fleet were half-deaf from the thunder of the big guns. The sound of the battle could be heard from Coffin Point to Daufuskie and as far inland as Lobeco. For a generation of freedmen on the sea islands, November 7 was remembered as the "Day of the Big Gun Shoot."

As the battle wore on, the fleet concentrated more and more of its firepower on Fort Walker and ignored the smaller battery at Fort Beauregard, which did not have the range to harm the ships. In Fort Walker, the damage was severe. The only truly big gun in the fort, the ten-inch Columbiad, was knocked off its carriage and out of action after the fourth round. By noon, most of the other guns were also out of action. By 12:30, General Drayton turned command of the fort over to Colonel Heyward and told him to return fire as long as he could. Drayton rode off to find General Ripley and seek reinforcements. Colonel Heyward had only three thirty-two-pound cannons and only ten or eleven rounds of shot left. The evacuation of Fort Walker was ordered with only the guncrews, commanded by Captain Bedon and Lieutenants Heape, Guerard, and Boyle, left as a rear guard. In the meantime, General Drayton and General Ripley determined they could not hold Hilton Head. General Drayton commandeered all the boats and barges on the island to move the infantry and the survivors of the

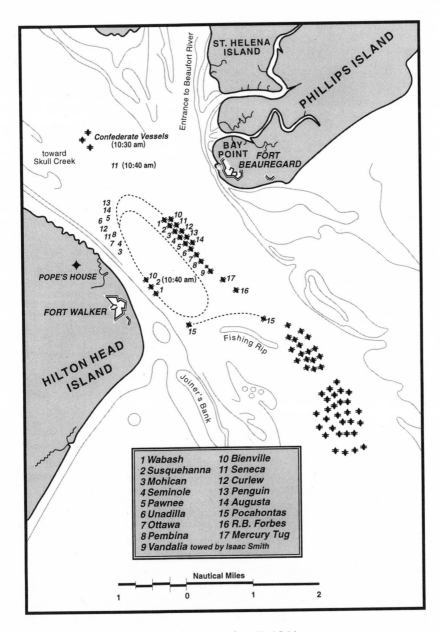

Battle of Port Royal Sound, November 7, 1861

Fort Walker garrison to the mainland. The evacuation of Hilton Head was hurried. All the heavy guns were spiked and abandoned. Supplies and knapsacks were dropped along the road to the ferry landing. Commodore Tattnall took his last load of troops to Bluffton at 1:30 and then retired to Savannah. Troops came wandering out of the woods from all directions converging on Ferry Point.[24]

The garrison of Fort Beauregard could only watch in dismay the destruction of Fort Walker across the sound. The day before, Colonel Dunovant had the foresight to send Reverend Stephen Elliott, father of Captain Stephen Elliott, along with William H. Cuthbert, to assemble enough barges and flatboats at Dr. Jenkins's landing on Station Creek to ferry his 640 troops to St. Helena Island. By midafternoon, when the guns of Fort Walker were silent, they spiked their cannons, marched four miles up the beach to the landing, boarded the boats, and made it to St. Helena Island by nightfall. Some stragglers who had lost their way did not get off Bay Point until the following day.[25]

At 2:30 the *Wabash* passed Fort Walker and fired a single shot into the fort. There was no return fire. Lookouts on the gunboat in Fish Haul Creek shortly afterward reported seeing the evacuation of the garrison. At 2:45, the *Wabash* signaled the cease fire. Commander John Gillis of the USS *Seminole* went ashore in a longboat under a flag of truce. Alone, he climbed the parapet, walked along the top of the earthen wall, and disappeared into the wreckage of the fort. A few minutes later he emerged atop the Pope family mansion that had been General Drayton's headquarters. He walked to the flagstaff, reached in his blue jacket, pulled out the stars and stripes, and raised the ensign to the top of the pole. Cheers erupted from the fleet and bands on several ships began simultaneously playing the "Star-Spangled Banner." The Battle of Port Royal Sound was over.

The naval victory allowed the 12,653 soldiers and marines of the expeditionary force to land on Hilton Head virtually without opposition. The Union surf boats assembled about the transports and ferried men ashore. If the weather had not been nearly perfect, the landing would have been much more hazardous on Hilton Head's exposed beaches. As it turned out, the landing of soldiers and marines was completed without a serious mishap. The first Union regiment to come ashore was the Seventh Connecticut. By nightfall, Hilton Head was securely in Union hands.[26] On November 8, General Alexander Lawton in Savannah reported to Judah P. Benjamin in Richmond, "The enemy has taken complete possession of Port Royal entrance and now controls the inland navigation at that point." General Lee arrived at Coosawhatchie to meet with General Ripley on November 8. He reported that all Confederate troops had evacuated Hilton Head, Bay Point, and most of the other islands. General Drayton had withdrawn to Coosawhatchie to guard the Charleston-Savannah Railroad and Colonel Dunovant had finally gotten his command from Bay Point to St. Helena Island, from St. Helena to Beaufort, and then across the Whale Branch River to the mainland. They were posted at Garden's Corner.[27]

Compared to what was to follow in the Civil War, the casualties from the Battle of Port Royal Sound were fairly light. The overwhelming firepower of the fleet kept Union losses to a minimum, and the earthen breastworks of Fort Walker and Fort Beauregard proved to be effective protection for the garrisons, if not for their guns. Union forces had eight dead and twenty-three wounded. Confederate defenders had fifty-nine killed and managed to withdraw their wounded, but Commodore DuPont received reports of an additional "twenty or thirty" bodies found among the wreckage of Fort Walker.[28] Despite the relatively light losses there were plenty of personal tragedies. On Bay Point, James Stuart recalled rushing to the side of his younger brother, Allan, whose body was shattered and thrown from the parapet at Fort Beauregard by the recoil of a cannon. Allan thought he was dying and told his brother to carry his goodbye to their mother and tell her that he "had died at his duty." Allan Stuart was successfully evacuated from Bay Point, but never fully recovered from his wounds. He served the Confederate Army in administrative capacities until his death in Aiken in 1864. He was twenty-nine years old, and, as his brother noted, "He was the best boy and . . . the truest Christian I ever knew."[29] On Hilton Head, when the Seventh Connecticut Regiment entered Fort Walker, they ceased their celebration and fell silent amongst the death and debris. Most poignant was the body of Dr. E. S. Buist, Confederate Army surgeon, who had been decapitated by an artillery shell while in the act of bandaging a wounded soldier. His body lay across his medicine chest. He was given a proper burial by the Union Army and his body later reclaimed by the Confederates under a flag of truce.

Tragedy did not escape the Union side. Confederate gunners had been very accurate, and when the fleet closed to within 600 yards, the artillery duel had been at almost point-blank range. The Union ships were hit often. One shell went right in a gunport of the *Wabash* and sent a sailor crashing across the deck, his legs almost torn off. He took out his knife and tried to amputate his own leg before dying of shock a few minutes later. The USS *Susquehanna* was hit ten times, and its rigging was shredded. The USS *Pawnee* was hit four times, and the gunboat *Bienville* received two direct hits, the second of which exploded between the decks and blew two sailors to bits.[30] On November 8, Union troops occupied Bay Point where one soldier tripped a mine placed in one of the beach cottages and was blown up along with the house.[31]

On Dr. Jenkins's veranda at Land's End, where the St. Helena Island planters had gathered to watch the battle, the realization of what had occurred began to sink in. By early afternoon, it was clear that the Union fleet commanded Port Royal Sound and that thousands of federal troops would soon overrun their islands. With urgent dismay, they mounted their horses and wagons, rode off down Seaside Road to spread the alarm among the planter households, and gathered their belongings for a hasty evacuation.

Some planters tried to take their slaves with them, but most refused to go. Some masters told the field hands that the Yankees would sell them to the particular rigors of the Cuban sugar plantations if they stayed. Other planters suggested shooting a few recalcitrant slaves to force the rest to leave. Threats and lies did not work. As the slave woman Susannah disingenuously asked her master Daniel Pope, "Why should they [Yankees] kill poor black folks who did no harm and could only be guided by white folks?" The slaves knew very well what was going on. On Datha Island, Dr. Berners Barnwell Sams ordered his slave Cupid to gather the slaves on the island at the "big landing" to be transported to the mainland, but Cupid and the other slaves took to the woods. Not all the planters tried to take their slaves. Captain John Fripp told his slaves to keep together, stay on the plantation, plant provisioning crops for their own sustenance, and forget the cotton. He wished them well and left St. Helena Island.[32]

Conveniently for the white population of Beaufort, a steamer was moored at the town dock on November 7. Many of the inhabitants who had not evacuated the night before put their belongings aboard the paddle wheeler and were taken directly to Charleston. Had the Union ships steamed up the Beaufort River, they would have captured much of the white population of the town. As it was, elements of the Union fleet came up the Beaufort River on November 8. Henry, the cook at Coffin Point on St. Helena Island, brought word to the overseer to flee. Henry reported that "all the Yankee ships were going in procession up to Beaufort, solemn as a funeral."[33] The army did not actually occupy the village until November 9, and, according to local tradition, they found only one white man left in town and he was stone drunk on Bay Street.

In the intervening two days between the flight of the white population and the arrival of federal troops, the slaves in town and those from the surrounding plantations had looted the village and occupied the fine mansions. Several local men stationed on the mainland made forays into Beaufort to burn the valuable cotton, collect personal belongings, and gather military intelligence. Captain James Stuart of the Beaufort Volunteer Artillery was dispatched to burn the cotton. He reported that the town was already plundered when he returned. Lieutenant Teddy Barnwell led a detachment of the Rutledge Mounted Rifles onto Port Royal Island the same day to gather military information. He reported that the town was "still as death," but from the fourth floor of the Barnwell Castle on Bay Street he could see the Union gunboats steaming up the Beaufort River.[34] When Thomas Elliott slipped into Beaufort on November 8, he found that the homes had already been ransacked by the plantation slaves and that the debris of

Secession House, Beaufort, was built by Milton Maxcy ca. 1810. It was remodeled by Edmund Rhett in the early 1850s and is shown here as it appeared during the Civil War. It was called Secession House because in the early 1850s it was the unofficial headquarters of Beaufort's secessionist faction (Beaufort County Public Library Collection).

Nathaniel Heyward House, Beaufort, built ca. 1820, as it appeared during the Civil War. It was later known as the Sea Island Hotel (Beaufort County Public Library Collection).

The Beaufort waterfront with cotton docks and warehouses in the foreground and Abram Cockcroft House (later the Customs House) in the rear. This photograph was taken during the Civil War, probably from the deck of a steamboat (Reed Collection, Beaufort County Public Library).

Intersection of Bay and Carteret Streets, Beaufort, looking west. The photograph dates from the Civil War (Beaufort County Public Library Collection).

furniture and household goods cluttered the streets. When he arrived at his own home, Elliott found several plantation slaves reveling in the house. "Chloe, Steven's wife seated at Phoebe's piano playing away like the very Devil and two damsels upstairs dancing away famously."[35]

On Hilton Head, the Union troops themselves at first engaged in looting the plantations which were so hurriedly abandoned. But General Sherman, enraged at the behavior of his own troops, soon put a stop to it. On November 11, he issued General Order Number 24 from his headquarters on Hilton Head. He ordered any troops or officers engaged in looting to cease their activity or be disciplined. He noted that "the right of citizens to be secure in their property must continue."[36] Despite General Sherman's best efforts and intentions, the sea island planters had already lost everything. Few ever recovered the land or possessions they left behind, and their most valuable property, the slaves, never returned. The planters were never fully compensated for this financial loss. The sea islands of the Beaufort District had changed forever.

As the planters began to absorb the magnitude of their loss, Union occupiers began to realize the importance of their conquest. On Port Royal Sound, Commodore DuPont mused to his wife in words reminiscent of Captain Jean Ribaut three hundred years before, and reflective of the opinions of hundreds of mariners over the centuries, "This is a wonderful sheet of water—the navies of the world could ride here."[37] Captain Rufus Saxton of the Quartermaster's Corps, in his report to General Sherman, saw Port Royal with the same vision that Ribaut, Menendez, Cardross, Nairne, and Barnwell had seen it centuries before: "We are now in possession of the finest harbor in the South, where the largest ships can enter and ride at anchor in safety. In the heart of the richest part of the cotton district with direct and easy communication by inland water with Charleston and Savannah, it possesses unrivaled advantages for a Quartermasters and Naval depot, and in the future a great commercial city must grow up here."[38]

The Battle of Port Royal Sound was not only the beginning of the end of the Old South, it was also, in many ways, the beginning of the New South. November 7, 1861, was the most important day in the four-hundred-year history of the Beaufort District. Beaufort was the first southern city to be captured by Union forces, and it was successfully occupied until the end of the war. Few of the planter families ever returned to the sea islands, and not until 1892 were they compensated by the federal government for their lands lost to conquest. Though the slaves were not immediately freed, they were never returned to their former status, and they were among the first slaves in America to be affected by the Emancipation Proclamation of September 22, 1862. The old order, almost two centuries in the making, had vanished in a single day, and the sea island community would never be the same again. It is doubtful if any community in

America ever experienced so violent, irrevocable, and immediate a reversal of fortune as the sea islands of the Beaufort District did on the "Day of the Big Gun Shoot."

NOTES

1. Thomas Cooper and David J. McCord, eds., *The Statutes at Large of South Carolina,* 10 vols. (Columbia: A. S. Johnston, 1836–1841), 10: 506–77.

2. Cooper and McCord, eds., *Statutes of South Carolina,* 10: 627.

3. Cooper and McCord, eds., *Statutes of South Carolina,* 10: 732–34.

4. Cooper and McCord, eds., *Statutes of South Carolina,* 10: 726–30.

5. Cooper and McCord, eds., *Statutes of South Carolina,* 10: 740–42, 744–45.

6. Stephen B. Barnwell, *The Story of an American Family* (Marquette, Mich.: Privately printed, 1969), 187–89.

7. Roy P. Basler et al., eds., *The Collected Works of Abraham Lincoln,* 9 vols. (New Brunswick: Rutgers University Press, 1953), 5:27.

8. Virginia Holmgren, *Hilton Head: A Sea Island Chronicle* (Hilton Head: Hilton Head Publishing Co., 1959), 80–86.

9. Barnwell, *Story of an American Family,* 189–90; Holmgren, *Hilton Head,* 83.

10. James M. Merrill, *DuPont, The Making of an Admiral: The Biography of Samuel Francis DuPont* (New York: Dodd, Mead, 1986), 258–60.

11. *The War of the Rebellion: A Compilation of the Official Records of the Union and Confederate Armies,* 128 vols. (Washington, D.C.: U.S. Government Printing Office, 1880–1901), series 1, vol. 6: 168–71.

12. Merrill, *DuPont,* 262.

13. James M. McPherson, *Battle Cry of Freedom* (New York: Oxford University Press, 1988), 370.

14. *War of the Rebellion,* series 1, 6:181–82.

15. Merrill, *DuPont,* 261–62.

16. Merrill, *DuPont,* 263.

17. John Abbott, *The History of the Civil War in America* (New York: H. Bill Pub., 1863–1866), 1: 226; Merrill, *DuPont,* 261–65; McPherson, *Battle Cry of Freedom,* 370–71.

18. *War of the Rebellion,* series 1, 6: 308–9.

19. *War of the Rebellion,* series 1, 6: 309.

20. Robert Carse, *Department of the South: Hilton Head and the Civil War* (Hilton Head: Impressions Printing, 1987), 9; Holmgren, *Hilton Head,* 85; Abbott, *History of Civil War in America,* 1: 227.

21. Carse, *Department of the South,* 10.

22. Barnwell, *Story of an American Family,* 189–91.

23. Willie Lee Rose, *Rehearsal For Reconstruction: The Port Royal Experiment* (Indianapolis: Bobbs-Merrill, 1964), 104.

24. Excellent compilations of eyewitness accounts and battlefield reports are in Holmgren, *Hilton Head,* 88–90; Carse, *Department of the South,* 10–17; Merrill, *DuPont,* 266–69; Abbott, *History of the Civil War in America,* 1: 227–28.

25. Barnwell, *Story of an American Family,* 194–95.

26. Carse, *Department of the South,* 20.

27. *War of the Rebellion,* series 1, 6: 311–12.

28. Carse, *Department of the South,* 22; Merrill, *DuPont,* 267.

29. Barnwell, *Story of an American Family,* 192, 201.

30. Carse, *Department of the South,* 17, 21.

31. Edith M. Dabbs, *Sea Island Diary: A History of St. Helena Island* (Spartanburg: Reprint Co., 1983), 118.

32. Rose, *Rehearsal for Reconstruction,* 104–5.

33. Rose, *Rehearsal for Reconstruction,* 105.

34. Barnwell, *Story of an American Family,* 194.

35. Rose, *Rehearsal for Reconstruction,* 106–7.

36. *War of the Rebellion,* series 1, 6: 187.

37. Merrill, *DuPont,* 268.

38. *War of the Rebellion,* series 1, 6: 186.

Bibliography

MANUSCRIPT, PRINTED PRIMARY, AND ARCHIVAL SOURCES

Baldwin, Agnes, "Savannah River Property Map," May 24, 1977, South Carolina Historical Society.

Barnwell, William Hazzard Wigg, Plantation Book, 1838–1857, South Carolina Historical Society.

Berrien, John McPherson, Papers, Georgia Historical Society.

British Public Record Office, transcripts of records relating to South Carolina, 1685–1790, South Carolina Department of Archives and History.

Butler, Pierce, Letterbook, South Caroliniana Library.

Calendar of the Stetson Collection, P. K. Yonge Library, Gainesville, Fla.

Carleton, Sir Guy, Papers, microfilm at South Carolina Department of Archives and History.

Charleston County Wills, South Carolina Department of Archives and History.

Charleston Inventories, South Carolina Department of Archives and History.

Cheves, Langdon I, Papers, South Carolina Historical Society.

Cheves, Langdon III, Papers, South Carolina Historical Society.

Cheves-Middleton Papers, South Carolina Historical Society.

Coffin, Thomas Aston, Plantation Book, South Carolina Historical Society.

Colcock, William Ferguson, "Autobiography of William Ferguson Colcock," South Carolina Historical Society.

DeSaussure, C. A., "The Story of My Life Before the War Between the States," Memphis, Tenn., 1927, family manuscript provided by Charles A. DeSaussure, Gainesville, Ga.

DeSaussure Papers, South Carolina Historical Society.

Dozier, Henrietta, Genealogy of the Screven Family, 1935, Georgia Historical Society.

Elliott, William, *Address to the People of St. Helena Parish.* Charleston: Charleston Press by William Estill, 1832, South Caroliniana Library.

Forman–Bryan–Screven Papers, Georgia Historical Society.

Fowles, M. A., "Recollections," South Carolina Historical Society.

Frederick, Jane, "An Investigation of the Origins of Prince William Parish Church," manuscript in possession of the author, Beaufort, S.C.

"Frogmore Plantation Journal, 1813–1816," Stapleton Papers, South Caroliniana Library.

Fuller, Richard, *Address before the American Colonization Society,* delivered at Washington, D.C., January 21, 1851. Baltimore: Office of the True Union, 1851, South Caroliniana Library.

General Assembly Papers, South Carolina Department of Archives and History.

Government Auction Pamphlet, 17 November 1862. N.Y.: C. C. Shelley, Printer, 1862, Beaufort County Public Library.

Great Britain Historical Manuscripts Commission, *The Manuscripts of the Duke of Roxburgh, Sir H. A. Campbell, Bart. and the Countess Dowager of Seafield.* London: HMSO, 1894.

Hamilton, James, Jr., Papers, South Caroliniana Library.

Inabinet, E. L., "The Lawton Family of Robertville, S. C.," paper delivered at Allendale, S.C., June 8, 1963, South Caroliniana Library.

Joyner, William, Account Book, South Caroliniana Library.

King, Rufus, Papers, New-York Historical Society.

Kirk Family Papers, South Carolina Historical Society.

Lawton Papers, South Caroliniana Library.

Lee, Charles, Letterbook, South Caroliniana Library.

Lincoln Papers, South Carolina Department of Archives and History.

Lipscomb, Terry W., "S.C. Revolutionary Battles, Part Nine," South Carolina Department of Archives and History.

Loyalist Claims, microfilm, South Carolina Department of Archives and History.

McConnell and Kennedy Papers, Lewis Library, University of Manchester, England.

Manigault, Charles, Letterbook, 1846–1848, South Carolina Historical Society.

Manigault, Louis, "Rice Lands Planted on the Savannah and Ogeechee Rivers," Manigault Papers, University of North Carolina, Chapel Hill, Southern Historical Collection.

Moore, Alexander, "Henry Woodward's Twenty Years among the Southeastern Indians," paper presented at the Society for American Ethnohistory Annual Meeting, Charleston, S.C., Nov. 1986, South Carolina Historical Society.

Parrish, Lydia Austin, "Records of Some Southern Loyalists," microfilm, Georgia Historical Society.

Pope Family Papers, South Carolina Historical Society.

Records of the Public Treasurer of South Carolina, 1725–1776, General Tax Receipts and Payments, 1761–1769, South Carolina Department of Archives and History.

Rhett, Edmund, "Who is the Producer?," address delivered to the Beaufort Agricultural Society, August 1840, Wragg Papers, South Carolina Historical Society.

"Rhett Family Genealogy," South Carolina Historical Society.

Rhett, Robert Barnwell, Papers, South Carolina Historical Society.

Rojas, Manrique de, "Report on the French Settlement in Florida in 1564," July 9, 1564, P. K. Yonge Library, Gainesville, Fla.

Ruidaz y Caravia, Eugenio, "La Florida, Su Conquista y Colonizacion por Pedro Menendez de Aviles," Madrid, 1893, P. K. Yonge Library, Gainesville, Fla.

———, "Juan Rogel's Account of the Florida Mission, 1569–1570," P. K. Yonge Library, Gainesville, Fla.

South Carolina Commons House Journals, 1717–1776, South Carolina Department of Archives and History.

Smith, Buckingham, Collection, P. K. Yonge Library, Gainesville, Fla.
Society for the Propagation of the Gospel in Foreign Parts, Papers, microfilm, South
    Carolina Department of Archives and History.
Stapleton Papers, 1790–1839, South Caroliniana Library.
U.S. Census, Agricultural Schedules, Beaufort District, 7th and 8th Census, microfilm,
    South Carolina Department of Archives and History.
U.S. Census, Population Schedules, Beaufort District, lst, 2nd 3rd, 4th, 5th, 6th, 7th, and
    8th Census, microfilm, South Carolina Department of Archives and History.
U. S. Census, Slave Schedules, Beaufort District, 5th, 6th, 7th and 8th Census, microfilm,
    South Carolina Department of Archives and History.

NEWSPAPERS

Charleston City Gazette, South Carolina Historical Society.
Charleston Courier, South Carolina Historical Society.
Daily Morning News, Savannah, Ga., Georgia Historical Society.
Gazette of State of South Carolina, South Carolina Historical Society.
Georgia Gazette, Georgia Historical Society.
Georgian, Georgia Historical Society.
Royal Georgia Gazette, Georgia Historical Society.
South Carolina and American General Gazette, South Carolina Historical Society.
South Carolina Gazette, South Carolina Historical Society.
South Carolina Gazette and Country Journal, South Carolina Historical Society.
Savannah Georgian, Georgia Historical Society.

PUBLISHED SOURCES

Articles

Alcorn, Wallace, "A Cavalry Chaplain's Farewell Sermon." *Military Chaplain* 61 (November–
    December 1988): 3.
Anderson, David G, "Mississippian in South Carolina," *Studies in South Carolina Archaeology,*
    ed. Albert C. Goodyear III and Glen Hanson. Columbia: South Carolina Institute of
    Archaeology and Anthropology, 1989.
Arnade, Charles W., "Cattle Raising in Spanish Florida, 1513–1763." *Agricultural History*
    35 (July 1961).
Barnwell, John, "Hamlet to Hotspur: Letters of Robert Woodward Barnwell to Robert
    Barnwell Rhett." *South Carolina Historical Magazine* 77 (October 1976): 236–56.
Barnwell, Joseph, and Mabel Webber, eds. "St. Helena's Parish Register" *South Carolina
    Historical Magazine* 23 (January–October 1922): 8–25, 46–71, 102–51, 171–204.
Barnwell, Joseph, W., ed. "Fort King George: Journal of Colonial John Barnwell in the
    Construction of the Fort on the Altamaha in 1721." *South Carolina Historical Magazine*
    27 (October 1926): 189–203.
Brooks, Mark J., Peter A. Stone, David J. Colquhoun, and Janice G. Brown, "Sea Level
    Change, Estuarine Development and Temporal Variability in Woodland Period

Subsistence Patterning on the Lower Coastal Plain of South Carolina," in *Studies in South Carolina Archaeology*, ed. Albert C. Goodyear III and Glen Hanson. Columbia: South Carolina Institute of Archaeology and Anthropology, 1989.

Brown, Phillip M., "Early Indian Trade in the Development of South Carolina: Politics, Economics and Social Mobility during the Proprietary Period, 1670–1719." *South Carolina Historical Magazine* 76 (July 1975): 118–128.

Carteret, Nicholas, "Mr. Carteret's Relation of Their Planting at Ashley River, '70," in *Narratives of Early Carolina 1650–1708*, ed. A.S. Salley. New York: Charles Scribner's Sons, 1911.

"Charleston, S. C., in 1774, as Described by an English Traveler." *Historical Magazine* 9 (1865).

Coon, David L., "Eliza Lucas Pinckney and the Reintroduction of Indigo Culture in South Carolina." *Journal of Southern History* 42 (February 1976): 61–76.

Covington, James W., "Stuart's Town, the Yamasee Indians and Spanish Florida." *Florida Anthropologist* 21 (March 1968): 8–13

DePratter, Chester B., "Cofitachequi: Ethnohistorical and Archaeological Evidence," in *Studies in South Carolina Archaeology*, ed. Albert C. Goodyear III and Glen Hanson. Columbia: South Carolina Institute of Archaeology and Anthropology, 1989.

———, "Explorations in Interior South Carolina by Hernando DeSoto (1540) and Juan Pardo (1566–1568)," *South Carolina Institute of Archaeology and Anthropology Notebook 19*. Columbia: South Carolina Institute of Archaeology and Anthropology, 1987.

DePratter, Chester, Charles Hudson, and Marvin Smith, "The Route of Juan Pardo's Explorations in the Interior Southeast, 1566–1568." *Florida Historical Quarterly* 61 (1982/83): 125–58.

Dunbar, Gary S., "Colonial Carolina Cowpens." *Agricultural History* 35 (July 1961): 125–31.

Dunlop, J. G., "Capt. Dunlop's Voyage to the Southward, 1687." *South Carolina Historical Magazine* 30 (July 1929): 127–33.

———, "Letters from John Stewart to William Dunlop." *South Carolina Historical Magazine* 32 (January–April 1931): 1–33, 81–114.

———"Paul Grimball's Losses by the Spanish Invasion in 1686." *South Carolina Historical Magazine* 29 (July 1928): 231–37.

———, "Spanish Depredations, 1686." *South Carolina Historical Magazine* 30 (April 1929): 81–89.

———, "William Dunlop's Mission to St. Augustine in 1688." *South Carolina Historical Magazine* 34 (1933): 1–30.

Easterby, J. H., "Shipbuilding on St. Helena Island in 1816: A Diary of Ebenezer Coffin." *South Carolina Historical Magazine* 47 (April 1946): 117–20.

Elliott, William, "Charles Davant," *Magnolia* 2, South Caroliniana Library.

Flanders, Ralph B., "Planters' Problems in Ante-Bellum Georgia." *Georgia Historical Quarterly* 14 (March 1930): 17–40.

Flynn, Jean Martin, "South Carolina's Compliance with the Militia Act of 1792." *South Carolina Historical Magazine* 69 (January 1968): 26–43.

Greene, Jack P., "Bridge to Revolution: The Wilkes Fund Controversy in South Carolina, 1769–1775." *Journal of Southern History* 29 (February 1963): 19–52.

Haan, Richard L., "'The Trade do's not flourish as formerly': The Ecological Origins of the Yamassee War of 1715." *Ethnohistory* 28 (Fall 1982): 341–58.

Harden, William, "The Screven Family." *Georgia Historical Quarterly* 1 (June 1917): 166–67.

Hilliard, Sam B., "Tidewater Rice Plantation: An Ingenious Adaptation to Nature." *Geoscience and Man* 12 (1975).

Hirsch, Arthur, "French Influence on American Agriculture in the Colonial Period with Special Reference to Southern Provinces." *Agricultural History* 4 (1930).

Hoffman, Paul E., "The Chicora Legend and Franco-Spanish Rivalry in La Florida." *Florida Historical Quarterly* 44 (1984): 419–38.

———, "Diplomacy and the Papal Donation, 1493–1585." *Americas* 30 (1973): 151–83.

———, "A New Voyage of Discovery: Pedro de Salazar's Visit to the 'Land of the Giants.'" *Florida Historical Quarterly* 58 (1979/80): 415–26.

Hudson, Charles, Marvin T. Smith, and Chester B. DePratter, "The Hernando DeSoto Expedition: From Apalachee to Chiaha," *South Carolina Institute of Archaeology and Anthropology Notebook 19.* Columbia: South Carolina Institute of Achaeology and Anthropology, 1987.

Hutson, R. W., ed., "Register Kept by Rev. William Hutson of Stoney Creek Independent Congregational Church and (Circular) Congregational Church in Charleston, 1743–1760." *South Carolina Historical Magazine* 38 (January 1937): 21–36.

Insh, George Pratt, "The *Carolina Merchant:* Advice of Arrival." *Scottish Historical Review* 25 (January 1928): 98–108.

Ivers, Larry E., "Scouting the Inland Passage." *South Carolina Historical Magazine* 73 (July 1972): 117–29.

Jackson, Harvey H., "Hugh Bryan and Great Awakening in South Carolina." *William and Mary Quarterly* 43 (October 1986): 594–614.

———, "The Carolina Connection: Jonathan Bryan, His Brothers and the Founding of Georgia." *Georgia Historical Quarterly* 68 (Summer 1984): 147–72.

Johnson, J. G., "The Spanish Period of Georgia and South Carolina History, 1566–1702." *Bulletin of the University of Georgia* (May 1923).

———, "A Spanish Settlement in Carolina, 1526." *Georgia Historical Quarterly* 7 (December 1923): 339–45.

Jones, George Fenwicke, "Compilation of Lists of German-speaking Settlers of Purrysburg." *South Carolina Historical Magazine* 92 (October 1991): 253–68.

———, "John Martin Bolzius' Trip to Charleston, October 1742." *South Carolina Historical Magazine* 82 (April 1981): 87–110.

Jones, Kenneth R., "'A Full and Particular Account' of the Assault on Charleston in 1706." *South Carolina Historical Magazine* 83 (January 1982): 1–11.

Kopperman, Paul E., "Profile of a Failure: The Carolana Project, 1639–1640." *North Carolina Historical Review* 59 (January 1982): 1–23.

Kovacik, Charles F., and Lawrence S. Rowland, "Images of Colonial Port Royal, South Carolina." *Annals of the American Association of Geographers* 63 (1973).

Landers, Jane, "Gracia Real de Santa Teresa de Mose: A Free Black Town in Spanish Colonial Florida." *American Historical Review* 95 (February–June 1990): 9–30.

Lanning, John Tate, "Don Miguel Wall and the Spanish Attempt against the Existence of Carolina and Georgia." *North Carolina Historical Review* 10 (July 1933): 186–213.

Lash, Jeffrey N., "The Rev. Martin Luther Hurlbut: Yankee President of Beaufort College, 1812–1814." *South Carolina Historical Magazine* 85 (October 1984): 305–16.

Lawson, Edward, "What Ever Happened to the Man Who Cut Off Jenkins' Ear?" *Florida Historical Quarterly* 37 (1958).

"Letters of John Rutledge." *South Carolina Historical Magazine* 18 (January 1917): 42–49.

Lowery, Woodbury, "Jean Ribaut and Queen Elizabeth." *American Historical Review* 9 (1904).

Mathews, Maurice, "Mr. Mathew's Relation of St. Katherina," in *Narratives of Early Carolina, 1650–1708,* ed. A. S. Salley. New York: Charles Scribner's Sons, 1911.

Michie, James L., "The Daws Island Shell Midden and its Significance during the Shell Mound Formative." *Studies in Southeastern Aboriginal Shell Rings.* Columbia: Department of Geological Sciences, University of South Carolina, 1989–1991.

———, "An Intensive Shoreline Survey of Archaeological Sites in Port Royal Sound and the Broad River Estuary, Beaufort County, South Carolina." *Research Manuscript Series No. 167.* Columbia: South Carolina Institute of Archeology and Anthropology, 1980.

Migliazzo, Arlin C., "A Tarnished Legacy Revisited: Jean Pierre Purry and the Settlement of the Southern Frontier, 1718–1736." *South Carolina Historical Magazine* 92 (October 1991): 232–52.

Moore, Alexander, "The Daniel Axtell Account Book and the Economy of Early South Carolina." *South Carolina Historical Magazine* 95 (October 1994): 280–301.

Moore, Clarence B., "Certain Aboriginal Mounds of the Coast of South Carolina." *Journal of the Academy of Natural Sciences of Philadelphia,* 2nd Series, vol. 11, part 2 (1899).

Morgan, Phillip D. "Work and Culture: The Task System in the World of Lowcountry Blacks, 1700–1880." *William and Mary Quarterly* 39 (October 1982): 563–99.

Naish, G. P. B., "Ships and Shipbuilding," in *A History of Technology,* 5 vols., ed. Charles Singer et al. Oxford: Clarendon Press, 1957.

Ochenkowski, J. P., "The Origins of Nullification in South Carolina." *South Carolina Historical Magazine* 83 (April 1982): 121–53.

Olsberg, R. Nicholas, "Ship Registers in the South Carolina Archives, 1734–1780." *South Carolina Historical Magazine* 74 (October 1973): 189–299.

Otto, John S., "The Origins of Cattle Ranching in Colonial South Carolina, 1670–1715." *South Carolina Historical Magazine* 87 (April 1986): 117–24.

"Papers of the First Council of Safety of the Revolutionary Party in South Carolina, June–November 1775." *South Carolina Historical Magazine* 1 (January–April, July 1900): 41–75, 119–35, 183–205.

Pease, Jane H., and William H. Pease, "Intellectual Life in the 1830's: The Institutional Framework and the Charleston Style," in *Intellectual Life in Antebellum Charleston,* ed. Michael O'Brien and David Moltke-Hansen. Knoxville: University of Tennessee Press, 1986.

Pennington, Edgar L., "The South Carolina Indian War of 1715, as Seen by the Clergymen." *South Carolina Historical Magazine* 32 (October 1931): 251–69.

Powell, William S., "Carolina in the Seventeenth Century: An Annotated Bibliography of Contemporary Publications." *North Carolina Historical Review* 41 (January 1964): 74–103.

Ribaut, Jean, "The Whole and True Discoverie of Terra Florida," in *New American World,* 5 vols., ed. David B. Quinn. New York: Arno, 1979.

Rodgers, George C., Jr., "Walking in the Footsteps of the Lords Proprietors," *Carologue* 10 (Autumn 1994): 8–12, 18–19.

Rowland, Lawrence S., "Alone on the River: The Rise and Fall of the Savannah River Rice Plantations of St. Peter's Parish, South Carolina." *South Carolina Historical Magazine* 88 (July 1987): 121–50.

Salley, A. S., ed., "Stock Marks Recorded in S.C., 1695–1721," *South Carolina Historical Magazine* 13 (July–October 1912): 119–31, 224–28.

Sandford, Robert, "A Relation of a Voyage on the Coast of Carolina, 1666," in *Narratives of Early Carolina, 1650–1708,* ed. A. S. Salley. New York: Charles Scribner's Sons, 1911.

Sayle, William, "Letter of Governor Sayle and Council," in *Narratives of Early Carolina, 1650–1708,* ed. A. S. Salley. New York: Charles Scribner's Sons, 1911.

Sharrar, Terry, "Indigo in Carolina, 1670–1796." *South Carolina Historical Magazine* 72 (April 1971): 94–103.

Smith, Henry A. M., "Beaufort: The Original Town and Earliest Settlers." *South Carolina Historical Magazine* 9 (July 1908): 141–60.

———, "Purrysburg." *South Carolina Historical Magazine* 10 (October 1909): 87–219.

Spieler, Gerhard, Lawrence Rowland, Larry Lepionka, Emmet Bufkin, and Arthur Wade, "Fortifications in the Beaufort Area, 1700–1900." Compiled for the 16th Annual Military History Conference of the Council on America's Military Past, Charleston, S.C., 1982.

"Statements Made in the Introduction to the Report on General Oglethorpe's Expedition to St. Augustine," in *Historical Collections of South Carolina,* 2 vols., ed. B. R. Carroll. New York: Harper, 1836.

Stevenson, Robert L., and Stanley South, "Bienvenido a Santa Elena: Report on the Santa Elena Site on Parris Island, S.C." Paper presented at 16th Annual Military History Conference of the Council on America's Military Past, Charleston, S. C., 1982.

TePaske, John J., "The Fugitive Slave," in *Eighteenth-Century Florida and Its Spanish Borderlands,* ed. Samuel Proctor. Gainesville: University Presses of Florida, 1975.

Thornton, John K., "African Dimensions of the Stono Rebellion: Notes and Comments." *American Historical Review* 91 (October 1991): 1101–13.

———, "On the Trail of Voodoo: African Christianity in Africa and the Americas." *Americas* 44 (January 1988): 261–78.

Trinkley, Michael B., "An Archaeological Overview of the South Carolina Woodland Period: It's the Same Old Riddle," in *Studies in South Carolina Archaeology,* ed. Albert C. Goodyear III and Glen Hanson. Columbia: South Carolina Institute of Archaeology and Anthropology, 1989.

Vargas, Ruben, "The First Jesuit Missions in Florida." *Historical Records and Studies: U.S. Catholic Historical Society.* New York: U.S. Catholic Historical Society, 1935.

Voigt, Gilbert, "The Periclean Age of Beaufort." *South Carolina Historical Magazine* 58 (October 1957): 218–23.

Waring, Joseph I., ed., "An Account of the Invasion of South Carolina by the French and Spaniards in August 1706." *South Carolina Historical Magazine* 66 (April 1965): 98–101.

Watson, Alan, "Beaufort Removal and the Revolutionary Impulse in South Carolina." *South Carolina Historical Magazine* 84 (July 1983): 121–135.

Webber, Mabel, ed., "Journal of Robert Pringle, 1746–1747." *South Carolina Historical Magazine* 26 (April 1925): 93–112.

Weir, Robert M., "Beaufort: The Almost Capital." *Sandlapper Magazine* (September 1976): 43–44.

———, "Muster Rolls of the S.C. Granville and Colleton County Regiments of Militia, 1756." *South Carolina Historical Magazine* 70 (October 1969): 226–39.

Whitefield, George, "A Journal of a Voyage from London to Savannah, Georgia," in *Our First Visit to America: Early Reports from Georgia,* ed. Trevor R. Reese. Savannah: Beehive Press, 1974.

Wilson, Samuel, "An Account of the Province of Carolina in America," in *Historical Collections of South Carolina,* 2 vols., ed. B. R. Carroll. New York: Harper, 1836.

Winberry, John J., "Reputation of Carolina Indigo." *South Carolina Historical Magazine* 80 (July 1979): 242–50.

Books

Abbott, John S. C., *The History of the Civil War in America,* 2 vols. New York: H. Bill, 1863–1866.

Acts of the General Assembly 1850–1859. Columbia: R. W. Gibbs, 1859.

Alden, John Richard, *John Stuart and the Southern Colonial Frontier: A Study of Indian Relations, War, Trade, and Land Problems in the Southern Wilderness, 1754–1775.* Ann Arbor: University of Michigan Press, 1944.

———, *The South in the Revolution, 1763–1789.* Baton Rouge: Louisiana State University Press, 1957.

Alderman, Edward and Joel Chandler Harris, eds., *Library of Southern Literature,* 16 vols. Atlanta: Martin and Hoyt, 1907–1913.

Arnade, Charles W., *Florida on Trial, 1593–1602.* Miami: University of Miami Press, 1959.

Ashley, Maurice, *England in the Seventeenth Century (1603–1714).* Baltimore: Pelican Books, 1963.

Bailey, N. Louise, et al. eds., *Biographical Directory of the South Carolina Senate, 1776–1985.* 3 vols. Columbia: University of South Carolina Press, 1986.

Baker, Steven G., *A Partial Biography of John Kean, South Carolinian.* Elizabeth, N.J.: Privately printed for Mrs. John Kean, 1971.

Barcia, Andreas Gonzalez, *Ensayo Cronologico, Para la Historia General de la Florida de Sole ano de 1512,* trans. Anthony Kerrigan. Gainesville: University of Florida Press, 1951.

Barnwell, Stephen B., *The Story of an American Family*. Marquette, Mich.: Privately printed, 1969.

Barrientos, Bartolome, *Pedro Menendez de Aviles: Founder of Florida*, trans. Anthony Kerrigan. Gainesville: University of Florida Press, 1965.

Basler, Roy P., et al., eds., *The Collected Works of Abraham Lincoln*, 9 vols. New Brunswick: Rutgers University Press, 1953–1955.

Bell, Malcolm, Jr., *Major Butler's Legacy: Five Generations of a Slaveholding Family*. Athens: University of Georgia Press, 1987.

Bennett, Charles E., *Laudonniere and Fort Caroline: History and Documents*. Gainesville: University of Florida Press, 1964.

————, *Twelve on the River St. Johns*. Jacksonville: University of Florida Press, 1989.

Biographical Directory of the American Congress 1774–1961. Washington, D.C.: U.S. Government Printing Office, 1961.

Blassingame, John W., *The Slave Community: Plantation Life in the Antebellum South*. New York: Oxford University Press, 1972.

Bolton, Herbert E., ed., *Arredondo's Historical Proof of Spain's Title to Georgia: A Contribution to the History of One of the Spanish Borderlands*. Berkeley: University of California Press, 1925.

Bolton, Herbert, and Mary Ross, *The Debatable Land: A Sketch of the Anglo-Spanish Contest for the Georgia Country*. Berkeley: University of California Press, 1925.

Bourne, Edward G., *Spain in America, 1450–1580*. New York: Harper, 1906.

Braund, Kathryn E. Holland, *Deerskins & Duffels: The Creek Indian Trade with Anglo-America, 1685–1815*. Lincoln and London: University of Nebraska Press, 1993.

Browne, Gary Lawson, *Baltimore in the New Nation*. Chapel Hill: University of North Carolina Press, 1980.

Calhoun, Richard J., ed., *Witness to Sorrow: The Autobiography of William J. Grayson*. Columbia: University of South Carolina Press, 1990.

Candler, Allen D., ed., *The Revolutionary Records of Georgia*, 3 vols. Atlanta: Franklin-Turner, 1908.

Carse, Robert, *Department of the South: Hilton Head and the Civil War*. Hilton Head: Impressions Printing, 1987.

Channing, Stephen, *Crisis of Fear: Secession in South Carolina*. New York: Simon and Schuster, 1970.

Chesnutt, David R., *South Carolina's Expansion into Colonial Georgia, 1720–1765*. New York: Garland, 1989.

Clark, William B., ed., *Naval Documents of the American Revolution*, 8 vols. Washington, D.C.: U.S. Government Printing Office, 1964–1981.

Clifton, James M., ed., *Life and Labor on Argyle Island: Letters and Documents of a Savannah River Rice Plantation, 1833–1867*. Savannah: Beehive Press, 1978.

Clowse, Converse D., *Economic Beginnings in Colonial South Carolina, 1670–1730*. Columbia: University of South Carolina Press, 1971.

Coleman, Kenneth, *The American Revolution in Georgia, 1763–1789*. Athens: University of Georgia Press, 1958.

Connor, Jeanette Thurber, ed. and trans., *Colonial Records of Spanish Florida: Letters and Reports of Governors and Secular Persons,* 2 vols. Deland: Florida State Historical Society, 1925–1930.

Cooper, Thomas, and David J. McCord, eds., *The Statutes at Large of South Carolina,* 10 vols. Columbia: A. S. Johnston, 1836–1841.

Courtenay, William A., ed., *The Genesis of South Carolina, 1562–1670.* Columbia: State Printing Co., 1907.

Crafford, John, *A New and Most Exact Account of the Fertiles* [sic] *and Famous Colony of Carolina on the Continent of America . . . Together with a Maritine* [sic] *Account of Its Rivers, Barrs, Soundings and Harbours: also of the Natives, Their Religion, Traffick and Commodities* . . . Dublin: N. Tarrant, 1683.

Crane, Verner Winslow, *The Southern Frontier, 1670–1732.* Durham: Duke University Press, 1928.

Creel, Margaret Washington, *A Peculiar People: Slave Religion and Community-Culture among the Gullahs.* New York: New York University Press, 1988.

Crum, Mason, *Gullah: Negro Life in the Carolina Sea Islands.* Durham: Duke University Press, 1940.

Cuthbert, J. H., *The Life of Richard Fuller, D.D.* New York: Sheldon, 1879.

Dabbs, Edith M., *Sea Island Diary: A History of St. Helena Island.* Spartanburg: Reprint Co., 1983.

Dalcho, Frederick, *An Historical Account of the Protestant Episcopal Church in South-Carolina from the First Settlement of the Province. . . .* Charleston: E. Thayer, 1820.

Davidson, Chalmers, *The Last Foray: The South Carolina Planters of 1860, A Sociological Study.* Columbia: University of South Carolina Press, 1971.

Davis, John, *Travels of John Davis in the United States of America, 1798–1802.* Boston: Privately printed, 1910.

De Brahm, John Gerar William, *Report of the General Survey of the Southern District of North America,* ed. Louis J. De Vorsey. Columbia: University of South Carolina Press, 1971.

Derting, Keith, Sharon Pekrul, and Charles J. Rinehart, *A Comprehensive Bibliography of South Carolina Archaeology, Research Manuscript Series, No. 211.* Columbia: South Carolina Institute of Archaeology and Anthropology, 1991.

De Vorsey, Louis J., *The Georgia-South Carolina Boundary Dispute: A Problem in Historical Geography.* Athens: University of Georgia Press, 1982.

Donnan, Elizabeth, ed., *Documents Illustrative of the History of the Slave Trade to America,* 4 vols. New York: Octagon Books, 1965.

Drayton, John, *Memoirs of the American Revolution in S.C.* 1821; rpt. ed. New York: Arno, 1969.

———, *A View of South Carolina, As Respects Her Natural and Civil Concerns.* 1802; rpt. ed. Spartanburg, S.C.: Reprint Co., 1972.

Dunbar, Gary S., *Historical Geography of the North Carolina Outer Banks.* Baton Rouge: Louisiana State University Press, 1958.

Easterby, J. H., ed., *Journal of the Commons House of Assembly, 1741–1742.* Columbia: Historical Commission of South Carolina, 1953.

——, *Journal of the Commons House of Assembly, 1744–1745.* Columbia: Historical Commission of South Carolina, 1955.

Eaton, Clement, *The Mind of the Old South.* Baton Rouge: Louisiana State University Press, 1967.

Edgar, Walter B., Louise N. Bailey, et al., eds., *Biographical Directory of South Carolina House of Representatives,* 5 vols. Columbia: University of South Carolina Press, 1974–1993.

Edwards, Adele, ed., *Journals of the Privy Council, 1783–1789.* Columbia: University of South Carolina Press, 1971.

Elliot, Jonathan, *Debates on the Adoption of the Federal Constitution.* 5 vols. Salem, N.H.: Ayer, 1987.

Elliott, William, *Carolina Sports by Land and Water.* 1846; rpt. ed. New York: Arno, 1967.

Erskine, John, of Carnock, *Journal of the Hon. John Erskine of Carnock, 1683–1687,* ed. Walter Macleod. Edinburgh: T. and A. Constable, 1893.

Fassett, Frederick Gardner. *The Shipbuilding Business in the United States of America,* 2 vols. New York: Society of Naval Architects and Marine Engineers, 1948.

Fleetwood, Rusty, *Tidecraft: An Introductory Look at the Boats of Lower South Carolina, Georgia, and Northeastern Florida, 1650–1950.* Savannah: Coastal Heritage Society, 1982.

Ford, Lacy K., *Origins of Southern Radicalism: The South Carolina Upcountry, 1800–1860.* New York: Oxford University Press, 1988.

Fortescue, J. W., ed., *Calendar of State Papers, Colonial Series, America and West Indies, Volume 12, 1685–1688.* London: HMSO, 1899.

Freehling, William W., *Prelude to Civil War: The Nullification Controversy in South Carolina, 1816–1836.* New York: Harper and Row, 1966.

French, B. F., ed., *Historical Collections of Louisiana and Florida.* New York: Albert Mason, 1875.

Friis, Herman R., *A Series of Population Maps of the Colonies and United States, 1625–1790.* New York: American Geographical Society, 1940.

Fuller, Richard, and Francis Wayland, *Domestic Slavery Considered as a Scriptural Institution: In a Correspondence between Rev. Richard Fuller of Beaufort, S.C., and Rev. Francis Wayland of Providence, R.I.* New York: Lewis Colby, 1845.

Gaffarel, Paul, *Histoire de la Floride Française.* Paris: Librarie de Fermin-Didot, 1875.

Gallay, Alan, *The Formation of a Planter Elite: Jonathan Bryan and the Southern Colonial Frontier.* Athens: University of Georgia Press, 1989.

Garden, Alexander, *Anecdotes of the Revolutionary War.* 1822; rpt. ed., Spartanburg: Reprint Co., 1972.

Geiger, Maynard, *The Franciscan Conquest of Florida, 1573–1618,* Catholic University of America Studies in Hispanic-American History, vol. 1. Washington, D.C.: Murray and Heister, 1936.

Gibbes, Robert Wilson, ed., *Documentary History of the American Revolution,* 3 vols. 1853–1857; rpt. ed. Spartanburg: Reprint Co., 1972.

Glen, Isabella, *Life on St. Helena Island.* New York: Carlton Press, 1980.

Goldenberg, Joseph A., *Shipbuilding in Colonial America*. Charlottesville: University of Virginia Press, 1976.

Goodyear, Albert C., III, and Glen Hanson, eds., *Studies in South Carolina Archaeology: Essays in Honor of Robert L. Stephenson*. Columbia: South Carolina Institute of Archaeology and Anthropology, 1989.

Granger, Mary, ed., *Savannah River Plantations*. Savannah: Georgia Historical Society, 1947.

Gray, Lewis Cecil, *History of Agriculture in the Southern United States to 1860*. 2 vols. Gloucester, Mass.: Peter Smith, 1958.

Greene, Jack P. *The Nature of Colony Constitutions: Two Pamphlets on the Wilkes Fund Controversy in S.C. by Sir Egerton Leigh and Arthur Lee*. Columbia: University of South Carolina Press, 1970.

————, *Selling a New World: Two Colonial South Carolina Promotional Pamphlets*. Columbia: University of South Carolina Press, 1989.

————, *Quest for Power: The Lower Houses of Assembly in the Southern Royal Colonies, 1689–1776*. Chapel Hill: University of North Carolina Press, 1963.

Hamer, Philip M., *The Secession Movement in South Carolina 1847–1852*. New York: DaCapo Press, 1971.

Harcourt, Malcolm, ed., *Historical Documents Relating to the Bahama Islands*. Nassau: Nassau Guardian, 1910.

Haring, C. H., *The Spanish Empire in America*. New York: Harcourt, Brace and World, 1947.

Harlow, Vincent Todd, *A History of the Barbadoes, 1625–1685*. Oxford: Clarendon Press, 1926.

Harmon, Joyce E., *Trading and Privateering in Spanish Florida, 1732–1763*. St. Augustine: St. Augustine Historical Society, 1969.

Hemphill, W. Edwin, Wylma Anne Wates, and R. Nicholas Olsberg, eds., *Journals of the General Assembly and House of Representatives, 1776–1780*. Columbia: University of South Carolina Press, 1970.

Heyward, Duncan Clinch, *Seed From Madagascar*. 1937; rpt. ed. Columbia: University of South Carolina Press, 1993.

Historic Beaufort: A Guide to the Gracious Homes, Churches, and Other Points of Interest of Beaufort, S.C. Beaufort: Historic Beaufort Foundation, 1977.

The History of the Parish Church of St. Helena, Beaufort, South Carolina. . . . Columbia: Privately printed, 1991.

Hoffman, Paul E. *New Andalucia and a Way to the Orient: The American Southeast during the Sixteenth Century*. Baton Rouge: Louisiana State University Press, 1990.

Hollis, Daniel W., *University of South Carolina*, vol. 1, *South Carolina College*. Columbia: University of South Carolina Press, 1951.

Holmgren, Virginia, *Hilton Head: A Sea Island Chronicle*. Hilton Head: Hilton Head Publishing Co., 1959.

Hough, Franklin, ed., *Siege of Savannah*. 1866; rpt. ed., Spartanburg: Reprint Co., 1975.

Hudson, Charles, and Paul E. Hoffman, *The Juan Pardo Expeditions: Explorations of the Carolinas and Tennessee, 1566–1568*. Washington, D.C.: Smithsonian Institution, 1990.

Huff, Archie Vernon, Jr., *Langdon Cheves of South Carolina*. Columbia: University of South Carolina Press, 1977.

Hurmence, Belinda, ed., *Before Freedom, When I Just Can Remember: Twenty-seven Oral Histories of Former South Carolina Slaves*. Winston-Salem: John F. Blair, 1989.

Insh, George Pratt, *Scottish Colonial Schemes, 1620–1686*. Glasgow: Maclehose, Jackson, 1922.

Ivers, Larry E., *British Drums on the Southern Frontier: The Military Colonization of Georgia, 1733–1749*. Chapel Hill: University of North Carolina Press, 1974.

——, *Colonial Forts of South Carolina, 1670–1775*. Columbia: University of South Carolina Press, 1970.

Johnson, Allen, et al., *Dictionary of American Biography*. 21 vols. New York: Charles Scribner's Sons, 1928.

Johnson, Guion Griffis, *Social History of the Sea Islands*. Chapel Hill: University of North Carolina Press, 1930.

Johnson, Joseph, *Traditions and Reminicences of the American Revolution in the South*. 1851; rpt. ed. Spartanburg: Reprint Co., 1972.

Johnson, Samuel A., *Battle Cry of Freedom: The New England Immigrant Aid Society in the Kansas Crusade*. Laurence: University of Kansas Press, 1984.

Johnston, Coy K., *Two Centuries of Lawtonville Baptists, 1775–1975*. Columbia: State Printing Co., 1974.

Jones, Charles C., Jr., *History of Savannah, Georgia, from Its Settlement to the Close of the Eighteenth Century*. Syracuse: D. Mason, 1890.

Jones, Katherine M., ed., *Port Royal Under Six Flags*. Indianapolis: Bobbs-Merrill, 1960.

Jones-Jackson, Patricia, *When Roots Die*. Athens: University of Georgia Press, 1987.

Jones, Newton, *Guide to the Records of the Public Treasurer of South Carolina, 1725–1776*. Columbia: South Carolina Department of Archives and History, 1969.

Journal of the Constitution Which Ratified the Constitution of the U.S., May 23, 1788. Atlanta: Foote & Davis Co., for the Historical Commission of South Carolina, 1928.

Joyner, Charles W., *Down by the Riverside: A South Carolina Slave Community*. Urbana: University of Illinois Press, 1984.

Julien, Charles Andre, *Les Voyages de Descouverte et les Premiers Etablissements*. Paris: Presses Universitaires de France, 1948.

Kennedy, Roger G., *Greek Revival America*. New York: Stuart, Tabori and Chang, 1989.

Kilgo, James, *Pipe Creek to Matthew's Bluff: A Short History of Groton Plantation*. N.p.: Privately printed for the Winthrop family, 1988.

Kovacik, Charles F., and John Winberry, *South Carolina: A Geography*. Boulder and London: Westview Press, 1987.

LaBorde, Maximilian, *History of the South Carolina College*. Columbia: Peter Glass, 1859.

Lanning, John Tate, *The Diplomatic History of Georgia: A Study of the Epoch of Jenkins' Ear*. Chapel Hill: University of North Carolina Press, 1936.

——, *The Spanish Missions of Georgia*. Chapel Hill: University of North Carolina Press, 1935.

Laudonniere, Rene de, *A Notable History Containing Four Voyages Made by Certain French*

Captains unto Florida, ed. Martin Basanier, trans. Richard Hakluyt. Facimile of the edition printed in London in 1587 with a survey by Thomas C. Adams. Larchmont, N.Y.: Henry Stevens and Sons, 1964.

Lawrence, David R., ed., *Studies in Southeastern Aboriginal Shell Rings, Five Parts.* Columbia: Department of Geological Sciences, University of South Carolina, 1989–1991.

Lesser, Charles H., *Relic of the Lost Cause: The Story of South Carolina's Ordinance of Secession.* Columbia: South Carolina Department of Archives and History, 1990.

Lichliter, Asselia Strobhar, *Pioneering with the Belville and Related Families in South Carolina, Georgia, and Florida: Their Lives, Times, and Descendants.* Washington, D.C.: Privately printed, 1982.

Littlefield, Daniel C., *Rice and Slaves: Ethnicity and the Slave Trade in Colonial South Carolina.* Baton Rouge: Louisiana State University Press, 1981.

Lloyd, Christopher, and J. Douglas Henry, *Ships and Seamen from Vikings to the Present Day.* London: Wiedenfeld and Nicolson, 1963.

A Longer Short History of Bluffton, South Carolina, and Its Environs. Hilton Head: Bluffton Historical Preservation Society, 1988.

Lorant, Stefan, ed., *The New World: The First Pictures of America Made by John White and Jacques Le Moyne and Engraved by Theodore De Bry with Contemporary Narratives of the Huguenot Settlements in Florida, 1562–1565, and the Virginia Colony, 1585–1590.* New York: Duell, Sloan and Pearce, 1946.

Loring, Jessica Stevens, *Auldbrass, the Plantation Complex Designed by Frank Lloyd Wright.* Greenville: Southern Historical Press, 1992.

Lowery, Woodbury, *The Spanish Settlements within the Present Limits of the United States, 1513–1561.* New York: Russell and Russell, 1959.

Lubbock, Francis Richard, *Six Decades in Texas: or Memoirs of Francis Richard Lubbock, Governor of Texas in Wartime: A Personal Experience in Business, War and Politics.* Austin: Ben C. Jones, 1900.

Lumpkin, Henry, *Savannah to Yorktown: The American Revolution in the South.* Columbia: University of South Carolina Press, 1981.

Lyons, Eugene, *The Enterprise of Florida: Pedro Menendez de Aviles and the Spanish Conquest of 1565–1568.* Gainesville: University of Florida Press, 1976.

McCrady, Edward, *The History of South Carolina in the Revolution.* 1901; rpt. ed., New York: Russell and Russell, 1969.

———, *The History of South Carolina under the Proprietary Government, 1670–1719.* 1897; rpt. ed., New York: Russell and Russell, 1969.

———, *The History of South Carolina under the Royal Government, 1719–1776.* 1899; rpt. ed., New York: Russell and Russell, 1969.

McDowell, William L., ed., *Journals of the Commissioners of the Indian Trade, September 20, 1710–August 29, 1718.* Columbia: University of South Carolina Press, 1955.

McPherson, James M., *Battle Cry of Freedom.* New York: Oxford University Press, 1988.

McTeer, J. E., *High Sheriff of the Lowcountry.* Beaufort: Beaufort Book Co., 1970.

Martyr, Peter, *De Orbe Novo*, 22 vols., trans. Augustus Francis MacNutt. New York: G. P. Putnam's, 1912.

Matthews, Donald G., *Religion in the Old South*. Chicago: University of Chicago Press, 1977.

Meats, Stephen, and Edwin T. Arnold., eds., *The Writings of Benjamin F. Perry*, 3 vols. Spartanburg: Reprint Co., 1980.

Meriwether, Robert L., *The Expansion of South Carolina, 1729–1865*. Kingsport, Tenn.: Southern Publishers, 1940.

Merrens, H. Roy, ed., *The Colonial South Carolina Scene*. Columbia: University of South Carolina Press, 1977.

Merrill, James M., *DuPont, The Making of an Admiral: The Biography of Samuel Francis DuPont*. New York: Dodd, Mead, 1986.

Miller, Annie Elizabeth, *Our Family Circle: Being a Reunion of Our House of Langrave Thomas Smith, House of Robert, House of Bostick, House of Lawton, House of Grimball, House of Erwin, House of Stafford, House of Maner, including Screvens, Jaudons, Rhodes, Daniels, Willinghams, Baynards, Polhills, Goldwires, and Caters*. Hilton Head: Lawton and Allied Families Association, 1987.

Milling, Chapman James, ed., *Colonial South Carolina: Two Contemporary Descriptions by Governor James Glen and Dr. George Milligen-Johnston*. Columbia: University of South Carolina Press, 1951.

———, *Red Carolinians*. Chapel Hill: University of North Carolina Press, 1940.

Mills, Robert, *Mills' Atlas of South Carolina, 1825*. Easley, S.C.: Southern Historical Press, 1980.

Milner, John and Associates, *The Beaufort Preservation Manual*. Westchester, Pa.: John Milner and Associates, 1979.

Montgomery, Sir Robert and John Barnwell, *The Most Delightful Golden Isles. Being a Proposal for the Establishment of a Colony in the Country to the South of Carolina*. 1717; rpt. ed. Atlanta: Cherokee Publishers, 1969.

Moultrie, William, *Memoirs of the American Revolution*, 2 vols. 1802; rpt. in one, New York: New York Times, 1968.

Myers, Robert M., ed., *The Children of Pride: A True Story of Georgia and the Civil War*. New Haven: Yale University Press, 1972.

Nadelhaft, Jerome, *Disorders of War: The Revolution in South Carolina*. Orono, Me.: University of Maine at Orono Press, 1981.

Nairne, Thomas, *Nairne's Muskhogean Journals: The 1708 Expedition to the Mississippi River*, ed. Alexander Moore. Jackson: University Press of Mississippi, 1988.

O'Brien, Michael and David Moltke-Hansen, eds., *Intellectual Life in Antebellum Charleston*. Knoxville: University of Tennessee Press, 1986.

Oliphant, Mary C. Simms, Alfred Taylor Odell, and T. C. Duncan Eaves, eds., *The Letters of William Gilmore Simms*, 6 vols. Columbia: University of South Carolina Press, 1952–1982.

Parker, Mattie E.E., *North Carolina Charters and Constitutions, 1578–1698*. Raleigh: North Carolina Tercentenary Commission, 1963.

Paton, Henry, ed., *Register of the Privy Council of Scotland*, third series, vol. 9. Edinburgh: H. M. Register House, 1924.

Peeples, Robert E. H., *Tales of Antebellum Hilton Head Island Families.* Hilton Head: Hilton Head Island Historical Society, 1970.

Perry, Grace Fox, *Moving Finger of Jasper.* Ridgeland, S.C.: Confederate Centennial Committee, 1947.

Phillips, Ulrich B., *American Negro Slavery: A Survey of the Supply, Employment and Control of Negro Labor as Determined by the Plantation Regime.* 1918; rpt. ed. Gloucester, Mass.: Peter Smith, 1959.

————, *Plantation and Frontier Documents, 1649–1863,* 2 vols. Cleveland: Arthur Clark, 1909.

Pinckney, Elise, ed., *The Letterbook of Eliza Lucas Pinckney.* Chapel Hill: University of North Carolina Press, 1972.

Pinckney, Josephine, *Hilton Head.* New York and Toronto: Farrar and Rinehart, 1941.

Powell, Mary Pinckney. *Over Home: The Heritage of Pinckneys of Pinckney Colony, Bluffton, South Carolina.* Columbia: R. L. Bryan, 1982.

Powell, William S., *The Proprietors of Carolina.* Raleigh: Carolina Charter Tercentenary, 1963.

Priestley, Herbert R., ed., *The Luna Papers. Documents Relating to the Expedition of Don Tristan de Luna y Arrellano for the Conquest of La Florida in 1559–1561.* 2 vols. Deland: Florida Historical Society, 1928.

————, *Tristan de Luna: Conquistador of the Old South.* Glendale, Calif.: Arthur Clark, 1936.

Proctor, Samuel, ed., *Eighteenth-Century Florida and Its Borderlands.* Gainesville: University Presses of Florida, 1975.

Quattlebaum, Paul, *The Land Called Chicora: The Carolinas under Spanish Rule with French Intrusions, 1520–1670.* Gainesville: University of Florida Press, 1956.

Quinn, David. B., *North America from Earliest Discovery to First Settlement: Norse Voyages to 1612.* New York: Harper and Row, 1975.

————, ed., *New American World: A Documentary History of North America to 1612,* 5 vols. New York: Arno, 1979.

————, ed., *The Roanoke Voyages, 1584–1590: Documents to Illustrate the English Voyages to North America under the Patent Granted to Walter Raleigh in 1584.* Nendeln, Liechtenstein: Kraus Reprint, 1955.

Raboteau, Albert J., *Slave Religion: An Invisible Institution in the Antebellum South.* New York: Oxford University Press, 1978.

Rahn, Ruby A., *River Highway for Trade: The Savannah.* Savannah: U.S. Army Corps of Engineers, 1968.

Ramsay, David, *History of South Carolina from Its Earliest Settlement in 1670 to the Year 1808.* 2 vols. Newberry, S.C.: N. J. Duffie, 1858.

Reese, Trevor R., ed., *Our First Visit to America: Early Reports from Georgia.* Savannah: Beehive Press, 1974.

Reynolds, Emily Bellinger, and Joan Reynolds Faunt, eds., *Biographical Directory of the Senate of the State of South Carolina.* Columbia: South Carolina Department of Archives and History, 1964.

Rivers, William J., *A Sketch of the History of South Carolina*. Charleston: McCarter, 1856.

Rogers, George C., Jr., *The History of Georgetown County, South Carolina*. Columbia: University of South Carolina Press, 1970.

———, *Evolution of a Federalist: William Loughton Smith of Charleston (1758–1812)*. Columbia: University of South Carolina Press, 1962.

———, et al., eds., *The Papers of Henry Laurens*, 14 vols. to date. Columbia: University of South Carolina Press, 1968–1994.

Rose, Willie Lee, *Rehearsal for Reconstruction: The Port Royal Experiment*. Indianapolis: Bobbs-Merrill, 1964.

Rosengarten, Theodore, *Tombee: Portrait of a Cotton Planter*. New York: Morrow, 1986.

Rowland, Lawrence S., *Window on the Atlantic: The Rise and Fall of Santa Elena, South Carolina's Spanish City*. Columbia: South Carolina Department of Archives and History, 1990.

Salley, A. S., ed., *Records in the British Public Records Office Relating to South Carolina*. 5 vols. Columbia: Historical Commission of South Carolina, 1928–1947.

———, *Minutes of the Vestry of St. Helena's Parish, South Carolina, 1726–1812*. Columbia: Historical Commission of South Carolina, 1919.

———, *Narratives of Early Carolina, 1650–1708*. New York: Charles Scribner's Sons, 1911.

———, *Warrants for Land in South Carolina, 1672–1711*. Columbia: University of South Carolina Press, 1973.

Sassaman, Kenneth E., *Early Pottery in the Southeast: Tradition and Innovation in Cooking Technology*. Tuscaloosa: University of Alabama Press, 1993.

Sauer, Carl O., *Sixteenth Century North America: The Land and the People as Seen by the Europeans*. Berkeley: University of California Press, 1971.

Schultz, Harold S., *Nationalism and Sectionalism in South Carolina, 1852–1860: A Study of the Movement for Southern Independence*. New York: DaCapo Press, 1969.

Seabrook, William., *A Memoir on the Sea Island Cotton Plant*. Charleston: Walker and Cogswell, 1844.

Sellers, Leila, *Charleston Business on the Eve of the American Revolution*. Chapel Hill: University of North Carolina Press, 1934.

Shepherd, James F., and Gary M. Walton, *Shipping, Maritime Trade and the Economic Development of Colonial North America*. Cambridge: Cambridge University Press, 1972.

Siebert, Wilbur Henry, *Loyalists in East Florida, 1774–1785*, 2 vols. Deland: Florida State Historical Society, 1929.

Sirmans, M. Eugene, *Colonial South Carolina: A Political History, 1663–1763*. Chapel Hill: University of North Carolina Press, 1966.

Skipper, Otis Clark, *J. D. B. DeBow: Magazinist of the Old South*. Athens: University of Georgia Press, 1958.

Smith, Henry A. M., *The Historical Writings of Henry A. M. Smith*. 3 vols. Spartanburg, S.C.: Reprint Co., 1988.

Smith, Julia Floyd, *Slavery and Rice Culture in Lowcountry Georgia, 1750–1860*. Knoxville: University of Tennessee Press, 1985.

Solis de Meras, Gonzalo, *Pedro Menendez de Aviles,* trans. Jeannette Thurber Connor. Gainesville: University of Florida Press, 1964.

Stafford, George M. G., *General Leroy Augustus Stafford: His Forebears and Descendants.* New Orleans: Pelican Publishers, 1943.

Stevens, Michael E., ed., *Journals of the House of Representatives, 1787–1788.* Columbia: University of South Carolina Press, 1981.

Stevens, William Bacon, *A History of Georgia, From Its First Discovery by Europeans to the Adoption of the Present Constitution in MDCCXCVIII,* 2 vols. 1847; rpt. ed. Savannah, Ga.: Beehive Press, 1972.

Swanton, John R., *Indians of the Southeastern United States.* Westwood, Conn.: Greenwood Press, 1946.

Syrett, Harold C., ed., *The Papers of Alexander Hamilton,* 27 vols. New York: Columbia University Press, 1962.

Tarleton, Lieutenant-General (Banastre), *A History of the Campaigns of 1780 and 1781 in the Southern Provinces of North America.* London: T. Cadell, 1787; rpt. ed. Spartanburg: Reprint Co., 1967.

TePaske, John J., *The Governorship of Spanish Florida, 1700–1763.* Durham: Duke University Press, 1964.

Terry, C. S., *The Pentland Rising and Rullion Green.* Glasgow, 1905.

Thompson, Theodora J., ed., *Journals of the House of Representatives, 1783–1784.* Columbia: University of South Carolina Press, 1977.

Todd, John R., and Francis M. Hutson, *Prince William Parish and Plantations.* Richmond: Garrett and Massie, 1935.

Townsend, Leah, *South Carolina Baptists, 1670–1805.* Baltimore: Genealogical Publishing, 1974.

Trueba, Alfonso, *Expediciones a la Florida.* Mexico City: Editoreal Campeador, 1955.

Uhlendorff, Bernard Alexander, ed., *Siege of Charleston.* Ann Arbor: University of Michigan Press, 1968.

U.S. Commerce Department, Bureau of the Census, *Historical Statistics of the United States: Colonial Times to 1957.* Washington, D.C.: U.S. Government Printing Office, 1960.

Vega, Garcilaso de la, *The Florida of the Inca: A History of the Adelantado, Hernando de Soto, Governor and Captain General of Florida and Other Heroic Spanish and Indian Cavaliers,* trans. and ed. John G. Varner and Jeanette J. Varner. Austin: University of Texas Press, 1951.

Waddell, Gene, *Indians of the South Carolina Lowcountry, 1562–1751.* Spartanburg: Reprint Co., 1980.

Waddell, Gene, and R. W. Liscombe, *Robert Mills's Courthouses and Jails.* Easley, S.C.: Southern Historical Press, 1981.

Wallace, David Duncan, *The History of South Carolina,* 4 vols. New York: American Historical Society, 1934.

Walsh, Richard, ed., *The Writings of Christopher Gadsden, 1746–1805.* Columbia: University of South Carolina Press, 1966.

The War of the Rebellion: A Compilation of the Official Records of the Union and Confederate Armies, 128 vols. Washington, D.C.: U.S. Government Printing Office, 1880.

Weir, Robert M., *Colonial South Carolina: A History*. Millwood, N.Y.: KTO Press, 1983.

White, Laura Amanda, *Robert Barnwell Rhett: Father of Secession*. New York: Century, 1931.

Wilder, Ellie Leland, *Henry Woodward, Forgotten Man of American History*. n. p., n. d.

Wilson, Clyde N., et al., eds., *The Papers of John C. Calhoun*, 22 vols. to date. Columbia: University of South Carolina Press, 1959–1995.

Wilson, James Grant, and John Fiske, eds., *Appleton's Cyclopedia of American Biography*, 7 vols. New York: D. Appleton and Co., 1887.

Wood, Peter H., *Black Majority: Negroes in Colonial South Carolina from 1670 through the Stono Rebellion*. New York: Knopf, 1974.

Wodrow, Robert, *History of the Sufferings of the Church of Scotland from the Restoration to the Revolution*, 4 vols. Glasgow: Blackie, 1836.

Wood, Virginia S., *Live Oaking: Southern Timbers for Tall Ships*. Boston: Northeastern University Press, 1981.

Woodward, C. Vann, ed., *Mary Chesnut's Civil War*. New Haven: Yale University Press, 1981.

Yonge, Francis, *A View of the Trade of South Carolina with Proposals Humbly Offer'd for Improving the Same*. London, 1722.

Zubillaga, Felix, *La Florida: La Mision Jesuitica y la Colonizacion Espanola*. Rome: Institutam Historicum, 1941.

DISSERTATIONS AND THESES

Bass, Marvin D., ed., "Autobiography of William J. Grayson." Ph.D. dissertation, University of South Carolina, 1933.

Calmes, Alan, "Indian Cultural Tradition and the European Conquest of the Georgia-S.C. Coastal Plain, 3000 B.C.–1733 A.D.: A Combined Archaeological and Historical Investigation." Ph.D. dissertation, University of South Carolina, 1967.

Cantrell, Clyde, "The Reading Habits of Antebellum Southerners." Ph.D. dissertation, University of Michigan, 1960.

Duncan, John Donald, "Servitude and Slavery in Colonial South Carolina, 1670–1776." Ph.D. dissertation, Emory University, 1971.

Fagg, Daniel W., Jr., "Carolina, 1663–1683: The Founding of a Proprietary Colony." Ph.D. dissertation, Emory University, 1970.

Glenn, Virginia L., "James Hamilton, Jr., of South Carolina: A Biography." Ph.D. dissertation, University of North Carolina, 1964.

Green, William G., "The Search for Altamaha: The Archaeology of an Early 18th Century Yamasee Indian Town." M.A. thesis, Columbia: University of South Carolina, 1991.

Honeycutt, Dwight, "The Economics of the Indigo Industry in South Carolina." M.A. thesis, University of South Carolina, 1948.

Johnson, David Lee, "The Yamasee War." M.A. thesis, University of South Carolina, 1980.

Matier, Robert A., "The Spanish Missions of Florida: The Friars vs. the Governors in the Golden Age." Ph.D. dissertation, University of Washington, 1972.

McKivergan, David Andrew, "Migration and Settlement among the Yamasee in South Carolina." M.A. thesis, University of South Carolina, 1991.

Roberts, Charles Arthur, "The Sea Island Cotton Industry as Revealed in the McConnell-Kennedy Letters, 1819–1825." M.A. thesis, University of South Carolina, 1965.

Stuckey, Heyward C., "The South Carolina Navy and the American Revolution." M.A. thesis, University of South Carolina, 1972.

Index

Fripp Island, 2
Fripp's Hunting Island, 169
Frogmore, S.C., 3, 338
Frogmore Plantation, 242–43,
   281–83, 338–39, 343, 349, 356,
   370, 401
Fruit, 33, 35, 37, 45, 60, 254–55,
   281, 381, 383, 403
Fuller, Charlotte Bull Stuart, 409
Fuller, Elizabeth, 287
Fuller, Elizabeth Middleton, 408
Fuller, Harriet, 409–11
Fuller, Henry, 408
Fuller, Henry M., 382
Fuller, Richard, 259, 286, 354–55,
   359, 372, 381, 398, 401, 408–16
Fuller, Thomas, 284, 292, 356, 372,
   382, 408
Fundamental Constitutions of
   Carolina, 68

Gadsden, Christopher, 197, 199–200,
   203–4, 211, 237, 272
Gaillard, Theodore, 271
Galt, John, 70
Garcia, Juan, 41
Garden, Alexander, 133, 229, 236
Garden, Benjamin, 203, 227
Garden's Corners, S.C., 231
Gardner, John, 71
Gardner, Nettle, 305
Gardner, Thomas, 262
Gardner, William, 216–18
Garnet, S.C., 102, 297
Garrison, William Lloyd, 343
Garvey, James, 268
Gascoyne, Joel, 68
Gates, Horatio, 232
Geddes, John, 291
Geffrey, Nicholas, 272

General Assembly, 12, 204–5, 219,
   237, 258, 273, 299–300, 310–11,
   317, 319, 333–34, 338, 340, 342,
   347–48, 383, 398, 404, 422–23,
   425, 431, 437, 438–43. *See also*
   Commons House of Assembly
George (ship), 58
George I of England, 119
George II of England, 117, 148, 175
George III of England, 195, 198
Georgetown (ship), 184
Georgetown, S.C., 2, 113, 148, 162,
   177, 183, 232, 265, 339, 443
Georgia, 4, 16, 23, 33–34, 38, 47,
   50, 72, 74, 95, 101, 103, 107,
   111, 119, 120, 128, 139, 145, 155,
   178, 181, 206–7, 209, 211–12,
   226, 242, 255, 266, 277, 289, 297,
   355, 398, 410
Georgia Gazette, 180, 181
Gibb, James, 118
Gibbes, Mary Anna, 223
Gibbes Island, 165
Gibson, James, 70–71
Gibson, John, 70
Gibson, Walter, 70–71
Gilbert (Indian), 100
Gilbert, Barnabas, 106
Gilbert, Edward, 130
Gilbert, Sir Humphrey, 45
Gilbert, William, 117
Gilcrest, Robert, 97
Gillet, Aaron, 238
Gillingham (captain), 212
Gillis, John, 454
Gillison, Derry, 385
Gillison, T. W., 385
Gillisonville, S.C., 259, 368, 373,
   380, 385, 420, 428
Gillon, Alexander, 247, 267–68

Smith, Thomas Laughton, 184

Smith, William, 70, 268, 421

Smithfield Plantation, 313, 319

Smiths, DeSaussure and Darrell
Company, 190, 245, 264–65

Smithsonian Institution, 287

smuggling, 96, 147–48, 155–56,
205–7, 244, 348

Society for the Propagation of the
Gospel, 120, 132

Soldiers' Relief Society, 449

Solis, Alonso, 36–38, 47–48

Solomon, Saul, 307

Solomons, Henry, 429

Somerset, Charles, Duke of
Beaufort, 90

Somerset, Henry, Duke of
Beaufort, 90–91

Somers Island Company, 58, 64

Sotil, Fernandez, 18

Soto, Hernando de, 9–10, 19

South Atlantic Blockading Squadron,
444–45

South Carolina (ship), 247

South Carolina Agricultural Society,
277, 403

*South Carolina and American General
Gazette*, 183

South Carolina Bank, 392

South Carolina College, 285–86,
318, 344, 382, 396, 399–400,
405–7, 422

South Carolina Constitutional
Convention (1852), 432, 433–34

South Carolina Gazette, 135, 149,
155–56, 162, 183–84, 186, 188–
89, 196, 203, 212, 218–19, 222,
229, 267, 269

South Carolina Land Company, 392

South Edisto Inlet, 142–43, 155

South Edisto River, 86, 224

Southern Agriculturist, 372, 403

*Southern Baptist and General
Intelligencer*, 416

Southern Baptist Convention, 354,
358–59

Southern Quarterly Review, 402, 404

Southern Review, 399

Southern Rights Association, 428,
432–33

Southern Rights Convention (1852),
439

South Wimbee Creek, 2–3

Spanish Point, 156, 175, 185, 215,
288, 449

Spanish Wells, Hilton Head
Island, 99

Spann, T. H., 381

Sparks, John, 105

Spaulding, James, 294n

Spaulding, Thomas, 290, 355

Speakman, John and Company, 290

Speedwell (ship), 149

Speights, A. M., 385

Speights, James, 310, 389, 391

Speight's Bay, Barbados, 59

Spring Island, 360, 373, 374, 420

SS *Altamaha*, 292

SS *Charleston*, 292

SS *Columbia*, 292

SS *Enterprise*, 292

SS *Georgia*, 292

SS *Headley*, 393

SS *Henry Shultz*, 293, 381

SS *Ockmulgee*, 292

SS *Samuel Howard*, 292

SS *Savannah*, 292

SS *South Carolina*, 92

Stafford, Edward, 298

Stafford, John, 303